Managerial Accounting

Ninth Edition

SUSAN L. KULP
George Washington University

AMIE L. DRAGOO

AL L. HARTGRAVES
Emory University

WAYNE J. MORSE
Rochester Institute of Technology

Cambridge Business Publishers

MANAGERIAL ACCOUNTING, Ninth Edition, by Susan Kulp, Amie Dragoo, Al Hartgraves, and Wayne Morse.

ISBN 978-1-61853-362-3

Bookstores & Faculty: to order this book, contact the company via email **customerservice@cambridgepub.com**.

Students & Retail Customers: to order this book, please visit the book's website and order directly online.

Printed in Canada.
10 9 8 7 6 5 4 3 2 1

my BusinessCourse

FREE WITH NEW COPIES OF THIS TEXTBOOK*

Start using my BusinessCourse Today: www.mybusinesscourse.com

my BusinessCourse is a web-based learning and assessment program intended to complement your textbook and faculty instruction.

Student Benefits

- **eLectures**: These videos review the key concepts of each Learning Objective in each chapter.
- **Guided examples**: These videos provide step-by-step solutions for select problems in each chapter.
- **Auto-graded assignments**: Provide students with immediate feedback on select assignments. (**with Instructor-Led course ONLY**).
- **Quiz and Exam preparation**: myBusinessCourse provides students with additional practice and exam preparation materials to help students achieve better grades and content mastery.

You can access my BusinessCourse 24/7 from any web-enabled device, including iPads, smartphones, laptops, and tablets.

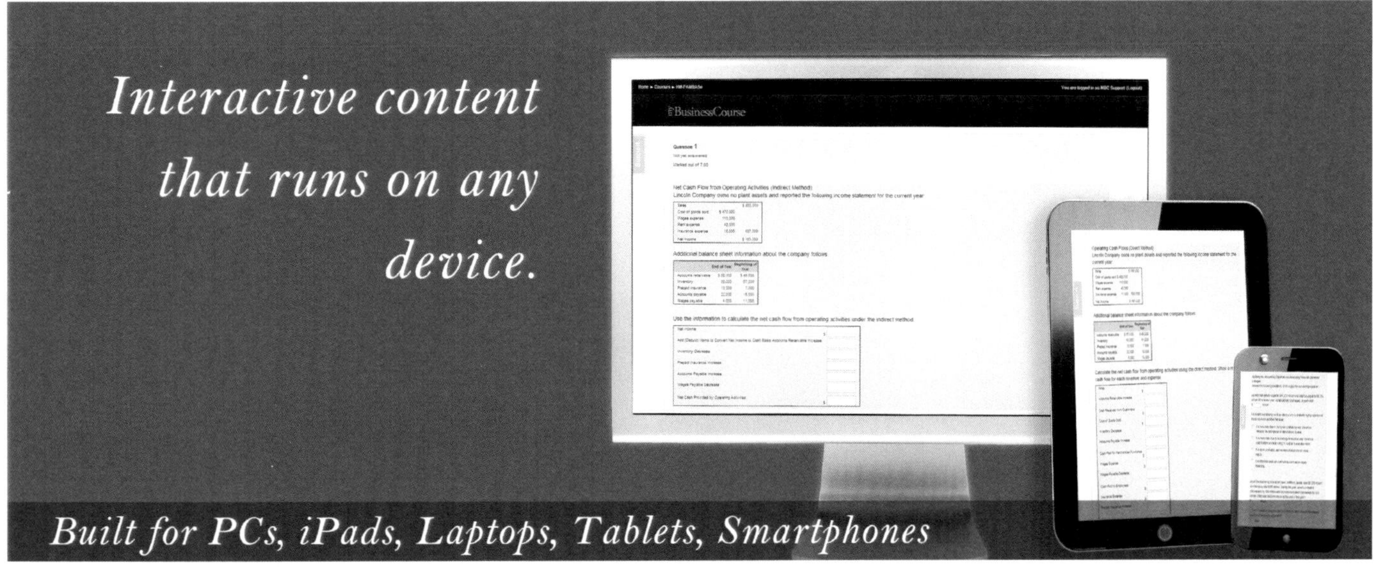

***Each access code is good for one use only.** If the textbook is used for more than one course or term, students will have to purchase additional my BusinessCourse access codes. In addition, students who repeat a course for any reason will have to purchase a new access code. If you purchased a used book and the protective coating that covers the access code has been removed, your code may be invalid.

Access to my BusinessCourse is free ONLY with the purchase of a new textbook.

About the Author

Susan L. Kulp is Professor of Accountancy at the George Washington University School of Business. She received her Ph.D. at Stanford University. Before joining the George Washington University faculty, Professor Kulp was a faculty member at Harvard Business School.

Professor Kulp's research focuses on performance measurement, incentive, and internal decision-making issues in inter-organizational relationships. The settings that she examines include supply chain relationships, private partnerships, and government entities. Her research highlights the conflicts between inter-organizational contracts and the control systems in place within the partnering firms. She has published research studies in both accounting and operations management journals, including the Journal of Accounting Research, The Accounting Review, Management Science, Production and Operations Research, and Review of Accounting Studies. Professor Kulp currently services as a Department Editor at Decision Sciences. In addition to her published research studies, Professor Kulp has published several Harvard Business School cases focused on management control.

Professor Kulp has taught managerial accounting to undergraduate, MBA, online MBA, and executive MBA students. Additionally, she teaches financial accounting to online MBA students. Professor Kulp has won several teaching awards.

Amie L. Dragoo is a Professor of Accounting and Educational Consultant. Former Accounting Department Chair and Associate Professor at Edgewood College, Dr. Dragoo earned her BA and MBA from Michigan State University, and her doctorate from Edgewood College. She holds a CPA license, and for nearly 15 years has been a Becker Professional Education faculty instructor. Prior to her experiences in higher education, she was a senior business assurance associate with PricewaterhouseCoopers LLP (formerly Coopers & Lybrand L.L.P.). Dr. Dragoo has extensive teaching experiences, including courses in Intermediate Accounting I and II, Cost Accounting, Advanced Cost Management, Strategic Financial Management, and other advanced courses in financial and managerial accounting. She has received a number of teaching awards including the School of Business Outstanding Faculty Award and the Estervig-Beaubien Excellence in Teaching and Mentoring Award. She has also worked as an independent consultant, including projects in higher education, and has worked with several corporate clients. Dr. Dragoo's research has been published in the *Journal of Education for Business* and the *Journal of Continuing Higher Education* and she has contributed to numerous articles published by organizations affiliated with the AICPA. She has been involved in many community-oriented programs including the Volunteer Income Tax Assistance (VITA) program.

Al L. Hartgraves is Professor Emeritus of Accounting at the Goizueta Business School at Emory University in Atlanta, Georgia. He has been a Guest Professor at Johannes Kepler University in Linz, Austria and at the Helsinki School of Economics and Business Administration and Aalto University in Finland. He is an honorary faculty member of the LIMAK Austrian Business School. He has also served as Senior Associate Dean, Acting Dean, and Director MBA Programs at Emory. His published scholarly and professional articles have appeared in *The Accounting Review, Accounting Horizons, Management Accounting, Journal of Accountancy, Journal of Accounting and Public Policy,* and many other journals. Students at Goizueta Business School selected him on six occasions to receive the Distinguished Educator Award. He is also the recipient of Emory University's highest teaching award, The Scholar/Teacher Award, and he was recognized as the Accounting Educator of the Year by the Georgia Society of CPAs. He has been recognized as an Outstanding Faculty Member in two editions of *The Business Week Guide to the Best Business Schools*. He is a Certified Public Accountant (inactive) and a Certified Management Accountant, having received the Certificate of Distinguished Performance on the CMA exam. He received his Ph.D. from Georgia State University, and in 2011 was granted an honorary doctorate by Johannes Kepler University.

Wayne J. Morse is Professor Emeritus at the Saunders College of Business at Rochester Institute of Technology. An author or co-author of more than fifty published papers, monographs, and textbooks, he was a founding member of the Management Accounting section of the American Accounting Association. His most notable writings are in the areas of learning curves, human resource accounting, and quality costs. He was a member of the IMA Committee on Research and an AICPA Board of Examiners subcommittee, and he has served on the editorial boards of *Advances in Accounting*, *Trends in Accounting Education*, *Issues in Accounting Education*, and *Management Accounting Research*. A Certified Public Accountant, he received his Ph.D. from Michigan State University. Prior to joining RIT, he was on the faculty of the University of Illinois, Duke University, the University of Tennessee, Clarkson University, and the University of Alabama-Huntsville.

Preface

Welcome to the Ninth Edition of Managerial Accounting. Our book presents managerial accounting in the context of a big-picture, decision oriented, business setting. It integrates traditional coverage with contemporary topics, and does so with an eye toward the general business student because a book is not useful if it is not read. An overriding aim of our book is to engage students to read further and understand the materials presented.

Much has changed in recent years, including the way education is delivered to and consumed by students. Online learning has become mainstream, and today's students expect extensive digital resources that facilitate learning. Similarly, instructors' needs have changed. Faculty are being asked to deliver courses online, which requires extensive digital content creation.

In the ninth edition, we embrace the power of technology in the learning process. This product is not so much a textbook as it is an integrated learning system. Although the print textbook can be used on its own, we created extensive digital resources that integrate with and complement the print book. The emphasis in our approach is to provide students with a review problem for each deliberately selected, key learning objective. In this way, students see the application of concepts through a step-by-step illustration and then have the opportunity to immediately practice similar assignments electronically in myBusinessCourse (MBC), our online homework platform. In addition, MBC contains many instructional videos that were created by one of the authors. The combination of textbook, videos, and online practice comprises an **active learning** system that recognizes and embraces how today's students prefer to learn and provides students with the tools to master managerial accounting.

Audience and Approach

Our book is written for all students—not just accounting students. We place managerial accounting in a broad business context, relating it to other business areas. Like the trunk of a tree, our book serves as a strong base for students' future knowledge growth and as a means of unifying the branches of business management.

Managerial accounting focuses on using financial and nonfinancial information by managers and associates of a firm to make strategic, organizational, and operational decisions. Our book provides a framework for identifying and analyzing decision alternatives and for evaluating success or failure in accomplishing such organizational goals. Although accountants are important in the managerial accounting process, managerial accounting is more about managerial tools than processes. In our era of global competition, continuous improvement, process reengineering, and employee empowerment, the tools of managerial accounting are used by decision makers at all levels, rather than just by "managers."

> *"An excellent presentation of difficult material for today's student. Excellent, well-written text aimed at the appropriate student level. Best limited use of journal entries of any other text."*
> **Theresa Tiggeman**
> University of the Incarnate Word

We emphasize the use of managerial accounting information for decision making within the context of organizational strategy. The organization and content of our book reflect our belief that students who understand the big picture are better learners, are better decision makers, and are better able to apply what they learn.

Ethics

Managerial ethics receives extensive coverage in this edition. For example, ethics is introduced in the context of measurement and management in Chapter 1 and discussed further in Chapters 4 and 9. "Business Insight" features and numerous end-of-chapter problems and cases in Chapters 1, 3, 8, 9, 10, and 11 include a variety of decision situations involving ethical dilemmas.

Technology that Improves Learning and Complements Instruction

95% of students who used MBC, responded that MBC helped them learn accounting.*

myBusinessCourse is an online learning and assessment program intended to complement your textbook and faculty instruction. Access to **myBusinessCourse** is FREE ONLY with the purchase of a new textbook, but access can be purchased separately.

MBC is ideal for faculty seeking opportunities to augment their course with an online component. MBC is also a turnkey solution for online courses. The following are some of the features of MBC.

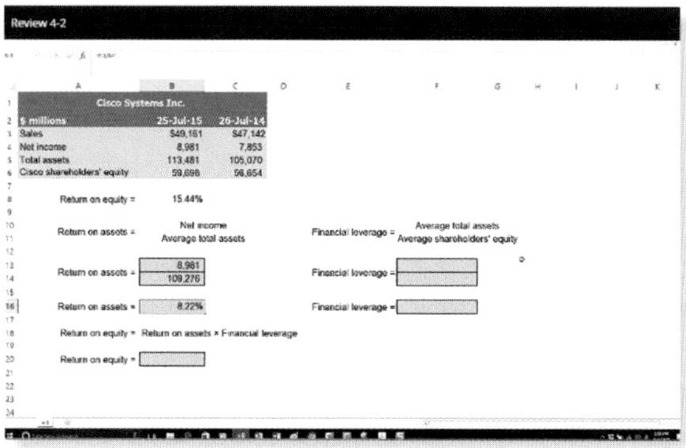

Increase Student Readiness

- **eLectures** cover each chapter's learning objectives and concepts. Consistent with the text and created by the authors, these videos are ideal for remediation and online instruction.
- **Reviews** are narrated video demonstrations created by the authors that show students how to solve the Review problems from the textbook.
- Immediate feedback is provided with **auto-graded homework**.
- **Test Bank** questions that can be incorporated into your assignments.
- Instructor **gradebook** with immediate grade results.

Make Instruction Needs-Based

- Identify where your students are struggling and customize your instruction to address their needs.
- Gauge how your entire class or individual students are performing by viewing the easy-to-use gradebook.
- Ensure your students are getting the additional reinforcement and direction they need between class meetings.

86% of students said they would encourage their professor to continue using MBC in future terms.*

Provide Instruction and Practice 24/7

- Assign homework from your Cambridge Business Publishers' textbook and have MBC grade it for you automatically.
- With our Videos, your students can revisit accounting topics as often as they like or until they master the topic.
- Make homework due before class to ensure students enter your classroom prepared.
- For an additional fee, upgrade MBC to include the eBook and you have all the tools needed for an online course.

The e-Lectures and Guided Examples are great learning tools and are much better than other publishers.
Ray Shaffer
Youngstown State University

Safeguard the Integrity of Online Exams

- myBusinessCourse comes with Respondus LockDown Browser®.
- LockDown Browser® protects the integrity of online testing and gives faculty confidence with their assessments.
- LockDown Browser® deters digital cheating.
- LockDown Browser® comes standard with myBusinessCourse at **no additional cost**.

Integrate with LMS

myBusinessCourse integrates with many learning management systems, including **Canvas**, **Blackboard**, **Moodle**, **Brightspace** (formerly D2L), **Schoology**, and **Sakai**. Your gradebooks sync automatically.

[1] These statistics are based on the results of two surveys in which 2,330 students participated.

Unique Pedagogy

Managerial Accounting includes several special features specifically designed to engage students and help them succeed in this course.

Road Maps

Each chapter opens with a grid that identifies each learning objective for the chapter, the related pages, eLecture and Guided Example videos, and end-of-chapter assignments. This allows students and faculty to quickly grasp the chapter contents and to efficiently navigate to the desired topic.

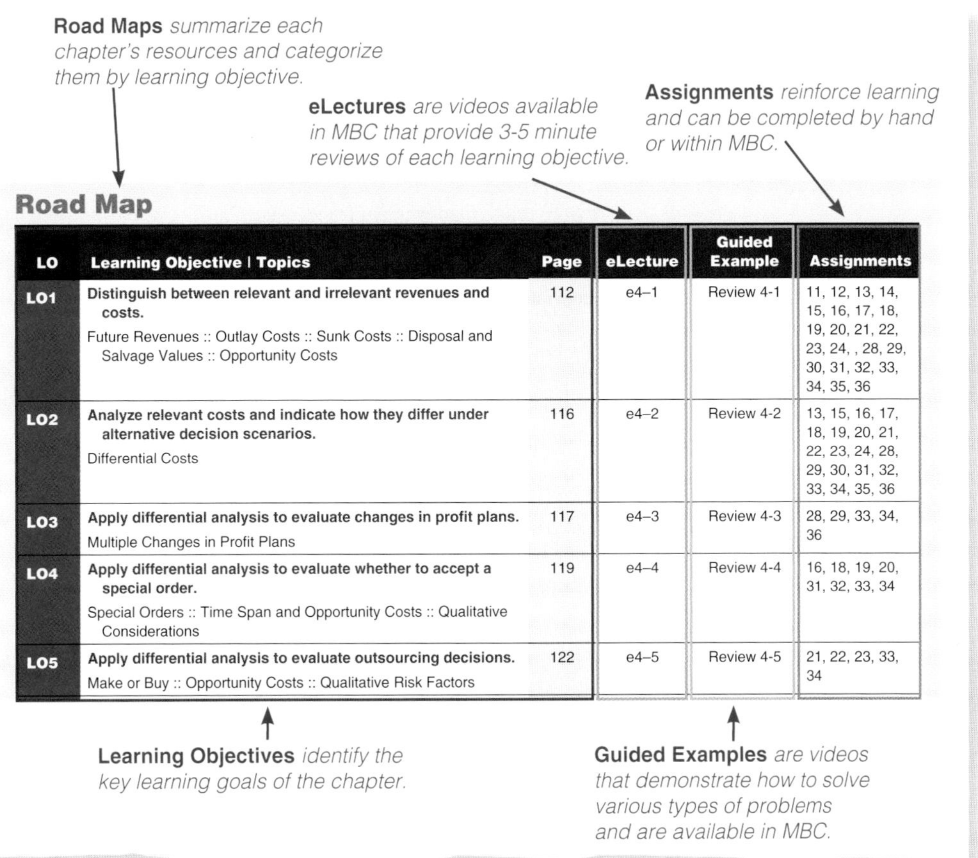
Road Maps *summarize each chapter's resources and categorize them by learning objective.*
eLectures *are videos available in MBC that provide 3-5 minute reviews of each learning objective.*
Assignments *reinforce learning and can be completed by hand or within MBC.*
Learning Objectives *identify the key learning goals of the chapter.*
Guided Examples *are videos that demonstrate how to solve various types of problems and are available in MBC.*

Road Map

LO	Learning Objective I Topics	Page	eLecture	Guided Example	Assignments
LO1	**Distinguish between relevant and irrelevant revenues and costs.** Future Revenues :: Outlay Costs :: Sunk Costs :: Disposal and Salvage Values :: Opportunity Costs	112	e4–1	Review 4-1	11, 12, 13, 14, 15, 16, 17, 18, 19, 20, 21, 22, 23, 24, , 28, 29, 30, 31, 32, 33, 34, 35, 36
LO2	**Analyze relevant costs and indicate how they differ under alternative decision scenarios.** Differential Costs	116	e4–2	Review 4-2	13, 15, 16, 17, 18, 19, 20, 21, 22, 23, 24, 28, 29, 30, 31, 32, 33, 34, 35, 36
LO3	**Apply differential analysis to evaluate changes in profit plans.** Multiple Changes in Profit Plans	117	e4–3	Review 4-3	28, 29, 33, 34, 36
LO4	**Apply differential analysis to evaluate whether to accept a special order.** Special Orders :: Time Span and Opportunity Costs :: Qualitative Considerations	119	e4–4	Review 4-4	16, 18, 19, 20, 31, 32, 33, 34
LO5	**Apply differential analysis to evaluate outsourcing decisions.** Make or Buy :: Opportunity Costs :: Qualitative Risk Factors	122	e4–5	Review 4-5	21, 22, 23, 33, 34

Decision Making Orientation

One primary goal of a managerial accounting course is to teach students the skills needed to apply their accounting knowledge to solve real business problems and make informed business decisions. With that goal in mind, Managerial Decision boxes in each chapter encourage students to apply the material presented to solving actual business scenarios. The following is a representative example:

Managerial Decision ■ You Are the Vice President of Manufacturing

You recently made the decision to purchase a very expensive machine for your manufacturing plant that used technology that was well established over several years. The purchase of this machine was a major decision supported by the chief financial officer, based solely on your recommendation. Shortly after making the purchase, you were attending a trade convention where you learned of new technology that is now available that essentially renders obsolete the machine you recently purchased. You feel that it may be best for the company to acquire the new technology since most of your competitors will be using it soon; however, you feel that this cannot be done now that you have recently purchased the new machine. What should you consider in making this decision? [Answer, p. 131]

"Well-organized, relevant examples."
Cathy Zishang Liu
University of Houston—Downtown

Business Insights

Students appreciate and become more engaged when they can see the relevance of what they are learning in the classroom. We have revised and added new Business Insight boxes throughout each chapter to bring the accounting to life for students through current, real-world examples. The following is a representative example:

Business Insight ■ Using CVP for Financial Analysis and Prediction

Microsoft Corporation is a technology company that develops and supports software, services, devices, and solutions. We can use historical data to predict future costs through the cost-volume-profit method. We used data from the condensed 2018 and 2017 income statements (in millions) to predict 2019 costs:

	For the Year Ending	
	June 30, 2018	**June 30, 2017**
Sales	$110,360	$ 96,571
Cost of sales and operating expenses	(75,302)	(67,546)
Operating profit	$ 35,058	$ 29,025

We can use the high-low method to understand Microsoft's cost-volume-profit relationships and forecast profits based on expected sales. The first step is to calculate variable costs as a percentage of sales:

$$\textbf{Variable cost ratio} = \frac{\$75{,}302 - \$67{,}546}{\$110{,}360 - \$96{,}571} = 0.5625$$

Next, use this ratio to estimate Microsoft's fixed costs by subtracting variable costs from total costs for either period. Based on 2018 revenues and variable costs, we can calculate fixed costs as:

Annual fixed costs = $75,302 – ($110,360 × 0.5625) = $13,225 million

Our estimate of Microsoft's cost function is:

Total annual costs = $13,225 million + (0.5625 × Sales)

Microsoft's break-even sales can be calculated using fixed cost and contribution margin (1 minus the variable cost ratio).

Break-even point = $13,225 million/(1 – 0.5625) = $30,229 million

In 2019 sales were $125,843 million and operating income was $42,959 million. Based on the CVP relationships developed above and 2019 sales, the predicted level of operating income is:

Predicted operating income = $125,843 – [($125,843 × 0.5625) + $13,225] = $41,831

The difference between the estimated operating income and actual results suggests that Microsoft's cost structure has changed slightly over the past three years.

Data Analytics

This edition includes a new appendix (Appendix B) that introduces students to data analytics and the tools that are used. Assignments require students to use Tableau and Excel to perform managerial accounting analysis. Versions of both tools, along with tutorials, are currently available online for free for student use. We also provide numerous videos on this book's website to support the use of these data analytics tools.

LO3, 4 **PB-14. Segment Reports Using Tableau (Descriptive and Diagnostic Analytics)**

Southern Comforts, Inc. is a department store chain with stores in North Carolina, Tennessee, Kentucky, and West Virginia. Its corporate headquarters are located in Charlotte, North Carolina.

In the past, the store owners only received financial reports for the company operations overall. They have recently asked for reports of costs and profitability by segment (Location and department). Southern Comforts' locations include the four stores (Charlotte, Nashville, Virginia Beach, and Louisville) and the corporate office (Charlotte HQ). Departments include the product lines (Mens, Womens, Kids, Shoes, and Home) and the overhead expense types (Facilities, Labor, and Other).

Research Insights

Academic research plays an important role in the way business is conducted, accounting is performed, and students are taught. It is important for students to recognize how modern research and modern business practice interact. Therefore, we periodically incorporate relevant research to help students understand the important relation between research and modern business. The following is a representative example:

Research Insight ■ Why Don't Managers Always Ignore Sunk Costs?

For decades, business school students have learned that sunk costs are irrelevant to decision making; however, managers still find these costs difficult to ignore. Researchers have shown that, far from ignoring sunk costs, many managers increase commitment to a project as sunk costs increase. Recent experimental research from a team at the University of Melbourne in Australia sheds more light on the precise motivations of managers who choose not to ignore sunk costs. The researchers found that the managers' personal motivations interact with the context of the specific project and the related sunk costs. Their study found that individuals who are focused on promotion become increasingly fixated on completion as the end of the project nears. While other managers are able to ignore fixed costs more consistently throughout the project life cycle, those who are focused on promotion are most likely to continue to invest in a project that should be abandoned when the project is close to completion. As managerial accountants advise executive teams, this type of bias should be kept in mind.

Source: Adam P. Barsky and Michael J. Zyphur, "Disentangling Sunk-Costs and Completion Proximity: The Role of Regulatory Focus," *Journal of Experimental Social Psychology* 65 (2016): 105-108.

Reviews

Managerial accounting can be challenging—especially for students lacking business experience or previous exposure to business courses. To reinforce concepts presented in each chapter and to ensure student comprehension, we include in-chapter reviews for each Learning Objective that require students to recall and apply the managerial accounting techniques and concepts just described. The following is a representative example:

Review 3-4 LO4 **Analyzing Profitability of a Multi-Product Firm**

Suppose the Coffee Bean has a new shop in a Cambridge village shopping center that sells high-end teas and coffees. Further, suppose it has added smoothie drinks to its product line. Below are the assumed sales and cost data for the company:

	Coffee	Tea	Smoothie
Sales price per (12 oz.) serving	$1.35	$1.25	$1.95
Variable cost per serving	0.60	0.45	0.75
Fixed costs per month $8,000			

Suppose the company sells each month an average of 6,000 servings of coffee, 3,750 servings of tea, and 2,250 servings of smoothies.

Required

a. Calculate the current before-tax profit, contribution margin ratio, and sales mix based on sales dollars.

b. Using a sales dollar analysis, calculate the monthly break-even point assuming the sales mix does not change.

Solution on p. 108.

Excellent Assignments

Excellent assignment material is a must-have component of any successful textbook (and class). We went to great lengths to create the best assignments possible. We tried to include assignments that reflect our belief that students should be trained in analyzing accounting information to make business decisions, as opposed to working on mechanical computations. Assignments encourage students to analyze accounting information, interpret it, and apply the knowledge gained to a business decision. There are five categories of assignments: **Questions**, **Mini Exercises**, **Exercises**, **Problems**, and **Cases and Projects**. The following is a representative example:

LO2 **P7-32. Budgeted Service Department Cost Allocation: Pricing a New Product**

Fit & Active Company is adding a new diet food concentrate called Body Fit & Healthy to its line of bodybuilding and exercise products. A plant is being built for manufacturing the new product. Management has decided to price the new product based on a 100% markup on total manufacturing costs. A direct cost budget for the new plant projects that direct department costs of $7,152,500 will be incurred in producing an expected normal output of 750,000 pounds of finished product. In addition, indirect costs for Administration and Technical Support will be shared by Body Fit & Healthy with the two exercise products divisions, Commercial Products and Retail Products. Budgeted annual data to be used in making the allocations are summarized here.

	Administration	Technical Support	Commercial Products	Retail Products	Body Fit & Healthy
Number of employees	10	4	70	60	20
Amount of technical support time (hours)	690	—	1,840	1,610	460

Direct costs are budgeted at $750,000 for the Administration Department and $500,000 for the Technical Support Department.

Changes To The 9th Edition

Many significant changes have been made in the 9th edition, including:

- Susan Kulp and Amie Dragoo have assumed authorship responsibility on the ninth edition. Al Hartgraves and Wayne Morse retired from academia and have decided to focus on other pursuits.
- Data Analytics: A new appendix (Appendix B) introduces students to data analytics and the tools that are used.
- Road Map: Each chapter opens with a grid that identifies each learning objective for the chapter, the related pages, eLecture and Guided Example videos, and end-of-chapter assignments. This allows students and faculty to quickly grasp the chapter contents and to efficiently navigate to the desired topic.
- Contemporary Topics and Examples: The authors have revised and added new Business Insight boxes throughout each chapter to bring the accounting to life for students using current, real-world examples.
- Several new Research Insight boxes have been incorporated throughout the text to emphasize the important relationship between research and modern business.
- Real Company Examples: Dozens of new, real company examples have been integrated throughout the text.
- Revised Assignments: Nearly two-thirds of the assignments in each chapter have been revised and updated.
- myBusinessCourse (MBC) is a complete learning and assessment program that accompanies the textbook and contributes to student success in this course. MBC has been expanded to include more assignments and resources.
- In addition, the Guided Examples and eLectures have been completely revised and new supporting videos have been created by the new authors.

Supplemental Materials

"The material is rich and thorough. The supports and supplements are helpful and useful for both you and your students."
Suzanne Kiess
Jackson College

Our book is part of a comprehensive and carefully prepared teaching package that includes various forms of assistance to both instructors and students.

For Instructors

- **myBusinessCourse:** A web-based learning and assessment program intended to complement your textbook and classroom instruction. This easy-to-use course management system grades homework automatically and provides students with additional help when you are not available. In addition, detailed diagnostic tools assess class and individual performance. myBusinessCourse is ideal for online courses or traditional face-to-face courses for which you want to offer students more resources to succeed. Assignments with the MBC in the margin are available in myBusinessCourse. eLecure videos are available for the chapter Learning Objectives, and the Guided Examples for the in-chapter Reviews are available for you to assign students.

- **Solutions Manual:** Prepared by the authors; contains detailed solutions to all assignments.
- **PowerPoint:** Prepared by the authors; instructional PowerPoint slides for each chapter enhance the classroom presentation of book materials.
- **Test Bank:** Prepared by the authors; a collection of multiple-choice questions, exercises, and problems designed to save time in preparing and grading periodic and final exams.
- **Website:** All instructor materials are accessible via the book's website (password protected) along with other useful links and marketing information. **www.cambridgepub.com**

For Students

- ***eLectures:*** Each of the chapters' Learning Objectives includes an eLecture video available in our online learning management system, myBusinessCourse (see below for more information).
- ***Guided Examples:*** Guided Example videos are available for each in-chapter Review, also in MyBusiness-Course (see below for more information).
- myBusinessCourse: A web-based learning and assessment program intended to complement your textbook and faculty instruction. This easy-to-use program provides you with additional help when your instructor is not available. Guided Example videos are available for all in-chapter Reviews, and eLecture videos are available for each Learning Objective. With Instructor-Led MBC courses, assignments with the in the margin are also available in myBusinessCourse and are automatically graded. Access is free with new copies of this textbook (look for page containing the access code towards the front of the book). If you buy a used copy of the book, you can purchase access at **www.mybusinesscourse.com**.

- **Website:** Useful links, including updates, are available to students free of charge on the book's website.

Acknowledgments

We are indebted to the following instructors who provided us with revision suggestions for this and prior editions of our book:

Helen Adams, *University of Washington*
Akinloye Akindayomi, *The University of Texas —Rio Grande Valley*
William David Albrecht, *Bowling Green State University*
Frank Beil, *University of Minnesota*
James L. Bierstaker, *Villanova University*
Susan Borkowski, *LaSalle University*
A. Faye Borthick, *Georgia State University*
Gary Bridges, *University of Texas—San Antonio*
Stephen Brown, *University of Maryland*
Gene Bryson, *University of Alabama—Hunstville*
Brian Cadman, *The University of Utah*
Kathryn Chang, *Sonoma State University*
Tom Clausen, *University of Illinois—Springfield*
Douglas Clinton, *Northern Illinois University*
Gary Colbert, *University of Colorado—Denver*
David Cooper, *Baker University*
Michael Dambra, *University at Buffalo*
Vicki Dickinson, *University of Mississippi*
Trish Driskill, *University of the Incarnate Word*
Andrew Felo, *Nova Southeastern University*
Paul M. Fischer, *University of Wisconsin—Milwaukee*
Benjamin P. Foster, *University of Louisville*
Thomas Francl, *National University*
David P. Franz, *San Francisco State University*
Mark Friedman, *University of Miami*
Peter Frischmann, *Idaho State University*
Margaret Gagne, *Marist College*
Karen Geiger, *Arizona State University*
John Giles, *North Carolina State University*
Sanjay Gupta, *Valdosta State University*
Judith Harris, *Nova Southeastern University*
John Hassell, *Indiana University—Indianapolis*
Eleanor G. Henry, *Southeast Missouri State University*
James W. Hesford, *Cornell University*
Jay S. Holmen, *University of Wisconsin—Eau Claire*
David R. Honodel, *University of Denver*
Ronald Huefner, *SUNY Buffalo*
Eric N. Johnson, *Indiana University—Indianapolis*
Paul Juras, *Wake Forest University*
Anthony Craig Keller, *Missouri State University*
Suzanne Kiess, *Jackson College*
Charles Kile, *Middle Tennessee State University*
Larry N. Killough, *Virginia Tech University*
John Koeplin, *University of San Francisco*
Mark Koscinski, *Moravian College*
William Lathen, *Boise State University*
James Ledwith, *San Diego State University*
Deborah Leitsch, *Goldey-Beacom College*
Elliot Levy, *Bentley College*
Cathy Zishang Liu, *University of Houston—Downtown*
Donna Losell, *University of Toronto*
Linda M. Marquis, *Northern Kentucky University*
Otto B. Martinson, *Old Dominion University*

Katie Matt, *SUNY Polytechnic*
Michael J. Meyer, *University of Notre Dame*
Robin Meyerink, *Black Hills State University*
Donald Minyard, *University of Alabama—Tuscaloosa*
Dale Morse, *University of Oregon*
Ramesh Narasimhan, *Montclair State University*
Jeanie O'Laughlin, *Pepperdine Unversity*
Stephen Owusu-Ansah, *Houston Baptist University*
Larry Paquette, *Francis Marion University*
Matthew Pickard, *University of New Mexico*
Lincoln Pinto, *Concordia University*
Kendell Poch, *University of Minnesota*
Gordon Potter, *Cornell University*
Barbara Reider, *University of Montana*
Maryanne Rouse, *University of South Florida*
Jack Ruhl, *Western Michigan University*
Jane Saly, *University of St. Thomas*
Jeffrey Schatzberg, *University of Arizona*
Lewis Shaw, *Suffolk University*
Arpita Shroff, *University of Houston—Downtown*
Andreas Simon, *Pepperdine University*
Henry Smith, III, *Otterbein College*
Charles Stanley, *Baylor University*
Audrey Taylor, *Western Washington University*
Theresa Tiggeman, *University of the Incarnate Word*
Pierre L. Titard, *Southeastern Louisiana State University*
Pamela Trafford, *University of Massachusetts*
Leslie Turner, *Northern Kentucky University*
Sheila Viel, *University of Wisconsin—Milwaukee*
Gayle Williams
Wallace Wood, *University of Cincinnati*
Kimberly Zahller, *University of Colorado—Colorado Springs*
Elisa Zuliani, *University of Toronto*

Special appreciation is extended to Jim Wallace and Gayle Williams for their significant contributions to the new Data Analytics appendix at the end of the text. We appreciate the tolerance and feedback of our students as we tested many of the new ideas and assignments for this book. Finally, we appreciate the encouragement, support, and detailed suggestions for improvement provided by George Werthman and his colleagues at Cambridge Business Publishers, including Marnee Fieldman, Lorraine Gleeson, Karen Carroll, Jocelyn Mousel, Dana Zieman, Deborah McQuade, and Terry McQuade.

Brief Contents

Contents

CHAPTER 12
Capital Budgeting Decisions

APPENDIX A
Managerial Analysis of Financial Statements

APPENDIX B
Data Analytics

Chapter 1

Managerial Accounting: Tools for Decision Making

Learning Objectives *identify the key learning goals of the chapter.*

Learning Objectives

LO1 Explain the importance of managerial accounting and how it differs from financial accounting. (p. 4)

LO2 Describe the three themes of strategic cost management and illustrate how strategic cost management can be used to create a long-term competitive advantage. (p. 7)

LO3 Examine how managerial accounting supports an organization's mission, goals, and strategies. (p. 8)

LO4 Analyze how trends in the business environment impact the role of management accounting. (p. 13)

LO5 Assess the nature of the ethical dilemmas managers and accountants confront. (p. 15)

LO6 Demonstrate the use of structural, organizational, and activity cost drivers. (p. 19)

A **Focus Company** *introduces each chapter and illustrates the relevance of managerial accounting in everyday business.*

In the last ten years, the percentage of sales made through e-commerce has more than doubled. In the first half of 2019 alone, retailers announced closures of 7,037 brick-and-mortar stores up from 5,864 closures in all of 2018.[1]

So who was the fastest growing retailer in the U.S. in 2018 according to *Business Insider*?[2] Primark, a subsidiary of Associated British Foods, is a European clothing chain that only sells its merchandise in brick-and-mortar stores. You can view Primark products online, but you have to physically go to a store to buy them.

Primark's remarkable growth (up 103% from 2017) is attributed to low retail prices, which average over 200% lower than other retailers in the United States.[3] The company keeps it costs down by buying in bulk and limiting its advertising costs.

Information provided by managerial accounting systems is critical in companies, like Primark, that operate on low gross profit margins. For example, Primark relied on information provided by the company's management accounting system in making the decision not to sell online. An analysis of the shipping and high return costs associated with e-commerce indicated that expanding into that market would simply drive sales prices too high for their customer base.

Primark also uses management accounting information to focus and evaluate its product line. Primark sells a large range of licensed products (Disney, Game of Thrones, Rolling Stones). The company has found that creating themed, in-store departments turns Primark into a "shopping destination," which results in higher revenues. Throughout this book, we will learn how management accounting provides useful information for making informed business decisions, such as the evaluation of product lines and segments.

---

[1] https://coresight.com/research/weekly-us-and-uk-store-openings-and-closures-tracker-2019-week-26-freds-set-to-close-more-stores/

[2] Jessica Tyler, "These Are the Fastest-Growing Retailers in America Right Now," *Business Insider*, 2018.

[3] Mary Hanbury, "An Irish Clothing Chain Is Suddenly the Fastest Growing Retailer in America. Here's What You Need to Know About It," *Business Insider*, 2018.

Chapter Road Maps *visually organize the textbook resources by Learning Objective and can be used as a quick reference guide by students. The resources include readings, videos, and assignments.*

Road Map

LO	Learning Objective | Topics	Page	eLecture	Guided Example	Assignments
LO1	**Explain the importance of managerial accounting and how it differs from financial accounting.** Financial Accounting :: Managerial Accounting :: Institute of Management Accountants	4	e1–1	Review 1-1	12, 13, 14, 21
LO2	**Describe the three themes of strategic cost management and illustrate how strategic cost management can be used to create a long-term competitive advantage.** Strategic Cost Management :: Strategic Position Analysis :: Cost Driver Analysis :: Value Chain Analysis	7	e1–2	Review 1-2	12
LO3	**Examine how managerial accounting supports an organization's mission, goals, and strategies.** Missions and Goals :: Strategic Position Analysis :: Cost Leadership :: Product or Service Differentiation :: Market Niche :: Goal Attainment :: Planning, Organizing and Controlling	8	e1–3	Review 1-3	12, 15, 16, 17, 22, 23, 24, 25, 27, 28, 34
LO4	**Analyze how trends in the business environment impact the role of management accounting.** Global Competition :: Big Data Analysis :: Robotics and Cognitive Technologies :: Enterprise Risk Management	13	e1–4	Review 1-4	18
LO5	**Assess the nature of the ethical dilemmas managers and accountants confront.** Ethical Dilemmas :: Codes of Ethics :: Corporate Governance and SOX :: Sustainability Accounting :: Corporate Social Responsibility	15	e1–5	Review 1-5	12, 29, 30, 31, 32
LO6	**Demonstrate the use of structural, organizational, and activity cost drivers.** Business Activities :: Structural, Organizational, and Activity Cost Drivers	19	e1–6	Review 1-6	12, 19, 20, 26, 33

Chapter Organization Charts visually depict the key topics and their sequence within the chapter.

Managerial Accounting: Tools for Decision Making

Uses of Accounting Information	Organizations: Missions, Goals, and Strategies	Changing Environment of Business	Ethics in Managerial Accounting	Cost Drivers
• Financial Accounting • Managerial Accounting • Strategic Cost Management	• Strategic Position Analysis • Managerial Accounting and Goal Attainment • Planning, Organizing, and Controlling	• Global Competition and Its Key Dimensions • Big Data and Analysis • Enterprise Risk Management (ERM)	• Codes of Ethics • Corporate Governance • Sustainability Accounting and Corporate Social Responsibility	• Structural Cost Drivers • Organizational Cost Drivers • Activity Cost Drivers

Managers of organizations such as Primark are required to make strategic decisions every day in order to remain competitive in the marketplace. These decisions might involve answering questions such as: What is our target market? What products should we offer and at what price? How many employees should we hire? How much should we pay our employees? Which suppliers should we use to fulfill our orders? And, how much money should we invest in capital resources? In order to make these decisions, and to achieve their organizations' goals, managers must have an understanding of, and access to, timely and reliable information.

Managerial accounting is defined as the activities carried out to provide managers and other employees with accounting information and control to assist management in the formulation and implementation of an organization's strategy. We begin our exploration of managerial accounting by discussing the differences between managerial and financial accounting and by investigating how strategy and operations affect the way organizations use managerial accounting information. Next, we explore how the emergence of global competition and changes in technology have increased the need to understand managerial accounting concepts. We also examine the interrelationships among measurement, management, and ethics. Finally, we provide an overview of factors that influence costs in an organization and how these factors have changed in recent years.

Uses of Accounting Information

LO1 Explain the importance of managerial accounting and how it differs from financial accounting.

eLecture *icons identify topics for which there are instructional videos in* **myBusinessCourse** *(MBC). See the Preface for more information on MBC.*

Accounting information attempts to satisfy the needs of a variety of individuals and agencies that make decisions about and for organizations. These decision makers can be classified by their relation to a business as either external users or internal users. **Financial accounting** is designed primarily for decision makers outside of the company, whereas managerial accounting is designed primarily for decision makers within the company.

Financial Accounting

Financial accounting is an information-processing system that generates general-purpose reports of financial operations (income statement and statement of cash flows) and financial position (balance sheet) for an organization. Although financial accounting is used by decision makers inside and outside the firm, financial accounting typically emphasizes external users, such as security investors, analysts, and lenders. Adding to this external orientation are external financial reporting requirements determined by law and generally accepted accounting principles (GAAP).

Financial accounting is also concerned with keeping records of the organization's assets, obligations, and the collection and payment of cash. An organization cannot survive without converting sales into cash, paying for purchases, meeting payroll, and keeping track of its assets.

Managers often use income statements and balance sheets as a starting point in evaluating and planning the firm's overall activities. Managers learn a great deal by performing a comparative analysis of their firm and competing firms. Corporate goals are often stated using financial accounting numbers such as net income, or ratios such as return on investment and earnings per common share. However, internal decision makers often find the information provided in financial statements of limited value in managing day-to-day operating activities. They often complain that financial accounting information is too aggregated, prepared too late, based on irrelevant past costs, constrained by rules, and not action oriented. For example, the costs of all items produced and sold or all services rendered are summarized in a single line in most financial statements, making it impossible to determine the costs of individual products or services. Financial accounting procedures, acceptable for costing inventories as a whole, often produce misleading information when applied to individual products. Even when they are accurately determined, the costs of individual products or services are rarely detailed enough in overall financial statements to provide the information needed for decisions concerning the factors that influence costs. Financial accounting reports, seldom prepared more than once a month, are not timely enough for use in the management of day-to-day activities that cause excess costs. Finally, financial accounting reports, to a great extent, are based on historical costs rather than on current or future costs. Managers are more interested in future costs than in historical costs such as last year's depreciation. While financial accounting information is useful in making some management decisions, its primary emphasis is not on internal decision making.

Managerial Accounting

As emphasized in our Primark example, managers are constantly faced with the need to understand and control costs, make important product decisions, coordinate resources, and guide and motivate employees. Managerial accounting provides an information framework to organize, evaluate, and report proprietary data in light of an organization's goals. This information is directed to managers and other employees within the organization. Managerial accounting reports should be designed to meet the information needs of internal decision makers. Top management may need only summary information prepared once a month for each business unit. An engineer responsible for hourly production scheduling may need continuously updated and detailed information concerning the cost of alternative ways of producing a product.

With the intensity of competition and the shorter life cycles of new products and services, managerial accounting is crucial to an organization's success. All managers must understand the financial implications of their decisions. While accountants are available to assist in obtaining and evaluating relevant information, individual managers are responsible for asking the right questions, requesting information, analyzing it, and ultimately making the final decisions.

Business Insights *offer recent examples from the business news and popular press.*

Business Insight ■ Strategic Thinking Requires a Company to Think Inside the Consumer's Sphere

Selling a used car can be difficult in any country, but prior to 2014 it was even more difficult in Russia where there were very few used car dealers located outside of major cities. CarPrice founders offered consumers a digital alternative when they opened the first Russian online, real-time auction for used cars in June 2014.

With CarPrice, sellers complete an online form and then take their car to a CarPrice location where it is inspected and rated. Once the paperwork is checked, CarPrice conducts a 30-minute online auction reaching over 30,000 dealers. If the seller accepts the winning bid, they immediately receive the agreed-upon payment. If the seller isn't satisfied with the price, they are free to leave with their car. There are no fees to the seller in either case. CarPrice boasts that the entire process can be completed in 1.5–2 hours.

Managerial accounting helps guide companies like CarPrice through the myriad of growth opportunities available to them, while providing information about their costs and profits. In order for this business model to be successful, accurate managerial accounting information must be available in a timely basis in order for the company to be able to offer an acceptable price to consumers that still allows the company to be profitable.

Sources: The Boston Consulting Group, "The 2018 BCG Local Dynamos: Emerging-Market Companies Up Their Game," October 2018; and carprice.ru.

Managerial accounting information exists to serve the needs of management, both in answering questions and contributing to solutions. Hence, it should be developed only if the perceived benefits exceed the costs of development and use. Also, while financial measures are often used in managerial accounting, they are not used to the exclusion of other measures. Money is simply a convenient way of expressing events in a form suitable to summary analysis. When this is not possible or appropriate, nonfinancial measures are used. Time, for example, is often an important element of quality or service. Hence, many performance measures focus on time, for example:

Real Companies *and* **Institutions** *are highlighted in bold, blue font.*

- Internet vendors such as **UPS** and **Amazon.com** track delivery time.
- Fire departments and police departments measure the response time to emergency calls.
- Airlines, such as **Delta Airlines** as well as the Federal Aviation Administration, monitor the number of on-time departures and arrivals.

About IMA® (Institute of Management Accountants)

No external standards (such as requirements of the Securities and Exchange Commission) are imposed on information provided to internal users. However the IMA®—the association of accountants and financial professionals in business—acts as a guide for defining the role and best practices of managerial accounting. Globally, IMA supports the profession through research, the CMA® (Certified Management Accountant) program, continuing education, networking, and advocacy of the highest ethical business practices. In 2019, the IMA updated its Management Accounting Competency Framework. The framework emphasizes the need for management accountants to partner in planning and decision making, to create performance management systems, and to provide expertise in financial reporting and control.[4]

The IMA's CMA program focuses specifically on the competencies required by organizations and CFOs to protect investors and drive business value. The CMA tests professional competency in financial planning and analysis, risk management and internal controls, strategic costing, decision support, performance management, corporate finance, ethics, and more. CMA-certified professionals work within organizations of all sizes, industries, and types, including manufacturing and services, public and private enterprises, not-for-profit organizations, academic institutions, government entities, and multinational corporations. To become certified, a qualified professional must be a member of IMA, pass a two-part exam, stay current through continuing education, and abide by IMA's *Statement of Ethical Professional Practice*. Based on a study cited by the CMA,[5] CMAs have a 55% salary advantage globally. That advantage increases to 70% for CMAs ages 20–29. For more information about IMA, please visit www.imanet.org.

The significant differences between financial and managerial accounting are summarized in **Exhibit 1.1**.

EXHIBIT 1.1 Differences Between Financial and Managerial Accounting

Financial Accounting	Managerial Accounting
Information for internal *and* external users	Information for internal users
General-purpose financial statements	Decision-driven, special-purpose information and reports
Statements are highly aggregated	Information is aggregated or detailed, depending on need
Relatively long reporting periods	Reporting periods are long or short, depending on need
Report on past decisions	Oriented toward current and future decision-making
Must conform to external standards (GAAP)	Not constrained by external standards
Emphasizes objective data	Incorporates relevant objective and subjective data

[4] http://www.imanet.org/career-resources/management-accounting-competencies

[5] Gregory L. Krippel PhD, and Sheila Mitchell CPA, "The CMA Advantage: An Update," *Strategic Finance*, September 2017, pp. 39-45.

Comparison of Financial to Managerial Accounting LO1 **Review 1-1**

The previous discussion has focused on understanding the difference between financial and managerial accounting and the broader context of managerial accounting within a company.

Required

Identify the statements and phrases from the following list as either primarily relevant to (1) managerial accounting or (2) financial accounting.

a. Preparing annual financial statements of a company
b. A company's strategic sales position
c. Calculation of a company's earnings per share of common stock
d. Reports based on generally accepted accounting principles
e. Reports not in conformance with external standards
f. Financial information to inform investor and lender decisions
g. Data analyzed to support a decision on a new product launch
h. Dashboard information updated daily on sales by individual product
i. Company-wide sales for the first quarter of the year
j. Report of customer satisfaction surveys for new products

Solution on p. 1-29.

Strategic Cost Management

LO2 Describe the three themes of strategic cost management and illustrate how strategic cost management can be used to create a long-term competitive advantage.

Most businesses are under constant pressure to reduce costs to remain competitive. A 2019 study by the accounting firm Deloitte reported that intensified competition within peer groups and the need for investment in growth areas were the primary drivers of cost management measures.[6]

During recent years, the rapid introduction of improved and new products and services has shortened the market lives of products and services. Some products, such as personal computers, can be obsolete within two or three years after introduction. At the same time, the increased use of complex automated equipment makes it difficult to change production procedures after production begins. Combining short product life cycles with automated production results in an environment where most costs are determined by decisions made before production begins (decisions concerning product design and production procedures).

In response to these trends, a strategic approach to managerial accounting, referred to as *strategic cost management* has emerged. Strategic cost management is a blending of three themes:

1. **Strategic position analysis**—an examination of an organization's basic way of competing to sell products or services.
2. **Cost driver analysis**—the study of factors that cause or influence costs.
3. **Value chain analysis**—the study of value-producing activities, stretching from basic raw materials to the final consumer of a product or service.[7]

We define **strategic cost management** as making decisions concerning specific cost drivers within the context of an organization's business strategy, internal value chain, and position in a larger value chain stretching from the development and use of resources to final consumers. Strategic position analysis is considered in this chapter as part of an organization's strategy. Cost driver analysis is also introduced in this chapter and examined further in Chapter 2. Value chain analysis is discussed in Chapter 8.

Review Problems *are self-study tools that require the application of the accounting topics covered in each section. To aid learning, solutions are provided at the end of the chapter.*

Management Accounting Information Used for Strategy Purposes LO2 **Review 1-2**

Consider the competitive environment of a manufacturer of a smart watch. Name three types of management accounting information that would help management compete more effectively.

Solution on p. 1-29.

Guided Examples *icons denote the availability of a demonstration video in* **myBusinessCourse** *(MBC) for each Review Problem—see the Preface for more on MBC.*

[6] "Save-to-Transform as a Catalyst for Embracing Digital Disruption," Deloitte's second biennial global cost survey, 2019.

[7] John K. Shank, "Strategic Cost Management: New Wine, or Just New Bottles?" *Journal of Management Accounting Research*, Fall 1989, p. 50.

Missions, Goals, and Strategies

An Organization's Mission and Goals

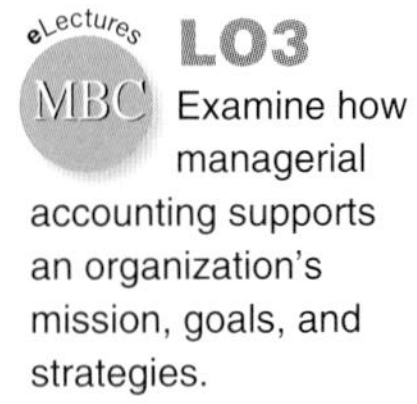

LO3 Examine how managerial accounting supports an organization's mission, goals, and strategies.

Learning Objectives *are highlighted at the start of the section covering that topic.*

An organization's **mission** is the basic purpose toward which its activities are directed. Although there is no published mission statement for Primark, one of the company's slogans, "Amazing Fashions, Amazing Prices," makes it clear that providing customers with inexpensive, trendy clothing is the mission. TED is a nonprofit devoted to spreading ideas, usually in the form of short, powerful talks (18 minutes or less). TED's mission statement is simply two words: "Spread ideas."[8] Organizations vary widely in their missions. One benefit of a mission statement is to help focus all the activities of an organization. For instance, the mission of The Coca-Cola Company is stated as follows on the company's website:

> **Our Purpose:**
> Refresh the world. Make a difference.
>
> **Our Vision:**
> Our vision is to craft the brands and choice of drinks that people love, to refresh them in body & spirit. And done in ways that create a more sustainable business and better shared future that makes a difference in people's lives, communities and our planet.[9]

The Chairman and CEO of Coca-Cola Company indicated that the company has continued to grow since its inception in 1886 with a purpose to refresh the world and make a difference. This applies beyond a physical sense to include a refreshment in spirit which expands to communities and to the environment in which it operates.[10]

Key Terms *are highlighted in bold, red font.*

We frequently distinguish between organizations on the basis of profit motive. **For-profit organizations** have profit as a primary objective, whereas **not-for-profit organizations** do not have profit as a core mission. Clearly, the Coca-Cola Company is a for-profit organization, whereas TED and United Way are not-for-profit organizations. (The term *nonprofit* is frequently used to refer to what we have identified as not-for-profit organizations.) Regardless of whether a profit motive exists, organizations must use resources wisely. Every dollar United Way spends for administrative salaries is a dollar that cannot be used to support charitable activities. Not-for-profit organizations, including governments, can go bankrupt if they are unable to meet their financial obligations. All organizations, for-profit and not-for-profit, should use managerial accounting concepts to ensure that resources are used wisely.

A **goal** is a definable, measurable objective. Based on the organization's mission, management sets a number of goals. For-profit organizations have some measure of profitability or shareholder value as one of their stated or implicit goals. The mission of a paper mill located in a small town is to provide quality paper products in order to earn a profit for its owners. The paper mill's goals might include earning an annual profit equal to 10% of average total assets, maintaining annual dividends of $2 per share of common stock, developing a customer reputation for above-average quality and service, providing steady employment for area residents, and meeting or exceeding environmental standards.

A clear statement of mission and well-defined goals provides an organization with an identity and unifying purpose, thereby ensuring that all employees are heading in the same direction. Having developed a mission and a set of goals, employees are more apt to make decisions that move the organization toward its defined purpose. Managerial accounting information supports decisions to ensure that a company's actions support its missions and goals.

[8] https://www.ted.com/about/our-organization

[9] https://www.coca-colacompany.com/company/purpose-and-vision

[10] https://www.coca-colacompany.com/content/dam/journey/us/en/our-company/purpose-and-vision/james-quincey-letter-to-employees-coca-cola-company-purpose-dec-2019.pdf

A **strategy** is a course of action that will assist in achieving one or more goals. Much of this text will focus on the financial aspects of selecting strategies to achieve goals. For example, if an organization's goal is to improve product quality, possible strategies for achieving this goal include investing in new equipment, implementing additional quality inspections, prescreening suppliers, reducing batch size, redesigning products, training employees, and rearranging the shop floor. Managerial accounting information will assist in determining which of the many alternative strategies for achieving the goal of quality improvement are cost effective. The distinction between mission, goals, and strategies is illustrated in **Exhibit 1.2**.

EXHIBIT 1.2 Mission, Goals, and Strategies

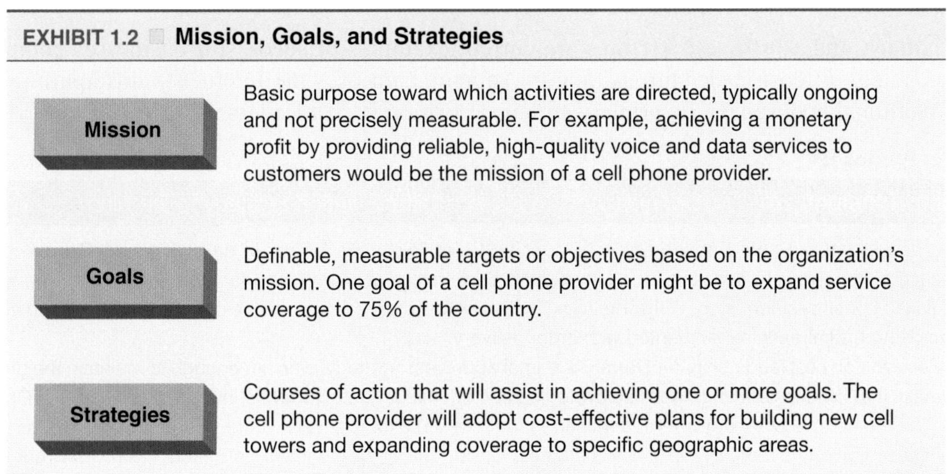

Mission
Basic purpose toward which activities are directed, typically ongoing and not precisely measurable. For example, achieving a monetary profit by providing reliable, high-quality voice and data services to customers would be the mission of a cell phone provider.
Goals
Definable, measurable targets or objectives based on the organization's mission. One goal of a cell phone provider might be to expand service coverage to 75% of the country.
Strategies
Courses of action that will assist in achieving one or more goals. The cell phone provider will adopt cost-effective plans for building new cell towers and expanding coverage to specific geographic areas.

Strategic Position Analysis

In competitive environments, managers must make a fundamental decision concerning their organization's goal for positioning itself in comparison to competitors. This goal is referred to as the organization's **strategic position**. Much of the organization's strategy depends on this strategic positioning goal. Michael Porter, a highly regarded expert on business strategy, has identified three possible strategic positions that lead to business success.[11]

Excerpts *from relevant accounting sources are used to illustrate and reinforce concepts.*

1. Cost leadership
2. Product or service differentiation
3. Market niche

According to Porter, cost leadership

> requires aggressive construction of efficient-scale facilities, vigorous pursuit of cost reductions from experience, tight cost and overhead control, avoidance of marginal customer accounts, and cost minimization in areas like R&D [research and development], service, sales force, advertising, and so on. A great deal of managerial attention to cost control is necessary to achieve these aims. Low cost relative to competitors becomes the theme running through the entire strategy, though quality, service, and other areas cannot be ignored.[12]

Achieving cost leadership allows an organization to achieve higher profits selling at the same price as competitors or by allowing the firm to aggressively compete on the basis of price while remaining profitable. One of the first companies to successfully use a cost leadership strategy was Carnegie Steel Company.

[11] Michael E. Porter, *Competitive Strategy* (New York: The Free Press, 1980), p. 35.

[12] Porter, p. 35.

> Carnegie's operating strategy was to push his own direct costs below his competitors so that he could charge prices that would always ensure enough demand to keep his plants running at full capacity. This strategy prompted him to require frequent information showing his direct costs in relation to those of his competitors. Possessing that information and secure in the knowledge that his costs were the lowest in the industry, Carnegie then mercilessly cut prices during economic recessions. While competing firms went under, he still made profits. In periods of prosperity, when customers' demands exceeded the industry's capacity to produce, Carnegie joined others in raising prices.[13]

Primark and Southwest Airlines are current examples of successful businesses competing with a strategy of cost leadership. Although Amazon.com uses the Internet to differentiate itself from traditional booksellers, its primary strategic position is cost leadership.

Business Insight ■ McDonald's Adds a Service Differentiation Strategy to the Mix

Three weeks before Steve Easterbrook took over as Chief Executive Officer in early 2015, McDonald's announced its worst year in decades. Consumer preferences were changing, and fast-food competitors were responding to consumer demands. Chipotle and Chick-fil-A were attracting new customers with new menu items. Burger King had already experimented with order delivery.

Focusing on cost leadership, McDonald's primary business strategy, was not enough to maintain the growth and profits that its investors and franchise owners expected. In 2017, McDonald's introduced its Velocity Growth Plan. Three growth accelerators were identified in that plan: Digital, Delivery, and Experience of the Future. All three focused on improved service for the customer. McDonald's entered into a partnership with Uber (and later with Door Dash) for delivery services, added mobile app ordering with curbside pickup, and installed touchscreen kiosks in upgraded restaurants for order customization. In 2019, McDonald's acquired two technology companies focused on making drive-through ordering faster and more accurate.

McDonald's adoption of service differentiation as a secondary strategy has proved to be worthwhile. Profit margin ratios increased from 19% in 2016 to 28.2% in 2018.

Sources: Thomas Buckely and Leslie Patton, "McDonald's CEO Wants Big Macs to Keep Up with Big Tech," *Bloomberg Business Week*, September 25, 2019.

Conversely, while an organization might compete primarily on the basis of price, management must take care to ensure their product or service remains attuned to changing customer needs and preferences. In the early twentieth century, General Motors employed a differentiation strategy, focusing on the rapid introduction of technological change in new automobile designs to overcome the market dominance of the Model T produced by Ford Motor Company. While successfully following a cost leadership strategy for years, Ford made the mistake of excluding other considerations such as vehicle performance and customer desires for different colors.

The third possible strategic position, according to Porter, focuses on a specific market niche such as a buyer group, segment of the product line, or geographic market and

> rests on the premise that the firm is thus able to serve its narrow strategic target more effectively or efficiently than competitors who are competing more broadly. As a result, the firm achieves either differentiation from better meeting the needs of the particular target, or lower costs in serving the target, or both. Even though the focus strategy does not achieve low costs or differentiation for the market as a whole, it does achieve one or both of these positions vis-à-vis its narrow market target.[14]

[13] H. Thomas Johnson and Robert S. Kaplan, *Relevance Lost: The Rise and Fall of Management Accounting* (Boston: Harvard Business School Press, 1987), pp. 33–34.

[14] Porter, pp. 38–39.

Business Insight ■ Managerial Accounting Is Key to Creating New Business Models

YY, one of the largest live-streaming companies in the world, has adopted a unique business model in the entertainment market. Instead of generating revenue from advertisers, the Chinese company collects fees from users who are allowed to buy gifts for their favorite performers (amateur singers, dancers, and comedians) and purchase virtual goods for use in online games. Users can also pay a monthly subscription fee, which gives them priority entrance to live-streamed performances and access to other enhanced features. To appeal to younger audiences, the company introduced participant-focused live streaming in 2017, where users can interact directly with the performers.

On average, over 90 million users per month were engaged with YY in the fourth quarter of 2018. Revenues for 2018 exceeded $2.2 billion.

Managerial accounting helps companies like YY understand the cost of delivering their services, and the costs of adapting their business model to access new markets.

Sources: The Boston Consulting Group, "The 2018 BCG Local Dynamos: Emerging-Market Companies Up Their Game," October 2018; and YY Inc. Form 20-F: *Annual Report Pursuant to Section 13 or 15(D) of the Securities Exchange Act of 1934* for the fiscal year ended December 31, 2018.

YY, highlighted in the Business Insight box above, is following a market niche strategy. It identified behaviors of its target market, and using management accounting information, is adapting its model to better fit its market's needs.

Managerial Accounting and Goal Attainment

A major purpose of managerial accounting is to support the achievement of goals. Hence, determining an organization's strategic position goal has implications for the operation of an organization's managerial accounting system.

Careful budgeting and cost control with frequent and detailed performance reports are critical with a goal of cost leadership. When the product is difficult to distinguish from that of competitors', price is the primary basis of competition. Under these circumstances, everyone in the organization should continuously apply managerial accounting concepts to achieve and maintain cost leadership. The managerial accounting system should constantly compare actual costs with budgeted costs and signal the existence of significant differences. A simplified version of a *performance report* for costs during a budget period is as follows:

Budgeted (planned) Costs	Actual Costs	Deviation from Budget	Percent Deviation
$560,000	$595,000	$35,000 unfavorable	6.25%

Frequent and detailed comparisons of actual and budgeted costs are less important when a differentiation strategy is followed. This is especially true when products have short life cycles or production is highly automated. In these situations, most costs are determined before production begins and there is little opportunity to undertake cost reduction activities thereafter.

With short product lives or automated manufacturing, exceptional care must go into the initial design of a product or service and the determination of how it will be produced or delivered. Here, detailed cost information assists in design and scheduling decisions. A simplified version of the predicted costs of producing one batch of a specialty product is as follows:

Engineering and scheduling (12 hours @ $70) . . .	$ 840
Materials (detail omitted)	3,500
Equipment setup (2.5 hours @ $100).	250
Machine operation (9.5 hours @ $90)	855
Materials movement.	150
Packing and shipping	675
Total	$6,270

When a differentiation strategy is followed, it often pays to work closely with customers to find ways to enhance the perceived value of a product or service. This leads to an analysis of costs from the customer's viewpoint. The customer may not want a costly feature. Alternatively, the customer may be willing to pay more for an additional feature that will reduce subsequent operating costs.

Planning, Organizing, and Controlling

The process of selecting goals and strategies to achieve these goals is often referred to as **planning**. The implementation of plans requires the development of subgoals and the assignment of responsibility to achieve subgoals to specific individuals or groups within an organization. This process of making the organization into a well-ordered whole is called **organizing**. In organizing, the authority to take action to implement plans is delegated to other managers and employees.

Developing an **organization chart** illustrating the formal relationships that exist between the elements of an organization is an important part of organizing. An organization chart for Crown Department Stores is illustrated in **Exhibit 1.3**. The blocks represent organizational units, and the lines represent relationships between the units. Authority flows down through the organization. Top management delegates authority to use resources for limited purposes to subordinate managers who, in turn, delegate to their subordinates more limited authority for accomplishing more structured tasks. Responsibility flows up through the organization. People at the bottom are responsible for specific tasks, but the president is responsible for the operation of the entire organization.

A distinction is often made between line and staff departments. *Line departments* engage in activities that create and distribute goods and services to customers. *Staff departments* exist to facilitate the activities of line departments. In **Exhibit 1.3**, we see that Crown Department Stores has two levels of staff organizations—corporate and store. The corporate staff departments are Purchasing, Advertising, Operations, Treasurer, and Controller. Staff departments at the store level are Personnel, Accounting,

EXHIBIT 1.3 Crown Department Stores' Organization Chart

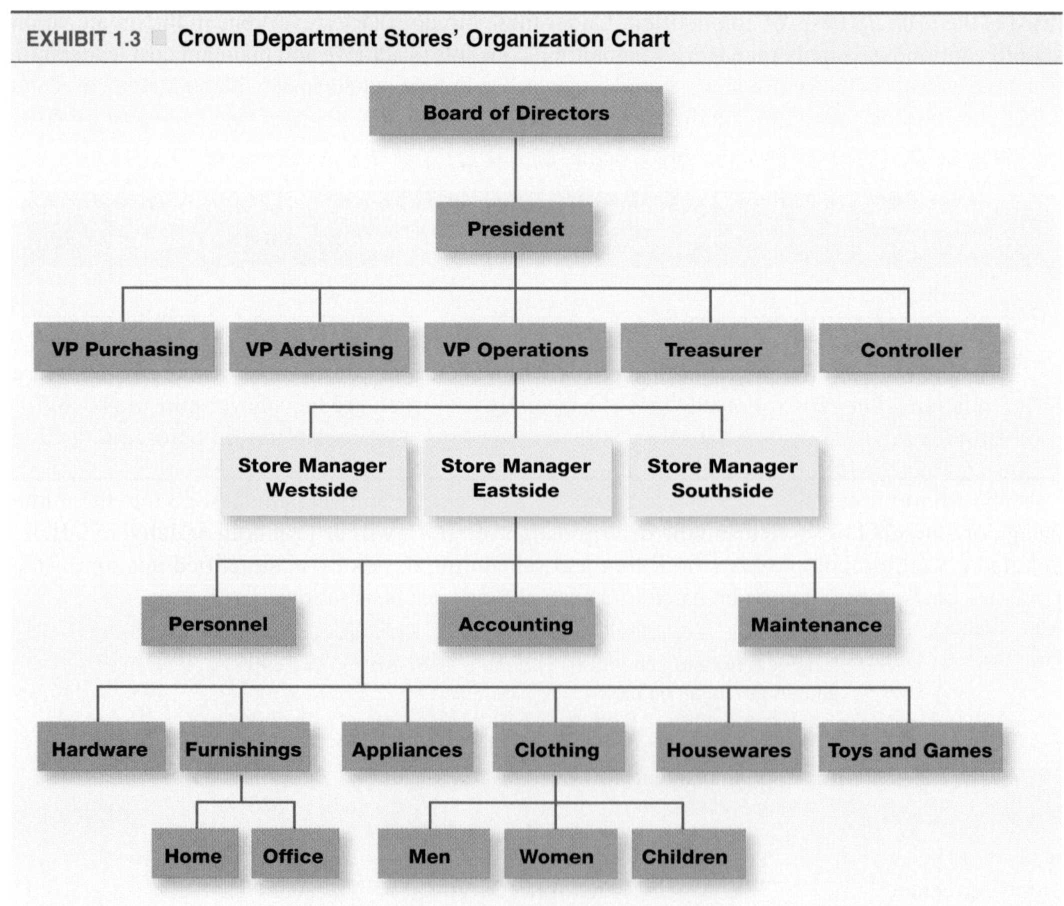

and Maintenance. All other units are line departments. A change in plans can necessitate a change in the organization. For example, Crown's plan to discontinue the sale of hardware and add an art department during the coming year will necessitate an organizational change.

Controlling is the process of ensuring that results agree with plans with no surprises. A brief example of a performance report for costs was presented previously on page 11. In the process of controlling operations, actual performance is compared with plans.

With a cost leadership strategy and long-lived products, if actual results deviate significantly from plans, an attempt is made to bring operations into line with plans, or the plans are adjusted. The original plan is adjusted if it is deemed no longer appropriate because of changed circumstances.

With a differentiation strategy and short-lived products, design and scheduling personnel will consider previous errors in predicting costs as they plan new products and services. Hence, the process of controlling feeds forward into the process of planning to form a continuous cycle coordinated through the management accounting system. This cycle is illustrated in **Exhibit 1.4**.

EXHIBIT 1.4 Planning, Organizing, & Control Cycle

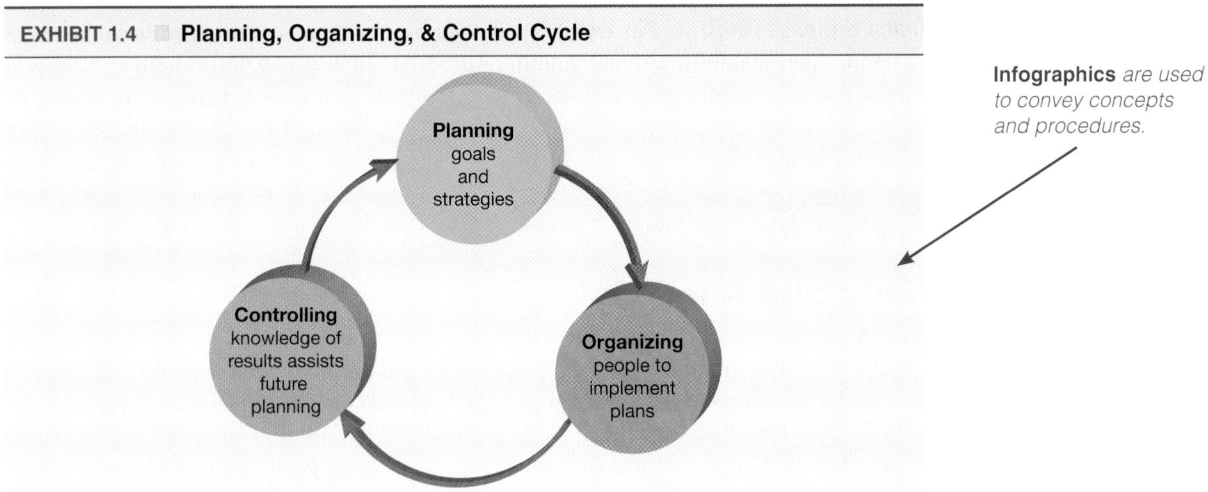

Infographics are used to convey concepts and procedures.

Managerial Accounting Supporting Strategic Position **LO3 Review 1-3**

Starbucks Coffee Company offers a variety of products including hot and cold drinks (coffees, teas, other) and limited food items including bakery, lunch, and snack items. The company's website indicates its mission is "to inspire and nurture the human spirit – one person, one cup, and one neighborhood at a time."[15] Based on your own experience at a Starbucks location and/or through research online, answer the following questions.

1. Which strategic position does Starbucks Coffee Company primarily follow: (a) cost leadership, (b) product or service differentiation, or (c) market niche?
2. Name three ways that managerial accountants can help support the goals of the position you identified in part (1).

Solution on p. 1-30.

Changing Environment of Business

eLectures MBC **LO4** Analyze how trends in the business environment impact the role of management accounting.

The changing environment of business includes trends such as the global economic system, big data and predictive analytics, robotics and cognitive technologies, and enterprise risk management (ERM). Additional items such as lean manufacturing and just-in-time inventory will be discussed later in Chapter 7.

Global Competition and Its Key Dimensions

The move away from isolated national economic systems toward an interdependent global economic system has become increasingly pronounced. International treaties, such as the North American Free Trade Agreement and the General Agreement on Tariffs and Trade, merely recognize an already

[15] https://www.starbucks.com/about-us/company-information

existing and inevitable condition made possible by advances in telecommunications (to move data), computers (to process data into information), and transportation (to move products and people).

The labels of origins on goods (Japan, Germany, Canada, Taiwan, China, and so forth) only scratch the surface of existing global relationships. Behind labels designating a product's final assembly point are components from all over the world.

The move toward a global economy has heightened competition and reduced selling prices to such an extent that there is little or no room for error in managing costs or pricing products. Moreover, customers are not just looking for the best price. Well-informed buyers routinely search the world for the product or service that best fits their needs on the three interrelated dimensions of price/cost, quality, and service; hence, these are the three key dimensions of competition.

To customers, *price/cost* includes not only the initial purchase price but also subsequent operating and maintenance costs. To compete on the basis of price, the seller must carefully manage costs. Otherwise, reduced prices might squeeze product margins to such an extent that a sale becomes unprofitable. Hence, price competition implies cost competition.

Quality refers to the degree to which products or services meet the customer's needs. *Service* includes things such as timely delivery, helpfulness of sales personnel, and subsequent support.

Managers of successful companies know they compete in a global market with instant communications. Because the competition is hungry and always striving to gain a competitive advantage, world-class companies must continuously struggle to improve performance on these three interrelated dimensions: price/cost, quality, and service. Throughout this text, we examine how firms successfully compete on these three dimensions.

Big Data and Analysis

Given recent advancements in technology, there is a vast amount of data available to organizations. However, it can be difficult to turn this data into useful and predictive information. Big data is unique in that it is so large or complex, traditional analysis methods are often inadequate. In 2016, IMA and Robert Half worked together to publish a report, *Building a Team to Capitalize in Big Data*. Based on their research, there is a shortage of finance and accounting professionals who have the skills to effectively analyze **big data**. "Finance leaders face significant shortages of accounting and finance professionals who possess the technical and nontechnical skills required for data analytics initiatives." Organizations are in need of employees who have the abilities to: identify key data trends, perform data mining and extraction, conduct operational and decision analysis, recommend process improvement, and conduct strategic thinking and execution.

Robotics and Cognitive Technologies

Robotic process automation (RPA) "is an application of technology, governed by business logic and structured inputs, aimed at automating business processes."[16] More than 420,000 robots, generating $16.5 billion in revenue worldwide, were installed in 2018.[17]

Artificial intelligence (AI) can be defined as technologies that "perform tasks that previously required human intelligence, such as extracting meaning from images, text or speech, detecting patterns and anomalies, and making recommendations, predictions, or decisions."[18]

Cognitive technologies (or intelligent automation) combine RPA with AI. Examples include machine learning applications that use algorithms to predict what a particular customer is likely to buy and natural language processing chatbots that provide customer support. A specific use in accounting might involve using machine learning applications to predict, based on past performance and current cash flows, when a loan covenant might be breached.[19]

In May 2019, Deloitte surveyed over 500 executives in 26 different countries. Fifty-eight percent of the executives reported that they had either already incorporated or were in the process of

[16] Clint Boulton, "What Is RPA? A Revolution in Business Process Automation," *CIO*, September 2018, https://www.cio.com/article/3236451/what-is-rpa-robotic-process-automation-explained.html

[17] Alexandre Tanzi, "Annual Investments in Robotics Rose to World Record $16.5 Billion," *Bloomberg*, September 2019.

[18] Deloitte Insights, "Automation with Intelligence: Reimagining the Organization in the 'Age of With,'" 2019.

[19] Katie Canell, "Accountancy and Technology: The Journey to Cognitive Intelligence," *AccountancyAge*, October 18, 2018.

incorporating cognitive technologies into their business operations. Increased productivity and cost reduction, greater accuracy, and an improved customer experience were seen as the greatest benefits of the new technologies. Those organizations that had successfully incorporated cognitive technologies reported a 27% reduction in costs with an average payback of nine months.

Incorporating new technologies doesn't come without challenges. Accountants will need to develop new skills to meet those challenges.

Enterprise Risk Management (ERM)

Organizations are constantly faced with uncertainty from the environment, competitors, and other factors that could result in significant risk or loss. The Committee of Sponsoring Organizations (COSO) defines **enterprise risk management (ERM)** as "the culture, capabilities and practices, integrated with strategy-setting and performance, that organizations rely on to manage risk in creating, preserving, and realizing value."[20] By better understanding the types and potential costs of these risks, management accountants can help their organizations devise strategies to better predict and minimize their exposures to risk. In Chapter 9 we will discuss how an organization's budgeting model is used to evaluate the financial impact of a risk and to determine, from a financial perspective, the best response to risk.

Big Data Analysis and Enterprise Risk Management LO4 **Review 1-4**

Big data analysis and ERM are of growing interest to leaders of organizations. Discuss briefly how the influence of each might affect the role of management accountants.

Solution on p. 1-30.

Ethics in Managerial Accounting

eLectures MBC **LO5** Assess the nature of the ethical dilemmas managers and accountants confront.

Ethics deals with the moral quality, fitness, or propriety of a course of action that can injure or benefit people. Ethics goes beyond legality, which refers to what is permitted under the law, to consider the moral quality of an action. Because situations involving ethics are not guided by well-defined rules, they are often subjective.

Although some actions are clearly ethical (working a full day in exchange for a full day's pay) and others are clearly unethical (pumping contaminants into an underground aquifer used as a source of drinking water), managers are often faced with situations that do not fall clearly into either category such as the following:

- Accelerating or decelerating shipments at the end of the quarter to meet current earnings forecasts.
- Keeping inventory that is unlikely to be used so as to avoid recording a loss.
- Purchasing supplies from a relative or friend rather than seeking bids.
- Basing a budget on an overly optimistic sales forecast.
- Assigning some costs of Contract A to Contract B to avoid an unfavorable performance report on Contract A.

Many ethical dilemmas involve actions that are perceived to have desirable short-run consequences and highly probable undesirable long-run consequences. The ethical action is to face an undesirable situation now to avoid a worse situation later, yet the decision maker prefers to believe that things will work out in the long run, is not overly concerned with the consequences of not doing well in

[20] *Enterprise Risk Management—Integrating with Strategy and Performance*, Committee of Sponsoring Organizations of the Treadway Commission, June 2017.

the short run, or simply does not care about the future because the problem will then belong to someone else. In a situation that is clearly unethical, the future consequences are known to be avoidable and undesirable. In situations involving questionable ethics, there is some hope that things will work out:

- Next year's sales will more than make up for the accelerated shipments.
- The obsolete inventory can be used in a new nostalgia line of products.
- The relative or friend may charge more but provides excellent service.
- Sales staff will be motivated by corporate optimism.
- Employees will make up for the cost shift by working extra hard and more efficiently with the remaining work on Contract B.

When forced to think about the situation, most employees want to act in an ethical manner. The problem faced by personnel involved in measurement and reporting is that while they may question the propriety of a proposed action, and the arguments may be plausible, they want to be team players, and their careers can be affected by "whistle-blowing." Of course, careers are also affected when individuals are identified as being involved in unethical behavior.

Major ethical dilemmas often evolve from a series of small compromises, none of which appears serious enough to warrant taking a stand on ethical grounds. WorldCom is such a case, in which managers deferred expenses inappropriately over several periods to meet profit forecasts, expecting to recognize them at a later time when sales improved. Unfortunately, these small compromises establish a pattern of behavior that is increasingly difficult to reverse. The key to avoiding these situations is recognizing the early warning signs of situations that involve questionable ethical behavior and taking whatever action is appropriate.

Codes of Ethics

Codes of ethics are often developed by professional organizations to increase members' awareness of the importance of ethical behavior and to provide a reference point for resisting pressures to engage in actions of questionable ethics. These professional organizations include the American Bar Association, the American Institute of Certified Public Accountants, the American Medical Association, and the Institute of Management Accountants (IMA).

Many corporations have established codes of ethics. Hershey's has a 31-page published document "In Good Company," which lists and explains Hershey's code of conduct. One of the important goals of corporate codes of ethics is to provide employees with a common foundation for addressing

Business Insight ■ Violations of Ethical Standards for Management Accountants at Toshiba

Toshiba is a 140-year-old company that started making telegraph equipment in 1875 and has since expanded into a diverse line of products. In 2015, Toshiba had over 200,000 employees worldwide and ranked as 356 in the list of the world's largest public companies.

At the end of 2015, Japanese regulators fined Toshiba Corporation with a record fine of ¥7.37 billion ($60 million). This fine was in response to accounting violations between 2008 and 2014 that inflated profits by $1.2 billion to meet unrealistic profit targets. Toshiba's accountants, under pressure from executives, delayed the recognition of losses.

The Institute of Management Accountants (IMA) has developed four standards of ethical conduct for management accountants and financial managers.

1. Competence: Perform their professional duties in accordance with relevant laws, regulations, and technical standards.
2. Confidentiality: Refrain from disclosing confidential information acquired in the course of their work except when authorized, unless legally obligated to do so.
3. Integrity: Refrain from engaging in or supporting any activity that would discredit the profession.
4. Credibility: Communicate information fairly and objectively.

Toshiba and its auditors violated all or part of each of these standards.

Sources: Pavel Alpeyev and Takashi Amano, "Toshiba Said to Face Biggest Fine by Japan's Financial Regulator," *Bloomberg Technology*, December 6, 2015.
Pavel Alpeyev and Takashi Amano, "Toshiba to Restate at Least 152 Billion Yen of Past Profits," *Bloomberg Technology*, July 20, 2015.
"Standards of Ethical Conduct for Management Accountants," *Accountingverse*, accessed July 19, 2016.

ethical issues. These codes provide a summary of a company's policies that define ethical standards of employee conduct, and they often include broad philosophical statements about behavior. Hershey's code states, "Every day provides new opportunities to do the right thing. Let this Code and your good judgment be your guide."[21]

Corporate Governance

Corporate governance refers to the system of policies, processes, laws, and regulations that affect the way a company is directed and controlled. At the highest level, the system of corporate governance for a company is the responsibility of the board of directors, but it affects all stakeholders, including employees, creditors, customers, vendors, and the community at large. The large number of corporate failures of the last decade brought the topic of corporate governance to the forefront.

The collapse of Enron, along with its independent auditor, Arthur Andersen, prompted the U.S. Congress to pass the Sarbanes-Oxley Act of 2002 (or SOX), which was intended to address weaknesses affecting U.S. capital markets. Although SOX deals primarily with issues pertaining to the relationship between publicly traded companies and the capital markets, some of its requirements have become a standard for corporate responsibility and governance affecting both public and private companies, as well as not-for-profit organizations.

SOX consists of 66 sections, including such topics as external auditing standards, auditor conflicts of interest, codes of ethics for financial officers, review of internal controls, and criminal penalties for fraud. Probably the most important provisions of SOX, from a managerial accounting standpoint, are those related to internal control systems. **Internal control systems** generally are made up of the policies and procedures that exist to ensure that company objectives are achieved with regard to (a) effectiveness and efficiency of operations, (b) reliability of financial reporting, and (c) compliance with laws and regulations.

SOX imposes the requirement that CEOs and CFOs annually review and assess the effectiveness of their company's internal controls over financial reporting, and issue a report of their assessment. Although many CEOs and CFOs have argued that the cost of SOX compliance is unjustified by the benefits to investors, the following Research Insight provides evidence that SOX is improving the quality of financial reporting. Even though SOX limits the internal control review to aspects of the system related to financial reporting, in practice there is very little that takes place in any organization that does not impact the financial statements. Therefore, if SOX is resulting in improvements in data that goes into financial reports, it is likely that data supporting managerial accounting is also enhanced by a more reliable internal control system.

Research Insight ■ SOX Gives Important Internal Control Information to Financial Markets

An important question that accounting researchers ask about any disclosure is whether the disclosure is useful to the financial markets. A team of researchers from Shanghai and Hong Kong have shown that information provided by SOX about internal controls directly influences the pricing of Credit Default Swaps (CDS), a transaction that allows lenders to hedge the risk of their loans. CDS provide the firm's owners with insurance if the firm goes bankrupt, so the connection between information about internal control and the price of this type of insurance suggests that SOX is releasing important information about the way the firm is run.

The impact of good internal control on annual debt interest expense is meaningful. Firms with good controls book, on average, $35.7 million less in annual debt interest expense than firms with material weaknesses in their internal controls. This study shows that the relationship between CDS pricing and internal control holds, not only for the material weakness disclosures, but also as internal controls deteriorate over time, leading up to the material weakness. To the extent that the firm is concerned about the cost of debt, SOX-mandated disclosures provide pressure for good internal controls. This may improve the information that is provided to management accounting systems.

Source: Dragon Yongjun Tang, Feng Tian, and Hong Yan, "Internal Control Quality and Credit Default Swap Spreads," *Accounting Horizons*, September 2015, Vol. 29, No. 3, pp. 603–629.

Research Insights *introduce relevant research findings on the topics presented.*

Many of the models and processes that we discuss in this text have either a direct or indirect impact on a company's financial statements; hence, they are likely subject to the SOX internal control

[21] https://www.thehersheycompany.com/content/dam/corporate-us/documents/investors/business-code-of-conduct.pdf

review. An overlap often exists between the systems that produce the data for the external financial statements and those that produce data for internal decision making. For example, cost data produced by the product costing system is often used for both financial reporting and managerial decision-making purposes. A more detailed discussion of SOX and internal control systems can typically be found in financial accounting and auditing textbooks.

Sustainability Accounting and Corporate Social Responsibility

Sustainability accounting and corporate social responsibility are increasingly important to managers. "Since the 1960s environmentalists have been concerned with the impact of economic growth and the increasingly rapid use of the world's resources. In recent years, these concerns have increased because of the impact of greenhouse gases, caused by the burning of fossil fuels, on global warming."[22] John Elkington introduced the concept of the Triple Bottom Line (TBL), which incorporates traditional financial performance and accountability to shareholders, as well as broader accountability through both environmental and social impacts.[23]

These concepts entail balancing the objective of profitability with the objective of giving proper attention to issues such as environmental sustainability and energy conservation, and avoiding actions that would lower the quality of life in the communities in which a company operates and sells its products or services. In earlier generations it would have meant giving a day's wage for a day's labor, not hiring underage children, or not dumping untreated waste into the local river.

Managerial accounting includes a variety of models that help managers determine the cost of a particular activity or product, or the benefits and costs of various decision alternatives. Although such models in their current state of development may not take into account all external social costs, accountants are more aware today than in the past of the need to consider such costs. For example, when calculating the cost of building a new capital asset that is going to last for 25 years, it is necessary to include in that calculation the present value of the cost of the ultimate disposal of the asset, including any environmental cleanup.

Being a socially responsible company does not mean abandoning the profit motive or the goal of providing an attractive return to investors. It means that while pursuing these essential objectives, a for-profit company attempts to measure the total benefits and costs of its actions and accepts the responsibility for those actions. Also, being a good competitor should not be confused with social responsibility. For example, many companies offer certain fringe benefits, such as on-site childcare, because it attracts better employees, not because they feel they have a social responsibility to provide such services. Obviously, the line between being a good competitor and being socially responsible is sometimes blurred.

Research Insight ■ Environmental Disclosures—Silence Is Not Golden

Various regulatory sources have been calling for increased disclosure regarding a firm's effect on the environment, including a report on the firm's carbon emissions. Shareholder activists have also driven increased reporting of climate-change risks to their investee firms. In 2004, only 14% of shareholder resolutions involved environmental initiatives, but that number had grown to 27% by 2009, according to a report by EY. The authors of a recent study note that firms with a reputation for environmental responsibility enjoy higher revenues, lower compliance costs, more motivated employees, and positive perceptions among customers and suppliers.

EY analyzed carbon emissions data from 2006 to 2008 for S&P 500 firms and found that for each additional thousand metric tons of carbon emissions produced by the firm, the firm's value (as measured by market value of equity) decreases by $212,000. The difference in value between the first and third quartiles of carbon emission levels correlates to a 1.4-billion-dollar difference in firm value. However, silence is not golden. The authors state that although all firms are penalized for their carbon emissions, those firms that do not disclose the information to the public are penalized to a larger extent by the stock market.

Source: Ella Mae Matsumura, Rachna Prakash, and Sandra Vera-Munoz, "Firm-Value Effects of Carbon Emissions and Carbon Disclosures," (June 21, 2013). *The Accounting Review*, March 2014, Vol. 89, No. 2, pp. 695–724.

[22] *The Evolution of Accountability Sustainability Reporting for Accountants*, IMA 2014.

[23] John Elkington, founder of "SustainAbility," 1987.

Corporate Social Responsibility LO5 **Review 1-5**

Provide three examples of how managerial accounting can help support corporate social responsibility?

Solution on p. 1-30.

Cost Drivers

eLectures MBC **LO6** Demonstrate the use of structural, organizational, and activity cost drivers.

The foundation for the managerial accounting concepts covered in this text is the ability to identify and measure the activities of an organization. In this chapter, we introduce the idea of business activities and what drives the costs related to those activities.

An **activity** is a unit of work. To serve a customer at a restaurant such as Fleming's Prime Steakhouse, a server might perform the following units of work:

- Seat customer and offer menu
- Take customer order
- Send order to kitchen
- Bring food to customer
- Serve and replenish beverages
- Determine and bring bill to customer
- Accept and process payment
- Clear and reset table

Each of these is an activity, and the performance of each activity consumes resources that cost money. To manage activities and their costs, it is necessary to understand how costs respond to **cost drivers**, which are the factors that cause or influence costs.

The most basic cost driver is customer demand. Without customer demand for products or services, the organization cannot exist. To serve customers, managers and employees make a variety of decisions and take numerous actions. These decisions and actions, undertaken to satisfy customer demand, drive costs. While these cost drivers may be classified in a variety of ways, we believe that dividing them into the three categories of structural, organizational, and activity cost drivers, as summarized in **Exhibit 1.5**, provides a useful foundation for the study of managerial accounting.

EXHIBIT 1.5 Structural, Organizational, and Activity Cost Drivers

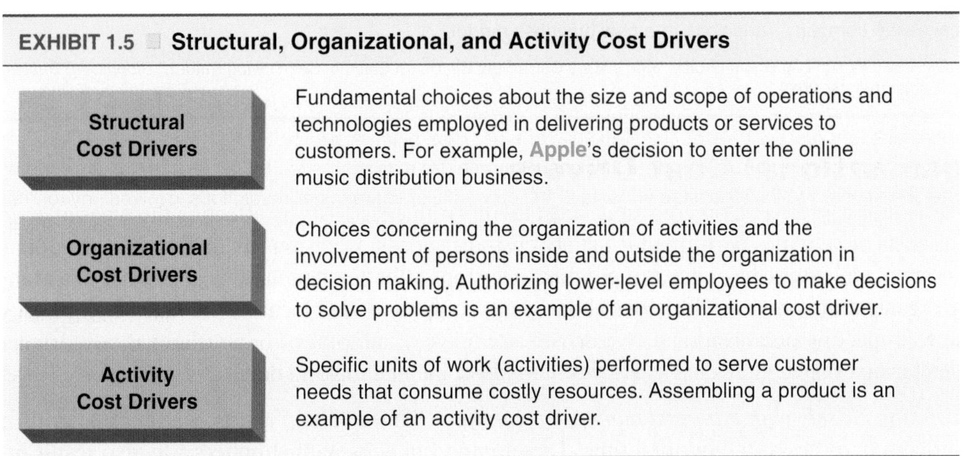

Structural Cost Drivers
Fundamental choices about the size and scope of operations and technologies employed in delivering products or services to customers. For example, Apple's decision to enter the online music distribution business.
Organizational Cost Drivers
Choices concerning the organization of activities and the involvement of persons inside and outside the organization in decision making. Authorizing lower-level employees to make decisions to solve problems is an example of an organizational cost driver.
Activity Cost Drivers
Specific units of work (activities) performed to serve customer needs that consume costly resources. Assembling a product is an example of an activity cost driver.

Structural Cost Drivers

The types of activities and the costs of activities performed to satisfy customer needs are influenced by an organization's size, its location, the scope of its operations, and the technologies used. Decisions affecting structural cost drivers are made infrequently, and once made, the organization is committed to a course of action that will be difficult to change. For a chain of retail stores such as Target, possible structural cost drivers include:

- *Determining the size of stores.* This affects the variety of merchandise that can be carried and operating costs.
- *Determining the type of construction.* While a lean warehouse type of construction is less expensive, it is not an appropriate setting for selling high-fashion clothing.
- *Determining the location of stores.* Locating in a shopping mall can cost more and subject the store to mall regulations but provides for more customer traffic and shared advertising.
- *Determining types of technology to employ in stores.* A computerized system for maintaining all inventory and sales data requires a large initial investment and fixed annual operating costs while providing more current information. However, the computerized inventory and sales systems can be less expensive at high sales volumes than a less costly system relying more on clerks taking physical inventory.

An important structural cost driver for many companies is the decision to redefine their company's product offering. The following Business Insight illustrates how the auto industry is rethinking what "product" they bring to market. Traditionally their product was manufacturing cars. Now they are thinking broader in terms of transportation. This has led to investments in ride hailing apps, the creation of their own driver services, and driverless car technology.

Business Insight ■ Auto Manufacturer Begins Structural Shift to Match Changing Car Culture

In November 2018, Mary Barra, chief executive officer of General Motors Co. (GM), announced the biggest layoff of employees since the company's bankruptcy in 2009. This layoff wasn't about declining sales or profits, though. GM had reported operating profits in all but one year since 2010. This layoff was part of GM's planned transition from the sales of sedans and small cars to the sale of electric vehicles and self-driving cars. In an interview, Barra said, "Once you start to believe in the science of global warming and look at the regulatory environment around the world, it becomes pretty clear that to win in the future, you've got to win" with electric and driverless vehicles.

The company had already invested $500 million in Lyft Inc. in 2016 with the intention of "marrying GM's self-drive technology with the ride-hailing brand." And in 2017, GM acquired Cruise Automation, a self-driving vehicle startup, to work on technical difficulties slowing down development of GM's own autonomous vehicles. GM management believes that it is the only company with the cash, the facilities, and the engineering talent to claim the lead position in a ride-sharing industry that is expected to generate $1.3 billion in revenue globally by 2030.

For now, sales of GM's electric car, the Chevrolet Bolt, generate losses of about $9,000 each and the expected 2019 rollout of its self-driving car, Cruise, has been postponed. This means Barra has to depend on sales in its traditional businesses to keep money flowing. Information from GM's management accounting system is critical as the company transitions to a new business model.

Sources: David Welch and Bryan Gruley, "GM's Mary Barra Bets Big on an Electric, Self-Driving Future," *Bloomberg Businessweek*, September 19, 2019.

Organizational Cost Drivers

Like structural cost drivers, organizational cost drivers influence costs by affecting the types of activities and the costs of activities performed to satisfy customer needs. Decisions that affect organizational cost drivers are made within the context of previous decisions affecting structural cost drivers. In a manufacturing organization, previous decisions about plant, equipment, and location are taken as a given when decisions impacting organizational cost drivers are made. Examples of organizational cost drivers at a manufacturing organization such as Harley-Davidson include making decisions regarding

- *Working closely with a limited number of suppliers.* This can help achieve proper materials in the proper quantities at the optimal time. Developing linkages with suppliers can also result in suppliers' initiatives that improve the profitability of both organizations.
- *Providing employees with cost information and authorizing them to make decisions.* This helps improve decision speed and reduce costs while making employees more customer oriented. Production employees may, for example, offer product design suggestions that reduce manufacturing costs or reduce defects.

- *Reorganizing the existing equipment in the plant so that sequential operations are closer.* This more efficient layout reduces the cost of moving inventory between workstations.
- *Designing components of a product so they can fit together only in the correct manner.* This can reduce defects as well as assembly time and cost.
- *Manufacturing a low-volume product on low-speed, general-purpose equipment rather than high-speed, special-purpose equipment.* Assuming the special-purpose equipment is more difficult and costly to set up for a new job, this decision can increase operating time and operating cost while reducing setup time and setup cost.

The following Business Insight illustrates how an innovative software startup managed a key organizational cost driver to keep down costs and achieve profitability.

Business Insight ■ Software Company Increases Sales at a Lower Cost Without Sales Department

Atlassian, a company without a commissioned direct salesforce, had revenues of $1,210 million in Fiscal 2019. The company, known for its team collaboration software, is valued at $26.6 billion and is competing with industry giants such as IBM, Microsoft, and Google. While unconventional, the benefit to Atlassian's approach shows up in its 19% revenue-to-sales/marketing cost ratio, where Atlassian beats its peers by 30% or more.

The decision to develop the business without a traditional sales department was an organic one. Launched while the founders Scott Farquhar and Mike Cannon-Brooks were in school, at first they simply lacked the time and resources for a formal sales department. Effort was focused on developing and delivering the product, not on selling it. Now customers are guided through the purchase process online, and requests for a sales rep visit are politely declined. As the company has matured, it has learned that this strategy has increased sales at a low cost.

As young firms develop, management accountants can help decision makers think carefully about the future organizational costs associated with structural decisions like those Cannon-Brooks and Farquhar faced as students.

Sources: Dina Bass, "This $5 Billion Software Company Has No Sales Staff," *Bloomberg Businessweek*, May 19, 2016; and Peter High, "Atlassian President Drives the Company North of $1 Billion in Revenue" *Forbes*, June 10, 2019.

Activity Cost Drivers

Activity cost drivers are specific units of work (activities) performed to serve customer needs that consume costly resources. Several examples of activities in a restaurant were mentioned previously. The customer may be outside the organization, such as a client of an advertising firm, or inside the organization, such as an accounting office that receives maintenance services. Because the performance of activities consumes resources and resources cost money, the performance of activities drives costs.

The basic decisions concerning which available activities will be used to respond to customer requests precede the actual performance of activities. At the activity level, execution of previous plans and following prescribed activities are important. All of the examples of structural and organizational cost drivers involved making decisions. In the following list of activity cost drivers for a manufacturing organization, note the absence of the decision-oriented words:

- Placing a purchase order for raw materials
- Inspecting incoming raw materials
- Moving items being manufactured between workstations
- Setting up a machine to work on a product
- Spending machine time working on a product
- Spending labor time working on a product
- Hiring and training a new employee
- Packing an order for shipment
- Processing a sales order
- Shipping a product

In managing costs, management makes choices concerning structural and organizational cost drivers. These decisions affect the types of activities required to satisfy customer needs. Because

Managerial Decisions *require you to assume various roles within a business and use your accounting knowledge to address an issue. Solutions are provided at the end of the chapter.*

different types of activities have different costs, management's decisions concerning structural and organizational cost drivers ultimately affect activity costs and profitability. Good decision making at the level of structural and organizational cost drivers requires an understanding of the linkages among the types of cost drivers and the costs of different activities.

Managerial Decision ■ You Are the CEO

How can you use information about structural, organizational, and activity cost drivers to help you in implementing the organization's strategy? [Answer, p. 22]

Review 1-6 LO6 — Classification of Cost Drivers

Classify each of the following as a structural, organizational, or activity cost driver.

a. Meals served to airplane passengers aboard Delta Airlines.
b. GM's decision to manufacture the Bolt, an all-electric automobile.
c. Zenith's decision to sell its computer operations and focus on the core television business.
d. Number of tax returns filed electronically by H&R Block.
e. Number of passenger cars in an Amtrak train.
f. Coors' decision to expand its market area east from the Rocky Mountains.
g. Boeing's decision to invite airlines to assist in designing the model 777 airplane.
h. Daimler Benz's decision to use cross-disciplinary teams to design a new automobile.
i. St. Jude Hospital's decision to establish review committees on the appropriateness and effectiveness of medical procedures for improving patient care.
j. Harley-Davidson's efforts to restructure production procedures to reduce inventories and machine setup times.

Solution on p. 1-30.

Guidance Answers

You Are the CEO

Pg. 22 It is important that an organization's cost structure be aligned with its strategy. If your goal is to be a cost leader (such as Wal-Mart or Costco), you will want to make sure that the structural cost drivers, such as the type of buildings acquired and the displays used, are consistent with this strategy. As the CEO of Wal-Mart, you would not permit many of the costs that would be incurred in an organization such as Tiffany or Nordstrom.

Key Terms *are listed for each chapter with references to page numbers within the chapter.*

Key Terms

activity, 19
activity cost drivers, 21
big data, 14
controlling, 13
corporate governance, 17
cost driver analysis, 7
cost drivers, 19
enterprise risk management (ERM), 15
ethics, 15
financial accounting, 4
for-profit organizations, 8
goal, 8
internal control systems, 17
managerial accounting, 4
mission, 8
not-for-profit organizations, 8
organization chart, 12
organizing, 12
planning, 12
strategic cost management, 7
strategic position, 9
strategic position analysis, 7
strategy, 9
sustainability accounting, 18
value chain analysis, 7

Multiple Choice *questions with answers are provided for each chapter.*

Multiple Choice

1. Which of the following is not a characteristic of Managerial Accounting?
   a. No external standards
   b. Reports primarily on past decisions
   c. Provides information for internal users
   d. Information is more detailed

2. Controlling is the process of
   a. Selecting goals and adopting strategies for achieving them
   b. Delegating authority to others to take action to implement plans
   c. Organizing employees into line and staff functions
   d. Ensuring that results agree with plans

3. Which of the following is not likely to be regarded as an action that has ethical implications in today's business environment?
   a. Purchasing supplies from a relative or friend rather than seeking bids
   b. Using different depreciation methods for calculating depreciation expense for the financial statements and the income tax return
   c. Failing to recognize obsolete inventory to avoid missing a profit forecast
   d. Shifting costs for one contract to another to make the profits of the contracts line up with initial forecasts

4. Which of the following is not a cost driver?
   a. The gender of the wait staff at a restaurant
   b. The number of customers in a restaurant
   c. The size of a restaurant
   d. The policy of empowering a server to make the decision to give a customer a free dessert because of the delay in delivering the main entrée

5. Which of the following is not one of the three basic types of cost drivers discussed in the text?
   a. Activity cost drivers
   b. Organizational cost drivers
   c. Direct cost drivers
   d. Structural cost drivers

Multiple Choice Answers
1. b 2. d 3. b 4. a 5. c

Questions

Q1-1. Contrast financial and managerial accounting on the basis of user orientation, purpose of information, level of aggregation, length of time period, orientation toward past or future, conformance to external standards, and emphasis on objective data.

Q1-2. What three themes are a part of strategic cost management?

Q1-3. Distinguish between a mission and a goal.

Q1-4. Describe the three strategic positions that Porter views as leading to business success.

Q1-5. Distinguish between how managerial accounting would support the strategy of cost leadership and the strategy of product differentiation.

Q1-6. Why are the phases of planning, organizing, and controlling referred to as a *continuous cycle*?

Q1-7. Identify three advances that have fostered the move away from isolated national economic systems toward an interdependent global economy.

Q1-8. What are the three interrelated dimensions of today's competition?

Q1-9. How can top management establish an ethical tone in an organization?

Q1-10. Describe how pressures to have desirable short-run outcomes can lead to ethical dilemmas.

Q1-11. Differentiate among structural, organizational, and activity cost drivers.

Assignments with the MBC logo in the margin are available in myBusinessCourse. See the Preface of the book for details.

MINI EXERCISES

LO1, 2, 3, 5, 6 **M1-12. Management Accounting Terminology**

Homework *icons indicate which assignments are available in* **myBusinessCourse** *(MBC). This feature is only available when the instructor incorporates MBC in the course.*

Match the following terms with the best descriptions. Each description is used only once.

Terms

1.	Ethics	9.	Strategic cost management
2.	Mission	10.	Financial accounting
3.	Controlling	11.	Activity cost driver
4.	Goal	12.	Structural cost driver
5.	Cost drivers	13.	Managerial accounting
6.	Quality	14.	Resources
7.	Balance sheet	15.	Product differentiation
8.	Income statement		

Description

a. Making decisions concerning specific cost drivers
b. Factors that influence costs
c. Reports a company's financial position
d. Accounting for external users
e. Increase year 2020 sales by 10% over year 2019 sales
f. Shows the results of operations for a period of time
g. Packing an order for shipment
h. Deciding to limit market focus to a region rather than the entire nation
i. The degree to which a new e-book reader meets a buyer's expectations
j. Used internally to make decisions
k. Consumed by activities
l. The propriety of taking some action
m. Reduces customer price sensitivity
n. Basic purpose toward which activities are directed
o. Comparing the budget with the actual results

LOs *link assignments to the Learning Objectives of each chapter.*

LO1 **M1-13. Financial and Managerial Accounting**

Indicate whether each phrase is more descriptive of financial accounting or managerial accounting.

a. May be subjective
b. Often used to obtain financing
c. Typically prepared quarterly or annually
d. May measure time or customer satisfaction
e. Future oriented
f. Has a greater emphasis on cost-benefit analysis
g. Keeps records of assets and liabilities
h. Highly aggregated statements
i. Must conform to external standards
j. Special-purpose reports
k. Decision-making tool
l. Income statement, balance sheet, and statement of cash flows

LO1 **M1-14. Institute of Managerial Accountants**

What is the role of managerial accounting according to the IMA, and how does the IMA try to influence the best practices of managerial accountants?

LO3 **M1-15. Missions, Goals, and Strategies**

Identify each of the following as a mission, goal, or strategy.

a. Budget time for study, sleep, and relaxation
b. Provide shelter for the homeless
c. Provide an above-average return to investors

d. Protect the public
e. Locate fire stations so that the average response time is less than five minutes
f. Overlap police patrols so that there are always police cars on major thoroughfares
g. Achieve a 12% market share
h. Lower prices and costs
i. Select the most scenic route to drive between Las Vegas and Denver
j. Graduate from college

M1-16. Line and Staff Organization

LO3

Target (TGT)

Presented are the names of several departments often found in a merchandising organization such as Target.

a. Maintenance
b. Home Furnishings
c. Store Manager
d. Payroll
e. Human Resources
f. Advertising

Required
Identify each as a line or a staff department.

M1-17. Line and Staff Organization

LO3

KraftHeinz (KHC)

Presented are the names of several departments often found in a manufacturing organization such as KraftHeinz.

a. Manager, Plant 2
b. Design Engineering
c. President
d. Controller
e. Property Accounting
f. Sales Manager, District 1

Required
Identify each as a line or a staff department.

M1-18. Changing Business Environment

LO4

Identify some trends that should be considered when developing the role and processes of an organization's managerial accounting strategy.

M1-19. Classifying Cost Drivers

LO6

Apple Inc. (AAPL)

Classify each of the following as structural, organizational, or activity cost drivers.

a. Apple Inc. reorganizes production facilities from a layout in which all similar types of machines are grouped together to a layout in which a set of machines is designated for the production of a particular product and that set of machines is grouped together.
b. A cable television company decides to start offering telephone service.
c. IBM decides to stop making personal computers.
d. Canon decides to start making high-volume photocopy equipment to compete head-to-head with Xerox.
e. The number of meals a cafeteria serves.
f. The number of miles a taxi is driven.
g. A company eliminates the position of supervisor and has each work group elect a team leader.
h. Tesla empowers employees to halt production if a quality problem is identified.
i. The number of tons of grain a ship loads.
j. Northbrook Mall decides to build space for 80 additional stores.

IBM (IBM)
Canon (CAJ)
Tesla Motors Inc. (TSLA)

M1-20. Classifying Cost Drivers

LO6

Henderson Construction managers provide design and construction management services for various commercial construction projects. Senior managers are trying to apply cost driver concepts to their firm to better understand Henderson's costs.

Required
Classify each of the following actions or decisions as structural, organizational, or activity cost drivers.

a. The decision to be a regional leader in computer-assisted design services.
b. The decision to allow staff architects to follow a specific project through to completion.
c. The daily process of inspecting the progress on various construction projects.
d. The process of conducting extensive client interviews to assess the exact needs for Henderson services.
e. The decision to expand the market area by establishing an office in another state.

f. The decision to use only Henderson staff rather than relying on subcontractors.
g. The process of receiving approval from government authorities along with appropriate permits for each project.
h. The decision to organize the workforce into project teams.
i. The decision to build a new headquarters facility with areas for design and administration as well as storage and maintenance of construction equipment.
j. The process of grading building sites and preparing forms for foundations.

EXERCISES

LO1 KraftHeinz (KHC)

Ticker *symbols are provided for companies so one can easily obtain additional information.*

E1-21. Financial and Managerial Accounting

Assume Katie Milling has just been promoted to product manager at KraftHeinz. Although she is an accomplished sales representative and well versed in market research, her accounting background is limited to reviewing her paycheck, balancing her checkbook, filing income tax returns, and reviewing the company's annual income statement and balance sheet. She commented that while the financial statements are no doubt useful to investors, she just doesn't see how accounting can help her be a good product manager.

Required

Based on her remarks, it is apparent that Katie's view of accounting is limited to financial accounting. Explain some of the important differences between financial and managerial accounting and suggest some ways managerial accounting can help Katie be a better product manager.

LO3

E1-22. Developing an Organization Chart

Develop an organization chart for a three-outlet bakery chain with a central baking operation and deliveries every few hours. Assume the business is incorporated and that the president has a single staff assistant. Also assume that the delivery truck driver reports to the bakery manager.

LO3 Stanford University; Good Samaritan Hospital; Walgreen Boots Alliance (WBA); Starwood Hotels and Resorts (HOT); United Parcel Service (UPS)

E1-23. Identifying Monetary and Nonmonetary Performance Measures

Identify possible monetary and nonmonetary performance measures for each of the following situations. One nonmonetary measure should relate to quality, and one should relate to time.

a. Stanford University wishes to evaluate the success of last year's graduating class.
b. Good Samaritan Hospital wishes to evaluate the performance of its emergency room.
c. Walgreen Boots Alliance wishes to evaluate the performance of its online order–filling operations.
d. Starwood Hotels wishes to evaluate the performance of registration activities at one of its hotels.
e. United Parcel Service wishes to evaluate the success of its operations in Knoxville.

LO3 EarthLink (ELNK); Comcast (CMCSA); Asustek Computer Inc.; Target Corporation (TGT); Emory University

E1-24. Identifying Monetary and Nonmonetary Performance Measures

Identify possible monetary and nonmonetary performance measures for each of the following situations. One nonmonetary measure should relate to quality, and one should relate to time.

a. EarthLink's evaluation of the performance of its Internet service in Chicago.
b. Comcast's evaluation of the performance of new customer cable installations in Springfield.
c. Asustek Computer's evaluation of the performance of its logistical arrangements for delivering computers to its U.S. customers.
d. Target's evaluation of the performance of its website.
e. Emory University's evaluation of the success of its freshman admissions activities.

LO3 Toyota (TM); General Motors (GM)

E1-25. Identifying Information Needs of Different Managers

Matt Parker operates a number of auto dealerships for Toyota and General Motors. Identify possible monetary and nonmonetary performance measures for each of the following situations. One nonmonetary measure should relate to quality, and one should relate to time.

a. An individual sales associate.
b. The sales manager of a single dealership.
c. The general manager of a particular dealership.
d. The corporate chief financial officer.
e. The president of the corporation.

E1-26. Activities and Cost Drivers LO6

For each of the following activities, select the most appropriate cost driver. Each cost driver may be used only once.

Activity		Cost Driver	
1.	Pay vendors	*a.*	Number of different raw material items
2.	Receive material deliveries	*b.*	Number of classes offered
3.	Inspect raw materials	*c.*	Number of machine hours
4.	Plan for purchases of raw materials	*d.*	Number of employees
5.	Packaging	*e.*	Number of maintenance hours
6.	Supervision	*f.*	Number of units of raw materials received
7.	Employee training	*g.*	Number of new customers
8.	Operating machines	*h.*	Number of deliveries
9.	Machine maintenance	*i.*	Number of checks issued
10.	Opening accounts at a bank	*j.*	Number of customer orders

Cases and Projects

C1-27. Goals and Strategies LO3

a. What is your instructor's goal for students in this course? What strategies has he or she developed to achieve this goal?

b. What is your goal in this course? What strategies will help you achieve this goal?

c. What is your goal for this semester or term? What strategies will help you achieve this goal?

d. What is your next career goal? What strategies will help you achieve this goal?

C1-28. Product Differentiation LO3

You are the owner of Lobster's Unlimited. You have no trouble catching lobsters, but you have difficulty in selling all that you catch. The problem is that all lobsters from all vendors look the same. You do catch high-quality lobsters, but you need to be able to tell your customers that your lobsters are better than those sold by other vendors.

Required

a. What are some possible ways of distinguishing your lobsters from those of other vendors?

b. Explain the possible results of this differentiation.

C1-29. Ethics and Short-Term Borrowing LO5

Rory, an administrative assistant, is in charge of petty cash for a local law firm. Normally, about $300 is kept in the petty cash box. When Rory is short on cash and needs some for lunch or to pay her babysitter, she sometimes takes a few dollars from the box. Because she is in charge of the box, nobody knows that she takes the money, and she always replaces it within a few days.

Required

a. Is Rory's behavior ethical?

b. Assume that Rory has recently had major problems meeting her bills. She also is in charge of purchasing supplies for the office from petty cash. Last week when she needed $50 for the babysitter, she falsified a voucher for the amount of $50. Is this behavior ethical?

C1-30. Ethics and Travel Reimbursement LO5

Jake takes many business trips throughout the year. All of his expenses are paid by his company. Last week he traveled to Rio De Janeiro, Brazil, and stayed there on business for five days. He is allowed a maximum of $50 per day for food and $150 per day for lodging. To his surprise, the food and accommodations in Brazil were much less than he expected. Being upset about traveling last week and having to sacrifice tickets he'd purchased to a Cubs baseball game, he decided to inflate his expenses a bit. He increased his lodging expense from $80 per day to $100 per day and his food purchased from $30 per day to $40 per day. Therefore, for the five-day trip, he overstated his expenses by $150 total. After all, the allowance was higher than the amount he spent.

Required

Assume that the company would never find out that he had actually spent less. Are Jake's actions ethical? Are they acceptable?

LO5 **C1-31. Ethical Issues with Supplier-Buyer Partnerships**

Tom Wopat was excited to learn of his appointment as Circuit Electronics Corporation's sales representative to Household Appliance Inc. For the past four years, Circuit Electronics has supplied all of the electric switches used in Household's washers and dryers. As Circuit Electronics' sales representative, Tom's job involves the following tasks.

1. Working with Household engineers to design electric switches that can be manufactured to meet Household's cost and quality requirements.
2. Assisting Household in resolving any problems related to electric switches.
3. Monitoring the inventory levels of electric switches at Household and placing orders for additional switches when appropriate.

This appointment will require Tom to move to Stuttgart, Germany, for two years. Although Tom has mixed feelings about the move, he is familiar with the success of the program in improving Circuit Electronics' financial performance. He is also very much aware of the fact that the two previous sales representatives received promotions at the end of their appointments.

As Tom toured the Household factory in Stuttgart with his predecessor, Catherine Bach, his excitement turned to concern. It became apparent that Circuit Electronics had not been supplying Household with the best available switches at the lowest possible costs. Although the switches were adequate, they were more likely to wear out after five or six years of use than would switches currently on the market (and being used by Household's competitors). Furthermore, taking into account the current number of switches in transit by ship from North America to Europe, it also appeared that the inventory level of electric switches would soon be more than enough to satisfy Household's needs for the next four months.

Required

If you were Tom, what would you do?

LO5 **C1-32. Expected Values of Questionable Decisions**

Exxon Mobil (XOM)

The members of the jury had to make a decision in a lawsuit brought by the State of Alabama against Exxon Mobil. The suit revolved around natural-gas wells that Exxon drilled in state-owned waters. After signing several leases obligating Exxon to share revenues with Alabama, company officials started questioning the terms of the agreement that prohibited deducting several types of processing costs before paying the state royalties.

Royal Dutch Shell (RDSB)

During the course of the trial, a memo by an in-house attorney of Exxon Mobil came to light. The memo noted that Royal Dutch Shell, which had signed a similar lease, interpreted it "in the same manner as the state." The memo then presented arguments the company might use to claim the deduction, estimated the probability of the arguments being successful (less than 50%), and proceeded to consider whether Exxon should obey the law using a cost-benefit analysis. According to the memo, "If we adopt anything beyond a 'safe' approach, we should anticipate a quick audit and subsequent litigation." The memo also observed that "our exposure is 12 percent interest on underpayments calculated from the due date, and the cost of litigation." Deducting the questionable costs did, indeed, result in an audit and a lawsuit.[24]

Required

If you were a member of the jury, what would you do? Why?

LO6 **C1-33. Management Decisions Affecting Cost Drivers**

An avid bicycle rider, you have decided to use an inheritance to start a new business to sell and repair bicycles. Two college friends have already accepted offers to work for you.

Required

a. What is the mission of your new business?
b. Suggest a strategic positioning goal you might strive for to compete with area hardware and discount stores that sell bicycles.
c. Identify two items that might be long-range goals.
d. Identify two items that might be goals for the coming year.
e. Mention two decisions that will be structural cost drivers.
f. Mention two decisions that will be organizational cost drivers.
g. Identify two activity cost drivers.

[24] Mike France, "When Big Oil Gets Too Slick," *Business Week*, April 9, 2001, p. 70.

C1-34. Success Factors and Performance Measurement LO3

Three years ago, Vincent Chow completed his college degree. The economy was in a depressed state at the time, and Vincent managed to get an offer of only $25,000 per year as a bookkeeper. In addition to its relatively low pay, this job had limited advancement potential. Since Vincent was an enterprising and ambitious young man, he instead started a business of his own. He was convinced that because of changing lifestyles, a drive-through coffee establishment would be profitable. He was able to obtain backing from his parents to open such an establishment close to the industrial park area in town. Vincent named his business The Cappuccino Express and decided to sell only two types of coffee: cappuccino and decaffeinated.

As Vincent had expected, The Cappuccino Express was very well received. Within three years, Vincent had added another outlet north of town. He left the day-to-day management of each site to a manager and turned his attention toward overseeing the entire enterprise. He also hired an assistant to do the record keeping and other selected chores.[25]

Required

a. Develop an organization chart for The Cappuccino Express.
b. What factors can be expected to have a major impact on the success of The Cappuccino Express?
c. What major tasks must Vincent undertake in managing The Cappuccino Express?
d. What are the major costs of operating The Cappuccino Express?
e. Vincent would like to monitor the performance of each site manager. What measure(s) of performance should he use?
f. If you suggested more than one measure, which of these should Vincent select if he could use only one?
g. Suppose that last year, the original site had yielded total revenues of $146,000, total costs of $122,000, and hence, a profit of $24,000. Vincent had judged this profit performance to be satisfactory. For the coming year, Vincent expects that due to factors such as increased name recognition and demographic changes, the total revenues will increase by 20% to $175,200. What amount of profit should he expect from the site? Discuss the issues involved in developing an estimate of profit.

Solutions to Review Problems

Review 1-1—Solution

a. financial accounting
b. managerial accounting
c. financial accounting
d. financial accounting
e. managerial accounting
f. financial accounting
g. managerial accounting
h. managerial accounting
i. financial accounting
j. managerial accounting

Review 1-2—Solution

There is a seemingly endless amount of managerial accounting information that can be compiled and used for management decision-making. Managers are responsible for asking the right questions, gathering the most relevant data, analyzing the information, and making the decisions. Examples of managerial accounting information that could help management better compete include:

1. Daily sales of product by different customer categories, by geographical location, by means of purchase, etc.
2. Sales forecasts (weekly, monthly, annual) with comparisons to actual results. Include information on sales of products and any associated revenue streams such as monthly app fees.
3. Detailed cost information for each product category and for any optional features.

[25] Based on Chee W. Chow, "Instructional Case: Vincent's Cappuccino Express—A Teaching Case to Help Students Master Basic Cost Terms and Concepts Through Interactive Learning," *Issues in Accounting Education*, Spring 1995, pp. 173–190.

Review 1-3—Solution

1. Product/service differentiation
2. Three ways that managerial accountants can help support the goals of product/service differentiation include:
   a. Track customer satisfaction information as it relates to pricing of products in order to determine whether products are priced in line with customer's value perceptions.
   b. Report timely sales data by product type in order to understand and to be able to quickly respond to changes in consumer trends.
   c. Analyze studies of the time it takes for customers to receive their product after ordering in person, through the drive thru, or through the store app.

Review 1-4—Solution

Big Data and Analysis—Given recent advancements in technology, there is a vast amount of data available to organizations. However, it can be difficult to turn this data into useful and predictive information. Organizations are in need of employees who have the abilities to: identify key data trends, perform data mining and extraction, conduct operational and decision analysis, recommend process improvement, and conduct strategic thinking and execution.

ERM—Organizations are constantly faced with uncertainty from the environment, competitors, and other factors that could result in significant risk of loss. By better understanding the types and potential costs of these risks, management accountants can help their organizations devise strategies to better predict and minimize exposure to risk.

Review 1-5—Solution

Corporate social responsibility is a balance of the objective of company profitability and of concern for the company's environmental and social impacts. Three examples of how managerial accounting can help support corporate social responsibility include:

1. Estimating disposal costs when purchasing new equipment or a building.
2. Providing a cost analysis of different recyclable packaging options.
3. Providing an analysis of the environmental impact of the company's operations.

Review 1-6—Solution

a. Activity cost driver
b. Structural cost driver
c. Structural cost driver
d. Activity cost driver
e. Activity cost driver
f. Structural cost driver
g. Organizational cost driver
h. Organizational cost driver
i. Organizational cost driver
j. Organizational cost driver

Chapter 2

Cost Behavior, Activity Analysis, and Cost Estimation

Learning Objectives

LO1 Identify basic patterns of how costs respond to changes in activity cost drivers. (p. 34)

LO2 Determine a linear total cost-estimating equation. (p. 37)

LO3 Calculate and compare three different approaches to cost estimation. (p. 42)

LO4 Identify and discuss problems encountered in cost estimation. (p. 48)

LO5 Describe and develop alternative classifications for activity cost drivers. (p. 49)

The creator of Twitter, Jack Dorsey, founded Square, Inc. in 2009 to address a void in payment processing services for small, portable businesses. Square makes a postage stamp-sized plastic card reader that attaches to smartphones, which gives businesses such as food trucks, kiosk boutiques, taxi drivers, and the like the ability to accept credit card payments. Square also has an online payment app, and in 2016, Square introduced Virtual Terminal, which enables sellers to accept payments from their computers through the Square Dashboard.

The San Francisco–based company has been so successful that it now processes over $90 billion in transactions each year. Square provides the card readers, the Dashboard App, and the Virtual Terminal to businesses free of charge but collects a per transaction fee to compensate for its services.

The cost of making the card readers is directly related to the number of new businesses adopting the technology. In other words, the hardware cost is driven by the number of new merchants in any given period. But the number of new adoptions is difficult to estimate in advance. The costs associated with processing payments are even more difficult to predict. Consider that the company remits most of the payments received from customers' credit card companies to the merchant, minus Square's fee. However, what is Square's cost of processing each payment? Does the cost of processing a payment differ based on volume or seasonality?

To predict processing costs, we must be able to predict merchant sales volume or number of transactions. If the processing costs vary proportionately with this activity, the processing costs are referred to as variable costs. What about the costs that do not vary with the number or type of transactions processed? Many of Square's employees are salaried engineers and software developers. These costs are likely to be unrelated to the number of card readers issued or payments processed. We call costs that do not vary with activity fixed costs. As we'll see throughout the chapter, many costs are neither variable nor fixed, but a mixture of the two. Mixed costs present a challenge to a company in estimating future costs. Square needs the ability to accurately predict its future costs if it is to maintain the financial flexibility necessary to remain competitive.

Road Map

LO	Learning Objective I Topics	Page	eLecture	Guided Example	Assignments
LO1	**Identify basic patterns of how costs respond to changes in activity cost drivers.** Cost Behavior Patterns :: Variable Costs :: Fixed Costs :: Mixed Costs :: Step Costs :: Factors Affecting Cost Behavior	34	e2–1	Review 2-1	11, 12, 13, 14, 21, 22
LO2	**Determine a linear total cost-estimating equation.** Total Cost Function :: Relevant Range :: Economic vs Accounting Cost Structures :: Additional Cost Behavior Patterns :: Committed and Discretionary Fixed Costs	37	e2–2	Review 2-2	13, 14, 15, 16, 17, 21, 22, 23, 24, 25
LO3	**Calculate and compare three different approaches to cost estimation.** High-Low Cost Estimation :: Scatter Diagrams :: Least Squares Regression	42	e2–3	Review 2-3	13, 14, 18, 19, 20, 21, 23, 24, 25, 29, 30, 33, 34, 35
LO4	**Identify and discuss problems encountered in cost estimation.** Additional Issues :: Changes in Technology and Prices :: Matching Activity and Costs :: Identifying Activity Cost Drivers	48	e2–4	Review 2-4	19, 20, 25, 31, 34
LO5	**Describe and develop alternative classifications for activity cost drivers.** Alternative Classifications :: Manufacturing Cost Hierarchy :: Customer Cost Hierarchy	49	e2–5	Review 2-5	26, 27, 28, 32

CHAPTER ORGANIZATION

Cost Behavior, Activity Analysis, and Cost Estimation

Cost Behavior Analysis	Cost Estimation	Additional Issues in Cost Estimation	Alternative Cost Driver Classifications
• Four Basic Cost Behavior Patterns • Factors Affecting Cost Behavior Patterns • Total Cost Function for an Organization or Segment • Relevant Range • Additional Cost Behavior Patterns • Committed and Discretionary Fixed Costs	• High-Low Cost Estimation • Scatter Diagrams • Least-Squares Regression	• Changes in Technology and Prices • Matching Activity and Costs • Identifying Activity Cost Drivers	• Manufacturing Cost Hierarchy • Customer Cost Hierarchy

Cost Behavior Analysis

LO1 Identify basic patterns of how costs respond to changes in activity cost drivers.

This chapter introduces **cost behavior**, which refers to the relationship between a given cost item and the quantity of its related cost driver. Cost behavior, therefore, explains how the total amount for various costs responds to changes in activity volume. Understanding cost behavior is essential for estimating future costs. In this chapter we examine several typical cost behavior patterns and methods for developing cost equations that are useful for predicting future costs.

Four Basic Cost Behavior Patterns

Although there are an unlimited number of ways that costs can respond to changes in activity cost drivers, as a starting point it is useful to classify cost behavior into four categories: **variable costs**, **fixed costs**, **mixed costs**, and **step costs**. Graphs of each are presented in **Exhibit 2.1**. Observe that total cost is measured on the vertical axis, and total activity is measured on the horizontal axis. Consider pizza franchise Domino's. Domino's specializes in quick delivery and online order tracking. Customers can pick from signature pies like ExtravaganZZa, or they can create their own and choose the type of dough, sauce, and toppings. Domino's has been the global pizza chain leader in revenue since 2017. To manage its growth, the company must understand the behavior underlying its cost structure. In the discussion that follows, we assume that the activity that drives cost is sales volume.

1. **Variable costs** change in total in direct proportion to changes in the number of units sold. Total variable cost increases as sales volume increases, equaling zero dollars when sales volume is zero and increasing at a constant amount per unit of sales. The higher the variable cost for each unit sold, the steeper the slope (incline) of the line representing total cost. With the number of pizzas served as the activity cost driver for Domino's locations, the cost of cheese is an example of a variable cost.
2. **Fixed costs** do not change in response to a change in sales volume. Hence, a line representing total fixed costs is flat with a slope of zero. With the number of Domino's pizzas sold as the activity cost driver, annual depreciation, property taxes, and property insurance are examples of fixed costs. While fixed costs may respond to structural and organizational cost drivers over time, they do not respond to short-run changes in activity cost drivers.
3. **Mixed costs** (sometimes called **semivariable costs**) contain a fixed and a variable cost element. Total mixed costs are positive (like fixed costs) when sales volume is zero, and they increase in a linear fashion (like total variable costs) as sales volume increases. With the number of pizzas sold as the cost driver for Domino's, the cost of electric power is an example of a mixed cost.

Exhibit 2.1 Cost Behavior Patterns

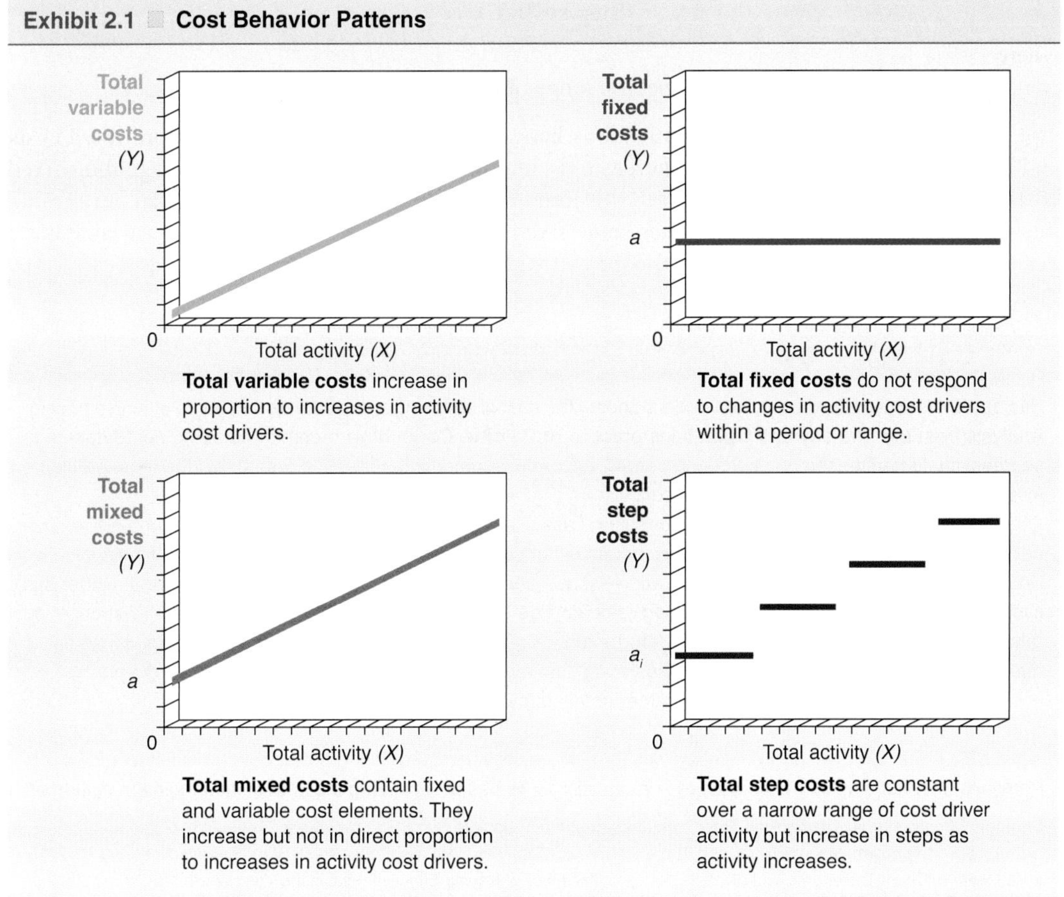

Total variable costs increase in proportion to increases in activity cost drivers.

Total fixed costs do not respond to changes in activity cost drivers within a period or range.

Total mixed costs contain fixed and variable cost elements. They increase but not in direct proportion to increases in activity cost drivers.

Total step costs are constant over a narrow range of cost driver activity but increase in steps as activity increases.

Some electricity is required to provide basic lighting (fixed cost), while an increasing amount of electricity is required to prepare food as the number of pizzas served increases (variable cost).

4. **Step costs** are constant within a narrow range of sales volume but shift to a higher level when sales volume exceeds the range. Total step costs increase in a steplike fashion as sales volume increases. With the number of pizzas served as the cost driver for Domino's, employee wages is an example of a step cost. Up to a certain number of pizzas, only a small staff needs to be on duty. Beyond that number, additional employees are needed for quality service and so forth.

The relationship between total cost (*Y* axis) and total activity (*X* axis) for the four cost behavior patterns is mathematically expressed as follows:

Variable cost: Y = bX

where

b = the variable cost per unit, sometimes referred to as the slope of the cost function.

Fixed cost: Y = a

where

a = total fixed costs. The slope of the fixed cost function is zero because fixed costs do not change with activity.

Mixed cost: Y = a + bX

where

a = total fixed cost element

b = variable cost element per unit of activity.

$$\textbf{Step cost: } Y = a_i$$

where

a_i = the step cost within a specific range of activity, identified by the subscript i.

The total cost function of most organizations has shifted in recent years toward more fixed costs and fewer variable costs, making it increasingly important for organizations to manage their fixed costs. Some organizations have reversed this trend by outsourcing activities rather than performing the activities internally. This eliminates some fixed costs in exchange for additional variable costs per unit of outsourced activity. The Business Insight box below provides a few examples of how understanding costs can lead to better pricing decisions.

Business Insight ■ Understanding Costs Is Key to Pricing

Pricing affects firm performance, and understanding the cost of servicing a customer is the key to effective pricing. Analysts from the Strategy and Operations practice of Deloitte Consulting recommend using rich datasets to segment customers based on needs and behavior. Careful segmenting allows the firm to find the most profitable match of customers with services and prices.

The auto insurance industry is an interesting case. The cost of service is driven by the risk of a claim. Traditionally, auto insurers collect a list of risk factors when calculating the cost of insuring a particular driver. This list includes factors such as age, gender, address, and sometimes an estimate of expected mileage. Under this system, a young driver with fewer estimated annual miles often receives a higher rate than a more experienced driver with more estimated annual miles. Unfortunately for traditional insurers, up to 70% of the variation in risk is due to the actual number of miles driven; so young, low-mile drivers subsidize more experienced drivers.

A new trend in auto insurance is to gather detailed mileage data and charge drivers a low monthly premium with a variable mileage charge. A pioneer of this approach, Metromile, uses a smartphone app and a thumbnail-sized device that users install in their vehicles to gather usage data. Gathering better data on mileage allows Metromile to offer substantially lower rates to drivers simply by better estimating the cost of insuring each customer.

Sources: Quentin Hardy, "Technology Transforms How Insurers Calculate Risk," *The New York Times*, April 6, 2016.
John Hagel, John Brown, Maggie Wooll, and Andrew de Maar, "Align Price with Use," *Deloitte University Press*, February 12, 2016.
Julie Meehan, Chuck Davenport, and Shruti R. Kahlon, "The Price of Pricing Effectiveness: Is the View Worth the Climb?" *Deloitte University Press*, July 1, 2012.

Factors Affecting Cost Behavior Patterns

The four cost behavior patterns presented are based on the fundamental assumption that a unit of final output is the primary cost driver. The implications of this assumption are examined later in this chapter.

Another important assumption is that the time period is too short to incorporate changes in structural cost drivers such as the scale of operations. Although this assumption is useful for short-range planning, for the purpose of developing plans for extended time periods, it is more appropriate to consider possible variations in the size and scope of operations. When this is done, many costs otherwise classified as fixed are better classified as variable.

Even the cost of depreciable assets can be viewed as variable if the time period is long enough. Assuming that the number of pizzas served is the cost driver, for a single month straight-line depreciation on all Domino's locations in the world is a fixed cost. Over several years, if sales are strong, a strategic decision will be made to open additional restaurants; if sales are weak, strategic decisions will likely be made to close some restaurants. Hence, over a multiple-year period, the number of restaurants varies with sales volume, making depreciation appear as a variable cost with sales revenue as the cost driver.

Fixed costs are easily identified. They are the same at each activity level. Variable and mixed costs can be determined by dividing total costs by monthly sales at two activity levels. The quotients of variable costs will be the same at both levels. The quotients of mixed costs will be lower at the higher activity level. This is because the fixed costs are spread over a larger number of units.

Identifying Cost Behavior **LO1 Review 2-1**

Assume a local Subway reported the following results for April and May:

	April	May
Sandwiches sold	2,100	2,700
Cost of food sold	$1,575	$2,025
Wages and salaries	1,525	1,675
Rent on building	1,500	1,500
Depreciation on equipment	200	200
Utilities	710	770
Supplies	225	255
Miscellaneous	113	131
Total	$5,848	$6,556

Required

Identify each cost as being fixed, variable, or mixed.

Solution on p. 2-66.

Total Cost Function for an Organization or Segment

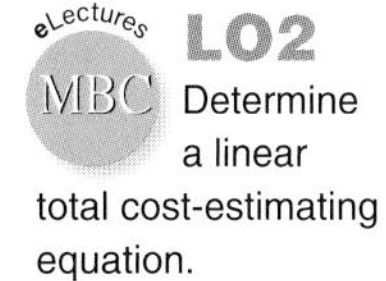

LO2 Determine a linear total cost-estimating equation.

To obtain a general understanding of an organization, to compare the cost structures of different organizations, or to perform preliminary planning activities, managers are often interested in how total costs respond to a single measure of overall activity such as units sold or sales revenue. This overview can be useful, but presenting all costs as a function of a single cost driver is seldom accurate enough to support decisions concerning products, services, or activities. Doing so implies that all of an organization's costs can be manipulated by changing a single cost driver. This is seldom true.

In developing a total cost function, the independent variable usually represents some measure of the goods or services provided customers, such as total student credit hours in a university, total sales revenue in a store, total guest-days in a hotel, or total units manufactured in a factory. The resulting cost function is illustrated in **Exhibit 2.2**.

Exhibit 2.2 Total Cost Behavior

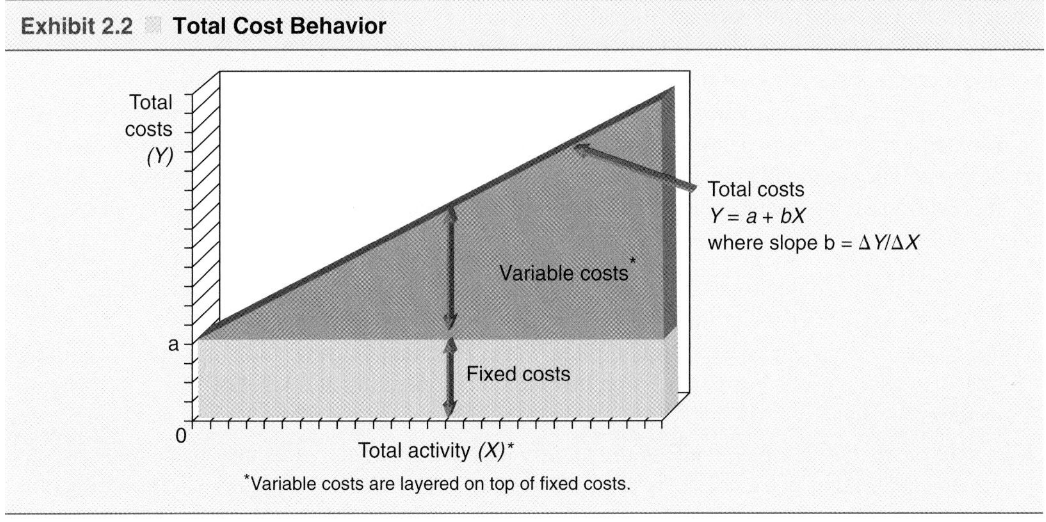

*Variable costs are layered on top of fixed costs.

The equation for total costs is:

$$Y = a + bX$$

where

Y = total costs
a = vertical axis intercept (an approximation of fixed costs)
b = slope (an approximation of variable costs per unit of X)
X = value of independent variable (activity level)

In situations where the variable, fixed, and mixed costs, and the related cost functions, can be determined, a total cost equation can be useful in predicting future costs for various activity levels. For example, assume that Coco Froyo frozen yogurt shop's only fixed cost is the depreciation on its frozen yogurt making machines. Coco Froyo's monthly depreciation is $1,200. Also assume that the variable cost per frozen yogurt served is $3.25. Therefore, the total cost equation for Coco Froyo is:

Y = $1,200 + $3.25 (number of yogurts served)

If the shop expects to serve 1,600 frozen yogurts in July, it can then estimate its total July costs to be:

$6,400 = $1,200 + $3.25 (1,600)

Relevant Range

Generally, a total cost equation is useful for predicting costs in only a limited range of activity. The **relevant range** of a total cost equation is that portion of the range associated with the fixed cost of the current or expected capacity. In our Coco Froyo example, it is able to produce a maximum of 50 gallons of frozen yogurt per day with a single machine. If it has four machines in operation, and if it can readily adjust its fixed capacity cost by increasing or decreasing the number of machines, the relevant range of activity for the shop's current total cost equation is 151 to 200 gallons. (The maximum number of gallons that can be produced with four machines producing 50 gallons per machine is 200 gallons. The minimum number of gallons of yogurt produced before one of the machines could be discontinued is 151 gallons.) In the future, if the shop expects to operate at more than 200 gallons per day, the current total cost equation would not predict total cost accurately, because fixed costs would have to be increased for additional machines. Conversely, if it expects to operate at 150 gallons or fewer, it may reduce the number of machines in the shop, thereby reducing total fixed costs.

The use of straight lines in accounting models of cost behavior assumes a linear relationship between cost and activity with each additional unit of activity accompanied by a uniform increment in total cost. This uniform increment is known as the *variable cost of one unit.*

Economic models show a nonlinear relationship between cost and activity with each incremental unit of activity being accompanied by a varying increment in total cost. Economists identify the varying increment in total cost as the **marginal cost** *of one unit*. For our Coco Froyo example, the marginal cost of one unit is specifically the additional costs incurred with each additional serving of yogurt sold.

It is useful to relate marginal costs to the following three levels of activity:

1. *Below the activity range for which the facility was designed,* the existence of excess capacity results in relatively high marginal costs. Having extra time, employees complete assignments at a leisurely pace, increasing the time and the cost to produce each unit above what it would be if employees were more pressed to complete work. Frequent starting and stopping of equipment may also add to costs. For Coco Froyo this would be operating at a level of 150 gallons per day or fewer.
2. *Within the activity range for which the facility was designed,* activities take place under optimal circumstances and marginal costs are relatively low. For Coco Froyo this would be operating within a range of 151 to 200 gallons per day.
3. *Above the activity range for which the facility was designed,* the existence of capacity constraints again results in relatively high marginal costs. Near capacity, employees may be paid overtime wages, less-experienced employees may be used, regular equipment may operate less efficiently,

and old equipment with high energy requirements may be placed in service. For Coco Froyo this would be operating at a level of more than 200 gallons per day.

Based on marginal cost concepts, the economists' short-run total cost function is illustrated in the first graph in **Exhibit 2.3**. To clarify the concept, we use the capacity information for Coco Froyo. The vertical axis intercept represents capacity costs. In this simple example, our only capacity, or fixed cost, is depreciation. Corresponding to the high marginal costs at low levels of activity, the initial slope is quite steep. In the normal activity range, where marginal costs are relatively low, the slope becomes less steep. Then, corresponding to high marginal costs above the normal activity range, the slope of the economists' total cost function increases again.

Exhibit 2.3 Economic and Accounting Total Cost Structures

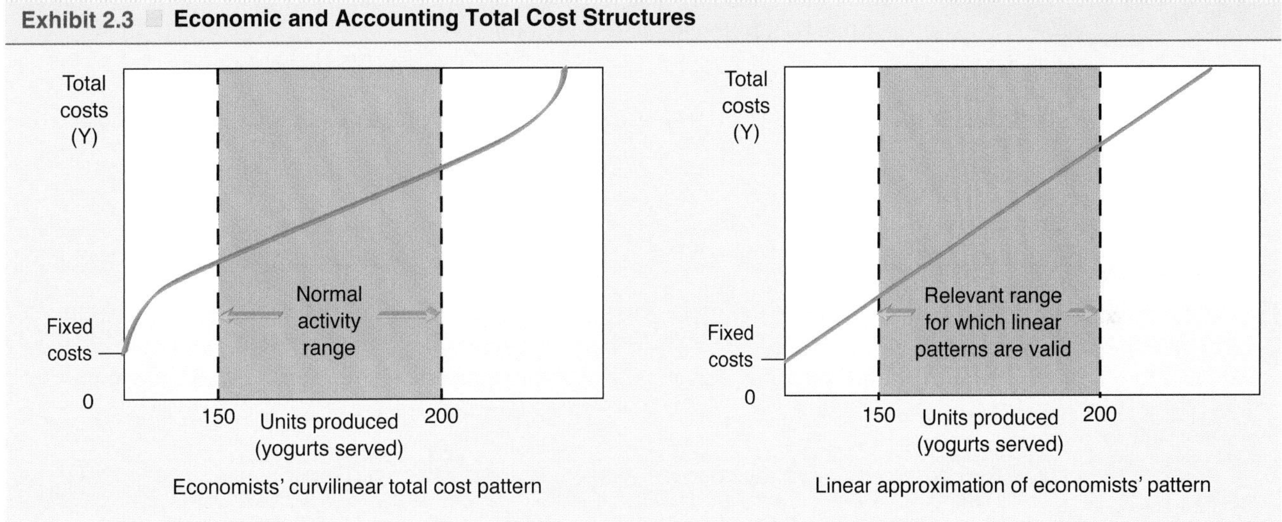

Business Insight ■ Firm Makes Warehouse Costs Variable

A warehouse is an essential but risky investment for many businesses. The risk is that actual activity will be above or below the level for which the facility was designed. The Raj India Trading Co., a Seattle-area importer, found itself in just this situation when changes to its product lines left it with a vastly underused warehouse. Rather than find a new, smaller warehouse, owner Jeff Lykins used the services of Flexe Inc. to rent out the unused space on a month-to-month basis.

While industrial real estate vacancy was low in 2015 (around 5% in key areas such as Seattle and Southern California), experts agreed that there was a surplus of warehouse space. Flexe Inc. carved out a niche by connecting companies in need of warehouse space and companies with unused space. Flexe let those who needed more space rent it by the pallet and helped those with too much space integrate the new pallets into their existing workflow. Flexe helped companies with fixed warehouse costs maintain usage and consume excess capacity.

Sources: David Morris, "This Startup Could Change the Game for Same-day Shipping," *Fortune*, October 9, 2015.
Erica E. Phillips, "Collaborative Logistics Comes to the Warehouse," *Wall Street Journal*, June 12, 2015.

If the economists' total cost curve is valid, how can we reasonably approximate it with a straight line? The answer to this question is in the notion of a *relevant range*. A linear pattern may be a poor approximation of the economists' curvilinear pattern over the entire range of possible activity, but a linear pattern as illustrated in the right-hand graph in **Exhibit 2.3** is often sufficiently accurate within the range of probable operations. The range of activity within which a linear cost function is valid is called the relevant range. Linear estimates of cost behavior are valid only within the relevant range. Extreme care must be exercised when making comments about cost behavior outside the relevant range.

Additional Cost Behavior Patterns

Although we have considered the most frequently used cost behavior patterns, remember that there are numerous ways that costs can respond to changes in activity. As illustrated by the preceding Business Insight box, it is important to think through each situation and then select a behavior pattern that seems logical and fits the known facts.

Particular care needs to be taken with the vertical axis. So far, all graphs have placed *total* costs on the vertical axis. Miscommunication is likely if one party is thinking in terms of *total* costs while the other is thinking in terms of *variable* or *average* costs. FIXthat4U is a smartphone and tablet repair store. FIXthat4U's monthly fixed costs include rent and depreciation on tools and furniture. Its variable costs include direct labor and any materials used up in the repair such as new screens. Consider FIXthat4U's following cost function:

Total costs = \$3,000 + \$5X

where

X = customer repairs

The total, variable cost per unit, and average cost per unit at various levels of activity are computed here and graphed in **Exhibit 2.4** on the following page. As the number of customer repairs increases, total costs increase, the variable costs of each repair remain constant, and the average cost decreases because fixed costs are spread over a larger number of repairs.

Customer Repairs	Total Costs	Average Cost*	Variable Costs per Repair
100	\$3,500	\$35.00	\$5.00
200	4,000	20.00	5.00
300	4,500	15.00	5.00
400	5,000	12.50	5.00
500	5,500	11.00	5.00

* Total costs/customer repairs

To predict total costs for the coming period, FIXthat4U's management will use the first graph in **Exhibit 2.4**. To determine the minimum price required to avoid a loss on each additional repair, management is interested in the variable costs per customer repair, yet if a manager inquired as to the cost of each customer repair, a financial accountant would probably provide average cost information, as illustrated in the third graph in **Exhibit 2.4**. The specific average cost would likely be a function of the number of customer repairs during the most recent accounting period.

Errors can occur if last period's average costs, perhaps based on a volume of 500 repairs, were used to predict total costs for a future period when the anticipated volume was some other amount, say 300 repairs. Using average costs, based on the 500 repairs, the predicted total costs of 300 repairs are \$3,300 (\$11 × 300). In fact, using the proper total cost function, a more accurate prediction of total costs is \$4,500 [\$3,000 + (\$5 × 300)]. The prediction error could cause a number of problems. If management budgeted \$3,300 to pay bills and the bills actually totaled \$4,500, the company might have to curtail activities or borrow under unfavorable terms to avoid running out of cash.

Because variable costs per unit remain constant within the relevant range, the average cost per unit will increase or decrease based on the change in the fixed cost per unit. To determine the number of customer repairs needed to lower the average cost to \$9, the average fixed cost must be \$4 (\$9 – \$5 variable cost per unit). That would occur when volume was 750 repairs (\$3,000/\$4).

Exhibit 2.4 Total Costs, Variable Costs, and Average Costs

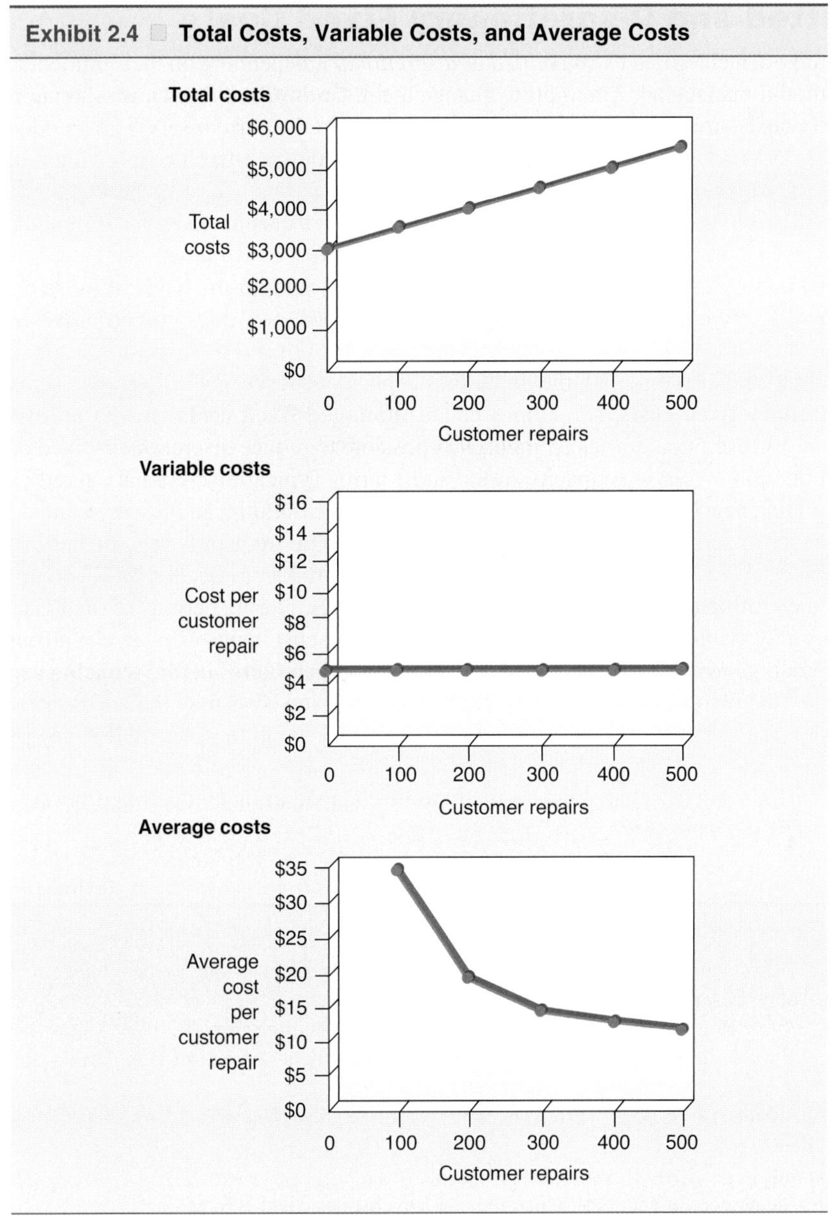

Research Insight ■ Managers Use Procurement to Control Risk

In a recent study of cost data from California Hospitals, researchers analyzed the way that firms adjust committed costs in response to external risk. The study shows that managers seek to mitigate the effects of both demand uncertainty and financial risk through procurement decisions. The study considers three procurement choices that affect committed costs:

1. Deliver new services through outsourcing or onsite.
2. Rent or purchase new equipment.
3. Structure labor costs to be more flexible versus fixed.

The researchers found that hospitals facing greater uncertainty limited committed costs, for example, limiting capital expenditures on equipment. This study highlights that managers can make cost-structure decisions that protect their organizations from the risk of demand uncertainty.

Source: Martin Holzhacker, Ranjani Krishnan, and Matthias D. Mahlendorf, "Unraveling the Black Box of Cost Behavior: An Empirical Investigation of Risk Drivers, Managerial Resource Procurement, and Cost Elasticity," *The Accounting Review* 90, no. 6 (2015): 2305-2335.

Committed and Discretionary Fixed Costs

Fixed costs are often classified as *committed* or *discretionary*, depending on their immediate impact on the organization if management attempts to change them. **Committed fixed costs**, sometimes referred to as **capacity costs**, are the fixed costs required to maintain the current service or production capacity or to fill previous legal commitments. Examples of committed fixed costs include depreciation, property taxes, rent, and interest on bonds.

Committed fixed costs are often the result of structural decisions about the size and nature of an organization. For example, years ago the management of Santa Fe Railroad made decisions concerning what communities the railroad would serve. Track was laid on the basis of those decisions and BNSF Railway, the company that acquired Santa Fe Railroad, now pays property taxes each year on the railroad's miles of track. These property taxes could be reduced by disposing of track. However, reducing track would also diminish the Santa Fe's capacity to serve.

Discretionary fixed costs, sometimes called **managed fixed costs**, are set at a fixed amount each period at the discretion of management. It is possible to reduce discretionary fixed costs without reducing production or service capacity in the short term. Typical discretionary fixed costs include advertising, maintenance, charitable contributions, employee training, and research and development.

Maintenance expenditures for discretionary fixed costs are frequently regarded as investments in the future. Research and development, for example, is undertaken to develop new or improved products that can be profitably produced and sold in future periods. During periods of financial well-being, organizations may make large expenditures on discretionary cost items. Conversely, during periods of financial stress, organizations likely reduce discretionary expenditures before reducing capacity costs. Unfortunately, fluctuations in the funding of discretionary fixed costs may reduce the effectiveness of long-range programs. A high-quality research staff may be difficult to reassemble if key personnel are laid off. Even the contemplation of layoffs may reduce the staff's effectiveness. In all periods, discretionary costs are subject to debate and are likely to be changed in the budgeting process.

Review 2-2 LO2 — Estimating Costs Using a Linear Total Cost Estimating Equation

The total monthly operating costs for a financial consulting firm is estimated to be $45,000 in fixed costs plus an additional $1,800 in variable costs per client. These estimates are valid as long as the number of clients does not exceed 50 clients per month.

1. Determine the linear total cost estimating equation for the consulting firm.
2. Determine the total monthly cost and the average cost per client if the firm is expecting the following number of clients for the month:
   a. 25 clients
   b. 30 clients
   c. 36 clients
3. Determine the number of clients at which the average cost per client is $2,925.

Solution on p. 2-66.

Cost Estimation

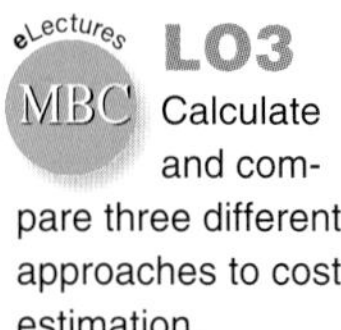

LO3 Calculate and compare three different approaches to cost estimation.

Cost estimation, the determination of the relationship between activity and cost, is an important part of cost management. In this section, we develop equations for the relationship between total costs and total activity.

To properly estimate the relationship between activity and cost, we must be familiar with basic cost behavior patterns and cost-estimating techniques. Costs known to have a variable or a fixed pattern are readily estimated by interviews or by analyzing available records. Sales commission per sales dollar, a variable cost, might be determined to be 15% of sales. In a similar manner, annual property taxes might be determined by consulting tax documents.

Mixed (semivariable) costs, which contain fixed and variable cost elements, are more difficult to estimate. According to a basic rule of algebra, two equations are needed to determine two unknowns. Following this rule, at least two observations are needed to determine the variable and fixed elements of a mixed cost.

High-Low Cost Estimation

The most straightforward approach to determining the variable and fixed elements of mixed costs is to use the **high-low method of cost estimation**. This method utilizes data from two time periods, a *representative* high-activity period and a *representative* low-activity period, to estimate fixed and variable costs. Assuming identical fixed costs in both periods, any difference in total costs between these two periods is due entirely to variable costs. The variable costs per unit are found by dividing the difference in total costs by the difference in total activity:

$$\textbf{Variable costs per unit} = \frac{\textbf{Difference in total costs}}{\textbf{Difference in activity}}$$

Once variable costs are determined, fixed costs, which are identical in both periods, are computed by subtracting the total variable costs of either the high or the low activity period from the corresponding total costs.

Fixed costs = Total costs – Variable costs

Assume a retailer such as Pottery Barn wants to develop a monthly cost function for its packaging department and that the number of shipments is believed to be the primary cost driver. The following observations are available for the first four months of the year.

		Number of Shipments	Packaging Costs
(Low-activity period)	January	6,000	$17,000
	February	9,000	26,000
(High-activity period)	March	12,000	32,000
	April	10,000	20,000

Equations for total costs for the packaging department in January and March (the periods of lowest and highest activity) follow:

January: $17,000 = a + b (6,000 shipments)
March: $32,000 = a + b (12,000 shipments)

where

a = fixed costs per month
b = variable costs per shipment

Solving for the estimated variable costs per shipment:

$$b = \frac{\textbf{Difference in total costs}}{\textbf{Difference in activity}}$$

$$b = \frac{\$32{,}000 - \$17{,}000}{12{,}000 - 6{,}000}$$

$$= \$2.50$$

Next, the estimated monthly fixed costs are determined by subtracting variable costs from total costs of *either* the January or March equation:

$$\textbf{a = Total costs} - \textbf{Variable costs}$$
$$\textbf{January : a = \$17,000} - \textbf{(\$2.50 per shipment} \times \textbf{6,000 shipments)}$$
$$= \textbf{\$2,000}$$

or

$$\textbf{March : a = \$32,000} - \textbf{(\$2.50 per shipment} \times \textbf{12,000 shipments)}$$
$$= \textbf{\$2,000}$$

The cost-estimating equation for total packaging department costs is:

$$\textbf{Y = \$2,000 + \$2.50X}$$

where

X = number of shipments

Y = total costs for the packaging department

The concepts underlying the high-low method of cost estimation are illustrated in **Exhibit 2.5**.

Cost prediction, the forecasting of future costs, is a common purpose of cost estimation. Previously developed estimates of cost behavior are often the starting point in predicting future costs. Continuing the Pottery Barn example, if 5,000 shipments are budgeted for June, the predicted June packaging department costs are $14,500 [$2,000 + ($2.50 per shipment × 5,000 shipments)].

Exhibit 2.5 High-Low Cost Estimation

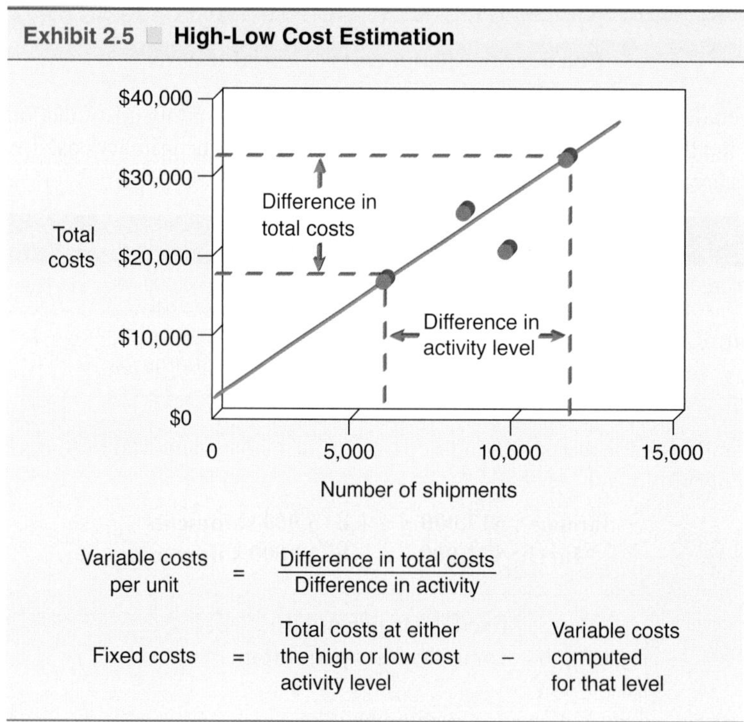

Scatter Diagrams

A **scatter diagram** is a graph of past activity and cost data, with individual observations represented by dots. Plotting historical cost data on a scatter diagram is a useful approach to cost estimation, especially when used in conjunction with other cost-estimating techniques. As illustrated in **Exhibit 2.6**, a scatter diagram helps in selecting high and low activity levels representative of normal operating conditions. The periods of highest or lowest activity may not be representative because of the cost of overtime, the use of less efficient equipment, strikes, and so forth. If the goal is to develop an equation to predict costs under normal operating conditions, then the equation should be based on observations of normal operating conditions. A scatter diagram is also useful in determining whether costs can be reasonably approximated by a straight line.

Exhibit 2.6 Selecting High and Low Activity Levels with a Scatter Diagram

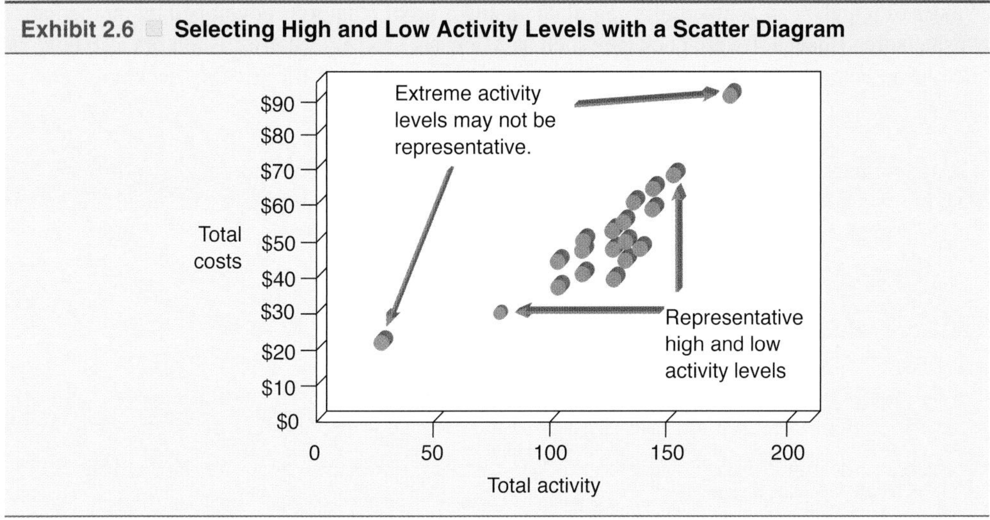

Scatter diagrams are sometimes used alone as a basis of cost estimation. This requires the use of professional judgment to draw a representative straight line through the plot of historical data. Typically, the analyst tries to ensure that an equal number of observations are on either side of the line while minimizing the total vertical differences between the line and actual cost observations at each value of the independent variable. Once a line is drawn, cost estimates at any representative volume are made by studying the line. Where the line crosses the Y axis represents total fixed costs. Variable cost per unit is calculated by solving the cost-estimating equation using total cost and activity from one of the points closest to the line. Alternatively, an equation for the line may be developed by applying the high-low method to any two points on the line.

Least-Squares Regression

Least-squares regression analysis uses a mathematical technique to fit a cost-estimating equation to the observed data. The technique mathematically accomplishes what the analyst does visually with a scatter diagram. The least-squares technique creates an equation that minimizes the sum of the vertical squared differences between the estimated and the actual costs at each observation. Each of these differences is an estimating error. Using the packaging department example, the least-squares criterion is illustrated in **Exhibit 2.7**. Estimated values of total monthly packaging costs are represented by the straight line, and the actual values of total monthly packaging costs are represented by the dots. For each dot, such as the one at a volume of 10,000 shipments, the line is fit to minimize the vertical squared differences.

Exhibit 2.7 Least-Squares Criterion

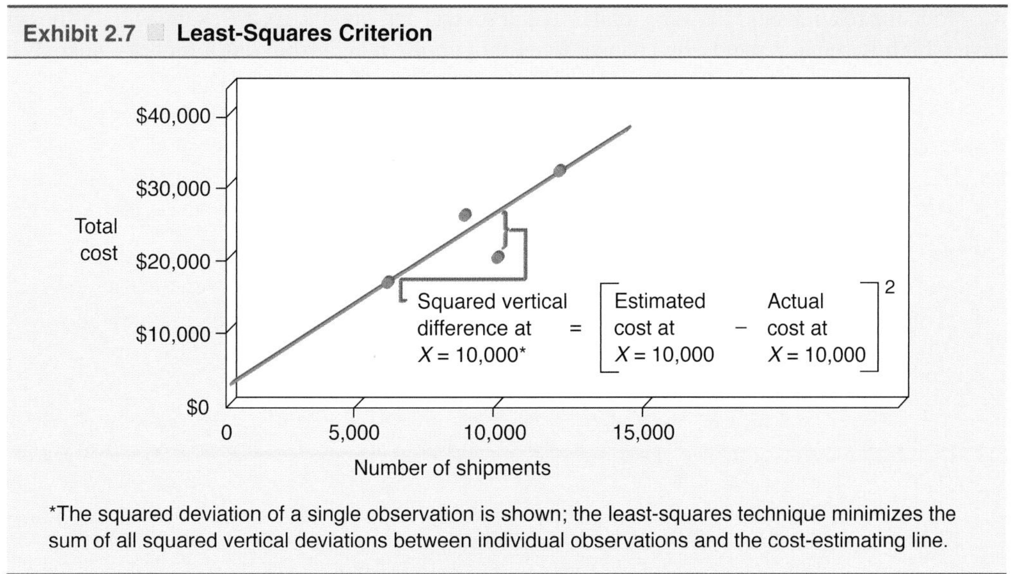

*The squared deviation of a single observation is shown; the least-squares technique minimizes the sum of all squared vertical deviations between individual observations and the cost-estimating line.

Values of *a* and *b* can be manually calculated using a set of equations developed by mathematicians or by using spreadsheet software packages such as Microsoft Excel®. Many calculators also have built-in functions to compute these coefficients. The least-squares equation for monthly packaging costs is:

$$Y = \$3{,}400 + \$2.20X$$

Using the least-squares equation, the predicted June packaging department costs with 5,000 budgeted shipments are $14,400 [$3,400 + ($2.20 per shipment × 5,000 shipments)]. Recall that the high-low method predicted June costs of $14,500. Although this difference is small, we should consider which prediction is more reliable.

Advantage of Least-Squares Regression

Mathematicians regard least-squares regression analysis as superior to both the high-low and the scatter diagram methods. It uses all available data, rather than just two observations, and does not rely on subjective judgment in drawing a line. Statistical measures are also available to determine how well a least-squares equation fits the historical data. These measures are often contained in the output of spreadsheet software packages.

In addition to the vertical axis intercept and the slope, least-squares regression calculates the coefficient of determination. The **coefficient of determination** is a measure of the percent of variation in the dependent variable (such as total packaging department costs) that is explained by variations in the independent variable (such as total shipments). Statisticians often refer to the coefficient of determination as R-squared and represent it as R^2.

The coefficient of determination can have values between zero and one, with values close to zero suggesting that the equation is not very useful and values close to one indicating that the equation explains most of the variation in the dependent variable. When choosing between two cost-estimating equations, the one with the higher coefficient of determination is generally preferred. The coefficient of determination for the packaging department cost-estimating equation, determined using least-squares regression analysis, is 0.68. This means that 68% of the variation in packaging department costs is explained by the number of shipments.

Managers, Not Models, Are Responsible

Although computers make least-squares regression easy to use, the generated output should not automatically be accepted as correct. Statistics and other mathematical techniques are tools to help managers make decisions. Managers, not mathematical models, are responsible for decisions. Judgment should always be exercised when considering the validity of the least-squares approach, the solution, and the data. If the objective is to predict future costs under normal operating conditions, observations reflecting abnormal operating conditions should be deleted. Also examine the cost behavior pattern to determine whether it is linear. Scatter diagrams assist in both of these judgments. Finally, the results should make sense. When the relationships between total cost and several activity drivers are examined, it is possible to have a high R-squared purely by chance. Even though the relationship has a high R-squared, if it "doesn't make sense" there is probably something wrong.

Simple and Multiple Regression

Least-squares regression analysis is identified as "simple regression analysis" when there is only one independent variable and as "multiple regression analysis" when there are two or more independent variables. The general form for simple regression analysis is:

$$Y = a + bX$$

The general form for multiple regression analysis is:

$$Y = a + \Sigma b_i X_i$$

In this case, the subscript i is a general representation of each independent variable. When there are several independent variables, i is set equal to 1 for the first, 2 for the second, and so forth. The total variable costs of each independent variable are computed as b_iX_i, with b_i representing the variable cost per unit of independent variable X_i. The Greek symbol sigma, Σ, indicates that the costs of all independent variables are summed in determining total variable costs.

As an illustration, assume that Staples' costs are expressed as a function of the unit sales of its two products: executive desks and task desks. Assume fixed costs are $18,000 per month and the variable costs are $250 per executive desk and $120 per task desk. The mathematical representation of monthly costs with two variables is:

$$Y = a + b_1X_1 + b_2X_2$$

where

$$\begin{aligned} a &= \$18{,}000 \\ b_1 &= \$250 \text{ per executive desk} \\ b_2 &= \$120 \text{ per task desk} \\ X_1 &= \text{unit sales of executive desks} \\ X_2 &= \text{unit sales of task desks} \end{aligned}$$

During a month if 105 executive desks and 200 task desks are sold, Staples' estimated total costs are:

$$\begin{aligned} Y &= \$18{,}000 + \$250(105) + \$120(200) \\ &= \$68{,}250 \end{aligned}$$

In addition to estimating costs, multiple regression analysis can be used to determine the effect of individual product features on the market value of a product or service. Multiple regression can be done in Excel or in data analysis applications like Tableau or Python. The following Research Insight reports on insurance companies that use lifestyle and health behaviors to predict future health issues using a model similar to multiple regression analysis. These predictions are used to motivate changes in behavior that will ultimately improve employee health and reduce costs.

Research Insight ■ Regression Modeling and Data Analytics

Regression analysis is one of the primary tools used in predictive analytics. Predictive analytics is the use of current and historical data to predict future outcomes and trends. The extensive amount of data that companies are now able to collect increases the use and value of predictive analytic models.

How can companies use data analytics to reduce costs? To lower costs of employee turnover, companies have used data analytics to analyze the potential fit of applicants for open positions and to monitor employee frustration levels.

Kaiser Permanente, a hospital and health-insurance company, has reduced readmission costs by using data to better monitor and assess patients recovering from a cardiac event (heart attacks, bypass surgery, and heart failure). Patients are given smartwatches to use over an eight-week rehab program. The smartwatch collects data such as steps taken and pulse levels. Patients send Kaiser details of exercise sessions and symptoms through a mobile app accessible through their watch. In return, reminders are sent to patients about medication and exercise. If the patient isn't meeting program goals, health-providers can follow up with phone calls. Kaiser is also able to use the data collected to determine the most effective program plans. In the first year, readmission rates for participating patients were less than 2%, compared to 10% to 15%, on average, for patients in-clinic rehab programs.

Source: Kayla Matthews, "6 Ways Companies Are Using Data Analytics to Reduce Expenses," *InsideBIGDATA*, February 24, 2019. Agam Shah, "Kaiser Permanente Bets on Smartwatches to Lower Costs," *Wall Street Journal*, January 15, 2020.

Managerial Decision ■ You Are the Purchasing Manager

Your department has been experiencing increased activity in recent periods as the company has grown, and you have observed that the average cost per purchase order processed has been declining, but not at a constant rate. You have been given an estimate by the production manager of the number of purchase orders that will be processed next period and have been asked by the accounting department to provide within one hour an estimate of the cost to process those orders. How can the scatter diagram method help you to meet this deadline? [Answer, p. 53]

Review 2-3 LO3 Using the High-Low Method to Estimate Costs

Assume a local Subway reported the following results for April and May:

	April	May
Sandwiches sold	2,100	2,700
Cost of food sold	$1,575	$2,025
Wages and salaries	1,525	1,675
Rent on building	1,500	1,500
Depreciation on equipment	200	200
Utilities	710	770
Supplies	225	255
Miscellaneous	113	131
Total	$5,848	$6,556

Required

a. Create an equation for each of the following costs in April: cost of food sold, wages and salaries, rent on building, and total monthly costs. Use the high-low method to create an equation for any mixed cost.

b. Predict total costs for monthly volumes of 1,000 and 2,000 sandwiches.

c. Predict the average cost per unit at monthly volumes of 1,000 and 2,000 sandwiches. Explain why the average costs differ at these two volumes.

Solution on p. 2-66.

Additional Issues in Cost Estimation

LO4 Identify and discuss problems encountered in cost estimation.

We have mentioned several items to be wary of when developing cost-estimating equations:

- Data that are not based on normal operating conditions.
- Nonlinear relationships between total costs and activity.
- Obtaining a high R-squared purely by chance.

Additional items of concern include

- Changes in technology or prices.
- Matching activity and cost within each observation.
- Identifying activity cost drivers.

Changes in Technology and Prices

Changes in technology and prices make cost estimation and prediction difficult. When telecommunications companies changed from using landlines to voice over internet protocol (VOIP) to place long-distance telephone calls, cost estimates based on the use of fiber optic cables were of little or no value in predicting future costs. Care must be taken to make sure that data used in developing cost estimates are based on the existing technology. When this is not possible, professional judgment is required to make appropriate adjustments.

Only data reflecting a single price level should be used in cost estimation and prediction. If prices have remained stable in the past but then uniformly increase by 20%, cost-estimating equations based on data from previous periods will not accurately predict future costs. In this case, all that is required is a 20% increase in the prediction. Unfortunately, adjustments for price changes are seldom this simple. The prices of various cost elements are likely to change at different rates and at different times. Furthermore, there are probably several different price levels included in the past data used to develop cost-estimating equations. If data from different price levels are used, an attempt should be made to restate them to a single price level.

Matching Activity and Costs

The development of accurate cost-estimating equations requires the matching of the activity to related costs within each observation. This accuracy is often difficult to achieve because of the time lag between an activity and the recording of the cost of resources consumed by the activity. Current activities usually consume electricity, but the electric bill won't be received and recorded until next month. Driving an automobile requires routine maintenance for items such as lubrication and oil, but the auto can be driven several weeks or even months before the maintenance is required. Consequently, daily, weekly, and perhaps even monthly observations of miles driven and maintenance costs are unlikely to match the costs of oil and lubrication with the cost-driving activity, miles driven.

In general, the shorter the time period, the higher the probability of error in matching costs and activity. The cost analyst must carefully review the database to verify that activity and cost are matched within each observation. If matching problems are found, it may be possible to adjust the data (perhaps by moving the cost of electricity from one observation to another). Under other circumstances, it may be necessary to use longer periods to match costs and activity.

Identifying Activity Cost Drivers

Identifying the appropriate activity cost driver for a particular cost requires judgment and professional experience. In general, the cost driver should have a logical, causal relationship with costs. In many cases, the identity of the most appropriate activity cost driver, such as miles driven for the cost of automobile gasoline, is apparent. In other situations, where different activity cost drivers might be used, scatter diagrams and statistical measures, such as the coefficient of determination, are helpful in selecting the activity cost driver that best explains past variations in cost. When scatter diagrams are used, the analyst can study the dispersion of observations around the cost-estimating line. In general, a small dispersion is preferred. If regression analysis is used, the analyst considers the coefficient of determination. In general, a higher coefficient of determination is preferred. The relationship between the activity cost driver and the cost must seem logical, and the activity data must be available.

Identifying Appropriate Cost Drivers **LO4 Review 2-4**

a. Identify potential activity drivers that would have logical and causal relations with costs in a manufacturing operation.

b. In deciding which activity driver is the most appropriate for a particular manufacturing cost, would the following items make the driver more desirable or less desirable? Consider each scenario separately.

1. A scatter plot reveals a small dispersion of points around the cost-estimating line.
2. The coefficient of determination is 0.65 which is less than the coefficient of the other options.
3. There is a logical relation between the activity and the cost but the activity data is not reliably available.
4. Observations on a scatter plot do not reasonably approximate a straight-line.
5. The cost changes with changes in the level of the activity driver.
6. The coefficient of determination is 0.88 which is greater than the coefficient of the other options.

Solution on p. 2-67.

Alternative Cost Driver Classifications

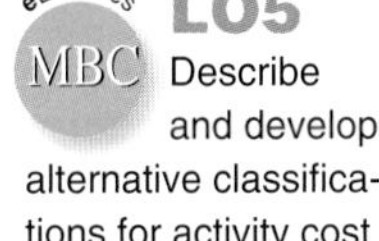

LO5 Describe and develop alternative classifications for activity cost drivers.

So far we have examined cost behavior and cost estimation using only a unit-level approach, which assumes changes in costs are best explained by changes in the number of units of product or service provided customers. This approach may have worked for Carnegie Steel Company, but it is inappropriate for multidimensional organizations, such as Square. The unit-level approach becomes increasingly inaccurate for analyzing cost behavior when organizations experience the following types of changes:

- From face-to-face customer interactions to web-based interface,
- From stand-alone products to products with multiple layers of customer interface, such as Square's hardware versus the processing of payments executed by Square for its customers, and

- From internet-based operations to mobile platforms, thus engaging a more geographically diverse set of customers.

Exhibit 2.8 illustrates the composition of total manufacturing costs for the past century, illustrating changes in the percentage of manufacturing costs for three major cost categories.

Exhibit 2.8 Changing Composition of Total Manufacturing Costs

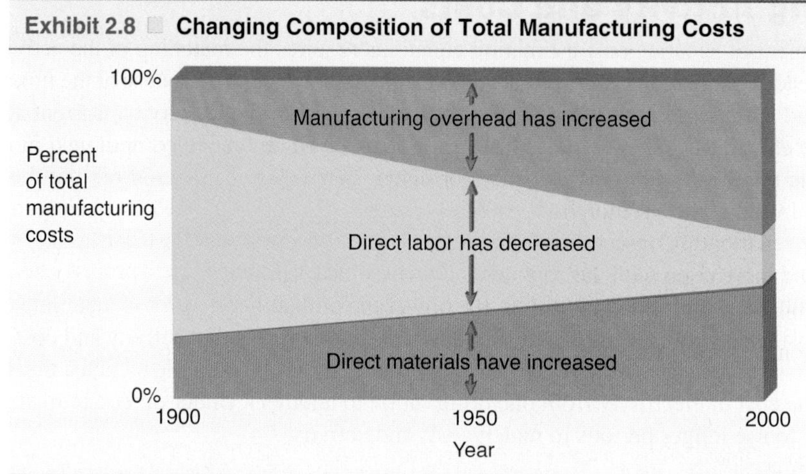

1. **Direct materials**, the cost of primary raw materials converted into finished goods, have increased slightly as organizations purchase components they formerly fabricated. The word "direct" is used to indicate costs that are easily or directly traced to a finished product or service.
2. **Direct labor**, the wages earned by production employees for the time they spend converting raw materials into finished products, has decreased significantly as employees spend less time physically working on products and more time supporting automated production activities.
3. **Manufacturing overhead**, which includes all manufacturing costs other than direct materials and direct labor, has increased significantly due to automation, product diversity, and product complexity.

Changes in the composition of manufacturing costs have implications for the behavior of total costs and the responsiveness of costs to changes in cost drivers. Because direct materials and direct labor vary directly with the number of units, they are easy to measure. In the past, when manufacturing overhead was relatively small, it was possible to assume units of product or service was the primary cost driver. This is no longer true. Units of final product is no longer an adequate explanation of changes in manufacturing overhead for many organizations.

The past tendency to ignore overhead, while focusing on direct materials and direct labor, led one researcher to describe overhead-causing activities as "the hidden factory."[1] To better understand the hidden factory, several researchers have developed frameworks for categorizing cost-driving activities. The crucial feature of these frameworks is the inclusion of nonunit cost drivers. Depending on the characteristics of a particular organization, as well as management's information needs, there are an almost unlimited number of cost driver classification schemes. We consider two frequently applied cost driver classification schemes: one based on a manufacturing cost hierarchy and a second based on a customer cost hierarchy. We also illustrate variations of each.

Manufacturing Cost Hierarchy

The most well-known framework, developed by Cooper[2] and Cooper and Kaplan[3] for manufacturing situations, classifies activities into the following four categories.

[1] Jeffrey G. Miller and Thomas E. Vollmann, "The Hidden Factory," *Harvard Business Review*, September-October 1985, pp. 142–150.

[2] Robin Cooper, "Cost Classification in Unit-Based and Activity-Based Manufacturing Cost Systems," *Journal of Cost Management*, Fall 1990, pp. 4–14.

[3] Robin Cooper and Robert S. Kaplan, "Profit Priorities from Activity-Based Costing," *Harvard Business Review*, May-June 1991, pp. 130–135.

1. A **unit-level activity** is performed *for each unit* of product produced. Christofle is a French manufacturer of high-end silver flatware. In the production of forks, the stamping of each fork into the prescribed shape is an example of a unit-level cost driver.
2. A **batch-level activity** is performed *for each batch* of product produced. At Christofle, a batch is a number of identical units (such as a fork of a specific design) produced at the same time. Batch-level activities include setting up the machines to stamp each fork in an identical manner, moving the entire batch between workstations (i.e., molding, stamping, and finishing), and inspecting the first unit in the batch to verify that the machines are set up correctly.
3. A **product-level activity** is performed *to support* the production of *each different type of product*. At Christofle, product-level activities for a specific pattern of fork include initially designing the fork, producing and maintaining the mold for the fork, and determining manufacturing operations for the fork.
4. A **facility-level activity** is performed *to maintain* general manufacturing capabilities. At Christofle, facility-level activities include plant management, building maintenance, property taxes, and electricity required to sustain the building.

Several additional examples of the costs driven by activities at each level are presented in **Exhibit 2.9**.

Exhibit 2.9 Hierarchy of Activity Costs

Activity Level	Reason for Activity	Examples of Activity Cost
1. Unit level	Performed for each unit of product produced or sold	• Cost of raw materials • Cost of inserting a component • Utilities cost of operating equipment • Some costs of packaging • Sales commissions
2. Batch level	Performed for each batch of product produced or sold	• Cost of processing sales order • Cost of issuing and tracking work order • Cost of equipment setup • Cost of moving batch between workstations • Cost of inspection (assuming same number of units inspected in each batch)
3. Product level	Performed to support each different product that can be produced	• Cost of product development • Cost of product marketing such as advertising • Cost of specialized equipment • Cost of maintaining specialized equipment
4. Facility level	Performed to maintain general manufacturing capabilities	• Cost of maintaining general facilities such as buildings and grounds • Cost of nonspecialized equipment • Cost of maintaining nonspecialized equipment • Cost of real property taxes • Cost of general advertising • Cost of general administration such as the plant manager's salary

When using a cost hierarchy for analyzing and estimating costs, total costs are broken down into the different cost levels in the hierarchy, and a separate cost driver is determined for each level of cost. For example, using the above hierarchy, the costs that are related to the number of units produced (such as direct materials or direct labor) may have direct labor hours or machine hours as the cost driver; whereas batch costs may be driven by the number of setups of production machines or the number of times materials are moved from one machine to another. Other costs may be driven by the number of different products produced. Facility-level costs are generally regarded as fixed costs and do not vary unless capacity is increased or decreased.

Customer Cost Hierarchy

The manufacturing hierarchy presented is but one of many possible ways of classifying activities and their costs. Classification schemes should be designed to fit the organization and meet user needs. A merchandising organization or the sales division of a manufacturing organization might use the following hierarchy.

1. **Unit-level activity**: performed for each unit sold.
2. **Order-level activity**: performed for each sales order.
3. **Customer-level activity:** performed to obtain or maintain each customer.
4. **Facility-level activity**: performed to maintain the general sales or store function.

This classification scheme assists in answering questions concerning the cost of individual orders or individual customers.

If an organization sells to distinct market segments (for profit, not for profit, and government), the cost hierarchy can be modified as follows:

1. Unit-level activity
2. Order-level activity
3. Customer-level activity
4. **Market-segment-level activity:** performed to obtain or maintain operations in a segment.
5. Facility-level activity

The market-segment-level activities and their related costs differ with each market segment. This classification scheme assists in answering questions concerning the profitability of each segment.

Finally, an organization that completes unique projects for different market segments (such as buildings for IBM and the U.S. Department of Defense) can use the following hierarchy to determine the profitability of each segment:

1. **Project-level activity**: performed to support the completion of each project.
2. Market-segment-level activity
3. Facility-level activity

The possibilities are endless. The important point is that both the cost hierarchy and the costs included in the hierarchy be tailored to meet the specific circumstances of an organization and the interests of management.

Review 2-5 LO5 — Classifying Costs Using a Customer Cost Hierarchy

Consider the pizza chain Blaze Pizza. It custom builds and cooks each pizza to order. Items 1–6 represent cost activities associated with a particular store.

1. Pepperoni on the pizza
2. Wood to fuel the fire used to cook the pizzas
3. Insurance on the building
4. The labor costs of the employee building and cooking each pizza
5. The cost of the sales calls made to local organizations to promote the pizzas for catering special events
6. The costs associated with employees taking pizza orders

Required

Classify each cost activity above, in the most appropriate level of the proposed customer cost hierarchy. Each cost activity may be used more than once.

______ *a.* Unit-level—performed for each unit sold
______ *b.* Order-level—performed for each sales order
______ *c.* Customer-level—performed to obtain or maintain each customer
______ *d.* Store(facility)-level—performed to maintain the general store functions

Solution on p. 2-67.

Guidance Answers

You Are the Purchasing Manager

Pg. 48 One of the quickest methods for gaining a general understanding of the relationship between a given cost and its cost driver is to graph the relationship using data from several recent periods. As purchasing manager you could probably quickly obtain information about the amount of the total purchasing department costs and number of purchase orders processed for each of the most recent eight or ten periods. By graphing these data with costs on the vertical axis and number of purchase orders on the horizontal axis, you should be able to visually determine if there is an obvious behavioral pattern (variable, fixed, or mixed). Since costs have been declining as volume has increased, this would suggest that there are some fixed costs, and that they have been declining on a per unit basis as they are spread over an increasing number of purchase orders. Using two representative data points in the scatter diagram, you can plot a cost curve on the graph, and then use the data for those two points to calculate the estimated fixed and variable costs using the high-low cost estimation method. Using these cost estimates, you can predict the total cost for next period. This method may not give you a precise estimate of the cost, but coupled with your subjective estimate of cost based on your experience as manager of the department, it should give you more confidence than merely making a best guess. Hopefully, you will have an opportunity before presenting your budget for the next period to conduct additional analyses using more advanced methods.

Key Ratios

Variable costs: $Y = bX$

Where b = the variable cost per unit, sometimes referred to as the slope of the cost function.

Fixed costs: $Y = a$

Where a = total fixed costs. The slope of the fixed cost function is zero because fixed costs do not change with activity.

Mixed costs: $Y = a + bX$

Where a = total fixed cost element and b = variable cost element per unit of activity.

Step cost: $Y = a_i$

Where a_i = the step cost within a specific range of activity, identified by the subscript i.

Total costs: $Y = a + bX$

Where Y = total costs, a = vertical axis intercept (an approximation of fixed costs), b = slope (an approximation of variable costs per unit of X), and X = value of independent variable.

$$\text{Variable costs per unit} = \frac{\text{Difference in total costs}}{\text{Difference in activity}}$$

Fixed costs = Total costs − Variable costs

General form for simple regression analysis: $Y = a + bX$

Where a = total fixed cost element and b = the variable cost per unit of independent variable X.

General form for multiple regression analysis is: $Y = a + \sum b_i X_i$

Where the subscript i is a general representation of each independent variable. When there are several independent variables, i is set equal to 1 for the first, 2 for the second, and so forth. The total variable costs of each independent variable are computed as $b_i X_i$, with b_i representing the variable cost per unit of independent variable X_i. The Greek symbol sigma, $\sum$, indicates that the costs of all independent variables are summed in determining total variable costs.

Key Terms

batch-level activity, 51
capacity costs, 42
coefficient of determination, 46
committed fixed costs, 42
cost behavior, 34
cost estimation, 42
cost prediction, 44
customer-level activity, 52
direct labor, 50
direct materials, 50
discretionary fixed costs, 42
facility-level activity, 51, 52
fixed costs, 34
high-low method of cost estimation, 43
least-squares regression analysis, 45
managed fixed costs, 42
manufacturing overhead, 50
marginal cost, 38
market-segment-level activity, 52
mixed costs, 34
order-level activity, 52
product-level activity, 51
project-level activity, 52
relevant range, 38
scatter diagram, 44
semivariable costs, 34
step costs, 34
unit-level activity, 50, 52
variable costs, 34

Multiple Choice

Multiple Choice Answers
1. a 2. d 3. d 4. c 5. c 6. c 7. d

Papa Murphy's (FRSH)

1. A graph of the total cost of ingredients used in Papa Murphy's pizzas most closely resembles this total cost behavior pattern:
   a. Variable cost
   b. Fixed cost
   c. Mixed cost
   d. Step cost

2. Increasing the length of the time period included in each observation of activity and cost will assist in overcoming this possible problem in cost estimation:
   a. Data not based on normal operations
   b. Nonlinear relationship between total costs and activity
   c. Changes in technology or prices
   d. Failure to match activity and costs within each observation

3. At a sales volume of 50 units the average cost is $410 per unit and the variable cost is $10 per unit. Assuming a linear cost behavior pattern, if sales double to 100 units the average cost will be
   a. $10
   b. $200
   c. $205
   d. $210

4. Employees of Chelsea, a financial consulting firm, often travel to client sites for project meetings. The firm's business manager is attempting to better understand the costs associated with the employees' company cars. Below is data for the first four months of the year related to miles incurred and costs associated with the cars, including leases, insurance, maintenance, and gas. Use the high-low method to calculate the fixed costs associated with the company cars.

	Mileage	Costs
Jan.	450	$29,300
Feb.	325	$22,550
Mar.	418	$27,572
Apr.	380	$25,520

   a. $0.54
   b. $3,215
   c. $5,000
   d. $4,500

5. Which of the following situations would cause concern when an analyst is developing a cost-estimating equation?

a. A relatively linear relationship exists between total costs and activity.
b. The data is based on normal operating conditions.
c. The industry incurs significant changes in technology.
d. The cost driver has a logical, causal relationship with costs.

6. Arch manufactures a product with the following manufacturing cost hierarchy for its only current product:

	Cost
Unit	$20/unit
Batch	$500/batch
Product	$10,000/year
Facility	$50,000/year

Next year Arch plans to manufacture 50,000 units of product in batches of 500 units. Arch's predicted manufacturing costs for next year are

a. $1,560,000
b. $1,500,000
c. $1,110,000
d. $660,000

7. West sells specialized products produced by electronics companies to 100 engineering firms. West sells these products at a price based on West's purchase price. West's customer cost hierarchy is as follows:

	Cost
Unit	80% of selling price
Batch	$200 per sales order
Customer	$1,000 per customer per year
Facility	$120,000 per year

Next year West plans to sell $4,000,000 of product to the 100 engineering firms it serves. It anticipates that each firm will place an average of 4 orders. West's predicted customer costs for next year are

a. $80,000
b. $300,000
c. $3,200,000
d. $3,500,000

Questions

Q2-1. Briefly describe variable, fixed, mixed, and step costs and indicate how the total cost function of each changes as activity increases within a time period.

Q2-2. Why is presenting all costs of an organization as a function of a single independent variable, although useful in obtaining a general understanding of cost behavior, often not accurate enough to make specific decisions concerning products, services, or activities?

Q2-3. Explain the term "relevant range" and why it is important in estimating total costs.

Q2-4. How are variable and fixed costs determined using the high-low method of cost estimation?

Q2-5. Distinguish between cost estimation and cost prediction.

Q2-6. Why is a scatter diagram helpful when used in conjunction with other methods of cost estimation?

Q2-7. Identify two advantages of least-squares regression analysis as a cost-estimating technique.

Q2-8. Why is it important to match activity and costs within each observation? When is this matching problem most likely to exist?

Q2-9. During the past century, how have direct materials, direct labor, and manufacturing overhead changed as a portion of total manufacturing costs? What is the implication of the change in manufacturing overhead for cost estimation?

Q2-10. Distinguish between the unit-, batch-, product-, and facility-level activities of a manufacturing organization.

Assignments with the MBC logo in the margin are available in myBusinessCourse. See the Preface of the book for details.

Mini Exercises

LO1 **M2-11. Classifying Cost Behavior**

Classify the total costs of each of the following as variable, fixed, mixed, or step. Sales volume is the cost driver.

a. Salary of the department manager
b. Memory chips in a computer assembly plant
c. Real estate taxes
d. Salaries of quality inspectors when each inspector can evaluate a maximum of 1,000 units per day
e. Wages paid to production employees for the time spent working on products
f. Electric power in a factory
g. Raw materials used in production
h. Automobiles rented on the basis of a fixed charge per day plus an additional charge per mile driven
i. Sales commissions
j. Straight-line depreciation on office equipment

LO1 **M2-12. Classifying Cost Behavior**

Classify the total costs of each of the following as variable, fixed, mixed, or step.

a. Straight-line depreciation on a building
b. Maintenance costs at a hospital
c. Rent on a photocopy machine charged as a fixed amount per month plus an additional charge per copy
d. Cost of goods sold in a bookstore
e. Salaries paid to temporary instructors in a college as the number of course sessions varies
f. Lumber used by a house construction company
g. The costs of operating a research department
h. The cost of hiring a dance band for three hours
i. Laser printer paper for a department printer
j. Electric power in a restaurant

LO1, 2, 3 **M2-13. Classifying Cost Behavior**

For each of the following situations, select the most appropriate cost behavior pattern (as shown in the illustrations following this problem) where the lines represent the cost behavior pattern, the vertical axis represents costs, the horizontal axis represents total volume, and the dots represent actual costs. Each pattern may be used more than once.

a. Variable costs per unit
b. Total fixed costs
c. Total mixed costs
d. Average fixed costs per unit
e. Total current manufacturing costs
f. Average variable costs
g. Total costs when employees are paid $15 per hour for the first 40 hours worked each week and $20 for each additional hour
h. Total costs when employees are paid $15 per hour and guaranteed a minimum weekly wage of $300
i. Total costs per day when a consultant is paid $200 per hour with a maximum daily fee of $1,000
j. Total variable costs
k. Total costs for salaries of social workers where each social worker can handle a maximum of 25 cases

l. A water bill where a flat fee of $800 is charged for the first 100,000 gallons and additional water costs $0.005 per gallon
m. Total variable costs properly used to estimate step costs
n. Total materials costs
o. Rent on exhibit space at a convention

Graphs for Mini Exercise 2-13

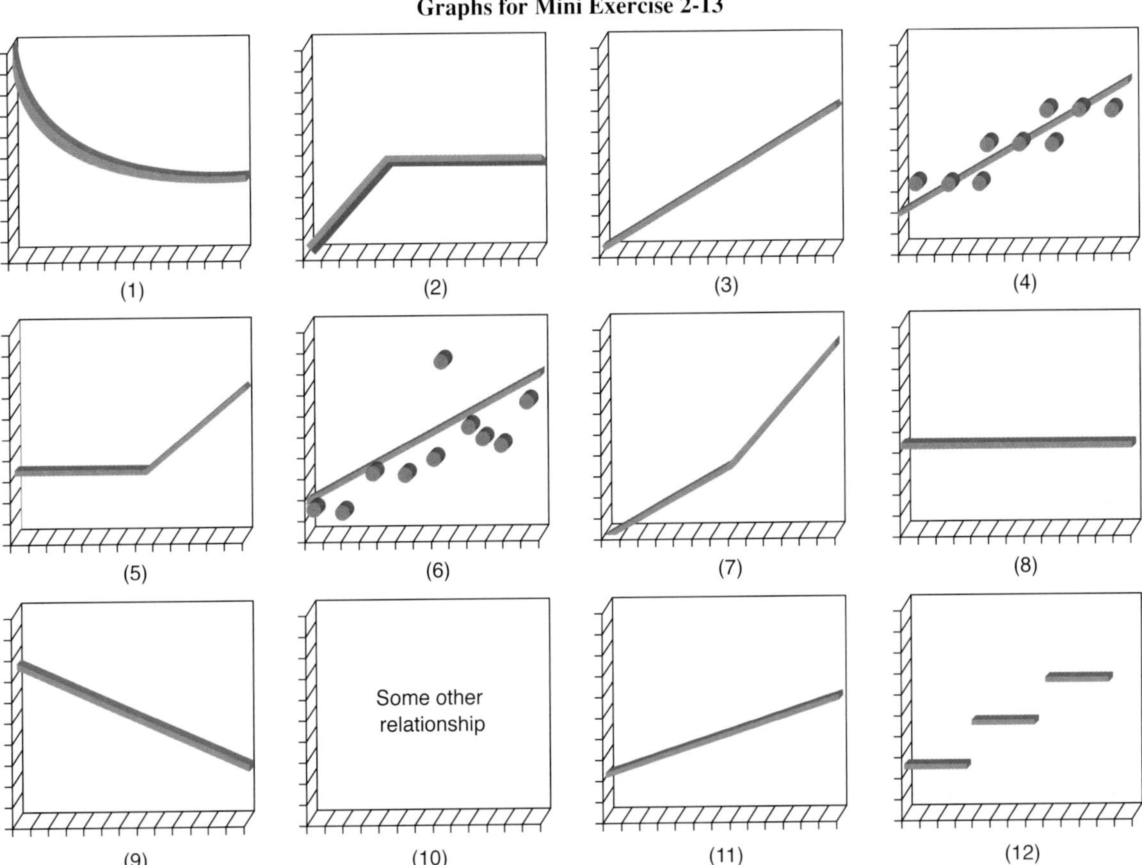

M2-14. Classifying Cost Behavior LO1, 2, 3

For each of the graphs displayed following this problem, select the most appropriate cost behavior pattern where the lines represent the cost behavior pattern, the vertical axis represents total costs, the horizontal axis represents total volume, and the dots represent actual costs. Each pattern may be used more than once.

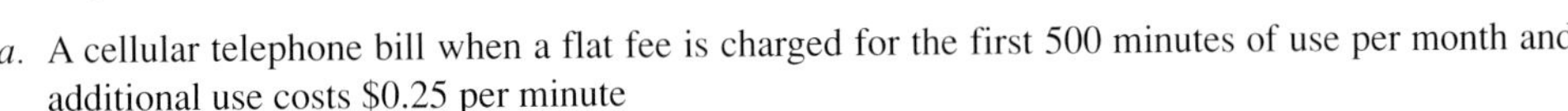

a. A cellular telephone bill when a flat fee is charged for the first 500 minutes of use per month and additional use costs $0.25 per minute
b. Total selling and administrative costs
c. Total labor costs when employees are paid per unit produced
d. Total overtime premium paid production employees
e. Average total cost per unit
f. Salaries of supervisors when each one can supervise a maximum of 10 employees
g. Total idle time costs when employees are paid for a minimum 40-hour week
h. Materials costs per unit
i. Total sales commissions
j. Electric power consumption in a restaurant
k. Total costs when high volumes of production require the use of overtime and obsolete equipment
l. A good linear approximation of actual costs
m. A linear cost estimation valid only within the relevant range

Graphs for Mini Exercise 2-14

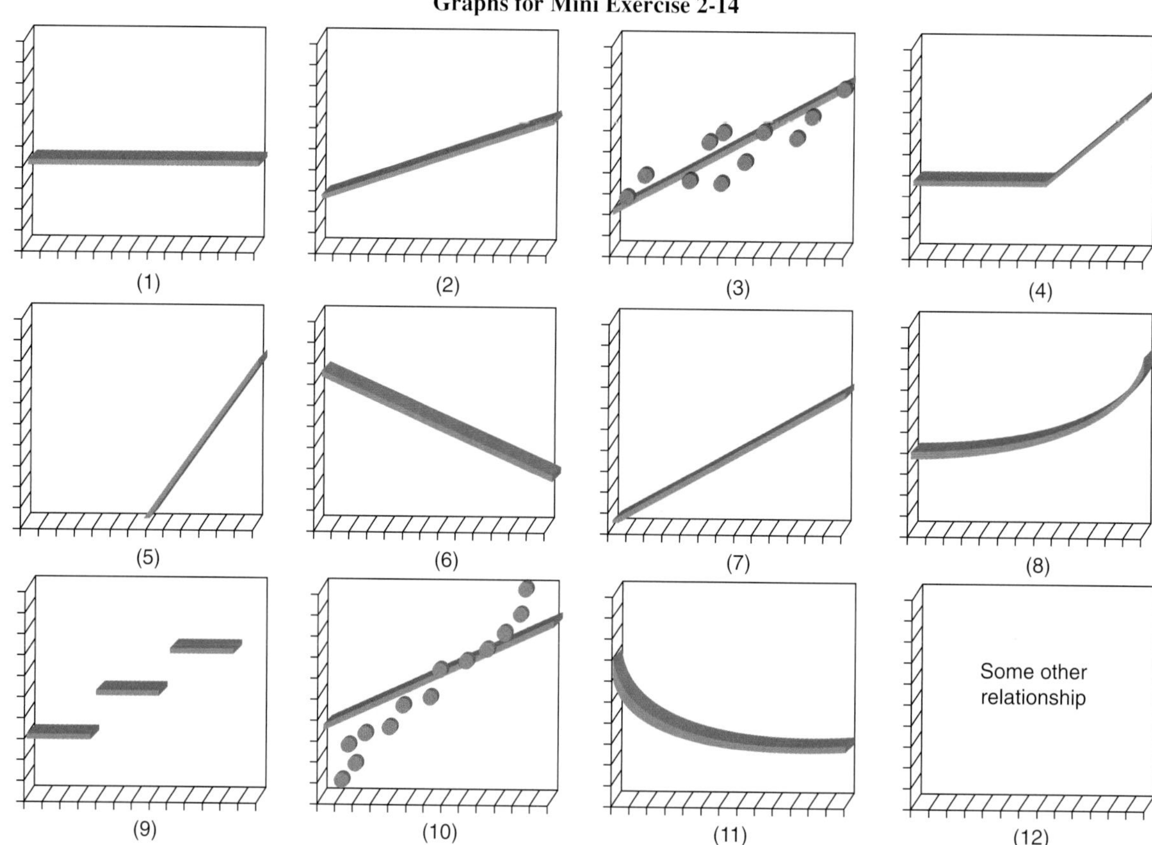

Exercises

LO2 McDonald's (MCD)

E2-15. Computing Average Unit Costs

Assume the total monthly operating costs of a McDonald's restaurant are:

$40,000 + $0.75X

where

X = Number of salad orders

Required

a. Determine the average cost per salad at each of the following monthly volumes: 1,000; 10,000; 50,000; 100,000.

b. Determine the monthly volume at which the average cost per serving is $2.35.

LO2 Bartell's

E2-16. Automatic versus Manual Processing

Bartell's, a Seattle area drug store, operates an in-store printing service for customers with digital cameras. The current service, which requires employees to download photos from customer cameras, has monthly operating costs of $5,500 plus $0.15 per photo printed. Management is evaluating the desirability of acquiring a machine that will allow customers to download and make prints without employee assistance. If the machine is acquired, the monthly fixed costs will increase to $7,000 and the variable costs of printing a photo will decline to $0.05 per photo.

Required

a. Determine the total costs of printing 10,000 and 25,000 photos per month:
   1. With the current employee-assisted process.
   2. With the proposed customer self-service process.

b. Determine the monthly volume at which the proposed process becomes preferable to (costs less than) the current process.

E2-17. Automatic versus Manual Processing

LO2 Office Depot (ODP)

Assume Office Depot processes 2,500,000 photocopies per month at its service center. Approximately 50% of the photocopies require collating. Collating is currently performed by high school and college students who are paid \$10 per hour. Each student collates an average of 5,000 copies per hour. Management is contemplating the lease of an automatic collating machine that has a monthly capacity of 6,000,000 photocopies, with lease and operating costs totaling \$3,000, plus \$0.05 per 1,000 units collated.

Required

a. Determine the total costs of collating 1,000,000 and 2,000,000 per month:
   1. With student help.
   2. With the collating machine.

b. Determine the monthly volume at which the automatic process becomes preferable to (costs less than) the manual process.

E2-18. High-Low Cost Estimation

LO3 YRC Worldwide (YRCW)

Assume the local YRC Worldwide delivery service hub has the following information available about fleet miles and operating costs:

Year	Miles	Operating Costs
Year 1	695,000	\$219,500
Year 2	855,000	267,500

Required

Use the high-low method to develop a cost-estimating equation for total annual operating costs.

E2-19. Scatter Diagrams and High-Low Cost Estimation

LO3, 4 Pearle Vision (LUX)

Assume the local Pearle Vision has the following information on the number of sales orders received and order-processing costs.

Month	Sales Orders	Order-Processing Costs
1	3,300	\$ 90,970
2	1,650	55,412
3	4,840	132,770
4	3,080	90,090
5	2,530	76,752
6	1,320	47,410
7	2,200	68,750

Required

a. Use information from the high- and low-volume months to develop a cost-estimating equation for monthly order-processing costs.

b. Plot the data on a scatter diagram. Using the information from representative high- and low-volume months, develop a cost-estimating equation for monthly production costs.

c. What factors might have caused the difference in the equations developed for requirements (*a*) and (*b*)?

E2-20. Scatter Diagrams and High-Low Cost Estimation

LO3, 4 Coles County Highway Department

From April 1 through October 31, Coles County Highway Department hires temporary employees to mow and clean the right-of-way along county roads. The County Road Commissioner has asked you to help her in determining the variable labor cost of mowing and cleaning a mile of road. The following information is available regarding current-year operations:

Month	Miles Mowed and Cleaned	Labor Costs
April	240	$6,800
May	305	7,680
June	325	8,310
July	275	7,200
August	220	6,550
September	200	5,760
October	75	4,960

Required

a. Use the information from the high- and low-volume months to develop a cost-estimating equation for monthly labor costs.

b. Plot the data on a scatter diagram. Using the information from representative high- and low-volume months, use the high-low method to develop a cost-estimating equation for monthly labor costs.

c. What factors might have caused the difference in the equations developed for requirements (*a*) and (*b*)?

d. Adjust the equation developed in requirement (*b*) to incorporate the effect of an anticipated 5% increase in wages.

LO1, 2, 3 Potbelly's (PBPB)

E2-21. Cost Behavior Analysis in a Restaurant: High-Low Cost Estimation

Assume a Potbelly's restaurant has the following information available regarding costs at representative levels of monthly sales (meals served):

	Monthly Sales in Units		
	5,000	7,000	10,000
Cost of food sold	$ 7,500	$10,500	$15,000
Wages and fringe benefits	5,900	5,940	6,000
Fees paid delivery help	6,000	8,400	12,000
Rent on building	3,500	3,500	3,500
Depreciation on equipment	850	850	850
Utilities	600	640	700
Supplies (soap, floor wax, etc.)	400	480	600
Administrative costs	1,200	1,200	1,200
Total	$25,950	$31,510	$39,850

Required

a. Identify each cost as being variable, fixed, or mixed.

b. Use the high-low method to develop a schedule identifying the amount of each cost that is mixed or variable per unit. Total the amounts under each category to develop an equation for total monthly costs.

c. Predict total costs for a monthly sales volume of 8,500 units.

LO1, 2 Tucker Pup's Pet Resort

Homework MBC

E2-22. Developing an Equation from Average Costs

Tucker Pup's Pet Resort offers dog boarding services in Chicago. Assume that in March, when dog-days occupancy was at an annual low of 150 days, the average cost per dog-day was $65. In July, when dog-days were at a capacity level of 600, the average cost per dog-day was $20.

Required

a. Develop an equation for monthly operating costs.

b. Determine the average boarding cost per dog-day at an annual volume of 4,500 dog-days.

E2-23. Selecting an Independent Variable: Scatter Diagrams

LO2, 3
Brenthaven

Brenthaven produces protective cases for mobile technology. The cases are sold internationally, online, and through retail partners. Presented is information on production costs and inventory changes for five recent months:

	January	February	March	April	May
Finished goods inventory in units:					
Beginning	20,000	30,000	20,000	5,000	35,000
Manufactured	35,000	45,000	40,000	50,000	60,000
Available	55,000	75,000	60,000	55,000	95,000
Sold	(25,000)	(55,000)	(55,000)	(20,000)	(65,000)
Ending	30,000	20,000	5,000	35,000	30,000
Manufacturing costs	$525,000	$615,000	$550,000	$745,000	$800,000

Required

a. With the aid of scatter diagrams, determine whether units sold or units manufactured is a better predictor of manufacturing costs.

b. Prepare an explanation for your answer to requirement (*a*).

c. Which independent variable, units sold or units manufactured, should be a better predictor of selling costs? Why?

E2-24. Selecting a Basis for Predicting Shipping Expenses (Requires Computer Spreadsheet*)

LO2, 3
Cambridge SoundWorks

Cambridge SoundWorks sell portable speakers systems and bluetooth headphones. In an effort to improve the planning and control of shipping expenses, management is trying to determine which of three variables—units shipped, weight shipped, or sales value of units shipped—has the closest relationship with shipping expenses. The following information is available:

Month	Units Shipped	Weight Shipped (lbs.)	Sales Value of Units Shipped	Shipping Expenses
May	10,000	7,500	$350,000	$38,000
June	12,000	8,760	432,000	42,000
July	15,000	9,200	420,000	50,100
August	20,000	10,500	400,000	72,500
September	12,000	7,600	300,000	41,000
October	8,000	6,000	320,000	35,600

Required

a. With the aid of a spreadsheet program, determine whether units shipped, weight shipped, or sales value of units shipped has the closest relationship with shipping expenses.

b. Using the independent variable that appears to have the closest relationship to shipping expenses, develop a cost-estimating equation for total monthly shipping expenses.

c. Use the equation developed in requirement (*b*) to predict total shipping expenses in a month when 14,000 units, weighing 9,380 lbs., with a total sales value of $420,000 are shipped.

Problems

P2-25. High-Low and Scatter Diagrams with Implications for Regression

LO2, 3, 4
Midnight Cookie Company

Midnight Cookie Company produces and delivers gourmet cookies and ice cream until 1:30 a.m. from its three Seattle area locations. Presented is monthly cost and sales information for cookies at one of Midnight's locations.

* This assignment requires the use of a computer spreadsheet such as Excel® to solve. This assignment assumes previous knowledge of computer spreadsheets.

Month	Sales (Dozens)	Total Costs
January	6,800	$30,650
February	7,800	35,336
March	5,500	29,700
April	1,000	25,000
May	6,100	30,600
June	4,500	28,670

Required

a. Using the high-low method, develop a cost-estimating equation for total monthly costs.

b. 1. Plot the equation developed in requirement (*a*).
 2. Using the same graph, develop a scatter diagram of all observations for the cookie shop. Select representative high and low values and draw a second cost-estimating equation.

c. Which is a better predictor of future costs? Why?

d. If you decided to develop a cost-estimating equation using least-squares regression analysis, should you include all the observations? Why or why not?

e. Mention two reasons that the least-squares regression is superior to the high-low and scatter diagram methods of cost estimation.

LO5
Newman's Own

P2-26. Multiple Cost Drivers

Newman's Own manufactures a variety of specialty salad dressings. Production runs are both high-volume and low-volume activities, depending on customer orders. Assume the following represents general manufacturing costs (manufacturing overhead) and each cost's related activity cost driver for Newman's Own.

Level	Total Cost	Units of Cost Driver
Unit	$600,000	20,000 machine hours
Batch	40,000	400 customer orders
Product	84,000	15 products

The lime vinaigrette dressing required 1,000 machine hours to fill 60 customer orders for a total of 4,000 cases.

Required

a. Assuming all manufacturing overhead is estimated and predicted on the basis of machine hours, determine the predicted total overhead costs to produce the 4,000 cases of lime vinaigrette.

b. Assuming manufacturing overhead is estimated and predicted using separate rates for machine hours, customer orders, and products (a multiple-level cost hierarchy), determine the predicted total overhead costs to produce the 4,000 cases of lime vinaigrette.

c. Calculate the error in predicting manufacturing overhead using machine hours versus using multiple cost drivers. Indicate whether the use of only machine hours results in overpredicting or underpredicting the costs to produce 4,000 cases of lime vinaigrette.

d. Looking just at batch level costs, calculate the error in predicting those costs using machine hours versus using customer orders. Indicate whether the use of only machine hours results in overpredicting or underpredicting the batch-level costs to produce 4,000 cases of lime vinaigrette.

e. Looking just at product-level costs, calculate the error in predicting those costs using machine hours versus using number of products. Indicate whether the use of only machine hours results in overpredicting or underpredicting the product-level costs to produce 4,000 cases of lime vinaigrette.

LO5
Kentucky Fried Chicken
Yum Brands Inc. (YUM)

Homework MBC

P2-27. Unit- and Batch-Level Cost Drivers

Kentucky Fried Chicken (a reportable operating segment of Yum Brands Inc.), a fast-food restaurant, serves fried chicken. The managers are considering an "all you can eat" promotion and want to know the costs before setting a price. Each batch must be 50 pieces. The chicken is precut by the chain headquarters and sent to the stores in 10-piece bags. Each bag costs $5. Preparing a batch of 50 pieces of chicken with KFC's special coating takes one employee two hours. The current wage rate is $10 per hour. Another cost driver is the cost of putting fresh oil into the fryers. New oil, costing $9, is used for each batch.

Required

a. Determine the cost of preparing one batch of 50 pieces.

b. If management projects that it will sell 150 pieces of fried chicken, determine the total cost and the cost per piece.

c. If management estimates the sales to be 350 pieces, determine the total costs.

d. How much will the batch costs increase if the government raises the minimum wage to $12 per hour?

e. If management decided to increase the number of pieces in a batch to 100, determine the cost of preparing 350 pieces. Assume that the batch would take twice as long to prepare, pay rate stays at $10 per hour, and management wants to replace the oil after 100 pieces are cooked. Assume no change in expected sales volume. Note that only full batches can be prepared.

P2-28. Optimal Batch Size LO5

This is a continuation of parts *c* and *e* of P2-27.

Required

Should management increase the batch size to 100? Why or why not?

Cases and Projects

C2-29. Significance of High R-Squared LO3

Drew Conner had always been suspicious of "newfangled mathematical stuff," and the most recent suggestion of his new assistant merely confirmed his belief that schools are putting a lot of useless junk in students' heads. It seems that after an extensive analysis of historical data, the assistant suggested that the number of pounds of scrap was the best basis for predicting manufacturing overhead. In response to Mr. Conner's rage, the slightly intimidated assistant indicated that of the 35 equations he tried, pounds of scrap had the highest coefficient of determination with manufacturing overhead.

Required

Comment on Conner's reaction. Is it justified? Is it likely that the number of pounds of scrap is a good basis for predicting manufacturing overhead? Is it a feasible basis for predicting manufacturing overhead?

C2-30. Estimating Machine Repair Costs LO3

In an attempt to determine the best basis for predicting machine repair costs, the production supervisor accumulated daily information on these costs and production over a one-month period. Applying simple regression analysis to the data, she obtained the following estimating equation:

Y = $800 − $2.60X

where

Y = total daily machine repair costs
X = daily production in units

Because of the negative relationship between repair costs and production, she was somewhat skeptical of the results, even though the R-squared was a respectable 0.765.

Required

a. What is the most likely explanation of the negative variable costs?

b. Suggest an alternative procedure for estimating machine repair costs that might prove more useful.

C2-31. Ethical Problem Uncovered by Cost Estimation LO4

Westfield owns and provides management services for several shopping centers. After five years with the company, James Heller was recently promoted to the position of manager of one of Westfield's smaller malls on the outskirts of a downtown area. When he accepted the assignment, James was told that he would hold the position for only a couple of years because that mall would likely be torn down to make way for a new sports stadium. James was also told that if he did well in this assignment, he would be in line for heading one of the company's new 200-store operations that were currently in the planning stage.

While reviewing the mall's financial records for the past few years, James observed that last year's oil consumption was up by 8%, even though the number of heating degree days was down by 4%. Somewhat curious, James uncovered the following information:

- The mall is heated by forced-air oil heat. The furnace is five years old and has been well maintained.
- Fuel oil is kept in four 5,000-gallon underground oil tanks. The oil tanks were installed 25 years ago.
- Replacing the tanks would cost $80,000. If pollution was found, cleanup costs could go as high as $2,000,000, depending on how much oil had leaked into the ground and how far it had spread.
- Replacing the tanks would add more congestion to the mall's parking situation.

Required

What should James do? Explain.

LO5 **C2-32. Activity Cost Drivers and Cost Estimation**

Market Street Soup Company produces ten varieties of soup in large vats, several thousand gallons at a time. The soup is distributed to several categories of customers. Some soup is packaged in large containers and sold to college and university food services. Some is packaged in half-gallon or small containers and sold through wholesale distributors to grocery stores. Finally, some is packaged in a variety of individual servings and sold directly to the public from trucks owned and operated by Market Street Soup Company. Management has always assumed that costs fluctuated with the volume of soup, and cost-estimating equations have been based on the following cost function:

Estimated costs = Fixed costs + Variable costs per gallon × Production in gallons

Lately, however, this equation has not been a very accurate predictor of total costs. At the same time, management has noticed that the volumes and varieties of soup sold through the three distinct distribution channels have fluctuated from month to month.

Required

a. What *relevant* major assumption is inherent in the cost-estimating equation currently used by Market Street Soup Company?

b. Why might Market Street Soup Company wish to develop a cost-estimating equation that recognizes the hierarchy of activity costs? Explain.

c. Develop the general form of a more accurate cost-estimating equation for Market Street Soup Company. Clearly label and explain all elements of the equation, and provide specific examples of costs for each element.

LO3 **C2-33. Multiple Regression Analysis for a Special Decision (Requires Computer Spreadsheet[*])**

Phoenix Family Medical Clinic

For billing purposes, assume Phoenix Family Medical Clinic classifies its services into one of four major procedures, X1 through X4. A local business has proposed that Phoenix provide health services to its employees and their families at the following set rates per procedure:

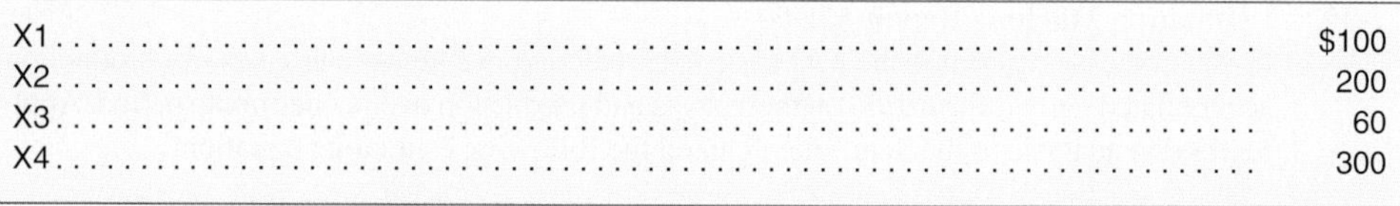

X1	$100
X2	200
X3	60
X4	300

Because these rates are significantly below the current rates charged for these services, management has asked for detailed cost information on each procedure. The following information is available for the most recent 12 months.

		Number of Procedures			
Month	**Total Cost**	**X1**	**X2**	**X3**	**X4**
1	$17,250	30	25	155	19
2	18,750	38	30	135	23
3	20,250	50	20	105	38
4	14,250	20	25	90	25
5	15,000	68	15	120	20
6	20,250	90	19	158	14
7	19,125	20	30	143	28
8	16,125	16	30	132	20
9	19,500	60	21	93	35
10	16,500	20	22	75	35
11	17,100	20	18	113	33
12	19,875	72	15	150	30

Required

a. Use multiple regression analysis to determine the unit cost of each procedure. How much variation in monthly cost is explained by your cost-estimating equation?

[*] This assignment requires the use of a computer spreadsheet such as Excel® to solve. This assignment assumes previous knowledge of computer spreadsheets.

b. Evaluate the rates proposed by the local business. Assuming Phoenix has excess capacity and no employees of the local business currently patronize the clinic, what are your recommendations regarding the proposal?

c. Evaluate the rates proposed by the local business. Assuming Phoenix is operating at capacity and would have to turn current customers away if it agrees to provide health services to the local business, what are your recommendations regarding the proposal?

C2-34. Cost Estimation, Interpretation, and Analysis (Requires Computer Spreadsheet*) **LO3, 4**

Kendrick Anderson Furniture Maker, LLC

Kendrick Anderson Furniture Maker, LLC creates custom tables in Atlanta. Assume that the following represents monthly information on production volume and manufacturing costs since the company started operations.

	Total Manufacturing Costs	Total Tables Produced	Living Room Tables Produced	Dining Room Tables Produced
June Year 1	$71,000	110	25	85
July	57,500	90	45	45
August	79,724	130	15	115
September	64,250	95	36	59
October	57,300	76	24	52
November	60,900	92	48	44
December	62,700	105	24	81
January Year 2	70,130	110	50	60
February	68,400	102	20	82
March	57,400	81	25	56
April	105,790	142	102	40
May	74,750	125	22	103
June	74,290	115	15	100
July	66,500	106	18	88
August	49,888	85	28	57
September	72,668	116	55	61
October	71,700	120	81	39
November	74,200	120	30	90
December	54,900	72	18	54

Required

a. Use the high-low method to develop a cost-estimating equation for total manufacturing costs. Interpret the meaning of the "fixed" costs and comment on the results.

b. Use the chart feature of a spreadsheet to develop a scatter graph of total manufacturing costs and total units produced. Use the graph to identify any unusual observations.

c. Excluding any unusual observations, use the high-low method to develop a cost-estimating equation for total manufacturing costs. Comment on the results, comparing them with the results in requirement (*a*).

d. Use simple regression analysis to develop a cost-estimating equation for total manufacturing costs. What advantages does simple regression analysis have in comparison with the high-low method of cost estimation? Why must analysts carefully evaluate the data used in simple regression analysis?

e. A customer has offered to purchase 50 dining room tables for $452 per table. Management has asked your advice regarding the desirability of accepting the offer. What advice do you have for management? Additional analysis is required.

C2-35. Simple and Multiple Regression (Requires Computer Spreadsheet*) **LO3**

Dan Mullen is employed by a mail-order distributor and reconditions used desktop computers, broadband routers, and laser printers. Dan is paid $12 per hour, plus an extra $6 per hour for work in excess of 40 hours per week. The distributor just announced plans to outsource all reconditioning work so Dan will need to start looking for a new job. Because the distributor is pleased with the quality of Dan's work, he has been asked to enter into a long-term contract to recondition used desktop computers at a rate of $50 per computer, plus all parts. The distributor also offered to rent all necessary equipment to Dan at a rate of $300 per month. Dan has been informed that he should plan on reconditioning as many computers as he can handle, up to a maximum of 20 per week.

* This exercise requires the use of a computer spreadsheet such as Excel® to solve. This assignment assumes previous knowledge of computer spreadsheets.

Dan has room in his basement to set up a work area, but he is unsure of the economics of accepting the contract, as opposed to working for a local computer repair shop at $14 per hour. Data related to the time spent and the number of units of each type of electronic equipment Dan has reconditioned in recent weeks is as follows:

Week	Laser Printers	Broadband Routers	Desktop Computers	Total Units	Total Hours
1	3	6	6	15	42
2	0	8	7	15	40
3	3	3	8	14	41
4	1	3	13	17	46
5	10	7	5	22	50
6	4	9	4	17	43
7	4	9	4	17	43
8	4	5	6	15	44
9	1	5	11	17	48
10	7	5	6	18	44
Total				167	441

Required

Assuming he wants to work an average of 40 hours per week, what should Dan do?

Solutions to Review Problems

Review 2-1—Solution

Fixed costs are easily identified. They are the same at each activity level. Variable and mixed costs are determined by dividing the total costs for an item at two activity levels by the corresponding units of activity. The quotients of the variable cost items will be identical at both activity levels. The quotients of the mixed costs will differ, being lower at the higher activity level because the fixed costs are being spread over a larger number of units.

Cost	April	May	Behavior
Cost of food sold	$1,575/2,100 = 0.750	$2,025/2,700 = 0.750	Variable
Wages and salaries	$1,525/2,100 = 0.726	$1,675/2,700 = 0.620	Mixed
Rent on building	NA	NA	Fixed
Depreciation on equipment	NA	NA	Fixed
Utilities	$710/2,100 = 0.338	$770/2,700 = 0.285	Mixed
Supplies	$225/2,100 = 0.107	$255/2,700 = 0.094	Mixed
Miscellaneous	$113/2,100 = 0.054	$131/2,700 = 0.049	Mixed

Review 2-2—Solution

1. Total costs = $45,000 + $1,800X
   X = number of clients
2. Total costs = $45,000 + $1,800X
   a. $45,000 + $1,800(25) = $90,000
   $90,000 ÷ 25 clients = $3,600 per client
   b. $45,000 + $1,800(30) = $99,000
   $99,000 ÷ 30 clients = $3,300 per client
   c. $45,000 + $1,800(36) = $109,800
   $109,800 ÷ 36 clients = $3,050 per client
3. $2,925 – $1,800 = $1,125 fixed costs per client
   $45,000 ÷ $1,125 = 40 clients

Review 2-3—Solution

a. The cost of food sold was classified as a variable cost. Variable cost per unit may be determined by dividing the total cost of food sold at either observation by the corresponding number of sandwiches.

$$b = \frac{\$1{,}575 \text{ total variable costs}}{2{,}100 \text{ units}}$$

$$= \$0.75$$

Wages and salaries were previously classified as a mixed cost. Hence, the high-low method is used to estimate the variable and fixed cost components.

$$b = \frac{\$1{,}675 - \$1{,}525}{2{,}700 - 2{,}100}$$
$$= 0.25$$
$$a = \$1{,}525 \text{ total cost} - (\$0.25 \times 2{,}100) \text{ variable cost}$$
$$= \$1{,}000$$

Rent on building was classified as a fixed cost.

$$a = \$1{,}500$$

Total monthly costs follow a mixed cost behavior pattern. Hence, the high-low method is used to estimate the variable and fixed cost components.

$$b = \frac{\$6{,}556 - \$5{,}848}{2{,}700 - 2{,}100}$$
$$= \$1.18$$
$$a = \$5{,}848 - (\$1.18 \times 2{,}100)$$
$$= \$3{,}370$$

Cost equation where X = Units sold	
(1) Cost of food sold	Y = $0.75X
(2) Wages and salaries.	Y = $1,000 + $0.25X
(3) Rent on building	Y = $1,500
(4) Total monthly costs	Y = $3,370 + $1.18X

b. and *c.*

Volume	Total Costs	Average Cost per Sandwich
1,000.	$3,370 + ($1.18 × 1,000) = $4,550	$\frac{\$4{,}550}{1{,}000} = \$4.550$
2,000.	$3,370 + ($1.18 × 2,000) = $5,730	$\frac{\$5{,}730}{2{,}000} = \$2.865$

The average costs differ at 1,000 and 2,000 units because the fixed costs are being spread over a different number of units. The larger the number of units, the smaller the average fixed cost per unit.

Review 2-4—Solution

a. Some common activity drivers for stating volume of activity in a manufacturing operation might include direct labor hours, machine hours, units of material produced, and units of finished product. The selection of the most appropriate basis requires judgment and professional experience. The relationship between the activity cost driver and the cost must seem logical and the activity data must be available.

b.
1. More desirable
2. Less desirable
3. Less desirable
4. Less desirable
5. More desirable
6. More desirable

Review 2-5—Solution

1. Unit-level
2. Store-level
3. Store-level
4. Unit-level
5. Customer-level
6. Order-level

Chapter 3

Cost-Volume-Profit Analysis and Planning

Learning Objectives

LO1 Describe the uses and limitations of traditional cost-volume-profit analysis. (p. 70)

LO2 Prepare and contrast contribution and functional income statements. (p. 74)

LO3 Apply cost-volume-profit analysis to find a break-even point and for preliminary profit planning. (p. 76)

LO4 Analyze the profitability and sales mix of a multiple-product firm. (p. 82)

LO5 Apply operating leverage ratio to assess opportunities for profit and the risks of loss. (p. 86)

LO6 Perform profitability analysis with unit and nonunit cost drivers (Appendix 3A). (p. 88)

Based in Cerritos, California, Razor USA, LLC designs and manufactures an array of rideable devices ranging from kick scooters to self-balancing hoverboards. Razor, as it is commonly known, was founded in 2000 and has experienced tremendous growth. Razor's first product, the model A kick scooter, sold over 5 million units within six months of its introduction and won the 2000 Toy of The Year award. By 2010, Razor had sold over 35 million scooters. Razor built on its kick scooter success and expanded its product line to include electric scooters, a modern version of the Scream Machine™, go-karts, electric motor bikes, and self-balancing hoverboards.

Razor is redefining the "ride on" category of toys and is well positioned for continued success, but how much should it charge for its products? How many units does Razor need to sell to break even? How many units does it need to sell to reach its target profit? These are questions that managers within Razor must answer.

Profitability analysis involves examining the relations between revenues, costs, and profits. Performing profitability analysis requires an understanding of selling prices, the behavior of activity cost drivers, and cost structure. Profitability analysis is widely used to make better decisions regarding existing or proposed products or services. Typically, it is performed before decisions are finalized in the operating budget for a future period.

If Razor is to accomplish its goals, it must generate profits, meaning that its revenues must exceed its costs. Razor's manufacturing processes consume energy and raw materials. The price of these inputs changes over time. By decomposing Razor's costs into its variable and fixed components, the company can perform profitability analyses to determine where to direct its future efforts. In fact, Razor can utilize the tools presented in this chapter to determine how much revenue it has to generate to achieve a desired profit.

Road Map

LO	Learning Objective | Topics	Page	eLecture	Guided Example	Assignments
LO1	**Describe the uses and limitations of traditional cost-volume-profit analysis.** CVP Analysis :: Key Assumptions :: Profit Formula	70	e3–1	Review 3-1	39
LO2	**Prepare and contrast contribution and functional income statements.** Contribution Income Statement :: Contribution Margin :: Unit Contribution :: Contribution Margin Ratio	74	e3–2	Review 3-2	17, 29, 41
LO3	**Apply cost-volume-profit analysis to find a break-even point and for preliminary profit planning.** Break-Even :: Profit Planning :: Cost-Volume-Profit Graph :: Profit-Volume Graph :: Impact of Taxes	76	e3–3	Review 3-3	11, 12, 13, 14, 15, 17, 18, 19, 20, 21, 22, 24, 25, 28, 29, 30, 31, 32, 33, 34, 36, 37, 40, 41
LO4	**Analyze the profitability and sales mix of a multiple-product firm.** Break-Even and Target Profit Sales Dollars :: Sales Mix Analysis	82	e3–4	Review 3-4	16, 23, 34, 35, 37, 38
LO5	**Apply operating leverage ratio to assess opportunities for profit and the risks of loss.** Operating Leverage :: Operating Leverage Ratio	86	e3–5	Review 3-5	21, 22, 40
LO6	**Perform profitability analysis with unit and nonunit cost drivers (Appendix 3A).** Multi-Level Contribution Income Statement :: Cost Hierarchy and Contribution Income Statement	88	e3–6	Review 3-6	26, 27

CHAPTER ORGANIZATION

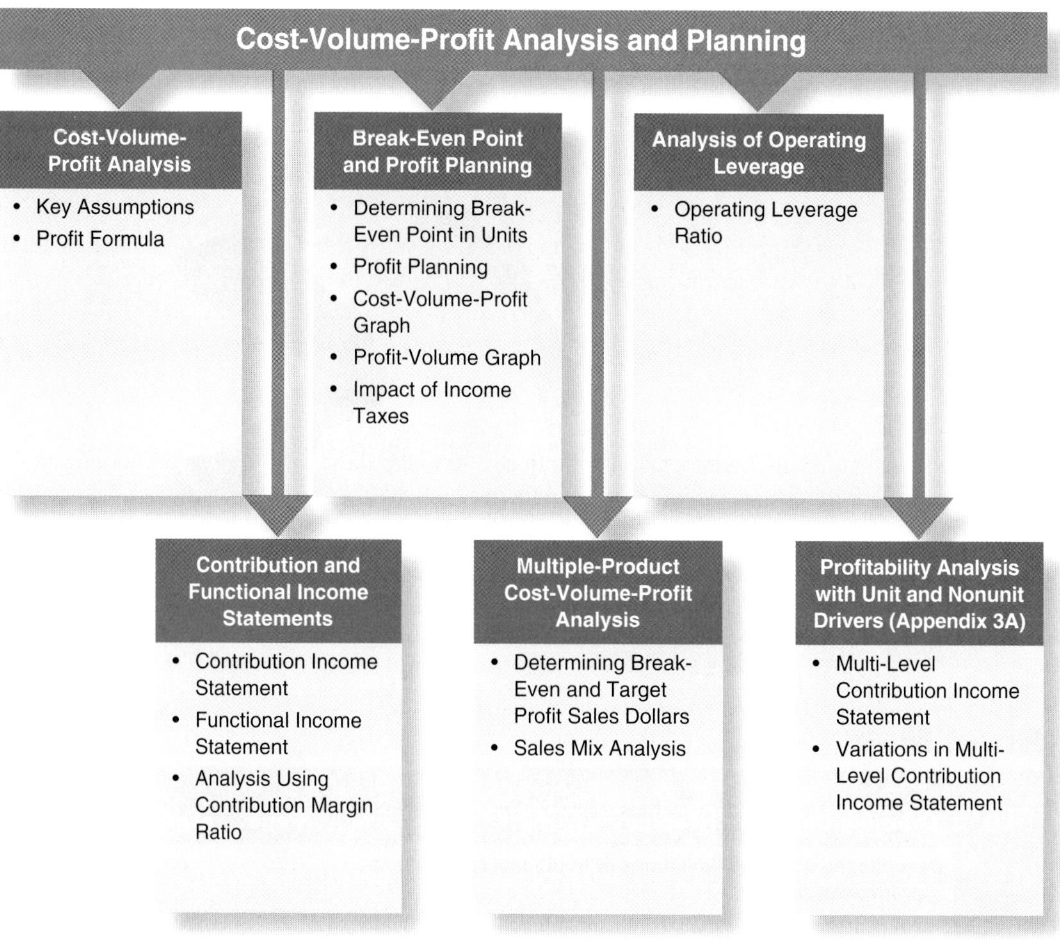

What fee should we charge for a subscription to our services? How many units do we need to sell to break even? How many units do we need to sell to reach our target profit?

Profitability analysis involves examining the relationships among revenues, costs, and profits. Performing profitability analysis requires an understanding of selling prices and the behavior of activity cost drivers. Profitability analysis is widely used to make better decisions regarding existing or proposed products or services. Typically, it is performed before decisions are finalized in the operating budget for a future period.

This chapter introduces basic approaches to profitability analysis and planning. We consider single-product, multiple-product, and service organizations; income taxes; sales mix; and the effects of cost structure on the relation between profit potential and the risk of loss.

Cost-Volume-Profit Analysis

eLectures MBC **LO1** Describe the uses and limitations of traditional cost-volume-profit analysis.

Cost-volume-profit (CVP) analysis is a technique used to examine the relationships among the total volume of an independent variable such as sales volume, total costs, total revenues, and profits for a time period (typically a quarter or year). With CVP analysis, volume refers to a single activity cost driver, such as unit sales, that is assumed to correlate with changes in revenues, costs, and profits.

Cost-volume-profit analysis is useful in the early stages of planning because it provides an easily understood framework for discussing planning issues and organizing relevant data. CVP analysis is widely used by for-profit as well as not-for-profit organizations. It is equally applicable to service, merchandising, and manufacturing firms.

In for-profit organizations, CVP analysis is used to answer such questions as these: How many photocopies must the local Staples store produce to earn a profit of $80,000? At what dollar sales volume will Whole Foods' total revenues and total costs be equal? What profit will Target earn at an annual sales volume of $75 billion? What will happen to the profit of Panera Bread if there is a 20% increase in the cost of food and a 10% increase in the average selling price of meals? The Research Insight box at the bottom of this page indicates how the role of managerial accounting is expanding. With greater availability of data, managers can efficiently perform more analyses to help guide CVP decisions.

In not-for-profit organizations, CVP analysis is used to establish service levels, plan fund-raising activities, and determine funding requirements. How many meals can the downtown Salvation Army serve with an annual budget of $600,000? How many tickets must be sold for the benefit concert to raise $20,000? Given the current cost structure, current tuition rates, and projected enrollments, how much money must DePaul University raise from other sources?

Key Assumptions

CVP analysis is subject to a number of assumptions. Although these assumptions do not negate the usefulness of CVP models, especially for a single product or service, they do suggest the need for further analysis before plans are finalized. Among the more important assumptions are

1. *All costs are classified as fixed or variable.* This assumption is most reasonable when analyzing the profitability of a specific event (such as a concert) or the profitability of an organization that produces a single product or service on a continuous basis.
2. *The total cost function is linear within the relevant range.* This assumption is often valid within a relevant range of normal operations, but over the entire range of possible activity, changes in efficiency are likely to result in a nonlinear cost function.
3. *The total revenue function is linear within the relevant range.* Unit selling prices are assumed constant over the range of possible volumes. This implies a purely competitive market for final products or services. In some economic models in which demand responds to price changes, the revenue function is nonlinear. In these situations, the linear approximation is accurate only within a limited range of activity.
4. *The analysis is for a single product, or the sales mix of multiple products is constant.* The **sales mix** refers to the relative portion of unit or dollar sales derived from each product or service. If products have different selling prices and costs, changes in the mix affect CVP model results.
5. *There is only one cost driver: unit or sales dollar volume.* In a complex organization it is seldom possible to represent the multitude of factors that drive cost with a single cost driver.

Research Insight ■ Data-Driven Planning Central to Management Accounting

The role of management accounting is expanding to include planning driven by data science. This work is often called financial planning and analysis (FP&A) and is used widely enough that a professional accrediting program has been launched by the Association for Financial Professionals (AFP).

The central function of the FP&A group within a company is to inform decisions with data. GoDaddy Inc. called on its FP&A group to help guide the domain-name seller's international expansion. The team developed purpose-built growth metrics to help executives allocate marketing dollars across the 40 countries where GoDaddy does business. By finding the correct metric to drive resource decisions, GoDaddy was able to increase the share of sales from foreign markets to 26% of total sales. Its CFO claims that the FP&A group's contribution tripled foreign growth.

At Dunkin Brands Group Inc., the FP&A group has influence in every department, helping managers and employees across the organization find ways to improve processes and practices. Dunkin's 36-member FP&A team took on the key job of mining loyalty data to find ways to get customers back into the store throughout the day and increasing the amount that the customers spent. This effort led to a 2.2% growth in same-store sales over nine months.

While Dunkin is deeply committed to FP&A (its CFO was the VP of FP&A), other firms are adopting this approach more slowly. The consulting firm CEB notes that 61% of FP&A directors do not feel that top managers take their contributions seriously. As this perception changes, accountants trained in management accounting principles will have the chance to influence companies with their analyses.

Source: Alix Stuart, "Metrics Sell Doughnuts and More," *Wall Street Journal*, December 21, 2015.

Business Insight ■ Amazon Explores New Customer Experience for In-Store Shopping

Amazon owns Whole Foods and is now exploring checkout-free convenience stores. Customers can go to an Amazon Go store and make in-store purchases. This shopping experience is truly unique in that shoppers do not "check out." They merely walk in, pick out what they want, and walk out. Amazon uses technology that can detect when products are moved between the shelf and the cart; and when you leave the store, your Amazon account is charged and you are sent a receipt.

The grocery store industry is already a low margin industry. How much will this cost? Although some overhead costs will go down such as in-store employees, the cost of creating and maintaining the complex technology required for this to work well is not cheap and the overall costs will likely be higher than those of a traditional bricks-and-mortar store. Will customers pay higher prices for the convenience of not having to wait in lines and not having to go through a checkout process?

Much is still to be determined, and in order for this to be a successful endeavor, Amazon must closely analyze its cost, volume, and profit implications. Regardless, this will be a significant learning experiment for the company.

Sources: Rob Lenihan, "Amazon Is Said to Plan Cashierless Go Supermarkets, Pop-Ups as Soon as Q1," https://www.thestreet.com/investing/stocks/amazon-looking-to-open-cashier-free-go-supermarkets-pop-up-stores-15174680?puc=yahoo&cm_ven=YAHOO&yptr=yahoo, November 20, 2019.

Rich Hardy, "Is Amazon Go's Checkout-Free Store the Future of Retail, or Just an Expensive Gimmick?" https://newatlas.com/amazon-go-future-retail-publicity-stunt/53077/, January 23, 2018.

When applied to a single product (such as pounds of potato chips), service (such as the number of pages printed), or event (such as the number of tickets sold to a banquet), it is reasonable to assume the single independent variable such as sales volume is the cost driver. The total costs associated with the single product, service, or event during a specific time period are often determined by this single activity cost driver.

Although cost-volume-profit analysis is often used to understand the overall operations of an organization or business segment, accuracy decreases as the scope of operations being analyzed increases.

Profit Formula

The profit associated with a product, service, or event is equal to the difference between total revenues and total costs as follows:

$$\textbf{Profit} = \textbf{Total revenues} - \textbf{Total costs}$$

The revenues are a function of the unit sales volume and the unit selling price, while total costs for a time period are a function of the fixed costs per period and the unit variable costs as follows:

$$\textbf{Total revenues} = \mathbf{pX}$$
$$\textbf{Total costs} = \mathbf{a + bX}$$

where

p = Unit selling price
a = Fixed costs
b = Unit variable costs
X = Unit sales

The equation for profit can then be expanded to include the above details of the total revenue and total cost equations as follows:

$$\textbf{Profit} = \mathbf{pX - (a + bX)}$$

Using information on the selling price, fixed costs per period, and variable costs per unit, this formula is used to predict profit at any specified activity level.

To illustrate, assume that Razor's only product is a standard kick scooter that it manufactures and sells to merchandisers at $60 per completed scooter. Applying inventory minimization techniques, Razor does not maintain inventories of raw materials or finished goods. Instead, newly purchased raw materials are delivered directly to the factory, and finished goods are loaded directly onto trucks for shipment. Razor's variable and fixed costs follow.

1. **Direct materials** refer to the cost of the primary raw materials converted into finished goods. Because the consumption of raw materials increases as the quantity of goods produced increases, *direct materials represents a variable cost.* Razor's raw materials consist primarily of nuts and bolts, rubber wheels, bearings, steel frames, and packaging materials. Razor also treats the costs of purchasing, receiving, and inspecting these materials as part of the cost of direct materials. Assume that all together, these costs are $20 per completed scooter.
2. **Direct labor** refers to wages earned by production employees for the time they spend working on the conversion of raw materials into finished goods. Based on Razor's manufacturing procedures, *direct labor represents a variable cost.* Further assume these costs are $10 per completed scooter.
3. **Variable manufacturing overhead** includes all other variable costs associated with converting raw materials into finished goods. Assume Razor's variable manufacturing overhead costs include the costs of lubricants for cutting and packaging machines, electricity to operate these machines, and the cost to move materials between receiving and shipping. These costs are $3 per completed scooter.
4. **Variable selling and administrative costs** include all variable costs other than those directly associated with converting raw materials into finished goods. Assume at Razor, these costs include sales commissions and transportation of finished goods to merchandisers. These costs are $5 per completed scooter.
5. **Fixed manufacturing overhead** includes all fixed costs associated with converting raw materials into finished goods. Suppose Razor's fixed manufacturing costs include the depreciation, property taxes, and insurance on buildings and machines used for manufacturing, the salaries of manufacturing supervisors, and the fixed portion of electricity used to light the factory. Further assume these costs are $35,000 per month.
6. **Fixed selling and administrative costs** include all fixed costs other than those directly associated with converting raw materials into finished goods. These costs include the salaries of Razor's divisional manager and many other staff personnel such as accounting and marketing. Also included are depreciation, property taxes, insurance on facilities used for administrative purposes, and any related utilities costs. Assume these costs are $15,000 per month.

Razor's hypothetical variable and fixed costs are summarized here.

Variable Costs per Scooter		
Manufacturing.		
Direct materials.	$20	
Direct labor	10	
Manufacturing overhead.	3	$33
Selling and administrative.		5
Total		$38

Fixed Costs per Month	
Manufacturing overhead.	$35,000
Selling and administrative.	15,000
Total	$50,000

The cost estimation techniques discussed in Chapter 2 can be used to determine many detailed costs. Least-squares regression, for example, might be used to determine the variable and monthly fixed amount of electricity used in manufacturing. Assume Razor manufactures and sells a single product on a continuous basis with all sales to merchandisers under standing contracts. Therefore, it is reasonable to assume that in the short run, Razor's total monthly costs respond to the number of scooters sold. Combining all this information, Razor's profit equation is assumed to be:

$$\textbf{Profit} = \$60X - (\$50{,}000 + \$38X)$$

where

$$X = \text{scooters sold}$$

Using this equation, Razor's profit at a volume of 5,400 units is $68,800, computed as ($60 × 5,400) − [$50,000 + ($38 × 5,400)].

Review 3-1 LO1 — Determining the Profit Equation

Benchmark Paper Company's only product is high-quality photocopy paper that it manufactures and sells to wholesale distributors at $14 per carton. Applying inventory minimization techniques, Benchmark does not maintain inventories of raw materials or finished goods. Newly purchased raw materials are delivered directly to the factory, and finished goods are loaded directly onto trucks for shipment. Benchmark's variable and fixed costs follow:

Variable Costs per Carton		
Manufacturing		
Direct materials	$1.25	
Direct labor	0.50	
Manufacturing overhead	2.50	$4.25
Selling and administrative		1.00
Total		$5.25

Fixed Costs per Month	
Manufacturing overhead	$ 2,000
Selling and administrative	8,000
Total	$10,000

Required

a. Determine Benchmark's profit equation.

b. Using your equation, calculate Benchmark's profit at a volume of 6,200 cartons.

Solution on p. 106.

Contribution and Functional Income Statements

Functional Income Statement

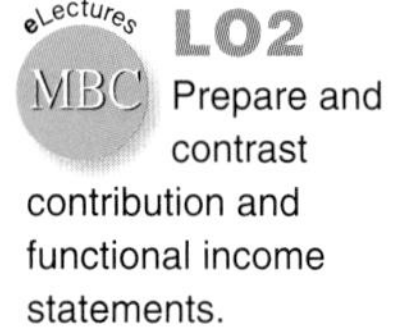

LO2 Prepare and contrast contribution and functional income statements.

The statement included in **Exhibit 3.1** is called a **functional income statement** because costs are classified according to function (rather than behavior), such as manufacturing, selling, and administrative. This is the type of income statement typically included in corporate annual reports.

Exhibit 3.1 Functional Income Statement

RAZOR COMPANY
Functional Income Statement
For a Monthly Volume of 5,400 Cartons

Sales (5,400 × $60)		$324,000
Less cost of goods sold		
Direct materials (5,400 × $20)	$108,000	
Direct labor (5,400 × $10)	54,000	
Variable manufacturing overhead (5,400 × $3)	16,200	
Fixed manufacturing overhead	35,000	(213,200)
Gross margin		110,800
Less other expenses		
Variable selling and administrative (5,400 × $5)	27,000	
Fixed selling and administrative	15,000	(42,000)
Profit		$ 68,800

Contribution Income Statement

Contrast the functional income statement in **Exhibit 3.1** with Razor's contribution income statement in **Exhibit 3.2**. To provide more detailed information on anticipated or actual financial results at a particular sales volume, a contribution income statement is often prepared. In a **contribution income statement**, costs are classified according to behavior as variable or fixed, and the **contribution margin** (the difference between total revenues and total variable costs) that goes toward covering fixed costs and providing a profit is emphasized.

The problem with a functional income statement is the difficulty of relating it to the profit formula in which costs are classified according to behavior rather than function. The relationship between sales volume, costs, and profits is not readily apparent in a functional income statement. Consequently, we emphasize contribution income statements because they provide better information to internal decision makers.

Exhibit 3.2 Contribution Income Statement

RAZOR COMPANY Contribution Income Statement For a Monthly Volume of 5,400 Scooters		
Sales (5,400 × $60)		$324,000
Less variable costs		
Direct materials (5,400 × $20)	$108,000	
Direct labor (5,400 × $10)	54,000	
Manufacturing overhead (5,400 × $3)	16,200	
Selling and administrative (5,400 × $5)	27,000	(205,200)
Contribution margin		118,800
Less fixed costs		
Manufacturing overhead	35,000	
Selling and administrative	15,000	(50,000)
Profit		$ 68,800

Analysis Using Contribution Margin Ratio

While the contribution income statement (shown in **Exhibit 3.1**) presents information on total sales revenue, total variable costs, and so forth, it is sometimes useful to present information on a per-unit or portion of sales basis.

	Total	Per Unit	Ratio to Sales
Sales (5,400 units)	$324,000	$60	1.0000
Variable costs	(205,200)	38	0.6333*
Contribution margin	118,800	$22	0.3667
Fixed costs	(50,000)		
Profit	$ 68,800		

* Rounded

The per-unit information assists in short-range planning. The **unit contribution margin** is the difference between the unit selling price and the unit variable costs. It is the amount, $22 in this case, that each unit contributes toward covering fixed costs and earning a profit.

The contribution margin is widely used in **sensitivity analysis** (the study of the responsiveness of a model to changes in one or more of its independent variables). Razor's income statement is an economic model of the firm, and the unit contribution margin indicates how sensitive Razor's income model is to changes in unit sales. If, for example, sales increase by 100 scooters per month, the increase in profit is readily determined by multiplying the 100-scooter increase in sales by the $22 unit contribution margin as follows:

100 (scooter sales increase) × $22 (unit contribution margin) = $2,200 (profit increase)

There is no increase in fixed costs, so the new profit level becomes $71,000 ($68,800 + $2,200) per month.

When expressed as a ratio to sales, the sales margin is identified as the **contribution margin ratio**. It is the portion of each dollar of sales revenue contributed toward covering fixed costs and earning a profit. In the abbreviated income statement above, the portion of each dollar of sales revenue contributed toward covering fixed costs and earning a profit is 0.3667 ($118,800 ÷ $324,000). This is Razor's assumed contribution margin ratio. If sales revenue increases by $6,000 per month, the increase in profits is computed as follows:

$6,000 (sales increase) × 0.3667 (contribution margin ratio) = $2,200 (profit increase)

The contribution margin ratio is especially useful in situations involving several products or when unit sales information is not available.

Review 3-2 LO2 — Preparing a Contribution Income Statement

Assume Solo Cup Company produces 16-ounce beverage containers. Further assume Solo sells the cups for $40 per box of 50 containers. Variable and fixed costs follow:

Variable Costs per Box			Fixed Costs per Month	
Manufacturing			Manufacturing overhead	$15,000
Direct materials	$15		Selling and administrative	10,000
Direct labor	3		Total	$25,000
Manufacturing overhead	10	$28		
Selling and administrative		2		
Total		$30		

Suppose in September, Solo produced and sold 3,000 boxes of beverage containers.

Required

a. Prepare a contribution income statement for September.

b. Determine Solo's unit contribution margin and contribution margin ratio.

Solution on p. 106.

Break-Even Point and Profit Planning

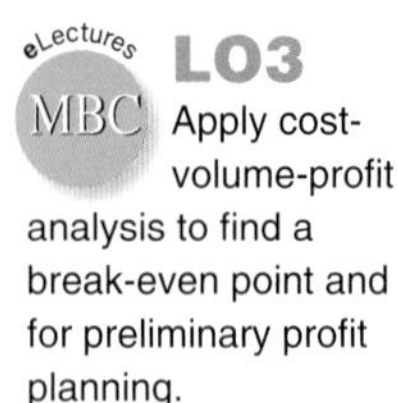

LO3 Apply cost-volume-profit analysis to find a break-even point and for preliminary profit planning.

The **break-even point** occurs at the unit or dollar sales volume when total revenues equal total costs. The break-even point is of great interest to management. Until break-even sales are reached, the product, service, event, or business segment of interest operates at a loss. Beyond this point, increasing levels of profits are achieved. Also, management often wants to know the **margin of safety**, the amount by which actual or planned sales exceed the break-even point. Other questions of interest include the probability of exceeding the break-even sales volume and the effect of some proposed change on the break-even point.

Determining Break-Even Point in Units

In determining the break-even point, the equation for total revenues is set equal to the equation for total costs and then solved for the break-even unit sales volume. Using the general equations for total revenues and total costs, the following results are obtained. Setting total revenues equal to total costs:

Total revenues = Total costs

$$pX = a + bX$$

Solving for the break-even unit sales volume:

$$pX - bX = a$$
$$(p - b)X = a$$
$$X = a/(p - b)$$

In words:

$$\textbf{Break-even unit sales volume} = \frac{\textbf{Fixed costs}}{\textbf{Selling price per unit} - \textbf{Variable costs per unit}}$$

Because the denominator is the unit contribution margin, the break-even point is also computed by dividing fixed costs by the unit contribution margin:

$$\textbf{Break-even unit sales volume} = \frac{\textbf{Fixed costs}}{\textbf{Unit contribution margin}}$$

With an assumed \$22 unit contribution margin and fixed costs of \$50,000 per month, Razor's break-even point is 2,273* units per month (\$50,000 ÷ \$22). Stated another way, at a \$22 per-unit contribution margin, 2,273 units of sales are required to cover \$50,000 of fixed costs. With a break-even point of 2,273 units, the monthly margin of safety for a sales volume of 5,400 units is 3,127 units (5,400 expected unit sales – 2,273 break-even unit sales). The expected profit at a sales volume of 5,400 units is \$68,794 (3,127 unit margin of safety × \$22 unit contribution margin). (The difference between the calculated \$68,794 and the profit of \$68,800 in **Exhibit 3.1** and 3.2 is due to rounding.)

* Rounded UP to the nearest whole unit

The break-even point concept is applicable to a wide variety of business and personal planning situations. The following Research Insight box illustrates how a personal financial planner might use break-even point concepts to assist a client making a retirement decision.

Research Insight ■ Determining the Cash Break-Even Point for Delaying Retirement

Social Security retirement benefits are a function of years worked, contributions to the Social Security System, and the age at which the recipient files for Social Security retirement benefits. Currently, persons retiring at age 67 are entitled to "full" retirement benefits, while those retiring at age 62 are eligible for only 70% of "full" benefits. A person contemplating retirement at age 62 might ask: (1) how large is the reduction in benefits and (2) what is the break-even age at which the benefits from delaying retirement until age 67 equals the cumulative benefits from retiring at age 62?

An individual with the analytic skills obtained from a managerial accounting course can readily determine the answers to these questions after consulting the Social Security website www.ssa.gov. Others might consult a personal financial planner.

(1) Assume the individual's full Social Security retirement benefits at age 67 are \$2,265 per month. If that person started receiving benefits at age 62, the monthly benefits are reduced by 30% or \$679.50 (\$2,265 × 0.30) to \$1,585.50.

(2) With retirement at age 62, the early retiree would receive total benefits of \$95,130 (\$1,585.50 × 12 months × 5 years) by age 67, the normal "full" age. Treating this as a fixed amount to be recovered by the subsequent incremental monthly benefits of \$679.50 from delaying the receipt of monthly benefits to age 67, the break-even age is computed as follows:

Months beyond age 67 = \$95,130/\$679.50 = 140 months or 11.67 years.
Hence, the break-even age is 78.67 years (67 + 11.67).

The analysis suggests that life expectancy is an important consideration in deciding when to start taking Social Security benefits.

Note that this analysis does not consider any return on the \$95,130 that might be earned by investing the benefits received during early retirement. Such returns would increase the break-even age. Nor does it consider the lost wages that could have been earned between age 62 and age 67.

Source: www.ssa.gov

Profit Planning

Establishing profit objectives is an important part of planning in for-profit organizations. Profit objectives are stated in many ways. They can be set as a percentage of last year's profits, as a percentage of total assets at the start of the current year, or as a percentage of owners' equity. They might be based on a profit trend, or they might be expressed as a percentage of sales. The economic outlook for the firm's products as well as anticipated changes in products, costs, and technology are also considered in establishing profit objectives.

Before incorporating profit plans into a detailed budget, it is useful to obtain some preliminary information on the feasibility of those plans. Cost-volume-profit analysis is one way of doing this. By manipulating cost-volume-profit relationships, management can determine the sales volume corresponding to a desired profit. Management might then evaluate the feasibility of this sales volume. If the profit plans are feasible, a complete budget might be developed for this activity level. The required sales volume might be infeasible because of market conditions or because the required volume exceeds production or service capacity, in which case management must lower its profit objective or consider other ways of achieving it. Alternatively, the required sales volume might be less than management believes the firm is capable of selling, in which case management might raise its profit objective.

Assume that Razor's management desires to know the unit sales volume required to achieve a monthly profit of $75,000. Using the profit formula, the required unit sales volume is determined by setting profits equal to $75,000 and solving for **X**, the unit sales volume.

$$\textbf{Profit} = \textbf{Total revenues} - \textbf{Total costs}$$
$$\$75{,}000 = \$60\mathbf{X} - (\$50{,}000 + \$38\mathbf{X})$$

Solving for **X**

$$\$60\mathbf{X} - \$38\mathbf{X} = \$50{,}000 + \$75{,}000$$
$$\mathbf{X} = (\$50{,}000 + \$75{,}000) \div \$22$$
$$= 5{,}682 \text{ units (rounded UP to the nearest whole unit)}$$

The total contribution must cover the desired profit as well as the fixed costs. Hence, the target sales volume required to achieve a desired profit is computed as the fixed costs plus the desired profit, all divided by the unit contribution margin.

$$\textbf{Target unit sales volume} = \frac{\textbf{Fixed costs + Desired profit}}{\textbf{Unit contribution margin}}$$

The Business Insight Box below discusses how Enjoy Technology plans to turn a profit through increased sales volume.

Business Insight ■ White-Glove, Same-Day Delivery

Ron Johnson definitely understands what attracts consumers. He helped Target create its "cheap-chic" identity and develop its popular product partnerships with designers and then moved to Apple where he pioneered the successful Genius Bars and free classes available at company retail stores.

He's now applying his knowledge of consumer preferences, combining the convenience of online shopping with the personal attention received at brick-and-mortar stores. Currently, Enjoy Technology, a company he co-founded in 2015, works with major telecom carriers [AT&T (US), British Telcom (UK), and Rogers (Canada)] to offer free delivery and setup of phones and other products to consumers in their homes or another location of their choice.

In an interview, Johnson said: "I've been watching e-commerce grow for 20 years. Every product has the same last mile. Apple creates a premium last-mile store. How should a premium brand go to market for customers buying online? We extend that online-purchasing experience and bring everything you do in the store to the home. It's smart last mile."

Enjoy employees visit on average seven to eight AT&T customers a day and in over 50% of those visits, customers have purchased additional products, services, or warranty plans. Enjoy gets paid a percentage of the additional profit created by Enjoy employees.

Johnson expects to turn a profit in 2020 when sales volume is expected to exceed the break-even point.

Source: Andria Cheng, "Ron Johnson Made Apple Stores the Envy of Retail and Target Hip, But This Startup May Be His Crowning Achievement," *Forbes*, January 17, 2020.

Cost-Volume-Profit Graph

A **cost-volume-profit graph** illustrates the relationships among activity volume, total revenues, total costs, and profits. Its usefulness comes from highlighting the break-even point and depicting revenue, cost, and profit relationships over a range of activity. This representation allows management to view the relative amount of important variables at any graphed volume. Razor's hypothetical monthly CVP graph is in **Exhibit 3.3**. Total revenues and total costs are measured on the vertical axis, with unit sales measured on the horizontal axis. Separate lines are drawn for total variable costs, total costs, and total revenues. The vertical distance between the total revenue and the total cost lines depicts the amount of profit or loss at a given volume. Losses occur when total revenues are less than total costs; profits occur when total revenues exceed total costs.

The total contribution margin is shown by the difference between the total revenue and the total variable cost lines. Observe that as unit sales increase, the contribution margin first goes to cover the fixed costs. Beyond the break-even point, any additional contribution margin provides a profit.

Exhibit 3.3 Cost-Volume-Profit Graph*

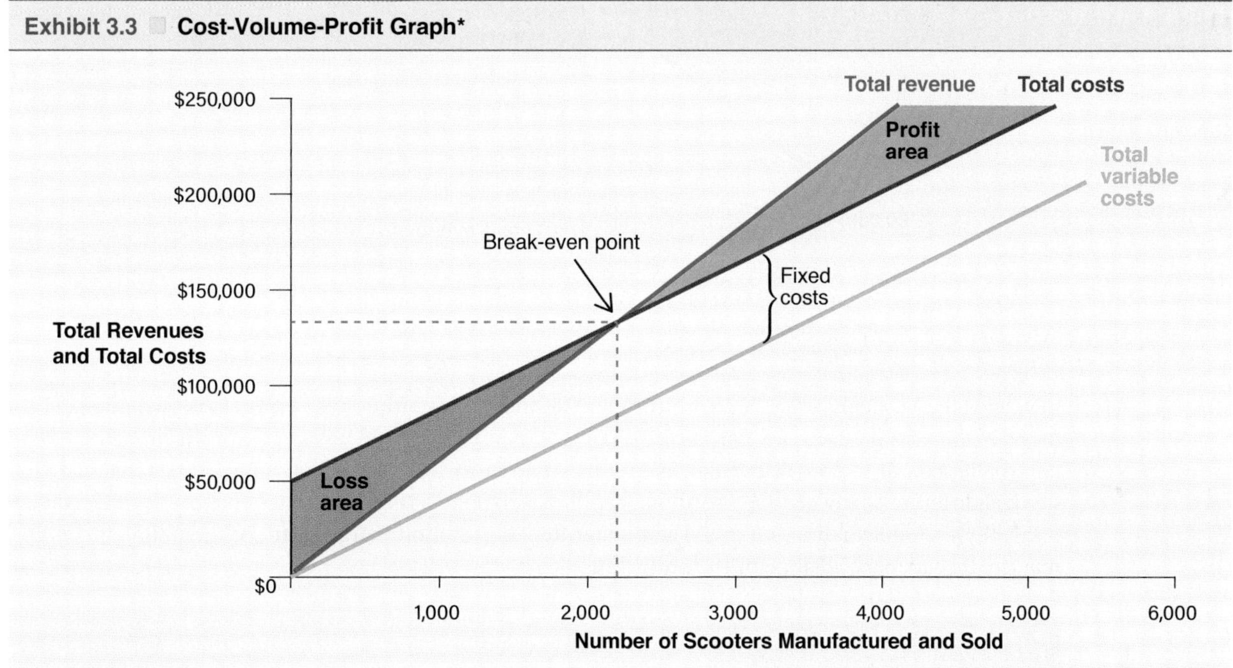

* The three lines are developed as follows:

1. **Total variable costs** line is drawn between the origin and total variable costs at an arbitrary sales volume. At 3,000 units, total variable costs are $114,000 (3,000 × $38).
2. **Total revenues** line is drawn through the origin and a point representing total revenues at some arbitrary sales volume. At 3,000 units, Razor's hypothetical total revenues are $180,000 (3,000 × $60).
3. **Total costs** line is computed by layering fixed costs, $50,000 in this case, on top of total variable costs. This gives a vertical axis intercept of $50,000 and total costs of $164,000 at 3,000 units.

Profit-Volume Graph

In cost-volume-profit graphs, profits are represented by the difference between total revenues and total costs. When management is primarily interested in the impact of changes in sales volume on profits, a **profit-volume graph** is sometimes used. A profit-volume graph illustrates the relationship between volume and profits; it does not show revenues and costs. Profits are read directly from a profit-volume graph, rather than being computed as the difference between total revenues and total costs. Profit-volume graphs are developed by plotting either unit sales or total revenues on the horizontal axis.

The Business Insight box on the following page discusses that GlaxoSmithKline expects a future reduction in its process costs. This would lead to a reduction in its required sales to breakeven.

Razor's assumed monthly profit-volume graph is presented in **Exhibit 3.4**. Profit or loss is measured on the vertical axis, and volume (total revenues) is measured on the horizontal axis, which

Exhibit 3.4 Profit-Volume Graph*

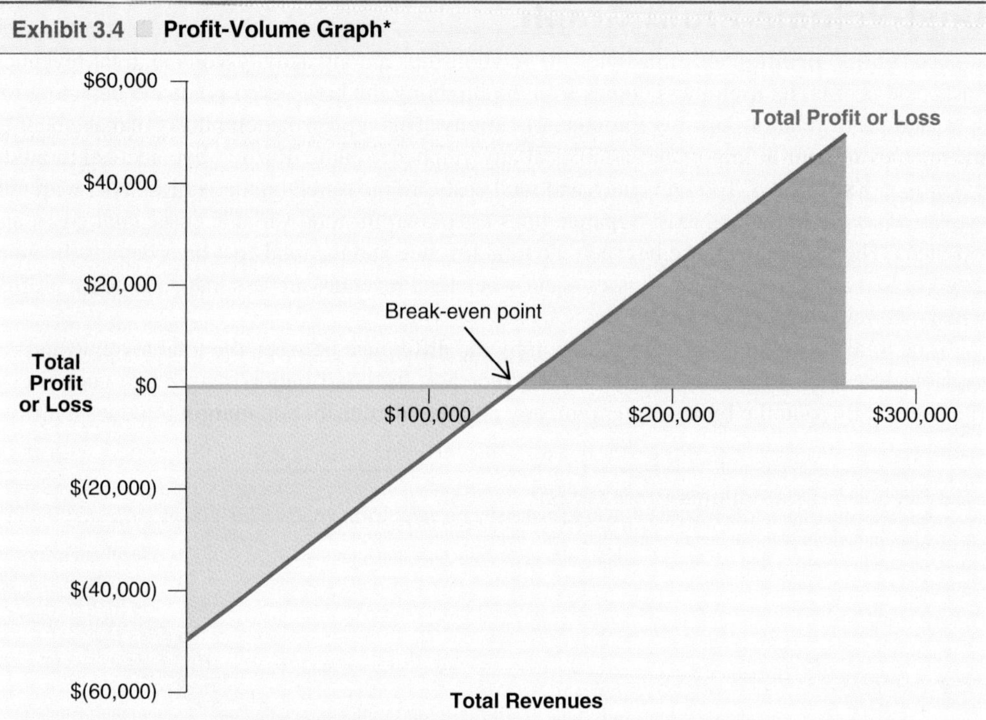

* The profit line is drawn by determining and plotting profit or loss at two different volumes and then drawing a straight line through the plotted values. Perhaps the easiest values to select are the loss at a volume of zero (with a loss equal to the fixed costs) and the volume at which the profit line crosses the horizontal axis (this is the break-even volume).

intersects the vertical axis at zero profit. A single line, representing total profit, is drawn intersecting the vertical axis at zero sales volume with a loss equal to the fixed costs. The profit line crosses the horizontal axis at the break-even sales volume. The profit or loss at any volume is depicted by the vertical difference between the profit line and the horizontal axis. The slope of the profit line is determined by the contribution margin. The greater the contribution margin ratio or the unit contribution margin, the steeper the slope of the profit line.

Business Insight ■ Drugmaker Looks to Bioelectronics to Change Cost Structure

At Galvani Bioelectronics (a partnership between GlaxoSmithKline (GSK) and Verily Life Sciences (a subsidiary of Alphabet, Inc.), treatments are not pills or serums delivering doses of chemicals to the entire body but rice-sized devices attached to nerve bundles. The innovation here is treating illness as a programming problem rather than as a chemical problem. The nervous system can be viewed as a communication system carrying messages about the body's operations. To the extent that problematic messages can be edited, many health problems can be solved by implanting and programming these devices. In addition to finding new solutions to old pathologies, GSK hopes to eventually change the cost structure of drug companies. GSK has started a venture capital effort worth $50 million that funds 100 independent researchers and 30 employees.

Development costs are exploding for conventional molecular drug therapies. The average drug takes 10 years and $2.6 billion to bring to market. GSK is betting that basic engineering innovations in bioelectronics will allow new therapies to be tested and implemented more quickly and at lower cost. This could potentially change some therapies into software problems rather than manufacturing problems, eliminating many of the process costs involved in manufacturing drugs under the current model. These investments remain risky, but GSK is hoping that its investment in this technology changes the cost structure of the drug business.

Source: Matthew Campbell, "Only One Big Drugmaker Is Working on a Nanobot Cure," *Bloomberg Businessweek*, June 9, 2016.

Impact of Income Taxes

Income taxes are imposed on individuals and for-profit organizations by government agencies. The amount of an individual's or organization's income tax is determined by laws that specify the calculation of taxable income (the income subject to tax) and the calculation of the amount of tax on taxable income. Income taxes are computed as a percentage of taxable income, with increases in taxable income usually subject to progressively higher tax rates. The laws governing the computation of taxable income differ in many ways from the accounting principles that guide the computation of accounting income. Consequently, taxable income and accounting income are seldom the same.

In the early stages of profit planning, income taxes are sometimes incorporated in CVP models by assuming that taxable income and accounting income are identical and that the tax rate is constant. Although these assumptions are seldom true, they are useful for assisting management in developing an early prediction of the sales volume required to earn a desired after-tax profit. Once management has developed a general plan, this early prediction should be refined with the advice of tax experts.

Assuming taxes are imposed at a constant rate per dollar of before-tax profit, income taxes are computed as before-tax profit multiplied by the tax rate. After-tax profit is equal to before-tax profit minus income taxes.

$$\textbf{After-tax profit} = \textbf{Before-tax profit} - (\textbf{Before-tax profit} \times \textbf{Tax rate})$$

After-tax profit can also be expressed as before-tax profit times 1 minus the tax rate.

$$\textbf{After-tax profit} = \textbf{Before-tax profit} \times (\textbf{1} - \textbf{Tax rate})$$

This formula can be rearranged to isolate before-tax profit as follows:

$$\textbf{Before-tax profit} = \frac{\textbf{After-tax profit}}{(\textbf{1} - \textbf{Tax rate})}$$

Since all costs and revenues in the profit formula are expressed on a before-tax basis, the most straightforward way of determining the unit sales volume required to earn a desired after-tax profit is to

1. Determine the required before-tax profit.
2. Substitute the required before-tax profit into the profit formula.
3. Solve for the required unit sales volume.

To illustrate, assume that Razor is subject to a 40% tax rate and that management desires to earn an after-tax profit of $75,000 for November. The required before-tax profit is $125,000 [$75,000 ÷ (1 – 0.40)], and the unit sales volume required to earn this profit is 7,955 units [($50,000 + $125,000) ÷ $22]. Rounded to the nearest whole unit.

Income taxes increase the sales volume required to earn a desired after-tax profit. A 40% tax rate increased the sales volume required for Razor to earn an after-tax profit of $75,000 from 5,682 to 7,955 units. These amounts are verified in **Exhibit 3.5**.

Another way to remember the computation of before-tax profit is shown on the right side of **Exhibit 3.5**. The before-tax profit represents 100% of the pie, with 40% going to income taxes and 60% remaining after taxes. Working back from the remaining 60% ($75,000), we can determine the 100% (before-tax profit) by dividing after-tax profit by 0.60.

Exhibit 3.5 Contribution Income Statement with Income Taxes

RAZOR COMPANY Contribution Income Statement Planned for the Month of November			
Sales (7,955 x $60)		$477,300	
Less variable costs			
Direct materials (7,955 x $20)	$159,100		
Direct labor (7,955 x $10)	79,550		
Manufacturing overhead (7,955 x $3)	23,865		
Selling and administrative (7,955 x $5)	39,775	(302,290)	
Contribution margin		175,010	
Less fixed costs			
Manufacturing overhead	35,000		
Selling and administrative	15,000	50,000	
Before-tax profit		125,000*	100%
Income taxes ($125,000 x 0.40)		(50,000)	(40)%
After-tax profit		$ 75,000	60%

*Calculated total is $125,010. Difference is due to rounding.

Review 3-3 LO3 Applying Cost-Volume-Profit Analysis

Assume Solo Cup Company produces 16-ounce beverage containers. Further assume Solo sells the cups for $40 per box of 50 containers. Variable and fixed costs follow:

Variable Costs per Box			Fixed Costs per Month	
Manufacturing			Manufacturing overhead	$15,000
Direct materials	$15		Selling and administrative	10,000
Direct labor	3		Total	$25,000
Manufacturing overhead	10	$28		
Selling and administrative		2		
Total		$30		

Suppose in September, Solo produced and sold 3,000 boxes of beverage containers.

Required

a. Prepare a cost-volume-profit graph with unit sales as the independent variable. Label the revenue line, total costs line, fixed costs line, loss area, profit area, and break-even point. The recommended scale for the horizontal axis is 0 to 5,000 units, and the recommended scale for the vertical axis is $0 to $200,000.

b. Determine Solo's monthly break-even point in units.

c. Determine the monthly dollar sales required for a monthly profit of $5,000 (ignoring taxes).

d. Assuming Solo is subject to a 40% income tax, determine the monthly unit sales required to produce a monthly after-tax profit of $4,500.

Solution on p. 107.

Multiple-Product Cost-Volume-Profit Analysis

LO4 Analyze the profitability and sales mix of a multiple-product firm.

Determining Break-Even and Target Profit Sales Dollars

Unit cost information is not always available or appropriate when analyzing cost-volume-profit relationships of multiple-product firms. Assuming the sales mix is constant, the contribution margin ratio (the portion of each sales dollar contributed toward covering fixed costs and earning a profit) can be used to determine the break-even dollar sales volume or the dollar sales volume required to achieve a desired profit. Treating a dollar of sales revenue as a unit, the break-even point in dollars is computed as fixed costs divided by the contribution margin ratio (the number of cents from each dollar of revenue contributed to covering fixed costs and providing a profit).

$$\textbf{Dollar break-even point} = \frac{\textbf{Fixed costs}}{\textbf{Contribution margin ratio}}$$

If unit selling price and cost information were not available, Razor's dollar break-even point could be computed as $136,351 ($50,000 ÷ 0.3667). Rounded to the nearest whole unit.

Corresponding computations can be made to find the dollar sales volume required to achieve a desired profit as follows.

$$\textbf{Target dollar sales volume} = \frac{\textbf{Fixed costs + Desired profit}}{\textbf{Contribution margin ratio}}$$

To achieve a desired profit of $82,000, Razor needs sales of $359,967 [($50,000 + $82,000) ÷ 0.3667]. Rounded to the nearest whole unit.

These relationships can be graphed by placing sales dollars, rather than unit sales, on the horizontal axis. The slope of the variable and total cost lines, identified as the **variable cost ratio**, presents variable costs as a portion of sales revenue. It indicates the number of cents from each sales dollar required to pay variable costs. The Business Insight box below demonstrates how CVP information can be developed from the published financial statements of a multiple-product firm.

Business Insight ■ Using CVP for Financial Analysis and Prediction

Microsoft Corporation is a technology company that develops and supports software, services, devices, and solutions. We can use historical data to predict future costs through the cost-volume-profit method. We used data from the condensed 2018 and 2017 income statements (in millions) to predict 2019 costs:

	For the Year Ending	
	June 30, 2018	**June 30, 2017**
Sales	$110,360	$ 96,571
Cost of sales and operating expenses	(75,302)	(67,546)
Operating profit	$ 35,058	$ 29,025

We can use the high-low method to understand Microsoft's cost-volume-profit relationships and forecast profits based on expected sales. The first step is to calculate variable costs as a percentage of sales:

$$\textbf{Variable cost ratio} = \frac{\$75{,}302 - \$67{,}546}{\$110{,}360 - \$96{,}571} = 0.5625$$

Next, use this ratio to estimate Microsoft's fixed costs by subtracting variable costs from total costs for either period. Based on 2018 revenues and variable costs, we can calculate fixed costs as:

Annual fixed costs = $75,302 – ($110,360 × 0.5625) = $13,225 million

Our estimate of Microsoft's cost function is:

Total annual costs = $13,225 million + (0.5625 × Sales)

Microsoft's break-even sales can be calculated using fixed cost and contribution margin (1 minus the variable cost ratio).

Break-even point = $13,225 million/(1 – 0.5625) = $30,229 million

In 2019 sales were $125,843 million and operating income was $42,959 million. Based on the CVP relationships developed above and 2019 sales, the predicted level of operating income is:

Predicted operating income = $125,843 – [($125,843 × 0.5625) + $13,225] = $41,831

The difference between the estimated operating income and actual results suggests that Microsoft's cost structure has changed slightly over the past three years.

Sales Mix Analysis

Sales mix refers to the relative portion of unit or dollar sales that are derived from each product. One of the limiting assumptions of the basic cost-volume-profit model is that the analysis is for a single product or a constant sales mix. When the sales mix is constant, managers of multiple-product organizations can use the average unit contribution margin, or the average contribution margin ratio, to determine the break-even point or the sales volume required for a desired profit. Often, however, management is interested in the effect of a change in the sales mix rather than a change in the sales volume at a constant mix. In this situation, it is necessary to determine either the average unit contribution margin or the average contribution margin ratio for each alternative mix.

Unit Sales Analysis

Assume that Hallmark Cards sells two kinds of greeting cards, regular and deluxe. At a 1:1 (one-to-one) unit sales mix in which Hallmark sells one box of regular cards for every box of deluxe cards, assume the following revenue and cost information is available:

	Regular Box	Deluxe Box	Average Box*
Unit selling price	$4	$12	$8
Unit variable costs	(3)	(3)	(3)
Unit contribution margin	$1	$ 9	$5
Fixed costs per month			$15,000

* At a 1:1 sales mix, the average unit contribution margin is $5[{($1 × 1 unit) + ($9 × 1 unit)} ÷ 2 units].

At a 1:1 mix, Hallmark's assumed monthly break-even sales volume is 3,000 units ($15,000 ÷ $5), consisting of 1,500 boxes of regular cards and 1,500 boxes of deluxe cards. The top line in **Exhibit 3.6** represents the current sales mix. Suppose management wants to know the break-even sales volume if the unit sales mix became 3:1; that is, on average, a sale of 4 units contains 3 regular units and 1 deluxe unit. With no changes in the selling prices or variable costs of individual products, the average contribution margin becomes $3[{($1 × 3 units) + ($9 × 1 unit)} ÷ 4 units], and the revised break-even sales volume is 5,000 units ($15,000 ÷ $3). The revised break-even sales volume includes 3,750 boxes of regular cards [5,000 × $\frac{3}{4}$] and 1,250 boxes of deluxe cards [5,000 × $\frac{1}{4}$].

Exhibit 3.6 Sales Mix Analysis: Unit Sales Approach

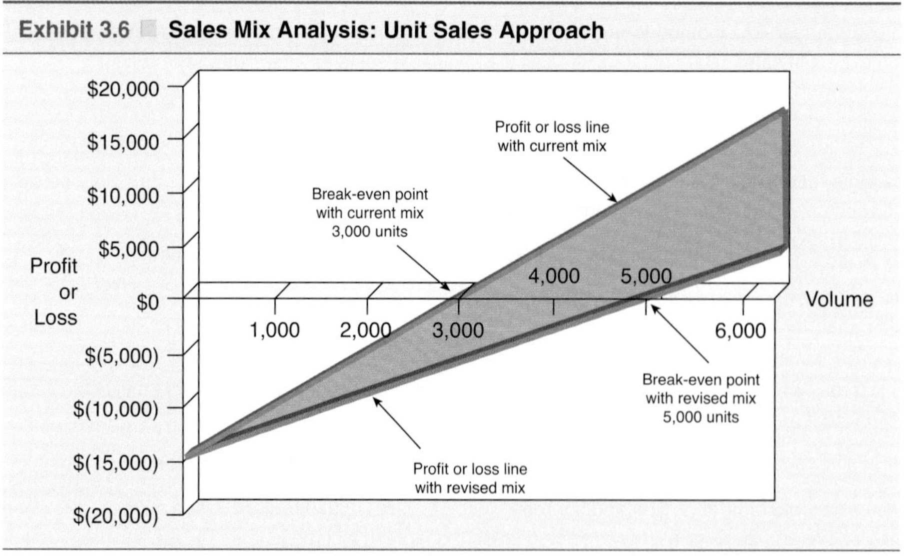

The bottom line in **Exhibit 3.6** represents the revised sales mix. Because a greater portion of the revised mix consists of lower contribution margin regular cards, the shift in the mix increases the break-even point.

Sales Dollar Analysis

The preceding analysis focused on units and the unit contribution margin. An alternative approach focuses on sales dollars and the contribution margin ratio. Following this approach, the sales mix is expressed in terms of sales dollars.

Assume Hallmark's current sales dollars are 25% from regular cards and 75% from deluxe cards. The following display indicates the contribution margin ratios at the current sales mix and monthly volume of 5,400 units.

	Regular	Deluxe	Total
Unit sales	2,700	2,700	
Selling price	$4.00	$12.00	
Sales	$10,800	$32,400	$43,200
Variable costs	8,100	8,100	16,200
Contribution margin	$ 2,700	$24,300	$27,000
Contribution margin ratio	0.25	0.75	0.625

If monthly fixed costs are $15,000, Hallmark's current break-even sales revenue is $24,000 ($15,000 ÷ 0.625), consisting of $6,000 from regular cards ($24,000 × 0.25) and $18,000 from deluxe cards ($24,000 × 0.75). The top line in **Exhibit 3.7** illustrates the current sales mix.

Now suppose management wants to know the break-even sales volume if the dollar sales mix became 70% regular and 30% deluxe. With no changes in the selling prices or variable costs of individual products, the total contribution margin ratio becomes 0.40 [(0.25 × 0.70) + (0.75 × 0.30)], and the revised break-even sales volume is $37,500 ($15,000 ÷ 0.40). The revised break-even sales volume includes $26,250 from regular cards ($37,500 × 0.70) and $11,250 from deluxe cards (37,500 × 0.30).

The bottom line in **Exhibit 3.7** represents the revised sales mix. Because a greater portion of the revised mix consists of lower contribution ratio regular cards, the shift in the mix increases the break-even point.

Exhibit 3.7 Sales Mix Analysis: Sales Dollar Approach

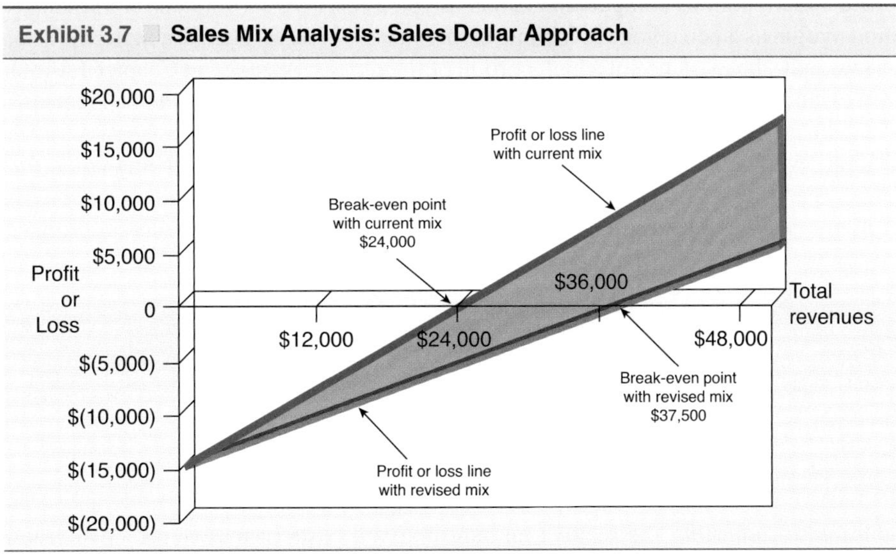

Sales mix analysis is important in multiple-product or multi-service organizations. Management is just as concerned with the mix of products as with the total unit or dollar sales volume. A shift in the sales mix can have a significant impact on the bottom line. Profits may decline, even when sales increase, if the mix shifts toward products or services with lower unit margins. Conversely, profits may increase, even when sales decline, if the mix shifts toward products or services with higher unit margins. Other things being equal, managers of for-profit organizations strive to increase sales of high-margin products or services.

Review 3-4 LO4 — Analyzing Profitability of a Multi-Product Firm

Suppose the Coffee Bean has a new shop in a Cambridge village shopping center that sells high-end teas and coffees. Further, suppose it has added smoothie drinks to its product line. Below are the assumed sales and cost data for the company:

	Coffee	Tea	Smoothie
Sales price per (12 oz.) serving	$1.35	$1.25	$1.95
Variable cost per serving	0.60	0.45	0.75
Fixed costs per month $8,000			

Suppose the company sells each month an average of 6,000 servings of coffee, 3,750 servings of tea, and 2,250 servings of smoothies.

Required

a. Calculate the current before-tax profit, contribution margin ratio, and sales mix based on sales dollars.

b. Using a sales dollar analysis, calculate the monthly break-even point assuming the sales mix does not change.

Solution on p. 108.

Analysis of Operating Leverage

LO5 Apply operating leverage ratio to assess opportunities for profit and the risks of loss.

Operating leverage refers to the extent that an organization's costs are fixed. The **operating leverage ratio** is computed as the contribution margin divided by before-tax profit as follows.

$$\textbf{Operating leverage ratio} = \frac{\textbf{Contribution margin}}{\textbf{Before-tax profits}}$$

The rationale underlying this computation is that as fixed costs are substituted for variable costs, the contribution margin as a percentage of income before taxes increases. Hence, a high degree of operating leverage signals the existence of a high portion of fixed costs. As noted in Chapter 1, the shift from labor-based to automated activities has resulted in a decrease in variable costs and an increase in fixed costs, producing an increase in operating leverage.

Operating leverage is a measure of risk and opportunity. Other things being equal, the higher the degree of operating leverage, the greater the opportunity for profit with increases in sales. Conversely, a higher degree of operating leverage also magnifies the risk of large losses with a decrease in sales.

	Operating Leverage	
	High	Low
Profit opportunity with sales increase	High	Low
Risk of loss with sales decrease	High	Low

In addition to indicating the relative amount of fixed costs in the overall cost structure of a company, the operating leverage ratio can be used to measure the expected change in net income resulting from a change in sales. The operating leverage ratio multiplied by the percentage change in sales equals the percentage change in income before taxes. For example, if Razor currently has an operating leverage ratio of 1.73, a change in sales of 12% will result in a 21% change in before-tax profit; whereas suppose Envy has an operating leverage ratio of 2.35, which will result in an increase in before-tax profit of 28%.

	Current		Projected	
	Razor	Envy	Razor	Envy
Unit selling price	$ 60	$ 60	$ 60	$ 60
Unit variable costs	(38)	(30)	(38)	(30)
Unit contribution margin	$ 22	$ 30	$ 22	$ 30
Unit sales	× 5,400	× 5,400	× 6,048	× 6,048
Contribution margin	$118,800	$162,000	$133,056	$181,440
Fixed costs	(50,000)	(93,200)	(50,000)	(93,200)
Before-tax profit	$ 68,800	$ 68,800	$ 83,056	$ 88,240
Contribution margin	$118,800	$162,000		
Before-tax profit	÷ 68,800	÷ 68,800		
Operating leverage ratio	1.73*	2.35*		
Percent increase in sales			12%	12%
Percent increase in income before taxes			21%*	28%*

* Rounded

Although both companies have identical before-tax profits at a sales volume of 5,400 units, assume Envy has a higher degree of operating leverage and its profits vary more with changes in sales volume.

If sales are projected to increase by 12%, from 5,400 to 6,048 units, the percentage of increase in each firm's profits is computed as the percent change in sales multiplied by the degree of operating leverage.

	Razor	Envy
Increase in sales	12%	12%
Degree of operating leverage	× 1.73	× 2.35
Increase in profits	21%*	28%*

* Rounded

As noted in the following Business Insight box, operating leverage is an important consideration when changes in demand, and consequently sales, occur.

Management is interested in measures of operating leverage to determine how sensitive profits are to changes in sales. Risk-averse managers strive to maintain a lower operating leverage, even if this results in some loss of profits. One way to reduce operating leverage is to use more direct labor and less automated equipment. Another way is to contract outside organizations to perform tasks that could be done internally. While operating leverage is a useful analytic tool, long-run success comes from keeping the overall level of costs down, while providing customers with the products or services they want at competitive prices.

Business Insight ■ Mining Companies Fight for Financial Flexibility When Prices Fall

While larger mining companies like BHP and Rio Tinto have the flexibility to maintain output when ore prices fall, smaller miners like the Australian Fortescue Metals Group struggle to deal with low prices. Cost cutting can only help so much when debt is nearly four times earnings. This makes Fortescue's profit exceptionally sensitive to sale price and volume; hence, China's slowdown in economic growth has corresponded to a 90% drop in profit for the company. As a result, Fortescue and other mid-sized mining firms are rushing to restructure their debt.

In response to the same pressures, other mining companies, like AngloAmerican, are selling assets to reduce operational leverage. In contrast, South32, a BHP spin-off, is less sensitive to demand fluctuations because its net debt is less than a quarter of pretax earnings. South32's more nimble financial structure makes it much easier for the company to deal with fluctuations in price and demand. Financial flexibility is an important consideration in industries such as mining, where fixed costs are high and demand is sensitive to macroeconomic fluctuations.

Source: "Miners: In Search of Flexibility," *Financial Times*, August 25, 2015, London edition, 14.

Managerial Decision ■ You Are the Division Manager

As manager of a division responsible for both production and sales of products and, hence, division profits, you are looking for ways to leverage the profits of your division to a higher level. You are considering changing your cost structure to include more fixed costs and less variable costs by automating some of the production activities currently performed by people. What are some of the considerations that you should keep in mind as you ponder this decision? [Answer, p. 91]

Review 3-5 LO5 — Applying Operating Leverage Ratio

Suppose the Coffee Bean has a new shop in a Cambridge village shopping center that sells high-end teas and coffees. Further, suppose it has added smoothie drinks to its product line. Below are the assumed sales and cost data for the company:

	Coffee	Tea	Smoothie
Sales price per (12 oz.) serving	$1.35	$1.25	$1.95
Variable cost per serving	0.60	0.45	0.75
Fixed costs per month $8,000			

Asssume the company sells each month an average of 6,000 servings of coffee, 3,750 servings of tea, and 2,250 servings of smoothies.

Required

Calculate Coffee Bean's operating leverage ratio. If sales increase by 20%, by how much will before-tax income be expected to change? If sales decrease by 20%, by how much will before-tax income be expected to change?

Solution on p. 108.

Appendix 3A: Profitability Analysis with Unit and Nonunit Cost Drivers

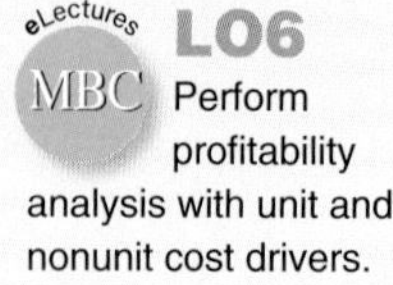

LO6 Perform profitability analysis with unit and nonunit cost drivers.

A major limitation of cost-volume-profit analysis and the related contribution income statement is the exclusive use of unit-level activity cost drivers. Even when multiple products are considered, the CVP approach either restates volume in terms of an average unit or in terms of a dollar of sales volume. Additionally, CVP analysis does not consider other categories of cost drivers.

We now expand profitability analysis to incorporate nonunit cost drivers. While the addition of multiple levels of cost drivers makes it difficult to develop graphical relationships (illustrating the impact of cost driver changes on revenues, costs, and profits), it is possible to modify the traditional contribution income statement to incorporate a hierarchy of cost drivers. The expanded framework is not only more accurate, but it encourages management to ask important questions concerning costs and profitability.

Multi-Level Contribution Income Statement

To illustrate the use of profitability analysis with unit and nonunit cost drivers, assume Anthropologie, a multiple-product merchandising organization, has the following cost hierarchy:

Unit-level activities	
Cost of goods sold	$0.80 per sales dollar
Order-level activities	
Cost of processing order.	$20 per order
Customer-level activities	
Mail, phone, sales visits, recordkeeping, etc.	$200 per customer per year
Facility-level costs	
Depreciation, manager salaries, insurance, etc..	$120,000 per year

Assume that Anthropologie is subject to a 40% income tax rate and has the following plans for next year:

Sales	$3,000,000
Number of sales orders	3,200
Number of customers	400

While Anthropologie's plans could be summarized in a functional income statement, we have previously considered the limitations of such statements for management. Contribution income statements are preferred because they correspond to the cost classification scheme used in CVP analysis. In this case, Anthropologie's cost structure (unit level, order level, customer level, and facility level) does not correspond to the classification scheme used in traditional contribution income statements (variable and fixed). The problem occurs because traditional contribution income statements consider only unit-level cost drivers. When a larger set of unit and nonunit cost drivers is used for cost analysis, an expanded contribution income statement should be used for profitability analysis.

A hypothetical multi-level contribution income statement for Anthropologie is presented in Exhibit 3A.1. Costs are separated using a cost hierarchy and there are several contribution margins, one for each level of costs that responds to a short-run change in activity. Suppose that in the case of Anthropologie, the contribution margins are at the unit level, order level, and customer level. Because the facility-level costs do not vary with short-run variations in activity, the final customer-level contribution goes to cover facility-level costs and to provide for a profit. If a company had a different activity cost hierarchy, it would use a different set of contribution margins.

Exhibit 3A.1 Multi-Level Contribution Income Statement with Taxes

ANTHROPOLOGIE
Multi-Level Contribution Income Statement
For Next Year

Sales	$3,000,000
Less unit-level costs	
Cost of goods sold ($3,000,000 × 0.80)	(2,400,000)
Unit-level contribution margin	600,000
Less order-level costs	
Cost of processing order (3,200 orders × $20)	(64,000)
Order-level contribution margin	536,000
Less customer-level costs	
Mail, phone, sales visits, recordkeeping, etc. (400 customers × $200)	(80,000)
Customer-level contribution margin	456,000
Less facility-level costs	
Depreciation, manager salaries, insurance, etc.	(120,000)
Before-tax profit	336,000
Income taxes ($336,000 × 0.40)	(134,400)
After-tax profit	$ 201,600

A number of additional questions of interest to management can be formulated and answered using the multi-level hierarchy. Consider the following examples:

- Holding the number of sales orders and customers constant, what is the break-even dollar sales volume? The answer is found by treating all other costs as fixed and dividing the total nonunit-level costs by the contribution margin ratio. Here the contribution margin ratio indicates how many cents of each sales dollar is available for profits and costs above the unit level.

$$\text{Unit-Level Break-Even Point in Dollars with No Changes in Other Costs} = \frac{\text{Current Order-Level Costs} + \text{Current Customer-Level Costs} + \text{Facility-Level Costs}}{\text{Contribution Margin Ratio}}$$

$$= (\$64{,}000 + \$80{,}000 + \$120{,}000) \div (1 - 0.80)$$

$$= \$1{,}320{,}000$$

- What order size is required to break even on an individual order? Answering this question might help management to evaluate the desirability of establishing a minimum order size. To break even, each order must have a unit-level contribution equal to the order-level costs. Any additional contribution is used to cover customer- and facility-level costs and provide for a profit.

Break-even order size = $20 ÷ (1 – 0.80)
= $100

- What sales volume is required to break even on an average customer? Answering this question might help management to evaluate the desirability of retaining certain customers. Based on the preceding information, an average customer places 8 orders per year (3,200 orders ÷ 400 customers). With costs of $20 per order and $200 per customer, the sales to an average customer must generate an annual contribution of $360 [($20 × 8) + $200]. Hence, the break-even level for an average customer is $1,800 [$360 ÷ (1 – 0.80)]. Management might consider discontinuing relations with customers with annual purchases of less than this amount. Alternatively, they might inquire as to whether such customers could be served in a less costly manner.

The concepts of multi-level break-even analysis and profitability analysis are finding increasing use as companies such as **FedEx**, **Best Buy**, and **Bank of America** strive to identify profitable and unprofitable customers. At FedEx, customers are sometimes rated as "the good, the bad, and the ugly." FedEx strives to retain the "good" profitable customers, turn the "bad" into profitable customers, and ignore the "ugly" who seem unlikely to become profitable.

Variations in Multi-Level Contribution Income Statement

Classification schemes should be designed to fit the organization and user needs. In Chapter 2, when analyzing the costs of a manufacturing company, we used a manufacturing cost hierarchy. While formatting issues can seem mundane and routine, format is important because the way information is presented encourages certain types of questions while discouraging others. Hence, management accountants must inquire as to user needs before developing management accounting reports, just as users of management accounting information should be knowledgeable enough to request appropriate information and know whether the information they are receiving is the information they need. With computers to reduce computational drudgery and to provide a wealth of available data, the most important issues involve identifying the important questions and presenting information to address those questions.

In the case of Anthropologie, we used a customer cost hierarchy with information presented in a single column. A multiple-column format is also useful for presenting and analyzing information. Assume that Anthropologie's management believes that the differences between the in-store and internet-based markets are such that these markets could be better served with separate marketing activities. They would have two market segments, one for the in-store customers and one for internet-based customers, giving the following cost hierarchy:

1. Unit-level activities
2. Order-level activities
3. Customer-level activities
4. Market segment activities
5. Facility-level activities

One possible way of presenting Anthropologie's hypothetical multi-level income statement with two market segments is shown in Exhibit 3A.2. The details underlying the development of this statement are not presented. In developing the statement, we assume the mix of units sold, their cost structure, and the costs of processing an order are unchanged. Finally, we present new market segment costs and assume that the addition of the segments allows for some reduction in previous facility-level costs.

The information in the total column is all that is required for a multi-level contribution income statement. The information in the two detailed columns for the government and private segments can, however, prove useful in analyzing the profitability of each. Observe that the facility-level costs, incurred for the benefit of both segments, are not assigned to specific segments. Depending on the nature of the goods sold, it may be possible to further analyze the profitability of each product (or type of product) sold in each market segment. The profitability analysis of business segments is more closely examined in Chapter 11.

Exhibit 3A.2 Multi-Level Contribution Income Statement with Segments and Taxes

ANTHROPOLOGIE Multi-Level Contribution Income Statement For Next Year	In-Store Segment	Internet Segment	Total
Sales	$1,500,000	$2,000,000	$3,500,000
Less unit-level costs			
Cost of goods sold (0.80)	(1,200,000)	(1,600,000)	(2,800,000)
Unit-level contribution margin	300,000	400,000	700,000
Less order-level costs			
Cost of processing order (1,000 × $20; 3,000 × $20)	(20,000)	(60,000)	(80,000)
Order-level contribution margin	280,000	340,000	620,000
Less customer-level costs			
Mail, phone, sales visits, recordkeeping, etc. (150 × $200, 300 × $200)	(30,000)	(60,000)	(90,000)
Customer-level contribution margin	250,000	280,000	530,000
Less market segment-level costs	(80,000)	(20,000)	(100,000)
Market segment-level contribution	$ 170,000	$ 260,000	430,000
Less facility-level costs			
Depreciation, manager salaries, insurance, etc.			(90,000)
Before-tax profit			340,000
Income taxes ($340,000 × 0.40)			(136,000)
After-tax profit			$ 204,000

Performing a Customer-Level Profitability Analysis

LO6 Review 3-6

7-Eleven operates a number of convenience stores worldwide. Assume that an analysis of operating costs, customer sales, and customer patronage reveals the following:

Fixed costs per store	$80,000/year
Variable cost ratio	0.80
Average sale per customer visit	$17.00
Average customer visits per week	1.50
Customers as portion of city population	0.05

Required

Determine the city population required for a single 7-Eleven to earn an annual profit of $40,000.

Solution on p. 109.

Guidance Answers

You Are the Division Manager

Pg. 88 Fixed costs represent a two-edged sword. When a company is growing its sales, fixed costs cause profits to grow faster than sales; however, if a company should experience declining sales, the rate of reduction in profits is greater than the rate of reduction in sales. When sales decline, variable costs decline proportionately, while fixed costs continue. For this reason, when a company faces serious declines that are expected to continue, one of the first steps its top management should consider is reducing capacity in order to reduce fixed costs. The automobile companies in the U.S. have been employing this technique in recent years to try to offset the effect of sales lost to importers.

Key Ratios

Profit = Revenues − Total costs

Revenues = Unit selling price × Unit sales volume

Total costs = Fixed costs + (Unit variable costs × Unit sales)

Profit: $\pi = pX - (a + bX)$
Where p = unit selling price, X = unit sales, a = fixed costs, b = unit variable costs.

$$\text{Break-even unit sales volume} = \frac{\text{Fixed costs}}{\text{Selling price per unit} - \text{Variable costs per unit}}$$

$$\text{Break-even unit sales volume} = \frac{\text{Fixed costs}}{\text{Unit contribution margin}}$$

$$\text{Target unit sales volume} = \frac{\text{Fixed costs} + \text{Desired profit}}{\text{Unit contribution margin}}$$

After-tax profit = Before-tax profit × (1 − Tax rate)

$$\text{Dollar break-even point} = \frac{\text{Fixed costs}}{\text{Contribution margin ratio}}$$

$$\text{Target dollar sales volume} = \frac{\text{Fixed costs} + \text{Desired profit}}{\text{Contribution margin ratio}}$$

$$\text{Operating leverage ratio} = \frac{\text{Contribution margin}}{\text{Before-tax profits}}$$

Key Terms

break-even point, 76
contribution income statement, 74
contribution margin, 74
contribution margin ratio, 76
cost-volume-profit (CVP) analysis, 70
cost-volume-profit graph, 79
direct labor, 73
direct materials, 73
fixed manufacturing overhead, 73
fixed selling and administrative costs, 73
functional income statement, 74
margin of safety, 76
operating leverage, 86
operating leverage ratio, 86
profitability analysis, 70
profit-volume graph, 79
sales mix, 71, 84
sensitivity analysis, 75
unit contribution margin, 75
variable cost ratio, 83
variable manufacturing overhead, 73
variable selling and administrative costs, 73

Multiple Choice

1. With fixed costs of $20,000/month and variable costs of $3/unit, Ace reported a monthly profit of $5,000 at a volume of 12,500 units. The unit selling price was
   a. $1.60
   b. $3.00
   c. $4.60
   d. $5.00

2. Presented is information from Wayne's contribution income statement:

Sales		$70,000
Less variable costs:		
Manufacturing	$20,000	
Selling and administrative	10,000	(30,000)
Contribution margin		40,000
Less fixed costs:		
Manufacturing	15,000	
Selling and administrative	8,000	(23,000)
Profit		$17,000

With a functional income statement Wayne would have reported a gross margin of

a. $35,000
b. $40,000
c. $47,000
d. $50,000

3. Based on the information in question 2, if Wayne had a $5,000 increase in sales, profits would increase by

a. $5,000
b. $3,570
c. $2,857
d. $2,500

4. Penn Company produces a product sold for $40 per unit. Variable and fixed cost information is presented below:

Variable Costs per Unit		Fixed Costs per Month	
Manufacturing	$ 8	Manufacturing	$29,000
Selling and administrative	2	Selling and administrative	16,000
Total	$10	Total	$45,000

The sales volume required for a monthly profit of $36,000 is

a. 900 units
b. 2,050 units
c. 2,700 units
d. 3,600 units

5. Based on the information in question 4, with an income tax rate of 40% the sales volume required for a monthly after-tax profit of $36,000 is

a. 2,000 units
b. 3,500 units
c. 3,700 units
d. 4,500 units

6. The Pitch sells 1 select style soccer ball for every 3 classic style balls. The select and classic style balls, respectively, sell for $40 and $20 and have unit variable costs of $20 and $10. Assuming a constant sales mix and total fixed costs for the company of $120,000, the break-even unit sales volume is

a. 7,200
b. 384,000
c. 9,600
d. 9,023

7. Each of the following is true *except*:

a. Operating leverage is a measure of a firm's fixed costs.
b. Operating leverage is a measure of risk and opportunity.
c. The lower the degree of operating leverage, the greater the opportunity for profit with increases in sales.
d. Operating leverage can be used to measure the expected change in net income resulting from a change in sales.

Multiple Choice Answers
1. d 2. a 3. c 4. c 5. b 6. c 7. c

Questions

Q3-1. What is cost-volume-profit analysis and when is it particularly useful?

Q3-2. Identify the important assumptions that underlie cost-volume-profit analysis.

Q3-3. When is it most reasonable to use a single independent variable in cost-volume-profit analysis?

Q3-4. Distinguish between a contribution and a functional income statement.

Q3-5. What is the unit contribution margin? How is it used in computing the unit break-even point?

Q3-6. What is the contribution margin ratio and when is it most useful?

Q3-7. How is the break-even equation modified to take into account the sales required to earn a desired profit?

Q3-8. How does a profit-volume graph differ from a cost-volume-profit graph? When is a profit-volume graph most likely to be used?

Q3-9. What impact do income taxes have on the sales volume required to earn a desired after-tax profit?

Q3-10. How are profit opportunities and the risk of losses affected by operating leverage?

Assignments with the MBC logo in the margin are available in myBusinessCourse.
See the Preface of the book for details.

Mini Exercises

LO3
Strands Salon

M3-11. Profitability Analysis
Assume Strands Salon, a San Diego hair salon, provides cuts, perms, and hairstyling services. Annual fixed costs are $225,000, and variable costs are 45% of sales revenue. Last year's revenues totaled $450,000.

Required

a. Determine its break-even point in sales dollars.
b. Determine last year's margin of safety in sales dollars.
c. Determine the sales dollar required for an annual pretax profit of $200,000.

LO3

Homework MBC

M3-12. Cost-Volume-Profit Graph: Identification and Sensitivity Analysis
A typical cost-volume-profit graph is presented below.

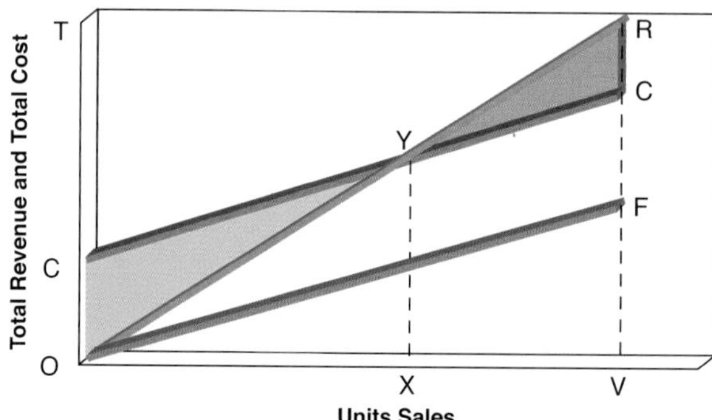

Required

a. Identify each of the following:
1. Line OF
2. Line OR
3. Line CC
4. The difference between lines OF and OV at any given number of unit sales
5. The difference between lines CC and OF at any given number of unit sales
6. The difference between lines CC and OV at any given number of unit sales
7. The difference between lines OR and OF at any given number of unit sales
8. Point X
9. Area CYO
10. Area RCY

b. Indicate the effect of each of the following independent events on lines CC, OR, and the break-even point:

1. A decrease in fixed costs
2. An increase in unit selling price
3. An increase in the variable costs per unit
4. An increase in fixed costs and a decrease in the unit selling price
5. A decrease in fixed costs and a decrease in the unit variable costs

M3-13. Profit-Volume Graph: Identification and Sensitivity Analysis LO3

A typical profit-volume graph follows.

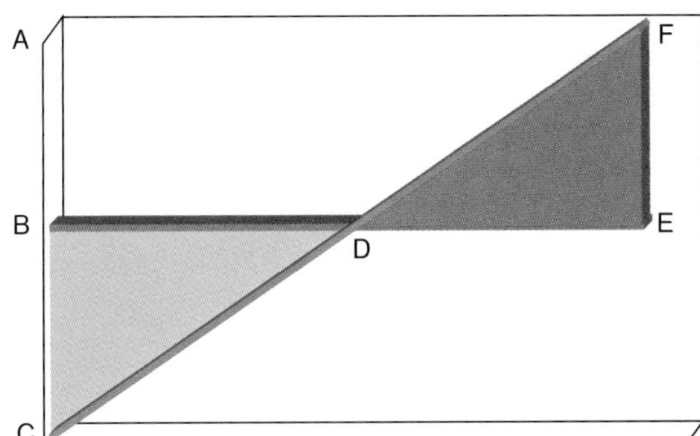

Required

a. Identify each of the following:

1. Area BDC
2. Area DEF
3. Point D
4. Line AC
5. Line BC
6. Line EF

b. Indicate the effect of each of the following on line CF and the break-even point:

1. An increase in the unit selling price
2. An increase in the variable costs per unit
3. A decrease in fixed costs
4. An increase in fixed costs and a decrease in the unit selling price
5. A decrease in fixed costs and an increase in the variable costs per unit

M3-14. Preparing Cost-Volume-Profit and Profit-Volume Graphs LO3 Connie's Pizza

Assume a Connie's Pizza shop has the following monthly revenue and cost functions:

Total revenues =	**\$20.00X**
Total costs =	**\$35,000 + \$6.00X**

Required

a. Prepare a graph (similar to that in **Exhibit 3.3**) illustrating Connie's cost-volume-profit relationships. The vertical axis should range from \$0 to \$120,000, in increments of \$20,000. The horizontal axis should range from 0 units to 6,000 units, in increments of 2,000 units.

b. Prepare a graph (similar to that in **Exhibit 3.4**) illustrating Connie's profit-volume relationships. The horizontal axis should range from 0 units to 6,000 units, in increments of 2,000 units.

c. When is it most appropriate to use a profit-volume graph?

M3-15. Preparing Cost-Volume-Profit and Profit-Volume Graphs LO3 Manu's Tacos

Manu's Tacos sells seven different burritos at a fixed price of \$9. Assume variable costs are \$6 per burrito and fixed operating costs are \$120,000 per year.

Required

a. Determine the annual break-even point in tacos.

b. Prepare a cost-volume-profit graph for the company. Use a format that emphasizes the contribution margin. The vertical axis should vary between \$0 and \$800,000 in increments of \$100,000. The horizontal axis should vary between 0 tacos and 80,000 tacos, in increments of 10,000 tacos. Label the graph in thousands.

c. Prepare a profit-volume graph for the company. The vertical axis should vary between $(150,000) and $150,000 in increments of $50,000. The horizontal axis should vary as described in requirement (b). Label the graph in thousands.

d. Evaluate the profit-volume graph. In what ways is it superior and in what ways is it inferior to the traditional cost-volume-profit graph?

LO4 Dick's Sporting Goods (DKS) Bauer Warrior CCM

M3-16. Multiple Product Break-Even Analysis

Assume Dick's Sporting Goods sells three types of youth hockey sticks: Bauer, Warrior, and CCM. Presented is information for Dick's three products.

	Bauer	Warrior	CCM
Unit selling price	$180	$120	$100
Unit variable costs	120	75	60
Unit contribution margin	$ 60	$ 45	$ 40

With monthly fixed costs of $150,000, the company sells two Bauer sticks for each Warrior, and three Warrior for each CCM.

Required

Determine the number of Warrior sticks sold at the monthly break-even point.

Exercises

LO2, 3 Picnic Time

E3-17. Contribution Income Statement and Cost-Volume-Profit Graph

Picnic Time produces a picnic basket that is sold for $100 per unit. Assume the company produced and sold 4,000 baskets during July. There were no beginning or ending inventories. Variable and fixed costs follow.

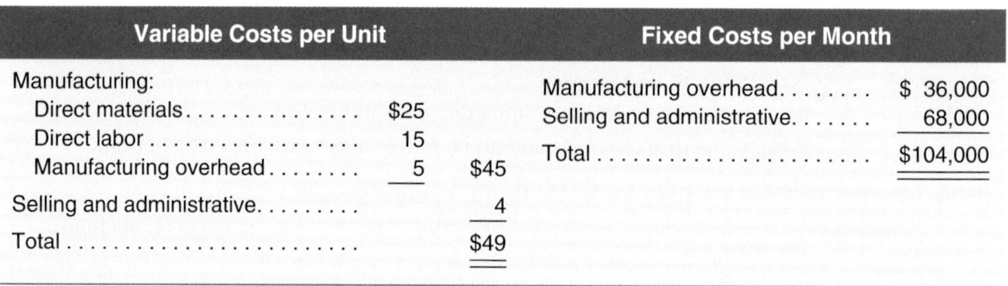

Variable Costs per Unit			Fixed Costs per Month	
Manufacturing:			Manufacturing overhead	$ 36,000
Direct materials	$25		Selling and administrative	68,000
Direct labor	15		Total	$104,000
Manufacturing overhead	5	$45		
Selling and administrative		4		
Total		$49		

Required

a. Prepare a contribution income statement for July.

b. Prepare a cost-volume-profit graph. Label the horizontal axis in units with a maximum value of 8,000. Label the vertical axis in dollars with a maximum value of $1,000,000. Draw a vertical line on the graph for the current (4,000) unit sales level, and label total variable costs, total fixed costs, and total profits at 4,000 units.

LO3 
DiPinto Electric Guitars & Basses

E3-18. Contribution Margin Concepts

DiPinto Electric Guitars & Basses sells musical instruments in Philadelphia. Assume the following information comes from the company's prior year records.

	Fixed	Variable	Total
Sales			$800,000
Costs			
Goods sold		$346,000	
Labor	$180,000	40,000	
Supplies	10,000	4,000	
Utilities	9,000	5,000	
Rent	48,000	—	
Advertising	10,000	—	
Miscellaneous	10,000	5,000	
Total costs	$267,000	$400,000	(667,000)
Net income			$133,000

Required

a. Determine the annual break-even dollar sales volume.

b. Determine the current margin of safety in dollars.

c. Prepare a cost-volume-profit graph for the guitar shop. Label both axes in dollars with maximum values of $1,000,000. Draw a vertical line on the graph for the current ($800,000) sales level, and label total variable costs, total fixed costs, and total profits at $800,000 sales.

d. What is the annual break-even dollar sales volume if management makes a decision that increases fixed costs by $50,000?

E3-19. Product Planning with Taxes LO3 Cliff Consulting

Assume that last year, Cliff Consulting, a firm in Berkeley, CA, had the following contribution income statement:

CLIFF CONSULTING Contribution Income Statement For the Year Ended September 30		
Sales revenue		$1,200,000
Variable costs		
Cost of services	$480,000	
Selling and administrative	60,000	540,000
Contribution margin		660,000
Fixed costs—selling and administrative		440,000
Before-tax profit		220,000
Income taxes 21%		46,200
After-tax profit		$ 173,800

Required

a. Determine the annual break-even point in sales revenue.

b. Determine the annual margin of safety in sales revenue.

c. What is the break-even point in sales revenue if management makes a decision that increases fixed costs by $80,000?

d. With the current cost structure, including fixed costs of $440,000, what dollar sales revenue is required to provide an after-tax net income of $250,000?

e. Prepare an abbreviated contribution income statement to verify that the solution to requirement (*d*) will provide the desired after-tax income.

E3-20. Not-for-Profit Applications LO3

Determine the solution to each of the following independent cases:

a. Collings College has annual fixed operating costs of $20,000,000 and variable operating costs of $2,400 per student. Tuition is $12,000 per student for the coming academic year, with a projected enrollment of 2,000 students. Expected revenues from endowments and federal and state grants total $400,000. Determine the amount the college must obtain from other sources.

b. The Collings College Student Association is planning a fall concert. Expected costs (renting a hall, hiring a band, etc.) are $15,000. Assuming 2,000 people attend the concert, determine the break-even price per ticket. How much will the association lose if this price is charged and only 1,500 tickets are sold?

c. City Hospital has a contract with the city to provide indigent health care on an outpatient basis for $125 per visit. The patient will pay $10 of this amount, with the city paying the balance ($115). Determine the amount the city will pay if the hospital has 5,000 patient visits.

d. A civic organization is engaged in a fund-raising program. On Civic Sunday, it will sell newspapers at $2.50 each. The organization will pay $1.75 for each newspaper. Costs of the necessary permits, signs, and so forth are $750. Determine the amount the organization will raise if it sells 3,000 newspapers.

e. Christmas for the Needy is a civic organization that provides Christmas presents to disadvantaged children. The annual costs of this activity are $10,000, plus $20 per present. Determine the number of presents the organization can provide with $30,000.

LO3, 5
Newell Brands (NWL)

E3-21. Alternative Production Procedures and Operating Leverage

Assume Sharpie, a brand of Newell Brands, is planning to introduce a new executive pen that can be manufactured using either a capital-intensive method or a labor-intensive method. The predicted manufacturing costs for each method are as follows:

	Capital Intensive	Labor Intensive
Direct materials per unit	$10.00	$12.00
Direct labor per unit	$ 4.00	$12.00
Variable manufacturing overhead per unit	$ 5.00	$ 2.00
Fixed manufacturing overhead per year	$1,800,000	$500,000

Sharpie's market research department has recommended an introductory unit sales price of $100. Selling costs under either method are predicted to be $250,000 per year, plus $4 per unit sold.

Required

a. Determine the annual break-even point in units if Sharpie uses the
   1. Capital-intensive manufacturing method.
   2. Labor-intensive manufacturing method.

b. Determine the annual unit volume at which Sharpie is indifferent between the two manufacturing methods.

c. Management wants to know more about the effect of each alternative on operating leverage.
   1. Explain operating leverage and the relationship between operating leverage and the volatility of earnings.
   2. Compute operating leverage for each alternative at a volume of 100,000 units.
   3. Which alternative has the higher operating leverage? Why?

LO3, 5
Willamette Valley Fruit Company

E3-22. Contribution Income Statement and Operating Leverage

Willamette Valley Fruit Company started as a small cannery-style operation in 1999. The company now processes, on average, 20 million pounds of berries each year. Flash-frozen berries are sold in 30 pound packs to retailers. Assume 650,000 packs were sold for $75 each last year. Variable costs were $42 per pack and fixed costs totaled $14,250,000.

Required

a. Prepare a contribution income statement for last year.

b. Determine last year's operating leverage.

c. Calculate the percentage change in profits if sales decrease by 10%.

d. Management is considering the purchase of several new pieces of packaging equipment. This will increase annual fixed costs to $15,500,000 and reduce variable costs to $40 per crate. Calculate the effect of this acquisition on operating leverage and explain any change.

LO4
TPG Tax & Accounting

E3-23. Multiple Product Break-Even Analysis

TPG Tax & Accounting is a full-service CPA firm located in Apache Junction, Arizona. Assume that tax return services are classified into one of three categories: standard, complex, and full-service (includes end-of-year bookkeeping with tax return preparation). Assume that TPG's fixed costs (rent, utilities, wages, and so forth) totaled $180,000 last year. Additional information from the prior year follows.

	Standard	Complex	Full-Service
Billing rate	$125.00	$250.00	$150.00
Average variable costs	(45.00)	(65.00)	(50.00)
Average contribution margin	$ 80.00	$185.00	$100.00
Number of returns prepared	1,000	200	800

Required

a. Using sales dollar analysis, determine TPG's break-even dollar sales volume.
b. Determine TPG's margin of safety in sales dollars. *Hint:* Use the weighted average billing rate.
c. Prepare a profit-volume graph for Joe's Tax Service.

E3-24. Cost-Volume-Profit Relations: Missing Data

LO3

Following are data from four separate companies.

	Case A	Case B	Case C	Case D
Unit sales	2,500	1,600	?	?
Sales revenue	$80,000	?	?	$240,000
Variable cost per unit	$20	$2	$24	?
Contribution margin	?	$1,600	?	?
Fixed costs	$14,000	?	$164,000	?
Net income	?	$900	?	?
Unit contribution margin	?	?	?	$30
Break-even point (units)	?	?	8,000	4,000
Margin of safety (units)	?	?	600	2,000

Required

Supply the missing data in each independent case.

E3-25. Cost-Volume-Profit Relations: Missing Data

Following are data from four separate companies.

	Case 1	Case 2	Case 3	Case 4
Sales revenue	$90,000	$150,000	?	?
Contribution margin	$45,000	?	$40,000	?
Fixed costs	$30,000	?	?	?
Net income	?	$15,000	$24,000	?
Variable cost ratio	?	0.40	?	0.60
Contribution margin ratio	?	?	0.25	?
Break-even point (dollars)	?	?	?	$150,000
Margin of safety (dollars)	?	?	?	$125,000

Required

Supply the missing data in each independent case.

E3-26. Customer-Level Planning

Circle K
Alimentation Couche-Tard (AID)

Circle K, a company of Alimentation Couche-Tard, operates a number of convenience stores worldwide. Assume that an analysis of operating costs, customer sales, and customer patronage reveals the following:

Fixed costs per store	$125,000
Variable cost ratio	0.60
Average sale per customer visit	$10.00
Average customer visits per week	2.00
Customers as portion of city population	.05

Required

Determine the city population required for a single Circle K to earn an annual profit of $75,000.

LO6 **E3-27. Multiple-Level Break-Even Analysis**

Kucera Associates provides marketing services for a number of small manufacturing firms. Kucera receives a commission of 10% of sales. Operating costs are as follows:

Unit-level costs	$0.05 per sales dollar
Sales-level costs	$400 per sales order
Customer-level costs	$1,000 per customer per year
Facility-level costs	$75,000 per year

Required

a. Determine the minimum order size in sales dollars for Kucera to break even on an order.
b. Assuming an average customer places five orders per year, determine the minimum annual sales required to break even on a customer.
c. What is the average order size in (*b*)?
d. Assuming Kucera currently serves 100 customers, with each placing an average of five orders per year, determine the minimum annual sales required to break even.
e. What is the average order size in (*d*)?
f. Explain the differences in the answers to (*a*), (*c*), and (*e*).

Problems

LO3 Carron Net Company **P3-28. Profit Planning with Taxes**

Carron Net Company manufactures sports nets for virtually every outdoor sport. Assume Carron sells nets for $50, on average, per unit. Last year, the company manufactured and sold 30,000 nets to obtain an after-tax profit of $275,000. Variable and fixed costs follow.

Variable Costs per Unit		Fixed Costs per Year	
Manufacturing	$20	Manufacturing	$232,250
Selling and administrative	4	Selling and administrative	204,000
Total	$24	Total	$436,250

Required

a. Determine the tax rate the company paid last year.
b. What unit sales volume is required to provide an after-tax profit of $400,000?
c. If the company reduces the unit variable cost by $4 and increases fixed manufacturing costs by $53,000, what unit sales volume is required to provide an after-tax profit of $400,000?
d. What assumptions are made about taxable income and tax rates in requirements (*a*) through (*c*)?

LO2, 3 Jail and Sail: Alcatraz Tour and Cruise **P3-29. Contribution Income Statement, Cost-Volume-Profit Graph, and Taxes**

Jail and Sail: Alcatraz Tour and Cruise provides sunset sightseeing tours of Alcatraz and the San Francisco Bay. Tickets cost $140 each. Assume 2,200 customers were served in July.

Variable Costs per Customer		Fixed Costs per Month	
Admission fees	$60	Operations	$50,000
Overhead	25	Selling and administration	12,500
Hors d'oeuvres	15		
Selling and administrative	2		
Total	$102	Total	$62,500

Jail and Sail is subject to an income tax rate of 21%.

Required

a. Prepare a contribution income statement for July.
b. Determine Jail and Sail's monthly break-even point in units.
c. Determine Jail and Sail's margin of safety in units for July.
d. Determine the unit sales required for a monthly after-tax profit of $20,000.
e. Prepare a cost-volume-profit graph. Label the horizontal axis in units with a maximum value of 4,000. Label the vertical in dollars with a maximum value of $600,000. Draw a vertical line on the graph for the current (2,200) unit level and label total variable costs, total fixed costs, and total before-tax profits at 2,200 units.

P3-30. High-Low Cost Estimation and Profit Planning LO3

Comparative income statements for Bismark Products Inc. follow:

BISMARK PRODUCTS INC.
Comparative Income Statements
For Years Ending December 31

	Year 1	Year 2
Unit sales	6,250	9,375
Sales revenue	$100,000	$150,000
Expenses	(85,000)	(105,000)
Pretax profit (loss)	$ 15,000	$ 45,000

Required

a. Determine the break-even point in units.
b. Determine the unit sales volume required to earn a pretax profit of $25,000.

P3-31. CVP Analysis and Special Decisions LO3 Smoothie Company

Smoothie Company produces fruit purees which it sells to smoothie bars and health clubs. Assume the most recent year's sales revenue was $5,800,000. Variable costs were 55% of sales and fixed costs totaled $1,560,000. Smoothie is evaluating two alternatives designed to enhance profitability.

- One staff member has proposed that Smoothie purchase more automated processing equipment. This strategy would increase fixed costs by $250,000 but decrease variable costs to 50% of sales.
- Another staff member has suggested that Smoothie rely more on outsourcing for fruit processing. This would reduce fixed costs by $250,000 but increase variable costs to 60% of sales.

Required

a. What is the current break-even point in sales dollars?
b. Assuming an income tax rate of 20%, what dollar sales volume is currently required to obtain an after-tax profit of $1,000,000?
c. In the absence of income taxes, at what sales volume will both alternatives (automation and outsourcing) provide the same profit?
d. Briefly describe one strength and one weakness of both the automation and the outsourcing alternatives.

P3-32. Break-Even Analysis in a Not-for-Profit Organization LO3

Melford Hospital operates a general hospital but rents space to separately owned entities rendering specialized services such as pediatrics and psychiatry. Melford charges each separate entity for patients' services (meals and laundry) and for administrative services (billings and collections). Space and bed rentals are fixed charges for the year, based on bed capacity rented to each entity. Melford charged the following costs to Pediatrics this year:

	Patient Services (Variable)	Bed Capacity (Fixed)
Dietary	$ 800,000	
Janitorial		$ 95,000
Laundry	375,000	
Laboratory	600,000	
Pharmacy	460,000	
Repairs and maintenance		40,000
General and administrative		1,750,000
Rent		2,000,000
Billings and collections	400,000	
Total	$2,635,000	$3,885,000

In addition to these charges from Melford Hospital, Pediatrics incurred the following personnel costs:

	Annual Salaries*
Supervising nurses	$135,000
Nurses	270,000
Assistants	240,000
Total	$645,000

* These salaries are fixed within the ranges of annual patient-days considered in this problem.

During the year, Pediatrics charged each patient $400 per day, had a capacity of 80 beds, and had revenues of $8,000,000 for 365 days. Pediatrics operated at 100% capacity on 90 days during this period. It is estimated that during these 90 days, the demand exceeded 100 beds.

Melford will have 20 additional beds available for rent next year. If Pediatrics rents the beds from Melford, the additional rental would proportionately increase Pediatrics' annual fixed charges that are based on bed capacity.

Required

a. Calculate the minimum number of patient-days required for Pediatrics to break even next year, if the additional beds are not rented. Patient demand is unknown, but assume that revenue per patient-day, cost per patient-day, cost per bed, and salary rates next year will be consistent with the current year.

b. Assume Pediatrics rents the extra 20-bed capacity from Melford during the busy 90-day period. Determine the net increase or decrease in earnings by preparing a schedule of increases in revenues and costs for next year. Assume that patient demand, revenue per patient-day, cost per patient-day, cost per bed, and salary rates remain the same as the current year.

(CPA adapted)

LO3 Converse Nike (NKE)

P3-33. CVP Analysis of Alternative Products

Assume Converse, a Nike company, plans to expand its manufacturing capacity to allow up to 30,000 pairs of a new shoe product each year. Because only one product can be produced, management is deciding between the production of the Roadrunner for backpacking and the Trail Runner for exercising. A marketing analysis indicates Converse could sell between 12,000 and 20,000 pairs of either product.

The accounting department has developed the following price and cost information:

	Product	
	Roadrunner	Trail Runner
Selling price per pair	$140	$125
Variable costs per pair	80	75
Fixed production costs	$150,000	$100,000

Additional annual facility costs, regardless of product, are estimated at $100,000. Assume Converse is subject to a 20% income tax rate.

Required

a. Determine the number of pairs of each product that Converse must sell to obtain an after-tax profit of $50,000.

b. Determine the number of pairs of each product Converse must sell to obtain identical before-tax profit.

c. For the solution to requirement (*b*), calculate Converse's after-tax profit or loss.

d. Which product should Converse produce if both products were guaranteed to sell at least 18,000 pairs? Verify your solution with calculations.

e. How much would the variable costs per pair of the product *not* selected in requirement (*d*) have to fall before both products provide the same profit at sales of 18,000 pairs? Verify your solution with calculations.

P3-34. CVP Analysis Using Published Financial Statements

LO3, 4
Microsoft (MSFT)

Condensed data in millions of dollars from Microsoft's 2019 and 2018 income statements follow:

	2019	2018
Revenues	$125,843	$110,360
Total cost of revenues and operating expenses	82,884	75,302
Operating income	$ 42,959	$ 35,058

Required

a. Develop a cost-estimation equation for Microsoft's annual cost of revenues and operating expenses using revenues as the activity.

b. Determine Microsoft's annual break-even point.

c. Predict operating profit for 2020, assuming 2020 sales of $150,000 million.

d. Identify the assumptions required to use the equations and amounts computed above.

P3-35. Multiple-Product Profitability Analysis, Multiple-Level Profitability Analysis

LO4
UCLA Store

Assume UCLA Store sells new college textbooks at the publishers' suggested retail prices and pays the publishers an amount equal to 70% of the suggested retail price. The store's other variable costs average 5% of sales revenue and annual fixed costs amount to $420,000.

Required

a. Determine the bookstore's annual break-even point in sales dollars.

b. Assuming an average textbook has a suggested retail price of $125, determine the bookstore's annual break-even point in units.

c. UCLA Store is planning to add used book sales to its operations. A typical used book costs the store 25% of the suggested retail price of a new book. The bookstore plans to sell used books for 75% of the suggested retail price of a new book. Assuming unit sales are unchanged, describe the effect on bookstore profitability of shifting sales toward more used and fewer new textbooks.

d. Chicago Publishers produces and sells new textbooks to college and university bookstores. Assume typical project-level costs total $285,000 for a new textbook. Production and distribution costs amount to 20% of the net amount the publisher receives from the bookstores. Textbook authors are paid a royalty of 15% of the net amount received from the bookstores. Determine the dollar sales volume required for Chicago to break even on a new textbook. This is the amount the bookstore pays the publisher, not the bookstore's sales revenue.

e. For a project with predicted sales of 10,000 new books at $125 each, determine

1. The bookstores' unit-level contribution.
2. The publisher's project-level contribution.
3. The author's royalties.

LO3 Spalding

P3-36. Multiple-Product Profitability Analysis

Spalding produces acrylic and polycarbonate basketball backboard and rim sets. Assume the following represents sales information for last year.

	Acrylic	Polycarbonate	Total
Units manufactured and sold	2,000	3,500	5,500
Sales revenue	$600,000	$735,000	$1,335,000
Variable costs	346,750	454,250	801,000
Contribution margin	$253,250	$280,750	$ 534,000
Fixed costs			(425,630)
Before-tax profit			108,370
Income taxes (20%)			(21,674)
After-tax profit			$ 86,696

Required

a. Determine the current break-even point in sales dollars.

b. With the current product mix and break-even point, determine the average unit contribution margin and unit sales.

c. Sales representatives believe that the total sales will increase to 5,750 units, with the sales mix likely shifting to 80% polycarbonate and 20% acrylic over the next few years. Evaluate the desirability of this projection.

LO3, 4

P3-37. Multiple-Product Break-Even Analysis

Currently, Corner Lunch Counter sells only Super Burgers for $5.50 each. During a typical month, the Counter reports a profit of $12,125 with sales of $68,750 and fixed costs of $36,000. Management is considering the introduction of a new Super Chicken Sandwich that will sell for $7.00 and have variable costs of $2.50. The addition of the Super Chicken Sandwich will require hiring additional personnel and renting additional equipment. These actions will increase monthly fixed costs by $5,400.

In the short run, management predicts that Super Chicken sales will average 7,500 sandwiches per month. However, almost all short-run sales of Super Chickens will come from regular customers who switch from Super Burgers to Super Chickens. Consequently, management predicts monthly sales revenue from Super Burgers will decline $27,500 (5,000 units). In the long run, management predicts that Super Chicken sales will increase to 9,000 sandwiches per month and that Super Burger sales will increase to 16,000 burgers per month.

Required

a. Determine each of the following:

1. The current monthly break-even point in sales dollars.
2. The short-run monthly profit and break-even point in sales dollars subsequent to the introduction of Super Chickens.
3. The long-run monthly profit and break-even point in sales dollars subsequent to the introduction of Super Chickens.

b. Based on your analysis, what are your recommendations?

LO4

P3-38. Multi-Level Profitability Analysis

AccuMeter manufactures and sells its only product (Z1) in lot sizes of 1,000 units. Because of this approach, lot (batch)-level costs are regarded as variable for CVP analysis. Presented is sales and cost information for the year:

Sales revenue (75,000 units at $65)	$4,875,000
Direct materials (75,000 units at $20)	1,500,000
Processing (75,000 units at $15)	1,125,000
Setup (150 lots at $2,500)	375,000
Batch movement (150 lots at $500)	75,000
Order filling (150 lots at $250)	37,500
Fixed manufacturing overhead	1,000,000
Fixed selling and administrative	450,000

Required

a. Prepare a traditional contribution income statement in good form.

b. Prepare a multi-level contribution income statement in good form. (*Hint:* First determine the appropriate cost hierarchy.)

c. What is the current contribution per lot (batch) of 1,000 units?

d. Management is contemplating introducing a limited number of specialty products. One product would sell for $80 per unit and have direct materials costs of $35 per unit. All other costs and all production and sales procedures will remain unchanged. What lot (batch) size is required for a contribution of $800 per lot?

Cases and Projects

C3-39. Ethics and Pressure to Improve Profit Plans LO1

Art Conroy is the assistant controller of New City Muffler, Inc., a subsidiary of New City Automotive, which manufactures tailpipes, mufflers, and catalytic converters at several plants throughout North America. Because of pressure for lower selling prices, New City Muffler has had disappointing financial performance in recent years. Indeed, Conroy is aware of rumblings from corporate headquarters threatening to close the plant.

One of Conroy's responsibilities is to present the plant's financial plans for the coming year to the corporate officers and board of directors. In preparing for the presentation, Conroy was intrigued to note that the focal point of the budget presentation was a profit-volume graph projecting an increase in profits and a reduction in the break-even point.

Curious as to how the improvement would be accomplished, Conroy ultimately spoke with Paula Mitchell, the plant manager. Mitchell indicated that a planned increase in productivity would reduce variable costs and increase the contribution margin ratio.

When asked how the productivity increase would be accomplished, Mitchell made a vague reference to increasing the speed of the assembly line. Conroy commented that speeding up the assembly line could lead to labor problems because the speed of the line was set by union contract. Mitchell responded that she was afraid that if the speedup were opened to negotiation, the union would make a big "stink" that could result in the plant being closed. She indicated that the speedup was the "only way to save the plant, our jobs, and the jobs of all plant employees." Besides, she did not believe employees would notice a 2% or 3% increase in speed. Mitchell concluded the meeting observing, "You need to emphasize the results we will accomplish next year, not the details of how we will accomplish those results. Top management does not want to be bored with details. If we accomplish what we propose in the budget, we will be in for a big bonus."

Required

What advice do you have for Art Conroy?

C3-40. CVP Analysis with Changing Cost Structure LO3, 5 Cincinnati Bell (CBB)

Cincinnati Bell was formed in the 1870s as a telegraph provider. In the 1890s it expanded, bringing telephone services to Cincinnati and surrounding areas. The early equipment was quite primitive by today's standards. All calls were handled manually by operators, and all customers were on party lines. By the 1970s, however, all customers were on private lines, and mechanical switching devices handled routine local and long distance calls. Operators remained available for directory assistance, credit card calls, and emergencies. In the 1990s Cincinnati Bell added local Internet connections as an optional service to its regular customers.

Required

a. Using a unit-level analysis, develop a graph with two lines, representing Cincinnati Bell's cost structure (1) in the 1970s and (2) in the late 1990s. Be sure to label the axes and lines.

b. With sales revenue as the independent variable, what is the likely impact of the changed cost structure on Cincinnati Bell's (1) contribution margin percent and (2) break-even point?

c. Discuss how the change in cost structure affected Cincinnati Bell's operating leverage and how this affects profitability under rising or falling sales scenarios.

LO2, 3 **C3-41. Cost Estimation and CVP Analysis**

Presented are the functional income statements of Regional Distribution Inc. for two recent years:

REGIONAL DISTRIBUTION INC. Functional Income Statements For Years Ending December 31, Year 1 and Year 2				
	Year 1		Year 2	
Sales		$1,800,000		$1,585,000
Expenses				
Cost of goods sold	$1,350,000		$1,188,750	
Shipping	68,500		65,250	
Sales order processing	20,650		19,850	
Customer relations	55,000		48,800	
Depreciation	30,000		30,000	
Administrative	90,500	(1,614,650)	90,000	(1,442,650)
Before-tax profit		185,350		142,350
Income taxes (20%)		(37,070)		(28,470)
After-tax profit		$ 148,280		$ 113,880

Required

a. Determine Regional Distribution's break-even point in sales dollars.

b. What dollar sales volume is required to earn an after-tax profit of $250,000?

c. Assuming sales of $4,000,000 next year, prepare a budgeted contribution income statement.

d. Discuss the reliability of the calculations in requirements (*a–c*), including the limitations of the CVP model and how they affect the reliability of the model.

Solutions to Review Problems

Review 3-1—Solution

a. Profit = $14X – ($10,000 + 5.25X)

b. At a volume of 6,200 cartons, Benchmark's profit is $44,250.

Computed as ($14 × 6,200) – [$10,000 + ($5.25 × 6,200)]

$86,800 – $42,550 = $44,250

Review 3-2—Solution

a.

SOLO CUP COMPANY Contribution Income Statement For the Month of September		
Sales (3,000 × $40)		$120,000
Less variable costs		
Direct materials (3,000 × $15)	$45,000	
Direct labor (3,000 × $3)	9,000	
Manufacturing overhead (3,000 × $10)	30,000	
Selling and administrative (3,000 × $2)	6,000	(90,000)
Contribution margin		30,000
Less fixed costs		
Manufacturing overhead	15,000	
Selling and administrative	10,000	(25,000)
Profit		$ 5,000

b.

Selling price	$40 per unit
Variable costs	(30) per unit
Contribution margin	$10 per unit

$$\textbf{Contribution margin ratio} = \frac{\textbf{Unit contribution margin}}{\textbf{Unit selling price}}$$
$$= \$10 \div \$40$$
$$= 0.25$$

Review 3-3—Solution

a.

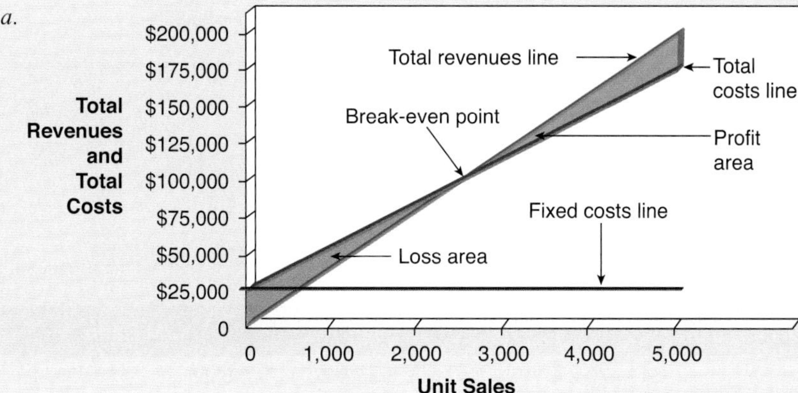

b.

$$\textbf{Break-even point} = \frac{\textbf{Fixed costs}}{\textbf{Unit contribution margin}}$$
$$= \$25{,}000 \div \$10$$
$$= 2{,}500 \text{ units}$$

c.

$$\textbf{Required dollar sales} = \frac{\textbf{Fixed costs + Desired profit}}{\textbf{Contribution margin ratio}}$$
$$= (\$25{,}000 + \$5{,}000) \div 0.25$$
$$= \$120{,}000$$

d.

$$\textbf{Required unit sales} = \frac{\textbf{Fixed costs + Desired before-tax profit}}{\textbf{Unit contribution margin}}$$

$$\textbf{Desired before-tax profit} = \$4{,}500 \div (1 - 0.40) = \$7{,}500$$

$$\textbf{Required unit sales} = (\$25{,}000 + \$7{,}500) \div \$10$$
$$= 3{,}250 \text{ units}$$

Review 3-4—Solution

a.

	Coffee	Tea	Smoothies	Total
Monthly unit sales	6,000	3,750	2,250	
Selling price	$1.35	$1.25	$1.95	
Sales	$8,100.00	$4,687.50	$4,387.50	$17,175.00
Variable costs	3,600.00	1,687.50	1,687.50	6,975.00
Contribution margin	$4,500.00	$3,000.00	$2,700.00	10,200.00
Fixed costs				8,000.00
Before-tax profit				$ 2,200.00
Contribution margin (CM) ratio	0.5556	0.6400	0.6154	0.5939
Current sales mix (based on sales dollars)	47.16%	27.29%	25.55%	

b.

$$\textbf{Break-even} = \frac{\textbf{Fixed costs}}{\textbf{Total contribution margin ratio}}$$

$$= \frac{\$8{,}000}{0.5939}$$

$$= \$13{,}470$$

Proof:			Sales				C/M Ratio
Coffee:	$13,470 × 47.16%	=	$ 6,352.45	×	0.5556	=	$3,529.42
Tea:	$13,470 × 27.29%	=	3,675.96	×	0.6400	=	2,352.62*
Smoothies:	$13,470 × 25.55%	=	3,441.59	×	0.6154	=	2,117.96*
			$13,470.00				
Total contribution margin							8,000.00
Fixed costs							8,000.00
Before-tax profit							–0–

* Amounts adjusted to correct for minor rounding error.

Review 3-5—Solution

The Coffee Bean has an operating leverage of 4.6364, calculated as a contribution margin of $10,200 divided by before-tax profit of $2,200. Therefore, if sales dollars increase by 20% to $20,610, before-tax profit should increase by 4.636 times 20%, or 92.73%, to $4,240. Because of the leverage caused by fixed costs, a 20% increase in sales results in a 92.73% increase in before-tax profit. Conversely, a 20% decrease in sales would result in a 92.73% decrease in before-tax profits to $160.

Proof:	20% Sales Increase	20% Sales Decrease
Sales	$20,610	$13,740
CM %	× 0.5939	× 0.5939
Total CM	12,240	8,160
Fixed costs	8,000	8,000
Before-tax profit	$ 4,240	$ 160

Current before-tax profit of $2,200 × (1 + 0.9273) = $4,240
Current before-tax profit of $2,200 × (1 – 0.9273) = $160

Review 3-6—Solution

Weekly contribution per average customer:

$17 sales per visit × (1 − 0.80) contribution ratio × 1.50 visits = $5.10

Annual contribution per customer = $5.10 × 52 weeks = $265.20

Customers required for desired profit = ($80,000 + $40,000)/$265.20 = 453 (rounded up to the next whole number)

Required population = 453 customers/0.05 customers in population = 9,060

Chapter 4

Relevant Costs and Benefits for Decision Making

Learning Objectives

LO1 Distinguish between relevant and irrelevant revenues and costs. (p. 112)

LO2 Analyze relevant costs and indicate how they differ under alternative decision scenarios. (p. 116)

LO3 Apply differential analysis to evaluate changes in profit plans. (p. 117)

LO4 Apply differential analysis to evaluate whether to accept a special order. (p. 119)

LO5 Apply differential analysis to evaluate outsourcing decisions. (p. 122)

LO6 Apply differential analysis to evaluate whether to sell or further process a product. (p. 126)

LO7 Allocate limited resources for purposes of maximizing short-run profit. (p. 128)

Every day companies, both large and small, are faced with making critical decisions that can drastically alter their likelihood of success. Some of these decisions are long term in nature, such as where a company should invest in property, plant, and equipment. Others are short-run decisions, such as whether or not to sell a product or service to a new customer at a price that is below the normal market price.

San Francisco startup company Uber got its start from pondering a common dilemma: how to get home from the club late at night. Founder Travis Kalanick explains that he and a friend joked, ". . . let's go buy 10 Mercedes S-Classes, let's go hire 20 drivers, let's get parking garages and let's make it so we could push a button and an S-Class would roll up, for only us, in the city of San Francisco, where you cannot get a ride." Shortly thereafter, an iPhone application called Uber was launched in 2010. Uber has now expanded to over 700 cities in 63 countries.

Uber's intent was to act as a broker by matching riders to available drivers with a summons via smartphones. But the company first had to decide whether it should purchase cars and pay for insurance, storage, and other associated costs or whether to contract with existing drivers, either limousine companies or individual drivers. In the end, Uber decided to contract with partners (limo companies or individuals) who had their own vehicles. These partners take responsibility for licensing, vehicle cost and maintenance, gas, auto insurance, and storage. In return, Uber trains the drivers on the software platform and pays them a percentage of the fare.

By acting as a broker instead of owning its own vehicles, Uber was able to minimize its fixed costs. This "operating leverage" results in a greater benefit from increases in customers, because the fixed costs don't need to increase to handle the higher capacity. However, the company's capacity is limited by how many drivers it has on contract. This limited resource can be maximized by minimizing the downtime of its drivers. Uber invested in engineers to build algorithms to manage its supply of drivers and demand of riders. The efficient management of this limited resource benefits both drivers (who are more likely to be engaged in fare-generating activity) and riders, who can use the software's tracking feature to see their car's progress toward the predetermined pickup destination.

Uber has successfully changed the way people think about transportation. It reported $11.3 billion in net revenue in 2018. However it also spent approximately $1.16 for every $1.00 of revenue it earned, with 2018 operating losses of $1.8 billion.

As Uber emphasizes growth over pofits, the company is betting that investing in areas such as mapping technology, food delivery, and autonomous vehicles will reduce the real cost of transportation.

In this chapter, we will learn how to incorporate the relevant revenues and costs to simplify decision making, even when operating in a complex, changing environment.

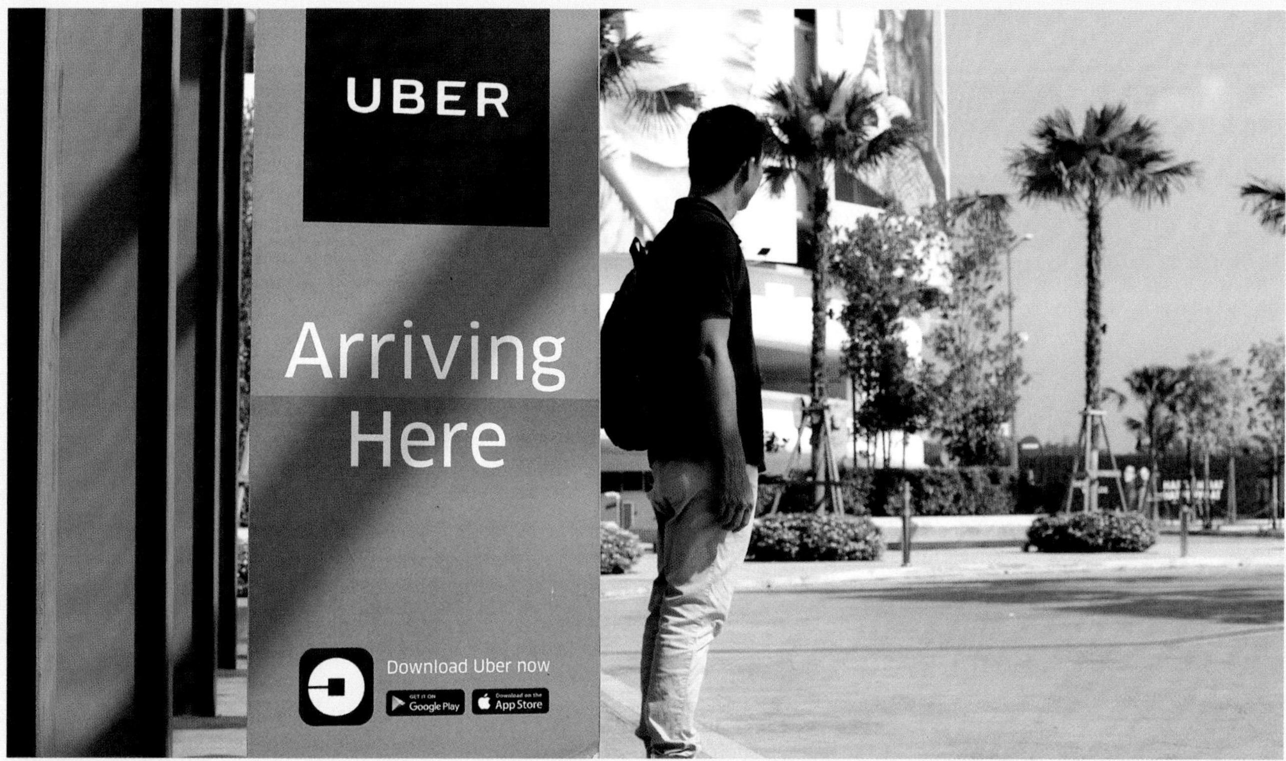

Road Map

LO	Learning Objective I Topics	Page	eLecture	Guided Example	Assignments
LO1	**Distinguish between relevant and irrelevant revenues and costs.** Future Revenues :: Outlay Costs :: Sunk Costs :: Disposal and Salvage Values :: Opportunity Costs	112	e4–1	Review 4-1	11, 12, 13, 14, 15, 16, 17, 18, 19, 20, 21, 22, 23, 24, , 28, 29, 30, 31, 32, 33, 34, 35, 36
LO2	**Analyze relevant costs and indicate how they differ under alternative decision scenarios.** Differential Costs	116	e4–2	Review 4-2	13, 15, 16, 17, 18, 19, 20, 21, 22, 23, 24, 28, 29, 30, 31, 32, 33, 34, 35, 36
LO3	**Apply differential analysis to evaluate changes in profit plans.** Multiple Changes in Profit Plans	117	e4–3	Review 4-3	28, 29, 33, 34, 36
LO4	**Apply differential analysis to evaluate whether to accept a special order.** Special Orders :: Time Span and Opportunity Costs :: Qualitative Considerations	119	e4–4	Review 4-4	16, 18, 19, 20, 31, 32, 33, 34
LO5	**Apply differential analysis to evaluate outsourcing decisions.** Make or Buy :: Opportunity Costs :: Qualitative Risk Factors	122	e4–5	Review 4-5	21, 22, 23, 33, 34
LO6	**Apply differential analysis to evaluate whether to sell or further process a product.** Single Product Decisions :: Joint Product Decisions	126	e4–6	Review 4-6	17, 24, 27
LO7	**Allocate limited resources for purposes of maximizing short-run profit.** Single Constraint :: Multiple Constraints :: Theory of Constraints :: Limitations of Decision Analysis Models	128	e4–7	Review 4-7	25, 26

CHAPTER ORGANIZATION

Relevant Costs and Benefits for Decision Making

Identifying Relevant Costs	Differential Analysis of Relevant Costs	Applying Differential Analysis	Use of Limited Resources
• Relevance of Future Revenues • Relevance of Outlay Costs • Irrelevance of Sunk Costs • Sunk Costs Can Cause Ethical Dilemmas • Relevance of Disposal and Salvage Values • Relevance of Opportunity Costs	• Differential Cost Analysis	• Multiple Changes in Profit Plans • Special Orders • Outsourcing Decisions • Sell or Process Further	• Single Constraint • Multiple Constraints • Theory of Constraints • Limitations of Decision Analysis Models

The purpose of this chapter is to examine approaches to identifying and analyzing revenue and cost information for specific decisions, such as the decision to outsource. Our emphasis is on identifying **relevant costs** (future costs that differ among competing decision alternatives) and distinguishing relevant costs from **irrelevant costs** that do not differ among competing decision alternatives. We consider a number of frequently encountered decisions: to make multiple changes in profit plans, to accept or reject a special order, to acquire a component or service internally or externally, to sell a product or process it further, and how to best use limited capacity. These decision situations are not exhaustive; they only illustrate relevant cost concepts. Once we understand these concepts, we can apply them to a variety of decision scenarios.

Although our focus in this chapter is on profit maximization, decisions should not be based solely on this criterion, especially maximizing profit in the short run. Managers must consider the implications decision alternatives have on long-run profit, as well as legal, ethical, social, and other nonquantitative factors. These factors can lead management to select a course of action other than that selected by financial information alone.

Identifying Relevant Costs

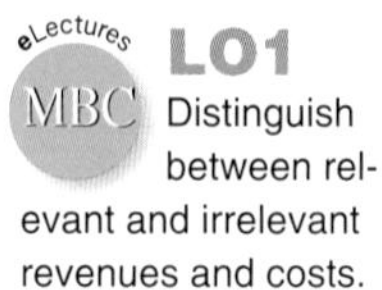

LO1 Distinguish between relevant and irrelevant revenues and costs.

For a specific decision, the key to relevant cost analysis is first to identify the relevant costs (and revenues) and then to organize them in a manner that clearly indicates how they differ under each alternative. Once we know what costs and revenues differ between the alternatives, we can assess quantitatively, what option is more favorable. Consider the following equipment replacement decision.

Beats by Dr. Dre (Beats), a subsidiary of Apple Inc., produces headphones and supplies high-quality components and equalizer software to HP for its line of personal computers. Assume that one of its components used in wireless headsets is forecasted to sell 10,000 units during the coming year at a price of $20 per unit. Further assume that each of Beats' components is manufactured with separate machines in a shared plant.

The machine used in the manufacture of headset components is two years old and has a remaining useful life of four years. Its purchase price was $90,000 (new), and it has an estimated salvage value of zero dollars at the end of its useful life. Its current book value (original cost less accumulated depreciation) is $60,000, but it could be sold today for only $35,000.

Headset component costs	
Direct materials	$3.00 per unit
Conversion	5.00 per unit
Selling and distribution	1.00 per unit
Inspection and adjustment	$500 per batch (1,000 units)

continued

continued from previous page

Depreciation on machines	$15,000 per year
Machine maintenance	$ 200 per month
Advertising	$ 5,000 per year
Common costs	
Administrative salaries	$65,000 per year
Building operations	23,000 per year
Building rent	24,000 per year

Management is evaluating the desirability of replacing the machine with a new machine. The new machine costs $80,000, has a useful life of four years, and a predicted salvage value of zero dollars at the end of its useful life. Although the new machine has the same production capacity as the old machine, its predicted operating costs are lower because it consumes less electricity. Further, because of a computer control system, the new machine allows production of twice as many units between inspections and adjustments, and the cost of inspections and adjustments is lower. The new machine requires only annual, rather than monthly, overhauls. Hence, machine maintenance costs are lower. Costs for the new machine are predicted as follows:

Conversion costs	$4.00 per unit
Inspection and adjustment	$ 300 per batch (2,000 units)
Machine maintenance	$ 200 per year

All other costs and all revenues remain unchanged.

The decision alternatives are to keep the old machine or to replace it with a new machine. An analysis of how costs and revenues differ under each alternative assists management in making the best choice. The first objective of this chapter is to study the distinction between relevant and irrelevant items. After evaluating the relevance of each item, we develop an analysis of relevant costs.

Relevance of Future Revenues

Revenues, which are inflows of resources from the sale of goods and services, are relevant to a decision only if they differ between alternatives. In this example, revenues are not relevant because they are identical under each alternative. Because revenues do not change no matter what choice we make, we ignore revenues in deciding between the two alternatives. Revenues would be relevant if the new machine had greater capacity or if management intended to change the selling price should it acquire the new machine. (The $35,000 disposal value of the old machine is an inflow. However, *revenues* refer to resources from the sale of goods and services to customers in the normal course of business. We include the sale of the old machine under disposal and salvage values.)

The hypothetical keep-or-replace decision facing Beats' management might be called a **cost reduction proposal** because it is based on the assumption that the organization is committed to an activity and that management desires to minimize the cost of activities. Here, the two alternatives are either to continue operating with the old machine or to replace it with a new machine.

Although this approach is appropriate for many activities, managers should remember that they have another alternative—discontinue operations. To simplify the analysis, managers normally do not consider the alternative to discontinue when operations appear to be profitable. However, if there is any doubt about an operation's profitability, this alternative should be considered. Because revenues change if an operation is discontinued, revenues are relevant whenever this alternative is considered.

Relevance of Outlay Costs

Outlay costs are costs that require future expenditures of cash or other resources. Outlay costs that differ under the decision alternatives are relevant; outlay costs that do not differ are irrelevant. In deciding whether to replace the machine, Beats classifies costs as relevant or irrelevant. The cost of the new machine is a relevant cost as well as the ongoing costs that are expected to change using the new machine: conversion costs, inspection and adjustment, and machine maintenance. The remaining costs are not expected to change with the purchase of the new machine, thus they are considered irrelevant. The relevant and irrelevant costs are listed in the following table.

Relevant Outlay Costs	Irrelevant Outlay Costs
Cost of New Machine	Direct Materials
Conversion Costs	Depreciation Selling and Distribution
Inspection and Adjustment Costs	Advertising
Machine Maintenance	Common Outlay Costs

Irrelevance of Sunk Costs

Sunk costs result from past decisions that cannot be changed. Suppose we purchased a car for $30,000 five years ago. Today we must decide whether to purchase another car or have major maintenance performed on our current car. In making this decision, the purchase price of our current car is a sunk cost.

Although the relevance of outlay costs is determined by the decision scenario, sunk costs are never relevant. The cost of the old machine is a sunk cost, not a future cost. This cost and the related depreciation result from the past decision to acquire the old machine. Even though all the outlay costs discussed earlier would be relevant to a decision to continue or discontinue operations, the sunk cost of the old machine is not relevant even to this decision.

If management elects to keep the old machine, its book value will be depreciated over its remaining useful life of four years. However, if management elects to replace the old machine, its book value is written off when it is replaced. Even if management elects to discontinue operations, the book value of the old machine must be written off.

Sunk Costs Can Cause Ethical Dilemmas

Although the book value of the old machine has no economic significance, the accounting treatment of past costs may make it psychologically difficult for managers to regard them as irrelevant. If management replaces the old machine, a $25,000 accounting loss is recorded in the year of replacement:

Book value	$60,000
Disposal value	(35,000)
Loss on disposal	$25,000

The possibility of recording an accounting loss can create an ethical dilemma for managers. Although an action may be desirable from the long-run viewpoint of the organization, in the short run, choosing the action may result in an accounting loss. Fearing the loss will lead superiors to question her judgment, a manager might prefer to use the old machine (with lower total profits over the four-year period) as opposed to replacing it and being forced to record a loss on disposal. Although this action may avoid raising troublesome questions in the near term, the cumulative effect of many decisions of this nature is harmful to the organization's long-run economic health.

From an economic viewpoint, the analysis should focus on future costs and revenues that differ. The decision should not be influenced by sunk costs. Although there is no easy solution to this behavioral and ethical problem, managers and management accountants should be aware of its potential impact.

Managerial Decision ■ You Are the Vice President of Manufacturing

You recently made the decision to purchase a very expensive machine for your manufacturing plant that used technology that was well established over several years. The purchase of this machine was a major decision supported by the chief financial officer, based solely on your recommendation. Shortly after making the purchase, you were attending a trade convention where you learned of new technology that is now available that essentially renders obsolete the machine you recently purchased. You feel that it may be best for the company to acquire the new technology since most of your competitors will be using it soon; however, you feel that this cannot be done now that you have recently purchased the new machine. What should you consider in making this decision? [Answer, p. 131]

Relevance of Disposal and Salvage Values

Beats' assumed revenues (inflows of resources from operations) from the sale of headset components were discussed earlier. The sale of fixed assets is also a source of resources. Because the sale of fixed assets is a nonoperating item, cash inflows obtained from these sales are discussed separately.

The disposal value of the old machine is a relevant cash inflow. It is obtained only if the replacement alternative is selected. Any salvage value available at the end of the useful life of either machine is also relevant. A loss on disposal can have a favorable tax impact if the loss can be offset against taxable gains or taxable income. To simplify the analysis, we ignore any tax implications at this point. The tax effects related to capital asset transactions are discussed in Chapter 12.

Relevance of Opportunity Costs

When making a decision between alternative courses of action, accepting one alternative results in rejecting the other alternative(s). Any benefit foregone as a result of rejecting one opportunity in favor of another opportunity is described as an **opportunity cost** of the accepted alternative. For example, if you are employed at a salary of $40,000 per year and you have the opportunity to continue to work or the opportunity to go back to school full-time for two years to earn a graduate degree, the cost of getting the degree includes not only all the outlay costs for tuition, books, and so forth, it also includes the salary foregone (or opportunity cost) of $40,000 per year. So, if your tuition and other outlay costs are going to be $25,000 per year for two years, the cost of earning the degree will be $50,000 of outlay costs and $80,000 of opportunity costs, for a total cost of earning the degree of $130,000. Opportunity costs are always relevant in making decisions among competing alternatives.

The following is a summary of all the relevant and irrelevant costs discussed in this section.

Relevant Costs		Irrelevant Costs	
Future costs that differ among competing alternatives		Future costs that do not differ among competing alternatives	
Opportunity Costs	**Relevant Outlay Costs**	**Irrelevant Outlay Costs**	**Sunk Costs**
Net benefits foregone of rejected alternatives	Future costs requiring future expenditures that differ	Future costs requiring future expenditures that do not differ	Historical costs resulting from past decisions

Research Insight ■ Why Don't Managers Always Ignore Sunk Costs?

For decades, business school students have learned that sunk costs are irrelevant to decision making; however, managers still find these costs difficult to ignore. Researchers have shown that, far from ignoring sunk costs, many managers increase commitment to a project as sunk costs increase. Recent experimental research from a team at the University of Melbourne in Australia sheds more light on the precise motivations of managers who choose not to ignore sunk costs. The researchers found that the managers' personal motivations interact with the context of the specific project and the related sunk costs. Their study found that individuals who are focused on promotion become increasingly fixated on completion as the end of the project nears. While other managers are able to ignore fixed costs more consistently throughout the project life cycle, those who are focused on promotion are most likely to continue to invest in a project that should be abandoned when the project is close to completion. As managerial accountants advise executive teams, this type of bias should be kept in mind.

Source: Adam P. Barsky and Michael J. Zyphur, "Disentangling Sunk-Costs and Completion Proximity: The Role of Regulatory Focus," *Journal of Experimental Social Psychology* 65 (2016): 105-108.

Review 4-1 LO1 Identifying Relevant and Irrelevant Costs

TaylorMade-Adidas Golf Company, a subsidiary of Adidas, manufactures golf clubs using "adjustable weight technology" or AWT. Suppose a European machine company has proposed to sell TaylorMade a new highly automated machine that would reduce significantly the labor cost of producing its golf clubs. The cost of the machine is $1,000,000, and would have an expected life of five years, at the end of which it would have a residual value of $100,000. It has an estimated operating cost of $10,000 per month. The direct labor cost savings per club from using the machine is estimated to be $5 per club. In addition, one monthly salaried manufacturing manager, whose salary is $6,000 per month would no longer be needed. Assume the Vice President of Manufacturing earns $10,000 per month. Also, the new machine would free up about 5,000 square feet of space from the displaced workers. Assume TaylorMade's building is held under a 10-year lease that has eight years remaining. The current lease cost is $1 per square foot per month. TaylorMade may be able to use the space for other purposes, and it has received an offer to rent it to a nearby related company for $3,500 per month.

Required

Identify all of the costs described above as either "relevant" or "irrelevant" to the decision to acquire the new machine.

Solution on p. 147.

Differential Analysis of Relevant Costs

eLectures MBC **LO2** Analyze relevant costs and indicate how they differ under alternative decision scenarios.

Differential cost analysis is an approach to the analysis of relevant costs that focuses on the costs that differ under alternative actions. A differential analysis of relevant costs for Beats' equipment replacement decision is in **Exhibit 4.1**. Replacement provides a net advantage of $17,800 over the life of both machines versus keeping the old machine.

An alternative analysis to that presented in **Exhibit 4.1** is to present all revenues and costs (relevant and irrelevant) for each alternative in separate columns, such that the bottom line of the analysis is the total profit or loss for each alternative. This method is preferred if the goal is to determine the total profitability of each alternative.

Exhibit 4.1 Differential Analysis for Beats' Equipment Replacement

	Four-Year Totals			
	Replace with New Machine		Keep Old Machine	Difference (effect of replacement on income)
Conversion				
Old machine (10,000 units × $5 × 4 years)			$200,000	
New machine (10,000 units × $4 × 4 years)	$160,000			($40,000)
Inspection and adjustment				
Old machine (10* setups × $500 × 4 years)			20,000	
New machine (5** setups × $300 × 4 years)	6,000			(14,000)
Machine maintenance				
Old machine ($200 per month × 12 months × 4 years)			9,600	
New machine ($200 per year × 4 years)	800			(8,800)
Disposal of old machine	(35,000)			(35,000)
Cost of new machine	80,000			80,000
Totals	$211,800		$229,600	($17,800)
Advantage of replacement		$17,800		

* Old machine: 10,000 units ÷ 1,000 units per batch

** New machine: 10,000 units ÷ 2,000 units per batch

Assuming the organization is committed to providing a particular product or service, a differential analysis of relevant costs (as shown in **Exhibit 4.1**) is preferred to a complete analysis of all costs and revenues for a number of reasons:

- A differential analysis focuses on only those items that differ, providing a clearer picture of the impact of the decision. Management is less apt to be confused by this analysis than by one that combines relevant and irrelevant items.
- A differential analysis contains fewer items, making it easier and quicker to prepare.
- A differential analysis can help to simplify complex situations (such as those encountered by multiple-product or multiple-plant firms), when it is difficult to develop complete firmwide statements to analyze all decision alternatives.

Before preparing a differential analysis, it is always desirable to reassess the organization's commitment to a product or service. This helps avoid "throwing good money after bad." If Beats currently had large annual losses, acquiring the new machine would merely reduce total losses over the next four years by $17,800. In this case, discontinuing operations (a third alternative) should also be considered.

Preparing a Differential Analysis of Relevant Costs **LO2 Review 4-2**

TaylorMade-Adidas Golf Company, a subsidiary of Adidas, manufactures golf clubs using "adjustable weight technology" or AWT. Suppose a European machine company has proposed to sell TaylorMade a new highly automated machine that would reduce significantly the labor cost of producing its golf clubs. The cost of the machine is $1,000,000, and would have an expected life of five years, at the end of which it would have a residual value of $100,000. It has an estimated operating cost of $10,000 per month. The direct labor cost savings per club from using the machine is estimated to be $5 per club. In addition, one monthly salaried manufacturing manager, whose salary is $6,000 per month would no longer be needed. Assume the Vice President of Manufacturing earns $10,000 per month. Also, the new machine would free up about 5,000 square feet of space from the displaced workers. Assume TaylorMade's building is held under a 10-year lease that has eight years remaining. The current lease cost is $1 per square foot per month. TaylorMade may be able to use the space for other purposes, and it has received an offer to rent it to a nearby related company for $3,500 per month.

Required

a. Assuming the new machine would be used to produce an average of 5,000 clubs per month, prepare a differential analysis of the relevant costs of buying the machine and using it for the next five years, versus continuing to use hand labor.

b. In addition to the quantitative analysis in requirement *a*, what qualitative considerations are important for making the right decision?

Solution on p. 148.

Applying Differential Analysis

Differential analysis is used to provide information for a variety of planning and decision-making situations. This section illustrates some of the more frequently encountered applications of differential analysis. To focus on differential analysis concepts, we will continue with the Uber discussion introduced in the opening vignette of this chapter. For the purposes of our example, we assume a simplified financial model, which consists of variable costs based on number of miles driven and costs that are fixed in the short run. As Uber is primarily a technology company, other than driver fees, its costs are generally related to the processing, storage, and communication of information. Also, for this example, we assume that the entire amount of the customer fees collected by the drivers is categorized as revenue for Uber and the fees paid out to the drivers are categorized as variable driver fees.

Multiple Changes in Profit Plans

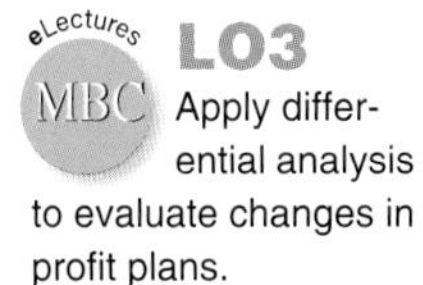

LO3 Apply differential analysis to evaluate changes in profit plans.

Assume Uber collects an average of $45 for every 10 miles of customer rides. Variable costs per every 10 miles and fixed costs per month are as follows:

Variable Costs*		Fixed Costs per Month	
Driver fees	$35.00	Platform and cloud-based data storage	$ 40,000
Platform and cloud-based data storage	1.50	Mapping technology	75,000
Mapping technology	2.00	Advertising	5,000
Customer service	0.50	Total	$120,000
Total	$39.00		

*Per every 10 miles

Assume the contribution margin per every 10 miles driven is $6 ($45 customer collection less $39 variable costs). Uber's hypothetical contribution income statement for April is presented in **Exhibit 4.2**. Assume the April operations are typical and monthly miles driven average 300,000 miles, with monthly profits averaging $60,000.

Management wants to know the effect that each of the following three mutually exclusive alternatives would have on monthly profits.

1. The introduction of a bonus program. For every 500 miles a driver completes within a month, the driver receives an additional $25. The bonus program is expected to result in a 10% increase in miles per month and a bonus payout of $10,000 per month.
2. Increasing the cost of the rides to the customers by an average of $1 per every 10 miles. The average payout to the drivers will remain constant at $35 per every 10 miles. This should result in a decrease of 50,000 in monthly miles.
3. Decreasing the cost of the rides to the customers by an average of $1 per every 10 miles. The average payout to the drivers will remain constant at $35 per every 10 miles driven. This should result in an increase of 60,000 in monthly miles. Uber faces a constraint of driver availability. To encourage its drivers to work more, Uber is offering to pay an extra $1 for every 10 miles, after a driver completes 1,200 miles within a one-week period. Assume that 30,000 miles will be paid out at the higher rate.

It is possible to develop contribution income statements for each alternative and then determine the profit impact of the proposed change by comparing the new income with the current income. A more direct approach is to use differential analysis and focus on only those items that differ under each alternative.

Alternative 1	
Profit increase from increased miles (3,000* × $6)	$18,000
Profit decrease from bonus	(10,000)
Increase in monthly profit	$ 8,000

*(300,000 × 10%) divided by 10

Alternative 2	
Profit decrease from reduced miles (5,000* × $6)	$(30,000)
Profit increase from increased price**	25,000
Decrease in monthly profit	$ (5,000)

*50,000 divided by 10

**[(300,000 current miles – 50,000 lost miles) divided by 10] × $1

Alternative 3	
Profit increase from increase in miles (6,000* × $6)	$36,000
Profit decrease from reduced selling price (36,000** × $1)	(36,000)
Profit decrease from increased driver fees (3,000*** × $1)	($3,000)
Decrease in monthly profit	($3,000)

*60,000 divided by 10

**(300,000 current miles + 60,000 increased miles) divided by 10

***30,000 divided by 10

Alternatives 2 and 3 are undesirable because they would each result in a decrease in monthly profit. Because Alternative 1 results in an increase in monthly profit, it is preferred to both Alternatives 2 and 3.

Applying Differential Analysis to Alternative Profit Scenarios — LO3 Review 4-3

Epson produces color cartridges for inkjet printers. Suppose cartridges are sold to mail-order distributors for $4.80 each and that manufacturing and other costs are as follows:

Variable Costs per Unit		Fixed Costs per Month	
Direct materials	$2.00	Factory overhead	$15,000
Direct labor	0.20	Selling and administrative	5,000
Factory overhead	0.25	Total	$20,000
Distribution	0.05		
Total	$2.50		

The variable distribution costs are for transportation to mail-order distributors. Also assume the current monthly production and sales volume is 15,000 and monthly capacity is 20,000 units.

Required

Determine the effect of the following separate situations on monthly profits.

a. A $1.50 increase in the unit selling price should result in an 1,800 unit decrease in monthly sales.

b. A $1.80 decrease in the unit selling price should result in a 6,000 unit increase in monthly sales. However, because of capacity constraints, the last 1,000 units would be produced during overtime, when the direct labor costs increase by 50%.

Solution on p. 148.

Special Orders

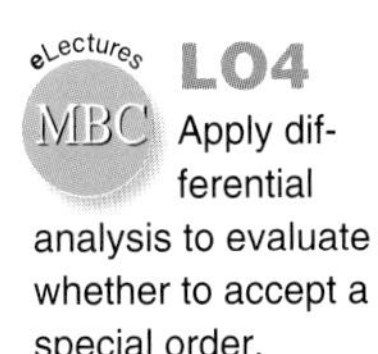

LO4 Apply differential analysis to evaluate whether to accept a special order.

Assume that a not-for-profit is hosting a fundraising dinner, and it would like to offer its attendees Uber rides home from the event at a reduced rate of $40 for every 10 miles. The total expected miles related to the fundraiser are 3,000. Uber drivers will not be called to the site via the online app as the drivers will be ready and waiting at the event when it is over. Therefore, the mapping technology fees can be reduced to $1.50 per every 10 miles. Also assume that the driver fees will remain constant at $35 per every 10 miles. Uber has sufficient driver capacity to handle the event without reducing its rides to other customers. Uber's management wants to know the profit impact of accepting the offer. The following analysis focuses on those costs and revenues that will differ if the offer is accepted.

Increase in revenues (300* × $40)		$12,000
Increase in costs		
Driver fees (300* × $35)	$10,500	
Platform and cloud-based data storage (300* × $1.50)	450	
Mapping technology (300* × $1.50)	450	
Customer service (300* × $0.50)	150	11,550
Increase in profits		$ 450

*3,000 divided by 10

Accepting the offer will result in a profit increase of $450. Although this is not a significant increase, management might consider this to be a great marketing opportunity and a chance to convert the attendees into future customers.

If management were unaware of relevant cost concepts, they might be tempted to compare the special event price of $40 to the average cost per every 10 miles as developed from the accounting reports. Based on Uber's hypothetical April contribution income statement in **Exhibit 4.2**, the average cost per every 10 miles was $43, calculated as follows:

Total variable costs	$1,170,000
Total fixed costs	120,000
Total costs	1,290,000
Total miles divided by 10 (300,000/10)	30,000
Average cost per every 10 miles	$ 43

Comparing the special event price of $40 per 10 miles to the average cost of $43, management might conclude the event would result in a loss of $3 per 10 miles.

It is apparent that the $43 figure encompasses variable costs of $39 per 10 miles (including irrelevant variable mapping technology costs of $0.50 per 10 miles) and irrelevant fixed costs of $120,000 spread over 3,000 miles. But remember, management may not have detailed cost information. To obtain appropriate information for decision-making purposes, management must ask its accounting staff for the specific information needed. Different configurations of cost information are provided for different purposes. In the absence of special instructions, the accounting staff might not supply relevant cost information.

Exhibit 4.2 Contribution Income Statement

UBER Contribution Income Statement For the Month of April		
Revenue (30,000* × $45.00)		$1,350,000
Less variable costs		
Driver fees (30,000* × $35.00)	$1,050,000	
Platform and cloud-based data storage (30,000* × $1.50)	45,000	
Mapping technology (30,000* × $2.00)	60,000	
Customer service (30,000* × $0.50)	15,000	(1,170,000)
Contribution margin		180,000
Less fixed costs		
Platform and cloud-based data storage	40,000	
Mapping technology	75,000	
Advertising	5,000	(120,000)
Profit		$ 60,000

*300,000 divided by 10

Importance of Time Span and Opportunity Costs

The special event is a one-time contract for 3,000 miles that will use current excess driver capacity. Because no special setups or technology are required to manage the event, it is appropriate to consider only variable costs in computing the event's profitability.

But what if the not-for-profit wanted Uber to sign a multiyear contract to provide 3,000 miles per month at $40 per every 10 miles? Under these circumstances, management would be well advised to reject the contract because there is a high probability that cost increases would make the order unprofitable in later years. At the very least, management should insist that a cost escalation clause be added to the agreement, specifying that the customer price would increase to cover any cost increases and detailing the cost computation.

Of more concern is the variable nature of all long-run costs. Given adequate time, management must replace fixed assets and may have to adjust the amount and quality of its equipment and technology. Accordingly, *in the long run, all costs (including costs classified as fixed in a given period) are relevant*. To remain in business in the long run, Uber must replace equipment, pay taxes, pay administrative salaries, and so forth. Consequently, management should consider *all costs*, fixed and variable, in evaluating a long-term contract.

Full costs include all costs, regardless of their behavior pattern or activity level. The average full cost per unit is sometimes used to approximate long-run variable costs. If accepting a long-term contract increases the monthly miles to 303,000, the average full cost per every 10 miles will be $42.97.

Driver fees	$35.00
Platform and cloud-based data storage	1.50
Mapping technology	2.00
Customer service support	0.50
Platform and cloud-based data storage (40,000/30,300*)	1.32**
Mapping technology (75,000/30,300*)	2.48**
Advertising (5,000/30,300*)	0.17**
Average full cost per every 10 miles	$42.97**

*303,000 divided by 10
**Rounded

In this case, the estimated long-run variable costs are $42.97 per every 10 miles. Many managers would say this is the minimum acceptable selling price, especially if the order extends over a long period of time.

Because Uber has excess productive driver capacity, no opportunity cost is associated with accepting the not-for-profit's one-time offer. There is no alternative use of the driving time related to the event, in the short run, so there is no opportunity cost.

But what if Uber was operating at driver capacity? In that case, accepting the special offer would require reducing regular miles. Assume hiring new drivers is not a possibility in the short run and there are safety concerns with having the current drivers driving too many miles. With an alternative use of the drivers' time, an opportunity cost is associated with using the drivers to drive for the fundraising event.

Every 10 miles driven at the event could otherwise generate a $6 contribution from regular customers. Accepting the special event would cause Uber to incur an opportunity cost of $1,800 for the contribution margin lost from foregoing rides to regular customers.

Lost fees to regular customers (3,000 miles/10)	300
Regular contribution margin per 10 miles	× $6
Opportunity cost of accepting special event	$1,800

Because this opportunity cost exceeds the $450 contribution derived from the special event, management might reject the special event. Accepting the event will reduce profits by $1,350 ($450 contribution – $1,800 opportunity cost). As discussed previously, there are also qualitative considerations. Even though there is a loss expected from accepting the special event, management might consider this a great marketing opportunity to reach out to new customers and decide that it is worthwhile to accept the order.

Qualitative Considerations

Although an analysis of cost and revenue information may indicate that a special order is profitable in the short run, management might still reject the order because of qualitative considerations. Any concerns regarding the order's impact on regular customers might lead management to reject the order even if there is excess capacity. If the order involves a special low price, regular customers might demand a similar price reduction and threaten to take their business elsewhere. Alternatively, management might accept the special order while operating at capacity if they believed there were long-term benefits associated with penetrating a new market. Legal factors must also be considered if the special order is from a buyer who competes with regular customers.

Review 4-4 LO4 Estimating the Profitability of Special Orders

Epson produces color cartridges for inkjet printers. Suppose cartridges are sold to mail-order distributors for $4.80 each and that manufacturing and other costs are as follows:

Variable Costs per Unit		Fixed Costs per Month	
Direct materials	$2.00	Factory overhead	$15,000
Direct labor	0.20	Selling and administrative	5,000
Factory overhead	0.25	Total	$20,000
Distribution	0.05		
Total	$2.50		

The variable distribution costs are for transportation to mail-order distributors. Also assume the current monthly production and sales volume is 15,000 and monthly capacity is 20,000 units.

Required

Determine the effect of the following independent situations on monthly profits.

a. A Russian distributor has proposed to place a special, one-time order for 4,000 units next month at a reduced price of $4.00 per unit. The distributor would pay all transportation costs. There would be additional fixed selling and administrative costs of $500.

b. An Austrian distributor has proposed to place a special, one-time order for 8,000 units at a special price of $4.00 per unit. The distributor would pay all transportation costs. There would be additional fixed selling and administrative costs of $500. Assume overtime production is not possible.

Solution on p. 149.

Outsourcing Decisions (Make or Buy)

LO5 Apply differential analysis to evaluate outsourcing decisions.

One of the most common applications of relevant cost analysis involves the make-or-buy decision. Virtually any service, product, or component that can be produced or manufactured internally can also be acquired from an external source. The procurement of services, products, or components from an external source is called **outsourcing**. For example, the management of the bookstore at your college or university is likely outsourced to Barnes and Noble or Follett, and the dining facilities may be outsourced to Compass Group North America or Aramark Corporation. Similarly, HP and, more recently, Samsung actually manufacture very few of the components of their computers. Instead the manufacture of components is outsourced to other firms such as Intel for computer chips and Seagate for storage devices. Virtually all computer manufacturers, with the exception of Apple, outsource their operating systems to Microsoft.

Any time you call a customer support call center, the representative reached is likely to be working in a different country. A growing number of companies even outsource employees from employee leasing companies. In the past 25 years, outsourcing of goods and services has expanded exponentially with the emergence of well-trained, low-cost labor forces in China and India and other parts of the world.

As the above discussion reveals, the decision to outsource rather than to produce a service or product internally involves a vast array of qualitative issues. The quantitative issues surrounding the outsourcing (or make-or-buy) decision are often less challenging. To illustrate, we continue the Uber example. Suppose a technology firm, DataTech, offers Uber a one-year contract to manage all of Uber's data storage service at a cost of $15,000 per month. Uber is now faced with the decision to continue to supply the data storage service internally or outsource the technology to DataTech. An analysis of the decision reveals that if Uber accepts the offer, it will be able to reduce the following:

- Variable platform and data storage costs by $0.20 per 10 miles.
- Fixed platform and data storage costs by $5,000.

Business Insight ■ When Being Liked Is Worth the Money

Comcast wants to be loved. After years of being enthusiastically anchored to the bottom of customer satisfaction surveys, Comcast is changing strategies. Finally faced with competition from on-demand services such as Netflix, Hulu, and Amazon, Comcast has decided that it is time to court its customers. This initiative has two parts. First, the company has begun to improve customer service by redesigning physical locations to feel more welcoming and Apple-like. Second, it has developed a new app to help customers plan around service visits, tracking the technician's estimated time of arrival to make the visit convenient for customers.

The second part of this effort also takes a page from the Apple playbook: make Internet, TV, and home-security devices that people can connect with. Fraser Stirling, head of hardware development at Comcast, says, "we are genuinely trying to create an emotional experience, whether that's love, or whatever, like you have with your phone. We want people to be able to put something from Comcast in their study or their living room and people can look at it and go 'Oof, what is that? It's amazing.'"

Differential analysis helps a company like Comcast weigh the increased costs associated with customer satisfaction and hardware design against the forecasted loss of customers to on-demand entertainment. This sort of analysis helps companies deal with the changing realities of their markets. For years Comcast had significant market power and, thus, sought to deliver cable at the lowest possible cost; now facing competition, the company finds it profitable to invest in the customer's experience. Ultimately, it may be the answer to managerial accounting questions that drive increased satisfaction.

Source: Felix Gillette, "Can a Company You Hate Make a Cable Box You Love?" *Bloomberg Businessweek*, June 23, 2016.

A differential analysis of Uber's decision to supply storage service internally or to outsource it is presented in **Exhibit 4.3**. Continuing to provide the service internally has a net advantage of $4,000.

Exhibit 4.3 Differential Analysis of Outsourcing Decision

	Cost to Do Internally		Cost to Outsource	Difference (income effect of outsourcing)
Cost to outsource data storage			$15,000	$(15,000)
Cost to do internally				
Variable costs related to data storage ($0.20 × 30,000*)	$ 6,000			6,000
Fixed costs related to data storage	5,000			5,000
Total	$11,000		$15,000	$ (4,000)
Advantage of providing service internally		$4,000		

*300,000 miles divided by 10

But what if the data storage capacity created by outsourcing to DataTech can be used to provide storage services to another company for $7,000 per month? In this case, the storage capacity has an alternative use, and the net cash flow from this alternative use is an opportunity cost of providing the service internally. Treating the revenue Uber will not receive if it continues to source data storage internally as an opportunity cost, the analysis in **Exhibit 4.4** indicates that outsourcing now has a net advantage of $3,000.

Although outsourcing has become widely accepted across virtually all industries, the results of outsourcing are not uniformly positive. Some companies that made a strong commitment to extensive outsourcing have discovered that there are many problems that can occur when they shift key processes and functions to other companies. It is usually easier to make major changes and to correct problems related to in-house functions and processes than for those outsourced to other companies, especially if they are located offshore. The following Business Insight discusses a peripheral issue in the aviation industry relating to outsourcing.

Exhibit 4.4 Differential Analysis of of Outsourcing Decision with Opportunity Cost

	Cost to Do Internally		Cost to Outsource	Difference (income effect of outsourcing)
Cost to outsource data storage			$15,000	$(15,000)
Cost to do internally				
Variable costs related to data storage ($0.20 × 30,000*)	$ 6,000			6,000
Fixed costs related to data storage	5,000			5,000
Opportunity cost of lost subscription revenue	7,000			7,000
Total	$18,000		$15,000	$ 3,000
Advantage of outsourcing		$3,000		

*300,000 miles divided by 10

Business Insight ■ Outsourcing in the Airline Industry

In 2019, third-party contractors provided about 30% of airport ground and passenger services, up from 19% in 2001. But while wages paid by airlines have been rising since 2009, wages paid by those subcontractors have not kept pace. In fact, wages for wheelchair service, cleaning, catering, and even some baggage handling workers have remained stagnant.

Members of three unions (Communications Workers of America, Service Employees International Union, and Unite Here) spoke at a House of Representatives' aviation subcommittee hearing in early 2020, asking for more scrutiny of working conditions for low-paid service providers at airports and that airline companies be encouraged to verify subcontractor compliance with federal, state, and local labor laws.

If future legislation increases the cost of ground and passenger service outsourcing or if growth in the aviation industry results in a tight market for service workers, airline companies will need to reassess the cost of outsourcing and may need to consider hiring internally.

Source: Ted Reed, "Labor Movement Eyes 'Dark Corner of the Airline Industry,'" *Forbes*, January 15, 2020.

Even if outsourcing appears financially advantageous in the short run, management should not decide to outsource before considering a variety of qualitative risk factors. Is the outside supplier interested in developing a long-term relationship or merely attempting to use some temporarily idle capacity? If so, what will happen at the end of the contract period? What impact would a decision to outsource have on the morale of a company's employees? Will it have to rehire laid-off employees after the contract expires? Will the outside supplier meet delivery schedules? Does the supplied part meet quality standards? Will it continue to meet them? Will the supplier continually improve its manufacturing operations in order to remain competitive? Organizations often manufacture products or provide services they can obtain elsewhere in order to control quality, to have an assured supply source, to avoid dealing with a potential competitor, or to maintain a core competency. Some of these issues are discussed in the Business Insight that follows.

Business Insight ■ Outsourcing Changes Cost Structure, Brings New Risks

Firms are finding that flexibility from outsourcing can come with significant costs, largely in holding the supplier to quality standards. Bert Ahill, who advises firms on outsourcing, feels that companies regularly forget the risks that they are exposing themselves to when outsourcing. Often firms forget to account for economic, political, and weather hazards that affect their international suppliers. Firms should take care to build redundancy into outsourced supply chains to control disruptions that could come from these sources.

Some firms are finding that the costs of monitoring outsourced contractors outweigh the benefits of outsourcing. Boston Scientific, a maker of medical devices, has been manufacturing its own batteries for 10 years. While companies like Boeing were making radical moves in the opposite direction, Boston Scientific found it more cost-effective to keep battery production in-house, as the quality and longevity of a battery implanted in a patient is of paramount importance. In addition to quality and stability, other supply chain issues arise with outsourcing. Taylor Guitars uses

continued

continued from previous page

exotic woods in its products, and when concerns arose about the sustainability of its suppliers' practices, it chose to purchase a Cameroonian mill to improve sourcing. The organic soap maker Dr. Bronner's ran into similar issues with its palm oil supply, so it formed a company to manage sustainable sourcing of palm oil in Ghana.

Careful analysis of the costs and benefits of both outsourcing and vertical integration should be undertaken on an ongoing basis to make sure that the company chooses the correct supply chain.

Sources: Alexis Bateman, "Guest Voices: New Supplier Strategies Revive Important Corporate Questions," *Wall Street Journal*, March 7, 2016; and Ben DiPietro, "When Manufacturing Means Building Supply-Chain Resilience," *Wall Street Journal*, October 21, 2015.

The qualitative risk factors discussed above are often magnified when a company goes global, either as an outsourcing buyer or provider. Global outsourcing is often motivated by the desire to get projects completed "on time" and "within budget." In the following Research Insight, PricewaterhouseCoopers views outsourcing as a way to focus resources on operations that truly differentiate the firm.

Research Insight ■ Role of Outsourcing in Operations

A PricewaterhouseCoopers's Global Operations Survey offers a narrower view of the role of outsourcing in operations. Rather than recommending outsourcing as a way to change the firm's cost structure, PwC views outsourcing as a way to focus on operations that truly differentiate the firm. The PwC study divides a company's capabilities into four groups:

1. Differentiating capabilities,
2. Competitive necessities,
3. Basic capabilities, and
4. Other activities.

PwC recommends focusing resources on those activities where being best-in-category offers greatest returns (item 1). Investments in attention, staff, and capital should center on these differentiating operations. PwC recommends aggressive cost management and efficiency in activities that are required for participation in the market sector, where excellence in these areas offers no advantage, but is required for participation in a market (item 2). For example, consumers expect all banks to have excellent security; thus, banks should find ways to meet the excellent security standards with the greatest efficiency. PwC recommends outsourcing basic capabilities (item 3). As there is no return for excelling in these areas, they are the areas in which cost minimization is the best strategy. Most firms outsource facilities maintenance and other operations that are unrelated to success in their sector but are required to function. All other activities that do not fit into the first three groups and deviate from the core business should be eliminated if possible (item 4).

Source: "2015 Global Operations Survey: Reimagining Operations," *PricewaterhouseCoopers*, 2015, p. 17. Link: http://operations-survey.pwc.com/PwC-2015-Global-Operations-Survey.pdf

Evaluating an Outsourcing Decision — LO5 Review 4-5

Epson produces color cartridges for inkjet printers. Suppose cartridges are sold to mail-order distributors for $4.80 each and that manufacturing and other costs are as follows:

Variable Costs per Unit		Fixed Costs per Month	
Direct materials	$2.00	Factory overhead	$15,000
Direct labor	0.20	Selling and administrative	5,000
Factory overhead	0.25	Total	$20,000
Distribution	0.05		
Total	$2.50		

continued

continued from previous page

The variable distribution costs are for transportation to mail-order distributors. Also assume the current monthly production and sales volume is 15,000 and monthly capacity is 20,000 units.

Required

Determine the effect of the following situation on monthly profits.

A Mexican manufacturer has offered a one-year contract to supply ink for the cartridges at a cost of $1.00 per unit. If Epson accepts the offer, it will be able to reduce variable manufacturing costs by 40% and rent some of its factory space to another company for $1,000 per month.

Solution on p. 149.

Sell or Process Further

LO6 Apply differential analysis to evaluate whether to sell or further process a product.

When a product is salable at various stages of completion, management must determine the product's most advantageous selling point. As each stage is completed, management must determine whether to sell the product then or to process it further. For example, petroleum companies have to determine how much crude oil to refine as diesel fuel and how much to process further as gasoline. We consider two types of sell or process further decisions: (1) for a single product and (2) for joint products.

Single Product Decisions

Assume that Scandinavian Furniture Inc. manufactures modular wood furniture from precut and shaped wood. Although all units are salable before they are sanded and painted, Scandinavian Furniture Inc. sands and paints all units before they are sold. Management wishes to know if this is the optimal selling point. For this example, we assume that the company could sell the same number of units either painted or unpainted.

A complete listing of unit costs and revenues for the alternative selling points for a low-end storage cabinet follows.

	Per Cabinet			
	Sell after Assembly		Sell after Painting	Difference (income effect of painting)
Selling price	$40		$75	$35
Assembly costs	(25)		(25)	
Sanding and painting costs	—		(12)	(12)
Contribution margin	$15		$38	$23
Advantage of painting		$23		

The sanding and painting operation has an additional contribution of $23 per unit. The storage cabinets should be sold after they are painted.

The assembly costs are the same under both alternatives. This illustrates that *all costs incurred prior to the decision point are irrelevant.* Given the existence of an assembled chair, the decision alternatives are to sell it now or to process it further. A differential analysis for the decision to sell or process further should include only revenues and the incremental costs of further processing as follows.

Increase in revenues		
Sell after painting	$75	
Sell after assembly	(40)	$35
Additional costs of sanding and painting		(12)
Advantage of sanding and painting		$23

The identical solution is obtained if the selling price without further processing is treated as an opportunity cost as follows.

Revenues after painting		$75
Additional costs of sanding and painting	$12	
Opportunity cost of not selling after assembly	40	(52)
Advantage of sanding and painting		$23

By processing a chair further, Scandinavian Furniture has foregone the opportunity to receive $40 from its sale. Since the chair is already assembled, and the cost of assembly is an irrelevant sunk cost, this $40 is the net cash inflow from the most desirable alternative; it is the opportunity cost of painting.

Joint Product Decisions

Two or more products simultaneously produced by a single process from a common set of inputs are called **joint products**. Joint products are often found in basic industries that process natural raw materials such as dairy, chemical, meat, petroleum, and wood products. In the petroleum industry, crude oil is refined into fuel oil, gasoline, kerosene, diesel, lubricating oil, and other products.

The point in the process where the joint products become separately identifiable is called the **split-off point**. Materials and conversion costs incurred prior to the split-off point are called **joint costs**. For external reporting purposes, a number of techniques are used to allocate joint costs among joint products. We do not discuss these techniques here (interested students should consult a cost accounting textbook), except to note that none of the methods provide information useful for determining what to do with a joint product once it is produced. Because joint costs are incurred prior to the decision point, they are sunk costs. Consequently, *joint costs are irrelevant to a decision to sell a joint product or to process it further*. The only relevant factors are the alternative costs and revenues subsequent to the split-off point.

Business Insight ■ Product Mix Decisions in Consumer Electronics

The changing consumer electronics landscape is driving changes in product mix at companies like Microsoft Corporation, Apple Inc., and Dell Technologies, Inc.

Microsoft, long a software company, is expanding its hardware products, like Surface desktop and computers, and its cloud-based services like Azure. Revenue from Azure, a cloud computing platform that can be used for services such as analytics, virtual computing, storage, and networking, increased 72% in the year ending June 30, 2019.

Increases in sales of AirPods and Apple Watches were the primary contributors to the 41% increase in sales in Apple's Wearables, Home and Accessories segment during the year ended September 28, 2019. Sales of Apple Mac computers increased 2% during the same period.

Dell Technologies Inc., the third-largest PC manufacturer, is expanding its Mobile Connect software application. Users will now be able to drag photos, videos, and other files from their iPhone or Android handsets to their PC.

The product mix decisions these companies are making rely on the decision relevance framework introduced in this chapter.

Sources: Mark Gurman, "Dell to Let Apple Users Control iPhones from Their Laptop", *Bloomberg Technology*, January 2, 2020. Dina Bass, "Microsoft Pushes Cloud Services to Retailers Anxious to Avoid Amazon," *Bloomberg Technology*, January 9, 2020. Microsoft Corporation Form 10-K for the year ended June 30, 2019. Apple Inc. Form 10-K for the year ended September 28, 2019.

Evaluating Whether to Sell or Process Further — LO6 Review 4-6

Epson produces color cartridges for inkjet printers. Suppose cartridges are sold to mail-order distributors for $4.80 each and that manufacturing and other costs are as follows:

Variable Costs per Unit		Fixed Costs per Month	
Direct materials.	$2.00	Factory overhead	$15,000
Direct labor	0.20	Selling and administrative.	5,000
Factory overhead	0.25	Total	$20,000
Distribution	0.05		
Total	$2.50		

continued

continued from previous page

The variable distribution costs are for transportation to mail-order distributors. Also assume the current monthly production and sales volume is 15,000 and monthly capacity is 20,000 units.

Required

The cartridges are currently unpackaged; that is, they are sold in bulk. Individual packaging would increase costs by $0.10 per unit. However, the units could then be sold for $5.05. Determine the effect on monthly profits if the company decided to process the cartridges.

Solution on p. 149.

Use of Limited Resources

LO7 Allocate limited resources for purposes of maximizing short-run profit.

All of us have experienced time as a limiting or constraining resource. With two exams the day after tomorrow and a paper due next week, our problem is how to allocate limited study time. The solution depends on our objectives, our current status (grades, knowledge, skill levels, and so forth), and available time. Given this information, we devise a work plan to best meet our objectives.

Managers must also decide how to best use limited resources to accomplish organizational goals. A supermarket may lose sales because limited shelf space prevents stocking all available brands of soft drinks. A manufacturer may lose sales because limited machine hours or labor hours prevent filling all orders. Managers of for-profit organizations will likely find the problems of capacity constraints less troublesome than the problems of excess capacity; nonetheless, these problems are real. Ultimately, the problem often boils down to a product-mix decision, in which we must decide the mix of products or services we are going to offer our customers with the limited resources available to us.

If the limited resource is not a core business activity, it may be appropriate to outsource additional units of the limited resource externally. For example, many organizations have a small legal staff to handle routine activities; if the internal staff becomes fully committed, the organization seeks outside legal counsel.

The long-run solution to the problem of limited resources to perform core activities may be to expand capacity. However, this is usually not feasible in the short run. Economic models suggest that another solution is to reduce demand by increasing the price. Again, this may not be desirable. A hotel, for example, may want to maintain competitive prices. A manufacturer might want to maintain a long-run price to retain customer goodwill to avoid attracting competitors, or to prevent accusations of "price gouging."

Single Constraint

The allocation of limited resources should be made only after a careful consideration of many qualitative factors. The following rule provides a useful starting point in making short-run decisions of how to best use limited resources: *To achieve short-run profit maximization, a for-profit organization should allocate limited resources in a manner that maximizes the contribution per unit of the limited resource.* The application of this rule is illustrated in the following example.

Assume Snap Fitness offers three different personal training packages (A, B, and C) to its customers. These packages vary from a personalized nutrition and exercise training to a one-time consultation. Suppose a limitation of 120 labor hours per week prevents Snap from meeting the demand for its services. Information for the three service packages is as follows.

	A	B	C
Unit selling price	$100	$80	$50
Unit variable costs	(60)	(35)	(25)
Unit contribution margin	$ 40	$45	$25
Hours per unit	4	3	1

Package A has the highest selling price and Package B has the highest unit contribution margin. Package C is shown below to have the highest contribution per hour.

	A	B	C
Unit contribution margin	$40	$45	$25
Hours per unit	÷ 4	÷ 3	÷ 1
Contribution per hour	$10	$15	$25

Following the rule of maximizing the contribution per unit of a single constraining factor (labor hours), Snap should use its limited labor hours to sell Package C. As shown in the following analysis, any other plan would result in lower profits.

	A Highest Selling Price per Unit	B Highest Contribution per Unit	C Highest Contribution per Constraining Factor
Hours available	120	120	120
Hours per unit	÷ 4	÷ 3	÷ 1
Weekly production in units	30	40	120
Unit contribution margin	× $40	× $45	× $25
Total weekly contribution margin	$1,200	$1,800	$3,000

Despite this analysis, management may decide on a product mix that includes some units of A or B or both to satisfy the requests of some "good" customers or to offer a full product line. However, such decisions sacrifice short-run profits.

Multiple Constraints

Continuing our illustration, assume a second constraint; that is, the maximum weekly demand for C is only 90 units, although the company is capable of producing 120 units of C each week. In this case, the limited labor resource should first be used to satisfy the demand for Package C, with any remaining capacity going to produce Package B, which has the next highest contribution per unit of constraining factor. This allocation provides a total weekly contribution of $2,700 as follows.

Available hours	120
Required for C (90 units × 1 hour)	(90)
Hours available for B	30
Labor hours per unit	÷ 3
Production of B in units	10
Unit contribution margin of B	× $45
Contribution from B	$ 450
Contribution from C ($25 per unit × 90 units)	2,250
Total weekly contribution margin	$2,700

When an organization has alternative uses for several limited resources, such as limited labor hours and limited space, the optimal use of those resources cannot be determined using the rule for short-run profit maximization. In these situations, techniques such as linear programming can be used to assist in determining the optimal mix of products or services.

Theory of Constraints

The **theory of constraints** states that every process has a bottleneck (constraining resource) and that production cannot take place faster than it is processed through that bottleneck. The goal of the theory of constraints is to maximize **throughput** (defined as sales revenue minus direct materials costs) in a constrained environment.[1] The theory has several implications for management.

- Management should identify the bottleneck. This is often difficult when several different products are produced in a facility containing many different production activities. One approach is to walk around and observe where inventory is building up in front of workstations. The bottleneck will likely have the largest piles of work that have been waiting for the longest time.
- Management should schedule production to maximize the efficient use of the bottleneck resource. Efficiently using the bottleneck resource might necessitate inspecting all units before they reach the bottleneck rather than after the units are completed. The bottleneck resource is too valuable to waste on units that may already be defective.
- Management should schedule production to avoid a buildup of inventory. Reducing inventory lowers the cost of inventory investments and the cost of carrying inventory. It also assists in improving quality by making it easier to identify quality problems that might otherwise be hidden in large piles of inventory. Reducing inventory will require a change in the attitude of managers who like to see machines and people constantly working. To avoid a buildup of inventory in front of the bottleneck, it may be necessary for people and equipment to remain idle until the bottleneck resource calls for additional input.
- Management should work to eliminate the bottleneck, perhaps by increasing the capacity of the bottleneck resource, redesigning products so they can be produced with less use of the bottleneck resource, rescheduling production procedures to substitute nonbottleneck resources, or outsourcing work performed by bottleneck resources.

The theory of constraints has implications for management accounting performance reports. Keeping people and equipment working on production full-time is often a goal of management. To support this goal, management accounting performance reports have traditionally highlighted underutilization as an unfavorable variance (see Chapter 10). This has encouraged managers to have people and equipment producing inventory, even if the inventory is not needed or cannot be further processed because of bottlenecks. The theory of constraints suggests that it is better to have nonbottleneck resources idle than it is to have them fully utilized. To support the theory of constraints, performance reports should

- Measure the utilization of bottleneck resources
- Measure factory throughput
- Not encourage the full utilization of nonbottleneck resources
- Discourage the buildup of excess inventory

While the theory of constraints is *similar* to our general rule for how to best use limited resources, it emphasizes throughput (selling price minus direct materials) rather than contribution (selling price minus variable costs) in allocating the limited resource. The exclusion of direct labor and variable manufacturing overhead yields larger unit margins, and it may affect resource allocations based on throughput rankings. The result will likely be a reduction in profits from those that could be achieved using our general rule for how to allocate limited resources. Although the theory of constraints has not been widely embraced by companies, many of its users are enthusiastic about its benefits.

Limitations of Decision Analysis Models

Analytical models, such as the relevant cost analysis model and applications presented in this chapter, are very useful in organizing information for purposes of determining the economics of a decision. However, it is important always to keep in mind that models do not make decisions—managers

[1] *The Goal*, by Eliyah M. Goldratt and Jeff Cox, presents the concepts underlying the theory of constraints in the form of a novel.

make decisions. The results of analytical models are an essential and necessary starting point in many decisions, but often there are other factors that weigh heavily on a decision that may cause the manager to go against the most economical alternative. There may be human resource, marketing, cultural, logistical, technological, or other factors that outweigh the analytics of a decision situation. It is in these situations where managers demonstrate leadership, problem-solving, and executive skill and potential, or the lack thereof.

Analyzing Profitability Considering a Scarce Resource — LO7 Review 4-7

Assume that Innovative Components Inc. produces only three different types of injection-molded knobs. It produces the Pointer Knob, which is used for on/off devices, the Instrument Knob, which is used for precision adjustment, and the Star Knob, which is used for snowblowers and lawnmowers. The factory machine capacity is the company's constraining resource. It operates at 90% capacity and management wants to devote the unused capacity to one of the products. The following data represents the current operations:

	Pointer Knob	Instrument Knob	Star Knob
Per-case data:			
Sales price	$20	$22	$6
Variable cost	8	16	2
Contribution margin	$12	$ 6	$4
Fixed costs*	6	2	1
Net income	$ 6	$ 4	$3

*Allocated on basis of machine hours at $1 per hour.

Required

Which product should management produce with its extra capacity?

Solution on p. 150.

Guidance Answers

You Are the Vice President of Manufacturing

Pg. 114 This is a decision that has both economic and ethical dimensions. Economically, the cost of the old machine is a sunk cost, since the expenditure to acquire it has already been made. If it can be sold to another company to recover part of the initial cost, that amount would be relevant to the decision regarding the new technology. However, you should ignore the cost of the recently purchased machine and consider only the outlay costs that will differ between keeping the recently purchased machine and purchasing the new technology, plus any opportunity costs that may be involved with disposing of the existing machine and acquiring the new machine. From an ethical standpoint, managers are often hesitant to recommend an action that reflects poorly on their past decisions. The temptation is to try to justify the past decision. If you have evaluated all of the relevant costs and have considered all of the qualitative issues associated with upgrading the machine, these should be the basis for making your recommendation, not what it will do to your reputation with your superiors.

Key Terms

cost reduction proposal, 113
differential cost analysis, 116
full costs, 121
irrelevant costs, 112
joint costs, 127
joint products, 127
opportunity cost, 115
outlay costs, 113
outsourcing, 122
relevant costs, 112
revenues, 113
split-off point, 127
sunk costs, 114
theory of constraints, 129
throughput, 130

Multiple Choice

Multiple Choice Answers
1. a 2. c 3. d 4. a 5. a

1. Jabo Inc. is considering a new bifro-spectra machine for its production plant to replace an old machine that originally cost $12,000 and has $9,000 of accumulated depreciation. The new machine can be purchased at a cash cost of $18,000, but the distributor of the new machine has offered to take the old machine in as a trade-in, thereby reducing the cost of the new machine to $16,000. Based only on this information, calculate the total relevant cost of acquiring the new machine.

   a. $16,000, or the net cash paid to the distributor
   b. $18,000, or the gross cost of the new machine
   c. $19,000, or the net cash paid plus the book value ($3,000) of the old machine
   d. $17,000, or the gross cost of the new machine minus the $1,000 loss on disposing of the old machine

2. Bruno Company is a Rhode Island company that sells a branded product regionally to retail customers in New England. It normally sells its product for $30 per unit; however, it has received a one-time offer from a private-brand company on the West Coast to buy 1,000 units at $19 per unit. Even though the company has excess capacity to produce the units, the president of the company immediately rejected the offer; however, the chief accountant stated that it might be a profitable opportunity for the company, even though $19 is below its unit cost of $21, calculated as follows:

Direct materials	$ 9.00
Direct labor	5.00
Variable overhead	4.00
Depreciation and other fixed overhead	3.00
Total unit cost	$21.00

   Also, the special order will save $1 per unit in packaging costs since the product will be bulk packaged instead of being individually packaged. Calculate the amount of profit or loss per unit if Bruno accepts the special order.

   a. $2 loss
   b. $1 loss
   c. $2 profit
   d. $1 profit

3. Sitro, LTD had been making a component for one of its products, but is now considering outsourcing the component to a Chinese company, which has offered to sell an unlimited quantity of components for $6 per unit. If Sitro outsources, it could shut down a whole department and rent the building for $2,000 per month. The cost of making the component is $5 per unit, which includes $1.50 of fixed costs, of which only $1.00 per unit can be avoided if the department is shut down. Sitro currently produces about 1,000 units per month. What is the cost advantage or disadvantage of per unit of outsourcing the component?

   a. $1.00 disadvantage
   b. $1.50 disadvantage
   c. $1.00 advantage
   d. $0.50 advantage

4. Mitrex Company makes a semi-finished machine component for the heavy equipment industry that has a unit contribution margin of $250 to Mitrex. A major customer has been purchasing 100 units per month from Mitrex for many years, but has indicated that it would prefer to purchase them already machined to its specifications. It has offered to pay an additional $50 per unit for the finished units. To meet those specifications, Mitrex would have to rent additional equipment at a cost of $2,000 per month and incur labor and other direct costs of $15 per unit. Calculate the per-unit advantage or disadvantage of further processing.

   a. $15 advantage
   b. $35 advantage
   c. $50 advantage
   d. $15 disadvantage

5. Giko, LTD makes three products (Abba, Babba, and Cabba), all of which use a very rare ingredient called Mecogen. Giko can purchase only 500 ounces of Mecogen per month from its East Asian source. Below are data for the three products:

	Abba	Babba	Cabba
Unit selling price	$80	$65	$100
Unit variable costs	45	40	60
Unit contribution margin	35	25	40
Mecogen (ounces per unit)	10	15	20

How should Giko allocate the 500 ounces of Mecogen assuming it can sell unlimited quantities of all three produces?

a. All 500 ounces should be allocated to Abba
b. All 500 ounces should be allocated to Babba
c. All 500 ounces should be allocated to Cabba
d. None of the above

Questions

Q4-1. Distinguish between relevant and irrelevant costs.

Q4-2. In evaluating a cost reduction proposal, what three alternatives are available to management?

Q4-3. When are outlay costs relevant and when are they irrelevant?

Q4-4. Relate the manufacturing cost hierarchy discussed in Chapter 2 to the concept of relevant costs. Under what conditions would product-level costs be relevant?

Q4-5. Why is a differential analysis of relevant items preferred to a detailed listing of all costs and revenues associated with each alternative?

Q4-6. When are opportunity costs relevant to the evaluation of a special order?

Q4-7. Identify some important qualitative considerations in evaluating a decision to make or buy a part.

Q4-8. In a decision to sell or to process further, of what relevance are costs incurred prior to the decision point? Explain your answer.

Q4-9. How should limited resources be used to achieve short-run profit maximization?

Q4-10. What should performance reports do in support of the theory of constraints?

Assignments with the MBC logo in the margin are available in myBusinessCourse. See the Preface of the book for details.

Mini Exercises

M4-11. Relevant Cost Terms: Matching

LO1 Astel&Kern

Astel&Kern produces three different versions of high-quality portable digital music players, the A@ultima, A@futura, and A@norma. Assume Astel&Kern is evaluating a proposal that will result in doubling the production of A@futura and disontinuing the production of A@norma. The facilities currently used to produce A@norma will be devoted to the production of A@futura. Furthermore, additional machinery will be acquired to produce A@futura. The production of A@ultima will not be affected. All products have a positive contribution margin.

Required

Presented below are a number of phrases related to the proposal followed by a list of cost terms. For each phrase, select the most appropriate cost term. Each term is used only once.

Phrases
1. Cost of equipment to produce A@norma
2. Increased variable costs of A@futura
3. Property taxes on the new machinery
4. Revenues from the sale of A@ultima
5. Increased revenue from the sale of A@futura
6. Contribution margin of A@norma
7. Variable costs of A@ultima
8. Company president's salary

Cost terms
a. Opportunity cost
b. Sunk cost
c. Irrelevant variable outlay cost
d. Irrelevant fixed outlay cost
e. Relevant variable outlay cost
f. Relevant fixed outlay cost
g. Relevant revenues
h. Irrelevant revenues

LO1
Tapestry, Inc.
(TPR)

M4-12. Relevant Cost Terms: Matching
Assume Coach, owned by Tapestry, Inc., produces and sells 4,000 specialty handbags per month and has the capacity to produce 5,000 units per month. Coach is evaluating a one-time, special order for 2,000 units from Bloomingdales. Accepting the order will increase variable manufacturing costs and certain fixed selling and administrative costs. It will also require the company to forego the sale of 1,000 units to regular customers.

Required
Presented below are a number of statements related to the proposal followed by a list of cost terms. For each statement, select the most appropriate cost term. Each term is used only once.

Statements
1. Increased revenues from special order
2. Lost contribution margin from foregone sales to regular customers
3. Revenues from 4,000 units sold to regular customers
4. Variable cost of 4,000 units sold to regular customers
5. Increase in fixed selling and administrative expenses
6. Cost of existing equipment used to produce special order
7. Salary paid to current supervisor who oversees manufacture of special order
8. Increased variable costs of special order

Cost terms
a. Irrelevant variable outlay cost
b. Irrelevant fixed outlay cost
c. Sunk cost
d. Relevant variable outlay cost
e. Relevant fixed outlay cost
f. Opportunity cost
g. Relevant revenues
h. Irrelevant revenues

LO1, 2
City of Hamilton
PJM Interconnection

M4-13. Identifying Relevant Costs and Revenues
The City of Hamilton operates a power plant on the Ohio River. The city uses some of this generated electricity to service Hamilton residents and sells the excess electricity to PJM Interconnection, manager of a wholesale electricity market serving nearby states. The city council is evaluating two alternative proposals:

- *Proposal A* calls for replacing the generators used in the plant with more efficient generators that will produce more electricity and have lower operating costs. The salvage value of the old generators is higher than their removal cost.
- *Proposal B* calls for raising the level of the dam to retain more water for generating power and increasing the force of water flowing through the dam. This will significantly increase the amount of electricity generated by the plant. Operating costs will not be affected.

Required

Presented are a number of cost and revenue items. Indicate in the appropriate columns whether each item is relevant or irrelevant to proposals A and B.

	Proposal A	Proposal B
1. Cost of new furniture for the city manager's office	_____	_____
2. Cost of old generators	_____	_____
3. Cost of new generators	_____	_____
4. Operating cost of old generators	_____	_____
5. Operating cost of new generators	_____	_____
6. The police chief's salary	_____	_____
7. Depreciation on old generators	_____	_____
8. Salvage value of old generators	_____	_____
9. Removal cost of old generators	_____	_____
10. Cost of raising dam	_____	_____
11. Maintenance costs of water plant	_____	_____
12. Revenues from sale of electricity	_____	_____

M4-14. Classifying Relevant and Irrelevant Items

LO1 Greenberg Traurig LLP

The law firm of Greenberg Traurig LLP has been asked to represent a local client. All legal proceedings will be held out of town in Boston.

Required

The law firm's accountant has asked you to help determine the incremental cost of accepting this client. Classify each of the following items on the basis of their relationship to this engagement. Items may have multiple classifications.

	Relevant costs		Irrelevant costs	
	Opportunity	Outlay	Outlay	Sunk
1. The case will require three attorneys to stay four nights in a Boston hotel. The predicted hotel bill is $3,600.	_____	_____	_____	_____
2. Greenberg Traurig LLP's professional staff is paid $2,000 per day for out-of-town assignments.	_____	_____	_____	_____
3. Last year, depreciation on Greenberg Traurig LLP's Philadelphia's office was $25,000.	_____	_____	_____	_____
4. Round-trip transportation to Boston is expected to cost $250 per person.	_____	_____	_____	_____
5. The firm has recently accepted an engagement that will require several partners to spend two weeks in Chicago. The predicted out-of-pocket costs of this trip are $25,000.	_____	_____	_____	_____
6. The firm has a maintenance contract on its computer equipment that will cost $2,200 next year.	_____	_____	_____	_____
7. If the firm accepts the client and sends attorneys to Boston, it will have to decline a conflicting engagement in Miami that would have provided a net cash inflow of $15,000.	_____	_____	_____	_____
8. The firm's variable overhead is $125 per client hour.	_____	_____	_____	_____
9. The firm pays $900 per year for a subscription to a law journal.	_____	_____	_____	_____
10. Last year the firm paid $22,500 to increase the insulation in its building.	_____	_____	_____	_____

M4-15. Relevant Costs for Equipment Replacement Decision

LO1, 2 Urgent Care

Assume Urgent Care paid $42,000 for X-ray equipment four years ago. The equipment was expected to have a useful life of 10 years from the date of acquisition with annual operating costs of $25,000. Technological advances have made the machine purchased four years ago obsolete with a zero salvage value. An improved X-ray device incorporating the new technology is available at an initial cost of

$50,000 and annual operating costs of $15,000. The new machine is expected to last only six years before it, too, is obsolete. Asked to analyze the financial aspects of replacing the obsolete but still functional machine, an Urgent Care accountant prepared the following analysis. After looking over these numbers, the company's manager rejected the proposal.

Six-year savings [($25,000 – $15,000) × 6]	$ 60,000
Cost of new machine	(50,000)
Undepreciated cost of old machine [($42,000/10) × 6]	25,200
Advantage (disadvantage) of replacement	$ 15,200

Required

Perform an analysis of relevant costs to determine whether the manager made the correct decision.

LO1, 2, 4
VideoSecu

M4-16. Special Order

VideoSecu produces wall mounts for flat panel television sets. Assume the forecasted income statement for next year is as follows.

VIDEOSECU Budgeted Income Statement For the Year	
Sales ($28 per unit)	$5,600,000
Cost of good sold ($19 per unit)	(3,800,000)
Gross profit	1,800,000
Selling expenses ($5 per unit)	(1,000,000)
Net income	$ 800,000

Additional Information

(1) Of the production costs and selling expenses, $1,520,000 and $750,000, respectively, are fixed.

(2) VideoSecu received a special order from a hospital supply company offering to buy 10,000 wall mounts for $15. If it accepts the order, there will be no additional fixed selling expenses, and there is currently sufficient excess capacity to fill the order. The company's sales manager argues for rejecting the order because "we are not in the business of paying $19 to make a product to sell for $15."

Required

Do you think the company should accept the special order? Should the decision be based only on the profitability of the sale, or are there other issues that VideoSecu should consider? Explain.

LO1, 2, 6
Beneteau

M4-17. Sell or Process Further

Assume Beneteau manufactures sailboat hulls at a cost of $7,500 per unit. The hulls are sold to boat-yards for $9,000. The company is evaluating the desirability of adding masts, sails, and rigging to the hulls prior to sale at an additional cost of $2,500. The completed sailboats could then be sold for $10,500 each.

Required

Determine whether the company should sell sailboat hulls or process them further into complete sailboats. Assume sales volume will not be affected.

Exercises

LO1, 2, 4
Full Belly Farm

E4-18. Special Order

Full Belly Farm grows organic vegetables and sells them to distributors and local restaurants after processing. Assume the farm's leading product for restaurant customers is a mixture of organic green salad ingredients prepared and ready to serve. The company sells a large bag to restaurants for $30. It calculates the variable cost per bag at $20 (including $1 for local delivery), and the average total cost per bag is $24. Growing conditions have been very good this season and Full Belly has extra capacity.

A representative of a restaurant association in another city has offered to buy fresh salad stock from the company to augment its regular supply during an upcoming international festival. The restaurant association wants to buy 3,000 bags during the next month for $22 per bag. Delivery to restaurants in the other city will cost the company $0.75 per bag. It can meet most of the order with excess capacity but would sacrifice 200 bags of regular sales to fill this special order. Please assist Full Belly Farm's management by answering the following questions.

Required

a. Using differential analysis, what is the impact on profits of accepting this special order?

b. What nonquantitative issues should management consider before making a final decision?

c. How would the analysis change if the special order were for 3,000 bags per month for the next five years? (Assume there would be no loss of regular sales.)

E4-19. Special Order

LO1, 2, 4
Denny's (DENN)

Denny's, just off the San Bernardino Freeway in Pomona, California, specializes in a Super Slam breakfast selling for $7. Assume daily fixed costs are $1,575, and variable costs are $5 per meal. With a capacity of 750 meals per day, the restaurant serves an average of 700 meals each day.

Required

a. Determine the current average cost per meal.

b. A busload of 30 Girl Scouts stops on its way home from the San Bernardino National Forest. The leader offers to bring them in if the scouts can all be served a meal for a total of $195. The owner refuses, saying he would lose $0.75 per meal if he accepted this offer. How do you think the owner arrived at the $0.75 figure? Comment on the owner's reasoning.

c. A local businessman on a break overhears the conversation with the leader and offers the owner a one-year contract to feed 100 of the businessman's employees one meal each day at a special price of $5.50 per meal. Should the restaurant owner accept this offer? Why or why not?

E4-20. Special Order: High-Low Cost Estimation

LO1, 2, 4
Autoliv (ALV)

Autoliv produces air bag systems that it sells to automobile manufacturers throughout the world. Assume the company has a capacity of 50 million units per year; it is currently producing at an annual rate of 40 million units. Autoliv has received an order from a Japanese manufacturer to purchase 100,000 units at $65 each. Budgeted costs for 40 million and 45 million units are as follows.

(in thousands, except costs per unit)	40 Million Units	45 Million Units
Manufacturing costs		
Direct materials	$ 560,000	$ 630,000
Direct labor	220,000	247,500
Factory overhead	1,780,000	1,822,500
Total	2,560,000	2,700,000
Selling and administrative	1,120,000	1,125,000
Total	$3,680,000	$3,825,000
Costs per unit		
Manufacturing	$64.00	$60.00
Selling and administrative	28.00	25.00
Total	$92.00	$85.00

Sales to auto manufacturers are priced at $120 per unit, but the sales manager believes the company should aggressively seek the Japanese business even if it results in a loss of $20 per unit. She believes obtaining this order would open up several new markets for the company's product. The general manager commented that the company cannot tighten its belt to absorb the $2,000,000 loss ($20 × 100,000) it would incur if the order is accepted.

Required

a. Determine the financial implications of accepting the order. (*Hint:* Use the high-low method to determine variable costs per unit.)

b. How would your analysis differ if the company were operating at capacity? Determine the advantage or disadvantage of accepting the order under full-capacity circumstances.

LO1, 2, 5
HP Inc. (HPQ)
Sanmina Corp. (SANM)

E4-21. Outsourcing (Make-or-Buy) Decision

Assume a division of HP Inc. currently makes 50,000 circuit boards per year used in producing diagnostic electronic instruments at a cost of \$50 per board, consisting of variable costs per unit of \$35 and fixed costs per unit of \$15. Further assume Sanmina Corporation offers to sell HP the 50,000 circuit boards for \$50 each. If HP accepts this offer, the facilities currently used to make the boards could be rented to one of HP's suppliers for \$75,000 per year. In addition, \$8 per unit of the fixed overhead applied to the circuit boards would be totally eliminated.

Required

Should HP outsource this component from Sanmina Corporation? Support your answer with relevant cost calculations.

LO1, 2, 5
Coway

E4-22. Outsourcing (Make-or-Buy) Decision

Coway manufactures a line of room air purifiers. Assume that management is currently evaluating the possible production of an air purifier for automobiles. Based on an annual volume of 50,000 units, the predicted cost per unit of an auto air purifier follows.

Direct materials	\$ 2.50
Direct labor	2.00
Factory overhead	12.00
Total	\$16.50

These cost predictions include \$450,000 in fixed factory overhead averaged over 50,000 units.

Also assume the completed air purifier units include a battery-operated electric motor, which Coway assembles with parts purchased from an outside vendor for \$2.00 per motor. Mini Motor Company has offered to supply an assembled battery-operated motor at a cost of \$5.25 per unit, with a minimum annual order of 5,000 units. If Coway accepts this offer, it will be able to reduce the variable labor and variable overhead costs of the auto air purifier by 50%.

Required

a. Determine whether Coway should continue to make the electric motor or outsource it from Mini Motor Company. (*Hint:* Analyze the relevant costs of making the "motors," not the entire air purifier.)

b. If it could otherwise rent the motor-assembly space for \$50,000 per year, should it make or outsource this component?

c. What additional factors should it consider in deciding whether to make or outsource the electric motors?

LO1, 2, 5

E4-23. Make or Buy

Priya Rahavy, M.D., is a general practitioner whose offices are located in the Lake Forest Professional Building. In the past, Dr. Rahavy has operated her practice with a nurse, a receptionist/secretary, and a part-time bookkeeper. Dr. Rahavy, like many small-town physicians, has billed her patients and their insurance companies from her own office. The part-time bookkeeper, who works 20 hours per week, is employed exclusively for this purpose.

North Avenue Physician's Service Center has offered to take over all of Dr. Rahavy's billings and collections for an annual fee of \$36,000. If Dr. Rahavy accepts this offer, she will no longer need the bookkeeper. The bookkeeper's wages and fringe benefits amount to \$25 per hour, and the bookkeeper works 50 weeks per year. With all the billings and collections done elsewhere, Dr. Rahavy will have three additional hours available per week to see patients. She sees an average of four patients per hour at an average fee of \$40 per visit. Dr. Rahavy's practice is expanding, and new patients often have to wait several weeks for an appointment. She has resisted expanding her office hours or working more than 50 weeks per year. Finally, if Dr. Rahavy signs on with the center, she will no longer need to rent a records storage facility for \$250 per month.

Required

Conduct a relevant cost analysis to determine if it is profitable to outsource the bookkeeping.

LO1, 2, 6
Ecolab (ECL)

E4-24. Sell or Process Further

Ecolab produces cleaning and sanitizing chemicals for commercial markets. Assume the company processes raw material D into joint products E and F. Raw material D costs \$8 per liter. It costs \$150 to convert 100 liters of D into 60 liters of E and 40 liters of F. Product F can be sold immediately for

$40 per liter or processed further into Product G at an additional cost of $12 per liter. Product G can then be sold for $55 per liter.

Required

Determine whether Product F should be sold or processed further into Product G.

E4-25. Limited Resources

LO7
Fender Musical Instruments Corp.

Assume Fender produces only three guitars: the Stratocaster, Telecaster, and Jaguar. A limitation of 960 labor hours per week prevents Fender from meeting the sales demand for these products. Product information is as follows.

	Stratocaster	Telecaster	Jaguar
Unit selling price	$1,200	$ 900	$1,400
Unit variable costs	(630)	(450)	(850)
Unit contribution margin	$ 570	$ 450	$ 550
Labor hours per unit	15	10	20

Required

a. Determine the weekly contribution from each product when total labor hours are allocated to the product with the highest
1. Unit selling price.
2. Unit contribution margin.
3. Contribution per labor hour.

(*Hint:* Each situation is independent of the others.)

b. What generalization can be made regarding the allocation of limited resources to achieve short-run profit maximization?

c. Determine the opportunity cost the company will incur if management requires the weekly production of 15 Jaguars. *Hint:* You want to maximize short-run profit. Think about which guitar is most profitable.

d. Give reasons why a company may not allocate resources in the most economical way in some situations.

E4-26. Limited Resources

LO7

Homework MBC

Maria Pajet, a regional sales representative for UniTec Systems Inc., has been working about 60 hours per week calling on a total of 85 regular customers each month. Because of family and health considerations, she has decided to reduce her hours to a maximum of 160 per month. Unfortunately, this cutback will require Maria to turn away some of her regular customers or, at least, serve them less frequently than once a month. Maria has developed the following information to assist her in determining how to best allocate time.

	Customer Classification		
	Large Business	Small Business	Individual
Number of customers	10	45	100
Average monthly sales per customer	$ 4,000	$2,500	$ 1,000
Commission percentage	5.0%	4.0%	3.0%
Hours per customer per monthly visit	4.0	2.5	1.5

Required

a. Develop a monthly plan that indicates the number of customers Maria should call on in each classification to maximize her monthly sales commissions.

b. Determine the monthly commissions Maria will earn if she implements this plan.

c. Give one or two reasons why Maria might decide not to follow the conclusions of the above analysis entirely.

E4-27 Sell of Process Further

LO6

Rose Hill, a soybean farm in northern Minnesota, has a herd of 25 dairy cows. The cows produce approximately 1,400 gallons of milk per week. The farm currently sells all its milk to a nearby processor for $1.25 per gallon, a significant drop from the $2.00 per gallon they were able to charge five years ago. It costs $1.60 per gallon to produce the milk.

The owners of Rose Hill are deciding whether to sell the dairy cows or expand into the artisan cheese market. Both owners have prior cheese-making experience and they already have all the needed equipment.

It takes .8 gallons of milk to make a pound of cheese. Costs to produce a pound of cheese are expected to total $7 per pound. Artisan cheeses are currently selling for $10 per pound at farmer's markets and upscale groceries.

Required

a. How much incremental profit would Rose Hill recognize if half the milk each week was used to make cheese?

b. How much, in total, would Rose Hill earn each week if half the milk was used to make cheese and half was sold to the processor?

c. How much of the milk would need to be used to make cheese each week in order for Rose Hill to break even on its dairy operations assuming no cows were sold? (*Note:* Any milk not used to make cheese would still be sold to a processor.)

d. What other factors should the owners of Rose Hill consider when deciding whether to sell the dairy cows or expand into cheese-making?

Problems

LO1, 2, 3 **P4-28. Multiple Changes in Profit Plans**

In an attempt to improve profit performance, Anderson Company's management is considering a number of alternative actions. An October contribution income statement for Anderson Company follows.

ANDERSON COMPANY Contribution Income Statement For Month of October		
Sales (12,000 units × $75)		$900,000
Less variable costs		
Direct materials (12,000 units × $10)	$120,000	
Direct labor (12,000 units × $10)	120,000	
Variable factory overhead (12,000 units × $4)	48,000	
Selling and administrative (12,000 units × $2)	24,000	(312,000)
Contribution margin (12,000 units × $49)		588,000
Less fixed costs		
Factory overhead	360,000	
Selling and administrative	240,000	(600,000)
Net income (loss)		$ (12,000)

Required

Determine the effect of each of the following independent situations on monthly profit.

a. Purchasing automated assembly equipment, which should reduce direct labor costs by $4 per unit and increase variable overhead costs by $1 per unit and fixed factory overhead by $12,000 per month.

b. Reducing the selling price by $5 per unit. This should increase the monthly sales by 3,000 units. At this higher volume, additional equipment and salaried personnel would be required. This will increase fixed factory overhead by $4,000 per month and fixed selling and administrative costs by $1,800 per month.

c. Buying rather than manufacturing a component of Anderson's final product. This will increase direct materials costs by $5 per unit. However, direct labor will decline $3 per unit, variable factory overhead will decline $1 per unit, and fixed factory overhead will decline $25,000 per month.

d. Increasing the unit selling price by $5 per unit. This action should result in a 2,000-unit decrease in monthly sales.

e. Combining alternatives (*a*) and (*d*).

P4-29. Multiple Changes in Profit Plans: Multiple Products LO1, 2, 3

Information on Guadalupe Ltd.'s three products follows:

	A	B	C
Unit sales per month	1,500	1,200	2,000
Selling price per unit	$20.00	$14.00	$30.00
Variable costs per unit	(22.00)	(10.00)	(18.00)
Unit contribution margin	$ (2.00)	$ 4.00	$12.00

Required

Determine the effect each of the following situations would have on monthly profits. Each situation should be evaluated independently of all others.

a. Product A is discontinued.
b. Product A is discontinued, and the subsequent loss of customers causes sales of Product B to decline by 150 units.
c. The selling price of A is increased to $25 with a sales decrease of 250 units.
d. The price of Product B is increased to $20 with a resulting sales decrease of 300 units. However, some of these customers shift to Product A; sales of Product A increase by 200 units.
e. Product A is discontinued, and the plant in which A was produced is used to produce D, a new product. Product D has a unit contribution margin of $2. Monthly sales of Product D are predicted to be 1,500 units.
f. The selling price of Product C is increased to $35, and the selling price of Product B is decreased to $10. Sales of C decline by 350 units, while sales of B increase by 400 units.

P4-30. Relevant Costs and Differential Analysis LO1, 2

Cornerstone Bank paid $90,000 for a check-sorting machine 10 years ago this month. The machine had an estimated life of 15 years and annual operating costs of $40,000, excluding depreciation. Although management is pleased with the machine, recent technological advances have made check-sorting machines obsolete. Consequently, the machine now has a book value of $30,000, a remaining operating life of five years, and a salvage value of $0.

The manager of operations is evaluating a proposal to acquire check scanning equipment for all branches. The new equipment would cost $50,000 and reduce annual operating costs to $20,000, excluding depreciation. Because of expected technological improvements, the manager believes the new machine will have an economic life of four years and no salvage value at the end of that life. Prior to signing the papers authorizing the acquisition of the new machine, the president of the bank prepared the following analysis:

Six-year savings [($40,000 – $20,000) × 4 years]	$80,000
Cost of new machine	(50,000)
Loss on disposal of old machine	(30,000)
Advantage (disadvantage) of replacement	$ 0

After looking at these numbers, the manager rejected the proposal and commented that he was "tired of looking at marginal projects. This bank is in business to make a profit, not to break even. If you want to break even, go work for the government."

Required

a. Evaluate the president's analysis.
b. Prepare a differential analysis of six-year totals for the old and the new machines.
c. Speculate on some limitations of the model or other issues that might be a factor in making a final decision.

P4-31. Special Order LO1, 2, 4 Razor USA

Razor USA produces a variety of electric scooters. Assume that Razor has just received an order from a customer (Pulse Cycles) for 500 Power Core scooters. The following price, based on cost plus a 60% markup, has been developed for the order:

Manufacturing costs	
Direct materials	$11,850
Direct labor	8,500
Factory overhead	15,800
Total	36,150
Markup (60%)	21,690
Selling price	$57,840

Pulse Cycles rejected this price and offered to purchase the 500 scooters at a price of $45,000. The following additional information is available:

- Razor has sufficient excess capacity to produce the scooters.
- Factory overhead is applied on the basis of direct labor dollars.
- Budgeted factory overhead is $8,000,000 for the current year. Of this amount, $6,000,000 is fixed. Of the $15,800 of factory overhead assigned to the Pulse Cycles order, only $3,950 is driven by the special order; $11,850 is a fixed cost.
- Selling and administrative expenses are budgeted as follows:

Fixed	$3,000,000 per year
Variable	$10 per unit manufactured and sold

Required

a. The president of Razor wants to know if he should allow Pulse Cycles to have the scooters for $45,000. Determine the effect on profits of accepting Pulse Cycles' offer.
b. Briefly explain why certain costs should be omitted from the analysis in requirement (*a*).
c. Assume Razor is operating at capacity and could sell the 500 scooters at its regular markup.
  1. Determine the opportunity cost of accepting Pulse Cycles' offer.
  2. Determine the effect on profits of accepting Pulse Cycles' offer.
d. What other factors should Razor consider before deciding to accept the special order?

LO1, 2, 4 **P4-32. Special Order**

Every Halloween, Peterson's Ice Cream Shop offers a trick-or-treat package of 25 coupons for $20. The coupons are redeemable by children 12 years or under, for a single-scoop cone, with a limit of one coupon per child per visit. Coupon sales average 600 books per year. The printing costs are $75. A single-scoop cone of Peterson's ice cream normally sells for $2.00. The variable costs of a single-scoop cone are $1.50.

Required

a. Determine the loss if all coupons are redeemed without any other effect on sales.
b. Assume all coupons will not be redeemed. With regular sales unaffected, determine the coupon redemption rate at which Peterson's will break even on the offer.
c. Assuming regular sales are not affected and one additional single-scoop cone is sold at the regular price each time a coupon is redeemed, determine the coupon redemption rate at which Peterson's will break even on the offer.
d. Determine the profit or loss incurred on the offer if the coupon redemption rate is 60% and:
  1. One-fourth of the redeemed coupons have no effect on sales.
  2. One-fourth of the redeemed coupons result in additional sales of two single-scoop cones.
  3. One-fourth of the redeemed coupons result in additional sales of three single-scoop cones.
  4. One-fourth of the redeemed coupons come out of regular sales of single-scoop cones.

LO1, 2, 3, 4, 5 **P4-33 Applications of Differential Analysis**
Moscot

Moscot manufactures high-end sunglasses that it sells in retail shops and online for $310, on average. Assume the following represent manufacturing and other costs.

Variable Costs per Unit		Fixed Costs per Month	
Direct materials	$ 80	Factory overhead	$450,000
Direct labor	50	Selling and administrative	375,000
Factory overhead	35	Total	$825,000
Distribution	10		
Total	$175		

The variable distribution costs are for transportation to retail partners. Assume the current monthly production and sales volume is 15,000 units. Monthly capacity is 20,000 units.

Required

Determine the effect of each of the following independent situations on monthly profits.

a. A $50 increase in the unit selling price should result in a 2,000-unit decrease in monthly sales.

b. A 10% decrease in the unit selling price should result in a 6,000-unit increase in monthly sales. However, because of capacity constraints, the last 1,000 units would be produced during overtime with the direct labor costs increasing by 50%.

c. A British distributor has proposed to place a special, one-time order for 1,000 units at a reduced price of $250 per unit. The distributor would pay all transportation costs. There would be additional fixed selling and administrative costs of $750.

d. A Swiss distributor has proposed to place a special, one-time order for 6,000 units at a special price of $250 per unit. The distributor would pay all transportation costs. There would be additional fixed selling and administrative costs of $1,000. Assume overtime production is not possible.

e. Assume Moscat provides a designer case for each pair of sunglasses that it manufactures. A Chinese manufacturer has offered a one-year contract to supply the cases at a cost of $10 per unit. If Moscat accepts the offer, it will be able to reduce variable manufacturing costs by 5%, reduce fixed costs by $5,000, and rent out some freed-up space for $4,000 per month.

f. The glasses also come with a choice of lens tint. Assume that eliminating that option would reduce variable costs by $5 and eliminate $50,000 in fixed factory overhead. The selling price would likely have to decrease to $290 per unit.

P4-34. Applications of Differential Analysis **LO1, 2, 3, 4, 5**

Adventure Expeditions offers guided back-country hiking/camping trips in British Columbia. Adventure provides a guide and all necessary food and equipment at a fee of $100 per person per day. Adventure currently provides an average of 600 guide-days per month in June, July, August, and September. Based on available equipment and staff, maximum capacity is 750 guide-days per month. Monthly variable and fixed operating costs (valued in Canadian dollars) are as follows.

Variable Costs per Guide-Day		Fixed Costs per Month	
Food	$ 6	Equipment rental	$10,000
Guide salary	20	Administration	12,000
Supplies	4	Advertising	2,500
Insurance	10	Total	$24,500
Total	$40		

Required

Determine the effect of each of the following situations on monthly profits. Each situation is to be evaluated independently of all others.

a. A $10 increase in the daily fee should result in a 100-unit decrease in monthly sales.

b. A $10 decrease in the daily fee should result in a 200-unit increase in monthly sales. However, because of capacity constraints, the last 50 guide-days would be provided by subcontracting to another firm at a cost of $50 per guide-day. (The $50 cost includes food, guides, supplies, and insurance.)

c. A French tour agency has proposed to place a special, one-time order for 100 guide-days at a reduced fee of $85 per guide-day. The agency would pay all insurance costs. There would be additional fixed administrative costs of $500.

d. An Italian tour agency has proposed to place a special, one-time order for 300 guide-days next month at a special fee of $80 per guide-day. The agency would pay all insurance costs. There would be additional fixed administrative costs of $500. Assume additional capacity beyond 800 guide-days is not available.

e. An Alberta outdoor supply company has offered to supply all necessary food and camping equipment at $7 per guide-day. This eliminates the current food costs and reduces the monthly equipment rental costs to $8,800.

f. Clients currently must carry a backpack and assist in camp activities such as cooking. Adventure is considering the addition of mules to carry all food and equipment and the hiring of college students to perform camp activities such as cooking. This will increase variable costs by $30 per guide-day and fixed costs by $5,000 per month. However, 600 full-service guide-days per month could now be sold at $150 each.

LO1, 2 **P4-35. Continue or Discontinue**

Westview Eye Clinic primarily performs three medical procedures: cataract removal, corneal implants, and laser keratotomy. At the end of the first quarter of this year, Dr. Rajan, president of Westview, expressed grave concern about the cataract sector because it had reported a loss of $150,000. He rationalized that "since the cataract market is losing $150,000, and the overall practice is making $300,000, if we eliminate the cataract market, our total profits will increase to $450,000."

Required

a. Is the president's analysis correct?

b. Will total profits increase if the cataract section is dropped?

c. Is it possible total profits will decline?

Cases and Projects

LO1, 2, 3 **C4-36. Assessing the Impact of an Incentive Plan**[2]

Overview

Ladbrecks is a major department store with 50 retail outlets. The company's stores compete with outlets run by companies such as Nordstrom, Macy's, Bloomingdales, and Saks Fifth Avenue. During the early nineties the company decided that providing excellent customer service was the key ingredient for success in the retail industry. Therefore, during the mid 1990s the company implemented an incentive plan for its sales associates in 20 of its stores. Your job is to assess the financial impact of the plan and to provide a recommendation to management to continue or discontinue the plan based on your findings.

Incentives in Retail

The past decade has evidenced a concerted effort by many firms to empower and motivate employees to improve performance. A recent *New York Times* article reported that more and more firms are offering bonus plans to hourly workers. An Ernst and Young survey of the retail industry indicates that virtually all department stores currently offer incentive programs such as straight commissions, base salary plus commission, and quota bonus programs. Although these programs can add to payroll costs, the survey respondents indicated that they believe these plans have contributed to major improvements in customer service.

Company's Background

Ladbrecks was founded by members of the Ladbreck family in the 1880s. The first store opened under the name Ladbreck Dry Goods. Growth was fueled through acquisitions as the industry consolidated during the 1960s. Over this hundred-year period, sales associates were paid a fixed hourly wage. Raises were based on seniority. Sales associates were expected to be neat and courteous to customers. The advent of specialty stores and the stated intention of an upscale west coast retailer to begin opening stores in the Midwest concerned Ladbreck's management. Building on its history of excellence in customer service, the company initiated its performance-based incentive plan to support its stated firm-wide strategy of

[2] Written to illustrate the use of relevant costs and revenues for decision making. This example is based on an actual company's experience with implementing an incentive plan. The company name and the financial numbers and key ratios have been altered.

"customer emphasis" with "employee empowerment." Management expected it to result in further enhancement of customer service and, consequently, in an increase in sales generated at its stores.

Incentive Plan

The plan was implemented in stores sequentially as company managers intended to examine and evaluate the plan's impact on sales and profitability. Initially, the firm selected one store from a group of similar stores in the same general area to begin the implementation. By the end of 1994, 10 stores had implemented the plan. In 1995, 10 more stores implemented the plan, bringing the total to 20 out of a total of 50.

The performance-based incentive plan is best described as a bonus program. At the time of the plan's implementation, sales associates received little in the form of annual merit increases, and promotions were rare. The bonus payment became the only significant reward for high performance. Each week sales associates are paid a base hourly rate times hours worked. In addition, under the plan sales associates could increase their compensation by receiving a bonus at the end of each quarter. The contract provides sales-force personnel with a cash bonus only if the actual quarterly sales generated by the employee exceed a quarterly sales goal. Individualized pre-specified sales goals were established for each employee based only on the individual's base hourly rate, hours worked, and a multiplier (multiplier = 1/bonus rate). The bonus is computed as a fixed percentage of the excess sales (actual sales minus a pre-specified sales goal) by the employee in a quarter (see Exhibit 1).

Employee's Bonus	=	**0.08**	×	**(Employee's actual sales for quarter – employee's targeted sales for quarter)**		
Where employee's targeted sales for quarter	=	**Employee's hourly wage**	×	**Hours worked in quarter**	×	**12.5**

Senior managers regarded the incentive plan as a major change for the firm and its sales force. Management expected that the new incentive scheme would motivate many changes in employee behavior that would enhance customer service. Sales associates were now expected to build a client base to generate repeat sales. Actions consistent with this approach include developing and updating customer address lists (including details of their needs and preferences), writing thank you notes, and contacting customers about upcoming sales and new merchandise that matched their preferences.

Consultant's Task

Management decided to call you in to provide an independent assessment. While the company thought that sales had increased with the plan's implementation, the human resources department did not know exactly how to quantify the plan's impact on sales and expenses. It suspected that employee salaries, cost of goods sold, and inventory carrying costs, as well as sales, may have changed due to the plan's implementation. You, therefore, requested information on these financial variables.

Sales Analysis: Because each of the 20 stores implemented the plan at different dates, and store sales fluctuated greatly with the seasons and the economy, you could not simply plot store sales. Instead, for each of the 20 stores, you picked another Ladbreck store as a control and computed for 48 months the following series of monthly sales:[3]

$$\text{Percent Change in Sales} = \frac{[(\text{Plan Store Sales in Month t} \div \text{Plan Store Sales in Month t-24}) -}{(\text{Control Store Sales in Month t} \div \text{Control Store Sales in Month t-24})] \times 100}$$

The plan's implementation was denoted as month 25, so you had 24 months prior to the plan and 24 months after the plan. Averages were then taken for the 20 stores. If the control procedure worked, then you expected that the first 24 months of the series would fluctuate around zero. The actual results are reported in Figure 1, page 146. Month 25 is denoted as the rollout month, the month the incentive plan began.

Expense Analysis: You then plotted wage expense/sales, cost of goods sold/sales, and inventory turnover for the 20 stores for the 24 months preceding the plan and the first 24 months after plan implementation. After pulling out seasonal effects, these monthly series are presented in Figures 2, 3, and 4. If the plan has no impact on these expenses, then you would expect no dramatic change in the series around month 25.

Figure 2 plots (wage expense in month t/sales in month t)

[3] For instance, assume sales for plan store were $2,200 this January and $2,000 two Januarys ago. Also assume that sales in the control store were $4,400 this January and $4,000 two Januarys ago. Percent change = 2,200/2,000 – 4,400/4,000 = 0.

Figure 3 plots (cost of goods sold in month t/sales in month t)
Figure 4 plots "annual" turnover computed as (12 × cost of goods sold in month t/inventory at beginning of month t)

For example, if monthly cost of sales is $100 and the annual inventory turnover ratio is 4, it suggests a monthly turnover of 0.333 with the firm holding an average inventory of $300 throughout the year. (Note that a monthly inventory turnover of .333 implies an annual turnover of 4 (from 12 × 0.333).

Financial Report for Store: A typical annual income statement for a pre-plan Ladbreck store before fixed charges, taxes, and incidentals looks as follows.

	Total	Percent
Sales.	10,000,000	100
Cost of goods sold	6,300,000	63
Gross profit.	3,700,000	37
Employee salaries	800,000	8
Profit before fixed charges	2,900,000	29

A store also has substantial charges for rent, management salaries, insurance, etc., but they are fixed with respect to the incentive plan.

Required

a. Suppose the goal of the firm is to now provide superior customer service by having the sales consultant identify and sell to the specific needs of the customer. What does this goal suggest about a change in managerial accounting and control systems?
b. Provide an estimate of the impact of the incentive plan on sales.
c. Did the sales impact occur all at once, or did it occur gradually?
d. What is the impact of the incentive plan on wage expense as a percent of sales?
e. What is the impact of the incentive plan on cost of good sold as a percent of sales?
f. What is the impact of incentive plan on inventory turnover (turnover = cost of goods sold ÷ inventory)? [If sales go up, then stores are selling more goods; therefore, more goods need to be on the floor or those goods on floor need to turn over faster.]
g. What is the additional dollar amount of inventory that must be held?
h. Using the information on sales and expenses for a typical store, provide an analysis of the additional store profit contributed by the plan. Assume that it costs 10% a year to carry the added inventory.
i. Look at Exhibit 1, which provides a partial listing of employee pay for one small department within a store. Which "type" of employee is receiving the bonus?
j. Should the company keep the plan? Explain your estimate of the financial impact of the plan and also incorporate any nonfinancial information you feel is relevant in justifying your decision.

Figure 1
Percentage Change in Sales

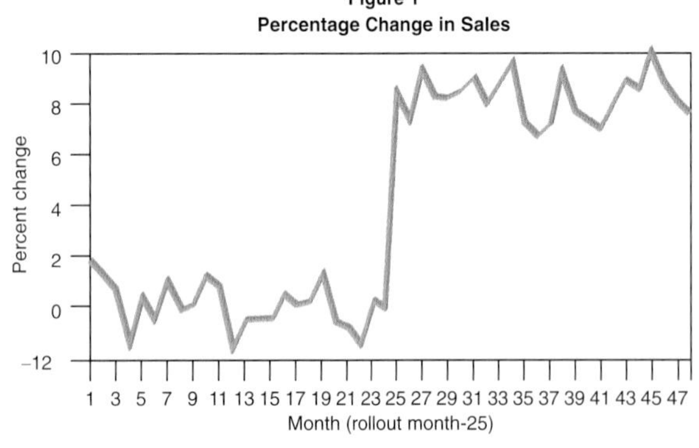

Figure 2
Wage Expense as a Percent of Sales

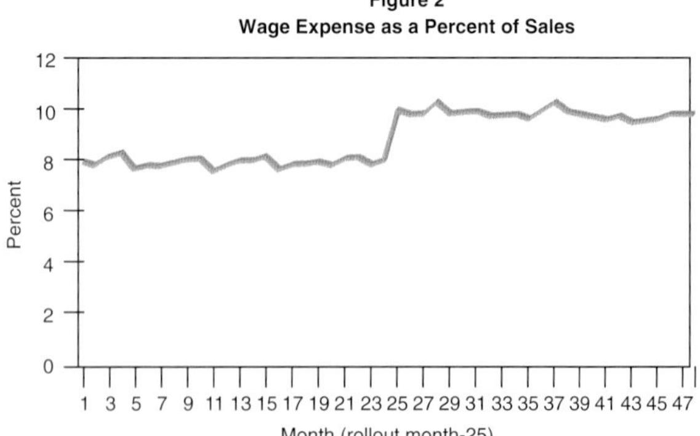

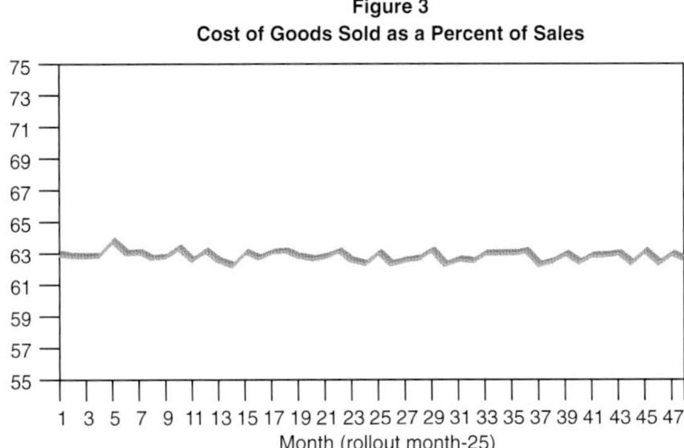

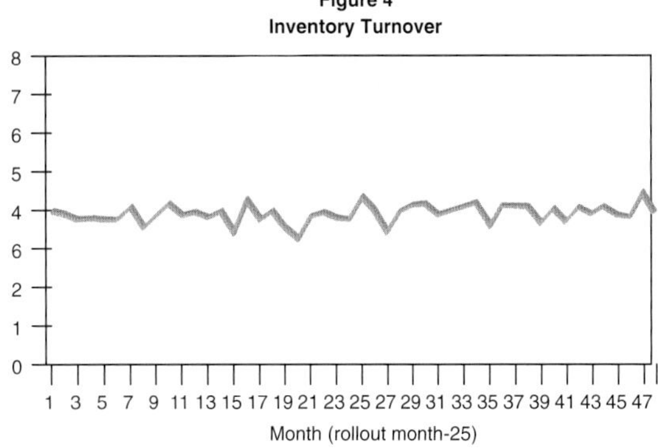

Exhibit 1 Wages by subset of employees in Ladbreck's fashion department

Name	Years of Service	Hourly Wage Rate	Hours Worked in Quarter	Regular Pay	Actual Sales for Quarter	Bonus	Total Pay Quarter
BOB MARLEY	2	4.00	400	1,600	25,000	400	2,000
JIMI HENDRIX	16	7.50	440	3,300	41,000	0	3,300
MILLIE SMALL	24	9.99	440	4,396	40,000	0	4,396
AL GREEN	11	6.00	400	2,400	36,000	480	2,880
BOB DYLAN	4	5.00	400	2,000	30,000	400	2,400
JANIS JOPLIN	10	6.00	400	2,400	30,000	0	2,400
WILSON PICKETT	16	7.50	440	3,300	50,000	700	4,000
BRUCE SPRINGSTEEN	23	9.99	440	4,396	30,000	0	4,396
MICHIGAN & SMILEY	13	7.00	400	2,800	38,000	240	3,040
RICHIE FURAY	22	9.90	400	3,960	30,000	0	3,960
JOHN LENNON	5	5.00	400	2,000	34,000	720	2,720
JULIO IGLESIAS	4	5.00	480	2,400	46,000	1,280	3,680
TOMMY PETTY	11	6.00	400	2,400	36,000	480	2,880
JOAN BAEZ	21	9.90	400	3,960	40,000	0	3,960
BB KING	8	6.00	400	2,400	38,000	640	3,040
GLADYS KNIGHT	14	8.00	480	3,840	46,000	0	3,840
NEIL YOUNG	15	8.00	480	3,840	36,000	0	3,840
BO DIDDLEY	4	5.00	400	2,000	30,000	400	2,400

Solutions to Review Problems

Review 4-1—Solution

Relevant Costs	Irrelevant Costs
Cost of machine	Building lease cost
Residual value of machine	Vice president's salary
Operating cost of machine	
Direct labor savings	
Cost of manager	
Opportunity cost of renting released space	

Review 4-2—Solution

a.

	Purchase Machine		Use Labor	Difference (in total cost of purchasing machine)
Cost of new machine	$1,000,000			$1,000,000
Residual value of machine	(100,000)			(100,000)
Operating cost of machine ($10,000 × 60 months)	600,000			600,000
Cost of direct laborers (5,000 clubs × $5 × 60 months)			$1,500,000	(1,500,000)
Cost of one manager ($6,000 × 60 months)			360,000	(360,000)
Rental value of freed-up space ($3,500 × 60 months)			210,000	(210,000)
Total costs	$1,500,000		$2,070,000	$ (570,000)
Advantage of purchasing machine		$570,000		

b. Even though the new machine would save estimated costs of $570,000 over the next five years, there are several qualitative questions that should be answered, including the following:

- Will the new machine provide the same quality product as the current workers?
- How important is it to have a cost structure that includes variable labor costs versus more fixed machine costs? If a business decline should occur, variable costs are often easier to eliminate than fixed costs.
- What is the expected effect on worker morale and community image of eliminating a significant number of jobs in the plant?
- How important is it for the sales staff to be able to promote the product as primarily handmade, versus machine made?

Review 4-3—Solution

Unit selling price	$4.80
Unit variable costs	(2.50)
Unit contribution margin	$2.30

a.

Profit decrease from reduced sales given no changes in prices or costs (1,800 units × $2.30)	$ (4,140)
Profit increase from increase in selling price [(15,000 units − 1,800 units) × $1.50]	19,800
Increase in monthly profit	$15,660

b.

Profit increase from increased sales given no changes in prices or costs (6,000 units × $2.30)	$13,800
Profit decrease from reduced selling price of all units [(15,000 units + 6,000 units) × $1.80]	(37,800)
Profit decrease from increased direct labor costs for the last 1,000 units [1,000 units × ($0.20 × 0.50)]	(100)
Decrease in monthly profit	$(24,100)

Review 4-4—Solution

a.

Increase in revenues (4,000 units × $4.00)		$16,000
Increase in costs		
Direct materials (4,000 units × $2.00)	$8,000	
Direct labor (4,000 units × $0.20)	800	
Factory overhead (4,000 units × $0.25)	1,000	
Selling and administrative	500	(10,300)
Increase in profits		$ 5,700

b.

Increase in revenues (8,000 units × $4.00)		$32,000
Increase in costs		
Direct materials (8,000 units × $2.00)	$16,000	
Direct labor (8,000 units × $0.20)	1,600	
Factory overhead (8,000 units × $0.25)	2,000	
Selling and administrative	500	
Opportunity cost of lost regular sales [(15,000 units + 8,000 units – 20,000 unit capacity) × $2.30]	6,900	(27,000)
Increase in profits		$ 5,000

Review 4-5—Solution

	Cost to Make	Cost to Buy
Cost to buy		$15,000
Direct materials	$30,000	18,000
Direct labor	3,000	1,800
Factory overhead	3,750	2,250
Opportunity cost	1,000	
Totals	$37,750	$37,050
Advantage of buying	$ 700	

Review 4-6—Solution

Increase in revenues		
Package individually (15,000 units × $5.05)	$75,750	
Sell in bulk (15,000 units × $4.80)	(72,000)	$3,750
Additional packaging costs (15,000 units × $0.10)		(1,500)
Advantage of individual packaging		$2,250

Review 4-7—Solution

Intuition suggests that the extra capacity should be devoted either to produce the Instrument Knob, which has the highest sales price, or the Pointer Knob, which has the highest per-unit contribution margin and net income. However, an analysis of the contribution margin of each product per unit of constraining factor reveals that the Star Knob should receive the extra capacity.

Note that fixed costs are allocated among products on the basis of machine hours—the constraining resource in our example. Furthermore, the unit allocations of fixed costs indicate that the Pointer Knob requires three times as many machine hours as the Instrument Knob and six times as many as the Star Knob. The contribution per unit of machine capacity for each product is as follows.

	Pointer Knob	Instrument Knob	Star Knob
Contribution margin per case	$12	$6	$4
Divided by units machine capacity required	6	2	1
Contribution margin per unit of machine capacity (the constraining resource)	$ 2	$3	$4

Use of the remaining capacity generates a greater contribution margin if devoted to the Star Knob.

Chapter **5**

Product Costing: Job and Process Operations

Learning Objectives

LO1 Describe inventory requirements and measurement issues for service, merchandising, and manufacturing organizations. (p. 154)

LO2 Explain the framework of inventory costing for financial reporting. (p. 156)

LO3 Describe the production environment as it relates to product costing systems. (p. 160)

LO4 Explain the operation of a job costing system. (p. 162)

LO5 Explain the operation of a process costing system. (p. 172)

LO6 Evaluate the differences between absorption and variable costing income (Appendix 5A). (p. 178)

Merchandising firms such as ModCloth have one type of inventory—the goods purchased from suppliers that will be resold to customers. However, the inventory of a manufacturing firm such as South Korea's Samsung Electronics is more complicated. Let's consider Samsung's smartphones. First, there are several components used in the manufacturing process of a smartphone, including external cases, batteries, SIM cards, circuit boards, motherboards, speaker assemblies, cameras, flash memory, controller chips, and numerous other elements. Of these components, some are purchased from outside vendors, whereas others are made internally by Samsung. In fact, one of Samsung's competitive advantages is that it makes everything from chips to screens in its own factories, thereby controlling the processing time and technological know-how that goes into its smartphones. This allows the company to bring its products to market more quickly than its competitors, especially because its competitors often buy their components from Samsung. Clearly, Samsung will satisfy its own demand for the components before selling its output to its competitors.

Given that Samsung makes many of its smartphone components internally, the company will have something called raw materials inventory. These are materials that will be transformed during the manufacturing process to become smartphone components. Examples of Samsung's raw materials include steel, glass, chemicals, wood, papers, metals, and polycarbonates. However, Samsung purchases some components from external vendors, for example, chips for Galaxy S10s come from Broadcomm. These components are also considered raw materials inventory until they are requisitioned into the manufacturing process.

Half of Samsung's smartphones (120 million phones per year) are manufactured in two facilities in Vietnam. The other half are manufactured in a single plant in India. Within each factory, employees assemble smartphones at a three-sided workbench that has all the needed tools and raw materials within arm's reach. As raw materials are requisitioned into this part of the facility and direct labor and overhead are added to the raw materials to manufacture the smartphones, these costs are accumulated in another type of inventory called work-in-process inventory. When the smartphones are completed, they are transferred into a third type of inventory called finished goods, where they will await sale to a customer. This means that for manufacturing companies, the line item "inventory" on the balance sheet may be the sum of three types of inventory: raw materials inventory, work-in-process inventory, and finished goods inventory.

This chapter will illustrate how the costs of products and services flow through these inventory accounts and how we allocate costs to individual products or services based on those products' or services' consumption of the resources. Sometimes, this allocation is straightforward; for example, we can track the amount of raw materials or direct labor hours that go into a product or service. Other times, however, this allocation is more complicated.

Road Map

LO	Learning Objective | Topics	Page	eLecture	Guided Example	Assignments
LO1	**Describe inventory requirements and measurement issues for service, merchandising, and manufacturing organizations.** Inventory Requirements :: Flow of Inventory Costs	154	e5–1	Review 5-1	
LO2	**Explain the framework of inventory costing for financial reporting.** Product Costs and Period Costs :: Direct Material :: Direct Labor :: Manufacturing Overhead :: Predetermined Overhead Rates	156	e5–2	Review 5-2	14, 15, 21, 24, 25, 34, 35, 36, 37, 44, 45
LO3	**Describe the production environment as it relates to product costing systems.** Production Environment :: Production Files and Records	160	e5–3	Review 5-3	
LO4	**Explain the operation of a job costing system.** Basic Production Cost Flows :: Job Costing Illustrated :: Statement of Cost of Goods Manufactured :: Overapplied and Underapplied Overhead :: Job Costing in a Service Organization	162	e5–4	Review 5-4	16, 17, 21, 22, 23, 24, 26, 27, 33, 34, 35, 36, 37, 44, 45
LO5	**Explain the operation of a process costing system.** Cost of Production Report :: Weighted Average :: First-In, First-Out :: Process Costing in Service Organizations	172	e5–5	Review 5-5	16, 17, 18, 28, 29, 38, 39, 40
LO6	**(Appendix 5A) Evaluate the differences between absorption and variable costing income.** Basic Concepts :: Income Under Absorption and Variable Costing :: Production Equals Sales :: Production Exceeds Sales :: Sales Exceed Production :: Evaluating Alternatives to Inventory Valuation	178	e5–6	Review 5-6	19, 20, 30, 31, 32, 41, 42, 43, 46

CHAPTER ORGANIZATION

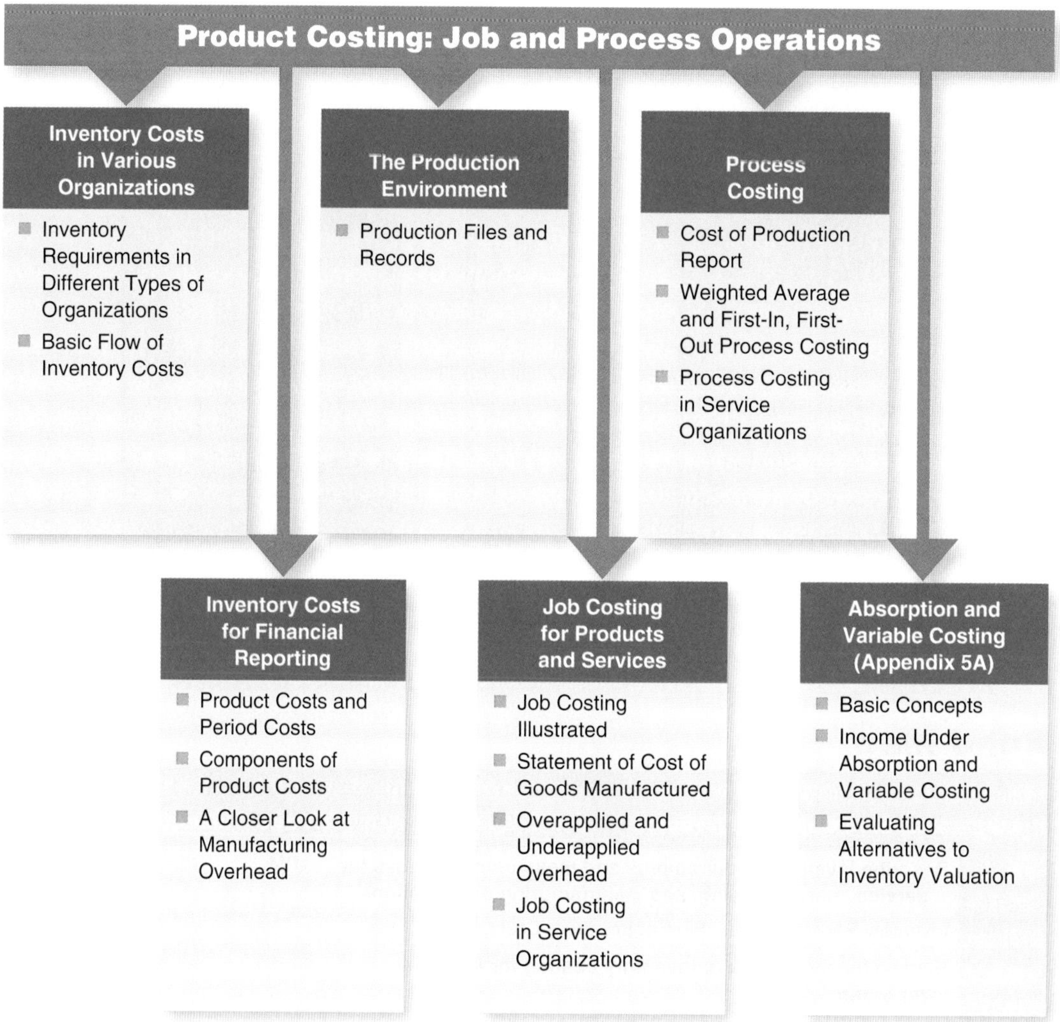

Product Costing: Job and Process Operations

Inventory Costs in Various Organizations
- Inventory Requirements in Different Types of Organizations
- Basic Flow of Inventory Costs

The Production Environment
- Production Files and Records

Process Costing
- Cost of Production Report
- Weighted Average and First-In, First-Out Process Costing
- Process Costing in Service Organizations

Inventory Costs for Financial Reporting
- Product Costs and Period Costs
- Components of Product Costs
- A Closer Look at Manufacturing Overhead

Job Costing for Products and Services
- Job Costing Illustrated
- Statement of Cost of Goods Manufactured
- Overapplied and Underapplied Overhead
- Job Costing in Service Organizations

Absorption and Variable Costing (Appendix 5A)
- Basic Concepts
- Income Under Absorption and Variable Costing
- Evaluating Alternatives to Inventory Valuation

This chapter provides an overview of product costing systems and a framework for understanding costs in a production environment. It also examines aspects of the production environment that can affect product costing systems and discusses costing issues related to the production of physical products versus the production of services.

Inventory Costs in Various Organizations

LO1 Describe inventory requirements and measurement issues for service, merchandising, and manufacturing organizations.

Organizations can be classified as service, merchandising, or manufacturing. **Service organizations**, such as SportClips hair salons, Shriners Hospitals for Children, The Cheesecake Factory restaurants, and Delta Air Lines, perform services for others. **Merchandising organizations**, such as Walmart, Urban Outfitters, and Best Buy, buy and sell goods. **Manufacturing organizations**, such as Garmin Ltd., The Boston Beer Company, and Hershey, process raw materials into finished products for sale to others.

Service organizations typically have a low percentage of their assets invested in inventory, which usually consists only of the supplies needed to facilitate their operations. In contrast, merchandising organizations usually have a high percentage of their assets invested in inventory. Their largest inventory investment is merchandise purchased for resale, but they also have supplies inventories.

Manufacturing organizations, like merchandisers, have a high percentage of their assets invested in inventories. However, rather than just one major inventory category, manufacturing organizations typically have three: raw materials, work-in-process, and finished goods. **Raw materials inventories** contain the physical ingredients and components that will be converted by machines and/or human labor into a finished product. **Work-in-process inventories** are the partially completed goods that are in the process of being converted into a finished product. **Finished goods inventories** are the completely manufactured products held for sale to customers. As of December 29, 2018, The Boston Beer Company reported the following current inventories:

Raw materials	$44.7 million
Work-in-process	8.3 million
Finished goods	17.3 million
Total current inventory	$70.3 million

Manufacturing organizations also have supplies inventories used to facilitate production and selling and administrative activities. **Exhibit 5.1** illustrates the flow of inventory costs in service, merchandising, and manufacturing organizations. In all three types of organizations, the financial accounting system initially records costs of inventories as assets; when they are eventually consumed or sold, inventory costs are recorded as expenses.

Exhibit 5.1 **Inventory Costs in Various Organizations**

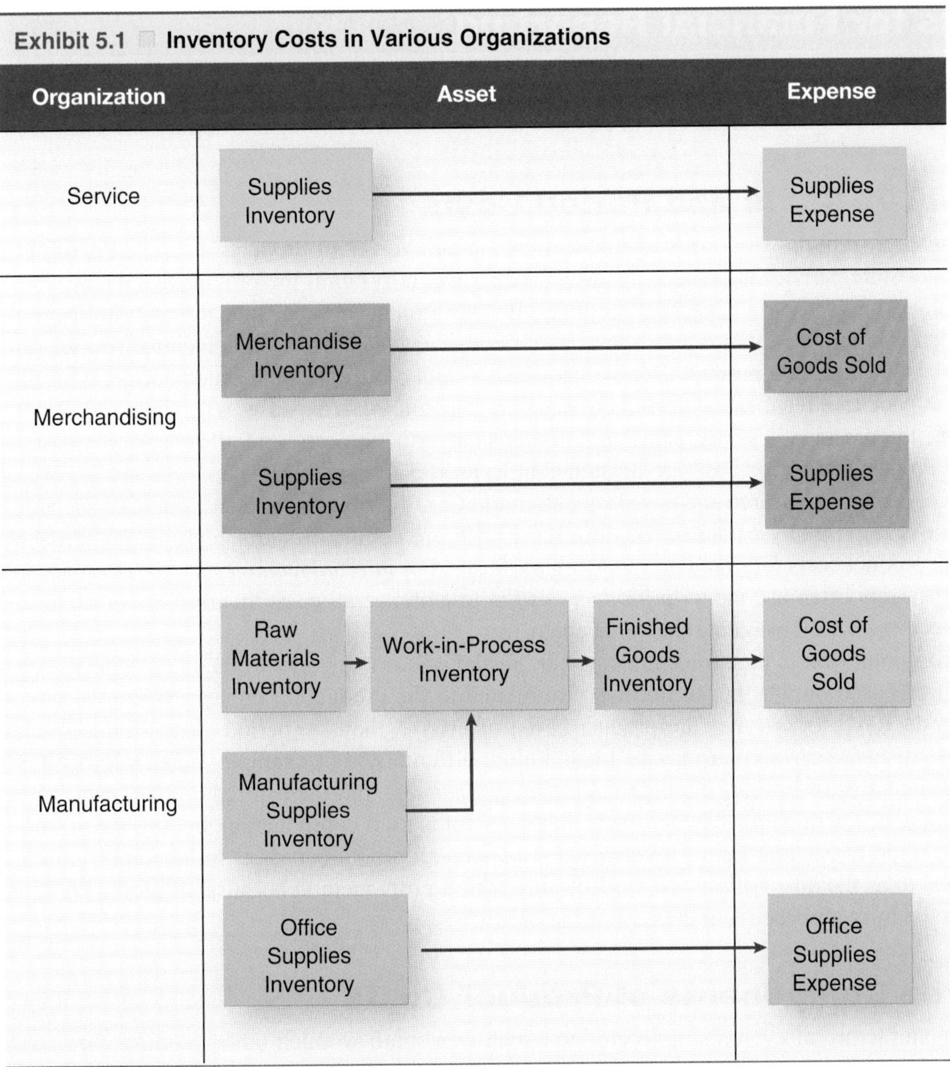

Most formal inventory costing systems are designed to provide information for general-purpose financial statements. Before the balance sheet and income statement are prepared, the cost of ending inventory and the cost of inventory sold or used during the period must be determined.

Review 5-1 LO1 Classifying Inventory Costs

Below is a list of asset accounts a company might maintain in its accounting records.

1. Office supplies inventory.
2. Merchandise inventory.
3. Finished goods inventory.
4. Work-in-process inventory.

Required

For each of the above accounts, identify which type of organization—service, merchandising, or manufacturing—is most likely to maintain the account in its records. You may list more than one organization type if it is relevant. Discuss where each of the above asset accounts would be presented in the organization's financial statements. As each of the above asset accounts is eventually consumed or sold, identify how it would be presented in the organization's financial statements.

Solution on p. 200.

Inventory Costs for Financial Reporting

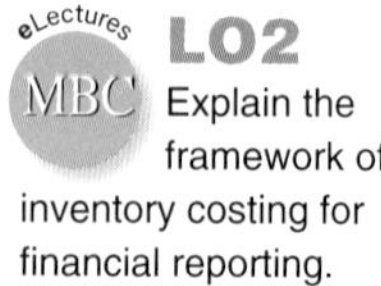

LO2 Explain the framework of inventory costing for financial reporting.

In financial reporting for manufacturing organizations, an important distinction is made between the cost of *producing* products and the cost of all other activities such as selling and administration.

Product Costs and Period Costs

For financial reporting, all costs incurred in the *manufacturing* of products are called **product costs**; these costs are carried in the accounts as an asset (inventory) until the product is sold, at which time they are recognized as an expense (cost of goods sold). Product costs include the costs of raw materials, production employee salaries and wages, and all other *manufacturing* costs incurred to transform raw materials into finished products. Costs that directly apply to the income statement period (other than costs of goods sold) are called **period costs** and are recognized as expenses when incurred. Period costs include the president's salary, sales commissions, advertising costs, and all other *nonmanufacturing* costs. Product and period costs are illustrated in **Exhibit 5.2**.

Costs such as research and development, marketing, distribution, and customer service are important for strategic analyses; however, since these costs are not incurred in the production process, they are not product costs for *financial reporting purposes*. For *internal managerial purposes*, accountants and managers often use the term *product costing* to embrace all costs incurred in connection with a product or service throughout the value chain.

To summarize, in the *product cost* versus *period cost* framework of *financial reporting*, costs are classified based on whether or not they are related to the production process. If they are related to the production process, they are product costs; otherwise, they are period costs. In this framework, costs that seem very similar may be treated quite differently. For example, note in **Exhibit 5.2** that the expired cost of insurance on the *plant* is a *product cost*, but the expired cost of insurance on the *showroom* is a *period cost*. The reason is that the plant is used in production, but the showroom is not. This method of accounting for inventory that assigns all production costs to inventory is sometimes referred to as the **absorption cost** (or **full absorption cost**) method because all production costs are said to be fully absorbed into the cost of the product.

Three Components of Product Costs

The manufacture of even a simple product, such as a small wooden table, requires three basic ingredients: materials (wood), labor (the skill of a worker), and production facilities (a building to work in, a saw, and other tools). Corresponding to these three basic ingredients of any product are three basic categories of product costs: direct materials, direct labor, and manufacturing overhead.

Direct materials are the costs of the primary raw materials converted into finished goods. Examples of primary raw materials include iron ore to a steel mill, coiled aluminum to a manufacturer of aluminum siding, cow's milk to a dairy, logs to a sawmill, and lumber to a builder. The finished product of one firm

Exhibit 5.2 Product Costs and Period Costs

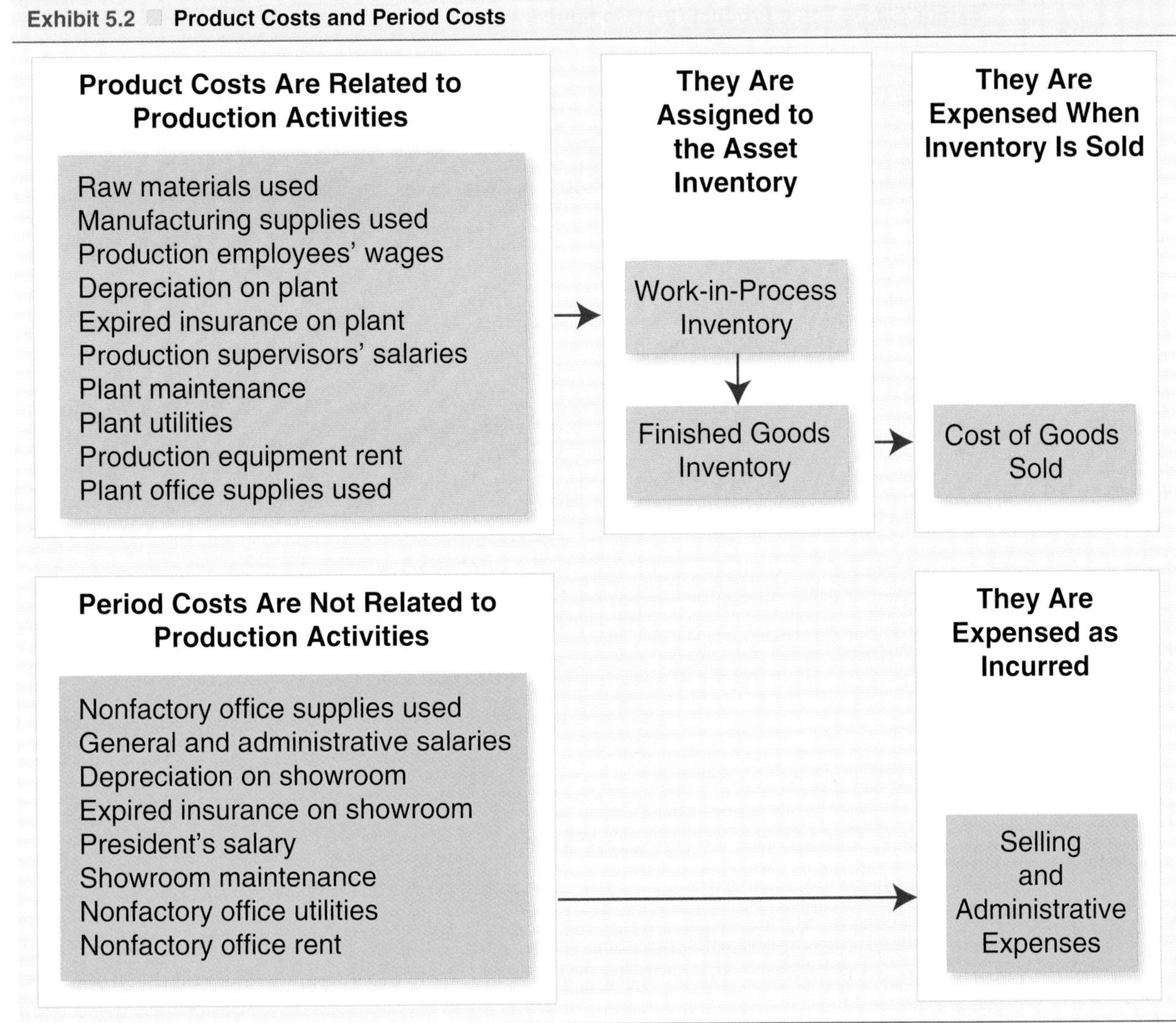

may be the raw materials of another firm down the value chain. For example, rolled steel is a finished product of U.S. Steel, but it is the raw material of the Whirlpool Corporation for the manufacture of washers and dryers. **Direct labor** consists of wages earned by *production employees for the time they actually spend working on a product,* and **manufacturing overhead** includes all manufacturing costs other than direct materials and direct labor. (Manufacturing overhead is also called *factory overhead, burden, manufacturing burden,* and just *overhead.* Merchandising organizations occasionally refer to administrative costs as *overhead.*) **Conversion cost** consists of the combined costs of direct labor and manufacturing overhead incurred to convert raw materials into finished goods.

Examples of manufacturing overhead are manufacturing supplies, depreciation on manufacturing buildings and equipment, and the costs of plant taxes, insurance, maintenance, security, and utilities. Also included are production supervisors' salaries and all other manufacturing-related labor costs for employees who do not work directly on the product (such as maintenance, security, and janitorial personnel).

Just as raw materials, labor, and production facilities are combined to produce a finished product, direct materials costs, direct labor costs, and manufacturing overhead costs are accumulated to obtain the total cost of goods produced. **Exhibit 5.3** illustrates that these product costs are accumulated in the general ledger in Work-in-Process Inventory (or just Work-in-Process) as production takes place and then are transferred to Finished Goods Inventory when production is completed. Product costs are finally assigned to Cost of Goods Sold when the finished goods are sold. (Account titles are capitalized to make it easier to determine when reference is being made to a physical item, such as work-in-process inventory, or to the account, Work-in-Process Inventory, in which costs assigned to the work-in-process inventory are accumulated.)

Exhibit 5.3 Three Product Cost Components

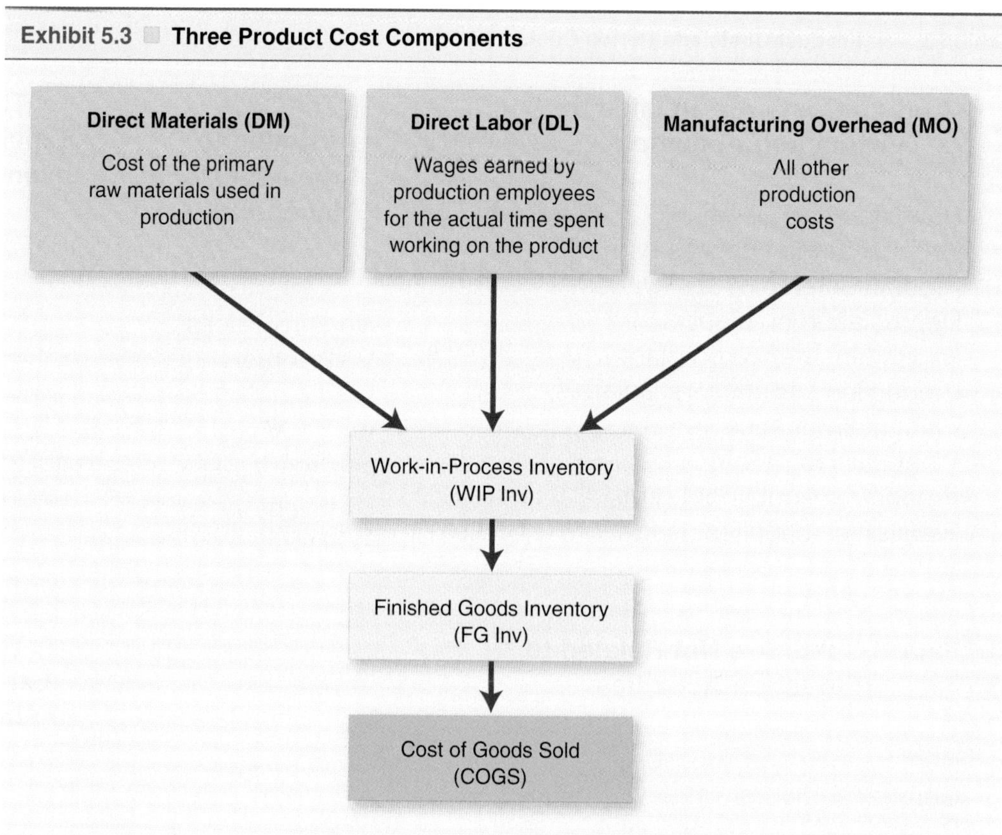

WIP Inv
DM XX | XX
DL XX |
MO XX |

FG Inv
XX | XX

COGS
XX |

A Closer Look at Manufacturing Overhead

The biggest challenge in measuring the cost of a product is determining the amount of overhead incurred to produce it. Direct materials cost is driven by the number of raw materials units used; hence, its cost is simply the number of units of raw materials used multiplied by the related cost per unit. Direct labor cost is driven by the number of directly traceable labor hours worked on the product; so its cost is the number of direct labor hours used times the appropriate rate per hour. But what about manufacturing overhead? Manufacturing overhead often consists of dozens of different cost elements, potentially with many different cost drivers. Electricity cost is based on kilowatt-hours and water cost on gallons used; depreciation is usually measured in years of service and insurance in premium dollars per thousand dollars of coverage; and supervisors' salaries are a fixed amount per month.

Historically, accountants have believed that, even when possible, it is not cost effective to try to separately measure the cost incurred for each manufacturing overhead item to produce a unit of finished product. Instead of identifying separate cost drivers for each individual cost component in manufacturing overhead, all overhead costs for a department or plant are frequently placed in a cost pool and a single unit-level cost driver is used to assign (or apply) overhead to products.

If a company produced only one product, it would be simple to assign (or apply) overhead to the units produced because it would merely involve dividing total manufacturing overhead cost incurred by the number of units produced to get a cost per unit. For example, if total manufacturing overhead costs were $100,000 for a period when 20,000 units of product were produced, the overhead cost assigned to each unit would be $5.

Selecting a Basis (or Cost Driver) for Assigning Overhead

When multiple products are manufactured in the same facilities, using a simple average of manufacturing overhead cost per unit seldom provides a good estimate of the overhead costs incurred to produce each product. Units requiring extensive manufacturing activity will have too little cost assigned to them, while others requiring only a small amount of manufacturing effort will absorb too much cost. In these cases, units of production is not an appropriate cost driver for manufacturing overhead.

To solve this allocation problem, an overhead application base (or cost driver) other than number of units produced is used. The overhead application base selected is typically a unit-level activity that is common to all products and has a causal relationship with the incurrence of overhead costs. For example, *machine hours* may be used to assign manufacturing overhead costs if the *number of machine hours used* is believed to be the primary cause of manufacturing overhead cost incurred.

Using Predetermined Overhead Rates

Although some organizations assign actual manufacturing overhead to products at the end of each period (normally a month), three problems often result from measuring product cost using "actual" manufacturing overhead costs:

1. Actual manufacturing overhead cost may not be known until days or weeks after the end of the period, delaying the calculation of unit product cost.
2. Some costs that are seasonal, such as property taxes, are not incurred each period, thus making the actual cost of a product produced in one month greater than that of another, even though non-seasonal costs may have been identical for both months.
3. When there is a significant amount of fixed manufacturing overhead, the costs assigned to each unit of product will vary from period to period, depending on the overall volume of activity for the period.

To overcome these problems, most firms use a **predetermined manufacturing overhead rate** to assign manufacturing overhead costs to products. A predetermined rate is established at the start of each year by dividing the *predicted overhead costs for the year* by the *predicted volume of activity in the overhead base* for the year. A predetermined manufacturing overhead rate based on direct labor hours is computed as follows:

$$\textbf{Predetermined manufacturing overhead rate per direct labor hour} = \frac{\textbf{Predicted total manufacturing overhead cost for the year}}{\textbf{Predicted total direct labor hours for the year}}$$

If management believes machine hours is the major driver of manufacturing overhead, the denominator should be predicted machine hours.

Using a predetermined manufacturing overhead rate based on direct labor hours, we compute the assignment of overhead to Work-in-Process Inventory as follows:

$$\textbf{Manufacturing overhead applied to Work-in-Process Inventory} = \textbf{Actual direct labor hours} \times \textbf{Predetermined manufacturing overhead rate per direct labor hour}$$

To illustrate, assume that at the beginning of the current year, one of Garmin's plants predicted an activity level of 25,000 direct labor hours with manufacturing overhead totaling \$187,500. Using this information, its predetermined overhead rate per direct labor hour for the year would have been computed as follows:

$$\textbf{Predetermined overhead rate} = \frac{\$187{,}500}{25{,}000 \text{ direct labor hours}}$$

$$= \$7.50 \text{ per direct labor hour}$$

If 2,000 direct labor hours were used in September of this year, the applied overhead for September would be \$15,000, as shown here:

$$2{,}000 \times \$7.50 = \$15{,}000$$

When a predetermined rate is used, monthly variations between actual and applied manufacturing overhead are expected because of the seasonality in costs and the variations in monthly activity. Hence, in some months overhead will be "overapplied" as applied overhead exceeds actual overhead; in other months overhead will be "underapplied" as actual overhead exceeds applied overhead. If the beginning-of-the-year estimates are accurate for annual overhead costs and annual activity, monthly over- and underapplied amounts during the year should offset each other by the end of the year. Later in this chapter, we consider accounting for any over- or underapplied manufacturing overhead balance that may exist at the end of the year.

Changing Cost Structures Affect the Basis of Overhead Application

By using a single overhead rate, we assume that overhead costs are primarily caused by a single cost driver. Historically, a single plantwide overhead application rate based on direct labor hours was widely used when direct labor was the predominant cost factor in production, and manufacturing overhead costs were driven by the utilization of direct labor.

Changes in manufacturing processes have produced major shifts in the composition of conversion costs, resulting in significantly less direct labor and significantly more manufacturing overhead. An example of this shift is the automobile industry where firms such as Ford and Toyota have spent billions of dollars on robotics and other technologies, thereby reducing direct labor in the production process. In many cases, direct labor hours are no longer an appropriate basis for assigning manufacturing costs to products. In others, these changes mean there is no longer a single cost driver that is appropriate for assigning manufacturing overhead to products.

Although some companies continue to use a single manufacturing overhead rate because it is convenient, many companies no longer use this approach. Instead, they have adopted multiple overhead rates based on either major departments or activities within the organization. One method for using multiple overhead rates is activity-based costing, discussed in Chapter 6.

Review 5-2 LO2 — Applying a Predetermined Overhead Rate

Assume that the following predictions were made at the beginning of the year for one of the plants of Milliken & Company:

Total manufacturing overhead for the year	$40,000,000
Total machine hours for the year	3,200,000

Actual results for February were as follows:

Manufacturing overhead	$4,410,000
Machine hours	410,000

Required

a. Determine the predetermined overhead rate per machine hour for the current year.

b. Using the predetermined overhead rate per machine hour, determine the manufacturing overhead applied to Work-in-Process during February.

c. As of February 1, actual overhead was underapplied by $400,000. Determine the cumulative amount of any overapplied or underapplied overhead at the end of February.

Solution on p. 201.

The Production Environment

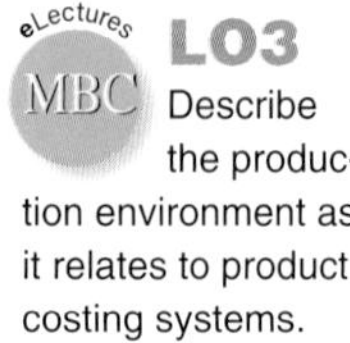

LO3 Describe the production environment as it relates to product costing systems.

Production personnel need to know the specific products to produce on specific machines on a daily or even hourly basis. The detailed scheduling of products on machines is performed by production scheduling personnel. Exactly how production is scheduled depends on whether process manufacturing or job production is used and whether production is in response to a specific customer sales order or for the company's inventory in anticipation of future sales.

In **process manufacturing**, production of identical units is on a *continuous* basis; a production facility may be devoted exclusively to one product or to a set of closely related products. Companies where you would likely find a process manufacturing environment include Exxon Mobil and Procter & Gamble. Process manufacturing is discussed later in this chapter.

In **job production**, also called **job order production**, products are manufactured in single units or in batches of identical units. Examples of single-unit jobs are found at Schumacher Homes, a builder of custom-designed homes, Bechtel Corporation, the largest commercial construction company in the U.S., and Cray Inc. (a subsidiary of Hewlett Packard Enterprise), which manufactures supercomputers. Examples of batches of identical units (multi-unit jobs) are found at True Religion Brand Jeans, a clothing manufacturer, and Herman Miller, a large producer of office chairs including the ergonomic Aeron model. Of course, the specific products included in different jobs or batches may vary considerably.

In a job production environment, when a customer's order is received, the marketing department forwards the order to production scheduling, where employees determine when and how the product is to be produced. Important scheduling considerations include the overall workload, raw materials availability, specific equipment or labor requirements, and the expected delivery date(s) of the finished product.

Important staff groups involved in production planning and control include engineering, scheduling, and accounting. Engineering is primarily concerned with determining how a product should be produced. Based on an engineering analysis and cost data, engineering personnel develop manufacturing specifications for each product. These manufacturing specifications are often summarized in two important documents: a bill of materials and an operations list. Each product's **bill of materials** specifies the kinds and quantities of raw materials required for one unit of product. The **operations list** (sometimes called an **activities list**) specifies the manufacturing operations and related times required for one unit or batch of product. The operations list should also include information on any machine setup time, movements between work areas, and other scheduled activities, such as quality inspections.

Scheduling personnel prepare a production order for each job. The **production order** contains a job's unique identification number and specifies such details as the quantity to be produced, raw materials requirements, manufacturing operations and other activities to be performed, and perhaps even the time when each manufacturing operation should be performed. In preparing a production order, scheduling personnel use the product's bill of materials and operations list to determine the materials, operations, and manufacturing times required for the job.

A **job cost sheet** is a document (usually an electronic document) used to accumulate the costs for a specific job. The job cost sheet serves as the basic record for recording actual progress on the job. As production takes place, the materials, labor, and machine resources utilized are recorded on the job cost sheet along with the related costs. When a job is completed, the final cost of the job is determined by totaling the costs on the job cost sheet.

Production Files and Records

Certain files in the cost system (typically in a computer database) provide the necessary detail for amounts maintained in total in the general ledger. For example, the raw materials inventory file contains separate records for each type of raw materials, indicating increases, decreases, and the available balance for both units and costs. Every time there is a change in the Raw Materials Inventory general ledger account, there must be an equal change in one or more individual inventory records. Therefore, at any given time, the total of the balances in the raw materials inventory file for all raw materials inventory items should equal the balance in the Raw Materials Inventory general ledger account. Because of this relationship between the raw materials inventory file and Raw Materials Inventory in the general ledger, Raw Materials Inventory is called a *control account* and the raw materials file of detailed records is called a *subsidiary ledger*. Other general ledger accounts related to the product cost system that have subsidiary files are Work-in-Process, Finished Goods Inventory, and Cost of Goods Sold.

Other records required to operate a job cost system include production orders, job cost sheets, materials requisition forms, and work tickets. Production orders and job cost sheets were previously discussed. The production order serves as authorization for production supervisors to obtain materials from the storeroom and to issue work orders to production employees, and the job cost sheet accumulates the cost of the job.

A **materials requisition form** indicates the type and quantity of each raw material issued to the factory. This form is used to record the transfer of responsibility for materials and to record materials changes on raw materials and job cost sheet records. The materials requisition form has a place to record the job number; the job cost sheet has a place to record the requisition number. If a question arises regarding the issuance of materials, the requisition number and job number provide a trail for tracing the destination and the source of the materials. The materials requisition form also identifies the materials warehouse employee who issued the materials and the production employee who received them.

A **work ticket** is used to record the time a job spends in a specific manufacturing operation. Each manufacturing operation performed on a job is documented by a work ticket. The completed work tickets for a job should correspond to the operations specified on the job production order. Time information on the work tickets is used by production scheduling or expediting personnel to determine whether the job is on schedule, and to assign costs to the job.

A production operation can involve a single employee, a group of employees, a machine, or even heating, cooling, or aging processes. When the operation involves a single employee, the rate recorded on the work ticket is simply the employee's wage rate. When it involves a group of employees, the rate is composed of the wage rates of all employees in the group. When the work involves a machine operation, the rate includes a charge for machine time, as well as the time of any machine operators. Other operations, such as heating, cooling, or aging, will also have a rate for each unit of time.

Review 5-3 LO3 — Defining Terms in a Production Environment

Which term below (*a–f*) is best associated with the following statements?

a. Process costing
b. Job order costing
c. Production order
d. Job cost sheet
e. Materials requisition
f. Work ticket

___1. Prepared by schedulers to specify the production requirements of a job.
___2. The accounting system most likely used to capture the costs of the production of rolls of paper that are sold as finished goods to print newspaper companies.
___3. Accumulates the costs of the job.
___4. The accounting system used to capture the costs of the production of custom-built boats.
___5. Records the time a job spends in a specific manufacturing operation.
___6. Authorizes the transfer of materials to a job.

Solution on p. 201.

Job Costing for Products and Services

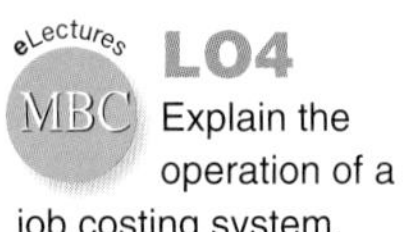

LO4 Explain the operation of a job costing system.

Exhibit 5.4 shows how inventory costs in a manufacturing organization flow in a logical pattern through the financial accounting system. Pay particular attention to the major inventory accounts (Raw Materials, Work-in-Process, and Finished Goods Inventory), Manufacturing Overhead, and the flow of costs through the inventory accounts. Each of the numbered items, representing a cost flow affecting an inventory account or Manufacturing Overhead, is explained here:

1. The costs of purchased raw materials and manufacturing supplies are recorded in Raw Materials and Manufacturing Supplies, respectively. An increase in Accounts Payable typically offsets these increases.

2. As primary raw materials are requisitioned to the factory, direct materials costs are transferred from Raw Materials to Work-in-Process.

3. Direct labor costs are assigned to Work-in-Process on the basis of the time devoted to processing raw materials. Indirect labor costs associated with production employees are initially assigned to Manufacturing Overhead.

4–6. Other indirect production related costs are also assigned to Manufacturing Overhead. Other Payables represents the incurrence of a variety of costs such as repairs and maintenance, utilities, and property taxes.

7. Costs assigned to Manufacturing Overhead are periodically reassigned (applied) to Work-in-Process, preferably with the use of a predetermined overhead rate such as direct labor hours, machine hours, or some other cost assignment base.
8. When products are completed, their accumulated product costs are totaled on a job cost sheet and transferred from Work-in-Process to Finished Goods Inventory.
9. When the completed products are sold, their costs are transferred from Finished Goods Inventory to Cost of Goods Sold.

Exhibit 5.4 Basic Production Cost Flows

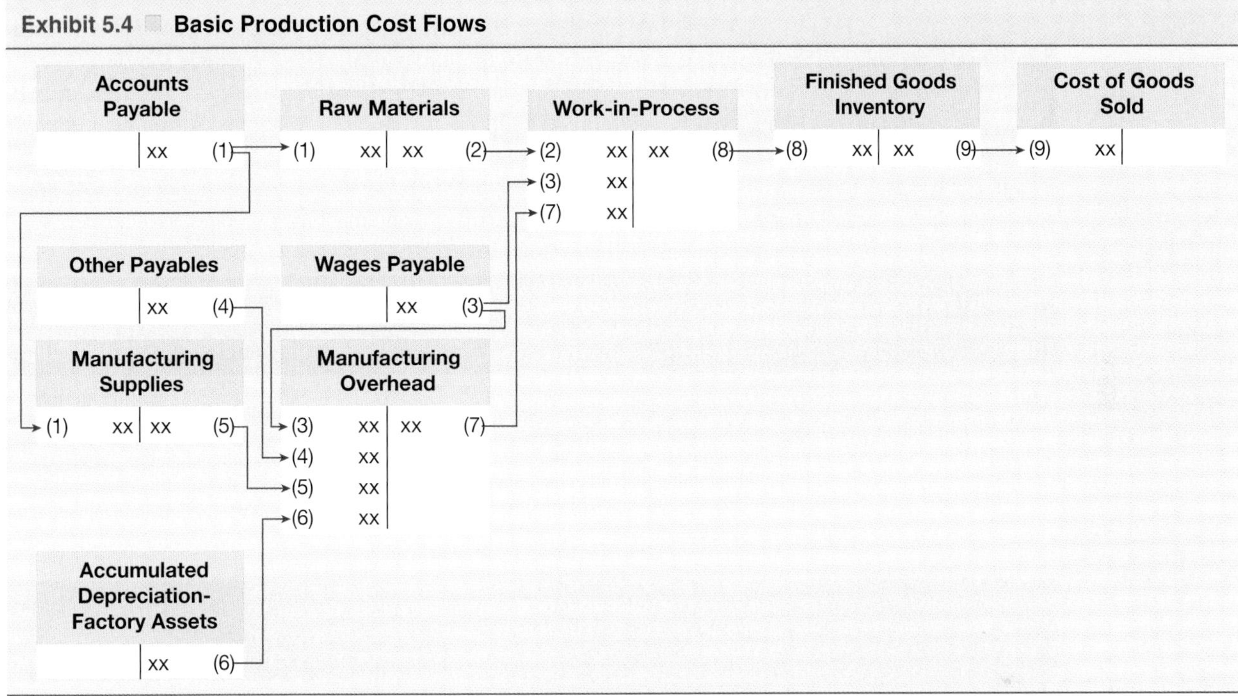

Business Insight ■ Job Costing Illustration

Technological advances have increased product choices for customers. One dimension of product choice that has increased with technology is customization. From custom bicycle brands like Seven Cycles to made-to-order shirts like Proper Cloth, customization is an increasing trend in retail.

Take the fashion brand Frilly. Frilly is a contemporary clothing brand "meant to empower you and encourage you to embrace your own style." Customers can choose a design, then customize it by selecting cuts, fabrics, detailing and more. Frilly claims that operating on a made-to-order model minimizes typical inventory issues that lead to pollution and waste. Of course customization demands a premium, and an accurate measure of costs is critical to any customization scheme. For example, different fabrics must be priced according to their cost, and more intricate stitching may result in upcharges for the customer.

Source: https://www.frilly.com/about-us

Job Costing Illustrated

Even though data are almost always processed with computerized systems, data processing procedures are best illustrated within the context of a paper-based manual system. Consider Frilly featured in the Business Insight box. Because variations in styles cause differences in costs, detailed records are kept concerning the costs assigned to specific jobs. Suppose raw materials consist of outer fabric, liner fabric, and thread.

Assume total inventory on August 1 included Raw Materials, \$71,000; Work-in-Process, \$109,900; and Finished Goods, \$75,000. In addition there were manufacturing supplies of \$1,600, consisting of various items such as thread, needles, sheers, and machine lubricant. The August 1 balance in Manufacturing Overhead was \$0.

Raw Materials			
Description	**Quantity**	**Unit Cost**	**Total Cost**
Fabric	3,000 square yards	$ 20	$60,000
Zippers	100 cases	50	5,000
Buttons	20 cases	150	3,000
Thread	150 spool sets	20	3,000
Total			$71,000

Manufacturing Supplies	
Item	**Total Cost**
Various	$1,600

Work-in-Process	
Job	**Total Cost**
425	$ 58,600
426	51,300
Total	$109,900

Finished Goods Inventory	
Job	**Total Cost**
424	$75,000

To illustrate manufacturing cost flows in a job cost system, "T" accounts are presented in the margin for the cost system transactions for Frilly, for August. Each cost assignment is supported by documented information that is recorded in subsidiary cost system records. The hypothetical manufacturing cost transactions for Frilly for August are discussed here. The numbered jobs combine orders that share the same style choices.

RM Inv

	Debit	Credit	
BB	71,000		
(1)	30,000		

Mfg. Supplies

	Debit	Credit	
BB	1,600		
(1)	1,000		

Accounts Payable

	Debit	Credit	
		31,000	(1)

1. Raw materials and manufacturing supplies are purchased on account. The vendor's invoice totals $31,000, including $1,000 of manufacturing supplies and $30,000 of raw materials. The cost of the raw materials must be assigned to specific raw materials inventory records:

Fabric	850 square yards	× $ 20 =	$17,000
Zippers	140 cases	× $ 50 =	7,000
Buttons	40 cases	× $150 =	6,000
Total			$30,000

WIP Inv

	Debit	Credit	
BB	109,900		
(2)	54,300		

RM Inv

	Debit	Credit	
BB	71,000	54,300	(2)
(1)	30,000		

2. Materials needed to complete Jobs 425 and 426 are requisitioned. Two new jobs, 427 and 428, were also started and direct materials were requisitioned for them. A total of $54,300 of raw materials was requisitioned:

	Job 425	Job 426	Job 427	Job 428	Total
Fabric					
975 sq. yds. × $20			$19,500		$19,500
955 sq. yds. × $20				$19,100	19,100
Zippers					
52 cases × $50	$2,600				2,600
30 cases × $50		$1,500			1,500
43 cases × $50			2,150		2,150
20 cases × $50				1,000	1,000
Buttons					
12 cases × $150	1,800				1,800
12 cases × $150		1,800			1,800
11 cases × $150			1,650		1,650
14 cases × $150				2,100	2,100
Thread					
20 spool sets × $20	400				400
15 spool sets × $20		300			300
10 spool sets × $20			200		200
10 spool sets × $20				200	200
Total	$4,800	$3,600	$23,500	$22,400	$54,300

3. Assume the August payroll liability was $41,650, including $34,450 for direct labor and $7,200 for indirect labor. Direct labor was assigned to the jobs as follows:

WIP Inv	Debit	Credit
BB	109,900	
(2)	54,300	
(3)	34,450	

MO	Debit	Credit
BB	–0–	
(3)	7,200	

Wages Payable	Debit	Credit
		41,650 (3)

	Job 425	Job 426	Job 427	Job 428	Total
Direct labor hours	600	900	1,000	945	
Direct labor rate	× $10	× $10	× $10	× $10	
Total	$6,000	$9,000	$10,000	$9,450	$34,450

Note: The $7,200 of indirect labor costs is assigned to products as part of applied overhead.

4–6. In addition to indirect labor, suppose Frilly incurred the following manufacturing overhead costs:

MO	Debit	Credit
BB	–0–	
(3)	7,200	
(4)	950	
(5)	2,400	
(6)	3,230	

Manufacturing Supplies	$ 950
Accumulated Depreciation—Factory Assets	2,400
Miscellaneous (Other Payables)	3,230

Mfg Supplies	Debit	Credit
BB	1,600	950 (4)
(1)	1,000	

Accum. Depr	Debit	Credit
		2,400 (5)

7. Assume manufacturing overhead is applied to jobs using a predetermined rate of $4 per direct labor hour. Assignments to individual jobs are as follows:

Other Payables	Debit	Credit
		3,230 (6)

	Job 425	Job 426	Job 427	Job 428	Total
Labor hours	600	900	1,000	945	
Overhead rate per labor hour	× $4	× $4	× $4	× $4	
Total	$2,400	$3,600	$4,000	$3,780	$13,780

MO	Debit	Credit
BB	-0-	13,780 (7)
(3)	7,200	
(4)	950	
(5)	2,400	
(6)	3,230	

WIP Inv	Debit	Credit
BB	109,900	
(2)	54,300	
(3)	34,450	
(7)	13,780	

8. Jobs 425, 426, and 427 are completed with the following costs:

	Job 425	Job 426	Job 427	Total
Beginning balance	$58,600	$51,300	$ 0	$109,900
Current costs				
Direct materials (entry 2)	4,800	3,600	23,500	31,900
Direct labor (entry 3)	6,000	9,000	10,000	25,000
Applied overhead (entry 7)	2,400	3,600	4,000	10,000
Total	$71,800	$67,500	$37,500	$176,800

FG Inv	Debit	Credit
BB	75,000	
(8)	176,800	

WIP Inv	Debit	Credit
BB	109,900	176,800 (8)
(2)	54,300	
(3)	34,450	
(7)	13,780	

Additional analysis for the completed jobs indicates the following:

	Job 425	Job 426	Job 427
Total cost of job	$71,800	$67,500	$37,500
Units in job	÷ 1,200	÷ 900	÷ 500
Unit cost	$ 59.83	$ 75.00	$ 75.00

COGS	
(9) 214,300	

FG Inv	
BB 75,000	214,300 (9)
(8) 176,800	

9. Jobs 424, 425, and 426 are delivered to customers for a sales price of $400,000. Determining the costs transferred from Finished Goods Inventory to Cost of Goods Sold requires summing the total cost of jobs sold:

Job 424	$ 75,000
Job 425	71,800
Job 426	67,500
Total	$214,300

At this point we can determine the gross profit on the completed jobs:

Sales	$400,000
Cost of goods sold	(214,300)
Gross profit	$185,700

If inventory were produced in anticipation of future sales rather than in response to specific customer orders, it is likely that not all units in a job would be sold at the same time. In this case, the unit cost information is used to determine the amount transferred from Finished Goods Inventory to Cost of Goods Sold.

Exhibit 5.5 shows the cost system records supporting the ending balances in the major inventory accounts and Cost of Goods Sold. Note the importance of the job cost sheets for determining cost transfers affecting Work-in-Process and Finished Goods Inventory. The job cost sheets are also used in determining the ending balances of these accounts.

Frilly's product costing system is adequate for determining the cost for each job for purposes of valuing ending inventories and cost of goods sold in its external financial statements. The costing system recognizes the differences in materials costs by carefully tracking each type of material as a separate cost pool. Assuming all direct labor employees are paid the same rate, it is necessary to maintain only one labor cost pool. Although there are three distinct operations in making clothing (cutting, sewing, and finishing), the various styles likely require the same proportionate times on each operation. Hence, even with only one plantwide manufacturing overhead cost pool applied on the basis of direct labor hours, individual product costs are reasonably accurate.

Although Frilly's assumed costing system may be adequate for inventory costing for financial statement purposes, the data it routinely generates will not provide management with information for many management decisions. To evaluate product or customer profitability, management needs additional information concerning marketing, distributing, selling, and customer service costs, which are not included in the product cost system. The following Business Insight illustrates the importance of distribution costs in decision making at Coca-Cola.

Furthermore, the cost system does not provide information for decisions concerning individual operations, such as cutting. To answer questions regarding how best to perform operations, Frilly's accountants should perform a special cost study to obtain relevant activity-cost information.

Exhibit 5.5 General Ledger Accounts and Subsidiary Records for Inventory Categories and Cost of Goods Sold

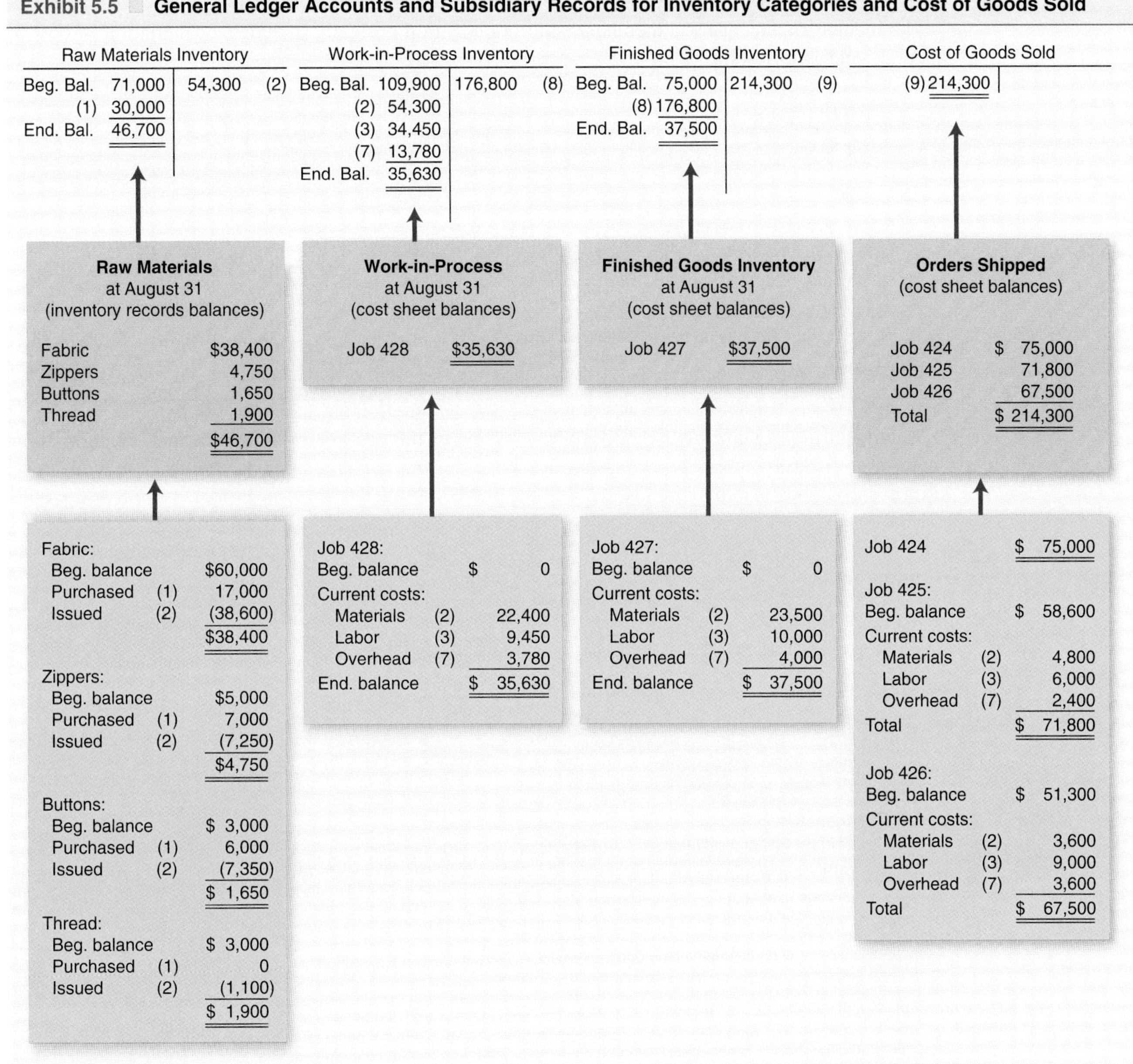

Business Insight ■ Coca-Cola Sheds Shipping and Production to Focus on Sales and Marketing

For a global brand like Coca-Cola, distribution costs can become quite large and can distract the company from its core business. Coca-Cola has announced that it is overhauling its U.S. supply chain by selling both production and distribution portions of the business to partner companies. Coca-Cola will focus on selling and marketing drink concentrate to production partners and bottlers.

This trend seems to be meaningful enough for logistics and distribution businesses to take note. FedEx and UPS have both announced acquisitions of logistics firms that offer supply chain tasks traditionally done in-house, such as processing returns and other distribution. In fact, Coyote Logistics, which UPS purchased in 2015, arranges shipping for 12,000 firms including beverage giant Heineken.

Sources: Mike Esterl, "Coke Plans to Sell Nine U.S. Production Plants," *Wall Street Journal*, September 24, 2015; Laura Stevens, "FedEx Pays $1.4 Billion for GENCO," *Wall Street Journal*, March 19, 2015; and Laura Stevens, "UPS Agrees to Buy Coyote Logistics for $1.8 Billion," *Wall Street Journal*, July 31, 2015.

Statement of Cost of Goods Manufactured

The income statement for a merchandising organization normally includes a calculation of cost of goods sold as follows:

Sales		$X,XXX
Less cost of goods sold		
Beginning inventory	$X,XXX	
Plus purchases	X,XXX	
Goods available for sale	X,XXX	
Less ending inventory	(X,XXX)	
Cost of goods sold		(X,XXX)
Gross profit		X,XXX
Less selling and administrative expenses		(X,XXX)
Net income		$X,XXX

Manufacturing organizations modify only one line of this income statement format, changing purchases to cost of goods manufactured. Since a manufacturer acquires finished goods from the factory, its cost of goods manufactured is the total cost transferred from Work-in-Process to Finished Goods Inventory during the period.

For internal reporting purposes, most companies prepare a separate **statement of cost of goods manufactured**, which summarizes the cost of goods completed and transferred into Finished Goods Inventory during the period. A hypothetical statement of cost of goods manufactured and an income statement for Frilly are presented in **Exhibit 5.6** for August.

Exhibit 5.6 Statement of Cost of Goods Manufactured and Income Statement

FRILLY
Statement of Cost of Goods Manufactured
August

Current manufacturing costs			
Cost of materials placed in production			
Raw materials, 8/1	$ 71,000		
Purchases	30,000		
Total available	101,000		
Raw materials, 8/31	(46,700)	$ 54,300	
Direct labor		34,450	
Manufacturing overhead		13,780	$102,530
Work-in-process, 8/1			109,900
Total costs in process			212,430
Work-in-process, 8/31			(35,630)
Cost of goods manufactured			$176,800

FRILLY
Income Statement
August

Sales		$400,000
Cost of goods sold		
Finished goods inventory, 8/1	$ 75,000	
Cost of goods manufactured	176,800	
Total goods available for sale	251,800	
Finished goods inventory, 8/31	(37,500)	214,300
Gross profit		185,700
Selling and administrative expenses*		(90,000)
Net income		$ 95,700

* Selling and administrative expenses for Frilly are assumed to be $90,000.

Overapplied and Underapplied Overhead

In the Frilly example, assume that the predetermined manufacturing overhead rate of $4 per direct labor hour was based on predicted manufacturing overhead for the year of $100,000 and predicted direct labor hours of 25,000. Assume further that it was determined that the company actually incurred $100,000 in manufacturing overhead during the year and that actual direct labor hours for the year were 25,000, resulting in applied overhead of $100,000 (25,000 hours × $4). The activity in Manufacturing Overhead is summarized as follows:

Manufacturing Overhead	
Beginning balance	$ 0
Actual overhead	100,000
Total	100,000
Applied overhead	(100,000)
Ending balance	$ 0

With identical amounts of actual and applied overhead, the ending balance in Manufacturing Overhead is zero. However, if either the actual overhead cost or the actual level of the production activity base differed from its predicted value, there would be a balance in Manufacturing Overhead representing overapplied or underapplied overhead.

Assume, for example, that the prediction of 25,000 direct labor hours was correct but that actual overhead cost was $105,000. In this case, Manufacturing Overhead shows a $5,000 positive balance, representing underapplied manufacturing overhead:

Manufacturing Overhead	
Beginning balance	$ 0
Actual overhead	105,000
Total	105,000
Applied overhead	(100,000)
Ending balance	$ 5,000*

* Underapplied; actual exceeds applied.

If actual manufacturing overhead were only $98,000, Manufacturing Overhead would be overapplied and show a $2,000 negative balance.

If the *prediction* of total manufacturing overhead cost is not accurate, there will be an underapplied or overapplied balance in Manufacturing Overhead at the end of the year. A similar result occurs when the *predicted* activity level used in computing the predetermined rate differs from the actual activity level. It is not uncommon for such differences to occur. Predictions are exactly that—predictions.

Month-to-month balances in Manufacturing Overhead are usually allowed to accumulate during the year. In the absence of evidence to the contrary, it is assumed that such differences result from seasonal variations in production or costs or both. However, any year-end balance in Manufacturing Overhead must be eliminated.

Theoretically, the disposition of any year-end balance in Manufacturing Overhead should be accomplished in a manner that adjusts every account to what its balance would have been if an actual, rather than a predetermined, overhead rate had been used. This involves adjusting the ending balances in Work-in-Process, Finished Goods Inventory, and Cost of Goods Sold. Procedures to do this are examined in cost accounting textbooks.

In most situations, the simple procedure of treating the remaining overhead as an adjustment to Cost of Goods Sold is adequate. Unless there are large ending balances in inventories and a large year-end balance in Manufacturing Overhead, this simple procedure produces acceptable results. Underapplied overhead indicates that the assigned costs are less than the actual costs, understating Cost of Goods Sold. Hence, disposing of an underapplied balance in Manufacturing Overhead increases the balance in Cost of Goods Sold.

Manufacturing Overhead		
Beginning balance	$ 0	
Actual overhead	105,000	
Total	105,000	
Applied overhead	(100,000)	
Ending balance	$ 5,000*	← Increase Cost of Goods Sold

* Underapplied; actual exceeds applied.

Conversely, overapplied overhead indicates that the assigned costs are more than the actual costs, overstating Cost of Goods Sold. Hence, disposing of an overapplied balance in Manufacturing Overhead decreases Cost of Goods Sold.

Job Costing in Service Organizations

Service costing, the assignment of costs to services performed, uses job costing concepts to determine the cost of filling customer service orders in organizations such as automobile repair shops, charter airlines, CPA firms, hospitals, and law firms. Many of these organizations bill clients on the basis of resources consumed. Consequently, they maintain detailed records for billing purposes. On the invoice sent to the client, the organization itemizes any materials consumed on the job at a selling price per unit, the labor hours worked on the job at a billing rate per hour, and the time special facilities were used at a billing rate per unit of time. Employees with different capabilities and experience often have different billing rates. In a CPA firm, for example, a partner or a senior manager has a higher billing rate than a staff accountant.

The prices and rates must be high enough to cover costs not assigned to specific jobs and to provide for a profit. To evaluate the contribution to common costs and profit from a job, a comparison must be made between the price charged the customer and the actual cost of the job. This is easily done when the actual cost of resources itemized on the customer's invoice is presented on a job cost sheet. A CPA firm, for example, should accumulate the actual hardware and software costs incurred in an accounting system installation for a client, along with the actual wages earned by employees while working on the job and any related travel costs. Comparing the total of these costs with the price charged, the client indicates the total contribution of the job to common costs and profit.

Although service organizations may identify costs with individual jobs for management accounting purposes, there is considerable variation in the way job cost information is presented in financial statements. Some organizations report the cost of jobs completed in their income statements using an account such as Cost of Services Provided. They use procedures similar to those outlined in **Exhibit 5.6**; the only major change involves replacing Cost of Goods Sold with Cost of Services Provided.

Business Insight ■ The Versatility of Job Costing—A Perfect Fit for Designers

FNDR, an adviser to startups, helps entrepreneurs identify their values and beliefs through a series of meetings. "The result is an 'intentional narrative' that can guide future decisions." The company worked with the founder of Iris, a company that has developed software that makes sound more immersive and has plans to release meditation apps, synthesize its narrative into two words, 'Listen well' that have become part of their brand design.

A new approach to focus groups was developed by Juliet, a Toronto-based agency. Instead of using groups to evaluate an already developed advertising campaign, Juliet assembles a group of people with strong interests in or connections to a product a client wants to promote. An advertising campaign is then developed using input from the focus group. Juliet's "Real Talk" process has been used successfully by a subsidiary of Signet Jewelers to increase sales of engagement rings to male customers.

By tracking resources to jobs, these firms have the flexibility to accurately adapt the costing system to the structure of the work being done for the client.

Sources: Stephanie Mehta, "How Brand Consultancy FNDR Helps Companies Such as Snap and Glossier Find Their Voices," *Fast Company*, December 16, 2019. Jeff Beer, "This Ad Agency Uses a Casting Agent to Create the Focus Group of the Future," *Fast Company*, November 5, 2019.

More often, however, service organizations do not formally establish detailed procedures to trace the flow of service costs. Instead, service job costs are left in their original cost categories such as materials expense, salaries and wages expense, travel expense, and so forth. Because all service costs are typically regarded as expenses rather than product costs, either procedure is acceptable for financial reporting. Regardless of the formal treatment of service costs in financial accounting records and statements, the managers of a well-run service organization need information regarding job cost and contribution. The previous Business Insight considers the importance of accurate cost estimation by service firms that focus on providing unique and customized service to each client.

All preceding examples of service costing involve situations in which the order is filled in response to a specific customer request. Job order costing can also be used to determine the cost of making services available even when the names of specific customers are not known in advance and the service is being provided on a speculative basis. A regularly scheduled airline flight, for example, could be regarded as a job. Management is interested in knowing the cost of the job in order to determine its profitability. This is but another example of the versatility of job order costing.

Managerial Decision ■ You Are the Chief Financial Officer

You have asked the accounting staff to provide you with cost information on each of the products manufactured by your company so you can conduct profitability analysis on each product. Accounting provided you with the costs that are used in the company's external financial statements. What additional information are you going to need before you can conduct a complete profitability analysis? [Answer p. 183]

Accounting for Costs of Jobs in a Job Costing System — LO4 Review 5-4

Stratasys, Ltd. is a manufacturer of 3D production systems. Assume that the company has a division that does custom prototypes for large clients. Production costs are accounted for using a job cost system. Suppose that at the beginning of June raw materials inventories totaled $7,000; manufacturing supplies amounted to $800; two jobs were in process—Job 225 with assigned costs of $13,750, and Job 226 with assigned costs of $1,800—and there were no finished goods inventories. There was no underapplied or overapplied manufacturing overhead on June 1. The following information summarized June manufacturing activities:

- Purchased raw materials costing $40,000 on account.
- Purchased manufacturing supplies costing $9,000 on account.
- Requisitioned materials needed to complete Job 226. Started two new jobs, 227 and 228, and requisitioned direct materials for them as follows:

Job 226	$ 2,600
Job 227	18,000
Job 228	14,400
Total	$35,000

- Incurred June salaries and wages as follows:

Job 225 (500 hours × $10 per hour)	$ 5,000
Job 226 (1,500 hours × $10 per hour)	15,000
Job 227 (2,050 hours × $10 per hour)	20,500
Job 228 (800 hours × $10 per hour)	8,000
Total direct labor	48,500
Indirect labor	5,000
Total	$53,500

continued

continued from previous page

- Used manufacturing supplies costing $5,500.
- Recognized depreciation on factory fixed assets of $5,000.
- Incurred miscellaneous manufacturing overhead cost of $10,750 on account.
- Applied manufacturing overhead at the rate of $5 per direct labor hour.
- Completed Jobs 225, 226, and 227.
- Delivered Jobs 225 and 226 to customers.

Required

a. Prepare "T" accounts showing the flow of costs through the Work-in-Process, Finished Goods, and Cost of Goods Sold accounts.

b. Show the job cost details to support the June 30 balances in Work-in-Process, Finished Goods, and Cost of Goods Sold.

c. Prepare a statement of cost of goods manufactured for June.

Solution on p. 201.

Process Costing

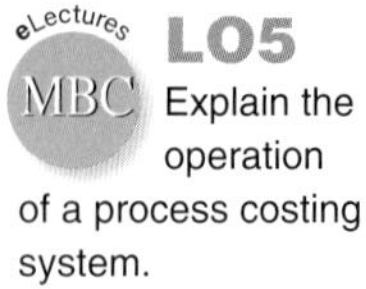

LO5 Explain the operation of a process costing system.

A job costing system works well when products are made one at a time (building houses) or in batches of identical items (making blue jeans). However, if products are produced in a continuous manufacturing environment, where production does not have a distinct beginning and ending (refining fossil fuels such as gasoline or diesel, for example), companies usually use a process costing system.

In job costing, the unit cost is the total cost of the "job" divided by the units produced in the job. Costs are accumulated for each job on a job cost sheet, and those costs remain in Work-in-Process until the job is completed, regardless of how long the job is in progress. A multiple-unit job is not considered completed until all units in the job are finished. The cost is not determined until the job is completed, which will not necessarily coincide with the end of an accounting period. Large jobs (such as construction projects) and jobs started near the end of the period frequently overlap two or more accounting periods.

In process costing, the cost of a single unit is equal to the total product costs assigned to a "process" or "department" during the accounting period (frequently a month) divided by the number of units produced. Since goods in the beginning and ending work-in-process inventory are only partially processed during the period, it is necessary to determine the total production for the period in terms of the equivalent number of completed units. For example, if 300 units were started but were only 40% completed during the period, then the equivalent of 120 fully completed units (300 units × 0.40) was produced. The average cost per unit is computed as total product costs divided by the number of equivalent units produced.

A good example of a process costing environment involving continuous production is the soft drink bottling process. At Coca-Cola's bottling facility in Wakefield, England, more than 4,000 twelve-ounce cans and 3,200 varying sized bottles of Coca-Cola can be produced each minute in a continuous process. The process adds the ingredients (concentrate syrup, water, sweetener, and the carbonation agent) at various points in the process.

In a job cost system, job cost sheets are used to collect cost information for each and every job. In a process costing system, cost accumulation requires fewer records because each department's production is treated as the only job worked on during the period. In a department that has just one manufacturing process, process costing is particularly straightforward because the Work-in-Process account is, in effect, the departmental cost record. If a department has more than one manufacturing process, separate records should be maintained for each process.

Business Insight ■ 3D Printing Builds Customization into the Production Process

Breakthroughs in technology are making customization available to the masses with customization built in as part of the production process. In the past, bespoke (custom-made) suit makers and automakers often had a lot in common. There was a time when automakers like Bugatti, Duesenberg, and Roller would build custom automobiles as personalized as any suit from Savile Row, a renowned street in London with custom-tailored suit offerings. The customer paid a lot of money and the producer made the product substantially to order. Skilled craftsmen were tasked with producing the customizations one job at a time. Cost management in the presence of dramatic customization was only possible through job costing.

3D printing and other new technology has made customization less costly, and brings changes to cost management. The custom knit wear manufacturer Unmade uses proprietary software and programmable machines to produce unique sweaters and scarves for clients. While each garment is unique, the variation in cost due to customization is largely captured by conventional drivers like direct materials (yarn), direct labor (programming), and machine hours. In addition, this business model saves costs by allowing Unmade to hold very little inventory while still delivering to the customer within 10 days. Similar changes have come to auto manufacturing. Daihatsu Copen, a Toyota subsidiary, uses 3D printing to allow customers to customize portions of their cars. Local Motors, an Arizona automaker, is more aggressive in its use of 3D printing. Olli, its self-driving shuttle, is 80% 3D printed and holds eight seated passengers.

Sources: Michael Pooler, "Makers Follow the Techies to Create a 'Nurture' Space of Their Own," *Financial Times*, December 17, 2015; and "Print My Ride," *Economist*, June 23, 2016.

Cost of Production Report

To illustrate process costing procedures, consider Intel, which manufactures memory chips for microcomputers using sophisticated machinery. Assume each finished unit requires one unit of raw materials added at the beginning of the manufacturing process. Hypothetical production and cost data for the month of July for Intel are as follows:

July Production Data	
Units in process, beginning of period (75% converted)	4,000
Units started	36,000
Completed and transferred to finished goods	35,000
Units in process, end of period (20% converted)	5,000

July Cost Data		
Beginning work-in-process		
Materials costs		$ 16,000
Conversion costs		9,000
Total		$ 25,000
Current manufacturing costs		
Direct materials (36,000 × $4)		$144,000
Conversion costs		
Direct labor	$62,200	
Manufacturing overhead applied	46,700	108,900
Total		$252,900

Developing a cost of production report is a useful way of organizing and accounting for costs in a process costing environment. A **cost of production report**, which summarizes unit and cost data for each department or process for each period, consists of the following sections:

- Summary of units in process
- Equivalent units
- Total cost to be accounted for and cost per equivalent unit
- Accounting for total costs

The cost of production report for Intel is shown in **Exhibit 5.7**, and its four sections are discussed next.

Exhibit 5.7 Cost of Production Report for Process Costing

INTEL
Cost of Production Report
For the Month Ending July 31

Summary of units in process	
Beginning	4,000
Units started	36,000
In process	40,000
Completed	(35,000)
Ending	5,000

Equivalent units in process	Materials	Conversion
Units completed	35,000	35,000
Plus equivalent units in ending inventory	5,000	1,000*
Equivalent units in process	40,000	36,000

Total cost to be accounted for and cost per equivalent unit in process	Materials	Conversion	Total
Beginning work-in-process	$ 16,000	$ 9,000	$ 25,000
Current cost	144,000	108,900**	252,900
Total cost in process	$160,000	$117,900	$277,900
Equivalent units in process	÷ 40,000	÷ 36,000	
Cost per equivalent unit in process	$ 4.00	$ 3.275	$ 7.275
Accounting for total costs			
Transferred out (35,000 × $7.275)			$254,625
Ending work-in-process			
Materials (5,000 × $4.00)		$20,000	
Conversion (1,000 × $3.275)		3,275	23,275
Total cost accounted for			$277,900

* 5,000 units, 20% converted
** Includes direct labor of $62,200 and applied manufacturing overhead of $46,700

Summary of Units in Process

This section of the cost of production report provides a summary of all units in the department during the period—both from an input and an output perspective—regardless of their stage of completion. From an input perspective, total units in process during the period consisted of the following:

- Units in process at the beginning of the period, **plus**
- Units started during the period.

From an output perspective, these units in process during the period were either

- Completed and transferred out of the department, **or**
- Still on hand at the end of the period.

In the summary of units in process, all units are treated the same, regardless of the amount of processing that took place on them during the period. The objective here is to account for all discrete units of product in process at any time during the period. In the summary of units in process in Exhibit 5.7, suppose 40,000 individual units were in process, including 4,000 partially completed units in the beginning inventory and 36,000 new units started during the month. During the period, 35,000 units were completed, and the remaining 5,000 were still in process at the end of the month.

Equivalent Units in Process

This section of the report translates the number of units in process during the period into equivalent completed units of production. The term **equivalent completed units** refers to the number of completed units that is equal, in terms of production effort, to a given number of partially completed units. For example, 80 units for which 50% of the expected total processing cost has been incurred is the equivalent of 40 completed units (80 × 0.50).

Frequently, direct materials costs are incurred largely, if not entirely, at the beginning of the process, whereas direct labor and manufacturing overhead costs are added throughout the production process. If direct labor and manufacturing overhead costs are added to the process simultaneously, it is common to treat them jointly as conversion costs. Assume Intel adds all materials at the beginning of the process; all conversion costs are added evenly throughout the process. Therefore, separate computations are made for equivalent units of materials and equivalent units of conversion. Although the department worked on 40,000 units during the period, the total number of equivalent units in process with respect to conversion costs was only 36,000 units, consisting of 35,000 finished units plus 1,000 equivalent units in ending inventory (5,000 units 20% converted). Because all materials are added at the start of the process, 40,000 equivalent units (35,000 finished and 5,000 in process) were in process during the period with respect to materials costs.

Total Cost to Be Accounted for and Cost per Equivalent Unit in Process

This section of the report summarizes total costs in Work-in-Process during the period and calculates the cost per equivalent unit for materials, conversion, and in total. Total cost consists of the beginning Work-in-Process balance (if any) plus current costs incurred. For our Intel example, the total cost to be accounted for during July was $277,900, consisting of $25,000 in Work-in-Process at the beginning of the period plus current costs of $252,900 incurred in July. **Exhibit 5.7** shows these amounts broken down between materials costs and conversion costs.

To compute cost per equivalent unit, total cost in process is divided by the equivalent units in process. This is done separately for materials cost and conversion cost. The total cost per equivalent unit is the sum of the unit costs for materials and conversion. Because the number of equivalent units in process was different for materials and conversion, it is not possible to get the total cost per unit by dividing total costs of $277,900 by some equivalent unit amount.

Accounting for Total Costs

This section shows the disposition of the total costs in process during the period divided between units completed (and sent to finished goods) and units still in process at the end of the period. As noted in the previous section, total cost in process is $277,900 and each equivalent unit in process has $4.00 of materials cost and $3.275 of conversion costs for a total of $7.275.

The first step in assigning total costs is to calculate the cost of units transferred out by multiplying the units completed during the period by the total cost per unit (35,000 units × $7.275). This assigns $254,625 of the total cost to units transferred out, leaving $23,275 ($277,900 – $254,625) to be assigned to ending Work-in-Process. To verify that $23,275 is the correct amount of cost remaining in ending Work-in-Process, the materials and conversion costs in ending Work-in-Process are calculated separately. Recall that the 5,000 units in process at the end of the period are 100% completed with materials costs, but only 20% completed with conversion costs. Therefore, in ending Work-in-Process, the materials cost component is $20,000 (5,000 × 1.00 × $4.00), the conversion cost component is $3,275 (5,000 × 0.20 × $3.275), and the total cost of ending Work-in-Process is $23,275 ($20,000 + $3,275).

The cost of production report summarizes manufacturing costs assigned to Work-in-Process during the period and provides information for determining the transfer of costs from Work-in-Process to Finished Goods Inventory. The supporting documents are similar to those previously illustrated for job costing, except that the single cost of production report replaces all the job cost sheets that flow through a department or process. The flow of costs through Work-in-Process is as follows:

Work-in-Process		
Beginning balance		$ 25,000
Current manufacturing costs		
Direct materials	$144,000	
Direct labor	62,200	
Applied overhead	46,700	252,900
Total		277,900
Cost of goods manufactured		(254,625)
Ending balance		$ 23,275

The reduction in Work-in-Process for the units completed during the period is determined in the cost of production report (see **Exhibit 5.7**). This amount is transferred to Finished Goods Inventory. The $23,275 ending balance in Work-in-Process is also determined in the cost of production report as the amount assigned to units in ending Work-in-Process.

Weighted Average and First-In, First-Out Process Costing

Because the costs of materials, labor, and overhead are constantly changing, unit costs are seldom exactly the same from period to period. Hence, if a unit is manufactured partially in one period and partially in the following period, its actual cost is seldom equal to the unit cost of units produced in either period.

In the cost of production report in **Exhibit 5.7**, we made no attempt to account separately for the completed units that came from beginning inventory and those that were started during the current period. The method illustrated in **Exhibit 5.7** is called the **weighted average method**, and it simply spreads the combined beginning inventory cost and current manufacturing costs (for materials, labor, and overhead) over the units completed and those in ending inventory on an average basis. For example, the total cost in process for conversion ($117,900) included both beginning inventory cost and current costs; the 36,000 equivalent units in process for conversion included both units from beginning inventory and units started during the current period. Hence, the average cost per unit of $3.275 (or $117,900 ÷ 36,000) is a weighted average cost of the partially completed units in beginning inventory (prior period costs) and units started during the current period. It is not a precise cost per unit for the current period's production activity but an average cost that includes the cost of partially completed units in beginning inventory carried over from the previous period.

An alternative, more precise process costing method is the **first-in, first-out (FIFO) method**. It accounts for unit costs of beginning inventory units separately from those started during the current period. Under this method, the first costs incurred each period are assumed to have been used to complete the unfinished units carried over from the previous period. Hence, the cost of the beginning inventory is partially based on the prior period's unit costs and partially based on the current period's unit costs.

If unit costs are changing from period to period and beginning inventories are large in relation to total production for the period, the FIFO method is more accurate. However, with the current trend toward smaller inventories, the additional effort and cost of the FIFO method may not be justified. Detailed coverage of the FIFO method is included in cost accounting textbooks. Unless stated otherwise, weighted average process costing is used in chapter assignments.

Process Costing in Service Organizations

There are many applications of process costing for service organizations. Process costing in service organizations is similar to that in manufacturing organizations, the primary purpose being to assign costs to cost objects. Generally, the use of process costing techniques for service organizations is easier than for manufacturing organizations because the raw materials element is not necessary. The applications for the labor and overhead costs are similar, if not identical, to those of a manufacturing firm.

Process costing for services is similar to job costing for batches in that an average cost for similar or identical services is determined. There are important differences, though, between batch and process costing. In a batch environment, a discrete group of services is identified, but in a process environment, services are performed on a continuous basis. Batch costing accumulates the cost for a specific group of services as the batch moves through the various activities that make up the service. Process service costing measures the average cost of identical or similar services performed each period (each month) in a department. An example of batch service costing is determining the cost of registering a student at your college during the fall term registration period; an example of process service costing is determining the cost each month of processing a check by a bank. If continuously performed services involved multiple processes, the total cost of the service would be the sum of the costs for each process.

After it is determined that process costing would be appropriate for a service activity, the actual decision to use it is generally contingent on two important factors about the items being evaluated. First, is average cost per unit acceptable as an input item to the decision process? For some activities, the answer is obvious. For instance, tracking the actual cost of processing each check through a bank would probably not be as useful as determining the average cost of processing checks for a given period; therefore, average cost is acceptable. For other activities, the answer is more difficult to determine. Should the decision model include average cost per patient-day or actual cost per individual patient?

The second issue relates to the benefits versus the costs of the resulting information. Normally, it is easier to track and record the cost of an activity or process than it is to track and record the cost of each individual item in the activity. Often actual cost tracking is impossible for practical reasons (the actual cost of processing a check through a banking system, for example). Although process costing will not work in every situation, it has many applications in service organizations. As illustrated in this text, there are many possibilities for applying either job or process costing to activities in service organizations.

Accounting for Costs in a Process Costing System — LO5 Review 5-5

Guided Examples MBC

SanDisk manufactures USB flash drives that are used in computing. Since there is little product differentiation between SanDisk's products, assume it uses a process costing system to determine inventory costs and that production and manufacturing cost data for one year are as follows:

Production Data (units)	
Units in process, beginning of period (60% converted)	3,000,000
Units started	27,000,000
Completed and transferred to finished goods	25,000,000
Units in process, end of period (30% converted)	5,000,000

Manufacturing Costs	
Work-in-Process, beginning of period (materials, $468,000; conversion, $252,000)	$ 720,000
Current manufacturing costs	
Raw materials transferred to processing	6,132,000
Direct labor for the period	1,550,000
Overhead applied for the period	3,498,000

Required

Prepare a cost of production report for SanDisk for the year.

Solution on p. 203.

Appendix 5A: Absorption and Variable Costing

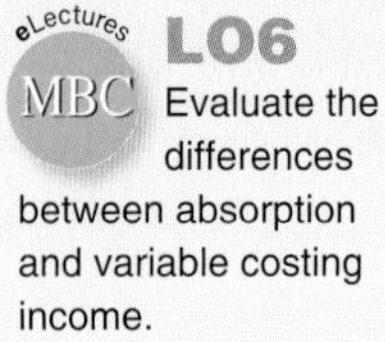

LO6 Evaluate the differences between absorption and variable costing income.

Product costing for inventory valuation is the link between financial and managerial accounting. Product costing systems determine the cost based valuation of the manufactured inventories used in making key financial accounting measurements (cost of goods sold and income on the income statement as well as inventory and total assets on the balance sheet). They also provide vital information to managers for setting prices, controlling costs, and evaluating management performance. The influence of financial accounting on product costing systems is apparent in the design of traditional job order and process costing systems. These systems reflect the requirement of financial accounting (i.e., generally accepted accounting principles) that all manufacturing costs be included in inventory valuations for external financial reporting purposes. In these systems, all other costs incurred, such as selling, general, and administrative costs, are treated as expenses of the period.

Basic Concepts

A debate exists over how to treat fixed manufacturing overhead costs in the valuation of inventory. The debate centers around whether fixed costs such as depreciation on manufacturing equipment should be considered an *inventoriable product cost* and treated as an asset cost until the inventory is sold, or as a *period cost* and recorded immediately as an operating expense. **Absorption costing** (also called **full costing**) treats fixed manufacturing overhead as a product cost, whereas **variable costing** (also called **direct costing**) treats it as a period cost. Therefore, fixed manufacturing overhead is recorded initially as an asset (inventory) under absorption costing but as an operating expense under variable costing.

Fixed manufacturing costs:

Absorption costing treats **fixed manufacturing costs** as **product costs.**

Variable costing treats **fixed manufacturing costs** as **period costs.**

Since fixed product costs are eventually recorded as expenses under both variable and absorption costing by the time the inventory is sold, why does it matter whether fixed overhead is treated as a product cost or a period cost? It matters because the way it is treated affects the measurement of income for a particular period and the valuation assigned to inventory on the balance sheet at the end of the period. Because absorption costing presents fixed manufacturing overhead as a cost per unit rather than a total cost per period, management's perceptions of cost behavior, and decisions based on perceptions of cost behavior, may also be affected.

Inventory Valuations

To illustrate the difference in inventory valuations between absorption and variable costing, assume the following cost data for a single component of a Trek bicycle at a monthly volume of 4,000 units:

Direct materials	$ 5	per unit
Direct labor	2	per unit
Variable manufacturing overhead	3	per unit
Total variable cost	$ 10	per unit
Fixed manufacturing overhead	$8,000	per month

To determine the unit cost of inventory using absorption costing, an average fixed overhead cost per unit is calculated by dividing the monthly fixed manufacturing overhead by the monthly volume. Even though fixed manufacturing overhead is not a variable cost, under absorption costing it is applied to inventory on a per-unit basis, the same as variable costs. At a monthly volume of 4,000 units, Trek's total component inventory cost per unit is $10 under variable costing and $12 under absorption costing.

The $2 difference in total unit cost is attributed to the treatment of fixed overhead of $8,000 divided by 4,000 units. The difference in the total component inventory valuation on the balance sheet between absorption and variable costing is the number of units in ending inventory times $2. So if 1,000 units are on hand at the end of the month, they are valued at $12,000 if absorption costing is used but at only $10,000 with variable costing.

Income Under Absorption and Variable Costing

The income statement formats used for variable and absorption costing are not the same. One benefit of variable costing is that it separates costs into variable and fixed costs, making it possible to present the income statement in a contribution format. As illustrated in Chapter 3, in a contribution income statement, variable costs are subtracted from revenues to compute contribution margin; fixed costs are then subtracted from contribution margin to calculate profit, also called net income or earnings.

When absorption costing is used, the income statement is usually formatted using the functional format, which classifies costs based on cost function, such as manufacturing, selling, or administrative. The functional income statement, used for financial reporting, subtracts manufacturing costs (represented by cost of goods sold) from revenues to calculate gross profit; selling and administrative costs are then subtracted from gross profit to calculate profit or income.

The contribution format provides information for determining the contribution margin ratio, which is calculated as total contribution margin divided by total sales. It also provides the total amount of fixed costs. These are the primary items of data needed to determine the break-even point and to conduct other cost-volume-profit analysis (see Chapter 3).

Not only is the income statement format different for absorption and variable costing methods, but also as illustrated in the following hypothetical examples for Trek, the amount of income reported on the income statement might not be the same because of the difference in the treatment of fixed manufacturing overhead. The following additional information is assumed for the Trek component examples:

Selling price	$30	per unit
Variable selling and administrative expenses	$3	per unit
Fixed selling and administrative expenses	$10,000	per month

Production Equals Sales

Assume Trek has no component inventory on June 1. Production and sales for the third quarter of the fiscal year ending November 30 are:

Month	Production	Sales
June	3,200 units	3,200 units
July	4,000 units	3,500 units
August	4,000 units	4,500 units
Third quarter	11,200 units	11,200 units

Production and sales both total 11,200 units for the third quarter. A summary of unit production, sales, and inventory levels is presented in Exhibit 5A.1. Using previously presented costs and a selling price of $30 per unit, monthly contribution (variable costing) and functional (absorption costing) income statements are presented in Exhibit 5A.1 parts B and C. An analysis of fixed manufacturing overhead with absorption costing is presented in part D.

In June, with 3,200 units produced and sold all $8,000 of fixed manufacturing overhead is deducted as a period cost under variable costing and expensed as part of the cost of goods sold under absorption costing. Since no inventory remained, no costs were deferred.

Production Exceeds Sales

July production of 4,000 units exceeded sales of 3,500 units by 500 units. The ending inventory under variable costing consisted of only the variable cost of production, $5,000 (500 × $10). The entire $8,000 of fixed manufacturing overhead is deducted as a period cost.

Under absorption costing, in addition to the variable cost of production, a portion of the fixed manufacturing overhead is assigned to the ending inventory. As shown in the July column of Exhibit 5A.1, part D, absorption costing assigns $1,000 of the month's fixed manufacturing overhead to the July ending inventory and $7,000 to the cost of goods sold. Consequently, under absorption costing the July ending inventory is $1,000 higher, the July expenses are $1,000 lower, and the July net income is $1,000 higher than under variable costing.

Exhibit 5A.1 Contribution (Variable Costing) and Functional (Absorption Costing) Income Statements with Variations in Production and Sales

	June (Production equals sales)	July (Production exceeds sales)	August (Sales exceed production)
A. Trek's Component: Summary of Unit Inventory Changes			
Beginning inventory	0	0	500
Production	3,200	4,000	4,000
Total available	3,200	4,000	4,500
Sales	(3,200)	(3,500)	(4,500)
Ending inventory	0	500	0
B. Contribution (Variable Costing) Income Statements			
Sales ($30/unit)	$96,000	$105,000	$135,000
Less variable expenses			
Cost of goods sold ($10/unit)	32,000	35,000	45,000
Selling & admin. ($3/unit)	9,600	10,500	13,500
Total	(41,600)	(45,500)	(58,500)
Contribution margin	54,400	59,500	76,500
Less fixed expenses			
Manufacturing overhead	8,000	8,000	8,000
Selling & admin.	10,000	10,000	10,000
Total	(18,000)	(18,000)	(18,000)
Net income	$36,400	$ 41,500	$ 58,500
C. Functional (Absorption Costing) Income Statements			
Sales ($30/unit)	$96,000	$105,000	$135,000
Cost of goods sold (Part D.)	(40,000)	(42,000)	(54,000)
Gross profit	56,000	63,000	81,000
Selling & admin. expenses			
Variable ($3/unit)	9,600	10,500	13,500
Fixed	10,000	10,000	10,000
Total	(19,600)	(20,500)	(23,500)
Net income	$36,400	$ 42,500	$ 57,500
D. Analysis of Fixed Manufacturing Overhead under Absorption Costing			
Fixed manufacturing overhead	$ 8,000	$ 8,000	$ 8,000
Units produced	÷ 3,200	÷ 4,000	÷ 4,000
Absorption fixed cost per unit*	$ 2.50	$ 2.00	$ 2.00
Units in ending inventory	× 0	× 500	× 0
Fixed costs in ending inv.	$ 0	$ 1,000 →	$ 0
Fixed cost of goods sold			
From beginning inventory	$ 0	$ 0	$ 1,000
June (3,200 units × $2.50)	8,000		
July (3,500 units × $2.00)		7,000	
August (4,000 × $2.00)			8,000
Total fixed	8,000	7,000	9,000
Variable cost of goods sold	32,000	35,000	45,000
Absorption cost of goods sold	$40,000	$ 42,000	$ 54,000

* To simplify the illustration, the example does not use a predetermined overhead rate. If a predetermined overhead rate were used, an increase or decrease in the balance of Manufacturing Overhead is treated as an adjustment to ending inventory.

Sales Exceed Production

In August just the opposite of July's situation occurred: sales of 4,500 units exceeded production of 4,000 units by 500 units. The additional units came from the July production. There was no inventory remaining on August 31. Under variable costing all current manufacturing costs (August costs) are expensed either as the variable cost of goods sold or as part of the fixed expense. Additionally, the August variable cost of goods sold includes variable costs assigned the July ending inventory.

Under absorption costing all current month manufacturing costs are expensed as part of the cost of goods sold. Additionally, the cost of goods sold includes the variable and fixed costs assigned the July ending inventory. The inclusion of the July fixed costs caused absorption costing net income to be $1,000 lower than the corresponding variable costing amount.

The above relationships between absorption and variable costing are summarized in Exhibit 5A.2.

Exhibit 5A.2 Comparative Effects of Absorption and Variable Costing

Relationship between period production and sales	Effect on inventory costs	Effect on operating income	Explanation
Production = Sales	No change in inventory costs.	Absorption costing income = Variable costing income	All current fixed manufacturing costs are expensed under both absorption and variable costing.
Production > Sales	Absorption costing ending inventory increases more than variable costing inventory.	Absorption costing income > Variable costing income	Under absorption costing some current fixed manufacturing costs are assigned to ending inventory. Under variable costing all current fixed manufacturing costs are expensed.
Sales > Production	Absorption costing ending inventory declines more than variable costing inventory.	Absorption costing income < Variable costing income	Under absorption costing fixed manufacturing costs previously assigned to ending inventory are expensed along with current fixed manufacturing costs. Under variable costing only current fixed manufacturing costs are expensed.

Exhibits 5A.1 and 5A.2 reveal several important relationships between absorption costing net income and variable costing net income, as well as the way net income responds to changes in sales and production under both methods.

For each period, the income differences between absorption and variable costing can be explained by analyzing the change in inventoried fixed manufacturing overhead under absorption costing net income. If fixed manufacturing cost per unit remains constant, the following relationship exists:

Variable costing net income + **Increase (or minus decrease) in inventoried fixed manufacturing overhead** = **Absorption costing net income**

Using Trek's July information, the equation is as follows:

$$\$41{,}500 + (500 \times \$2.00) = \$42{,}500$$

For any given time period, regardless of length, if total units produced equals total units sold, net income is the same for absorption costing and variable costing, all other things being equal. Under absorption costing, all fixed manufacturing overhead is released as a product cost through cost of goods sold when inventory is sold. Under variable costing, all fixed manufacturing overhead is reported as a period cost and expensed in the period incurred. Consequently, over the life of a product, the income differences within periods are offset since they occur only because of the timing of the release of fixed manufacturing overhead to the income statement.

Evaluating Alternatives to Inventory Valuation

The issue in the variable costing debate is whether or not fixed manufacturing costs add value to products. Proponents of variable costing argue that these costs do not add value to a product. They believe that fixed costs are incurred to provide the capacity to produce during a given period, and these costs expire with the passage of time regardless of whether the related capacity was used. Variable manufacturing costs, on the other hand, are incurred only if production takes place. Consequently, these costs are properly assignable to the units produced.

Proponents of variable costing also argue that inventories have value only to the extent that they avoid the necessity of incurring costs in the future. Having inventory available for sale avoids the necessity of incurring some future variable costs, but the availability of finished goods inventory does not avoid the incurrence of future fixed manufacturing costs. Proponents conclude that inventories should be valued at their variable manufacturing cost, and fixed manufacturing costs should be expensed as incurred.

Opponents of variable costing argue that fixed manufacturing costs are incurred for only one purpose, namely, to manufacture the product. Because they are incurred to manufacture the product, they should be assigned to the product. It is also argued that in the long run all costs are variable. Consequently, by omitting fixed costs, variable costing understates long-run variable costs and misleads decision makers into underestimating true production costs.

On a pragmatic level, the central arguments for variable costing center around the fact that use of variable costing facilitates the development of contribution income statements and cost-volume-profit analysis. With costs accumulated on an absorption costing basis, contribution income statements are difficult to develop, and cost-volume-profit analysis becomes very complicated unless production and sales are equal.

The Research Insight below discusses recent inventory levels and how these might impact variable and absorption costing.

Research Insight ■ Inventory Levels and Inventory Costing

Inventory levels are currently higher than they were prior to 2014. As of September 2019, the Total Business Inventories to Sales Ratio is 1.40, up 2.94 from the prior year. Inventories can build for a number of reasons including an economic slowdown (resulting in a reduction of sales); or, a positive economic outlook (resulting in aggressive inventory production). Increasing inventory levels create greater financial differences between absorption and variable costing methods. Using absorption costing, the building inventories will result in more fixed manufacturing costs sitting on the balance sheet. While using variable costing will flow these fixed manufacturing costs through the income statement as an expense in the period of their production.

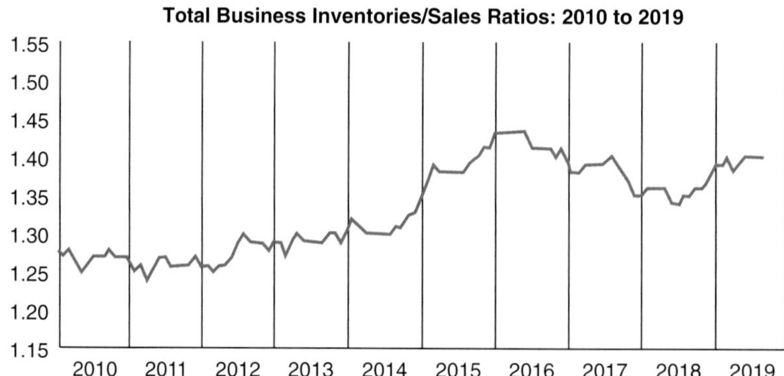

Source: U.S. Census Bureau, Manufacturing and Trade Inventories and Sales, October 16, 2019. (Data adjusted for seasonal, holiday and trading day differences but not for price changes)

Computing Inventory Costs Under Absorption and Variable Costing

LO6 Review 5-6

Boxtel Inc. has a highly automated assembly line that uses very little direct labor. Therefore, direct labor is part of variable overhead. For October, assume that it incurred the following unit costs:

Direct materials	$250
Variable overhead	220
Fixed overhead	80

The 100 units of beginning inventory for October had an absorption costing value of $45,000 and a variable costing value of $38,000. For October, assume that Boxtel Inc. produced 500 units and sold 540 units.

Required

a. Compute Boxtel's October amount of ending inventory under both absorption and variable costing if the FIFO inventory method was used.

b. Compute Boxtel's October Cost of Goods Sold using both the variable and absorption costing methods.

Solution on p. 203.

Guidance Answers

You Are the Chief Financial Officer

Pg. 171 Inventory costs that are provided for financial statement purposes for external stockholders and lenders are required by generally accepted accounting principles to include only the manufacturing costs of the product for direct materials, direct labor, and manufacturing overhead. To conduct a complete profitability analysis, the CFO will need to gather data for all other costs that relate to the marketing, sales, and distribution of each product, as well as any costs related to providing service to customers who buy the products.

Key Ratios

$$\text{Predetermined manufacturing overhead rate per direct labor hour} = \frac{\text{Predicted total manufacturing overhead cost for the year}}{\text{Predicted total direct labor hours for the year}}$$

$$\text{Manufacturing overhead applied to Work-in-Process Inventory} = \text{Actual direct labor hours} \times \text{Predetermined manufacturing overhead rate per direct labor hour}$$

$$\text{Variable costing net income} + \text{Increase (or minus decrease) in inventoried fixed manufacturing overhead} = \text{Absorption costing net income}$$

Key Terms

absorption cost, 156
absorption costing, 178
activities list, 161
bill of materials, 161
conversion cost, 157
cost of production report, 173
direct costing, 178
direct labor, 157
direct materials, 156
equivalent completed units, 175
finished goods inventories, 155
first-in, first-out (FIFO) method, 176
full absorption cost, 156
full costing, 178
job cost sheet, 161
job order production, 161
job production, 161
manufacturing organizations, 154
manufacturing overhead, 157
materials requisition form, 161
merchandising organizations, 154
operations list, 161
period costs, 156
predetermined manufacturing overhead rate, 159
process manufacturing, 160
product costs, 156
production order, 161
raw materials inventories, 154
service costing, 170
service organizations, 154
statement of cost of goods manufactured, 168
variable costing, 178
weighted average method, 176
work-in-process inventories, 155
work ticket, 162

Multiple Choice

Multiple Choice Answers
1. c 2. b 3. c 4. c 5. b 6. d 7. a 8. d

1. Which of the following statements best represents manufacturing organizations?

a. A manufacturing organization always uses process costing.
b. A manufacturing organization typically has a low percentage of its assets invested in inventory.
c. A manufacturing organization typically has three major inventory categories.
d. A manufacturing organization is the only type of organization that has a cost of goods sold account reported on the income statement.

2. Kay Company's formula for annual manufacturing overhead is:

Y = \$120,000 + \$10X, where X is direct labor dollars

The predicted activity for the year is 50,000 direct labor hours and the actual activity for January was 4,000 direct labor hours. Using a predetermined overhead rate, the applied January overhead is

a. \$40,000
b. \$49,600
c. \$160,000
d. \$169,600

3. Which of the following statements best represents job order costing?

a. Job order costing works best when there is production of identical units on a continuous basis.
b. Job order costing works best for companies like Kraft Heinz and SanDisk.
c. In job order costing, scheduling personnel prepare a production order for each job.
d. In job order costing, a process cost sheet is used to accumulate the costs for each job.

4. Presented is selected information from Took's April income statement and statement of cost of goods manufactured:

Cost of goods sold	$230,000
Cost of goods manufactured	$210,000
Finished goods inventory, April 30	$ 40,000

Took's finished goods inventory on April 1 was

a. \$20,000
b. \$40,000
c. \$60,000
d. \$80,000

5. Presented is selected information from Fred's January statement of cost of goods manufactured.

Predetermined overhead rate	80% of direct labor dollars
Direct materials	$ 60,000
Cost of goods manufactured	$150,000

Fred's January direct labor was

a. $40,000
b. $50,000
c. $75,000
d. $90,000

6. The beginning inventory consisted of 10,000 units, 30% complete and the ending inventory consisted of 8,000 units, 40% complete. There were 22,000 units started during the period. Determine the equivalent units of conversion in process.

a. 17,800
b. 20,800
c. 25,200
d. 27,200

7. Presented is selected information from Micro Systems cost of production report:

Cost per equivalent unit in process	$ 20
Units completed	30,000
Total costs in process	$664,000
Equivalent units of materials in ending inventory	4,000
Cost per equivalent unit of materials	$ 12

The ending inventory of work-in-process is complete as to materials. The cost of conversion in the ending inventory is

a. $16,000
b. $32,000
c. $48,000
d. $64,000

8. Chandler Company sells its product for $100 per unit. Variable manufacturing costs per unit are $40, and fixed manufacturing costs at the normal operating level of 12,000 units are $240,000. Variable expenses are $16 per unit sold. Fixed administration expenses total $104,000. Chandler had no beginning inventory. During the year, the company produced 12,000 units and sold 9,000. What would the operating income be for Chandler Company for the year using both variable costing and absorption costing?

a. Variable costing $60,000; absorption costing $60,000
b. Variable costing $112,000; absorption costing $52,000
c. Variable costing $112,000; absorption costing $125,000
d. Variable costing $52,000; absorption costing $112,000

Questions

Q5-1. Distinguish among service, merchandising, and manufacturing organizations on the basis of the importance and complexity of inventory cost measurement.

Q5-2. Distinguish between product costing and service costing.

Q5-3. When is depreciation a product cost? When is depreciation a period cost?

Q5-4. What are the three major product cost elements?

Q5-5. How are predetermined overhead rates developed? Why are they widely used?

Q5-6. Briefly distinguish between process manufacturing and job order production. Provide examples of products typically produced under each system.

Q5-7. Briefly describe the role of engineering personnel and production scheduling personnel in the production planning process.

Q5-8. Identify the primary records involved in the operation of a job cost system.

Q5-9. Describe the flow of costs through the accounting system of a labor-intensive manufacturing organization.

Q5-10. Identify two reasons that a service organization should maintain detailed job cost information.

Q5-11. What are the four major elements of a cost of production report?

Q5-12. What are equivalent completed units?

Q5-13. Under what conditions will equivalent units in process be different for materials and conversion costs?

Assignments with the MBC logo in the margin are available in myBusinessCourse. See the Preface of the book for details.

Mini Exercises

LO2

M5-14. Classification of Product and Period Costs

Classify the following costs incurred by a manufacturer of golf clubs as product costs or period costs. Also classify the product costs as direct materials or conversion costs.

a. Depreciation on computer in president's office
b. Salaries of legal staff
c. Graphite shafts
d. Plant security department
e. Electricity for the corporate office
f. Rubber grips
g. Golf club heads
h. Wages paid assembly line maintenance workers
i. Salary of corporate controller
j. Subsidy of plant cafeteria
k. Wages paid assembly line production workers
l. National sales meeting in Orlando
m. Overtime premium paid assembly line workers
n. Advertising on national television
o. Depreciation on assembly line

LO2
Milliken & Company

M5-15. Developing and Using a Predetermined Overhead Rate

Assume that the following predictions were made last year for one of the plants of Milliken & Company:

Total manufacturing overhead for the year.	$15,000,000
Total machine hours for the year	1,200,000

Actual results for February were as follows:

Manufacturing overhead.	$1,238,500
Machine hours	98,500

Required

a. Determine the predetermined overhead rate per machine hour.
b. Using the predetermined overhead rate per machine hour, determine the manufacturing overhead applied to Work-in-Process during February.
c. As of February 1, actual overhead was overapplied by $35,000. Determine the cumulative amount of any overapplied or underapplied overhead at the end of February.

M5-16. Job Order Costing and Process Costing Applications

LO4, 5

For each of the following manufacturing situations, indicate whether job order or process costing is more appropriate and why.

a. Manufacturer of chocolate candy bars
b. Manufacturer of carbonated beverages
c. Manufacturer of high-quality men's suits
d. Manufacturer of subway cars
e. Printer of a variety of history books

M5-17. Job Order Costing and Process Costing Applications

LO4, 5

For each of the following situations, indicate whether job order or process costing is more appropriate and why.

a. Building contractor for residential dwellings
b. Manufacturer of nylon yarn (single weight) that it sells to fabric-making textile companies
c. Evening gown manufacturer that makes gowns in several different fabrics, colors, styles, and sizes
d. Hosiery mill that manufactures a one-size-fits-all product
e. Vehicle battery manufacturer that has just received an order for 400,000 identical batteries

M5-18. Process Costing

LO5
Snooz

Snooz makes a single model of its white noise sound machine. Assume the product is produced on a continuous basis in one department. All materials are added at the beginning of production. The total cost per equivalent unit in process in March was $56, consisting of $32 for materials and $24 for conversion. During the month, 12,000 units of product were transferred to finished goods inventory; on March 31, 5,000 units were in process, 10% converted. The company uses weighted average costing.

Required

a. Determine the cost of goods transferred to finished goods inventory.
b. Determine the cost of the ending work-in-process inventory.
c. What was the total cost of the beginning work-in-process inventory plus the current manufacturing costs?

M5-19. Absorption and Variable Costing; Inventory Valuation

LO6

Bondware Inc. has a highly automated assembly line that uses very little direct labor. Therefore, direct labor is part of variable overhead. For March, assume that it incurred the following unit costs:

Direct materials	$450
Variable overhead	250
Fixed overhead	550

The 1,200 units of beginning inventory for March had an absorption costing value of $1,500,000 and a variable costing value of $840,000. For March, assume that Bondware Inc. produced 3,000 units and sold 3,500 units.

Required

Compute Bondware's March amount of ending inventory under both absorption and variable costing if the FIFO inventory method was used.

M5-20. Absorption and Variable Costing; Cost of Goods Sold

LO6

Use data from Mini Exercise 5-19.

Required

Compute Bondware's March Cost of Goods Sold using both the variable and absorption costing methods.

Exercises

LO2, 4 Steger Designs

E5-21. Analyzing Activity in Inventory Accounts

Steger Designs makes winter boots and moccasins at its factory in northern Minnesota. Assume the following represents data related to Steger operations last year:

Raw materials used	$400,000
Total manufacturing costs charged to production during the year (includes raw materials, direct labor, and manufacturing overhead applied at a rate of 200% of direct labor costs)	850,000
Cost of goods available for sale	958,000
Selling and general expenses	280,000

	Inventories	
	Beginning	Ending
Raw materials	$110,000	$105,000
Work-in-process	75,000	92,000
Finished goods	125,000	135,000

Required

Determine each of the following:

a. Cost of raw materials purchased
b. Direct labor costs charged to production
c. Cost of goods manufactured
d. Cost of goods sold

LO4

E5-22. Statement of Cost of Goods Manufactured and Income Statement

Information from the records of the Bridgeview Manufacturing Company for August follows:

Sales	$250,000
Selling and administrative expenses	98,600
Purchases of raw materials	32,000
Direct labor	22,000
Manufacturing overhead	38,600

	Inventories	
	August 1	August 31
Raw materials	$ 6,000	$ 6,500
Work-in-process	4,600	5,800
Finished goods	12,000	15,000

Required

Prepare a statement of cost of goods manufactured and an income statement for August.

LO4 Homework MBC

E5-23. Statement of Cost of Goods Manufactured from Percent Relationships

Information about Blue Line Products Company for the year ending December 31 follows:

- Sales equal $580,000.
- Direct materials used total $105,000.
- Manufacturing overhead is 200% of direct labor dollars.
- The beginning inventory of finished goods is 25% of the cost of goods sold.
- The ending inventory of finished goods is 1.5 times beginning inventory.
- The gross profit is 20% of sales.
- There is no beginning or ending work-in-process.

Required

Prepare a statement of cost of goods manufactured for the year. (*Hint:* Prepare an analysis of changes in Finished Goods Inventory.)

E5-24. Account Activity and Relationships LO2, 4

	Case A	Case B	Case C	Case D
Sales	$42,000	$ (b)	$82,500	$ (b)
Direct materials	7,500	31,500	(f)	42,000
Direct labor	3,000	(c)	15,000	(c)
Total direct costs	(a)	48,000	(e)	60,000
Conversion cost	(b)	39,000	(g)	(g)
Manufacturing overhead	4,000	(d)	7,500	(f)
Current manufacturing costs	(c)	(e)	71,250	158,000
Work-in-process, beginning	3,500	15,000	(d)	42,000
Work-in-process, ending	2,500	(f)	15,750	(e)
Cost of goods manufactured	(d)	48,000	(c)	164,000
Finished goods inventory, beginning	4,500	12,000	5,250	24,000
Finished goods inventory, ending	3,000	(g)	6,000	(d)
Cost of goods sold	(e)	52,500	(b)	160,000
Gross profit	(f)	(a)	13,500	30,000
Selling and administrative expenses	10,000	22,500	(a)	(a)
Net income	(g)	33,000	9,000	12,000

Required

Each case is independent. Solve for missing data in alphabetical order. (*Hint:* Refer to **Exhibit 5.6**, p. 168 and the WIP table, p. 176.)

E5-25. Developing and Using a Predetermined Overhead Rate: High-Low Cost Estimation LO2

For years, Mattoon Components Company has used an actual plantwide overhead rate and based its prices on cost plus a markup of 30%. Recently the marketing manager, Holly Adams, and the production manager, Sue Walsh, confronted the controller with a common problem. The marketing manager expressed a concern that Mattoon's prices seem to vary widely throughout the year. According to Adams, "It seems irrational to charge higher prices when business is bad and lower prices when business is good. While we get a lot of business during high-volume months because we charge less than our competitors, it is a waste of time to even call on customers during low-volume months because we are raising prices while our competitors are lowering them." Walsh also believed that it was "folly to be so pushed that we have to pay overtime in some months and then lay employees off in others." She commented, "While there are natural variations in customer demand, the accounting system seems to amplify this variation."

Required

a. Evaluate the arguments presented by Adams and Walsh. What suggestions do you have for improving the accounting and pricing procedures?

b. Assume that the Mattoon Components Company had the following total manufacturing overhead costs and direct labor hours in the last two years.

	Year 1	Year 2
Total manufacturing overhead	$325,000	$380,500
Direct labor hours	34,000	40,000

Use the high-low method (see Chapter 2) to develop a cost-estimating equation for total manufacturing overhead.

c. Develop a predetermined rate for next year, assuming 35,000 direct labor hours are budgeted for next year.

d. Assume that the actual level of activity next year was 36,000 direct labor hours and that manufacturing overhead was $341,550. Determine the underapplied or overapplied manufacturing overhead at the end of the year.

e. Describe two ways of handling any underapplied or overapplied manufacturing overhead at the end of the year.

LO4 E5-26. Manufacturing Cost Flows with Machine Hours Allocation

On April 1, Telecom Manufacturing Company's beginning balances in manufacturing accounts and finished goods inventory were as follows:

Raw materials	$35,000
Manufacturing supplies	3,500
Work-in-process	12,000
Manufacturing overhead	0
Finished goods	50,000

During April, Telecom Manufacturing completed the following manufacturing transactions:

1. Purchased raw materials costing $60,000 and manufacturing supplies costing $2,000 on account.
2. Requisitioned raw materials costing $52,000 to the factory.
3. Incurred direct labor costs of $18,000 and indirect labor costs of $6,500.
4. Used manufacturing supplies costing $3,800.
5. Recorded manufacturing depreciation of $11,000.
6. Miscellaneous payables for manufacturing overhead totaled $8,500.
7. Applied manufacturing overhead, based on 2,500 machine hours, at a predetermined rate of $10 per machine hour.
8. Completed jobs costing $90,500.
9. Finished goods costing $95,750 were sold.

Required

a. Prepare "T" accounts showing the flow of costs through all manufacturing accounts, Finished Goods Inventory, and Cost of Goods Sold.

b. Calculate the balances at the end of April for Work-in-Process Inventory and Finished Goods Inventory.

LO4 E5-27. Service Cost Flows

Cutwater, an advertising agency with offices in San Francisco and New York, develops marketing campaigns for companies in the United States and overseas. To achieve cost control, assume Cutwater uses a job cost system similar to that found in a manufacturing organization. It uses some different account titles:

Account	Replaces
Jobs-in-Process	Work-in-Process
Job Supplies Inventory	Manufacturing Supplies Inventory
Cost of Jobs Completed	Cost of Goods Sold
Accumulated Depreciation, Agency Assets	Accumulated Depreciation, Factory Assets
Production Overhead	Manufacturing Overhead

Cutwater does not maintain Raw Materials or Finished Goods Inventory accounts. Materials, such as props needed for video shoots, are purchased as needed from outside sources and charged directly to Jobs-in-Process and the appropriate job. The April 1 balances were as follows:

Job Supplies Inventory	$ 10,000	
Jobs-in-Process	200,000	
Production Overhead	2,850	underapplied

During April, Cutwater completed the following production transactions:

1. Purchased job supplies costing $4,500 on account.
2. Purchased materials for specific jobs costing $150,000 on account.
3. Incurred direct labor costs of $225,000 and indirect labor costs of $155,000.
4. Used production supplies costing $2,200.
5. Recorded equipment depreciation of $12,000.
6. Incurred miscellaneous payables for production overhead of $78,000.
7. Applied production overhead at a predetermined rate of $100 per production hour, based on 2,500 production hours.
8. Completed jobs costing $622,000.

Required

a. Prepare "T" accounts showing the flow of costs through all service accounts and Cost of Jobs Completed.

b. Calculate the cost incurred as of the end of April for the incomplete jobs still in process.

E5-28. Cost of Production Report: No Beginning Inventories

LO5
Port Townsend Paper

Port Townsend Paper (PTPC) produces paper by blending recycled corrugated cardboard with other fibers. Assume the following represent production and cost data for October. There was no inventory on hand on October 1.

Units of product started in process during October	20,000 tons
Units completed and transferred to finished goods	19,000 tons
Machine hours operated	3,410
Direct materials costs incurred	$134,000
Direct labor costs incurred	$185,000

Raw materials are added at the beginning of the process for each unit of product produced, and labor and manufacturing overhead are added evenly throughout the manufacturing process. Manufacturing overhead is applied to Work-in-Process at the rate of $50 per machine hour. Units in process at the end of the period were 75% converted.

Required

Prepare a cost of production report for PTPC for October.

E5-29. Cost of Production Report: No Beginning Inventories

LO5

Howell Paving Company manufactures asphalt paving materials for highway construction through a one-step process in which all materials are added at the beginning of the process. During April, the company accumulated the following data in its process costing system:

Production data	
Work-in-process, 4/1	0 tons
Raw materials transferred to processing	35,000 tons
Work-in-process, 4/30 (60% converted)	5,000 tons
Cost data	
Raw materials transferred to processing	$440,000
Conversion costs	
Direct labor cost incurred	$95,000
Manufacturing overhead applied	?

Manufacturing overhead is applied at the rate of $15 per equivalent unit (ton) processed.

Required

Prepare a cost of production report for April.

E5-30. Absorption and Variable Costing Comparisons: Production Equals Sales

LO6
The J.M. Smucker Company (SJM)

Assume that Smuckers manufactures and sells 45,000 cases of peanut butter each quarter. The following data are available for the third quarter of the year.

Total fixed manufacturing overhead	$ 675,000
Fixed selling and administrative expenses	1,225,000
Sales price per case	85
Direct materials per case	20
Direct labor per case	10
Variable manufacturing overhead per case	4

Required

a. Compute the cost per case under both absorption costing and variable costing.

b. Compute net income under both absorption costing and variable costing.

c. Reconcile any differences in income. Explain.

LO6 **E5-31. Absorption and Variable Costing Income Statements: Production Exceeds Sales**

Glenview Company sells its product at a unit price of $20. Unit manufacturing costs are direct materials, $5.00; direct labor, $2.00; and variable manufacturing overhead, $1.00. Total fixed manufacturing costs are $255,000 per year. Selling and administrative expenses are $1.00 per unit variable and $185,000 per year fixed. Though 60,000 units were produced during the year, only 54,000 units were sold. There was no beginning inventory.

Required

a. Prepare a functional income statement using absorption costing for the year.
b. Prepare a contribution income statement using variable costing for the year.

LO6 **E5-32. Absorption and Variable Costing Comparisons: Sales Exceed Production**

Wright Development purchases, develops, and sells commercial building sites. As the sites are sold, they are cleared at an average cost of $8,000 per site. Storm drains and driveways are also installed at an average cost of $10,000 per site. Selling costs are 6% of sales price. Administrative costs are $600,000 per year. Two years ago, the company bought 2,000 acres of land for $7,500,000 and divided it into 200 sites of equal size. During that year, 95 sites were sold at an average price of $150,000. Last year, the company purchased and developed another 2,000 acres, divided into 200 sites. The purchase price was again $7,500,000. Sales totaled 250 sites last year at an average price of $150,000.

Required

a. Prepare functional income statements using absorption costing for each of the two years.
b. Prepare contribution income statements using variable costing for each of the two years.

Problems

LO4 **P5-33. Cost of Goods Manufactured and Income Statement**

Following is information from the records of the Savoy Company for July.

Purchases	
Raw materials	$150,000
Manufacturing supplies	2,500
Office supplies	1,000
Sales	583,500
Administrative salaries	46,000
Direct labor	105,000
Production employees' fringe benefits*	10,500
Sales salaries and commissions	45,000
Production supervisors' salaries	10,000
Plant depreciation	12,000
Office depreciation	3,000
Plant maintenance	8,000
Plant utilities	7,500
Office utilities	2,500
Office maintenance	4,200
Production equipment rent	4,000
Office equipment rent	1,000

* Classified as manufacturing overhead

Inventories	July 1	July 31
Raw materials	$25,000	$28,000
Manufacturing supplies	4,000	3,500
Office supplies	1,500	1,000
Work-in-process	18,000	15,000
Finished goods	90,450	88,600

Required

Prepare a statement of cost of goods manufactured and an income statement. Actual overhead costs are assigned to products.

P5-34. Cost of Goods Manufactured and Income Statement with Predetermined Overhead and Labor Cost Classifications LO2, 4

Bauer Hockey, LLC

Assume information pertaining to Bauer Hockey for April of the current year follows.

Sales	$745,500
Purchases	
Raw materials	225,000
Manufacturing supplies	12,000
Office supplies	2,200
Salaries (including fringe benefits)	
Administrative	102,600
Production supervisors	24,500
Sales	105,000
Depreciation	
Plant and machinery	24,000
Office and office equipment	8,000
Utilities	
Plant	15,000
Office	6,000

Inventories	April 1	April 30
Raw materials	$50,350	$52,500
Manufacturing supplies	6,200	7,400
Office supplies	1,800	1,500
Work-in-process	38,500	40,200
Finished goods	90,000	88,000

Additional information follows:

- Manufacturing overhead is applied to products at 125% of direct labor dollars.
- Employee base wages are $15 per hour.
- Employee fringe benefits amount to 20% of the base wage rate. They are classified as manufacturing overhead.
- During April, production employees worked 6,500 hours, including 5,200 regular hours and 400 overtime hours spent working on products. There were 900 indirect labor hours.
- Employees are paid a 50% overtime premium. Any overtime premium is treated as manufacturing overhead.

Required

a. Prepare a statement of cost of goods manufactured and an income statement for April.
b. Determine underapplied or overapplied overhead for April.
c. Recompute direct labor and actual manufacturing overhead assuming employee fringe benefits for direct labor hours are classified as direct labor.

P5-35. Actual and Predetermined Overhead Rates LO2, 4

Custom Crate Engines

Custom Crate Engines assembles custom designed high-performance engines for classic American cars. Assume the following events occurred during the month of January:

- Materials costing $8,000 were purchased on account.
- Direct materials costing $6,000 were placed in process.
- A total of 450 direct labor hours was charged to individual jobs at a rate of $20 per hour.
- Overhead costs for the month were as follows:

Depreciation on building and equipment	$2,425
Indirect labor	2,700
Utilities	450
Property taxes on automotive shop	375
Insurance on building	350

- There were no jobs in process on January 1.
- On January 31, only one job (A06) was in process with materials costs of $1,800, direct labor charges of $1,000 for 50 direct labor hours, and applied overhead.

- The building and equipment were purchased before operations began and the insurance was prepaid. All other costs will be paid during the following month.

Note: Predetermined overhead rates are used throughout the chapter. An alternative is to accumulate actual overhead costs for the period in Manufacturing Overhead, and apply actual costs at the close of the period to all jobs in process during the period.

Required

a. Assuming Custom Crate assigned actual monthly overhead costs to jobs on the basis of actual monthly direct labor hours, prepare an analysis of the activity in Work-in-Process for the month of January.

b. Assuming Custom Crate uses a predetermined overhead rate of $15 per direct labor hour, prepare an analysis of Work-in-Process for the month of January. Describe the appropriate treatment of any overapplied or underapplied overhead for the month of January.

c. Assume that utilities and indirect labor are variable costs with respect to direct labor hours and that depreciation and property taxes are fixed costs. Predict the actual overhead rates for months when 250 and 750 direct labor hours are used. Assuming jobs similar to A06 were in process at the end of each month, determine the costs assigned to these jobs.

d. Why do you suppose predetermined overhead rates are preferred to actual overhead rates?

LO2, 4 Kubota Corporation (KUBTY)

P5-36. Job Costing with Predetermined Overhead Rate

Kubota Corporation manufactures equipment in batches for inventory stock. Assume that Kubota's production costs are accounted for using a job cost system. At the beginning of April raw materials inventories totaled $9,350,000, manufacturing supplies amounted to $1,320,000, and finished goods inventories totaled $6,600,000. Two jobs were in process: Job 522 with assigned costs of $6,440,000 and Job 523 with assigned costs of $2,750,000. The following information summarizes April manufacturing activities:

- Purchased raw materials costing $27,500,000 on account.
- Purchased manufacturing supplies costing $3,300,000 on account.
- Requisitioned materials needed to complete Job 523. Started two new jobs, 524 and 525, and requisitioned direct materials for them.

Direct materials	
Job 523	$ 3,300,000
Job 524	14,190,000
Job 525	10,560,000
Total	$28,050,000

- Recorded April salaries and wages as follows:

Direct labor	
Job 522 (150,000 hours × $25 per hour)	$ 3,750,000
Job 523 (950,000 hours × $25 per hour)	23,750,000
Job 524 (1,350,000 hours × $25 per hour)	33,750,000
Job 525 (875,000 hours × $25 per hour)	21,875,000
Total direct labor	83,125,000
Indirect labor	7,100,000
Total	$90,225,000

- Used manufacturing supplies costing $2,475,000.
- Recognized depreciation on factory fixed assets of $5,800,000.
- Incurred miscellaneous manufacturing overhead costs of $7,250,000 on account.
- Applied manufacturing overhead at the rate of $6.25 per direct labor hour.
- Completed Jobs 522, 523, and 524.

Required

Prepare a complete analysis of all activity in Work-in-Process. Be sure to show the beginning and ending balances, all increases and decreases, and label each item. Provide support information on decreases with job cost sheets.

P5-37. Job Costing with Predetermined Overhead Rate LO2, 4

SnoBlo Company manufactures a variety of gasoline-powered snow blowers for discount hardware and department stores. SnoBlo uses a job cost system and treats each customer's order as a separate job. The primary snow blower components (motors, chassis, and wheels) are purchased from three different suppliers under long-term contracts that call for the direct delivery of raw materials to the production floor as needed. When a customer's order is received, a raw materials purchase order is electronically placed with suppliers. The purchase order specifies the scheduled date that production is to begin as the delivery date for motors and chassis; the scheduled date production is to be completed is specified as the delivery date for the wheels. As a consequence, there are no raw materials inventories; raw materials are charged directly to Work-in-Process upon receipt. Upon completion, goods are shipped directly to customers rather than transferred to finished goods inventory. At the beginning of July SnoBlo had the following work-in-process inventories:

Job 365	$ 40,000
Job 366	29,800
Job 367	30,600
Job 368	17,000
Total	$117,400

During July, the following activities took place:

- Started Jobs 369, 370, and 371.
- Ordered and received the following raw materials for specified jobs:

Job	Motors	Chassis	Wheels	Total
366	$ 0	$ 0	$ 1,600	$ 1,600
367	0	0	2,400	2,400
368	0	0	3,050	3,050
369	28,000	10,000	2,100	40,100
370	18,000	7,000	1,800	26,800
371	17,000	7,200	0	24,200
Total	$63,000	$24,200	$10,950	$98,150

- Incurred July manufacturing payroll:

Direct labor	
Job 365	$ 2,450
Job 366	7,600
Job 367	6,500
Job 368	8,300
Job 369	5,850
Job 370	5,050
Job 371	3,000
Total	38,750
Indirect labor	6,850
Total	$45,600

- Incurred additional manufacturing overhead costs for July:

Manufacturing supplies purchased on account and used	$ 5,700
Depreciation on factory fixed assets	11,800
Miscellaneous payables	9,500
Total	$27,000

- Applied manufacturing overhead using a predetermined rate based on predicted annual overhead of $405,000 and predicted annual direct labor of $450,000.
- Completed and shipped Jobs 365 through 370.

Required

Prepare a complete analysis of all activity in Work-in-Process. Be sure to show the beginning and ending balances, all increases and decreases, and label each item. Provide support information on decreases with job cost sheets.

LO5 **P5-38. Weighted Average Process Costing**

Minot Processing Company manufactures one product on a continuous basis in two departments, Processing and Finishing. All materials are added at the beginning of work on the product in the Processing Department. During November, the following events occurred in the Processing Department:

Units started	20,000 units
Units completed and transferred to Finishing Department	21,000 units

Costs assigned to processing	
Raw materials	$350,000
Manufacturing supplies used	25,000
Direct labor costs incurred	182,000
Supervisors' salaries	15,000
Other production labor costs	18,000
Depreciation on equipment	12,000
Other production costs	95,000

Additional information follows:

- Minot uses weighted average costing and applies manufacturing overhead to Work-in-Process at the rate of 90% of direct labor cost.
- Ending inventory in the Processing Department consists of 3,000 units that are one-fourth converted.
- Beginning inventory contained 4,000 units, one-half converted, with a cost of $57,950 ($34,000 for materials and $23,950 for conversion).

Required

a. Prepare a cost of production report for the Processing Department for November.
b. Prepare an analysis of all changes in Work-in-Process.

LO5 **P5-39. Weighted Average Process Costing**

JIF
The J.M. Smucker Company (SJM)

Assume that JIF, which is part of The J.M. Smucker Company, processes its only product, 12-ounce jars of peanut butter, in a single process and uses weighted average process costing to account for inventory costs. All materials are added at the beginning of production. Assume the following inventory, production, and cost data are provided for September:

Production data	
Beginning inventory (25% converted)	200,000 units
Units started	600,000 units
Ending inventory (75% converted)	225,000 units

Manufacturing costs	
Beginning inventory in process	
Materials cost	$182,000
Conversion cost	44,600
Raw materials cost added at beginning of process	578,000
Direct labor cost incurred	401,900
Manufacturing overhead applied	446,000

Required

a. Prepare a cost of production report for September.
b. Prepare a statement of cost of goods manufactured for September.

LO5 **P5-40. Weighted Average Process Costing with Error Correction**

Capital Manufacturing Company began operations on December 1. On December 31 a new accounting intern was assigned the task of calculating and costing ending inventories.

The intern estimated that the ending work-in-process inventory was 40% complete as to both materials and conversion, resulting in 6,000 equivalent units of materials and conversion. The ending work-in-process was then valued at $60,000, including $30,000 for materials and $30,000 for conversion. A subsequent review of the intern's work revealed that although the materials portion of the ending inventory was correctly estimated to be 40% complete, the units in ending inventory, on average, were only 25% complete as to conversion.

Required

a. Determine the number of units in the ending inventory.
b. How many equivalent units of conversion were in the ending inventory?
c. What cost per unit did the intern calculate for conversion?
d. Assuming 12,000 units were completed during the month of December, determine the correct cost per equivalent unit. (*Hint:* Find the total conversion costs in process.)
e. Determine the corrected cost of the ending inventory.
f. By how much was the cost of goods manufactured misstated as a result of the intern's error? Indicate whether the cost of goods manufactured was overstated or understated.

P5-41. Absorption and Variable Costing Comparisons LO6 Otabo

Otabo is a shoe manufacturer. Assume the company is concerned with changing to the variable costing method of inventory valuation for making internal decisions. Functional income statements using absorption costing for January and February follow.

OTABO
Functional (Absorption Costing) Income Statements
For January and February

	January	February
Sales (10,000 units)	$800,000	$800,000
Cost of goods sold	(490,000)	(586,000)
Gross profit	310,000	214,000
Selling and administrative expenses	(235,000)	(235,000)
Net operating income	$ 75,000	$ (21,000)

Production data follow.

Production units	12,000	8,000
Variable costs per unit	$25	$25
Fixed overhead costs	$288,000	$288,000

The preceding selling and administrative expenses include variable costs of $2 per unit sold.

Required

a. Compute the absorption cost per unit manufactured in January and February.
b. Explain why the net operating income for January was higher than the net operating income for February when the same number of units was sold in each month.
c. Prepare contribution income statements for both months using variable costing.
d. Reconcile the absorption costing and variable costing net operating income figures for each month. (Start with variable costing net operating income.)

P5-42. Absorption and Variable Costing Comparisons LO6

Red Arrow Blueberries manufactures blueberry jam. Because of bad weather, its blueberry crop was small. The following data have been gathered for the summer quarter of last year:

Beginning inventory (cases)	0
Cases produced	8,000
Cases sold	7,000
Sales price per case	$115
Direct materials per case	$25
Direct labor per case	$40
Variable manufacturing overhead per case	$10
Total fixed manufacturing overhead	$192,000
Variable selling and administrative cost per case	$2
Fixed selling and administrative cost	$38,000

Required

a. Prepare a functional income statement for the quarter using absorption costing.
b. Prepare a contribution income statement for the quarter using variable costing.
c. What is the value of ending inventory under absorption costing?
d. What is the value of ending inventory under variable costing?
e. Reconcile the difference in ending inventory under absorption costing and variable costing.

LO6 **P5-43. Variable and Absorption Costing with High-Low Cost Estimation and CVP Analysis Including Taxes**

Presented are the Charger Company's functional income statements for January and February.

CHARGER COMPANY
Functional (Absorption Costing) Income Statements
For the Months of January and February

	January	February
Production and sales	35,000	40,000
Sales Revenue	$2,450,000	$2,800,000
Cost of goods manufactured and sold	(1,470,000)	(1,540,000)
Gross profit	980,000	1,260,000
General and administrative expenses	(650,000)	(650,000)
Net operating income	330,000	610,000
Income taxes at 0.21	(69,300)	(128,100)
Net income after taxes	$ 260,700	$ 481,900

Required

a. Using the high-low method (see Chapter 2), develop a cost-estimating equation for total monthly manufacturing costs.
b. Determine Charger Company's monthly break-even point.
c. Determine the unit sales required to earn a monthly after-tax income of $600,000.
d. Prepare a January contribution income statement using variable costing.
e. If the January net income amounts differ using absorption and variable costing, explain why. If they are identical, explain why.

Cases and Projects

LO2, 4 Walgreens Boots Alliance (WBA)

C5-44. Cost Data for Financial Reporting and Special Order Decisions

Harman Greeting Card Company produces a full range of greeting cards sold through pharmacies and department stores. Each card is designed by independent artists. A production master is then prepared for each design. The production master has an indefinite life. Product designs for popular cards are deemed to be valuable assets. If a card sells well, many batches of the design will be manufactured over a period of years. Hence, Harman Greeting maintains an inventory of production masters so that cards may be periodically reissued. Cards are produced in batches that may vary by increments of 1,000 units. An average batch consists of 10,000 cards. Producing a batch requires placing the production master on the printing press, setting the press for the appropriate paper size, and making other adjustments for colors and so forth. Following are facility-, product-, batch-, and unit-level cost information:

Product design and production master per new card	$ 3,500
Batch setup (typically per 10,000 cards)	300
Materials per 1,000 cards	150
Conversion per 1,000 cards	200
Shipping (per batch)	15
Selling and administrative	
Companywide	306,000
Per product design marketed	675

Information from previous year:

Product designs and masters prepared for new cards	125
Product designs marketed	150
Batches manufactured	800
Cards manufactured and sold	8,000,000

Required

You may need to review materials in Chapter 4 to complete the requirements.

a. Describe how you would determine the cost of goods sold and the value of any ending inventory for financial reporting purposes. (No computations are required.)

b. You have just received an inquiry from Walgreens department stores to develop and manufacture 10 special designs for sale exclusively in Walgreens stores. The cards would be sold for $3.00 each, and Walgreens would pay Harman Greeting $0.70 per card. The initial order is for 30,000 cards of each design. If the cards sell well, Walgreens plans to place additional orders for these and other designs. Because of the preestablished sales relationship, no marketing costs would be associated with the cards sold to Walgreens. How would you evaluate the desirability of the Walgreens proposal?

c. Explain any differences between the costs considered in your answer to requirement (a) and the costs considered in your answer to requirement (b).

C5-45. Continue or Discontinue: Plantwide Overhead with Labor- and Machine-Intensive Operations **LO2, 4**

When Dart Products started operation five years ago, its only product was a radar detector known as the Bear Detector. The production system was simple, with Bear Detectors manually assembled from purchased components. With no ending work-in-process inventories, unit costs were calculated once a month by dividing current manufacturing costs by units produced.

Last year, Dart Products began to manufacture a second product, code-named the Lion Tamer. The production of Lion Tamers involves both machine-intensive fabrication and manual assembly. The introduction of the second product necessitated a change in the firm's simple accounting system. Dart Products now separately assigns direct material and direct labor costs to each product using information contained on materials requisitions and work tickets. Manufacturing overhead is accumulated in a single cost pool and assigned on the basis of direct labor hours, which is common to both products. Following are last year's financial results by product:

	Bear Detector		Lion Tamer	
Sales				
Units		7,500		3,000
Dollars		$ 750,000		$ 450,000
Cost of goods sold				
Direct materials	$165,000		$ 97,500	
Direct labor	281,250		90,000	
Applied overhead	393,750		126,000	
Total		(840,000)		(313,500)
Gross profit		$ (90,000)		$ 136,500

Management is concerned about the mixed nature of last year's financial performance. It appears that the Lion Tamer is a roaring success. The only competition, the Nittney Company, has been selling a competing product for considerably more than Dart's Lion Tamer; this company is in financial difficulty and is likely to file for bankruptcy. The management of Dart Products attributes the Lion Tamer's success to excellent production management. Management is concerned, however, about the future of the Bear Detector and is likely to discontinue that product unless its profitability can be improved. You have been asked to help with this decision and have obtained the following information:

- The labor rate is $15 per hour.
- Dart has two separate production operations, fabrication and assembly. Bear Detectors undergo only assembly operations and require 2.5 assembly hours per unit. Lion Tamers undergo both fabrication and assembly and require 1.5 fabrication hours and 0.5 assembly hour per unit.
- The annual Fabricating Department overhead cost function is:

$184,500 + $6 (labor hours)

- The annual Assembly Department overhead cost function is:

$62,250 + $12 (labor hours)

Required

You may need to review materials in Chapters 3 and 4 to complete this case. Evaluate the profitability of Dart's two products and make any recommendations you believe appropriate.

LO6 **C5-46. Absorption Costing and Performance Evaluation**

On July 2, Maddon Financial acquired 90% of the outstanding stock of Kluber Industries in exchange for 2,000 shares of its own stock. Maddon Financial has a reputation as a "high flier" company that commands a high price-to-earnings ratio because its management team works wonders in improving the performance of ailing companies.

At the time of the acquisition, Kluber was producing and selling at an annual rate of 100,000 units per year. This is in line with the firm's average annual activity. Fifty thousand units were produced and sold during the first half of the year.

Immediately after the acquisition Maddon Financial installed its own management team and increased production to practical capacity. One-hundred thousand units were produced during the second half of the year.

At the end of the year, the new management declared another dramatic turnaround and a $100,000 cash dividend when the following set of income statements was issued:

KLUBER INDUSTRIES
Income Statement
For the first and second half of the year

	First	Second	Total
Sales	$2,800,000	$2,800,000	$5,600,000
Cost of goods sold*	(2,400,000)	(1,400,000)	(3,800,000)
Gross profit	400,000	1,400,000	1,800,000
Selling and administrative expenses	(400,000)	(800,000)	(1,200,000)
Net income	$ 0	$ 600,000	$ 600,000

* Absorption costing with any underabsorbed or overabsorbed overhead written off as an adjustment to cost of goods sold. Kluber applies manufacturing overhead using a predetermined overhead rate based on predicted annual fixed overhead of $2,000,000 and annual production of 200,000 units.

Required

As the only representative of the minority interest on the board of directors, evaluate the performance of the new management team.

Solutions to Review Problems

Review 5-1—Solution

1. **Office supplies inventory**
   Each of the three types of organizations might include an office supplies inventory account on its balance sheet. Office supplies will typically be classified on the balance sheet as "other current asset." A manufacturing organization is most likely to have a supplies inventory account including the term "office" in order to distinguish it from manufacturing supplies. As the office supplies are consumed, they will move to the income statement and be classified as supply expense.
2. **Merchandise inventory**
   Merchandise inventory is an inventory account in the current asset section of the balance sheet of a merchandising company. As the inventory is sold, it moves to the income statement and is reported as a cost of goods sold expense.
3. **Finished goods inventory**
   Finished goods inventory is an inventory account in the current asset section of the balance sheet of a manufacturing company. As the inventory is sold, it moves to the income statement and is reported as a cost of goods sold expense.

4. **Work-in-process inventory**
   Work-in-process inventory is an inventory account in the current asset section of the balance sheet of a manufacturing company. As the work-in-process inventory is completed, it moves on to the finished goods inventory account in the current asset section of the balance sheet. Then, as discussed above, as the finished goods inventory is sold, it moves to the income statement and is reported as a cost of goods sold expense.

Review 5-2—Solution

a. Predetermined overhead rate per machine hour = $40,000,000/3,200,000 = $12.50
b. Applied overhead = $12.50 × 410,000 = $5,125,000
c. February overhead:

Actual	$4,410,000
Applied	(5,125,000)
Overapplied for February	(715,000)
Underapplied overhead, February 1	400,000
Overapplied overhead, end of February	$ (315,000)

Review 5-3—Solution

1. *c*: Production order
2. *a*: Process costing
3. *d*: Job cost sheet
4. *b*: Job order costing
5. *f*: Work ticket
6. *e*: Material requisition

Review 5-4—Solution

a.

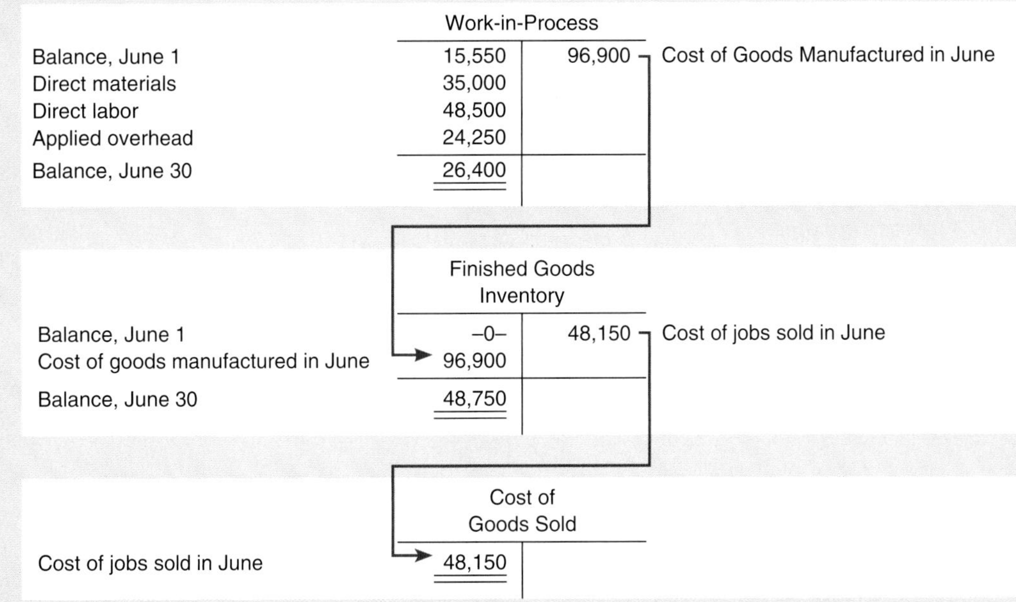

b. Job in Work-in-Process at June 30:

	Job 228
Direct materials	$14,400
Direct labor	8,000
Applied overhead (800 × $5)	4,000
Total	$26,400

Job in Finished Goods at June 30:

	Job 227
Direct materials	$18,000
Direct labor	20,500
Applied overhead (2,050 × $5)	10,250
Total	$48,750

Jobs sold in June:

	Job 225	Job 226	Total
Costs assigned from prior period	$13,750	$ 1,800	$15,550
June Costs: Direct materials	–0–	2,600	2,600
Direct labor	5,000	15,000	20,000
Applied overhead (500 & 1,500 × $5)	2,500	7,500	10,000
Total	$21,250	$26,900	$48,150

c. Statement of cost of goods manufactured for June:

STRATASYS LTD.
Statement of Cost of Goods Manufactured
June

Current manufacturing costs			
Cost of materials placed in production			
Raw materials, 6/1	$ 7,000 ^		
Purchases	40,000 ^		
Total available	47,000		
Raw materials, 6/30	(12,000)	$35,000 ^	
Direct labor		48,500	
Manufacturing overhead applied		24,250 *	$107,750
Work-in-process, 6/1			15,550 **
Total costs in process			123,300
Work-in-process, 6/30			(26,400)***
Cost of goods manufactured			$ 96,900

*Manufacturing Overhead Applied

Job 225:	500 hrs. × $5 = $ 2,500
Job 226:	1,500 hrs. × $5 = $ 7,500
Job 227:	2,050 hrs. × $5 = $10,250
Job 228:	800 hrs. × $5 = $ 4,000
	$24,250

**Work-in-process, 6/1

Job 225:	$13,750^
Job 226:	$ 1,800^
	$15,550

***Work-in-process, 6/30 (see part *b.*)

^ Given

Review 5-5—Solution

SANDISK
Cost of Production Report
For the Year

Summary of units in process			
Beginning	3,000,000		
Units started	27,000,000		
In process	30,000,000		
Completed	(25,000,000)		
Ending	5,000,000		
Equivalent units in process	**Materials**	**Conversion**	
Units completed	25,000,000	25,000,000	
Plus equivalent units in ending inventory	5,000,000	1,500,000	
Equivalent units in process	30,000,000	26,500,000	
Total costs to be accounted for and cost per equivalent unit in process	**Materials**	**Conversion**	**Total**
Work-in-Process, beginning	$ 468,000	$ 252,000	$ 720,000
Current cost	6,132,000	5,048,000	11,180,000
Total cost in process	$ 6,600,000	$ 5,300,000	$11,900,000
Equivalent units in process	÷ 30,000,000	÷26,500,000	
Cost per equivalent unit in process	$0.22	$0.20	$0.42
Accounting for total costs			
Transferred out (25,000,000 × $0.42)			$10,500,000
Work-in-Process, ending			
Materials (5,000,000 × $0.22)		$ 1,100,000	
Conversion (1,500,000 × $0.20)		300,000	1,400,000
Total cost accounted for			$11,900,000

Review 5-6—Solution

a. Ending inventory = 100 BI + 500 PROD − 540 SOLD = 60

Absorption costing	
Direct materials ($250 × 60)	$15,000
Variable overhead ($220 × 60)	13,200
Fixed overhead ($80 × 60)	4,800
Total	$33,000

Variable costing	
Direct materials ($250 × 60)	$15,000
Variable overhead ($220 × 60)	13,200
Total	$28,200

b.

Absorption costing		
Beginning inventory		$ 45,000
Production		
Direct materials (500 × $250)	$125,000	
Variable overhead (500 × $220)	110,000	
Fixed overhead (500 × $80)	40,000	275,000
Goods available for sale		320,000
Less ending inventory ($275,000/500 × 60)		33,000
Cost of goods sold		$287,000
Variable costing		
Beginning inventory		$ 38,000
Production		
Direct materials (500 × $250)	$125,000	
Variable overhead (500 × $220)	110,000	235,000
Goods available for sale		273,000
Less ending inventory ($235,000/500 × 60)		28,200
Cost of goods sold		$244,800

Chapter 6

Activity-Based Costing, Customer Profitability, and Activity-Based Management

Learning Objectives

LO1 Explain the changes in the modern production environment that have affected cost structures. (p. 208)

LO2 Outline the concept of activity-based costing and how it is applied. (p. 209)

LO3 Perform product costing using both traditional and activity-based costing methods. (p. 212)

LO4 Compare activity-based costing to traditional methods. Assess implementation issues involved in activity-based costing systems. (p. 218)

LO5 Analyze customer profitability using activity-based costing. (p. 221)

LO6 Explain the difference between activity-based costing and activity-based management. (p. 224)

We learned in the last chapter that indirect product costs need to be allocated to units of products or services based on a cost driver—a measure of activity that causes that cost to increase. However, the choice of one activity driver over another may result in widely differing costs for the same unit. In this chapter, we will address which driver is the correct driver; in many instances, product costing will be improved if we incorporate multiple drivers into the computation, choosing the drivers based on the activities undertaken to produce the good or service.

Consider the Anglo-Dutch company Unilever, one of the largest fast moving consumer goods (FMCG) companies in the world. Over 2.5 billion people in over 190 countries use Unilever products each day. The company operates through three divisions. The largest (by revenue) is Beauty & Personal Care, followed by Foods & Refreshment, and then Home Care. Unilever's nearly 400 household brands include Popsicle, Ben & Jerry's, Dove Beauty Products, Vaseline, and Seventh Generation.

Unilever operational strategies differ for each division. Beauty & Personal Care has been successful in offering premium products in the high-growth segment of the industry. Expansion of products for emerging markets has been a successful strategy in the Home Care division. More than 58% of Unilever's overall revenues are from emerging markets with the strongest growth in Southeast Asia. Operations in Foods & Refreshments are consolidated—bringing more scale and allowing for faster response to changes in consumer demand.

Overall, Unilever has focused on developing products that meet the consumer demand for more natural products and purpose-driven brands in recent years.

Twenty-six of the company's brands qualified as Sustainable Living brands, including B-Corp certified brands such as Ben & Jerry's, Seventh Generation, and Pukka Herbs. Certified B Corporations are businesses that meet high standards of social and environmental performance, public transparency, and legal accountability. In 2018, Sustainable Living brands grew 46% faster than other Unilever products and represented more than 70% of the company's growth.

Although still one of the top 10 global plastic polluters, the company recently adopted a "Less, Better, No" framework to transform its approach to plastic packaging. New ways of packaging and delivering products (including concentrates and refill stations for shampoo and laundry detergents in Southeast Asia) have reduced the amount of plastic used. Bottles made from recycled plastic are used in a variety of personal care products with a goal of at least 25% recycled plastic content in all packaging by 2025. Unilever also sells shampoo bars, refillable toothpaste tablets, and bamboo toothbrushes, which include no plastic.

In 2019, Unilever committed to cutting its use of virgin plastic by 50% and to helping collect and process more plastic packaging than it sells by 2025. The company expects all plastic packaging to be fully reusable, recyclable, or compostable.

When we break down our costs by activity and then allocate those costs based on the set of activities a product or service consumes, we provide the basis by which a company such as Unilever can make broad strategic and operational changes to its business. This chapter will demonstrate how to develop and implement costing systems based on activity consumption, which will lead to better decision making regarding product, geographic, and customer selection.

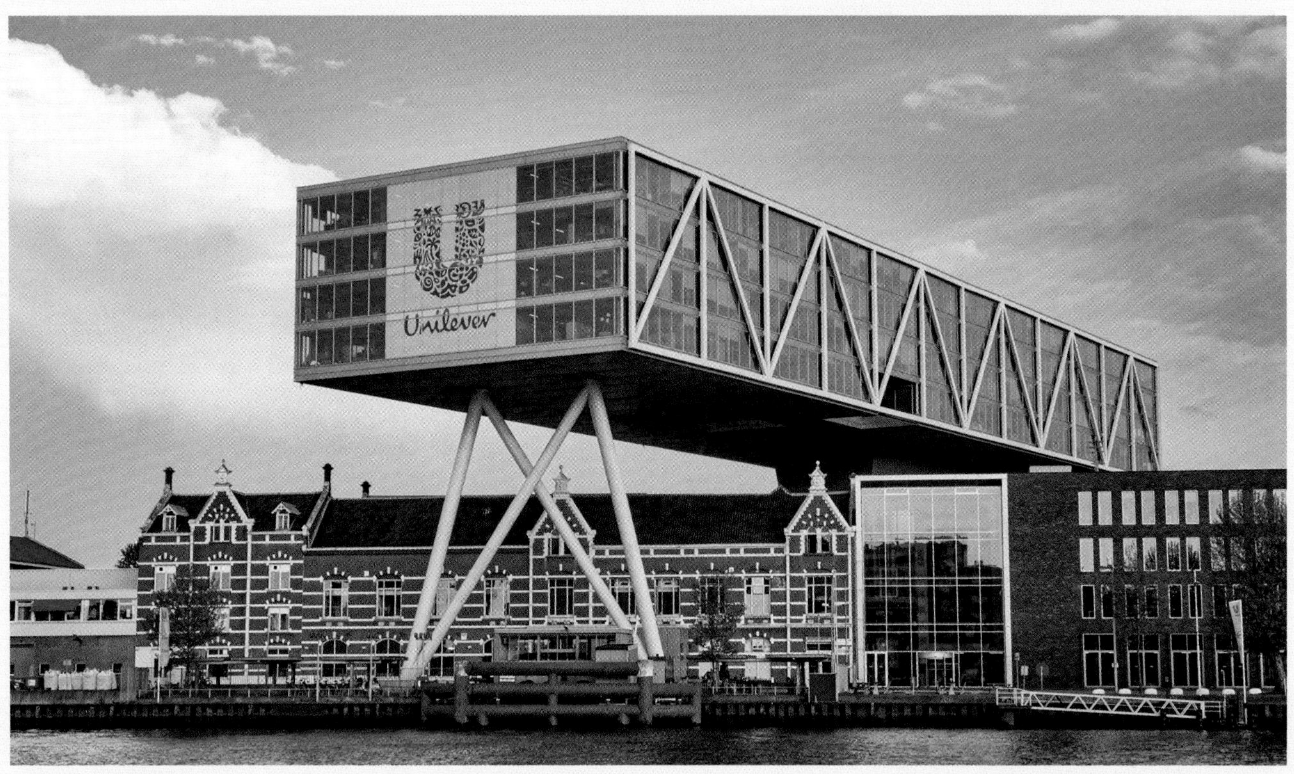

Road Map

LO	Learning Objective | Topics	Page	eLecture	Guided Example	Assignments
LO1	**Explain the changes in the modern production environment that have affected cost structures.** Changing Cost Environment :: ABC Product Costing Model	208	e6–1	Review 6-1	23
LO2	**Outline the concept of activity-based costing and how it is applied.** Cost of Activities :: Cost Objects :: Two-Stage ABC Model	209	e6–2	Review 6-2	10, 11, 12, 13, 14, 15, 16, 17, 19, 21, 22, 24, 25, 28, 29, 30, 31, 33, 34, 35, 36
LO3	**Perform product costing using both traditional and activity-based costing methods.** Plantwide Rate :: Department Rates :: ABC Activity Rates	212	e6–3	Review 6-3	20, 21, 22, 23, 24, 25, 28, 29, 30, 31, 32, 36
LO4	**Compare activity-based costing to traditional methods. Assess implementation issues involved in activity-based costing systems.** Limitations of ABC :: Traditional vs. ABC Methods :: Implementation Issues	218	e6–4	Review 6-4	20, 21, 22, 23, 24, 25, 28, 29, 30, 31, 32, 35, 36
LO5	**Analyze customer profitability using activity-based costing.** Customer Profitability Profile :: Customer Profitability Analysis	221	e6–5	Review 6-5	14, 18, 26, 27, 33, 34
LO6	**Explain the difference between activity-based costing and activity-based management.** Maximizing Value	224	e6–6	Review 6-6	26, 31, 33, 34, 35, 36

CHAPTER ORGANIZATION

Activity-Based Costing, Customer Profitability, and Activity-Based Management

Activity-Based Costing (ABC)	Traditional Product Costing and ABC Compared	Implementation of ABC	ABC and Customer Profitability Analysis	Activity-Based Management
• Changing Cost Environment • ABC Concepts • ABC Product Costing Model	• Applying Overhead with Plantwide Rate • Applying Overhead with Department Rates • Applying Overhead with ABC	• Limitations of ABC • Comparing Traditional and ABC Models • Implementation Issues	• Customer Profitability Profile • ABC Customer Profitability Analysis	• The Difference Between ABC and Activity-Based Management

Activity-Based Costing (ABC)

What are appropriate prices for our products and services? What are the current activities that contribute to our firm's costs? Does each of our activities add value for our customers? Which customers contribute the most to our profitability and which customers are unprofitable?

In a competitive business environment, it is imperative that a firm understand its costs in order to make good business decisions. It has become increasingly difficult to appropriately link overhead (indirect) costs to the products and services they support. In this chapter we will discuss some of the reasons behind the growing complexity of appropriately costing products and services and how activity-based costing can provide better information for decision making.

Changing Cost Environment

LO1 Explain the changes in the modern production environment that have affected cost structures.

As technology has advanced and competition has intensified over the last century, there has been a fundamental shift in manufacturing organizations from labor-intensive to automated assembly techniques. These changes have influenced the activities performed to meet customer needs and, consequently, the costs of producing goods and services.

At the beginning of the twentieth century, products had long life cycles, production procedures were relatively straightforward, production was labor based, and only a limited number of related products were produced in a single plant. It was said of the Model T Ford that "you could have any color you wanted, as long as it was black." The largest cost elements of most manufactured goods were the cost of raw materials and the wages paid to production employees. Manufacturing overhead was a relatively small portion of the overall cost of manufacturing products.

The twentieth century saw an accelerating shift from traditional labor-based activities to production procedures requiring large investments in automated equipment. In the past, production employees used equipment to assist them in performing their jobs. Now employees spend considerable time scheduling, setting up, maintaining, and moving materials to and from equipment. They spend relatively little time on actual production. The equipment does the work, and the employees keep it running efficiently. Increased complexity of production procedures and an increase in the variety of products produced in a single facility have also caused a shift toward more support personnel and fewer production employees. The result is a significant increase in manufacturing overhead as a percentage of total product cost. This change in the typical production cost structure over the past century is illustrated in **Exhibit 6.1**.

In the "low-tech," labor-intensive manufacturing environment, factors related to direct labor were often the primary drivers of manufacturing overhead costs; however, in today's "high-tech" automated environment there are many other factors that drive manufacturing overhead costs, and the specific set of cost drivers differs from organization to organization.

Exhibit 6.1 Changing Production Cost Structures

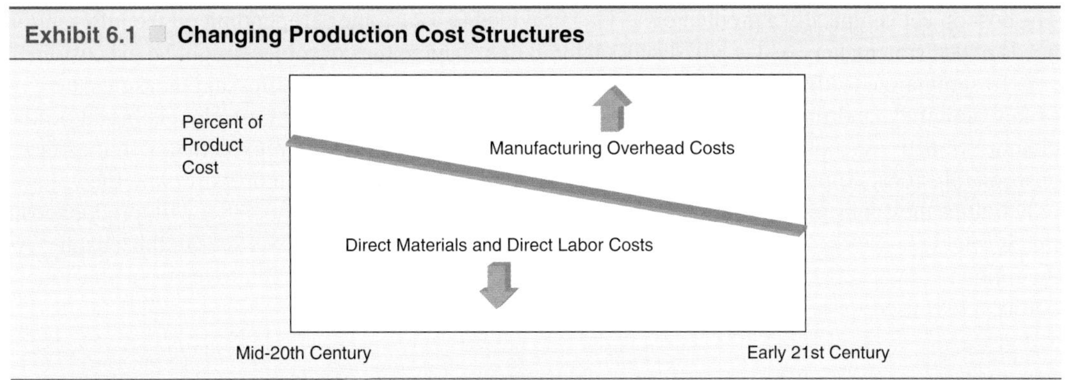

The previous chapter on product costing illustrated a simplified traditional system for allocating manufacturing overhead to products using a single, volume-based cost driver, such as direct labor hours. The following section introduces activity-based costing, which recognizes the multiple activities that drive manufacturing overhead costs in today's production environment.

Identifying Environment Changes that Impact Cost Structures **LO1 Review 6-1**

In a competitive business environment, it is imperative that a firm understand its costs in order to make good business decisions. These decisions might include: What are appropriate prices? What current activities contribute to a firm's costs? Which customers contribute the most to profitability?

Required

Discuss some of the factors in the U.S. economy that make it increasingly difficult to accurately assign costs to products and services.

Solution on p. 243.

Activity-Based Costing Concepts

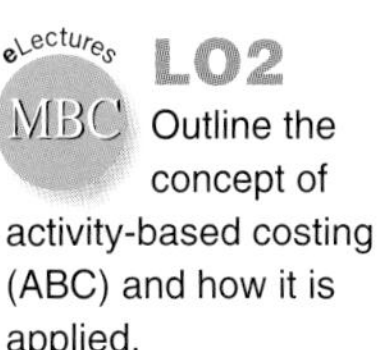

LO2 Outline the concept of activity-based costing (ABC) and how it is applied.

The manufacturing overhead cost pool has been referred to as a "blob" or "bucket" of common costs. The constant growth of costs classified as overhead has forced us to search for increasingly detailed methods to analyze these costs. If overhead costs are low in comparison with other costs and if factories produce few products in large production runs, the use of an overhead rate based on direct labor hours or machine hours may be adequate. However, as the amount of overhead costs continues to grow, as manufacturing facilities produce a wider variety of products, and as competition intensifies, the inadequacies of a single overhead rate based on a single cost driver such as direct labor hours become evident. In these cases, a single cost driver may not adequately represent how resources are consumed.

The shift from labor intensive to an automated manufacturing environment has resulted in the need for the identification of alternative cost drivers. Fortunately, advances in information technology and the declining costs of computerized information systems have facilitated the development and maintenance of increasingly detailed databases that support the use of multiple cost drivers. The increased complexity of the production environment, coupled with faster and cheaper computing technology, gave rise to the emergence and development of activity-based costing during the 1980s and 1990s.

Activity-based costing (ABC) involves determining the cost of activities and tracing their costs to cost objects on the basis of the cost object's utilization of units of activity.

The concepts underlying ABC can be summarized in the following two statements and illustrations:

1. Activities performed to fill customer needs consume resources that cost money.

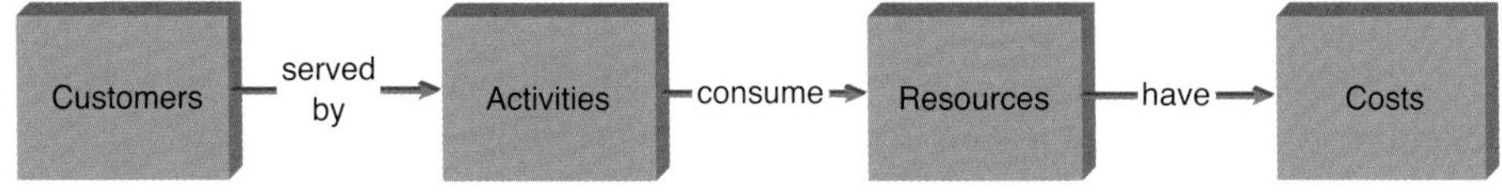

2. The cost of resources consumed by activities should be assigned to cost objects on the basis of the units of activity consumed by the cost object.

*Based on units of activity utilized by the cost object.

The cost object is typically a product or service provided to a customer. Depending on the information needs of decision makers, as we will discuss later in this chapter, the cost object might be the customer.

To summarize, activity-based costing is a system of analysis that identifies and measures the cost of key activities, and then traces these activity costs to products or other cost objects based on the quantity of activity consumed by the cost objects. ABC is based on the premise that activities drive costs and that costs should be assigned to products (or other cost objects) in proportion to the volume of activities they consume. Although activity cost analysis is most often associated with product costing, it offers many benefits for controlling and managing costs, as we will see later in this chapter. As the following Research Insight box explains, ABC was actually used first to improve cost management before it was used for product costing.

Research Insight ■ The History of ABC

ABC came to the forefront in the 1980s and 1990s; however, it was beginning to evolve as early as the 1960s when General Electric's (GE) finance and accounting staff attempted to improve the usefulness of accounting information in controlling ever-increasing indirect costs. The GE staff noted that indirect costs were often the result of "upstream" decisions, such as engineering design and change orders, which were made long before the costs were actually incurred. Frequently, the engineering department was not informed of the consequences their actions had on the other parts of the organization.

The second phase of the development of ABC was accomplished by business consultants, professors, and manufacturing companies during the 1970s and early 1980s. By generating more accurate cost and profitability measures for the various products offered by companies, these consultants and professors hoped to improve product cost information used in pricing and product mix decisions. ABC has since been extended to assess customer profitability.

In the late 1980s and 1990s, ABC was being promoted by many of the leading consulting firms, and it almost became a fad, much as TQM and JIT had become before it. Consequently, many companies that jumped on the ABC bandwagon early in its life later determined that it was not for them. Most of the companies that abandoned ABC probably adopted it initially for the wrong reasons.

Knowledge of the historical development of activity-based costing is important in order to clearly understand what ABC analysis was intended to accomplish, as well as what it was not intended to accomplish.

Source: Craig A. Latshaw and Teresa M. Cortese-Danile, "Activity-Based Costing: Usage and Pitfalls," *Review of Business*, Winter, 2002.

ABC Product Costing Model

Traditional costing considers the cost of a product to be its direct costs for materials and labor plus some allocated portion of factory overhead, using overhead rates typically based on direct labor or machine hours. Activity-based costing is based on the notion that companies incur costs because of the activities they conduct in pursuit of their goals and objectives and these activities are not necessarily unit-based. For example, various activities take place to produce a particular product, such as setting up, maintaining, or monitoring the machines to make the product, physically moving raw materials and work in process, and so forth. Each of these activities has a cost; therefore, the total cost of producing a product using ABC is the sum of the direct materials and direct labor costs of that product, plus the cost of other activities conducted to produce that product.

The general two-stage ABC product cost model is illustrated in **Exhibit 6.2**. The first stage includes the assignment of manufacturing overhead resource costs, such as indirect labor, depreciation, and utilities, to activity cost pools for the key activities identified. Typical activity cost pools in a manufacturing environment include pools for machine setup, material movement, and engineering. The second stage assigns those activity cost pools to products.

Notice in **Exhibit 6.2** that direct product costs, such as direct materials and direct labor, are directly assigned to products and are excluded from the activity cost pools. Only indirect product costs (manufacturing overhead) are assigned to products via activity cost pools.

Probably the most critical step in ABC is identifying activities and determining cost drivers. The activity cost driver for a particular cost (or cost pool) is the characteristic selected for measuring the quantity of the activity for a particular period of time. For example, if an activity cost pool is established for machine setup, it is necessary to select some basis for measuring the quantity of machine setup activity associated with the costs in the pool. The quantity of setup activity could be measured by the number of different times machines are set up to produce a different product, the amount of time used in completing

Exhibit 6.2 Two-Stage Activity-Based Costing Model

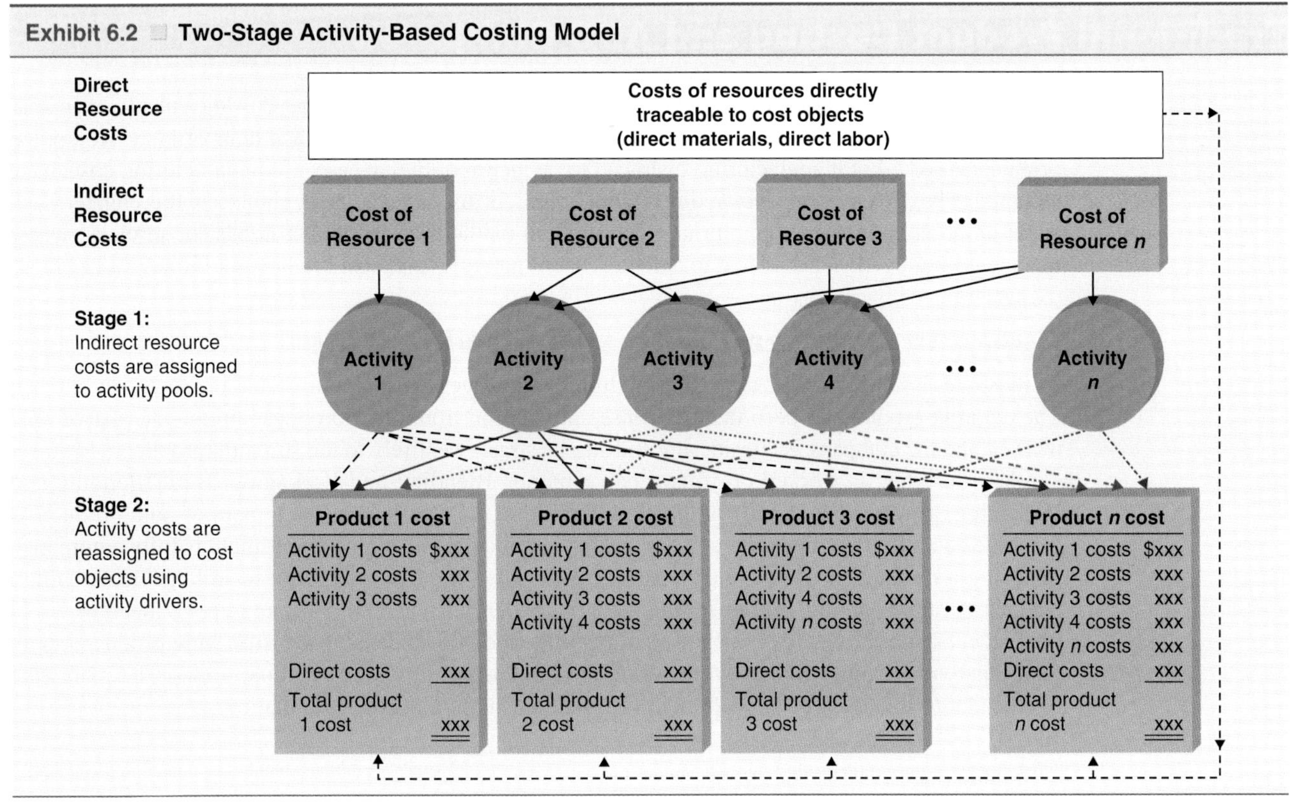

machine setups, the number of staff working on setups, or some other measure. It is critical that the activity measure used has a logical causal relationship to the costs in the pool and that the quantity of the activity is highly correlated with the amount of cost in the pool. Statistical methods, such as regression analysis and correlation analysis, can be very useful in selecting activity cost drivers.

Once the total cost in the activity pool and the activity cost driver have been determined, the cost per unit of activity is calculated as the total cost divided by the total amount of activity. For example, if total costs assigned to the setup activity pool in July were $100,000 and 200 setups were completed in July, the cost per setup for the month would be $500. If during July machines were set up 10 times to make product JX2, the total setup cost that would be assigned to product JX2 would be $5,000 ($500 × 10).

Identifying Relevant Cost Drivers — LO2 Review 6-2

Mobile Health Screening (MHS) offers onsite general health screening services for a flat rate of $35 per screening. MHS typically provides its services to businesses that offer fitness and health programs as a benefit to their employees. A representative of MHS arrives at a business early in the morning and sets up a room with the necessary equipment and supplies. The rooms are stocked with kits based on the expected number of participants. MHS sees participating employees throughout the day and screens for basic health measures such as blood pressure, weight, blood screening, and health behaviors. MHS sends samples to an outside lab for testing. MHS then compiles the results of all the tests and provides employees access to their individual results via a logon identification and password on the website. Participating employees may consult with a physician with questions on test results. Physicians are contracted by MHS and paid for time spent with the participants.

Required

For MHS, match each of the six activities to a likely related cost driver. A cost driver may be used more than once.

Activities

______ 1. Room setup
______ 2. Reception and admission of participating employees
______ 3. Administration of tests
______ 4. External lab processing
______ 5. Compiling, processing, and electronic posting of test results
______ 6. Consultations with MHS physician

Cost Drivers

a. Number tests
b. Number of participating employees
c. Number of minutes of consultation services

Solution on p. 243.

Traditional Product Costing and ABC Compared

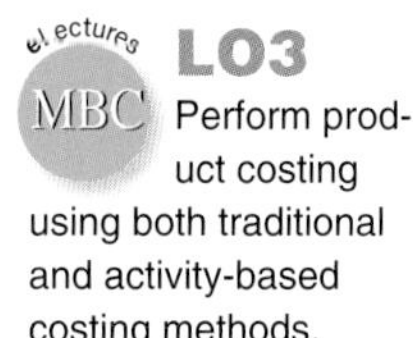

LO3 Perform product costing using both traditional and activity-based costing methods.

Recall that we assumed Frilly in Chapter 5 recognized manufacturing overhead using a plantwide manufacturing overhead rate of $4 per direct labor hour. It was assumed that each hour of labor worked on product caused $4 of manufacturing overhead to be incurred. In that case, all manufacturing costs were assumed to be driven by one factor, direct labor hours. As discussed at the beginning of this chapter, such an assumption is often not appropriate with modern methods of producing goods (or services) where manufacturing overhead is related to a diverse set of activities and cost drivers.

Applying Overhead with a Plantwide Rate

To illustrate, assume that Silk, a division of Danone, produces two alternative milk products, soy and oat. The oat milk product has been facing intense competition from other producers in the alternative milk market, and the company is considering shifting its strategy entirely to the soy milk product.

Each product is worked on in two departments, Blending and Packaging. Both Blending and Packaging operations are highly automated; therefore, the most common element of both products is machine hours in Blending and Packaging. Also assume the Packaging department is fully automated, incurring only machine hours and no labor hours. The products are produced in large 1,000-gallon batches. Assume oat milk requires 3 machine hours per batch and soy milk requires 2 machine hours per batch. Suppose for July, 232 batches of oat milk and 400 batches of soy milk were produced, with total plantwide manufacturing overhead of $187,000 and 1,496 total machine hours. The plantwide overhead rate is calculated as $125 per machine hour in the following tabulation.

Total plantwide manufacturing overhead	$187,000
Total plantwide machine hours	÷ 1,496
Plantwide overhead rate per machine hour	$ 125

Assigning $125 to each machine hour used is the simplest method of assigning manufacturing overhead to the products and, as the tabulation below shows, results in a total cost per batch of $610 for oat milk and $400 for soy milk after adding the direct materials and direct labor costs.

	Unit Costs	
	Oat Milk	Soy Milk
Direct materials	$125	$120
Direct labor	110	30
Manufacturing overhead		
Oat milk: 3 machine hours × $125	375	
Soy milk: 2 machine hours × $125		250
Total unit cost	$610	$400

A plantwide overhead allocation method is often used in situations where companies produce only one product in a plant, or where multiple products are very similar in regard to the cost of and use of resources, such as machine or labor hours, that drive most of the overhead costs. If multiple products are produced that consume varying levels of activities in multiple production departments, departmental overhead allocation rates will produce a more accurate allocation of overhead costs to the various products.

Applying Overhead with Department Rates

For Silk to establish separate overhead allocation rates for each of the two production departments, it is necessary first to assign the $187,000 of total overhead costs for the plant to the two production departments, some of which is directly assignable to the departments. For example, the departmental supervisors' salaries could be directly assignable to the departments. Other manufacturing overhead costs, such as support costs for maintenance, payroll, and so forth, are allocated to the production departments. Assume that after these allocations, the total costs assigned to the departments were $59,100 for Blending and $127,900 for Packaging.

The next step in the product costing process is to assign the departmental costs to the products. For this example, assume that the manufacturing process in the Blending Department is labor intensive, while the process in the Packaging Department is fully automated. Manufacturing overhead is applied to products as follows:

Department	Manufacturing Overhead Application Base
Blending	Direct labor hours
Packaging	Machine hours

During the month of July, 500 direct labor hours were worked in Blending. Packaging used 800 machine hours. Assume oat milk requires a total of 3 machine hours per batch with 1 of those hours incurred in Packaging. Soy milk requires a total of 2 machine hours per batch with 1.42 of those hours incurred in Packaging. The department manufacturing overhead rates based on actual costs for July and the total product costs using departmental overhead rates are calculated in the following tables:

Department manufacturing overhead rates for July	Blending	Packaging
Total department manufacturing overhead		
(direct department costs plus allocated costs)	$59,100	$127,900
Quantity of overhead application base		
Direct labor hours	÷ 500	
Machine hours		÷ 800
Department manufacturing overhead rates	$118.20	$159.875
	Per direct labor hour	Per machine hour

	Unit Costs per Batch	
Total costs per unit for July using department rates	Oat Milk	Soy Milk
Direct materials	$125	$120
Direct labor	110	30
Manufacturing overhead		
Blending: 1 labor hr. × $118.20	118	
0.67 labor hrs. × $118.20		79
Packaging: 1 machine hr. × $159.875	160	
1.42 machine hrs. × $159.875		227
Total costs	$513	$456

Allocating factory overhead costs based on department rates (rather than on a plantwide rate of $125 per machine hour) causes a shift in costs from oat to soy milk because oat milk's overhead activity is incurred evenly in both Blending and Packaging (1.00 hour each) while soy milk incurs more of its overhead activity in Packaging (1.42 hours versus 0.67 hour).

The per-unit costs with multiple allocations are substantially different from the per-unit costs when using plantwide rates and, in fact, show the cost of oat milk to be slightly below a competitor's bid of $525 that was offered to one of soy milk's customers. Assume that based on the plantwide rate, the cost of $610 for oat milk was higher than the competitor's price.

By creating separate manufacturing overhead cost allocation pools, allocation bases, and overhead application rates for Blending and Packaging, it is possible to recognize overhead cost differences in various products based on differences in Blending Department labor hours used and Packaging Department machine hours used for each product. In most multiproduct manufacturing environments, this approach represents a cost system improvement over using a single, plantwide overhead rate, and it reduces the likelihood of cost cross-subsidization, which occurs when one product is assigned too much cost as a result of another being assigned too little cost. While department overhead rates may improve product costing results for many organizations, and in fact may be satisfactory, this method does not attempt to reflect the actual activities used in producing the different product.

Applying Overhead with Activity-Based Costing

An even more precise method of measuring the cost of products than plantwide or departmental rates is the activity-based costing method. As stated earlier, activity-based costing involves determining the cost of activities associated with a particular cost object. Unlike traditional costing, activities are not limited to unit-level activities but can include for example, batch level and product level activities. ABC for product costing identifies and measures the cost of activities used to produce the various products and sums the cost of those activities to determine the cost of the products. The following Business Insight compares three key benefits regarding the accuracy of cost systems for ABC users and non-ABC users.

For Danone's Silk division, assume Blending and Packaging have overhead costs of $59,100 and $127,900, respectively. The overhead rates for each department were determined in the last section as $118.20 and $159.875, respectively, per relevant hour of use. The easiest way to assign these costs to products is by using one base and one rate for all products going through a given process (e.g., blending). However, different products typically use different amounts of resources from a given process and using the same base and overhead rate for all may distort the cost for some or all products.

Overhead costs in the Blending and Packaging departments consisted of two types of costs: direct department costs and allocated costs from other support departments. Direct department overhead costs are costs that are incurred directly by the department such as indirect labor, indirect materials, depreciation on equipment, supervisory wages, and so forth. Allocated support costs are costs allocated from other departments (specifically, engineering, support services, and building and grounds) that provide services to both Blending and Packaging. Danone's accountants determined that the *direct* department overhead costs in Blending were driven primarily by labor hours, whereas *direct* department overhead costs in Packaging were driven primarily by machine hours. It was also determined that each component of engineering, support services, and building and grounds represents a separate activity cost pool, and that these costs support both the Blending and Packaging Departments. Therefore, these costs should be assigned to the products based on specific cost drivers rather than a single department cost driver.

The following is a detailed analysis of overhead cost data for July's operations:

Overhead Activity	Total Activity Cost	Activity Cost Driver	Quantity of Activity	Unit Activity Rates
Direct departmental overhead costs				
Blending	$ 25,000	Labor hours	500	$ 50.00
Packaging	105,000	Machine hours	800	$131.25
Common overhead costs				
Support Services				
Receiving	14,000	Purchase orders	100	140.00
Inventory control	13,000	Units produced	632	20.57
Engineering Resources				
Production setup	12,000	Production runs	20	600.00
Engineering and testing	8,000	Machine hours	1,496	5.35
Building and Grounds				
Maintenance, machines	4,000	Machine hours	1,496	2.67
Depreciation, machines	6,000	Units produced	632	9.49
Total	$187,000			

Business Insight ■ Key Benefits of Using ABC

A 2009 study of 348 manufacturing and service companies worldwide indicated that activity-based costing continues to provide strategic and operational benefits. Although the study showed that there has been a decline in ABC users since the 1990s, when it was first widely adopted, the following graphics from the study report support the conclusion that users of ABC have a higher level of confidence than non-ABC users that their cost system provides more accurate cost measurements.

Comparisons of ABC to Non-ABC Users on Three Key Benefits

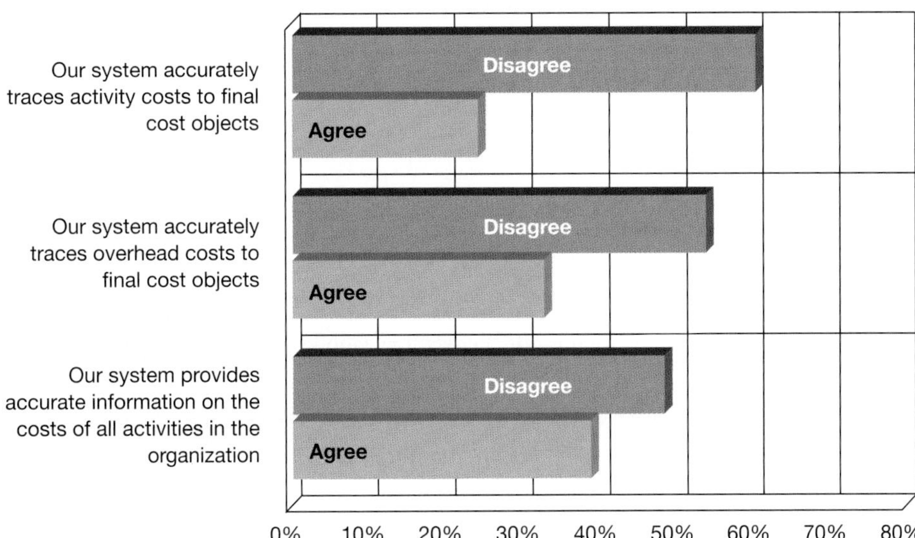

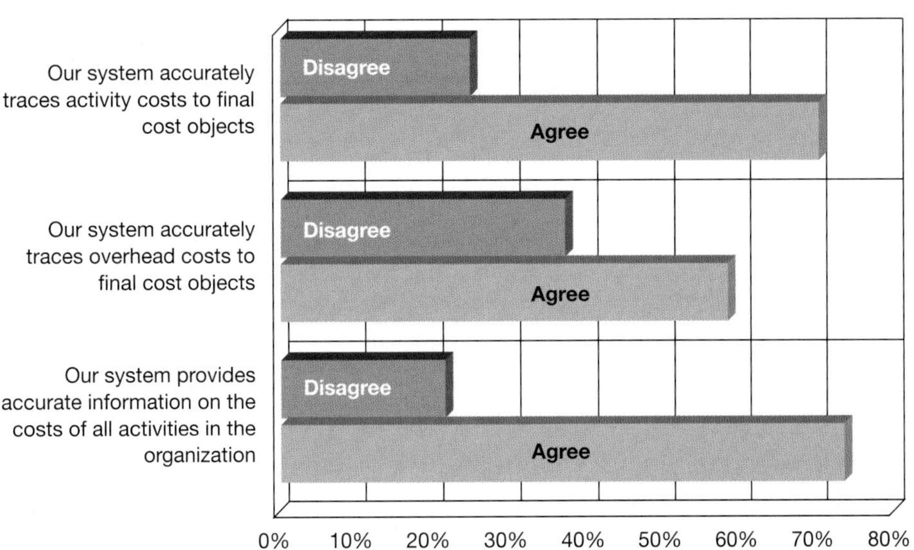

Source: William O. Stratton, Denis Desroches, Raef Lawson, and Toby Hatch, "Activity-Based Costing: Is It Still Relevant?" *Management Accounting Quarterly*, Spring 2009, Vol. 10, No. 3, pp. 31–40.

Assume that the amounts of activity attributed to oat and soy milk and the factory overhead cost per unit based on ABC costs are in the table that follows. This analysis outlines the activities in the production process, the amount spent on each activity, and the amount of activity used for each product line.

Activity (cost per unit of driver activity)	Oat Milk		Soy Milk	
	Quantity of Activity	Cost of Activity	Quantity of Activity	Cost of Activity
Blending ($50.00 per labor hour)	232	$11,600	268	$ 13,400
Packaging ($131.25 per machine hour)	232	30,450	568	74,550
Receiving ($140.00 per order)	40	5,600	60	8,400
Inventory control ($20.57 per unit produced)	232	4,772	400	8,228
Production setup ($600.00 per run)	5	3,000	15	9,000
Engineering and testing ($5.35 per machine hour)	696	3,724	800	4,280
Maintenance, machines ($2.67 per machine hour)	696	1,858	800	2,136
Depreciation, machines ($9.49 per unit produced)	232	2,202*	400	3,796
Total factory overhead product cost		$63,206		$123,790
Units produced		÷ 232		÷ 400
Factory overhead cost per unit of product*		$ 272		$ 309
Direct materials cost per unit of product		125		120
Direct labor cost per unit of product		110		30
Total unit product cost using ABC		$ 507		$ 459

The following table summarizes the total product costs for Danone's two products using the three different overhead cost assignment methods:

	Oat Milk	Soy Milk
Plantwide overhead rate	$610	$400
Departmental overhead rates	513	456
ABC	507	459

ABC product costing reveals a different cost picture. Using either a plantwide overhead rate or departmental rates, the oat milk product is bearing more than its share of total overhead costs. Using either of these methods could lead the company into a potentially poor strategy of abandoning the oat milk market. With an actual per-batch cost of $507, rather than $513 or $610, the company clearly has more latitude to compete on price with other companies in this market and remain profitable. Inaccurate costing can affect management's assessment of product profitability and its decisions regarding which products to continue to produce and which products to discontinue. Flawed product costing information can cause management mistakenly to decide to keep products that are losing money, while deciding to discontinue products that are profitable. Using a plantwide or departmental overhead allocation method could have led Danone's management to shift its emphasis from the oat milk to the soy milk market, a decision that could have been a poor decision for the company.

ABC often reveals product cross-subsidization problems. This is when ABC produces costs for some products that are higher, and costs for other products that are lower, than costs produced by traditional costing methods. This is referred to as cross-subsidization. For example, the cost of soy milk (oat milk) is higher (lower) under ABC than under traditional costing. Failing to assign and allocate costs by activity results in oat milk subsidizing soy milk. This can lead to ineffective business decisions such as product pricing decisions.

Business Insight ■ ABC and Software-as-Service

Changes in distribution have altered the business model and cost structure of the software industry. When software was distributed on physical discs, both the business model and cost structure of the software industry were rather traditional, dominated by direct labor and shipping costs. With the rise of the Internet and cloud-based computing, the software industry's business model is changing rapidly. Oracle has been particularly aggressive in switching its business from traditional software-as-product to software-as-service (SAS) and platform-as-service. According to Oracle's annual report, cloud-based and license support service business represents 83% of total revenue in fiscal 2019, up from 81% in 2018. Total revenue was $32.6 billion for fiscal year 2019.

continued

continued from previous page

Providing SAS requires both production of the software product and ongoing hardware and networking support as the product is delivered and maintained on a subscription basis. Each customer will have different service needs and require different amounts of various services from storage to support, as well as added functionality to make the services meet their needs on an ongoing basis. ABC is particularly useful in this type of business where units sold offer a very incomplete picture of the costs of serving the client.

Source: Mamta Badkar and Eric Platt, "Oracle Tops the S&P 500 Leaderboard," *Financial Times*, March 20, 2015.

Managerial Decision ■ You Are the Controller

You have heard about companies that have adopted ABC and experienced significant differences in product costs compared with previous cost calculations using traditional costing methods. Consequently, you were surprised when your newly implemented ABC system provided product costs that were almost identical to those from the old costing system. You are, therefore, thinking about abandoning the ABC system, since it is quite costly to maintain. Should you abandon your ABC system? [Answer, p. 225]

Determining Product Costs Using Traditional and Activity-Based Costing

LO3 Review 6-3

Assume that one of Illinois Tool Works Inc's (ITW) divisions has the following predicted indirect costs and cost drivers for the year for the given activity cost pools:

	Fabrication Department	Finishing Department	Cost Driver
Maintenance	$ 20,000	$10,000	Machine hours
Materials handling	30,000	15,000	Material moves
Machine setups	70,000	5,000	Machine setups
Inspections	—	25,000	Inspection hours
	$120,000	$55,000	

The following activity predictions were also made for the year:

	Fabrication Department	Finishing Department
Machine hours	10,000	5,000
Materials moves	3,000	1,500
Machine setups	700	50
Inspection hours	—	1,000

It is assumed that the cost per unit of activity for a given activity does not vary between departments.

Suppose ITW's divisional manager is trying to evaluate the company's product mix strategy regarding two of its five product models, Cobra Latch and GrimLoc. The company has been using a plantwide overhead rate based on machine hours but is considering switching to either department rates or activity-based rates. The production manager has provided the following data for the production of a batch of 100 units for each of these models:

	Cobra Latch	GrimLoc
Direct materials cost	$12,000	$18,000
Direct labor cost	$5,000	$4,000
Machine hours (Fabrication)	500	700
Machine hours (Finishing)	200	100
Materials moves	30	50
Machine setups	5	9
Inspection hours	30	60

continued

continued from previous page

Required

a. Determine the cost of one unit each of Cobra Latch and GrimLoc, assuming a plantwide overhead rate is used based on total machine hours.

b. Determine the cost of one unit of Cobra Latch and GrimLoc, assuming department overhead rates are used. Overhead is assigned based on machine hours in both departments.

c. Determine the cost of one unit of Cobra Latch and GrimLoc, assuming activity-based overhead rates are used for maintenance, materials handling, machine setup, and inspection activities.

Solution on p. 243.

Implementation of ABC

Limitations of ABC Illustration

eLectures MBC **LO4** Compare activity-based costing to traditional methods. Assess implementation issues involved in activity-based costing systems.

Several limitations of Danone's Silk division illustration should be mentioned. For the sake of simplicity, the example was limited to manufacturing cost considerations. A complete analysis would also require considerations of nonmanufacturing costs, such as marketing, distribution, and customer service, before a final determination of product profitability could be made. Finally, in calculating the activity cost per unit of activity, it is necessary to decide how to measure the total quantity of activity. For example, for the Silk division, the receiving cost per purchase order was calculated as $140.00 based on the actual quantity of 100 purchase orders for the period. Alternatively, the receiving cost could have been calculated based on **practical capacity**, which is the maximum possible volume of activity, while allowing for normal downtime for repairs and maintenance. If the plant has a practical capacity to prepare 140 purchase orders per period, the cost per purchase order based on the practical capacity is $100 per purchase order, or $14,000 ÷ 140. Using this overhead rate in costing product, only $10,000 would have been assigned to the two products, which required only 100 purchase orders, and the remaining $4,000 for the 40 purchase orders of excess (or idle) capacity not used would be written off as an operating expense of the period as underapplied overhead. Practical capacity is generally regarded as better than actual capacity for calculating activity costs because it does not hide the cost of idle capacity within product costs, and it gives a truer cost of the activities used to produce the product.

Comparing Traditional and Activity-Based Costing

Procedurally, ABC is not a new method for assigning costs to cost objects. Traditional costing systems have used a two-stage allocation model (similar to the ABC model) to assign costs to cost pools (such as departments) and subsequently assign those cost pools to products using an allocation base. In most traditional costing systems, overhead is assigned to one or more cost pools based on departments and functional characteristics (such as labor-related, machine-related, and space-related costs) and then reassigned to products using a unit-level allocation base such as direct labor hours or machine hours. ABC is different in that it divides the overall manufacturing processes into activities. ABC accumulates costs in cost pools for the major activities and then assigns the costs of these activities to products or other cost objects that benefit from these activities. *Conceptually,* ABC is different because of the way it views the operations of the company; *procedurally,* it uses a methodology that has been around for a long time.

The challenge in using ABC is specifying the model; that is, determining how many activity pools should be established for a given cost measurement purpose, which costs should be assigned to each activity pool, and the appropriate activity driver for each pool. Specifying the model also includes determining the resource cost drivers for assigning indirect resource costs to the various activity cost pools.

When evaluating whether to implement an ABC model, management must weigh the value of more accurate information against the administrative efforts of producing it. This can be complicated by the fact that it is often more difficult to measure the benefits of a process than it is to measure tangible costs. Further, once a company makes the decision to implement an ABC system, it also needs to assess the level of accuracy it wants the system to provide. In his article, "Implementing Activity-Based Costing," Gary Cokins emphasizes that the "quest for perfection is expensive," and that a reasonable level of accuracy might be sufficient.[1]

Business Insight ■ Batch Size Matters

Two trends are pushing American businesses to Maker's Row, a matchmaker for firms and factories in the United States. The rise of crowdfunding platforms like Kickstarter and IndieGogo has produced a large and growing number of small firms with a product and the cash required to produce it. Since these firms do not have the scale or resources to consider overseas production, they need local factories. At the same time, global manufacturing is shifting homeward. Large firms are trading lower labor costs and weaker regulatory environments at foreign plants for better supervision, more control, and lower shipping costs at U.S. plants. The crowdfunding and the "re-shoring" trends are both driving demand for domestic production, and Maker's Row is helping to match firms with factories that fit their needs.

According to Maker's Row cofounder Tanya Menendez, part of the problem with finding a factory is that the factory operators consider much of what they do to be a trade secret. Simple Internet searches yield little information of value, and even larger companies have difficulty finding the best option for their production. Maker's Row is a kind of online dating site for these manufacturers, allowing them to share information with potential clients and partners without making too much information public. By delivering information about factories to firms, Maker's Row helps firms make better production decisions about potential products.

Source: T.J. McCue, "80,000 Businesses Receive Manufacturing Help from Maker's Row," *Forbes*, September 3, 2015.

ABC Implementation Issues

The distortion in product costs for Danone's Silk division from using traditional cost systems based on plantwide or departmental rates, while hypothetical, is not uncommon. Studies have shown that distortions of this type occur regularly in traditional systems in which a significant variation exists in the volume and complexity of products and services produced.[2] Traditional systems tend to overcost high-volume, low-complexity products, and they tend to undercost low-volume, high-complexity products. These studies indicate that the typical amount of overcosting is up to 200% for high-volume products with low complexity and that the typical undercosting can be more than 1,000% for low-volume, highly complex products. In companies with a large number of different products, traditional costing can show that most products are profitable. After changing to ABC, however, these companies might find that 10% to 15% of the products are profitable while the remainder are unprofitable. Adopting ABC often leads to increased profits merely by changing the product mix to minimize the number of unprofitable products.

Most companies initially do not abandon their traditional cost system and move to a system that uses ABC for management and financial reporting purposes because financial statements must withstand the scrutiny of auditors and tax authorities. This scrutiny typically implies more demands on the cost accounting system for consistency, objectivity, and uniformity than required when the system is used only for management purposes. In addition, ABC systems must be built facility by facility rather than being embedded in a software program that can be used by all facilities within the company.[3] Often companies maintain traditional costing for external reporting purposes and ABC for pricing and other internal decision-making purposes.

Once an ABC system has been developed for a production facility, including an activities list (sometimes called an activities dictionary), identification of activity cost drivers, and calculation of cost per unit of driver activity, the activity costs of a current or proposed product can be readily determined. In ABC, as illustrated for Danone, manufacturing a product is viewed simply as the combination of activities selected to make it; therefore, the activity cost of a product or service is the sum of the costs of those activities. This approach to viewing a product enables management to evaluate the importance of each of the activities consumed in making a product. Possibly some activities can be eliminated or a lower cost activity substituted for a more costly one without reducing the quality or performance of the product.

[1] Gary Cokins, "Implementing Activity-Based Costing" (Institute of Management Accountants, 2014).

[2] Gary Cokins, Alan Stratton, and Jack Helbling, *An ABC Manager's Primer* (Montvale, NJ: Institute of Management Accountants, 1993).

[3] Robert S. Kaplan and Robin Cooper, *Cost and Effect* (Boston: Harvard Business School Press, 1998), p. 105.

In the 1980s, the Coca-Cola Company used ABC to determine that it was less costly—and thus, more profitable—to deliver soft drink concentrate to some fountain drink retailers (such as fast-food restaurants) in nonreturnable, disposable containers rather than in returnable stainless steel containers, which had been standard in the industry for many years.

Although an ABC system may be complex, it merely mirrors the complexity of an organization's design, manufacturing, and distribution systems. If a firm's products are diverse and its production and distribution procedures complex, the ABC system will also be complex; however, if its products are homogeneous and its production environment relatively simple, its ABC system should also be relatively simple. Even in highly complex manufacturing environments, ABC systems usually have no more than 10 to 20 cost pools. Many ABC experts in practice have observed that creating a large number of activity cost pools for a given costing application normally does not significantly improve cost accuracy above that of a smaller number of cost pools. As with any information system design, the costs of developing and maintaining the system must not exceed its benefits; hence, although adding more activity cost pools may result in some small amount of increased accuracy, it may be so small as not to be cost effective.

In addition to using ABC for product costing purposes, other important uses for ABC have also been found. One of the most useful applications for ABC discussed in the next section is in evaluating customer costs and distribution channel costs. Other applications include costing administrative functions such as processing accounts receivable or accounts payable; costing the process of hiring and training employees; and costing such menial tasks as processing a letter or copying a document. Any process, function, or activity performed in an organization, whether it is related to production, marketing and sales, finance and accounting, human resources, or even research and development, is a candidate for ABC analysis. In short, almost any cost object that has more than an insignificant amount of indirect costs can be more effectively measured using ABC.

Research Insight ■ A Time-Based Refinement of ABC for Health Care

ABC's complexity is both a strength and a weakness. To successfully implement ABC, an organization must be able to model and measure its production process in great detail. In industries such as health care this is all but impossible. Kaplan and his colleagues introduced a refinement to ABC in 2004 and tested its application to health care in 2011 with the help of several hospitals. Time-Driven Activity-Based Costing (TDABC) makes the patient and the diagnoses the unit of analysis. Rather than defining complex sets of activities and their rates, TDABC uses historical data to estimate two relationships—the cost of each resource used in treatment and the amount of time the patient spends with each resource.

These estimated relationships allow hospitals and other organizations to implement ABC without completely characterizing their activities. It also allows hospitals to determine which resources are particularly costly and focus on those resources for cost control. Thus, the benefits of ABC can be realized without the implementation issues discussed in this chapter. TDABC integrates easily with existing resource planning processes. The Mayo Clinic is a successful example of the benefits of TDABC implementation. It treats the TDABC process like it would any other improvement in medical care—as a scientific inquiry. It assembles a project team from every level of the organization and the group uses Kaplan's principles to estimate time/resource cost relationships. These relationships lead to experiments for improvement where they test the changes suggested in the TDABC process. Their findings are then shared with the whole organization.

Sources: Derek Haas, Richard Helmers, March Rucci, Meredith Brady, and Robert Kaplan, "The Mayo Clinic Model for Running a Value-Improvement Program," *Harvard Business Review*, October 22, 2015; Robert Kaplan and Michael Porter, "The Big Idea: How to Solve the Cost Crisis in Health Care," *Harvard Business Review*, September 2011; Alex Santana and Paulo Afonso, "Analysis of Studies on Time-Driven Activity Based Costing," *International Journal of Management Science & Technology Information 15* (2015): 133–157.

Review 6-4 LO4 **Comparing Product Costs Using Traditional and Activity-Based Costing**

Solution on p. 245.

Refer to Review 6-3 on page 217 and review your unit cost calculations in parts *a*, *b*, and *c*.

Required

Based on your calculations, compare and contrast the unit costs of the Cobra Latch and GrimLoc using the plantwide, department, and activity-based rates to assign manufacturing overhead.

ABC and Customer Profitability Analysis

LO5 Analyze customer profitability using activity-based costing.

One of the most beneficial applications of activity-based costing is in the analysis of the profitability of customers. Companies that have a large number of diverse customers also usually have widely varied profits from serving those customers. Many companies never attempt to calculate the profit earned from individual customers. They merely assume that if they are selling products above their costs, and that overall the company is earning a profit, then each of the customers must be profitable. Unfortunately, the cost incurred to sell goods and services, and to provide service, to individual customers is not usually proportionate with the gross profits generated by those sales. Customers with high sales volume are not necessarily the most profitable. Profitability of individual customers depends on whether the gross profits from sales to those customers exceed the customer-specific costs of serving those customers. Some customers are simply more costly than others, and some may even be unprofitable, and the unprofitable customers are eating away at the total profits of the company. In an ideal world, only profitable customers would be retained, and unprofitable customers would be either converted to a profitable status or they would be dropped as customers, unless there is a strategic reason for maintaining the relationship.

Customer Profitability Profile

If a company knows the amount of profits (or losses) generated by each of its customers, a **customer profitability profile** can be prepared similar to the one illustrated in **Exhibit 6.3**.

This hypothetical company has 350 customers and has current total profits of $5 million, but only 200 of its customers are profitable. Cumulative profits reach $7.5 million when the 200th customer is added to the graph, but the 201st through the 350th customers cause cumulative profits to decline to $5 million because they are unprofitable. Once a company has profitability data on each of its customers (or categories of customers), only then can it proceed to try to convert them to profitability, or seek to terminate the relationship with those customers. Just as we saw that ABC provided a model for producing more accurate product cost data, ABC is also a valuable tool for generating customer profitability data.

Exhibit 6.3 **Customer Profitability Profile Graph**

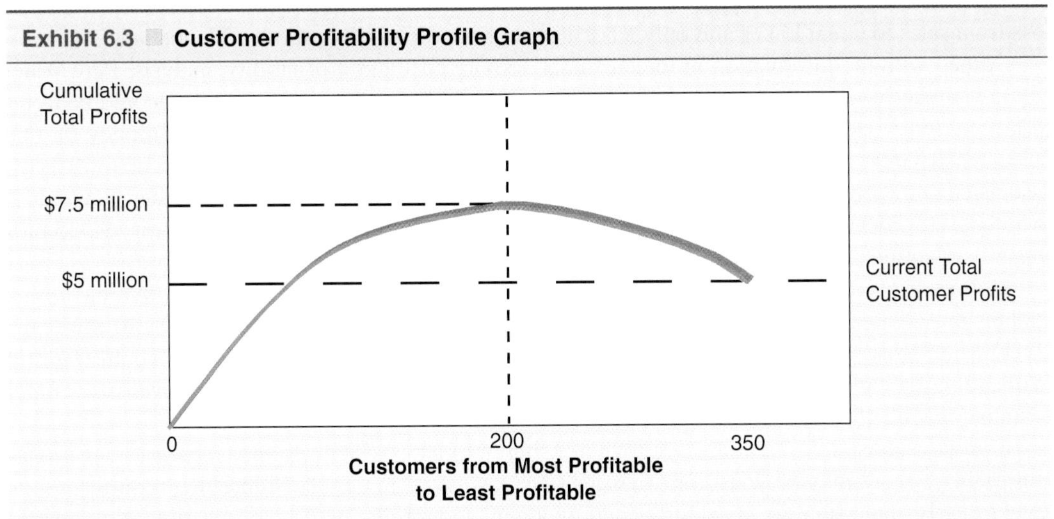

ABC Customer Profitability Analysis Illustrated

Pure Water Company is a "green" company located in the Midwest that manufactures and sells all-natural compounds for purifying water distributed through large public water systems. The CEO and founder of Pure Water personally developed the compounds using natural materials obtained from remote regions of the world. He knows that he has a product that is far superior to the traditional processes based on synthetic chemicals that have been used for generations to purify water. After five years in business, Pure Water has built a solid and growing customer base, but it has to invest significant time and expense servicing customers, especially those who have recently embraced its approach to water purification. Some customers require a lot of "hand-holding" with frequent visits and telephone calls, and they tend to purchase frequently in small amounts, often requiring repackaging. Other customers require little attention and support, and many of them purchase in large amounts once a year.

Although the company is making money, there is concern that profits could be higher if sales and other customer-related costs could be decreased. Pure Water's accountant has decided to conduct a customer profitability analysis using activity-based costing. As a first step, she determined that there were five primary activities related to serving customers: visits of customers by sales representatives, remote contacts (phone, email, fax), processing and shipping of customer orders, repackaging, and billing and collection. After extensive analysis, including numerous interviews and statistical analyses of activity and cost data, the accountant determined the following cost drivers and cost per unit of activity for the five customer-related activities:

Activity	Activity Cost Driver	Cost per Unit of Driver Activity
Visits to customers	Visits	$800
Remote contacts	Number of contacts	75
Processing & shipping	Customer orders	450
Repackaging	Number of requests	250
Billing & collection	Invoices	90

After collecting activity driver data on each of these activities for its major customers, the accounting group prepared the customer activity cost and profitability analysis presented in **Exhibit 6.4** for its five largest customers (in terms of sales dollars) in the order of greatest to least profit for the most recent year.

Since Pure Water is selling only one product to all of its customers, and has the same pricing policy for all customers, there is a constant 40% gross profit ratio across all customers, and the combined net profitability of these customers is 11.6% of sales. However, all customers are not equally profitable. The high level of support required by Manhattan and Great Lakes resulted in a net customer loss from sales to Great Lakes and only a 6.8% customer profitability ratio for Manhattan.

Armed with the information in the customer activity cost and profitability analysis, Pure Water can take proactive steps to increase its overall profitability ratio. An obvious option would be to try to terminate its relationship with Great Lakes since the company is clearly losing money on that customer. If Great Lakes were terminated as a customer, and assuming that all of the activity costs associated with Great Lakes could be avoided by the termination, Pure Water's total sales would drop to $68,750 (or $80,750 minus $12,000), but its total profit would increase to $11,785 (or $9,335 plus $2,450), resulting in a profitability ratio on the remaining four customers of 17.1%.

A more proactive approach would be to work with Great Lakes and Manhattan that have high support requirements, such as repackaging, frequent visits, and phone contacts to try to lower the level of high-cost support activities without reducing sales to those customers. This could result in maintaining the current level of gross profit, but generating a significantly higher level of total net customer profitability.

Two caveats should be considered when using activity cost data to manage customer profitability. First, there may be justifiable reasons (such as having a new customer that requires a high level of early-stage support, trying to penetrate a new geographic market, or existing relationships with other more profitable customers) for keeping customers that have lower profitability, or even customers that are not profitable. If so, these customers should be managed intensely to attempt to reduce the activities devoted to their support. Another caveat is that eliminating a customer may not immediately translate into an immediate reduction of activity costs. Some activity costs may not have a variable cost behavior pattern, and eliminating customers may merely create excess capacity in the short term. Of course, as stated previously, activity-based costing views virtually all costs

Exhibit 6.4 Pure Water Company

Customer Activity Cost and Profitability Analysis

	Seattle Water District	Manhattan Water Authority	Great Lakes Utility	Gulf Coast Utilities	Consolidated Water, Inc.	Total
Customer Activity Cost Analysis						
Activity Cost Driver Data						
Visits to customers	3	5	4	1	1	
Remote contacts	5	7	8	2	3	
Processing & shipping	3	3	5	4	1	
Repackaging	0	2	3	0	0	
Billing & collection	3	3	5	4	1	
Customer Activity Cost						
Visits to customers	$ 2,400	$ 4,000	$ 3,200	$ 800	$ 800	
Remote contacts	375	525	600	150	225	
Processing & shipping	1,350	1,350	2,250	1,800	450	
Repackaging	0	500	750	0	0	
Billing & collection	270	270	450	360	90	
Total Activity Cost	$ 4,395	$ 6,645	$ 7,250	$ 3,110	$ 1,565	
Customer Profitability Analysis						
Customer sales	$17,500	$20,000	$12,000	$15,000	$16,250	$80,750
Less cost of goods sold	10,500	12,000	7,200	9,000	9,750	48,450
Gross profit on sales	7,000	8,000	4,800	6,000	6,500	32,300
Less activity costs	4,395	6,645	7,250	3,110	1,565	22,965
Customer profitability	$ 2,605	$ 1,355	$ (2,450)	$ 2,890	$ 4,935	$ 9,335
Customer profitability ratio*	14.9%	6.8%	(20.4%)	19.3%	30.4%	11.6%

* Customer profitability ÷ Sales

as variable in the longer term. As the following Business Insight illustrates, despite these limitations, customer profitability analysis can provide valuable information to help keep an organization focused on its most profitable customers. In the case of General Growth Properties, understanding its customer profitability profile allowed it to adjust its leasing strategy to meet the changing needs of the retail industry.

Business Insight ■ Teams at Zappos Operate like Small Businesses

Zappos, a subsidiary of Amazon.com, has a unique management structure. Instead of a centralized, top-down corporate structure, Zappos operates in more of a marketplace system. Zappos "teams" (around 460 in early 2020) are operated like small businesses.

Each team is expected to manage its own profit-and-loss statement. Revenues are earned in most teams by selling their products to external customers or by selling their skills and services to other teams at market rates. Teams not focused on short-term profits, like research and development, are expected to fund their expenses through sponsorships from other teams.

Recently, the focus at Zappos has been to expand its offerings. CEO Tony Shieh said, "People can only wear so many shoes, the market is only so big." Employees are now being asked to consider possible services that Zappos could offer to entrepreneurs, similar to the way Amazon moved from selling books to selling just about everything to providing cloud computing services. Services could include anything from legal support to data analysis. Ideas that are considered promising receive $5,000 in seed funding as well as coaching and mentoring from Zappos employees.

The belief at Zappos is that encouraging "an entrepreneurial spirit and high degree of self-sovereignty" will result in revenue-producing or cost-cutting innovations that more than offset the costs related to self-direction and internal negotiations.

ABC can help Zappos teams analyze the relative profits of their current products and services and determine the profitability of new products and services.

Source: Aimee Growth, "Zappos Has Quietly Backed Away from Holacracy," *QUARTZ at WORK*, January 29, 2020.

Review 6-5 LO5 — Analyzing Customer Profitability

Suppose SAP is a systems design and implementation firm that serves five different types of customers. Assume SAP's design and installation projects are fairly standardized and routine; hence, the pricing is also standardized for all customers. While the company is profitable overall, the CFO thinks the net margins should be higher. She is concerned that customer support costs are eating up some of the margin and has decided to do a customer profitability analysis based on the five different types of customers to see if some of the customer groups may actually be less profitable than others. The following data for the most recent period have been collected to support the analysis.

Support Activity	Driver	Cost per Driver Unit
A. Minor systems maintenance	Hours on jobs	$160
B. Visits to customer	Number of visits	$300
C. Communication	Number of calls	$ 50

Customer Group	Activity A	Activity B	Activity C	Profit Before Support Costs
1	69	25	128	$80,000
2	141	42	205	85,000
3	74	19	99	83,000
4	61	28	106	90,000
5	136	39	189	78,000

Required

a. Calculate the customer profitability for each customer group taking into account the support activity required for each customer group.

b. Comment on the usefulness of this type of analysis. What reasonable actions might the company take as a result of this analysis?

Solution on p. 245.

Activity-Based Management

The Difference Between ABC and Activity-Based Management

LO6 Explain the difference between activity-based costing and activity-based management.

Activity-based costing has been highly touted as a technique for improving the measurement of the cost and profitability of products, customers, and other cost objects. In the early development of ABC, it was discovered that a by-product of accurately measuring the cost using ABC is that management invariably gains a much better understanding of the processes and activities that are used to create cost objects, such as products. Although ABC could be justified on the basis of its value as a tool in helping produce more accurate cost measurements for various cost objects, its greatest potential value may be in its by-products. The access to ABC data enables managers to engage in **activity-based management (ABM)**, defined as the identification and selection of activities to maximize the value of the activities while minimizing their cost from the perspective of the final consumer. In other words, ABM is concerned with how to efficiently and effectively manage activities and processes to provide value to the final consumer.

Defining processes and identifying key activities helps management better understand the business and to evaluate whether activities being performed add value to the customer. ABM focuses managerial attention on what is most important among the activities performed to create value for customers.

A helpful analogy in understanding what ABC can do for a company is to compare a company's operations with a large retail store, such as a Home Depot store. In a Home Depot store there is a clearly marked price on each of the tens of thousands of individual items that customers may decide to purchase. Similarly, every activity that takes place in any organization has a cost that can be determined and that management can use to make a judgment about the activity's value. In an ideal world, a manager could walk through the business and evaluate the cost of every activity being performed—maybe thousands of different activities—and then decide which ones are worth the cost and which ones are not adding value. Since generating ABC data has a cost, management must decide which ABC data are likely to be useful and cost beneficial. Our discussion here is only an introduction to activity-based costing and some of its applications. As the following Research Insight points out, over the past quarter of a century, ABC has matured well beyond merely accurately measuring cost of products and customers. More advanced topics such as those shown in the graphic are covered in advanced managerial accounting (or cost accounting) courses.

Research Insight ■ The Maturing of Activity-Based Costing

One of the leading thinkers and authors on the topic of activity-based costing over the past 25 years has been Peter B. B. Turney. He recently traced the evolution of ABC within the context of a product life cycle showing how ABC functionality has expanded since it was first introduced in the 1980s. As this graphic shows, ABC is now in its fourth generation, where it has become "an integral part of business performance management solutions, including profitability management, performance measurement, financial management, sustainability, and human capital management." In its current state of development, a single ABC model can support a number of needs, including historical cost measurement, resource planning, performance measurement, and other analyses.

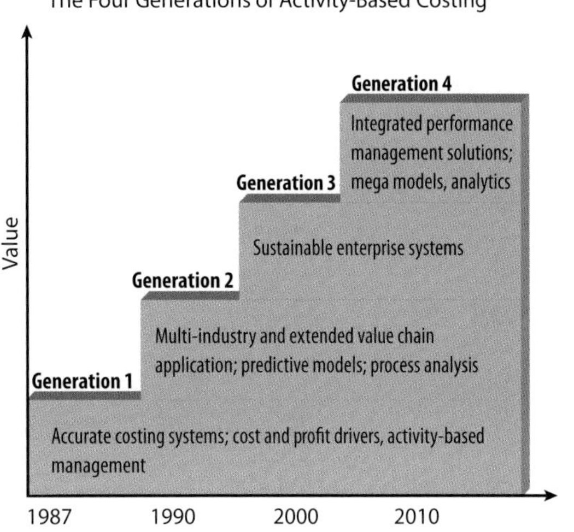

Source: Peter B. B. Turney, "Activity-Based Costing: An Emerging Foundation for Performance Management," *Cost Management*, July/August 2010, pp. 33–42.

Explaining Activity-Based Management LO6 **Review 6-6**

Although ABC could be justified on the basis of its value as a tool in helping produce more accurate cost measurements for various cost objects, its greatest potential value may be in its by-products.

Required

Discuss the relationship between activity-based management and activity-based costing.

Solution on p. 245.

Guidance Answers

You Are the Controller

Pg. 217 It probably is not the right decision to abandon the ABC system because there are many benefits to using ABC other than just calculating product costs. Indeed, in cases where companies produce multiple products that are fairly homogeneous in terms of the use of resources, ABC may not produce more accurate costs than traditional methods; however, there are many uses of ABC information beyond just calculating the cost of products. Having detailed information about activities and their costs can significantly improve the management of those activities. Identifying key activities and measuring their costs often cause companies to seek more efficient processes, possibly considering outsourcing activities that are currently performed internally, or even looking for ways to eliminate activities altogether. Activity cost information can also be used to identify best practices within an organization, or to benchmark internal activity costs with other organizations.

Key Terms

Multiple Choice

Multiple Choice Answers
1. c 2. b 3. b 4. d 5. a

1. Assume that Arco, Inc. has three activity pools which have the following costs: Machine Setups, $30,000; Material Moves, $45,000; and Machine Operations, $28,000. The activity cost drivers (and driver quantity) for the three pools are, respectively, number of setups (200), number of material moves (450), and number of machine hours (350). Product XJ3 used the following quantity of activity drivers to produce 100 units of final product: 25 setups, 40 material moves, and 75 machine hours. The total ABC cost and unit ABC cost assigned to Product XJ3 is

a. $103,000 total ABC cost and $1,030 unit ABC cost
b. $103,000 total ABC cost and $103 unit ABC cost
c. $13,750 total ABC cost and $137.50 unit ABC cost
d. $3,300 total ABC cost and $330 unit ABC cost

2. Marko Company produces two products, Xeon and Zeon, in a small manufacturing plant which had total manufacturing overhead of $45,000 in January and used 600 direct labor hours. The factory has two departments, Preparation, which incurred $25,000 of manufacturing overhead, and Processing which incurred $20,000 of manufacturing overhead. Preparation used 400 hours of direct labor and Processing used 160 machine hours. During January, 300 direct labor hours were used in making 100 units of Xeon, and 300 were used in making 100 units of Zeon. If Marko uses a plantwide rate based on direct labor hours to assign manufacturing costs to products, the total manufacturing overhead assigned to each unit of Xeon and Zeon in January were

a. $22,500 for Xeon and $22,500 for Zeon
b. $225 for Xeon and $225 for Zeon
c. $25,000 for Xeon and $20,000 for Zeon
d. $107.14 for Xeon, and $42.86 for Zeon

3. Refer to the previous question. Assume that instead of using a plantwide overhead rate, Marko used departmental rates based on direct labor hours for the Preparation Department and machine hours for the Processing Department. The departmental overhead rates for the Preparation and Processing Departments were

a. $75 per direct labor hour for both Preparation and Processing
b. $62.50 per direct labor hour for Preparation, and $125 per machine hour for Processing
c. $125 per direct labor hour for Preparation, and $62.50 per machine hour for Processing
d. $80.35 per direct labor hour for Preparation, and $80.35 per machine hour for Processing

4. Refer to the previous questions regarding Marko Company. Assume that Xeon used 175 direct labor hours and Zeon used 225 direct labor hours in the Preparation Department. Also, assume that Xeon used 100 machine hours and Zeon used 60 machine hours in the Processing Department. The overhead costs assigned to each unit of Xeon and Zeon were

a. $253.50 for Xeon and $196.50 for Zeon
b. $62.50 for Xeon and $125 for Zeon
c. $215.63 for Zeon and $215.63 for Xeon
d. $234.38 for Xeon and $215.63 for Zeon

5. Refer to the previous questions regarding Marko Company. Assume that Marko used an ABC product costing system and that its total manufacturing overhead costs of $45,000 were assigned to the following ABC cost pools:

Material inspections & preparation ($20,000)	$20 per pound of raw materials
Material moves ($5,000)	$50 per move
Machine setups ($6,000)	$300 per setup
Machine operations ($14,000)	$87.50 per machine hour

Xeon and Zeon used the following quantities of the four activity drivers:

	Xeon	Zeon
Pounds of raw materials	500	500
Material moves	60	40
Setups	12	8
Machine hours	100	60

The overhead costs assigned to each unit of Xeon and Zeon were

a. $253.50 for Xeon and $196.50 for Zeon
b. $62.50 for Xeon and $125 for Zeon
c. $215.63 for Xeon and $234.63 for Zeon
d. $234.38 for Xeon and $215.63 for Zeon

Questions

Q6-1. Summarize the concepts underlying activity-based costing in two sentences.

Q6-2. What steps are required to implement the two-stage activity-based costing model?

Q6-3. Define activity cost pool, activity cost driver, and cost per unit of activity.

Q6-4. Name two possible activity cost drivers for each of the following activities: maintenance, materials movement, machine setup, inspection, materials purchases, and customer service.

Q6-5. What is the premise of activity-based costing for product costing purposes?

Q6-6. In what ways does ABC product costing differ from traditional product cost methods?

Q6-7. Explain why ABC often reveals existing product cost cross-subsidization problems.

Q6-8. How can ABC be used to improve customer profitability analysis?

Q6-9. Explain activity-based management and how it differs from activity-based costing.

Assignments with the MBC logo in the margin are available in myBusinessCourse. See the Preface of the book for details.

Mini Exercises

M6-10. Activities and Cost Drivers LO2

For each of the following activities, select the most appropriate cost driver. Each cost driver may be used only once.

Activity	Cost Driver
1. Pay vendors	*a.* Number of different kinds of raw materials
2. Evaluate vendors	*b.* Number of classes offered
3. Inspect raw materials	*c.* Number of tables
4. Plan for purchases of raw materials	*d.* Number of employees
5. Packaging	*e.* Number of operating hours
6. Supervision	*f.* Number of units of raw materials received
7. Employee training	*g.* Number of moves
8. Clean tables	*h.* Number of vendors
9. Machine maintenance	*i.* Number of checks issued
10. Move in-process product from one workstation to the next	*j.* Number of customer orders

M6-11. Developing a List of Activities for Baggage Handling at an Airport LO2 Southwest Airlines (LUV)

Assume you have been asked to determine the activities involved in the baggage-handling process of Southwest Airlines' Chicago-Midway hub. Prior to conducting observations and interviews, you decide that a list of possible activities would help you to better observe key activities and ask meaningful questions.

Required

For incoming aircraft only, develop a sequential list of baggage-handling activities. Your list should contain between 8 and 10 activities.

LO2
University of Texas

M6-12. Stage 1 ABC at a College: Assigning Costs to Activities

Assume an accounting professor at the University of Texas devotes 60% of her time to teaching, 30% of her time to research and writing, and 10% of her time to service activities such as committee work and curriculum development. The professor teaches two semesters per year. During each semester, she teaches one section of an introductory financial accounting course (with a maximum enrollment of 60 students) and one section of a graduate financial accounting course (with a maximum enrollment of 30 students). Including course preparation, classroom instruction, and appointments with students, each course requires an equal amount of time. The accounting professor is paid $150,000 per year.

Required

Determine the activity cost of instruction per student in both the introductory and the graduate financial accounting courses.

LO2

M6-13. Stage 1 ABC for a Machine Shop: Assigning Costs to Activities

As the chief engineer of a small fabrication shop, Christine Sanders refers to herself as a "jack-of-all-trades." When an order for a new product comes in, Christine must do the following:

1. Design the product to meet customer requirements.
2. Prepare a bill of materials (a list of materials required to produce the product).
3. Prepare an operations list (a sequential list of the steps involved in manufacturing the product).

Each time the foundry manufactures a batch of the product, Christine must perform these activities:

1. Schedule the job.
2. Supervise the setup of machines that will work on the job.
3. Inspect the first unit produced to verify that it meets specifications.

Christine supervises the production employees who perform the actual work on individual units of product. She is also responsible for employee training, ensuring that production facilities are in proper operating condition, and attending professional meetings. Christine's estimates (in percent) of time spent on each of these activities last year are as follows:

Designing product	15%
Preparing bills of materials	5
Preparing operations lists	9
Scheduling jobs	12
Supervising setups	6
Inspecting first units	7
Supervising production	25
Training employees	8
Maintaining facility	3
Attending professional meetings	10
	100%

Required

Assuming Christine Sanders' salary is $115,000 per year, determine the dollar amount of her salary assigned to unit-, batch-, product-, and facility-level activities. (You may need to review Chapter 2 before answering this question.)

LO2, 5
Charlie's Produce

M6-14. Stage 2 ABC for a Wholesale Company

Charlie's Produce is a West Coast distributor of fresh produce. Assume the following information represents activity costs for the Los Angeles distribution center.

Activity	Cost per Unit of Activity Driver
Customer relations	$110.00 per customer per month
Selling	0.05 per sales dollar
Accounting	7.50 per order
Warehousing	0.60 per case shipped
Packing	0.30 per case shipped
Shipping	0.05 per pound shipped

The following information pertains to June operations for the Los Angeles distribution center of Charlie's Produce.

Number of orders	3,220
Sales revenue	$2,150,000
Cost of produce sold	$1,405,000
Number of customers	432
Cases shipped	57,850
Pounds shipped	1,250,000

Required

Determine the profitability of sales in the Los Angeles distribution center for June.

M6-15. Stage 2 ABC for Manufacturing: Reassigning Costs to Cost Objects LO2

Woodland Corporation has developed the following activity cost information for its manufacturing activities:

Activity	Activity Cost
Machine setup	$120.00 per batch
Movement	15.00 per batch move
	0.10 per pound, per move
Drilling	6.00 per hole
Welding	4.00 per inch
Shaping	22.00 per hour
Assembly	18.00 per hour
Inspection	2.00 per unit

Filling an order for a batch of 125 fireplace inserts (each insert weighing 50 pounds) required the following:

- Four batch moves
- Three sets of inspections
- Drilling eight holes in each unit
- Completing 100 inches of welds on each unit
- Forty-five minutes of shaping for each unit
- One hour of assembly per unit

Required

Determine the activity cost of converting the raw materials into 125 fireplace inserts.

M6-16. Two-Stage ABC for Manufacturing LO2 The Vollrath Company

Vollrath Manufacturing, a division of The Vollrath Company, manufactures restaurant equipment. Assume the company has determined the following activity cost pools and cost driver levels for the year:

Activity Cost Pool	Activity Cost	Activity Cost Driver
Machine setup	$750,000	18,750 setup hours
Material handling	121,600	3,800 tons of materials
Machine operation	552,500	16,250 machine hours

The following data are for the production of single batches of two products, Equipment Stands and Charbroilers during the month of August:

	Equipment Stands	Charbroilers
Units produced	100	50
Machine hours	8	25
Direct labor hours	400	1,200
Direct labor cost	$10,000	$30,000
Direct materials cost	$48,000	$125,000
Tons of materials	4	14
Setup hours	6	36

Required

Determine the unit costs of Equipment Stands and Charbroilers using ABC.

LO2 Sherwin-Williams (SHW)

M6-17. Two-Stage ABC for Manufacturing

Assume Sherwin-Williams, a large paint manufacturer, has determined the following activity cost pools and cost driver levels for the latest period:

Activity Cost Pool	Activity Cost	Activity Cost Driver
Machine setup	$210,000	3,500 setup hours
Material handling	468,000	6,500 material moves
Machine operation	1,026,270	12,670 machine hours

The following data are for the production of single batches of two of its products, Cashmere and Emerald:

	Cashmere	Emerald
Gallons produced	20,000	25,000
Direct labor hours	200	220
Machine hours	100	120
Direct labor cost	$5,000	$5,500
Direct materials cost	$282,940	$299,090
Setup hours	24	26
Material moves	35	40

Required

Determine the batch and unit costs per gallon of Cashmere and Emerald using ABC.

LO5

M6-18. Customer Profitability Analysis

Elite Services, Inc. provides residential painting services for three home building companies, Brookside, Edgewater, and Hillrose, and it uses a job costing system for determining the costs for completing each job. The job cost system does not capture any cost incurred by Elite for return touchups and refinishes after the homeowner occupies the home. Elite paints each house on a square footage contract price, which includes painting as well as all refinishes and touchups required after the homes are occupied. Each year, the company generates about one-third of its total revenues and gross profits from each of the three builders. The Elite owner has observed that the builders, however, require substantially different levels of support following the completion of jobs. The following data have been gathered:

Support Activity	Driver	Cost per Driver Unit
Major refinishes	Hours on jobs	$150
Touchups	Number of visits	$100
Communication	Number of calls	$ 30

Builder	Major Refinishes	Touchups	Communication
Brookside	120	260	900
Edgewater	70	205	530
Hillrose	80	220	590

Required
Assuming that each of the three customers produces gross profits of $150,000, calculate the profitability from each builder after taking into account the support activity required for each builder.

Exercises

E6-19. Two-Stage ABC for Manufacturing LO2

Thornton Company has determined its activity cost pools and cost drivers to be the following:

Cost pools	
Setup	$ 55,000
Material handling	10,050
Machine operation	242,400
Packing	67,200
Total indirect manufacturing costs	$374,650
Cost drivers	
Setups	550
Material moves	670
Machine hours	20,200
Packing orders	1,400

One product made by Thornton, metal casements, used the following activities during the period to produce 500 units:

Setups	45
Material moves	112
Machine hours	2,400
Packing orders	195

Required
a. Calculate the cost per unit of activity for each activity cost pool for Thornton Company.
b. Calculate the manufacturing overhead cost per metal casement manufactured during the period.

E6-20. Calculating Manufacturing Overhead Rates LO3, 4

Windsor Company accumulated the following data from last year's operations.

Milling Department manufacturing overhead	$450,000
Finishing Department manufacturing overhead	$150,000
Machine hours used	
Milling Department	15,000 hours
Finishing Department	5,000 hours
Labor hours used	
Milling Department	2,000 hours
Finishing Department	2,000 hours

In the Milling department, grooves are cut into aluminum and steel rods using computer-controlled equipment. In the Finishing department, the rods are individually cleaned and polished.

Required
a. Calculate the plantwide manufacturing overhead rate using machine hours as the allocation base.
b. Calculate the plantwide manufacturing overhead rate using direct labor hours as the allocation base.
c. Calculate department overhead rates using machine hours in Milling and direct labor hours in Finishing as the allocation bases.
d. Calculate department overhead rates using direct labor hours in Milling and machine hours in Finishing as the allocation bases.
e. Which of these allocation systems seems to be the most appropriate? Explain.

LO2, 3, 4

E6-21. Calculating Activity-Based Costing Overhead Rates

Assume that manufacturing overhead for Windsor Company in the previous exercise consisted of the following activities and costs:

Setup (2,500 setup hours)	$125,000
Production scheduling (150 batches)	75,000
Production engineering (20,000 machine hours)	265,000
Supervision (4,000 direct labor hours)	85,800
Machine maintenance (1,025 repair requests)	49,200
Total activity costs	$600,000

The following additional data were provided for Job 845:

Direct materials costs	$1,450
Direct labor cost (5 Milling direct labor hours; 15 Finishing direct labor hours)	$ 500
Setup hours	2 hours
Production scheduling	1 batch
Machine hours used (15 Milling machine hours; 5 Finishing machine hours)	20 hours
Machine maintenance	1 repair request

Required

a. Calculate the cost per unit of activity driver for each activity cost category.

b. Calculate the cost of Job 845 using ABC to assign the overhead costs.

c. Calculate the cost of Job 845 using the plantwide overhead rate based on machine hours calculated in the previous exercise.

d. Calculate the cost of Job 845 using a machine hour departmental overhead rate for the Milling Department and a direct labor hour overhead rate for the Finishing Department (see E6-20).

LO2, 3, 4

E6-22. Activity-Based Costing and Traditional Costs Compared

Cuisinart, a Conair Corporation, manufactures outdoor gas cookers and charcoal smokers. Assume that Cuisinart only makes a single model of each product and that the following information pertains to the total manufacturing costs for the products in the current month.

	Gas Cooker	Charcoal Smoker
Units	4,000	3,500
Number of batches	80	35
Number of machine hours	16,000	3,000
Direct materials	$225,500	$108,500
Direct labor	$100,683	$50,341

Manufacturing overhead follows:

Activity	Cost	Cost Driver
Materials acquisition and inspection	$ 50,100	Amount of direct materials cost
Product assembly	123,500	Number of machine hours
Scheduling	15,180	Number of batches
	$188,780	

Required

a. Determine the total and per-unit costs of manufacturing the Gas Cooker and Charcoal Smoker for the month, assuming all manufacturing overhead related to these two products is assigned on the basis of direct labor dollars.

b. Determine the total and per-unit costs of manufacturing the Gas Cooker and Charcoal Smoker for the month, assuming manufacturing overhead is assigned using activity-based costing.

E6-23. Activity-Based Costing Versus Traditional Costing LO1, 3, 4

Refer to the previous exercise in E6-22 for Cuisinart.

Required

a. Comment on the differences between the solutions to requirements (a) and (b). Which is more accurate? What errors might managers make if all manufacturing overhead costs are assigned on the basis of direct labor dollars?

b. Cuisinart's manufacturing process has become increasingly automated over the past few years. Discuss how this will likely impact its ability to accurately measure product costs.

c. Comment on the adequacy of the preceding data to meet management's needs.

E6-24. Traditional Product Costing versus Activity-Based Costing LO2, 3, 4 Panasonic Corporation (PCRFY)

Assume that Panasonic Corporation has determined its estimated total manufacturing overhead cost for one of its plants to be $436,000, consisting of the following activity cost pools for the current month:

Activity Centers	Activity Costs	Cost Drivers	Activity Level
Assembly setups	$124,000	Setup hours	4,000
Materials handling	57,000	Number of moves	600
Assembly	225,000	Assembly hours	12,500
Maintenance	30,000	Maintenance hours	1,200
Total	$436,000		

Total direct labor hours used during the month were 16,000. Panasonic produces many different electronic products, including the following two products produced during the current month:

	Model X301	Model Z205
Units produced	2,000	2,000
Direct materials costs	$18,550	$18,550
Direct labor costs	$5,000	$5,000
Direct labor hours	200	200
Setup hours	30	60
Materials moves	75	150
Assembly hours	500	750
Maintenance hours	25	45

Required

a. Calculate the total per-unit cost of each model using direct labor hours to assign manufacturing overhead to products.

b. Calculate the total per-unit cost of each model using activity-based costing to assign manufacturing overhead to products.

c. Comment on the accuracy of the two methods for determining product costs.

d. Discuss some of the strategic implications of your answers to the previous requirements.

E6-25. Traditional Product Costing versus Activity-Based Costing LO2, 3, 4

Ridgeland Inc. makes backpacks for large sporting goods chains that are sold under the customers' store brand names. The Accounting Department has identified the following overhead costs and cost drivers for next year:

Overhead Item	Expected Costs	Cost Driver	Maximum Quantity
Setup costs	$175,000	Number of setups	1,750
Ordering costs	120,000	Number of orders	15,000
Assembly	910,000	Number of machine hours	14,000
Finishing	208,000	Number of direct labor hours	104,000

The following data are for two recently completed jobs:

	Job 201	Job 202
Cost of direct materials	$12,000	$14,000
Cost of direct labor	$20,500	$40,000
Number of units completed	1,000	850
Number of setups	15	18
Number of orders	200	100
Number of machine hours	200	225
Number of direct labor hours	820	1,600

Required

a. Determine the unit cost for each job using a traditional plantwide overhead rate based on machine hours.

b. Determine the unit cost for each job using ABC. (Round answers to two decimal places.)

c. As the manager of Ridgeland, is there additional information that you would want to help you evaluate the pricing and profitability of Jobs 201 and 202?

d. Assuming the company has been using the method required in part *a*, how should management react to the findings in part *b*?

LO5, 6 **E6-26. Customer Profitability Analysis**

Leahy Inc. has 10 customers that account for all of its $1,472,000 of net income. Its activity-based costing system is able to assign all costs, except for $200,000 of general administrative costs, to key activities incurred in connection with serving its customers. A customer profitability analysis based on activity costing produced the following customer profits and losses:

Customer	#1	$ 350,000
	#2	262,000
	#3	(75,000)
	#4	240,000
	#5	50,000
	#6	375,000
	#7	(100,000)
	#8	325,000
	#9	225,000
	#10	(180,000)
Total		$1,472,000

Required

Prepare a customer profitability profile like the one in **Exhibit 6.3**.

LO5 **E6-27. Customer Profitability Analysis**

Refer to the previous exercise E6-26 for Leahy Inc.

Required

a. If Leahy were to notify customers 3, 7, and 10 that it will no longer be able to provide them services in the future, will that increase company profits by $355,000? Why or why not?

b. What is the primary benefit of preparing a customer profitability analysis?

Problems

LO2, 3, 4 **P6-28. Two-Stage ABC for Manufacturing with ABC Variances**

Meade Manufacturing developed the following activity cost pool information for its current year manufacturing activities:

	Budgeted Activity Cost	Activity Cost Driver at Practical Capacity
Purchasing and materials handling	$ 475,000	950,000 kilograms
Setup	225,000	1,500 setups
Machine operations	1,540,000	14,000 machine hours
First unit inspection	280,000	1,600 batches
Packaging	100,000	200,000 units

Actual production information for three of Meade's products during the year is as follows:

	Standard Product A	Standard Product B	Specialty Products
Units	35,000	15,000	10,000
Batches	140	50	400
Setups*	150	45	800
Machine hours	1,200	650	800
Kilograms of raw materials	175,000	65,000	95,000
Direct materials costs	$58,000	$44,350	$27,000
Direct labor costs	$95,500	$64,900	$45,000

* Some products require setups on two or more machines.

Required

a. Determine the unit cost of each product for Meade Manufacturing under activity-based costing.

b. Explain why the unit cost of the specialty products is so much higher than the unit cost of Standard Product A or Standard Product B.

P6-29. ABC—A Service Application LO2, 3, 4

Grand Haven is a senior living community that offers a full range of services including independent living, assisted living, and skilled nursing care. The assisted living division provides residential space, meals, and medical services (MS) to its residents. The current costing system adds the cost of all of these services (space, meals, and MS) and divides by total resident days to get a cost per resident day. Recognizing that MS tends to vary significantly among the residents, Grand Haven's accountant recommended that an ABC system be designed to calculate more accurately the cost of MS provided to residents. She decided that residents should be classified into four categories (A, B, C, D) based on the level of services received, with group A representing the lowest level of service and D representing the highest level of service. Two cost drivers being considered for measuring MS costs are number of assistance calls and number of assistant contacts. A contact is registered each time an assistance professional provides medical services or aid to a resident. The accountant has gathered the following data for the most recent annual period:

Resident Classification	Annual Resident Days	Annual Assistance Hours	Number of Assistance Contacts
A	18,000	9,100	27,000
B	10,000	22,500	31,000
C	5,500	23,000	27,500
D	3,000	18,400	24,000
	36,500	73,000	109,500

Other data	
Total cost of medical services for the period	$4,927,500
Total cost of meals and residential space	$2,591,500

Required (round answers to the nearest dollar):

a. Determine the total cost of a resident day using the current system.

b. Determine the ABC cost of a resident day for each category of residents using assistance hours as the cost driver for medical services and resident days as the cost driver for meals and residential space.

c. Determine the ABC cost of a resident day for each category of residents using assistance contacts as the cost driver for medical services and resident days as the cost driver for meals and residential space.

d. Which cost driver do you think provides the more accurate measure of the cost per day for a Grand Haven resident?

LO2, 3, 4 Molitor Financial Group

P6-30. ABC Costing for a Service Organization

Molitor Financial Group is a full-service residential mortgage company in the Chicago area that operates in a very competitive market. Assume management is concerned about operating costs associated with processing mortgage applications and has decided to install an ABC costing system to help them get a handle on costs. Although labor hours seem to be the primary driver of the cost of processing a new mortgage, the labor cost for the different activities involved in processing new loans varies widely. The Accounting Department has provided the following data for the company's five major cost pools for the current year:

Activity Cost Pools		Activity Drivers	
Taking customer applications	$ 306,000	Time—assistant managers	3,600 hours
Conducting credit investigations	378,000	Time—credit managers	5,400 hours
Underwriting	405,000	Time—Underwriting Department	5,400 hours
Preparing loan packages	594,000	Time—Processing Department	10,800 hours
Closing loans	396,000	Time—Legal Department	3,600 hours
	$2,079,000		28,800 hours

During the year, the company processed and issued 900 new mortgages, two of which are summarized here with regard to activities used to process the mortgages:

	Loan 7023	Loan 8955
Application processing hours	2.00	4.00
Credit investigating hours	3.00	5.00
Underwriting hours	6.00	6.00
Processing hours	9.00	18.00
Legal hours	4.00	6.00
Total hours	24.00	39.00

Required

a. Determine the cost per unit of activity for each activity cost pool.

b. Determine the cost of processing loans 7023 and 8955.

c. Determine the cost of preparing loans 7023 and 8955 assuming that an average cost per hour for all activities is used.

d. Compare and discuss your answers to requirements (*b*) and (*c*).

LO2, 3, 4, 6

P6-31. Activity-Based Costing in a Service Organization

Banctronics Inc. has 10 automatic teller machines (ATMs) spread throughout the city maintained by the ATM Department. You have been assigned the task of determining the cost of operating each machine. Management will use the information you develop, along with other information pertaining to the volume and type of transactions at each machine, to evaluate the desirability of continuing to operate each machine and/or changing security arrangements for a particular machine.

The ATM Department consists of a total of six employees: a supervisor, a head cashier, two associate cashiers, and two maintenance personnel. The associate cashiers make between two and four daily trips to each machine to collect and replenish cash and to replenish supplies, deposit tickets, and so forth. Each machine contains a small computer that automatically summarizes and reports transactions to the head cashier. The head cashier reconciles the activities of the two associate cashiers to the computerized reports. The supervisor, who does not handle cash, reviews the reconciliation. When an automatic teller's computer, a customer, or a cashier reports a problem, the two maintenance employees and one cashier are dispatched immediately. The cashier removes all cash and transaction records, and the maintenance employees repair the machine.

Maintenance employees spend all of their time on maintenance-related activities. The associate cashiers spend approximately 25% of their time on maintenance-related activities and 75% on daily trips. The head cashier's time is divided, with 60% directly related to daily trips to each machine and 40% related to supervising cashiers on maintenance calls. The supervisor devotes 20% of the time to daily trips to each machine and 80% to the equal supervision of each employee. Cost information for a recent month follows:

Salaries	
Supervisor	$ 8,000
Head cashier	6,000
Other ($3,000 each for other cashiers; $3,500 each for maintenance employees)	13,000
Lease and operating costs	
Cashiers' service vehicle	2,400
Maintenance service vehicle	4,800
Office rent and utilities	12,000
Machine lease, space rent, and utilities ($2,000 each machine)	20,000
Total	$66,200

Related monthly activity information for this month follows:

Machine	Daily Trips	Maintenance Call Hours
1	40	22
2	50	20
3	40	18
4	80	20
5	40	22
6	80	18
7	80	24
8	30	14
9	20	16
10	40	16
Total	500	190

Additional information follows:

- The office is centrally located with about equal travel time to each machine.
- Maintenance hours include travel time.
- The cashiers' service vehicle is used exclusively for routine visits.
- The office space is divided equally between the supervisor and the head cashier.

Required

a. Determine the monthly operating costs of machines 7 and 8 when cost assignments are based on the number of machines.

b. Determine the activity cost of a routine trip and a maintenance hour for the month given. Round answers to the nearest cent.

c. Determine the operating costs assigned and reassigned to machines 7 and 8 when activity-based costing is used.

d. How can ABC cost information be used by Banctronics Inc. to improve the overall management of monthly operating costs?

P6-32. Product Costing: Plantwide Overhead versus Activity-Based Costing LO3, 4

Sterling Industries produces machine parts as a contract provider for a large manufacturing company. Sterling produces two particular parts, shafts and gears. The competition is keen among contract producers, and Sterling's top management realizes how vulnerable its market is to cost-cutting competitors. Hence, having a very accurate understanding of costs is important to Sterling's survival.

Sterling's president, Sheila Hudson, has observed that the company's current cost to produce shafts is $23.35, and the current cost to produce gears is $14.30. She indicated to the controller that she suspects some problems with the cost system because Sterling is suddenly experiencing extraordinary competition on shafts, but it seems to have a virtual corner on the gears market. She is even considering dropping the shaft line and converting the company to a one-product manufacturer of gears. She asked the controller, George Coleman, to conduct a thorough cost study and to consider whether changes in the cost system are necessary. The controller collected the following data about the company's costs and various manufacturing activities for the most recent month:

	Shafts	Gears
Production units	50,000	18,000
Selling price	$34.95	$25.50
Overhead per unit (based on direct labor hours)	$12.50	$6.25
Materials and direct labor cost per unit.	$10.85	$8.05
Number of production runs	20	30
Number of purchasing and receiving orders processed	50	98
Number of machine hours	43,000	6,500
Number of direct labor hours	25,000	4,500
Number of engineering hours	2,500	2,500
Number of material moves	62	33

The controller was able to summarize the company's total manufacturing overhead into the following pools:

Setup costs	$ 40,000
Machine costs	198,000
Purchasing and receiving costs	218,300
Engineering costs	209,000
Materials handling costs	72,200
Total	$737,500

Required

a. Calculate Sterling's current plantwide overhead rate based on direct labor hours.

b. Verify Sterling's calculation of overhead cost per unit of $12.50 for shafts and $6.25 for gears.

c. Calculate the manufacturing overhead cost per unit for shafts and gears using activity-based costing, assuming each of the five cost pools represents a separate activity pool. Use the most appropriate activity driver for assigning activity costs to the two products.

d. Comment on Sterling's current cost system and the reason the company is facing fierce competition for shafts but little competition for gears.

LO2, 5, 6
Boeing (BA)
Airbus (AIR)

P6-33. Customer Profitability Analysis

Remington Aeronautics LTD is a British aeronautics subcontract company that designs and manufactures electronic control systems for commercial airlines. The vast majority of all commercial aircraft are manufactured by Boeing in the U.S. and Airbus in Europe; however, there is a relatively small group of companies that manufacture narrow body commercial jets. Assume for this exercise that Remington does contract work for the two major manufacturers plus three companies in the second tier.

Because competition is intense in the industry, Remington has always operated on a fairly thin 20% gross profit margin; hence, it is crucial that it manage nonmanufacturing overhead costs effectively in order to achieve an acceptable net profit margin. With declining profit margins in recent years, Remington Aeronautics' CEO, John Remington, has become concerned that the cost of obtaining contracts and maintaining relations with its five major customers may be getting out of hand. You have been hired to conduct a customer profitability analysis.

Remington Aeronautics' nonmanufacturing overhead consists of $2 million of general and administrative (G&A) expense (including, among other expenses, the CEO's salary and bonus and the cost of operating the company's corporate jet) and selling and customer support expenses of $3.15 million (including 5% sales commissions and $750,000 of additional costs).

The accounting staff determined that the $750,000 of additional selling and customer support expenses related to the following four activity cost pools:

Activity	Activity Cost Driver	Cost per Unit of Activity
1. Sales visits	Number of visit days	$1,000
2. Product adjustments	Number of adjustments	1,600
3. Phone and email contacts	Number of calls/contacts	100
4. Promotion and entertainment events	Number of events	3,000

Financial and activity data on the five customers follow (Sales and Gross Profit data in millions):

			Quantity of Sales and Support Activity			
Customer	Sales	Gross Profit	Activity 1	Activity 2	Activity 3	Activity 4
A	$19	$3.8	90	10	160	21
B	14	2.8	105	20	200	20
C	5	1.0	95	18	100	17
D	6	1.2	30	8	35	12
E	4	0.8	30	4	25	14
	$48	$9.6	350	60	520	84

In addition to the above, the sales staff used the corporate jet at a cost of $1,000 per hour for trips to customers as follows:

Customer A	16 hours
Customer B	32 hours
Customer C	8 hours
Customer D	0 hours
Customer E	5 hours

The total cost of operating the airplane is included in general and administrative expense; none is included in selling and customer support costs.

Required

a. Prepare a customer profitability analysis for Remington Aeronautics that shows the gross profits less all expenses that can reasonably be assigned to the five customers.

b. Now assuming that the remaining general and administrative costs are assigned to the five customers based on relative sales dollars, calculate net profit for each customer.

c. Discuss the merits of the analysis in part *a* versus part *b*.

Cases and Projects

C6-34. Designing an ABC System for a Country Club LO2, 5, 6

The Reserve Club is a traditional private golf and country club that has three different categories of memberships: golf, tennis & swimming, and social. Golf members have access to all amenities and programs in the club, Tennis & Swimming members have access to all amenities and programs except use of the golf course, and Social members have access to only the social activities of the club, excluding golf, tennis, and swimming. All members have clubhouse privileges, including use of the bar and restaurant, which is operated by an outside contractor. During the past year, the average membership in each category, along with the number of club visits during the year, was:

	Members	Visits
Golf	500	15,000
Tennis & Swimming	110	2,200
Social	250	5,000

Some members of the club have been complaining that heavy users of the club are not bearing their share of the costs through their membership fees. Dess Rosmond, General Manager of the Reserve Club, agrees that monthly fees paid by the various member groups should be based on the annual average amount of cost-related activities provided by the club for the three groups, and he intends to set fees on that basis for the coming year. The annual direct costs of operating the golf course, tennis courts, and swimming pool have been calculated by the club's controller as follows:

Golf course	$1,250,000
Swimming pool	75,000
Tennis courts	45,000

The operation of the bar and restaurant and all related costs, including depreciation on the bar and restaurant facilities, are excluded from this analysis. In addition to the above costs, the club incurs general overhead costs in the following amounts for the most recent (and typical) year:

General Ledger Overhead Accounts	Amounts
Indirect labor for the club management staff (the general manager, assistant general manager, membership manager, and club controller)	$375,000
Utilities (other than those directly related to golf, swimming, and tennis)	34,000
Website maintenance	8,000
Postage	2,500
Computers and information systems maintenance	10,000
Clubhouse maintenance & depreciation	32,000
Liability insurance	6,000
Security contract	15,000
	$482,500

Dess believes that the best way to assign most of the overhead costs to the three membership categories is with an activity-based system that recognizes four key activities that occur regularly in the club:

- Recruiting and providing orientation for new members
- Maintaining the membership roster and communicating with members
- Planning, scheduling, and managing club events
- Maintaining the financial records and reporting for the club

Required

a. Identify and explain which overhead costs can reasonably be assigned to one or more of the four key activities, and suggest a basis for making the assignment.

b. Identify a cost driver for each activity cost pool that would seem to be suitable for assigning the activity cost pool to the three membership categories.

c. Suggest a method for assigning any overhead costs to the three membership categories that cannot reasonably be assigned to activity pools.

d. Comment on the suitability of ABC to this cost assignment situation.

LO2, 4, 6 C6-35. **Product Costing: Department versus Activity-Based Costing for Overhead**

Advertising Technologies, Inc. (ATI) specializes in providing both published and online advertising services for the business marketplace. The company monitors its costs based on the cost per column inch of published space printed in print advertising media and based on the cost per minute of online advertising time delivered on "The AD Line," a computer-based, online advertising service. ATI has one new competitor, Tel-a-Ad, in its local online advertising market; and with increased competition, ATI has seen a decline in sales of online advertising in recent years. ATI's president, Robert Beard, believes that predatory pricing by Tel-a-Ad has caused the problem. The following is a recent conversation between Robert and Jane Minnear, director of marketing for ATI.

Jane: I just received a call from one of our major customers concerning our advertising rates on "The AD Line" who said that a sales rep from another firm (it had to be Tel-a-Ad) had offered the same service at $1 per minute, which is $0.75 per minute less than our price.

Robert: It's costing about $1.40 per minute to produce that product. I don't see how they can afford to sell it so cheaply. I'm not convinced that we should meet the price. Perhaps the better strategy is to emphasize producing and selling more published ads, which we're more experienced with and where our margins are high and we have virtually no competition.

Jane: You may be right. Based on a recent survey of our customers, I think we can raise the price significantly for published advertising and still not lose business.

Robert: That sounds promising; however, before we make a major recommitment to publishing, let's explore other possible explanations. I want to know how our costs compare with our competitors. Maybe we could be more efficient and find a way to earn a good return on online advertising.

After this meeting, Robert and Jane requested an investigation of production costs and comparative efficiency of producing published versus online advertising services. The controller, Tim Gentry, indicated that ATI's efficiency was comparable to that of its competitors and prepared the following cost data:

	Published Advertising	Online Advertising
Estimated number of production units	100,000	5,000,000
Selling price	$210	$1.75
Direct product costs	$10,500,000	$2,500,000
Overhead allocation*	$5,100,000	$4,500,000
Overhead per unit	$51	$0.90
Direct costs per unit	$105	$0.50
Number of customers	90,000	12,500
Number of salesperson days	14,250	1,750
Number of art and design hours	17,500	2,500
Number of creative services subcontract hours	50,000	12,500
Number of customer service calls	36,000	4,000

* Based on direct labor costs

Upon examining the data, Robert decided that he wanted to know more about the overhead costs since they were such a high proportion of total production costs. He was provided the following list of overhead costs and told that they were currently being assigned to products in proportion to direct labor costs.

Selling costs	$4,200,000
Visual and audio design costs	1,700,000
Creative services costs	2,950,000
Customer service costs	750,000

Required

Using the data provided by the controller, prepare analyses to help Robert and Jane in making their decisions. (*Hint:* Prepare cost calculations for both product lines using ABC to see whether there is any significant difference in their unit costs.) Should ATI switch from the fast-growing, online advertising market back into the well-established published advertising market? Does the charge of predatory pricing seem valid? Why are customers likely to be willing to pay a higher price to get published services? Do traditional costing and activity-based costing lead to the same conclusions?

C6-36. Unit-Level and Multiple-Level Cost Assignments with Decision Implications **LO2, 3, 4, 6**

CarryAll Company[4] produces briefcases from leather, fabric, and synthetic materials in a single production department. The basic product is a standard briefcase made from leather and lined with fabric. CarryAll has a good reputation in the market because the standard briefcase is a high-quality item that has been produced for many years.

Last year, the company decided to expand its product line and produce specialty briefcases for special orders. These briefcases differ from the standard in that they vary in size, contain both leather and synthetic materials, and are imprinted with the buyer's logo (the standard briefcase is simply imprinted with the CarryAll name in small letters). The decision to use some synthetic materials in the briefcase was made to hold down the materials cost. To reduce the labor costs per unit, most of the cutting and

[4] The CarryAll Company case, prepared by Professors Harold Roth and Imogene Posey, was originally published in the *Management Accounting Campus Report*.

stitching on the specialty briefcases is done by automated machines, which are used to a much lesser degree in the production of the standard briefcases. Because of these changes in the design and production of the specialty briefcases, CarryAll management believed that they would cost less to produce than the standard briefcases. However, because they are specialty items, they were priced slightly higher; standards are priced at $30 and specialty briefcases at $32.

After reviewing last month's results of operations, CarryAll's president became concerned about the profitability of the two product lines because the standard briefcase showed a loss while the specialty briefcase showed a greater profit margin than expected. The president is wondering whether the company should drop the standard briefcase and focus entirely on specialty items. Units and cost data for last month's operations as reported to the president are as follows:

	Standard	Specialty
Units produced	10,000	2,500
Direct materials		
Leather (1 sq. yd. × $15.00; ½ sq. yd. × $15.00)	$15.00	$ 7.50
Fabric (1 sq. yd. × $5.00; 1 sq. yd. × $5.00)	5.00	5.00
Synthetic		5.00
Total materials	20.00	17.50
Direct labor (½ hr. × $12.00, ¼ hr. × $12.00)	6.00	3.00
Manufacturing overhead (½ hr. × $8.98; ¼ hr. × $8.98)	4.49	2.25
Cost per unit	$30.49	$22.75

Factory overhead is applied on the basis of direct labor hours. The rate of $8.98 per direct labor hour was calculated by dividing the total overhead ($50,500) by the direct labor hours (5,625). As shown in the table, the cost of a standard briefcase is $0.49 higher than its $30 sales price; the specialty briefcase has a cost of only $22.75, for a gross profit per unit of $9.25. The problem with these costs is that they do not accurately reflect the activities involved in manufacturing each product. Determining the costs using ABC should provide better product costing data to help gauge the actual profitability of each product line.

The manufacturing overhead costs must be analyzed to determine the activities driving the costs. Assume that the following costs and cost drivers have been identified:

- The Purchasing Department's cost is $6,000. The major activity driving these costs is the number of purchase orders processed. During the month, the Purchasing Department prepared the following number of purchase orders for the materials indicated:

Leather	20
Fabric	30
Synthetic material	50

- The cost of receiving and inspecting materials is $7,500. These costs are driven by the number of deliveries. During the month, the following number of deliveries were made:

Leather	30
Fabric	40
Synthetic material	80

- Production line setup cost is $10,000. Setup activities involve changing the machines to produce the different types of briefcases. Each setup for production of the standard briefcases requires one hour; each setup for specialty briefcases requires two hours. Standard briefcases are produced in batches of 200, and specialty briefcases are produced in batches of 25. During the last month, there were 50 setups for the standard item and 100 setups for the specialty item.
- The cost of inspecting finished goods is $8,000. All briefcases are inspected to ensure that quality standards are met. However, the final inspection of standard briefcases takes very little time because the employees identify and correct quality problems as they do the hand cutting and stitching. A survey of the personnel responsible for inspecting the final products showed that 150 hours were spent on standard briefcases and 250 hours on specialty briefcases during the month.

- Equipment-related costs are $6,000. Equipment-related costs include repairs, depreciation, and utilities. Management has determined that a logical basis for assigning these costs to products is machine hours. A standard briefcase requires 1/2 hour of machine time, and a specialty briefcase requires 2 hours. Thus, during the last month, 5,000 hours of machine time relate to the standard line and 5,000 hours relate to the specialty line.
- Plant-related costs are $13,000. These costs include property taxes, insurance, administration, and others. For the purpose of determining average unit costs, they are to be assigned to products using machine hours.

Required

a. Using activity-based costing concepts, what overhead costs should be assigned to the two products?
b. What is the unit cost of each product using activity-based costing concepts?
c. Reevaluate the president's concern about the profitability of the two product lines.
d. Discuss the merits of activity-based management as it relates to CarryAll's ABC cost system.

Solutions to Review Problems

Review 6-1—Solution

Indirect expenses are displacing direct expenses. This may be attributed to the advancement of technology and equipment. It may also be largely related to an increase in the number of different types of products and services that companies offer. As companies move away from one simple product, the need for more indirect costs such as equipment design, changeover, and even the movement of products can increase. As the pool of indirect expenses becomes a more significant part of product costs, it is increasingly difficult yet important to come up with methods to reasonably assign indirect costs to products.

Review 6-2—Solution

Answers may vary but likely activities and related drivers might include:

- Reception and admission of participating employees/number of participating employees
- Consultations with physician/number of minutes of consultation services
- Administration of tests/number of tests
- Processing and distributing test results/number of participating employees
- Room setup/number of participating employees
- External lab processing/number of tests
- Technology support for website/number of participating employees

Review 6-3—Solution

a. **Plantwide overhead rate = Total manufacturing overhead ÷ Total machine hours**
= ($120,000 + $55,000) ÷ (10,000 + 5,000)
= $175,000 ÷ 15,000
= $11.67 per machine hour

	Cobra Latch	GrimLoc
Product costs per unit		
Direct materials	$12,000	$18,000
Direct labor	5,000	4,000
Manufacturing overhead		
700 machine hours × $11.67	8,169	
800 machine hours × $11.67		9,336
Total cost per batch	$25,169	$31,336
Number of units per batch	÷ 100	÷ 100
Cost per unit	$251.69	$313.36

b. **Departmental overhead rates = Total departmental overhead ÷ Dept. allocation base**

Fabrication = \$120,000 ÷ 10,000 machine hours

= \$12 per machine hour

Finishing = \$55,000 ÷ 5,000 machine hours

= \$11 per machine hour

	Cobra Latch	GrimLoc
Product costs per unit		
Direct materials	\$12,000	\$18,000
Direct labor	5,000	4,000
Manufacturing overhead		
Fabrication Department		
500 machine hours × \$12	6,000	
700 machine hours × \$12		8,400
Finishing Department		
200 machine hours × \$11	2,200	
100 machine hours × \$11		1,100
Total cost per batch	\$25,200	\$31,500
Number of units per batch	÷ 100	÷ 100
Cost per unit	\$252.00	\$315.00

c. **Activity-based overhead rates = Activity cost pool ÷ Activity cost driver**

Maintenance = \$30,000 ÷ 15,000 machine hours

= \$2 per machine hour

Materials handling = \$45,000 ÷ 4,500 materials moves

= \$10 per materials move

Machine setups = \$75,000 ÷ 750 setups

= \$100 per machine setup

Inspections = \$25,000 ÷ 1,000 inspection hours

= \$25 per inspection hour

	Cobra Latch	GrimLoc
Product costs per unit		
Direct materials	\$12,000	\$18,000
Direct labor	5,000	4,000
Manufacturing overhead		
Maintenance activity		
700 machine hours × \$2	1,400	
800 machine hours × \$2		1,600
Materials handling activity		
30 materials moves × \$10	300	
50 materials moves × \$10		500
Machine setups activity		
5 machine setups × \$100	500	
9 machine setups × \$100		900
Inspections activity		
30 inspection hours × \$25	750	
60 inspection hours × \$25		1,500
Total cost per batch	\$19,950	\$26,500
Number of units per batch	÷ 100	÷ 100
Cost per unit	\$199.50	\$265.00

Review 6-4—Solution

Following is a summary of product costs for Cobra Latch and GrimLoc assigning overhead costs based on a plantwide rate, department rates, and activity-based rates:

	Cobra Latch	GrimLoc
Plantwide rate	$251.69	$313.36
Department rates	$252.00	$315.00
Activity-based rates	$199.50	$265.00

Changing from a plantwide rate to department rates had little effect on unit costs because the department rates per machine hour are close to the plantwide rate per machine hour. Based on machine hours, both departments have similar cost structures.

When using activity-based rates, however, the cost of these two products drops dramatically because they use only a small portion (less than 2%) of the activities of setup (14 of 750) and materials moves (80 of 4,500). Neither a plantwide rate nor department rates recognize this fact, resulting in a large amount of cost cross-subsidization of other products by Cobra Latch and GrimLoc for these costs. Although this problem did not include cost analysis of the other three products, it shows that they are less profitable and that Cobra Latch and GrimLoc are much more profitable than management previously thought.

Review 6-5—Solution

a. Activity A—Minor systems maintenance
Activity B—Visits to customers
Activity C—Communications via phone

Activity	1	2	3	4	5
A (@ $160)	$11,040	$22,560	$11,840	$ 9,760	$21,760
B (@ $300)	7,500	12,600	5,700	8,400	11,700
C (@ $50)	6,400	10,250	4,950	5,300	9,450
Total support costs	$24,940	$45,410	$22,490	$23,460	$42,910
Profit before support costs	80,000	85,000	83,000	90,000	78,000
Customer profits	$55,060	$39,590	$60,510	$66,540	$35,090
Ratio of support costs to profit before support costs	31%	53%	27%	26%	55%

b. This analysis is beneficial to SAP because it shows that Groups 2 and 5 are outliers among the five customer groups in terms of support services required. Groups 2 and 5 are significantly larger consumers of activities for all three of the support activities. Note also that Group 4 customers are relatively light users of minor systems maintenance, and Group 3 are relatively light users of phone communications. Calculating the ratio of total support costs to profit before support costs provides additional insight into the relative profitability of the customer groups. All five customer groups are profitable; however, this analysis provides useful information for improving profits by working with Groups 2 and 5 to control support activities and related costs and attempt to bring their support costs in line with the other customer groups.

Review 6-6—Solution

Activity-based costing requires a company to understand, identify, and measure the activities it engages in in order to deliver its products or services. Activity-based management is the process of assessing those activities to make sure they align with companies' goals and objectives. It allows for a review of activities to identify which ones ultimately add value for its customers and can change or remove those activities that do not add value. It may also wish to make changes to activities that add value, to further a company's initiative. For example, Safety-Kleen is a subsidiary of Clean Harbors. Safety-Kleen states, "We are committed to continually examining our own operations to identify areas where we can reduce energy consumption, as well as determine innovative ways to drive enhancements across our entire network."[5] A firm is not in a position to do this effectively and profitably if it does not have a grasp of the costs and values of each of its activities.

[5] http://www.safety-kleen.com/about-us/sustainability

Chapter 7

Additional Topics in Product Costing

Learning Objectives

LO1 Differentiate between production and service department costs and direct and indirect department costs. (p. 248)

LO2 Describe the allocation of service department costs under the direct, step, and linear algebra methods. (p. 249)

LO3 Understand lean production and just-in-time inventory management. (p. 255)

LO4 Explain how lean production and just-in-time affect performance evaluation and recordkeeping. (p. 258)

LO5 Evaluate ways in which the increasing availability of data might change the roles and responsibilities of managerial accountants. (p. 261)

Whole Foods, a subsidiary of Amazon.com, Inc., tried to shed its nickname "Whole Paycheck" for years without success. However, since being purchased by Amazon in 2017, attitudes about the company have improved, according to YouGov, a market research company. The main reasons for the change in perception? Expanded grocery delivery, online ordering, price cuts on selected items, and regular discounts for Amazon's Prime members.

To increase grocery delivery and online ordering volume, Whole Foods has been expanding, geographically, into areas previously unserved. Leasing and startup costs can be minimized by looking at sites previously occupied by struggling retailers like Sears and Kmart. These larger sites can also be used to accommodate Amazon delivery and pickup from online orders. Whole Foods now has over 500 retail locations. Although in-store revenue decreased slightly between 2018 and 2019, grocery deliveries in the fourth quarter of 2019 doubled from the same period in 2018.

To maintain profitability while cutting prices, Whole Foods has been moving away from local vendors and stocking larger national brands, including its own brand, 365 Everyday Value. Private labels typically have higher profit margins. 365 products are sold at Whole Foods and are one of the best-selling private label brands on Amazon.com.

A grocery operation has numerous support departments—areas that are necessary to the operation of the store, but not directly attributable to any one product or group of products. Examples of support departments include human resources, accounting, and custodial services. Whole Foods must develop a system of service cost allocation that will minimize distortions in profitability across grocery departments. The company must also operate as efficiently as possible; however, that efficiency shouldn't come at the expense of the quality that has become Whole Foods' bedrock.

The last, but perhaps most important factor for the company is its inventory management. Holding inventory is costly due to storage and insurance costs; and in the case of a grocer, perishable inventory is prone to spoilage and waste. This chapter discusses how companies such as Whole Foods assign the cost of their internal service departments to their products, and how they can benefit from adopting a lean operations philosophy in managing their inventory levels.

Road Map

LO	Learning Objective | Topics	Page	eLecture	Guided Example	Assignments
LO1	**Differentiate between production and service department costs and direct and indirect department costs.** Direct Department Costs :: Indirect Department Costs	248	e7–1	Review 7-1	
LO2	**Describe the allocation of service department costs under the direct, step, and linear algebra methods.** Direct Method :: Step Method :: Linear Algebra Method :: Dual Rates	249	e7–2	Review 7-2	17, 18, 19, 22, 23, 29, 30, 31, 32, 33, 34, 37
LO3	**Understand lean production and just-in-time inventory management.** Value Chain Approach to Inventory Management :: Just-in-Time :: Lean Production	255	e7–3	Review 7-3	20, 21, 24, 35, 38, 39
LO4	**Explain how lean production and just-in-time affect performance evaluation and recordkeeping.** Dysfunctional Effects of Traditional Performance Measures :: Performance Measures under Lean and JIT :: Simplified Recordkeeping	258	e7–4	Review 7-4	20, 21, 24, 25, 26, 28, 35, 36, 38, 39
LO5	**Evaluate ways in which the increasing availability of data might change the roles and responsibilities of managerial accountants.** Correlation vs Causation :: Technical Skills Gap	261	e7–6	Review 7-5	27

CHAPTER ORGANIZATION

Additional Topics in Product Costing

Production and Service Department Costs	Service Department Cost Allocation	Lean Production and Just-in-Time Inventory Management	Performance Evaluation and Recordkeeping with Lean Production and JIT	Increased Focus on Data-Driven Decision Making
• Direct and Indirect Department Costs	• Direct Method • Step Method • Linear Algebra Method • Dual Rates	• Reducing Incoming Materials Inventory • Reducing Work-in-Process Inventory • Reducing Finished Goods Inventory	• Performance Evaluation • Simplified Recordkeeping	• Changing Landscape of Managerial Accounting • Risks Associated with Data-Driven Decision Making • Skills Required of Managerial Accountants

Production and Service Department Costs

LO1 Differentiate between production and service department costs and direct and indirect department costs.

In Chapter 5, we discussed two basic methods (job order costing and process costing) for accumulating, measuring, and recording the costs of producing goods. In Chapter 6, we discussed both traditional and activity-based methods for assigning indirect costs to products. We now look in more detail at another aspect of assigning indirect costs.

In addition to *production* departments that actually perform work on a product, many companies have production *support* departments, such as payroll, human resources, information technology, security, and facilities, that provide support services for all of the production departments, and sometimes even for each other. These departments are typically called **service departments**. The cost of producing products, therefore, includes the costs incurred within production departments, as well as the cost of services received from service departments.

A **direct department cost** is a cost assigned directly to a department (production or service) when it is incurred. For a production department, direct department costs include both *direct* product costs (direct materials and direct labor) as well as *indirect* product costs (such as indirect labor and indirect materials) incurred directly in the department. An **indirect department cost** is a cost assigned to a department as a result of an indirect allocation, or reassignment, from another department, such as a service department.

The product costing system must include a policy for assigning to products the cost of services received from service departments. For companies that use a plantwide overhead rate, the costs of all service departments are added to the indirect product costs incurred within all of the producing departments to get total plantwide manufacturing overhead, which is then assigned to products using a single overhead rate based on a common factor such as direct labor hours. For companies that use departmental overhead rates, service department costs are allocated to the production departments that utilize their services, and the allocated service department costs are added to the indirect costs incurred within the department to arrive at total departmental overhead and allocation rates. Also, as illustrated in Chapter 6, service department costs may also be assigned to products using activity-based costing. As discussed in the following Business Insight, service department cost allocation can impact the amount of revenue received for some organizations.

Business Insight ■ Cost Allocations in a Large University Setting

A major research university, such as Emory University, encounters numerous cost allocation situations where the cost allocation system can substantially impact the university's financial well-being. Two examples are (1) cost allocation of various overhead costs for purposes of billing governmental and private insurance systems for services rendered to patients in university hospitals and clinics, and (2) cost allocations for indirect costs when seeking research and other grants. Failing to properly allocate service department costs can result in large revenue losses to such organizations. During times of economic recession, it is even more important to accurately measure the indirect service costs that are being passed on to other organizations to ensure maximum cost recovery.

Discussing Policies for Allocating Service Costs

LO1 Review 7-1

Most companies have production support departments, such as payroll, human resources, and information technology that provide support services for multiple production departments. To create meaningful product and service cost information, the costs associated with support departments must be allocated to the ultimate products or services in a meaningful way.

Required

Discuss how a company using each of the product costing systems—plantwide overhead rate, department overhead rate, and activity-based costing—would handle the allocation of support department costs.

Solution on p. 274.

Service Department Cost Allocation

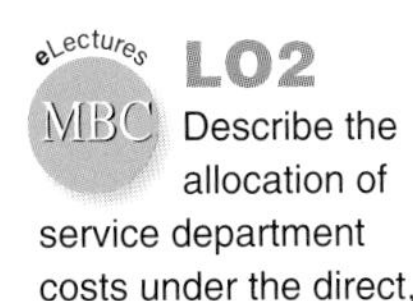

LO2 Describe the allocation of service department costs under the direct, step, and linear algebra methods.

As discussed above, service departments (maintenance, administration, information technology, security, etc.) provide a wide range of support functions, primarily for one or more production departments. These departments, which are considered essential elements in the overall manufacturing process, do not work directly on the "product" but provide auxiliary support to the producing departments. In addition to providing support for the various producing departments, some service departments also provide services to *other service departments*. For example, the payroll and personnel departments typically provide services to all departments (producing and service), and engineering may provide services to only the producing departments. Services provided by one service department to other service departments are called **interdepartment services**.

To illustrate service department cost allocations, suppose the Dasani Division of The Coca-Cola Company has two producing departments, three service departments, and two products. The service departments and their respective service functions and cost allocation bases are as follows:

Department	Service Functions	Allocation Base
Support Services	Receiving and inventory control	Total amount of department capital investment
Engineering Resources	Production setup and engineering and testing	Number of employees
Building and Grounds	Machinery maintenance and depreciation	Amount of square footage occupied

Difficulty in choosing an allocation base for service department costs is not uncommon. For example, Dasani may have readily determined the appropriate allocation bases for the Engineering Resources and the Building and Grounds Departments but may have found the choice for Support Services to be less clear. Perhaps after conducting correlation studies, the most equitable base for allocating Support Services costs to other departments was determined to be total capital investment in the departments because they included expensive computer-tracking equipment, both manual and automated forklifts, and other material-moving equipment.

Assume direct department costs and allocation base information used to illustrate Dasani's July service department cost allocations are summarized as follows:

	Direct Department Costs	Number of Employees		Amount of Square Footage Occupied		Total Amount of Department Capital Investment	
Service departments							
Support Services.	$ 27,000	15	15%	4,000	8%	—	—
Engineering Resources. . . .	20,000	—	—	2,000	4	$ 45,000	8%
Building and Grounds	10,000	5	5	—	—	50,000	9
Producing departments							
Mixing	40,000*	24	24	11,000	22	180,000	33
Bottling	90,000*	56	56	33,000	66	270,000	50
	$187,000	100	100%	50,000	100%	$545,000	100%

*Direct department overhead

The preceding information omitted the amount of capital investment in the Support Services Department, the number of employees in the Engineering Resources Department, and the amount of square footage used by the Building and Grounds Department. These data were omitted because a department does not allocate costs to itself; it allocates costs only to the departments it serves.

The three methods commonly used for service department cost allocations—direct, step, and linear algebra—are discussed in this section. Each of these methods eventually results in all service department costs being assigned to the production departments. Once this is done, Dasani can then use either department overhead rates or activity-based costing to further assign the indirect costs that are accumulated in the producing departments to the actual products. If Dasani were to use a plantwide overhead rate to allocate indirect costs, the service department costs would not be allocated to the producing departments; they would merely be added to the one plantwide indirect cost pool and allocated directly to the product using one plantwide overhead rate.

Direct Method

The **direct method** allocates all service department costs based only on the amount of services provided to the producing departments. **Exhibit 7.1** shows the flow of costs using the direct method. All arrows depicting the cost flows extend directly from service departments to producing departments; under the direct method there are no cost allocations between the service departments.

Exhibit 7.1 Flow of Costs—Direct Method

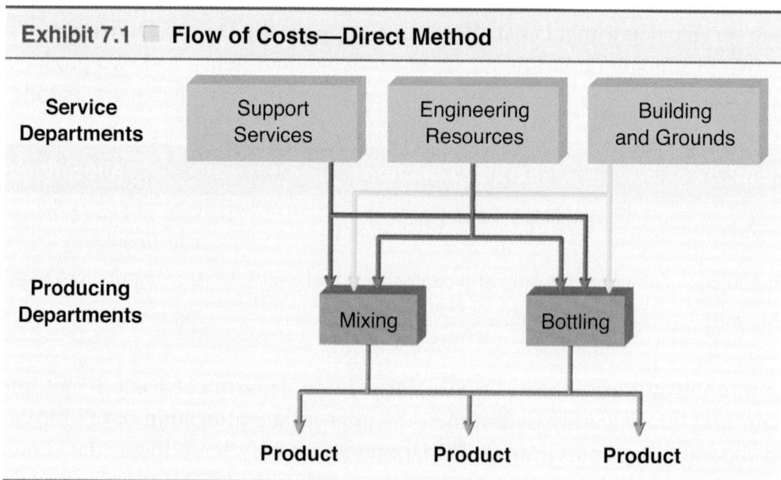

Exhibit 7.2 shows the service department cost allocations for the direct method. Notice the allocation base used to allocate Engineering Resources costs; only the employees in the producing departments are considered in computing the allocation percentages—24 in Mixing and 56 in Bottling, for a total of 80 employees in the allocation base. Thirty percent (24 ÷ 80) of the producing department employees work in Mixing; therefore, 30% of Engineering Resources costs are allocated

Exhibit 7.2 Service Department Cost Allocations—Direct Method

	Total	Mixing	Bottling
Support Services Department			
Allocation base (capital investment)	$450,000	$180,000	$270,000
Percent of total base	100%	40%	60%
Cost allocations	$ 27,000	$ 10,800	$ 16,200
Engineering Resources Department			
Allocation base (number of employees)	80	24	56
Percent of total base	100%	30%	70%
Cost allocations	$ 20,000	$ 6,000	$ 14,000
Building and Grounds Department			
Allocation base (square footage occupied)	44,000	11,000	33,000
Percent of total base	100%	25%	75%
Cost allocations	$ 10,000	$ 2,500	$ 7,500

Cost Allocation Summary

	Support Services	Engineering Resources	Building and Grounds	Mixing	Bottling	Total
Department cost before allocations	$27,000	$20,000	$10,000	$40,000	$ 90,000	$187,000
Cost allocations						
Support Services	(27,000)			10,800	16,200	—
Engineering Resources		(20,000)		6,000	14,000	—
Building and Grounds			(10,000)	2,500	7,500	—
Department costs after allocations	$ 0	$ 0	$ 0	$59,300	$127,700	$187,000

to Mixing. Applying the same reasoning, 70% of Engineering Resources costs are allocated to Bottling. Similar logic is followed in computing the cost allocations for Building and Grounds and Support Services.

The cost allocation summary at the bottom of **Exhibit 7.2** shows that all service department costs have been allocated, decreasing the service department costs to zero and increasing the producing department overhead balances by the amounts of the respective allocations. Also, total costs are not affected by the allocations; the total of $187,000 was merely redistributed so that all costs are reassigned to the producing departments. Total department overhead costs of the producing departments after allocation of service costs are $59,300 for Mixing and $127,700 for Bottling.

The advantage of the direct method of allocating service department costs is that it is easy and convenient to use. Its primary disadvantage is that it does not recognize the costs for interdepartment services provided by one service department to another. Instead, any costs incurred to provide services to other service departments are passed directly to the producing departments. The step method improves on the allocation procedure by redirecting some of the costs to other service departments before they are finally allocated to the production departments.

Step Method

The **step method** gives partial recognition of interdepartmental services by using a methodology that allocates the service department costs *sequentially* both to the remaining service departments and the producing departments. Any indirect costs allocated to a service department in this process are added to that service department's direct costs to determine the total costs to allocate to the remaining departments. Through this procedure, all service department costs are assigned to the production departments and ultimately to the products.

To illustrate a problem that can result from using the direct method, assume that Prestige Company has two service departments, S1 and S2, and two producing departments, P1 and P2, that provide services as follows:

Provider of Services	Receiver of Services			
	S1	S2	P1	P2
S1	0%	0%	70%	30%
S2	50%	0%	25%	25%

If the direct method is used to allocate service department costs to the producing departments, S2 total costs will be allocated equally to the producing departments because they use the same amount of S2 services (25% each). Is this an equitable allocation of S2 costs? S2 actually provides half of its services to the other service department (S1), which, in turn, provides the majority of its services to P1. Assume that S2 has total direct department costs of $100,000. If the direct method is used to allocate service department costs, the entire $100,000 will be divided equally between the two producing departments, each being allocated $50,000, with no allocation to S1.

	S1	S2	P1	P2
Direct method allocation of S2 to P1 and P2	$0	$(100,000)	$50,000	$50,000

Consider the following alternative allocation of the $100,000 of S2 costs that takes into account interdepartment services. First, 25%, or $25,000, is allocated to each of the producing departments, and 50%, or $50,000, is allocated to S1. Next, the $50,000 allocated to S1 from S2 is reallocated to the producing departments in proportion to the amount of services provided to them by S1: 70% and 30%, respectively. In this scenario, the $100,000 of S2 costs is ultimately allocated $60,000 to P1 and $40,000 to P2 as follows:

	S1	S2	P1	P2
Step 1:				
Allocate S2 costs to S1, P1, and P2	$50,000	$(100,000)	$25,000	$25,000
Step 2:				
Reallocate S1 costs to P1 and P2	(50,000)	0	35,000	15,000
Total allocation of S2 costs via step method	$ 0	$ 0	$60,000	$40,000

This calculation shows only the ultimate allocation of S2 costs. Of course, any S1 direct department costs would also have to be allocated to P1 and P2 on a 70:30 basis. If interdepartmental services are ignored, P1 is allocated only $50,000 of S2 costs; by considering interdepartmental services, P1 is allocated $60,000. Certainly, a more accurate measure of both the direct and indirect services received by P1 from S2 is $60,000, not $50,000.

As long as all producing departments use approximately the same percentage of services of each service department, the direct method provides a reasonably accurate cost assignment. In this example, the percentages of services used by the producing departments were quite different: 70% and 30% for S1, and 50% and 50% for S2. In such situations, the direct method can result in significantly different allocations.

The step method is illustrated graphically in **Exhibit 7.3** for Dasani. Notice the sequence of the allocations: Engineering Resources, Support Services, and Building and Grounds.

When using the step method, the sequence of allocation is typically based on the relative percentage of services provided to other service departments, with the largest provider of interdepartmental services allocated first and the smallest provider of interdepartmental services allocated last. For Dasani, Engineering Resources is allocated first because, of the three service departments, it provides the largest percentage (20%) of its services to other service departments: 15% to Support Services and 5% to Building and Grounds (see previous cost allocation data). Building and Grounds is allocated last because it provides the least amount (12%) of its services to other service departments: 8% to Support Services and 4% to Engineering Resources. The service department cost allocations for Dasani using the step method are shown in **Exhibit 7.4**.

Exhibit 7.3 Flow of Costs—Step Method

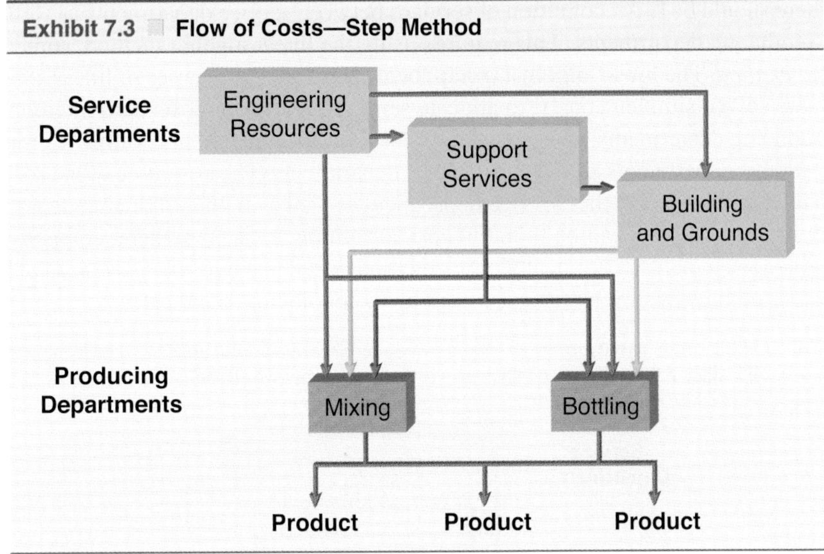

Exhibit 7.4 Service Department Cost Allocations—Step Method

	Total	Support Services	Building and Grounds	Mixing	Bottling
Engineering Resources Department					
Allocation base (number of employees)	100	15	5	24	56
Percent of total base	100%	15%	5%	24%	56%
Cost allocations	$20,000	$3,000	$1,000	$4,800	$11,200
Support Services Department					
Allocation base (capital investment)	$500,000		$50,000	$180,000	$270,000
Percent of total base	100%		10%	36%	54%
Cost allocations	$30,000		$3,000	$10,800	$16,200
Building and Grounds Department					
Allocation base (square footage occupied)	44,000			11,000	33,000
Percent of total base	100%			25%	75%
Cost allocations	$14,000			$3,500	$10,500

Cost Allocation Summary

	Engineering Resources	Support Services	Building and Grounds	Mixing	Bottling	Total
Department costs before allocations	$ 20,000	$ 27,000	$ 10,000	$40,000	$ 90,000	$187,000
Cost allocations						
Engineering Resources	(20,000)	3,000	1,000	4,800	11,200	—
Support Services		(30,000)	3,000	10,800	16,200	—
Building and Grounds			(14,000)	3,500	10,500	—
Department costs after allocations	$ 0	$ 0	$ 0	$59,100	$127,900	$187,000

Linear Algebra (Reciprocal) Method

The disadvantage of the step method is that it provides only partial recognition of interdepartmental services. For Dasani, the step method recognizes Engineering Resources services provided to the other two service departments; however, no services received by Engineering Resources from the other two departments are recognized. Similarly, services from Support Services to Building and Grounds are recognized, but not the reverse. To achieve the most mathematically accurate service department cost allocation, there should be full recognition of services between service departments as well as between service and producing departments. This requires using the linear algebra method, sometimes called the *reciprocal method*. The **linear algebra (reciprocal) method** uses a series of linear algebraic equations, which are solved simultaneously, to allocate service department costs both interdepartmentally and to the producing departments. This method is illustrated graphically in **Exhibit 7.5** for a company that has two service departments and two producing departments. The cost allocation arrows run from each service department to the other service department as well as to the producing departments. Further discussion of this method can be found in cost accounting texts. Whether a company should use the direct method, step method, or linear algebra method depends on the extensiveness of interdepartmental services and how evenly services are used by the producing departments.

Exhibit 7.5 Flow of Costs—Linear Algebra Method

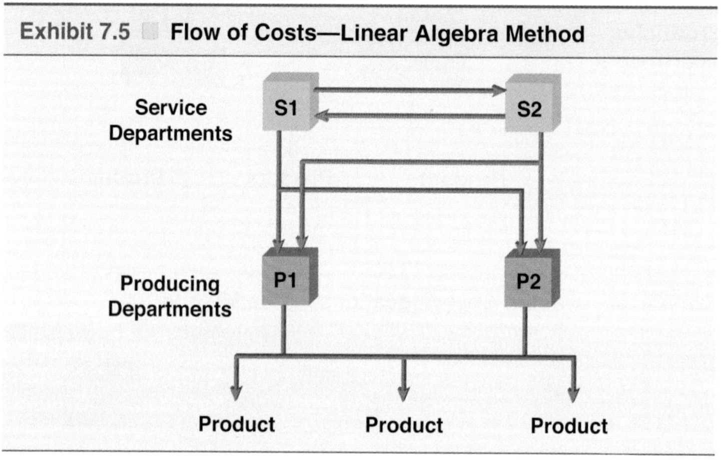

Managerial Decision ■ You Are the Controller

As the person responsible for the product costing system, you are trying to decide which method is best to use in allocating service department costs to the producing departments and to the products. Some of the service departments provide services only to producing departments, whereas others provide services to both producing and service departments. You would like to use the method that provides reliable cost measurements, but without creating more costs than the benefits derived. Which method do you recommend? [Answer, p. 262]

Dual Rates

When allocating service department costs, it can be useful to provide separate allocations for fixed costs and variable costs. This first requires the separation of indirect costs into the categories of fixed costs and variable costs, which is not always practical to do. Separately analyzing costs however, results in cost allocations that more accurately reflect the factors that drive costs. The capacity provided most often drives fixed costs, whereas some type of actual activity usually drives variable costs. Dual rates involve establishing separate bases for allocating fixed and variable costs. Dual rates may be used for one or all service departments, depending on the size and nature of the costs in each service department. They may also be used in conjunction with the direct, step, or linear algebra methods.

It is important to remember the relationship between capacity and cost when selecting the allocation method. Total variable costs change as activity changes. Fixed costs, however, are the same whether the activity is at or below capacity. Fixed costs should usually be allocated based on the relative capacity provided the benefiting department, while variable costs should be allocated on the basis of actual usage. The allocation methods and bases also may be different for variable and fixed costs.

Fixed costs based on capacity provided eliminates the possibility that the amount of the cost allocation to one department is affected by the level of services utilized by other departments. When fixed service department costs are allocated based on the capacity provided to the user department, managers of the user departments are charged for that capacity whether they use it or not, and their use of services has no effect on the amount of costs allocated to other departments. A benefit of this allocation system is that it reduces the temptation for managers to avoid or delay services to minimize fixed cost allocations to their departments. Dual rates are examined in more detail in most cost accounting texts.

Allocating Service Department Costs Using the Direct and Step Methods

LO2 Review 7-2

Suppose a Buckle retail store is organized into four departments: Women's Apparel, Men's Apparel, Administrative Services, and Facilities Services. The first two departments are the primary producing departments; the last two departments provide services to the producing departments as well as to each other. Top management has decided that, for internal reporting purposes, the cost of service department operations should be allocated to the producing departments. Administrative Services costs are allocated on the basis of the number of employees, and Facilities Services costs are allocated based on the amount of square footage of floor space occupied. Hypothetical data pertaining to the cost allocations for February are as follows:

Department	Direct Department Cost	Number of Employees	Square Footage Occupied
Women's Apparel	$ 60,000	15	15,000
Men's Apparel	50,000	9	7,500
Administrative Services	18,000	3	2,500
Facilities Services	12,000	2	1,000
Total	$140,000	29	26,000

Required

a. Determine the amount of service department costs to be allocated to the producing departments under the *direct method* of service department cost allocation.

b. Determine the percentage of total Administrative Department services that was provided to the Facilities Department.

c. Determine the percentage of total Facilities Department services that was provided to the Administrative Department.

d. Determine the amount of service department costs to be allocated to the producing departments under the *step method* of service department cost allocation.

Solution on p. 275.

Lean Production and Just-in-Time Inventory Management

LO3 Understand lean production and just-in-time inventory management.

Previously, our discussions about inventories have centered around how to measure the cost of products. A related issue is how to manage the production process and physical inventory levels. Cost accounting textbooks, as well as operations management textbooks, usually discuss models that have been used for decades to determine the economic order quantities for products, given the particular level of inventory a company wants to maintain. Although these models are still relevant in many situations, managing the production process and inventory levels has changed dramatically for companies that have adopted a value chain approach to management. No longer do most managers consider only their company's strategies, goals, and objectives in deciding the characteristics and quantities of inventory that should be acquired or produced and maintained.

A value chain approach to inventory management requires that managers consider their suppliers' and customers' strategies, goals, and objectives as well if they hope to compete successfully in a global marketplace. Computer technology has affected the way inventories are manufactured and handled (using robotics, fully computerized manufacturing and product handling systems, bar code identification systems, etc.), and it is changing the way companies relate to other parties in the value chain. It has spawned worldwide use of alternative inventory production and management techniques and processes including just-in-time (JIT) inventory management and lean production methods.

Just-in-time (JIT) inventory management is a comprehensive inventory management philosophy that emerged in the 1970s that stresses policies, procedures, and attitudes by managers and other workers that result in the efficient production of high-quality goods while maintaining the minimum level of inventories. JIT is often described simply as an inventory model that maintains only the level of inventories required to meet current production and sales requirements, but it is, in reality, much more than that. The key elements of the JIT philosophy, which has come to be known as the "lean production" philosophy, include increased coordination throughout the value chain, reduced inventory, reduced production times, increased product quality, and increased employee involvement and empowerment.

In sum, the concept of a JIT/lean approach is that in a manufacturing environment, the customers pull the production through the system with customer orders. Instead of the business making the decisions of what and when to produce, the customer does. JIT/lean production is a system aimed at reducing or eliminating waste, increasing cost efficiency, and securing a competitive advantage. Accordingly, it emphasizes a nimble production process with small lot sizes, short setup and changeover times, effective and efficient quality controls, a minimum number of bottlenecks and backups, and maximum efficiency of people.

Reducing Incoming Materials Inventory

The JIT/lean approach to reducing incoming materials includes these elements:

1. Developing long-term relationships with a limited number of vendors.
2. Selecting vendors on the basis of service and material quality, as well as price.
3. Establishing procedures for key employees to order materials for current needs directly from approved vendors.
4. Accepting vendor deliveries directly to the shop floor, and only as needed.

When fully implemented, these steps minimize or eliminate many materials inventories. Sufficient materials would be on hand to meet only immediate needs, and the materials inventories in the manufacturing setting are located on the shop floor.

To achieve this reduction, it is apparent that vendors and buyers must work as a team and that key employees must be involved in decision making. The goal of the JIT approach to purchasing is not to shift materials carrying costs to vendors. A close, long-term working relationship between purchasers and vendors should be beneficial to both. Purchasers' scheduling information is provided to vendors so that vendors also can reduce inventories and minimize costs. Vendors are therefore able to manufacture small batches frequently, rather than manufacturing large batches infrequently. Further, vendors are more confident of future sales.

Business Insight ■ Costs of Mismanaged Inventories

Forever 21 was founded in 1984 by Do Won Chang and his wife, Jin Sook. In 2014, revenues were $4 billion. By 2016, the company operated over 700 stores in 44 countries. However, in September 2019, the company declared bankruptcy, and, in January 2020, Forever 21 asked a bankruptcy court to approve plans to sell "substantially" all of its assets to an unnamed buyer.

There is more than one reason for the company's decline, but inventory mismanagement was one of the primary factors.

The company ordered too much inventory one year, and too little the next. Excess inventory was sent to store managers who stacked boxes of clothes in dressing rooms and then ended up returning items to the distribution centers when styles changed. Inventory shortages required replacement stock to be shipped overnight to stores, which resulted in higher than usual shipping costs. Errors were also made in the choice of items sent to specific stores. For example, down coats were sent to all stores in late fall even though it was almost summer in South America.

In the end, Forever 21's failure to anticipate changes in the industry and manage its inventory appropriately contributed to the company's need to file bankruptcy.

Sources: Susan Berfield, Eliza Ronalds-Hannon, and Lauren Coleman-Lochner, "The Failure of the Forever 21 Empire," *Bloomberg Businessweek*, January 17, 2020.
Eliza Ronalds-Hannon, "Forever 21 Proposed Auction to Keep Fashion Chain in Business," *Bloomberg*, January 30, 2020.

Reducing Work-in-Process Inventory

Reducing the total time required to complete a process, or the **cycle time**, is the key to reducing work-in-process inventories and is central to a lean production approach. In a manufacturing organization, cycle time is composed of the time needed for setup, processing, movement, waiting, and inspection. **Setup time** is the time required to prepare equipment to produce a specific product, or to change from producing one product to another product. **Processing time** is the time spent working on units. **Movement time** is the time units spend moving between work or inspection stations. **Waiting time** is the time units spend in temporary storage waiting to be processed, moved, or inspected. **Inspection time** is the amount of time it takes units to be inspected. Of the five elements of cycle time, only processing time adds value to the product. Efforts to reduce cycle time are appropriate for both continuous and batch production.

Devising means of reducing setup times will directly reduce the cycle time for batch production and thus reduce setup costs. Setup times can also be reduced by shifting from batch to continuous production whenever practical. Rearranging the shop floor to eliminate unnecessary movements of materials can help reduce movement time for both continuous and batch production.

Many companies have created **quality circles**, which are groups of employees involved in production who have the authority, within certain parameters, to address and resolve quality problems as they occur, without seeking management approval. Giving employees more authority and responsibility for quality, including the right to stop production whenever quality problems are noted, can reduce the need for separate inspection time.

Waiting time can be reduced by moving from a materials push to a materials pull approach to production. Under a traditional **materials push system**, employees work to reduce the pile of inventory building up at their workstations. Workers at each station remove materials from an in-process storage area, complete their operation, and place the output in another in-process storage area. Hence, they *push* the work to the next workstation. The emphasis is on production efficiency at each station. In a push system, one of the functions of work-in-process inventory is to help make workstations independent of each other. Inventories are large enough to allow for variations in processing speeds, for discarding defective units without interrupting production, and for machine downtime.

Under a **materials pull system** (often called a **Kanban system**), employees at each station work to provide inventory for the next workstation only as needed. (*Kanban*, the Japanese word for *card*, is a system created in Japan that originally used cards to indicate that a department needed additional components.) The building of excess inventories is strictly prohibited. When the number of units in inventory reaches a specified limit, work at the station stops until workers at a subsequent station pull a unit from the in-process storage area. Hence, the *pull* of inventory by a subsequent station authorizes production to continue.

A pull, or Kanban, system's low inventory levels require a team effort. To avoid idle time, processing speeds must be balanced and equipment must be kept in good repair. Quality problems are identified immediately, and the low inventory levels require immediate correction of quality problems. To make a pull system work, management must accept the notion that it is better to have employees idle than to have them building excess inventory. A pull system also requires careful planning by management and active participation in decision making by employees. A lean production process involves minimizing cycle time, eliminating waste, producing inventory only as needed, and ensuring the highest level of quality and efficiency. To achieve these results on a continuing basis, there is a strong emphasis on continuous improvement programs (see Chapter 8).

Business Insight ■ Inventory Management and Supply Chain Risk

Toyota's just-in-time inventory system is central to the company's global manufacturing success; however, this system also creates vulnerabilities. Toyota keeps as little inventory on site as possible—it holds only several hours' worth of parts, working with suppliers to maintain a steady supply of parts for production. This lowers cost and increases quality control, as defects are noticed immediately. However, Toyota is vulnerable to events affecting its suppliers.

In 1997, a fire at a supplier halted Toyota's production for five days. A 2007 earthquake left the Toyota plants unscathed but still stopped production due to damage at the site of their supplier of piston rings. The massive 2011 earthquake affected 660 of Toyota's suppliers. Since 2011 Toyota has aggressively sought to manage this risk. While some earthquake risk is inherent in manufacturing in Japan, Toyota has worked with suppliers to diversify geographically. These measures should reduce the supply chain effects of future disasters.

Source: Yoko Kubota, "Japan Earthquakes Rattle Toyota's Vulnerable Supply Chain," *Wall Street Journal*, April 19, 2016.
Link: http://www.wsj.com/articles/japan-earthquakes-rattle-toyotas-supply-chain-1460986805

Reducing Finished Goods Inventory

Finished goods inventory can be reduced by reducing cycle time and by better predicting customer demand for finished units. Lowering cycle times reduces the need for speculative inventories. If finished goods can be replenished quickly, the need diminishes for large inventory levels to satisfy customer needs and to provide for unanticipated fluctuations in customer orders. Anticipating customers' demand for goods can be improved by adopting a value chain approach to inventory management by which the manufacturer or supplier is working as a partner with its customers to meet their inventory needs. This frequently involves having online computer access to customers' inventory levels on a real-time basis and being able to synchronize changes in production with changes in customers' inventory levels as they occur.

Sharing this type of information obviously requires an enormous amount of mutual trust between a manufacturer or supplier and its customers, but it is becoming increasingly common among world-class organizations. An example of this type of vendor-customer relationship is the relationship between Procter & Gamble, one of the world's largest consumer products companies, and its largest customer, Walmart. By having access to Walmart's computer inventory system, Procter & Gamble is better able to determine and fill Walmart's specific needs for products, such as disposable diapers.

Review 7-3 LO3 — Distinguishing Lean Production from a Traditional Inventory Model

1. An element of lean production and just-in-time inventory management.
2. An element of a traditional inventory model that focuses on maintaining specified levels of inventory.

Required

For each of the statements *a–g* below, identify which of the two concepts listed above is more relevant.

_____ *a.* Nimble production process with small lot sizes and short setup and changeover times.
_____ *b.* Material push system.
_____ *c.* Reduction of cycle time.
_____ *d.* Finished goods inventory is stored in warehouses until needed.
_____ *e.* Selecting vendors on the basis of service and material quality, as well as price.
_____ *f.* Accepting vendor deliveries directly to the shop floor, and only as needed.
_____ *g.* Employees at each station work to provide inventory for the next workstation only as needed.

Solution on p. 276.

Performance Evaluation and Recordkeeping with Lean Production and JIT

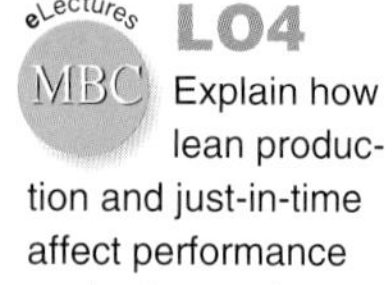

LO4 Explain how lean production and just-in-time affect performance evaluation and recordkeeping.

Movement toward a JIT/lean production philosophy requires changes in performance evaluation procedures and offers opportunities for significant reductions in recordkeeping costs. These changes are discussed in this section.

Performance Evaluation

JIT regards inventory as something to be eliminated. Hence, in a manufacturing organization, inventories are kept as small as possible. Under the JIT ideal, inventories do not exist because vendors deliver raw materials in small batches directly to the shop floor. JIT also strives to minimize, or eliminate, work-in-process inventory by minimizing the nonprocessing elements of cycle time and by having processing times as short as possible.

Dysfunctional Effects of Traditional Performance Measures

A potential conflict exists between the goals of JIT and lean production and those of traditional performance measures applied at the level of the department or cost center. Although lean production emphasizes overall efficiency, many traditional performance measures emphasize local (departmental) cost savings and local (departmental) efficiency. The following represent examples of cost and quality issues that may arise when management decisions are based solely on meeting departmental performance measures.

- To achieve quantity discounts and favorable prices, a purchasing agent might order excess inventory, thereby increasing subsequent storage, obsolescence, and handling costs.
- To obtain a low price, a purchasing agent might order from a supplier whose goods have not been certified as meeting quality specifications, thereby causing subsequent inspection, rework, and spoilage costs, and perhaps, dissatisfied customers further down the value chain.
- To avoid having idle employees and equipment, a supervisor might refuse to halt production to determine the cause of a quality problem, thereby increasing inspection, rework, and spoilage costs.
- To obtain low fixed costs per unit under absorption costing, a supervisor might produce in excess of current needs (preferably in long production runs), thereby causing subsequent increases in storage, obsolescence, and handling costs.

Performance Measures Under Lean Production and JIT

The selection of performance measures used by a company should align with the company's goals and objectives. In accordance with the goal of eliminating inventory and reducing cycle time to processing time, JIT supportive performance measures emphasize inventory turnover, cycle time, and **cycle efficiency** (the ratio of value-added to non-value-added manufacturing activities).

When applied to a specific item of raw materials or finished goods, **inventory turnover** is computed as the annual demand in units divided by the average inventory in units:

$$\textbf{Inventory turnover (in units)} = \frac{\textbf{Annual demand in units}}{\textbf{Average inventory in units}}$$

The selection of performance measures used by a company should align with the company's goals and objectives. Progress toward the goal of reducing inventory is measured by comparing successive inventory turnover ratios. Generally, the higher the inventory turnover, the better.

When measured with inventory dollars instead of inventory units, inventory turnover can be used as a measure of the organization's overall success in reducing inventory, or in increasing sales in relation to inventories. This financial measure can be derived directly from a firm's financial statements.

$$\textbf{Inventory turnover (in dollars)} = \frac{\textbf{Cost of goods sold}}{\textbf{Average inventory (in dollars)}}$$

Another ratio often used to monitor the effectiveness of inventory levels in retail organizations, such as Whole Foods or Macy's, is gross margin return on inventory investment (GMROI), calculated as follows:

$$\textbf{GMROI} = \frac{\textbf{Gross margin (in dollars)}}{\textbf{Average inventory (in dollars)}}$$

Cycle time is a measure of the total time required to produce one unit of a product:

$$\textbf{Cycle time} = \textbf{Setup time} + \textbf{Processing time} + \textbf{Movement time} + \textbf{Waiting time} + \textbf{Inspection time}$$

Under ideal circumstances, cycle time would consist of only processing time, and processing time would be as low as possible. Only processing time adds value to the product; hence, the time required for all other activities should be driven toward zero. The use of flexible manufacturing systems, properly sequencing jobs, and properly placing tools will minimize setup time. If the shop floor is optimally arranged, workers pass products directly from one workstation to the next. If production is optimally scheduled, inventory will not wait in temporary storage between workstations. If raw materials are of high quality and products are manufactured so that they always conform to specifications, separate inspection activities are not needed.

Cycle efficiency is computed as the ratio of processing time to total cycle time:

$$\textbf{Cycle efficiency} = \frac{\textbf{Processing time}}{\textbf{Cycle time}}$$

The highest cycle efficiency possible is always sought. If all non-value-added activities are eliminated, this ratio equals one.

Simplified Recordkeeping

Lean production and JIT enable significant reductions in the number of accounting transactions required for purchasing and production activities. This results in cost savings for bookkeeping activities and in shifting accounting resources from detailed bookkeeping to the development of more useful activity cost data.

Purchasing

In a traditional accounting system, every purchase results in the preparation of several documents. Additional documents are prepared for the issuance of raw materials to the factory. JIT, on the other hand, attempts to minimize inventory levels and stresses long-term relationships with a limited number of vendors who have demonstrated their ability to provide quality raw materials on a timely basis, as well as at a competitive price. Under a JIT inventory system, a company often has standing purchase orders for specified materials from specified vendors at specified prices. Production personnel are authorized to requisition materials directly from authorized vendors, who deliver limited quantities of materials as needed directly to the shop floor. Production personnel verify receipt of the raw materials. Periodically, each vendor sends an invoice for several shipments, which the company acknowledges and pays.

Product Costing

Another advantage of a lean production system is that it reduces the amount of detailed bookkeeping required for financial accounting purposes. If ending inventories are nonexistent, or so small that the costs assigned to them are insignificant in comparison with the costs assigned to Cost of Goods Sold, it makes little sense to track product costs through several inventory accounts. Instead of using a traditional product cost accounting system (as illustrated in Chapter 5), firms that have implemented JIT often use what is sometimes referred to as a backflush approach to accounting for product costs.

Under **backflush costing**, all costs of direct materials, direct labor, and manufacturing overhead are assigned as incurred to Cost of Goods Sold. If there are no inventories on hand at the end of the period, no additional steps are required. However, if there are inventories on hand at year-end, costs are backed out of Cost of Goods Sold and assigned to the appropriate inventory accounts. For a complete discussion of backflush costing, refer to a cost accounting text.

Also under a JIT inventory approach, many of the distinctions and arguments regarding absorption versus variable costing are moot (see Appendix 5A). If the quantity of inventory is insignificant, it matters little whether inventory cost includes only variable manufacturing costs or both variable and fixed manufacturing costs. Whether absorption or variable costing is used, the total cost assigned to inventory on the balance sheet will be small, and there is little difference in the amount of profit reported on the income statement.

As we discussed in previous chapters, traditional product costing systems go to great lengths to calculate the materials, labor, and manufacturing overhead cost per unit for each unit produced. Overhead is typically assigned to inventory using a predetermined overhead rate based on an assumed volume-based driver such as direct labor hours or machine hours. If actual production is less than budgeted production, there will be underapplied overhead, which is usually written off as an expense of the period. To avoid this expense, managers are often motivated to overproduce product in order to ensure that all overhead is allocated to product. Also, by budgeting a large amount of produced units, fixed overhead cost is spread over more units, resulting in a lower cost per unit. Such overproduction is equivalent to a cardinal sin in a lean production company.

As we will see in Chapter 10, many companies also adopt standard cost systems where they account for product cost components on both an actual and budgeted cost basis, with variances between actual cost and standard (or allowed) costs reported on the internal performance reports as increased expenses if they are unfavorable and as a reduction of expenses if they are favorable. In such cases, managers are motivated to maximize favorable variances and minimize or eliminate unfavorable variances. Such systems of reporting often lead managers to actions that are contrary to the lean production philosophy.

Analyzing Performance in Lean Manufacturing — LO4 Review 7-4

Assume Titleist is trying to decide which automated production line to use to produce its new Pro VI golf balls. Suppose the two best systems under consideration have the following estimated performance characteristics, based on minutes per 1,000 balls produced:

	System A	System B
Setup time	25	10
Movement time from start to finish	10	14
Waiting time	3	16
Inspection time	5	7
Processing time	40	30
Total time in minutes	83	77

Required

a. Determine the cycle time per batch for each system.

b. Determine the cycle efficiency for each system.

c. Assuming Titleist is a "lean" manufacturer, what improvements may be possible in the two systems?

Solution on p. 276.

Increased Focus on Data-Driven Decision Making

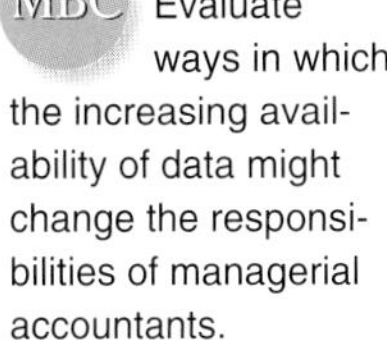

LO5 Evaluate ways in which the increasing availability of data might change the responsibilities of managerial accountants.

Increased access to data is changing the landscape of managerial accounting. Business leaders should be able to increasingly rely on data to answer difficult questions. Which products or services are most profitable? What are the best prices to charge for our services? Which manufacturing process is the most efficient? When business leaders can rely on data to answer these types of questions, they can then focus efforts on understanding which questions to ask. What is our business's core competency? What is our organization's strategic position (as discussed in Chapter 1)? Which products or services should we offer, or in which markets should we compete?

In order to rely on data, it must be accurate and timely. Costing models such as ABC, step, and linear algebra can help provide more accurate information on product costs. However, the accuracy of this data relies on management choosing relevant activity cost pools and cost drivers, and reasonable additional assumptions. Further, employees throughout the organization must understand and support the costing model. The concept of GIGO (garbage in, garbage out) refers to the idea that incorrect information going into a system results in incorrect data coming out. The system does not magically fix the information.[1]

Even when analysts have reliable and timely data, there are risks associated with data-driven decision making. A common issue is the misunderstanding of correlation versus causation. The idea behind big data analytics is to uncover hidden patterns and correlation among activities, and then to use this information to make decisions and to predict outcomes.[2] Often, just because there is a high correlation between two events, it does not mean that one caused the other. Using this information to then extrapolate further outcomes will be inaccurate. An example often referenced to demonstrate

[1] Rod Koch, "Big Data or Big Empathy," *Strategic Finance*, December 1, 2015.

[2] http://www.sas.com/en_us/insights/analytics/big-data-analytics.html

this issue is the windmill. The faster the windmill rotates, the more wind can be observed. Can we conclude that windmills cause wind? As ice cream sales increase, the rate of drowning increases. Does ice cream consumption cause drowning? These examples make it fairly obvious that one event does not cause the other, even though they are correlated. However, as managers are inundated with data, it may not always be so easy to understand the distinction between correlation and causation, resulting in poor decision making.

As the environment changes in terms of the availability of managerial accounting information, so too do the skills required of managerial accountants. **Exhibit 7.6** summarizes the research conducted by the IMA to better understand the talent gap between the skills business leaders perceive as important factors of success and the skills their finance teams possess.[3] Finance professionals seem to be reasonably prepared with the more traditional skills such as financial analysis; budgeting, planning, and forecasting; and operations analysis. However, a more significant talent gap exists related to data skills such as technological acumen; identifying key data trends; data mining and extraction; and statistical modeling and data analysis skills. The study also emphasizes that softer skills are also increasingly sought. Business leaders expect finance teams to be capable of using data to improve business performance through skills such as process improvement, strategic thinking and execution, adaptability to change, and communications.

Exhibit 7.6 Technical Skills Gap

	Important to Success	Possessed by Your Team	Talent Gap
Financial analysis	87%	69%	18%
Budgeting, planning, and forecasting	85%	63%	22%
Operational analysis	82%	54%	28%
Cost management	81%	61%	20%
Technological acumen	77%	50%	27%
Identifying key data trends	75%	46%	29%
Data mining and extraction	71%	43%	28%
Statistical modeling and data analysis	62%	35%	27%
Enterprise resource planning (ERP) systems	61%	40%	21%
Customer lifetime value (CLV)	55%	32%	23%

Review 7-5 LO5 Discussing Risks and Concerns of Access to Big Data

Increased access to data can help business leaders make better and more timely decisions. This can also allow them to focus more of their efforts toward more strategic analysis and thinking. Even though there are many benefits to the increasing availability of data, there are also risks and concerns.

Required

Discuss some accompanying risks and concerns of growing access to big data.

Solution on p. 276.

Guidance Answers

You Are the Controller

Pg. 254 Designing any information processing system is a matter of weighing benefits with the costs of designing and operating the system. The same is true for a cost allocation system. Also, you have to decide how the cost information will be used. If it is used only for external financial reporting purposes, a high degree of precision may not be necessary. However, if it is used to determine the most profitable product mix, it may be crucial to have the most precise cost information. For the service departments that provide only services to producing departments and that receive no services from other service departments, a direct allocation method might be adequate. For departments that provide and/or receive interdepartmental services, you should consider using either a step or linear algebra approach to assigning costs. Whether you use a direct, step, or linear algebra approach, you will have to decide whether to assign the costs using a single volume-based cost driver (such as square footage or number of employees) or using multiple cost drivers that reflect the actual activities performed. In most cases, the ABC approach (discussed in Chapter 6) will give a higher level of precision, but at considerably greater cost.

[3] Kip Krumweide, "Building a Team to Capitalize on the Promise of Big Data," *IMA*, January 2016.

Key Ratios

$$\text{Inventory turnover} = \frac{\text{Annual demand in units}}{\text{Average inventory in units}}$$

$$\text{Inventory turnover} = \frac{\text{Cost of goods sold}}{\text{Average inventory (in dollars)}}$$

$$\text{Gross margin return on inventory investment} = \frac{\text{Gross margin (in dollars)}}{\text{Average inventory (in dollars)}}$$

$$\text{Cycle time} = \text{Setup time} + \text{Processing time} + \text{Movement time} + \text{Waiting time} + \text{Inspection time}$$

$$\text{Cycle efficiency} = \frac{\text{Processing time}}{\text{Cycle time}}$$

Key Terms

backflush costing, 260
cycle efficiency, 259
cycle time, 256
direct department cost, 248
direct method, 250
indirect department cost, 248
inspection time, 257
interdepartment services, 249
inventory turnover, 259
just-in-time (JIT) inventory management, 255
Kanban system, 257
linear algebra (reciprocal) method, 254
materials pull system, 257
materials push system, 257
movement time, 257
processing time, 257
quality circles, 257
service departments, 248
setup time, 257
step method, 251
waiting time, 257

Multiple Choice

1. Which of the following statements regarding production and service department costs is incorrect?
  a. For a production department, direct department costs include both direct and indirect product costs.
  b. An indirect department cost is a cost assigned to a department as a result of a reassignment from another service department.
  c. Companies that use departmental overhead rates likely allocate service department costs to production departments.
  d. Companies that use activity-based costing likely do not allocate service department costs to production departments.

2. The following budgeted information pertains to Trawbing Company:

	Service Departments		Producing Departments	
	Human Resources	Facilities	Mixing	Molding
Direct department costs	$75,000	$50,000	$520,000	$860,000
Direct labor hours	6,000	4,000	20,000	36,000
Square footage	2,000	3,000	24,000	36,000
# of employees	3	2	18	12

The direct department costs for Mixing and Molding represent the direct department overhead costs of those departments, not including any direct material or direct labor. Human Resource Department costs are assigned to other departments based on the number of employees, and Facilities Department costs are assigned to other departments based on square footage occupied. If the direct method is used to allocate

Multiple Choice Answers
1. d 2. a 3. c 4. c 5. d 6. d 7. c

service department costs to the producing departments, the total budgeted overhead for the Molding Department after service department costs are allocated is

a. $920,000.00
b. $585,000.00
c. $584,062.50
d. $920,937.50

3. Refer to the previous question. If the step method is used to allocate service departments to the producing departments, the total budgeted overhead for the Mixing Department after service department costs are allocated is (round all calculations to two decimal places)

a. $920,000.00
b. $585,000.00
c. $584,062.50
d. $920,937.50

4. Refer to question 2 above. Assume that the Molding Department uses a predetermined overhead rate for assigning overhead costs to products based on budgeted total overhead after service department costs are allocated using the direct allocation method. The predetermined overhead rate for the Molding Department is (round all calculations to two decimal places)

a. $26.88 per direct labor hour
b. $23.89 per direct labor hour
c. $25.56 per direct labor hour
d. $29.25 per direct labor hour

5. The key elements of JIT/lean production include which of the following?

a. Increased coordination throughout the value chain
b. Reduced inventories and production times
c. Increased product quality and employee empowerment
d. All of the above are elements of JIT/lean production

6. Topaz Company sold and produced 40,000 units of product at a cost of $1,200,000 for a sales price of $60 per unit during the most recent year. Throughout the year its average inventory was 4,000 units with an average cost of $120,000. Based on this information, which of the following cannot be determined about Topaz's inventory management performance?

a. Topaz's inventory turnover in units was 10 times.
b. Topaz's gross margin return on average inventory investment was 1,000%.
c. Topaz's inventory turnover in dollars was 10 times.
d. Topaz's production cycle efficiency was 100%.

7. Which of the following is not a characteristic of a business environment with increasing availability of data?

a. There is potential risk of misinterpretation between correlation and causation.
b. It is increasingly important that data be accurate and timely.
c. There is decreasing reliance on the softer skills such as strategic analysis and communication.
d. The largest technical skills talent gaps occur in areas of identifying key data trends and data mining and extraction.

Questions

Q7-1. Distinguish between the following sets of terms:

a. Direct product costs and indirect product costs.
b. Direct department costs and indirect department costs.

Q7-2. Define the terms direct cost and indirect cost.

Q7-3. Differentiate between cost assignment and cost allocation.

Q7-4. Explain how a cost item can be both a direct cost and an indirect cost.

Q7-5. What is the primary advantage of separately allocating fixed and variable indirect costs?

Q7-6. Define interdepartmental services.

Q7-7. To what extent are interdepartmental services recognized under the direct, step, and linear algebra methods of service department cost allocation?

Q7-8. Is it feasible to assign interdepartmental services to production departments using ABC?

Q7-9. Explain the concept of just-in-time inventory management.

Q7-10. What are the major elements of lean production?

Q7-11. What is the relationship between JIT and the lean production concept?

Q7-12. Explain how computer technology has affected the way companies approach JIT inventory management and lean production methods.

Q7-13. What elements of the JIT approach contribute to reducing materials inventories?

Q7-14. Define and identify the elements of cycle time. Which of these elements adds value to the product?

Q7-15. Explain briefly how JIT/lean production benefits organizations that take a value-chain approach to management.

Q7-16. Explain how traditional performance evaluation systems using standard costs conflict with the lean production concept.

Assignments with the MBC logo in the margin are available in myBusinessCourse. See the Preface of the book for details.

Mini Exercises

M7-17. Allocating Service Department Costs: Allocation Basis Alternatives LO2 Genzink Steel

Assume Genzink Steel, a metal fabrication company, has two producing departments, P1 and P2, and one service department, S1. Estimated overhead costs per month are as follows:

P1	$2,000,000
P2	750,000
S1	1,000,000

Other data follow:

	P1	P2
Number of employees	50	30
Production capacity (units)	75,000	20,000
Space occupied (square feet)	57,600	22,400
Five-year average percent of S1's service output used	60%	40%

Required

a. For each of the following allocation bases, determine the total estimated overhead cost for P1 and P2 after allocating S1 cost to the producing departments.

1. Number of employees
2. Production capacity in units
3. Space occupied
4. Five-year average percentage of S1 services used
5. Estimated overhead costs (Round your answer to the nearest dollar.)

b. For each of the five allocation bases, explain the circumstances (including examples) under which each allocation base might be most appropriately used to allocate service department cost in a manufacturing plant such as Genzink Steel. Also, discuss the advantages and disadvantages that might result from using each of the allocation bases.

M7-18. Indirect Cost Allocation: Direct Method LO2

Charlie Manufacturing Company has two production departments, Melting and Molding. Direct general plant management and plant security costs benefit both production departments. Charlie allocates general plant management costs on the basis of the number of production employees and plant security costs on the basis of space occupied by the production departments using the direct method of overhead allocation. In November, the following overhead costs were recorded:

Melting Department overhead	$500,000
Molding Department overhead	400,000
General plant management	200,000
Plant security	100,000

Other pertinent data follow:

	Melting	Molding
Number of employees	60	40
Space occupied (square feet)	20,000	80,000
Machine hours	1,056	3,200
Direct labor hours	10,560	7,200

Required

a. Prepare a schedule allocating general plant management costs and plant security costs to the Melting and Molding Departments.

b. Determine the total departmental overhead costs for the Melting and Molding Departments.

c. Assuming the Melting Department uses machine hours and the Molding Department uses direct labor hours to apply overhead to production, calculate the overhead rate for each production department.

LO2 **M7-19. Interdepartment Services: Direct Method**

Wilhelm Manufacturing Company has five operating departments, two of which are producing departments (P1 and P2) and three of which are service departments (S1, S2, and S3). All costs of the service departments are allocated to the producing departments. The following table shows the distribution of services from the service departments.

	Services Provided to				
Services provided from	S1	S2	S3	P1	P2
S1	—	10%	20%	28%	42%
S2	5%	—	15%	52%	28%
S3	7%	3%	—	27%	63%

The direct operating costs of the service departments are as follows:

S1	$150,000
S2	80,000
S3	106,000

Required

Using the direct method, prepare a schedule allocating the service department costs to the producing departments.

LO3, 4 Tesla, Inc. (TSLA) **M7-20. Inventory Ratio Calculations**

Tesla reported the following data for 2017 and 2018, in millions:

Inventory	
December 31, 2017	$ 2,067
December 31, 2018	2,264
December 31, 2019	3,113
Cost of automotive sales	
2018	$ 6,725
2019	13,686
Gross margin	
2018	$ 1,810
2019	3,946

Required

(round all calculations to two decimal places)

a. Calculate the inventory turnover ratio for 2018 and 2019.

b. Calculate the gross margin return on inventory investment for 2018 and 2019.

M7-21. Inventory Ratio Calculations

LO3, 4
Dell Technologies Inc. (DELL)

Dell Technologies reported the following data for 2018 and 2019 (in millions):

Inventory	
February 3, 2017	$ 2,538
February 2, 2018	2,678
February 1, 2019	3,649
Cost of products sold	
Year ended February 2, 2018	$51,433
Year ended February 1, 2019	57,889
Gross margin	
Year ended February 2, 2018	$ 9,818
Year ended February 1, 2019	13,398

Required

(round all calculations to two decimal places)

a. Calculate the inventory turnover ratio for the years ended in February 2018 and February 2019.

b. Calculate the gross margin return on inventory investment for the years ended in February 2018 and February 2019.

Exercises

E7-22. Interdepartment Services: Step Method

LO2

Refer to the data in Mini Exercise M7-19. Using the step method, prepare a schedule for Wilhelm Manufacturing Company allocating the service department costs to the producing departments. (Round calculations to the nearest dollar.)

E7-23. Interdepartment Services: Step Method

LO2
Wilson's Department Store

Assume that Wilson's, a department store in Massachusetts, allocates the costs of the Personnel and Payroll departments to three retail sales departments, Housewares, Clothing, and Toys. In addition to providing services to the operating departments, Personnel and Payroll provide services to each other. Wilson's allocates Personnel Department costs on the basis of the number of employees and Payroll Department costs on the basis of gross payroll. Cost and allocation information for June is as follows:

	Personnel	Payroll	Housewares	Clothing	Toys
Direct department cost	$25,000	$30,340	$50,174	$60,830	$45,156
Number of employees	3	5	12	20	10
Gross payroll	$12,960	$17,280	$36,000	$43,200	$34,560

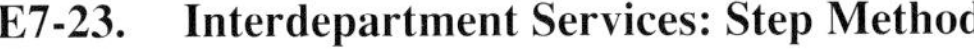

Required

a. Determine the percentage of total Personnel Department services that was provided to the Payroll Department.

b. Determine the percentage of total Payroll Department services that was provided to the Personnel Department.

c. Prepare a schedule showing Personnel Department and Payroll Department cost allocations to the operating departments, assuming Wilson's uses the step method. (Round calculations to the nearest dollar.)

E7-24. Product Costing in a JIT/Lean Environment

LO3, 4

Johanna Computer manufactures laptop computers under its own brand, but acquires all the components from outside vendors. No computers are assembled until the order is received online from customers, so there is no finished goods inventory. When an order is received, the bill of materials required to fill the order is prepared automatically and sent electronically to the various vendors. All components are received from vendors within three days and the completed order is shipped to the customer immediately when completed, usually on the same day the components are received from vendors. The number of units in process at the end of any day is negligible.

The following data are provided for the most recent month of operations:

Actual components costs incurred	$1,200,000
Actual conversion costs incurred	$1,850,000
Units in process, beginning of month	0
Units started in process during the month	4,000
Units in process, end of month	0

Required

a. Assuming Johanna uses traditional cost accounting procedures:
1. How much cost was charged to Work-in-Process during the month?
2. How much cost was charged to cost of goods sold during the month?

b. Assuming Johanna is a lean production company and uses the backflush costing method:
1. How much cost was charged to Work-in-Process during the month?
2. How much cost was charged to cost of goods sold during the month?

LO4 Costco (COST) Target (TGT)

E7-25. Inventory Management Metrics

Large retailers like Costco and Target typically use gross margin ratio (gross margin ÷ sales), inventory turnover (sometimes referred to as inventory turns), and gross margin return on investment (GMROI) to evaluate how well inventory has been managed. The goal is to maximize profits while minimizing the investment in inventory. Below are data for four scenarios, a base scenario (A) followed by three modifications (B, C, and D) to the base scenario.

	Scenario A	Scenario B	Scenario C	Scenario D
Sales	$50,000	$75,000	$60,000	$50,000
Cost of goods sold	35,000	35,000	30,000	35,000
Gross profit	$15,000	$40,000	$30,000	$15,000
Average inventory	$ 6,000	$ 6,000	$ 6,000	$ 4,000

Required

For each scenario calculate the gross margin percent, the inventory turnover, and GMROI.

LO4 **E7-26. Evaluating Inventory Management Metrics**

Refer to E7-25.

Required

a. For Scenarios B through D, explain what change occurred relative to Scenario A to cause GMROI to change. For example, was the change in GMROI caused by a change in inventory turns, a change in gross margin percent, or by reducing inventory levels?

b. What general conclusions can be made from the calculations and observations regarding the factors that influence GMROI?

LO5 **E7-27. Technical Skills Gap**

Katie Dempsey works as a recruiter, placing accounting and finance professionals. Katie's current project is to fill an open managerial accounting position at PepsiCo. Identify the technical skills that Katie will be looking for in the applicant's resume and application materials that will likely lead to success in the position. Do you think these skills will be difficult to find in candidates? If so, what are some ways PepsiCo might be able to develop these skills in-house?

LO4 **E7-28. Cycle Efficiency**

Clarion Scooters, Inc. runs one 8-hour shift per day. Three different machines are used in the production of electric scooters, Clarion's sole product.

The operations manager at Clarion is looking at ways to be more efficient and has gathered the following information:

Manufacturing time per batch of 50 scooters	
Function	**Time**
Actual processing time on the machines for one batch of scooters	3.75 hours
Time spent moving a batch of scooters from one station to the next	2 hours
Time spent on quality control testing, per batch	45 minutes
Time spent setting up equipment, for batch processing	30 minutes

The operations manager also noted that, on average, there was about one hour of downtime per batch. (Downtime occurred when employees were unavailable to move or test the scooters.)

a. What is the cycle time per batch, in hours?
b. What is Clarion's cycle efficiency?
c. What are some practical steps Clarion could take to improve its efficiency?

Problems

P7-29. Selecting Cost Allocation Bases and Direct Method Allocations LO2

Seattle Company has three producing departments (P1, P2, and P3) for which direct department costs are accumulated. In January, the following indirect costs of operation were incurred.

Plant manager's salary and office expense	$20,500
Plant security	6,000
Plant nurse's salary and office expense	7,000
Factory depreciation (building)	20,000
Equipment depreciation	15,000
Machine maintenance	7,000
Plant cafeteria cost subsidy	5,000
	$80,500

The following additional data have been collected for the three producing departments:

	P1	P2	P3
Number of employees	20	30	10
Space occupied (square feet)	12,000	6,000	6,000
Direct labor hours	3,400	5,000	1,600
Machine hours	1,500	600	900
Number of nurse office visits	25	20	5

Required

a. Group the indirect cost items into cost pools based on their common basis for allocation. Identify the most appropriate allocation basis for each cost pool and determine the total January costs in the pool. (*Hint:* A cost pool may consist of one or more cost items.)
b. Allocate the cost pools directly to the three producing departments using the allocation bases selected in requirement (*a*).
c. How much indirect cost would be allocated to each producing department if Seattle Company were using a plantwide rate based on direct labor hours? Based on machine hours?
d. Comment on the benefits of allocating costs in pools compared with using a plantwide rate.

P7-30. Evaluating Allocation Bases and Direct Method Allocations LO2

Brahtz Company has two service departments, Maintenance and Information Technology (IT), that serve two producing departments, Mixing and Packaging. The following data have been collected for these departments for the current year:

	IT	Maintenance	Mixing	Packaging
Direct department costs	$210,000	$185,000	$1,200,000	$550,000
Number of employees			40	20
Number of ethernet connections			50	30
Number of maintenance hours used			1,500	1,000
Number of maintenance orders			120	180

Required

a. Using the direct method, allocate the service department costs under the following independent assumptions:

1. IT costs are allocated based on the number of employees, and Maintenance costs are allocated based on the number of maintenance hours used.
2. IT costs are allocated based on the number of ethernet connections served, and Maintenance costs are allocated based on the number of maintenance orders.

b. Comment on the reasonableness of the bases used in the calculations in requirement (*a*). What considerations should determine which bases to use for allocating IT and Maintenance costs?

LO2 P7-31. Cost Reimbursement and Step Allocation Method

Hope Clinic is a not-for-profit outpatient facility that provides medical services to both fee-paying patients and low-income government-supported patients. Reimbursement from the government is based on total actual costs of services provided, including both direct costs of patient services and indirect operating costs. Patient services are provided through two producing departments, Medical Services and Ancillary Services (includes X-ray, therapy, etc.). In addition to the direct costs of these departments, the clinic incurs indirect costs in two service departments, Administration and Facilities. Administration costs are allocated first based on the number of full-time employees, and Facilities costs are then allocated based on space occupied. Costs and related data for the current month are as follows:

	Administration	Facilities	Medical Services	Ancillary Services
Direct costs	$65,000	$30,750	$745,700	$350,000
Number of employees	6	4	8	4
Amount of space occupied (square feet)	2,000	600	7,500	2,500
Number of patient visits	—	—	7,975	3,000

Required

a. Using the step method, prepare a schedule allocating the common service department costs to the producing departments.

b. Determine the amount to be reimbursed from the government for each low-income patient visit.

LO2 P7-32. Budgeted Service Department Cost Allocation: Pricing a New Product

Fit & Active Company is adding a new diet food concentrate called Body Fit & Healthy to its line of bodybuilding and exercise products. A plant is being built for manufacturing the new product. Management has decided to price the new product based on a 100% markup on total manufacturing costs. A direct cost budget for the new plant projects that direct department costs of $7,152,500 will be incurred in producing an expected normal output of 750,000 pounds of finished product. In addition, indirect costs for Administration and Technical Support will be shared by Body Fit & Healthy with the two exercise products divisions, Commercial Products and Retail Products. Budgeted annual data to be used in making the allocations are summarized here.

	Administration	Technical Support	Commercial Products	Retail Products	Body Fit & Healthy
Number of employees	10	4	70	60	20
Amount of technical support time (hours)	690	—	1,840	1,610	460

Direct costs are budgeted at $750,000 for the Administration Department and $500,000 for the Technical Support Department.

Required

a. Using the step method, determine the total direct and indirect costs of Body Fit & Healthy. (Administration costs are allocated based on number of employees; Technical Support costs are allocated based on technical support time.)

b. Determine the selling price per pound of Body Fit & Healthy. (Round calculations to the nearest cent.)

P7-33. Allocation and Responsibility Accounting

LO2 Timberland Company (TBL)

Assume that Timberland Company uses a responsibility accounting system for evaluating its managers, and that abbreviated performance reports for the company's three divisions for the month of March are as follows (amounts in thousands).

	Total	East	Central	West
Operating income before service department cost allocations	$480,000	$200,000	$170,000	$110,000
Less allocated costs:				
Information Technology	(250,000)	(96,154)	(76,923)	(76,923)
Personnel	(160,000)	(71,111)	(53,333)	(35,556)
Division income	$ 70,000	$ 32,735	$ 39,744	$ (2,479)

The West Division manager is very disturbed over his performance report and recent rumors that his division may be closed because of its failure to report a profit in recent periods. He believes that the reported profit figures do not fairly present operating results because his division is being unfairly burdened with service department costs. He is particularly concerned over the amount of Information Technology costs charged to his division. He believes that it is inequitable for his division to be charged with one-third of the total cost when it is using only 20% of the services. He believes that the Personnel Department's use of the Information Technology Department should also be considered in the cost allocations. Cost allocations were based on the following distributions of service provided:

	Services Receiver				
Services Provider	Personnel	Computer Services	East	Central	West
Information Technology	35%	—	25%	20%	20%
Personnel	—	10%	40%	30%	20%

Required

a. What method is the company using to allocate Personnel and Information Technology costs?

b. Recompute the cost allocations using the step method. (Round calculations to the nearest dollar.)

c. Revise the performance reports to reflect the cost allocations computed in requirement (*b*).

d. Comment on the complaint of the West Division's manager.

P7-34. Allocating Service Department Costs: Direct and Step Methods; Department and Plantwide Overhead Rates

LO2 Brown Jordan

Assume that Brown Jordan, a manufacturer of fine casual outdoor furniture, allocates Human Resources Department costs to the producing departments (Cutting and Welding) based on number of employees; Facilities Department costs are allocated based on the amount of square footage occupied. Direct department costs, labor hours, and square footage data for the four departments for October are as follows:

	Human Resources	Facilities	Cutting	Welding
Direct department overhead costs	$150,000	$450,000	$2,662,500	$1,102,500
Number of employees	12	20	60	90
Number of direct labor hours	—	—	12,000	15,000
Amount of square footage	15,000	4,500	225,000	75,000

Assume that two jobs, A1 and A2, were completed during October and that each job had direct materials costs of $3,000. Job A1 used 75 direct labor hours in the Cutting Department and 25 direct labor hours in the Welding Department. Job A2 used 25 direct labor hours in the Cutting Department and 75 direct labor hours in the Welding Department. The direct labor rate per hour, including benefits, is $50 in both departments.

Required

a. Find the cost of each job using a plantwide rate based on direct labor hours.
b. Find the cost of each job using department rates with *direct* service department cost allocation.
c. Find the cost of each job using department rates with *step* service department cost allocation.
d. Explain the differences in the costs computed in requirements (*a*)–(*c*) for each job. Which costing method is best for product pricing and profitability analysis?

LO3, 4 **P7-35. JIT/Lean Production and Product Costing**

Presented is information pertaining to the standard or budgeted unit cost of a product manufactured in a JIT/Lean Production environment at CNN Systems Inc.:

Direct materials	$30
Conversion	60
Total	$90

All materials are added at the start of the production process. All raw materials purchases and conversion costs are directly assigned to Cost of Goods Sold. At the end of the period, costs are backed out and assigned to Raw Materials in Process (only for materials still in the plant) and Finished Goods Inventory (for materials and conversion costs for completed units). Costs assigned to inventories are based on the standard or budgeted cost multiplied by the number of units in inventory. Conversion costs are assigned to inventories only for fully converted units. Since inventory levels tend to be small in this JIT environment, partially completed units are assigned no conversion costs. CNN Systems had no beginning inventories on August 1. During the month, it incurred the following manufacturing-related costs:

Purchase of raw materials on account	$500,000
Factory wages	100,000
Factory supervision salaries	25,000
Facilities costs	75,000
Factory supplies purchased	15,000
Depreciation	35,000

The end-of-month inventory included raw materials in process of 150 units and finished goods of 250 units. One hundred units of raw materials were 0% converted; the other 50 units averaged 40% converted.

Required

a. Calculate the total cost debited to Cost of Goods Sold during August.
b. Calculate the balances in Raw Materials in Process, Finished Goods Inventory, and Cost of Goods Sold at the end of August.
c. Assuming that August is a typical month, is it likely that using the company's shortcut backflush accounting procedures will produce misleading financial statements? Explain.

LO4 **P7-36. Just-in-Time Performance Evaluation**

To control operations, Sirius Company makes extensive and exclusive use of financial performance reports for each department. Although all departments have been reporting favorable cost variances in most periods, management is perplexed by the firm's low overall return on investment. You have been asked to look into the matter. Believing the purchasing department is typical of the company's operations, you obtained the following information concerning the purchases of parts for a product it started producing five years ago:

Year	Purchase Price Variance	Quantity Used (units)	Average Inventory (units)
Year 1	$ 1,500 F	10,000	1,500
Year 2	10,500 F	15,000	2,500
Year 3	12,000 F	17,500	3,000
Year 4	20,000 U	12,500	2,500
Year 5	8,000 F	18,000	2,250
Current year	9,500 F	14,500	2,900

Required

a. Compute the inventory turnover for each year. What conclusions can be drawn from a yearly comparison of the purchase price variance and the inventory turnover?

b. Identify problems likely to be caused by evaluating purchasing only on the basis of the purchase price variance.

c. Offer whatever recommendations you believe appropriate.

P7-37. Dual Allocation Approach and Charging for Services

LO2 Embassy Suites Hilton Worldwide (HLT)

Assume that the Maintenance Department of one of Embassy Suites properties, a Hilton Worldwide franchise has fixed costs of $750,000 a year. It also incurs $75 in out-of-pocket expenses for every hour of work. During the year the Rooms Department used 35,000 maintenance hours. The Food and Beverage (F&B) Department used 15,000 maintenance hours. When the Maintenance Department was established, the Rooms and F&B departments estimated they would need 35,000 and 25,000 maintenance hours, respectively. It turns out F&B cut back on maintenance hours used to insure it would meet its budget.

Required

a. Calculate the amount of Maintenance Department costs to allocate to Rooms and F&B based entirely on actual usage.

b. Calculate the amount of Maintenance Department costs to allocate to Rooms and F&B using a dual allocation approach where fixed cost is allocated based on estimated capacity needed and variable cost is allocated based on actual usage.

c. Which of the two methods applied in parts *a* and *b* is more fair to the two departments?

d. Assume that the Maintenance Department allocates costs to the producing departments using a user charge. What amount would you suggest for the user charge? Is it a good idea to use a user charge for allocating costs?

Cases and Projects

C7-38. Materials Push and Materials Pull Systems

LO3, 4

Data Storage Inc. produces three models of external storage devices for personal computers. Each model is produced on a separate assembly line. Production consists of several operations in separate work centers. Because of a high demand for Data's products, management is most interested in high-production volume and operating efficiency. Each work center is evaluated on the basis of its operating efficiency. To avoid idle time caused by defective units, variations in machine times, and machine breakdowns, significant inventories are maintained between each workstation.

At a recent administrative committee meeting, the director of research announced that the firm's engineers have made a dramatic breakthrough in designing a low-cost, read/write optical storage device. Data Storage's president is very enthusiastic, and the vice president of marketing wishes to add an assembly line for optical storage devices as soon as possible. The equipment necessary to manufacture the new product can be purchased and installed in less than 60 days. Unfortunately, all available plant space is currently devoted to the production of conventional storage devices, and expansion is not possible at the current plant location. It appears that adding the new product will require dropping a current product, relocating the entire operation, or manufacturing the optical storage devices at a separate location.

The vice president of marketing is opposed to dropping a current product. The vice president of finance is opposed to relocating the entire operation because of financing requirements and the associated financial risks. The vice president of production is opposed to splitting up production activities because of the loss of control and the added costs for various types of overhead.

Required

Explain how switching to a materials pull (Kanban) system can help solve Data Storage's space problems while improving quality and cycle time. Describe how a materials pull system works and the changes required in management attitude toward inventory and efficiency to make it work.

LO3, 4 C7-39. **Product Costing Using Activity-Based Costing and Just-in-Time: A Value Chain Approach** Wearwell Carpet Company is a small residential carpet manufacturer started by Don Stegall, a longtime engineer and manager in the carpet industry. Stegall began Wearwell in the early 1990s after learning about ABC, JIT, total quality management, and several other manufacturing concepts being used successfully in Japan and other parts of the world. Although it was a small company, he believed that with his many years of experience and by applying these advanced techniques, Wearwell could very quickly become a world-class competitor.

Stegall buys dyed carpet yarns for Wearwell from three different major yarn manufacturers with which he has done business for many years. He chose these companies because of their reputation for producing high-quality products and their state-of-the-art research and development departments. He has arranged for two carpet manufacturing companies to produce (tuft) all of his carpets on a contractual basis. Both companies have their own brands, but they also do contract work for other companies. For each manufacturer, Stegall had to agree to use the full output of one manufacturing production line at least one day per month. Each production line was dedicated to producing only one style of carpet, but each manufacturer had production lines capable of running each type of carpet that Wearwell sold.

Stegall signed a contract with a large transport company (CTC), which specializes in carpet-related shipping, to pick up and deliver yarn from the yarn plants to the tufting mills. This company will then deliver the finished product from the tufting mills to Wearwell's ten customers, which are carpet retailers in the ten largest residential building markets in the country. These retailers pay the shipping charges to have the carpets delivered to them. Wearwell maintains a small sales staff (which also doubles as a customer service staff) to deal with the retailers and occasionally with the end customers on quality problems that arise.

Wearwell started selling only one line of carpet, a medium-grade plush, but as new carpet styles were developed, it added two additional lines, a medium-grade berber carpet and a medium-grade textured carpet. Three colors are offered in each carpet style. By selling only medium grades with limited color choices, Stegall felt that he would reach a very large segment of the carpet market without having to deal with a large number of different products. As textured (trackless) carpets have become more popular, sales of plush have diminished substantially.

Required

a. Describe the value chain for Wearwell Carpet Company, and identify the parties who compose this value chain.

b. Identify and discuss the cost categories that would be included in the cost of the product for financial reporting purposes.

c. Identify and discuss the cost categories that would be included in the cost of the product for pricing and other management purposes.

d. Discuss some of the challenges that Stegall will have trying to apply JIT to regulate the levels of control at Wearwell. Suggest changes that might be necessary to make JIT work.

e. Does Wearwell seem to be an appropriate setting for implementing ABC? If so, what are likely to be the most important activities and related cost drivers?

Solutions to Review Problems

Review 7-1—Solution

Plantwide overhead rate—The costs of all service departments are added to the indirect product costs incurred within all the producing departments to get total plantwide manufacturing overhead, which is then assigned to products using a single overhead rate based on a common factor such as direct labor hours.

Department overhead rate—Service department costs are allocated to the production departments that use their services, and the allocated service department costs are added to the indirect costs incurred within the department to arrive at total department overhead and allocation rates.

Activity-based costing—Service department costs are assigned to activity cost pools; then the activity cost pools are assigned to the product based on an activity driver allocation rate.

Review 7-2—Solution

Service Department Cost Allocation

a. Direct Method

	Total	Women's	Men's
Administrative Services Department			
Allocation base (number of employees)	24	15	9
Percent of total base	100%	62.5%	37.5%
Cost allocation	$18,000	$11,250	$6,750
Facilities Services Department			
Allocation base (square footage)	22,500	15,000	7,500
Percent of total base	100%	66.67%	33.33%
Cost allocation	$12,000	$ 8,000	$4,000

Cost Allocation Summary

	Administrative	Facilities	Women's	Men's	Total
Departmental costs before allocation	$18,000	$12,000	$60,000	$50,000	$140,000
Cost allocations					
Administrative	(18,000)	—	11,250	6,750	0
Facilities	—	(12,000)	8,000	4,000	0
Departmental costs after allocation	$ 0	$ 0	$79,250	$60,750	$140,000

b. and *c.*

Allocation Sequence

	Administrative	Facilities
Allocation base	Number of employees	Amount of square footage
Total base for other service and producing departments (a)	26	25,000
Total base for other service departments (b)	2	2,500
Percent of total services provided to other service departments (b ÷ a)	7.7%	10.0%
Order of allocation	Second	First

d. Step Method

Step Allocations

	Total	Administrative	Women's	Men's
Facilities Services Department				
Allocation base (square footage)	25,000	2,500	15,000	7,500
Percent of total base	100%	10%	60%	30%
Cost allocation	$12,000	$1,200	$ 7,200	$3,600
Administrative Services Department				
Allocation base (number of employees)	24	—	15	9
Percent of total base	100%	—	62.5%	37.5%
Cost allocation ($18,000 + $1,200)	$19,200	—	$12,000	$7,200

Cost Allocation Summary	Facilities	Administrative	Women's	Men's	Total
Departmental costs before allocation	$12,000	$18,000	$60,000	$50,000	$140,000
Cost allocations					
Facilities	(12,000)	1,200	7,200	3,600	0
Administrative	—	(19,200)	12,000	7,200	0
Departmental costs after allocations	$ 0	$ 0	$79,200	$60,800	$140,000

Review 7-3—Solution

1 *a.* Nimble production process with small lot sizes and short setup and changeover times.
2 *b.* Material push system.
1 *c.* Reduction of cycle time.
2 *d.* Finished goods inventory is stored in warehouses until needed.
1 *e.* Selecting venders on the basis of service and material quality, as well as price.
1 *f.* Accepting vendor deliveries directly to the shop floor, and only as needed.
1 *g.* Employees at each station work to provide inventory for the next workstation only as needed.

Review 7-4—Solution

a. Cycle time is the total time required to produce one batch, including both value-added and non-value-added activities: System A = 83; System B = 77

b. The cycle efficiency is the percent of total time used in value-added activities. In this case, only the processing time is adding value to the product. Cycle efficiency: System A = 40/83 = 0.48; System B = 30/77 = 0.39

c. In a lean environment, management and all employees involved will be seeking ways to reduce the cycle time while maintaining a high-quality product. For A, the company could reduce non-value-added time, especially setup time. The company should also evaluate why the processing time is higher than in System B. For B, the most likely opportunity for significant reduction is to reduce the large amount of movement and waiting time. If these components of total cycle time can be reduced, B becomes even more attractive.

Review 7-5—Solution

Students will have a variety of answers. Here are a few possible responses.

1. The data must be timely and reliable. Incorrect or misleading data can result in bad information and lead to incorrect and poor decisions.
2. Softer skills such as communication, strategic thinking, and execution are also of growing importance as organizations focus more on the need to communicate and execute business strategies.
3. Analysts must be careful when drawing conclusions based on data. Often, events may seem to be linked when there may be no causal relationship driving the correlation. The cause may be inverted as in the windmill example. The machine does not cause the wind, but the wind causes the windmill to move. Or there may be additional factors to consider as in the ice cream/drowning relationship. The missing link here is that higher temperatures likely lead to more swimming and therefore, more drowning, and higher temperatures also lead to more ice cream consumption.

Chapter 8

Pricing and Other Product Management Decisions

Learning Objectives

LO1 Explain the importance of the value chain in managing products and describe the key components of an organization's internal and external value chain. (p. 280)

LO2 Distinguish between economic and cost-based approaches to pricing. (p. 284)

LO3 Explain target costing and discuss its acceptance in highly competitive industries. (p. 289)

LO4 Illustrate the relation between target costing and continuous improvement costing. (p. 294)

LO5 Explain how benchmarking enhances quality management, continuous improvement, and process reengineering. (p. 296)

Roku, Inc. has been a dominant player in streaming media since 2008, when it introduced its first set-top streaming media device. The Roku Stick was introduced in 2012. Roku devices stream content from most major content providers (Netflix, Amazon Prime, Disney+, and Apple TV+, for example). The company also launched its own streaming channel in 2017, although the free Roku Channel includes no original content. Roku started selling its own branded smart TVs in 2014, manufactured by companies like Hitachi, Magnavox, and Sharp. All Roku products are built on the Roku OS. The company also licenses Roku OS to other television manufacturers and distributors.

In 2019, over 44% of all connected-TV viewing hours were streamed through Roku devices. By the end of 2019, Roku's software was embedded in one-third of all smart TVs sold in the U.S.

That's the good news. The bad news is that Roku has yet to report any profits from operations. However, its most lucrative business, advertising, has substantial upside. The television advertising market is around $70 billion annually. Over-the-top (OTT) advertising revenue (streamed through media devices) was about $4 billion in 2019. As consumers move from cable and satellite television to streamed content, advertising dollars are expected to move as well.

In an industry as dynamic and fast-moving as video streaming, staying competitive means continuing to grow and adapt as the technology and the market change. Roku's primary media device competitors are Apple's Apple TV, Alphabet's Google Chromecast, and Amazon's Fire TV. All three are actively pursuing the growing advertising revenues, and, although most content providers are currently allowing streaming on all media devices, that may change. CBS's decision to block Dish Network from retransmitting CBS stations in various markets, after a contract dispute, affected 3 million Dish subscribers. Although the situation was resolved, the sheer number of consumer options increases the risks to Roku.

Other companies are looking to limit the use of Roku devices. For example, Samsung sells more than a dozen smart TVs that don't use Roku's operating system, Amazon is exploring deals with smart TV manufacturers, and Comcast and AT&T are offering streaming devices to subscribers.

Given the fledgling industry's vast uncertainty, we must assume that product life-cycle stages will be abbreviated either from competition or regulation. To maximize its sales and profits in the short run, a company like Roku must compete on the functionality, quality, and continuous improvement of its products and services. The managerial tools discussed throughout this chapter are increasingly important for managers involved in the development, production, and marketing of products and services that compete in contested environments. A company that truly understands the value chain of its production and delivery systems will remain nimble and flexible in the face of a changing regulatory and competitive landscape.

Road Map

LO	Learning Objective | Topics	Page	eLecture	Guided Example	Assignments
LO1	**Explain the importance of the value chain in managing products and describe the key components of an organization's internal and external value chain.** Understanding the Value Chain :: Usefulness of the Value Chain :: Supplier-Buyer Partnerships :: Focus on Core Competencies :: Value Add	280	e8–1	Review 8-1	13, 14, 15, 16
LO2	**Distinguish between economic and cost-based approaches to pricing.** The Pricing Decision :: Economic Approach :: Cost-Based Approach :: Critique of Cost-Based Pricing	284	e8–2	Review 8-2	17, 18, 19, 21, 22, 23, 24, 25, 27, 31, 32, 33
LO3	**Explain target costing and discuss its acceptance in highly competitive industries.** Target Costing :: Cost Management :: Design for Production :: Benefits of Target Costing :: Managing Life-Cycle Costs	289	e8–3	Review 8-3	26, 28, 34
LO4	**Illustrate the relation between target costing and continuous improvement costing.** Kaizen Costing :: Continuous Improvement	294	e8–4	Review 8-4	29, 30
LO5	**Explain how benchmarking enhances quality management, continuous improvement, and process reengineering.** Benchmarking :: Setting Goals :: Six Steps	296	e8–5	Review 8-5	20

CHAPTER ORGANIZATION

Pricing and Other Product Management Decisions

Understanding the Value Chain	The Pricing Decision	Target Costing	Other Costing Techniques
• Usefulness of a Value Chain Perspective • Value-Added and Value Chain Perspectives	• Economic Approaches to Pricing • Cost-Based Approaches to Pricing	• Target Costing and Cost Management • Target Costing and Design • Target Costing and Product Life Cycles	• Continuous Improvement Costing • Benchmarking

Strategic cost management techniques, such as *target costing* and *continuous improvement costing*, represent important concepts for product management professionals involved in the development, manufacture, and marketing of products and services. Virtually all such techniques are grounded in the notion of managing the value chain. This chapter examines pricing, the interrelation between price and cost, and the role of benchmarking in meeting customer needs at the lowest possible price.

We begin with a discussion of the value chain, followed by an overview of the pricing model economists use to explain price equilibrium. Given the limitations of this long-run equilibrium model for determining price of a product or service, we consider the widely used cost-plus approach to identifying initial prices. We then examine how intense competition (such as that for the green car market) has inverted the cost-plus pricing model into one that starts with an acceptable market price and subtracts a desired profit to determine a target cost. We also consider *life-cycle costs* from the perspectives of both the seller, who increasingly plans for all costs before production begins, and the buyer, who regards subsequent operating, maintenance, repair, and disposal costs as important as price. Finally, we consider how *benchmarking* can assist in improving competitiveness and profitability.

Understanding the Value Chain

eLectures MBC **LO1** Explain the importance of the value chain in managing products and describe the key components of an organization's internal and external value chain.

The **value chain** for a product or service is the set of value-producing activities that stretches from basic raw materials to the final consumer. Each product or service has a distinct value chain, and all entities along the value chain depend on the final customer's perception of the value and cost of a product or service. It is the final customer who ultimately pays all costs and provides all profits to all organizations along the entire value chain. Consequently, *the goal of every organization is to maximize the value, while minimizing the cost, of a product or service to final customers.*

The value chain provides a viewpoint that encompasses all activities performed to deliver products and services to final customers. Depending on the needs of management, value chains are developed at varying levels of detail. Analyzing a value chain from the perspective of the final consumer requires working backward from the end product or service to the basic raw materials entering into the product or service. Analyzing a value chain from the viewpoint of an organization that is in the middle of a value chain requires working forward (downstream) to the final consumer and backward (upstream) to the source of raw materials. The paper industry provides a convenient context for illustrating the value chain concept.

Exhibit 8.1 presents the value chain for the paperboard cartons used to package beverages, such as Coca-Cola, Pepsi, or Evían products. The value chain is presented at three levels, with each successive level containing additional details. The first level depicts the various business entities in the value chain:

- Timber producers grow the pulp wood (usually pine) used as the basic input into paper products. Some paper companies, such as International Paper (the leading producer of paperboard), harvest much of their pulp wood from timberlands that they manage. Other companies, including Georgia Pacific, do not manage their own timberlands, but purchase pulp for their mills on the open market through pulp intermediaries.
- Pulp mills produce the kraft (unbleached) paper used to produce the paperboard. Companies such as International Paper and Georgia Pacific own pulp mills which produce the kraft paper. Other paperboard manufacturers can purchase pulp and kraft paper from companies such as Domtar.

Exhibit 8.1 Value Chain for a Beverage-Packaging Product

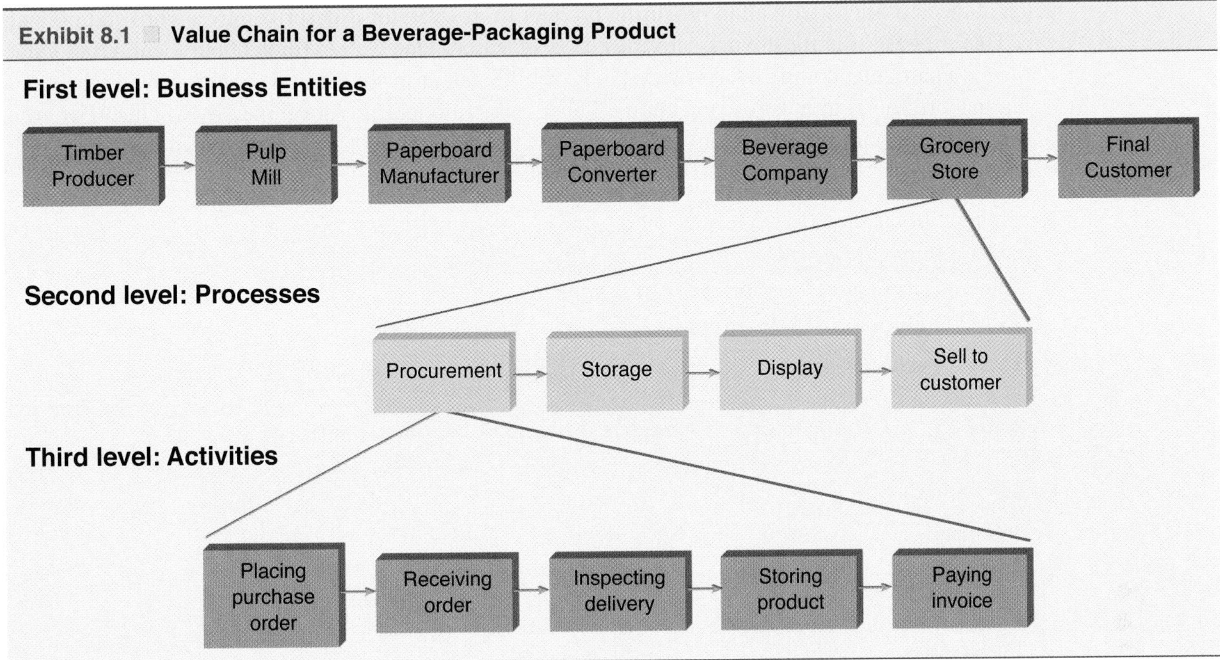

- Paperboard manufacturers perform a laminating process of coating paperboard material used to produce beverage packages. The layers of coating give the top surface a high gloss finish that is water resistant and suitable for multicolor printing.
- The paperboard converter uses manufactured paperboard to print and produce the completed beverage packaging product, such as the cartons used to package the Diet Coca-Cola 12-pack.
- Beverage distributors, such as Coca-Cola Enterprises and Anheuser-Busch, purchase the completed paperboard packages from companies like Graphic Packaging to package their many different brands in various package sizes and shapes.
- Grocery and convenience stores, such as Publix and 7-Eleven, display and sell beverages packaged in the paperboard containers.
- The final customer purchases beverages packaged in paperboard packages and uses the packages to carry the beverages and to store them until consumed. The packages not only perform a transport and storage function but also serve as an advertising medium for the beverage company. The beverage company's advertising on the paperboard packages is intended to entice customers to purchase the beverage company's product and to help create a sense of satisfaction for the customer.

To better understand how business entities within the chain add value and incur costs, management might further refine the value chain into **processes**, collections of related activities intended to achieve a common purpose. The second level in **Exhibit 8.1** represents major processes concerning the procurement and sale of Coca-Cola products by a grocery store. To simplify our illustration, we show only the processes for the grocery store related to the purchase and sale of Coca-Cola products packaged in paperboard packages. These processes include procuring Coca-Cola products from the bottling company, storing and displaying the product, and selling the product to the final consumer.

An **activity** is a unit of work. In the third level of **Exhibit 8.1**, the grocery store process to procure Coca-Cola products is further broken up into the following activities:

- *Placing* a purchase order for Coca-Cola products packaged in paperboard packages.
- *Receiving* delivery of the Coca-Cola products in paperboard packages.
- *Inspecting* the delivery to make sure it corresponds with the purchase order and to verify that the products are in good condition.
- *Storing* Coca-Cola products in paperboard packages until needed for display.
- *Paying* for Coca-Cola products acquired after the invoice arrives.

Each of the activities involved in procuring product from a vendor is described by a word ending with *ing*. This suggests that most work activities involve action. One way to think about the internal value chain for a particular company is provided in **Exhibit 8.2** in terms of the basic components of the value chain that are found in most organizations. This generic model, first developed by Michael Porter, is a good starting point in identifying the internal value chain links for a particular organization. The primary processes are made up of five key activities:

- Inbound logistics: Receiving, warehousing and distributing inputs
- Marketing and sales: Targeting customer for product/service
- Operations: Converting inputs into the finished product/service
- Outbound logistics: Delivering final product/service to the customer
- Service: Maintaining the value of the product/service to the customer

Exhibit 8.2 Generic Internal Processes of the Internal Value Chain

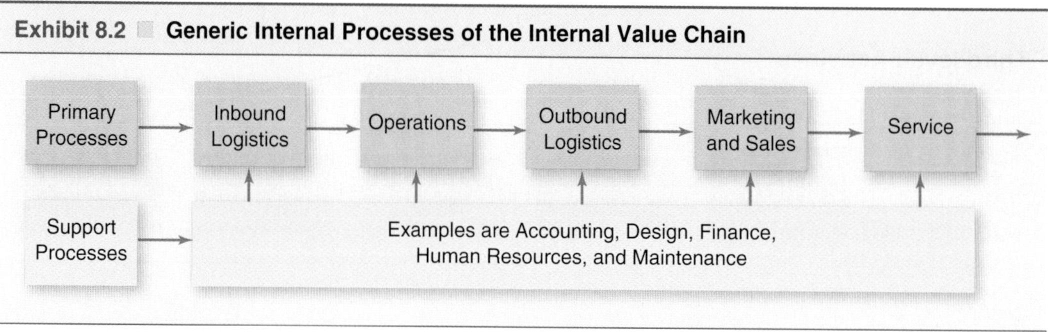

Usefulness of a Value Chain Perspective

The goal of maximizing final customer value while minimizing final customer cost leads organizations to examine *internal* and *external links* in the value chain rather than the departments, processes, or activities independently. From a value chain perspective, it is total cost across the entire value chain, not the cost of individual businesses, departments, processes, or activities that is most important.

Value Chain Perspective Fosters Supplier–Buyer Partnerships

In the past, relationships between suppliers and buyers were often adversarial. Contact between suppliers and buyers was solely through the selling and purchasing departments. Suppliers attempted merely to meet purchasing contract specifications at the lowest possible cost. Buyers encouraged competition among suppliers with the primary—and often single—goal of obtaining the lowest purchase price.

As discussed in Chapter 7 with JIT and lean production, exploiting cost reduction and value-enhancing opportunities in the value chain has led many buyers and suppliers to view each other as partners rather than as adversaries. Buyers have reduced the number of suppliers they deal with, often developing long-term partnerships with a single supplier. Once they establish mutual trust, both proceed to share detailed information on internal operations and help each other solve problems. Partners work closely to examine mutual opportunities by studying their common value chain. Supplier engineers might determine that a minor relaxation in buyer specifications would significantly reduce supplier manufacturing costs with only minor increases in subsequent buyer processing costs. Working together, they determine how best to modify processes to reduce overall costs and share increased profits.

Companies such as Hewlett-Packard and Boeing involve suppliers in design, development, and manufacturing decisions. Motorola has even developed a survey asking suppliers to assess Motorola as a buyer. Among other questions, the survey asks sellers to evaluate Motorola's performance in helping suppliers to identify major cost drivers and to increase their profitability. These questions represent the concerns of a partner rather than those of an adversary. Michael Dell, at Dell Computers, stated that "rather than closely guarding our information databases, which took us years to develop, we used Internet browsers to essentially give that information to our customers and suppliers—bringing them into our business."[1] The following Business Insight box describes how General Motors is strengthening its relationships with its suppliers, in the hopes of working together to develop cost-cutting strategies.

---

[1] *Direct from Dell*, Michael Dell with Catherine Fredman, Harper Collins Publishers, 1999.
Also, see http://money.cnn.com/magazines/fortune/fortune500/2007/full_list/index.html

Business Insight ■ Cost Control: For Starters, Your Suppliers Don't Need to Hate You

General Motors is seeking to improve historically poor supplier relationships. The company's purchasing chief, Steve Kiefer, says that the company is now negotiating parts contracts that span two vehicle generations—up to a decade. North America's largest automaker hopes that this will give them access to both lower costs and advanced technology. Strengthening relationships with suppliers and then partnering on cost cutting is a new approach for GM. In the past, GM's suppliers saw the automaker's planning and cost-cutting processes as heavy handed, which made suppliers unwilling to give GM access to new technologies. Kiefer hopes that long-term commitments to suppliers will lead to more attention and productive partnerships for the company.

Source: Jeff Bennett, "GM Seeks Longer-Term Supplier Contracts in Bid to Cut Costs," *Wall Street Journal*, April 15, 2015.

On a smaller scale, the grocery store in **Exhibit 8.1** should examine its external links. It may be willing to pay more for Coca-Cola products if the distributors cooperate to help reduce costs such as the following:

- Making more frequent deliveries in small lots would reduce storage costs.
- Being responsible for maintaining and changing the product displays would relieve store workers of these tasks.
- Streamlining ordering and payment procedures would reduce bookkeeping costs.

If partnership arrangements with upstream suppliers enable the grocery store to reduce its total costs, the store can enhance or maintain its competitive position by reducing prices charged to its consumers. Remember that competitors are also striving to reduce costs and enhance their competitive position. Hence, failing to strive for improvements will likely result in reduced sales and profits.

Value Chain Perspective Fosters Focus on Core Competencies

Using value chain concepts, relationships with suppliers often begin to represent an extended family, allowing companies to focus on core competencies; this capability provides a distinct competitive advantage. In addition, a new breed of contract manufacturers, such as Sanmina has emerged. Sanmina promotes itself as an end-to-end solution. It partners with customers across a variety of industries to design and make complex optical, electronic, and mechanical products. This allows Sanmina's customers to focus on marketing and product development while Sanmina focuses on efficient, low-cost manufacturing.

Interestingly, because their facilities are available to all innovators with the necessary financing, the emergence of contract manufacturers may speed innovation. Toyota attributes much of its rapid growth and profitability to virtual integration with suppliers. **Virtual integration** is the use of information technology and partnership concepts to allow two or more entities along a value chain to act as if they were a single economic entity.

Business Insight ■ The Search for Little Chickens

More chicken is eaten in America than in any other country in the world; approximately 93.5 pounds per person according to the National Chicken Council. To meet demand, chicken producers have focused on raising bigger birds through improvements in breeding and nutrition. In the last hundred years, the average weight of broiler chickens has increased from 2.5 pounds to over 6 pounds.

When it comes to fast-food sandwiches, though, smaller is better. Smaller chicken breasts fit better on the sandwich and consumers prefer the juicier, more tender chicken from birds less than 4.25 pounds.

By 2019, demand for the smaller birds was beginning to outstrip supply. Popeyes dramatically under-forecasted consumer demand for its new chicken sandwich and ran out of chicken two weeks after its introduction in August. It took two months before the sandwich was available again.

McDonald's and Wendy's are both expected to introduce new chicken sandwiches and sales at Popeyes and Chick-fil-A remain strong. The companies with a value chain perspective are likely looking seriously at developing strong partnerships with top poultry producers.

Source: Leslie Patton and Lydia Mulvany, "Chick-fil-A's War with Popeyes Drains Little-Chicken Supply," *Bloomberg*, January 28, 2020.

Value-Added and Value Chain Perspectives

The value chain perspective is often contrasted with a value-added perspective. Under a value-added perspective, decision makers consider only the cost of resources to their organization and the selling price of products or services to their immediate customers. Using a value-added perspective, the goal is to maximize the value added (the difference between the selling price and costs) by the organization. To do this, the value-added perspective focuses primarily on internal activities and costs. Under a value chain perspective, the goal is to maximize value and minimize cost to final customers, often by developing linkages or partnerships with suppliers and customers.

Although initial efforts to enhance competitiveness might start with a value-added perspective, it is important to expand to a value chain perspective. World-class competitors utilize both a value-added and a value chain perspective. These firms always keep the final customer in mind and recognize that the profitability of each entity in the value chain depends on the overall value and cost of the products and services delivered to final customers.

The value-added perspective is the foundation of the make or buy (outsourcing) decision considered in Chapter 4. The key differences between the partnering decisions considered here and the make or buy decision in Chapter 4 concern time frame, perspective, and attitude. The make or buy decision is a stand-alone decision, often in the short run, that does not view vendors and customers as partners. In contrast, characteristics of the value chain perspective are as follows:

- Comprehensive
- Focused on the final customers
- Strategic
- Basis for partnerships between vendors and customers

Enhancing or maintaining a competitive position requires an understanding of the entire system used to develop and deliver value to final customers, including interactions among organizations along the value chain. All organizations in the value chain are in business together and should work together as partners rather than as adversaries.

Review 8-1 LO1 — Classifying Activities Using a Generic Internal Value Chain

Using Michael Porter's generic model presented in **Exhibit 8.2**, classify each of the following activities of Starbucks' (corporate website at https://www.starbucks.com) as (a) inbound logistics, (b) operations, (c) outbound logistics, (d) marketing and sales, or (e) service.

_____ 1. Remaking any food or beverage item that a customer is not satisfied with at no additional cost to the customer
_____ 2. Managing stores owned and operated by the company
_____ 3. Offering online sales for limited products
_____ 4. Sourcing unroasted coffee beans from growers in farming communities in key coffee-growing regions
_____ 5. Increasing the company budget for promotions, advertising, and public relations activities
_____ 6. Maintaining storage sites and regional distribution centers
_____ 7. Offering a limited selection of products for sale in leading supermarket chains
_____ 8. Investing in innovative equipment that quickly brews high-quality coffee

Solution on p. 305.

The Pricing Decision

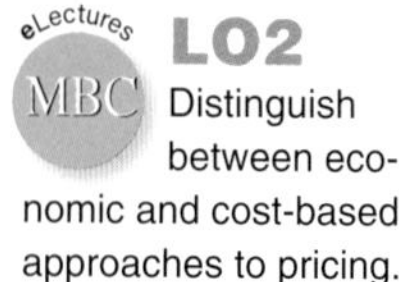

LO2 Distinguish between economic and cost-based approaches to pricing.

Pricing products and services is one of the most important and complex decisions facing management. Pricing decisions directly affect the salability of individual products or services, as well as the profitability, and even the survival, of the organization. Many economists have spent their entire careers examining the foundations of pricing. To respond to the needs of pricing hundreds or thousands of individual items, managers have developed pricing guidelines that are typically based on costs. More recently, global competition has turned cost-based approaches upside down. Managers of world-class organizations increasingly start with a price that customers are willing to pay and then determine allowable costs.

Economic Approaches to Pricing

In economic models, the firm has a profit-maximizing goal and known cost and revenue functions. Typically, increases in sales quantity require reductions in selling prices, causing **marginal revenue** (the varying increment in total revenue derived from the sale of an additional unit) to decline as sales increase.

Increases in production cause an increase in **marginal cost** (the varying increment in total cost required to produce and sell an additional unit of product). In economic models, profits are maximized at the sales volume at which marginal revenues equal marginal costs. Firms continue to produce as long as the marginal revenue derived from the sale of each additional unit exceeds the marginal cost of producing that unit.

Economic models provide a useful framework for considering pricing decisions. The ideal price is the one that will lead customers to purchase all units a firm can provide up to the point at which the last unit has a marginal cost exactly equal to its marginal revenue.

Despite their conceptual merit, economic models are seldom used for day-to-day pricing decisions. Perfect information and an indefinite time period are required to achieve equilibrium prices at which marginal revenues equal marginal costs. In the short run, most for-profit organizations attempt to achieve a target profit rather than a maximum profit. One reason for this is an inability to determine the single set of actions that will lead to profit maximization. Furthermore, managers are more apt to strive to satisfy a number of goals (such as profits for investors, job security for themselves and their employees, and being a "good" corporate citizen) than to strive for the maximization of a single profit goal. In any case, to maximize profits, a company's management would have to know the cost and revenue functions of every product the firm sells. For most firms, this information cannot be developed at a reasonable cost.

Cost-Based Approaches to Pricing

Although cost is not the only consideration in pricing, it has traditionally been the most important for several reasons.

- *Cost data are available.* When hundreds or thousands of different prices must be set in a short time, cost could be the only feasible basis for product pricing.
- *Cost-based prices are defensible.* Managers threatened by legal action or public scrutiny feel secure using cost-based prices. They can argue that prices are set in a manner that provides a "fair" profit.
- *Revenues must exceed costs if the firm is to remain in business.* In the long run, the selling price must exceed the full cost of each unit.

Cost-based pricing is illustrated in **Exhibit 8.3**. The process begins with market research to determine customer wants. If the product requires components to be designed and produced by vendors, the process of obtaining prices can be time consuming. When some costs, such as those fixed costs

Exhibit 8.3 Cost-Based Pricing for a New Product

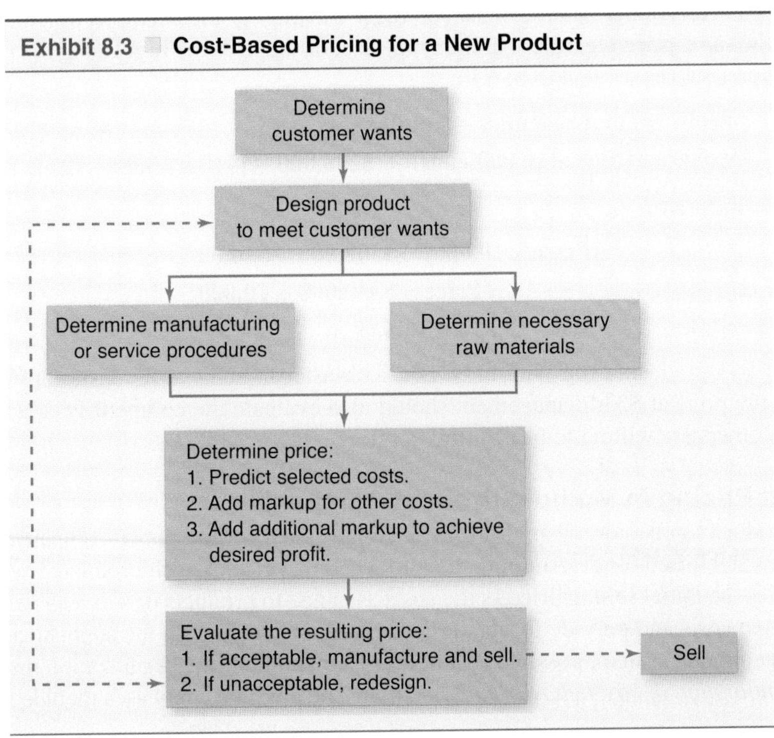
Determine customer wants
Design product to meet customer wants
Determine manufacturing or service procedures
Determine necessary raw materials
Determine price:
1. Predict selected costs.
2. Add markup for other costs.
3. Add additional markup to achieve desired profit.
Evaluate the resulting price:
1. If acceptable, manufacture and sell.
2. If unacceptable, redesign.
Sell

at the facility level, are not assigned to specific products, a markup is added to cover these costs. An additional markup is added to achieve a desired profit. The selling price is then set as the sum of the assigned costs, the markup to cover unassigned costs, and the markup to achieve the desired profit.

The proposed selling price should be evaluated with regard to competitive information and what customers are willing to pay. If the price is acceptable, the product or service is produced. If the price is too high, the product might be redesigned, manufacturing procedures might be changed, and different types of materials might be considered until either an acceptable price is achieved or it is determined that the product cannot be produced at an acceptable price. On the other hand, as the Business Insight below shows, the price can sometimes be a major driver of a company's growth.

Business Insight ■ For a Better Price, Make a Better Product

While traditional media companies and advertising firms are struggling to adapt to the Internet age, Vice Media has cracked the code. Vice has found a way to connect with millennial viewers, born between 1980 and 2000. Vice Media's unique foothold in the millennial market allows the company to change the way ads are delivered and allows Vice to name its price.

Vice's partnership with A&E, called Viceland, airs on the A&E network but is not a part of traditional ad buys. Companies must pay a premium to access the Vice audience. For example, instead of a traditional spot on a website or before a BuzzFeed or YouTube video, Vice charges between $83,000 and $413,000 per episode to sponsor any one of its 70 original video series. Vice's advertising is often integrated into its content in a way that differs dramatically from traditional commercial-break or sidebar ads. Vice programs are marketed as being "produced with" the sponsor rather than simply showing an ad. By accessing a new group of consumers in new ways, Vice has changed the price the market will bear for its ads.

Sources: Mike Shields, "Vice, BuzzFeed Tread on Madison Avenue's Turf," *Wall Street Journal*, June 22, 2016.
Aaron Taube, "How Vice Media Will Make $500 Million This Year," *Business Insider*, June 21, 2014.
Jason Lynch, "Viceland Is Shaking Up TV Advertising by Running More Native Ads That Look Editorial," *ADWEEK*, March 1, 2016.
Jane Martinson, "The Virtues of Vice: How Punk Magazine Was Transformed into Media Giant," *The Guardian*, January 1, 2015.

Cost-Based Pricing in Single-Product Companies

Implementing cost-based pricing in a single-product company is straightforward if everything is known but the selling price. In this case, all known data are entered into the profit formula, which is then solved for the variable price. ServiceMaster provides residential and commercial cleaning and restoration services. Assume that a ServiceMaster location's annual fixed facility-level costs are $200,000 and the unit cost of cleaning a rug is $10. Suppose management desires to achieve an annual profit of $30,000 at an annual volume of 10,000 rugs. To simplify the example, assume that management charges the same price regardless of the type, size, or shape of the rug. Using the profit formula, the cost-based price is determined to be $33:

Profit = Total revenues − Total costs

$30,000 = (Price × 10,000 rugs) − ($200,000 + [$10 × 10,000 rugs])

Solving for the price:

(Price × 10,000) = $300,000 + $30,000

Price = $330,000 ÷ 10,000

= $33

A price of $33 to clean a rug will allow ServiceMaster to achieve its desired profit. However, before setting the price at $33, management should also evaluate the competitive situation and consider what customers are willing to pay for this service.

Cost-Based Pricing in Multiple-Product Companies

In multiple-product companies, desired profits are determined for the entire company, and standard procedures are established for determining the initial selling price of each product. These procedures typically specify the initial selling price as the costs assigned to products or services plus a markup to cover unassigned costs and provide for the desired profit. Depending on the sophistication of the organization's accounting system, possible cost bases in a manufacturing organization include markups based on a *combination of cost behavior and function*. The possible cost bases include the following:

- Direct materials costs
- Variable manufacturing costs
- Total variable costs (manufacturing, selling, and administrative)
- Full manufacturing costs

Regardless of the cost base, the general approach to developing a markup is to recognize that the markup must be large enough to provide for costs not included in the base plus the desired profit.

$$\textbf{Markup on cost base} = \frac{\textbf{Costs not included in the base + Desired profit}}{\textbf{Costs included in the base}}$$

First we illustrate a pricing decision with variable costs as the cost base; full manufacturing costs is the cost base in the second illustration.

1. When the markup is based on variable costs, it must be large enough to cover all fixed costs and the desired profit. Assume that the predicted annual variable and fixed costs for one of Roku's divisions are are as follows:

Variable		Fixed	
Manufacturing	$600,000	Manufacturing	$300,000
Selling and administrative	200,000	Selling and administrative	100,000
Total	$800,000	Total	$400,000

Furthermore, assume that Roku's division has total assets of $1,250,000; management believes that an annual return of 16% on total assets is appropriate in Roku's industry. A 16% return translates into a desired annual profit of $200,000 ($1,250,000 × 0.16). Assuming all cost predictions are correct, obtaining a profit of $200,000 requires a 75% markup on variable costs:

$$\textbf{Markup on variable costs} = \frac{\$400{,}000 + \$200{,}000}{\$800{,}000} = 0.75$$

If the predicted variable costs for Product A1 are $12 per unit, the initial selling price for Product A1 is $21:

$$\textbf{Initial selling price} = \$12 + (\$12 \times 0.75) = \$21$$

2. When the markup is based on full manufacturing costs, it must be large enough to cover selling and administrative expenses and to provide for the desired profit. Again, it is necessary to determine the desired profit and predict all costs for the pricing period. The initial prices of individual products are then determined as their unit manufacturing costs plus the markup. For Roku, the markup on manufacturing costs would be 55.6%:

$$\textbf{Markup on manufacturing costs} = \frac{(\$200{,}000 + \$100{,}000) + \$200{,}000}{\$900{,}000} = 0.556$$

If the predicted manufacturing costs for Product B1 are $10, the initial selling price for Product B1 is $15.56:

$$\textbf{Initial selling price} = \$10 + (\$10 \times 0.556) = \$15.56$$

Cost-Based Pricing for Special Orders

Many organizations use cost-based pricing to bid on unique projects. If the project requires dedicated assets, the acquisition of new fixed assets, or an investment in employee training, the desired profit on the special order or project should allow for an adequate return on the dedicated assets or additional investment.

Critique of Cost-Based Pricing

Cost-based pricing has four major drawbacks:

1. Cost-based pricing requires accurate cost assignments. If costs are not accurately assigned, some products could be priced too high, losing market share to competitors; other products could be priced too low, gaining market share but being less profitable than anticipated.
2. The higher the portion of unassigned costs, the greater is the likelihood of over- or under-pricing individual products.
3. Cost-based pricing assumes that goods or services are relatively scarce and, generally, customers who want a product or service are willing to pay the price.
4. In a competitive environment, cost-based approaches increase the time and cost of bringing new products to market.

Cost-based pricing became the dominant approach to pricing during an era when products were relatively long-lived and there was relatively little competition. Also, these systems tend to focus on organizational units such as departments, plants, or divisions and not on activities or cost drivers. While easy to implement, reflecting the need to recover costs and earn a return on investment, and easily justified, cost-based prices might not be competitive. Competition puts intense downward pressure on prices and removes slack from pricing formulas. There is little margin for error in pricing. In a highly competitive market, small variations in pricing make significant differences in success.

Review 8-2 LO2

Applying Cost-Based Approaches to Pricing

Assume that Prince, a tennis equipment manufacturer, has the following current year contribution income statement:

PRINCE Contribution Income Statement For Year Ended December		
Sales (100,000 units at $12 per unit)		$1,200,000
Less variable costs		
Manufacturing	$300,000	
Selling and administrative	150,000	(450,000)
Contribution margin		750,000
Less fixed costs		
Manufacturing	400,000	
Selling and administrative	200,000	(600,000)
Net income		$ 150,000

Assume Prince has total assets of $2,000,000 and management desires an annual return of 10% on total assets.

Required

a. Determine the dollar amount by which Prince exceeded or fell short of the desired annual rate of return for the year.

b. Given the current sales volume and cost structure, determine the unit selling price required to achieve an annual profit of $250,000.

continued

continued from previous page

c. Given your answer to requirement (*b*) and the current sales volume and cost structure, determine (1) the selling price as a percentage of variable manufacturing costs and (2) the markup as a percentage of variable manufacturing costs.

d. Restate your answer to requirement (*c*) for the markup as a percentage of variable manufacturing costs, dividing into two separate markup percentages:

1. The markup on variable manufacturing costs required to cover unassigned costs.
2. The additional markup on variable manufacturing costs required to achieve an annual profit of $250,000.

Solution on p. 306.

Target Costing

LO3 Explain target costing and discuss its acceptance in highly competitive industries.

Economists argue that cost-based prices are not realistic, because in the real world prices are determined by the confluence of supply and demand. However, when a new product is introduced into the market for which there is no previously existing supply or demand, there has to be a starting point. As discussed above, cost has often been the baseline for determining initial selling prices. All too often, however, companies introduce new products into the market based on what the designers and engineers "think" the market wants (or based on inadequate market research), only to find out later that either the market does not want the product, or it is not willing to buy the new product at a price sufficient to cover its cost plus an acceptable profit to the producer. This often leads to costly redesign, or in many cases, complete abandonment of the product, typically resulting in substantial financial losses.

Toyota, which has pioneered many innovations in manufacturing systems, adopted and expanded price-based costing, referred to as target costing in the 1960s. Toyota determined that before a new product is introduced into the market, it must be able to be produced at a cost that will make it profitable when sold at a price acceptable to customers. The acceptable selling price to the marketplace determines the acceptable cost of producing the product.

Target Costing Is Proactive for Cost Management

Target costing starts with determining what customers are willing to pay for a product or service and then subtracts a desired profit on sales to determine the allowable, or target, cost of the product or service. This target cost is then communicated to a cross-functional team of employees representing such diverse areas as marketing, product design, manufacturing, and management accounting. Reflecting value chain concepts and the notion of partnerships up and down the value chain, suppliers of raw materials and components are often included in the teams. The target costing team is assigned the task of designing a product that meets customer price, function, and quality requirements while providing a desired profit. Its job is not completed until the target cost is met, or a determination is made that the product or service cannot be profitably introduced under the current circumstances. See **Exhibit 8.4** for an overview of target costing.

Although a formula can be used to determine a markup on cost, it is not possible to develop a formula indicating how to achieve a target cost. Hence, target costing is not a technique. It is more a philosophy or an approach to pricing and cost management. It takes a proactive approach to cost management, reflecting the belief that costs are best managed by decisions made during product development. This contrasts with the more passive cost-plus belief that costs result from design, procurement, and manufacture. Like the value chain, target costing helps orient employees toward the final customer and reinforces the notion that all departments within the organization and all organizations along the value chain must work together. Target costing also empowers employees who will be assigned the responsibility for carrying out activities necessary to deliver a product or service with the authority to determine what activities will be selected. Like process mapping, it helps employees to better understand their role in serving the customer. The following Research Insight discusses how target costing can improve margins for companies engaged in global sourcing.

Exhibit 8.4 Target Costing in a Competitive Environment

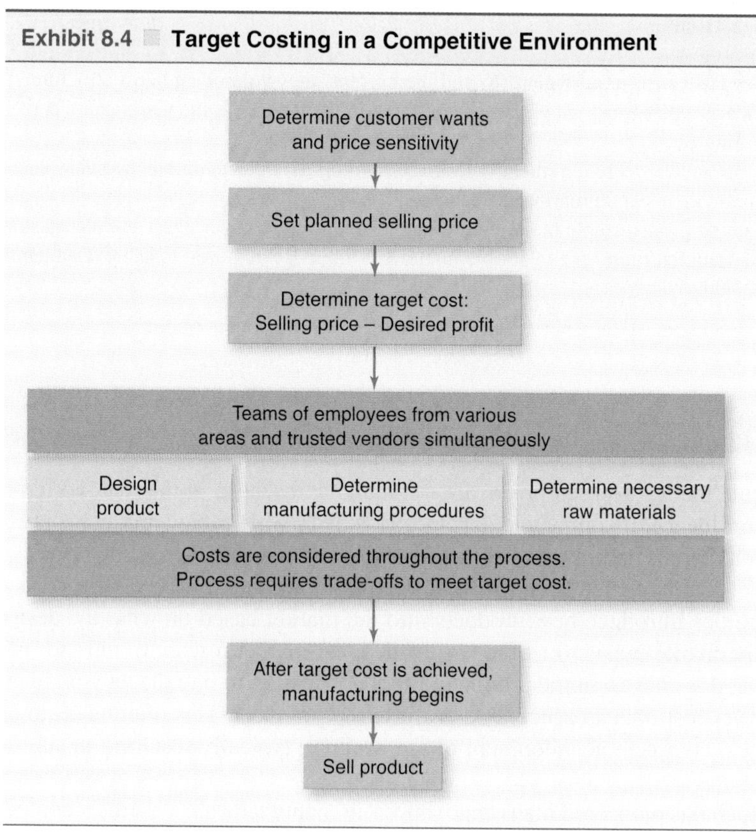

Research Insight ■ Target Costing and Global Sourcing

Creating and meeting cost targets in an age of global supply and distribution is fundamentally an information technology problem. Researchers with the Deloitte Consulting LLP Supply Chain Strategy Practice point to Toyota's response to the 2011 tsunami as an example of evolution toward modern supply chain management. Toyota's supply system now anticipates the impact of catastrophes on each part used in production. Parts are now designed to allow flexibility in sourcing. This focus is a shift from the optimization and cost minimization of the past. Toyota has adjusted its cost targets to build flexibility and durability into the supply chain, which requires data collection and analysis capabilities that are new for many organizations.

To meet these needs, Nordstrom Inc. has purchased a minority stake in the supply-chain software firm DS Co., a move specifically intended to help the retail giant manage inventories among its department stores, online business, and suppliers. This allows the company to maintain its traditional storefront business while also shipping directly from its suppliers to its online customers.

Information technology helps firms meet cost targets and manage inventories in a global marketplace.

Sources: Kelly Marchese and Bill Lam, "Anticipatory Supply Chains," Deloitte University Press, March 31, 2014.
Loretta Chao, "Nordstrom Buys Stake in Software Firm," *Wall Street Journal*, July 8, 2016.

Target Costing Encourages Design for Production

In the absence of a target costing approach, design engineers are apt to focus on incorporating leading-edge technology and the maximum number of features in a product. Target costing keeps the customer's function, quality, and price requirements in the forefront at all times. If customers do not want leading-edge technology (which could be expensive and untested) and several product features, they will resist paying for them. Focusing on achieving a target cost keeps design engineers tuned in to the requirements of the final customer.

Left on their own, design engineers might believe that their job ends when they design a product that meets the customer's functional requirements. The tendency is to simply pass on the design to manufacturing and let manufacturing determine how best to produce the product. Further down the line, if the product needs servicing, it becomes the service department's responsibility to determine how best to service the product. A target costing approach forces design engineers to explicitly consider the costs of manufacturing and servicing a product while it is being designed. This is known as **design for manufacture**.

Minor changes in design that do not affect the product's functioning can often produce dramatic savings in manufacturing and servicing costs. Examples of design for manufacture include the following:

- Using molded plastic parts to avoid assembling several small parts.
- Designing two parts that must be fit together so that joining them in the correct manner is obvious to assembly workers.
- Placing an access panel in the side of an appliance so service personnel can make repairs quickly.
- Using standard-size parts to reduce inventory requirements, to reduce the possibility of assembly personnel inserting the incorrect part, and to simplify the job of service personnel.
- Ensuring that tolerance requirements for parts that must fit together can be met with available equipment.
- Using manufacturing procedures that are common to other products.

The successful implementation of target costing requires employees from all involved disciplines to be familiar with costing concepts and the notions of value-added and non-value-added activities. When considering the manufacturing process, team members should minimize non-value-added activities such as movement, storage, inspection, and setup. They should also select the lowest-cost value-added activities that do the job properly.

Target Costing Reduces Time to Introduce Products

By designing a product to meet a target cost (rather than evaluating the marketability of a product at a cost-plus price and having to recycle the design through several departments), target costing reduces the time required to introduce new products. Involving vendors in target costing design teams makes the vendors aware of the necessity of meeting a target cost. This facilitates the concurrent engineering of components to be produced outside the organization and reduces the time required to obtain components.

Target Costing Requires Cost Information

Implementing target costing requires detailed information on the cost of alternative activities. This information allows decision makers to select design and manufacturing alternatives that best meet function and price requirements. Tables that contain detailed databases of cost information for various manufacturing variables are occasionally used in designing products and selecting processes to meet target costs.

Target Costing Requires Coordination

Limitations of target costing are employee and supplier attitudes and the many meetings required to coordinate product design and to select manufacturing processes. All people involved must have a basic understanding of the overall processes required to bring a product to market and an appreciation of the cost consequences of alternative actions. They must also respect, cooperate, and communicate with other team members and be willing to engage in a negotiation process involving trade-offs. Finally, they must understand that although the total time required to bring a new product to market can be reduced, the countless coordinating meetings could be quite intrusive on the individuals' otherwise orderly schedules. See **Exhibit 8.5** for an evaluation of target costing.

Exhibit 8.5 Pros and Cons of Target Costing

Pros
- Takes proactive approach to cost management.
- Orients organization toward customer.
- Breaks down barriers between departments.
- Enhances employee awareness and empowerment.
- Fosters partnerships with suppliers.
- Minimizes non-value-added activities.
- Encourages selection of lowest-cost value-added activities.
- Reduces time to market.

Cons
- To be effective, requires the development of detailed cost data.
- Requires willingness to cooperate.
- Requires many meetings for coordination.

This aspect of the process is even more difficult when suppliers must be brought in as part of the coordination process. This concept is frequently referred to as **chained target costing** because the supply chain's support is critical for the product to be both competitively priced and delivered to the final customer in a timely manner. When multiple suppliers are required, the organization must obtain everyone's support or the process will probably not be successful due to gaps in the reliability of delivery, quality, and cost control. Each organization and unit must understand that if the product is not brought to market within the defined constraints, all will lose. They must make firm commitments for the project undertaken and to have faith that each participant will carry out whatever part of the supply chain it has promised to fulfill. Coordination across the supply chain is vital in the overall process of continuous improvement as discussed later in this chapter.

Target Costing Is Key for Products with Short Life Cycles

From a traditional marketing perspective, products with a relatively long life go through four distinct stages during their life cycle:

1. *Start-up*. Sales are low when a product is first introduced. Traditionally, initial selling prices are set high, and customers tend to be relatively affluent trendsetters.
2. *Growth*. Sales increase as the product gains acceptance. Traditionally, prices have remained high during this stage because of customer loyalty and the absence of competitive products.
3. *Maturity*. Sales level off as the product matures. Because of increased competition, pressure on prices is increasing; some price reductions could be necessary.
4. *Decline*. Sales decline as the product becomes obsolete. Significant price cuts could be required to sell remaining inventories.

Target costing is more important for products with a relatively short market life cycle. Products with a long life cycle present many opportunities to continuously improve design and manufacturing procedures that are not available when a product has a short life cycle. Hence, extra care must go into the initial planning for short-lived products. This is especially true when short product life cycles are combined with increased worldwide competition. It is important to introduce a product first and at a price that ensures rapid market penetration.

Business Insight ■ **Raise Prices or Cut Costs?**

When Britain decided to leave the European Union, the pound decreased in value. This created a problem for foreign companies selling products into the British market. The cost to make the product remained the same but the amount of money received from the sale decreased. To maintain the same profit margin, the importer had to either increase the price to Britain or decrease the cost.

Researchers have found that, in general, companies are averse to increasing prices. Instead, the more common approach is to lower costs. After the drop in the British pound's value, many companies reduced costs by decreasing the size of the item. Toilet rolls and toothpaste tubes became smaller. The Toblerone candy bar suddenly contained fewer peaks of chocolate.

This phenomenon is especially true during long periods of low inflation. If inflation has been high year after year, consumers are more willing to accept a price increase. If inflation has been low for a number of years, companies are more apt to redesign a product (reducing the size or the quality) to lower manufacturing costs rather than risk a price increase.

Source: The Economist Staff, "Prices for Many Goods Do Not Move the Way Economists Think They Should," *The Economist*, August 8, 2019.

Target Costing Helps Manage Life-Cycle Costs

An awareness of the impact of today's actions on tomorrow's costs underlies the notion of **life-cycle costs**, which include all costs associated with a product or service ranging from those incurred with the initial conception through design, preproduction, production, and after-production support.

The lower line in **Exhibit 8.6** illustrates the cumulative expenditure of funds over the life of a product. For low-technology products with relatively long product lives, decisions committing the organization to spend money are made at approximately the same time the money is spent. However, for high-technology products with relatively short product lives, most of the critical decisions affecting cost, such as product design and the selection of manufacturing procedures, are made before production begins. The top line in **Exhibit 8.6** represents decisions committing the organization to expenditures for a product.

Exhibit 8.6 **Commitment and Expenditure for High-Technology Products with Relatively Short Product Lives**

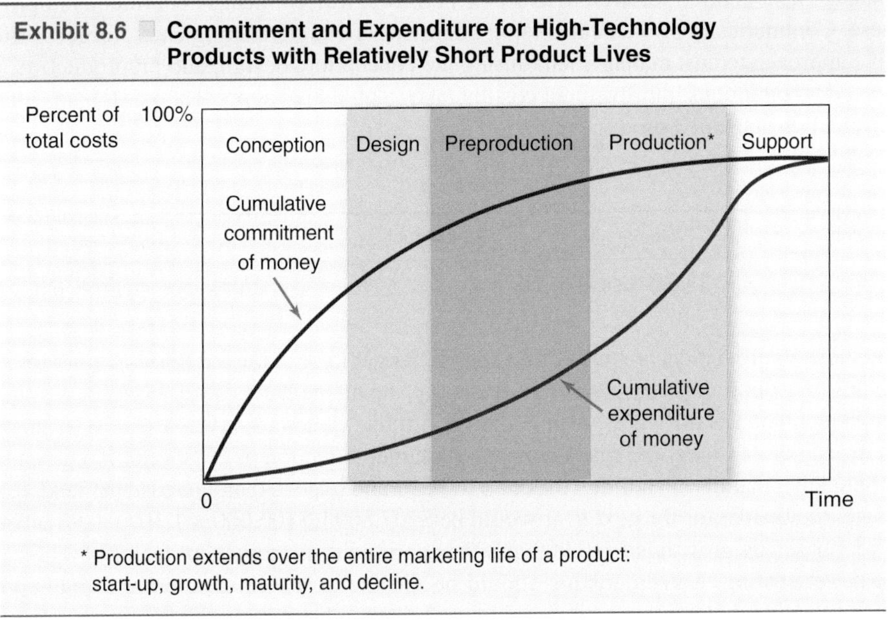

* Production extends over the entire marketing life of a product: start-up, growth, maturity, and decline.

Life-cycle cost concepts have also been usefully applied to low-technology issues, such as repair versus replace decisions. The New York State Throughway Authority uses life-cycle concepts to determine the point at which it is more expensive to repair than to replace bridges.

Managerial Decision ■ You Are the Vice President of Product Development

As head of new product development for your electronics company, you are concerned that so many of the ideas for new products coming from your research and development group are not succeeding in the market. Many recent attempts to take new products to market have failed, not because of technological deficiencies in the products, but because the market would not support the high prices for new products that were necessary to produce a satisfactory profit. What should you do to try to reverse this trend of new product failures? [Answer, p. 297]

Review 8-3 LO3 — Applying Target Costing

Chrysler has been conducting early-stage research on hydrogen-powered automobiles and is nearing the point where product development will soon begin. In order to determine the feasibility of the product, assume Chrysler has conducted marketing research that indicates that the price target for the product must be no more than $35,000 if it is to appeal to a large enough market segment to sell a minimum of 150,000 automobiles in the first year of production. The CFO has indicated that the new product must meet a 15% minimum profit margin requirement.

Required

a. Calculate the target cost per unit to produce the hydrogen-powered automobile.
b. How would Chrysler go about determining whether the target cost can be achieved?
c. What should Chrysler do if the estimated cost to produce the product exceeds the target cost?

Solution on p. 306.

Continuous Improvement Costing

eLectures MBC **LO4** Illustrate the relation between target costing and continuous improvement costing.

Continuous improvement (Kaizen) costing calls for establishing cost reduction targets for products or services that an organization is currently providing to customers. Developed in Japan, this approach to cost management is often referred to as *Kaizen costing. Kaizen* means "continuous improvement" in Japanese. Continuous improvement costing begins where target costing ends. Target costing takes a proactive approach to cost management during the conception, design, and preproduction stages of a product's life; continuous improvement costing takes a proactive approach to cost management during the production stage of a product's life:

Time →			
Conception	Design	Preproduction	Production
	Target costing		Continuous improvement costing

Continuous improvement costing adds a specific target to be achieved during a time period to the target costing concept previously discussed. Basically, the mathematics of the concept is quite simple, but its implementation is difficult. Assume that Walmart wanted to reduce the cost of merchandise handling in each of its stores, and management set a target reduction of 2% a year. If a given store had current annual merchandise handling costs of $100,000 and expected an increase the next year due to 10% growth, the budget for the next year would be $107,800 [($100,000 × 1.10) × 0.98]. The budget for next year based on growth is $110,000 less the continuous improvement factor of 0.02.

Like target costing, Kaizen costing should be viewed as a serious attempt to make processes more efficient, while maintaining or improving quality, thereby making the company more competitive and profitable. In Kaizen costing, cost reductions can be achieved both internally and externally through continuous redesign and improved internal processes, and by working with vendors to improve their designs and processes. Kaizen is a team effort involving everyone who has an influence on costs. Kaizen is typically found in companies that have adopted a lean production philosophy. The following Business Insight discusses Daisin's use of Kaizen to compete with Japanese suppliers for Toyota's business.

Business Insight ■ Thai Manufacturer Uses *Kaizen* to Compete

Thai auto component manufacturer Daisin uses the Japanese concept of *Kaizen*, or continual improvement, to compete with Japanese suppliers for Toyota's business. The firm was founded as a joint venture with Japanese brake parts maker Nissin Kogyo. Since the firm became independent in 2000, it has focused on developing production efficiency and quality control skills to rival other Toyota suppliers. To differentiate itself from other suppliers, the company has developed design capabilities. This allows Toyota to delegate important design steps to Daisin and to look to the supplier for design improvements. Daisin's efforts to differentiate fit with its effort to apply continuous improvement to costing. The firm's factory is designed to optimize use of time and space. The company produces jigs and molds in-house so that it can improve production of these expensive and time-consuming tools. At the same time, bringing these tooling steps in-house makes its design focus possible. Daisin's application of Kaizen has helped it carve out a place in Toyota's highly competitive supply chain.

Source: Kohei Fujimura and Natsuko Katsuki, "Thai Car Parts Makers Muscle into Supply Chains, Venture Abroad," *Nikkei Asian Review*, December 31, 2015.

Successful companies use continuous improvement costing to avoid complacency. Competitors are constantly striving to win market share through better quality or lower prices. Hewlett-Packard studied Epson to determine its strengths and weaknesses. To fend off competition, prices and costs must be continuously reduced. To maintain its competitive position, Hewlett-Packard has reduced the list price of the basic inkjet printer from nearly $400 when first introduced to less than $50 today. This could not have been done without continuous reductions in costs.

The "Toyota Way" describes Toyota's method to set Kaizen cost reduction targets for each cost element, including purchased parts per car, direct materials per car, labor hours per car, and office utilities. Performance reports developed at the end of each month compare targeted and actual cost reductions. If actual cost reductions are more than the targeted cost reductions, the results are favorable; if the actual cost reductions are less than the targeted cost reductions, the results are unfavorable.

Because cost reduction targets are set before it is known how they will be achieved, continuous improvement costing can be stressful to employees. A critical element in motivating employee cooperation and teamwork in aggressive cost management techniques, such as target and continuous improvement costing, is to avoid using performance reports to place blame for failure. The proper response to an unfavorable performance report must be an offer of assistance to correct the failure.

Analyzing the Impact of Continuous Improvement Initiatives — LO4 Review 8-4

Patel Company contracts manufacturing of compact video cameras. At its Pacific plant, cost control has become a concern of management. The actual costs per unit for the last two years were as follows:

	Year 1	Year 2
Direct materials		
Plastic case	$ 4.50	$ 4.40
Lens set	17.00	17.20
Electrical component set	6.60	5.70
Film track	11.00	10.00
Direct labor	32.00 (1.6 hours)	30.00 (1.5 hours)
Indirect manufacturing costs		
Variable	7.50	7.10
Fixed	3.00 (100,000 unit base)	2.85 (120,000 unit base)

The company manufactures all of the camera components except the lens sets, which it purchases from several vendors. The company has used target costing in the past but has not been able to meet the very competitive global pricing. Beginning in Year 2, the company implemented a continuous improvement program that requires cost reduction targets.

Required

If continuous improvement (Kaizen) costing sets a target of a 5% reduction of the Year 1 variable costs per unit, how successful was the company in meeting its per unit cost reduction targets in Year 2? Assume that the company sets a target for fixed costs to remain constant in total. Support your answer with appropriate computations.

Solution on p. 307.

Benchmarking

LO5 Explain how benchmarking enhances quality management, continuous improvement, and process reengineering.

When Hewlett-Packard studies Epson to identify Epson's strengths and weaknesses, each company is engaging in *benchmarking*, a practice that has been around for centuries. In recent years, however, as globalization and increased competitiveness have forced businesses to more aggressively compete on the bases of cost, quality, and service, benchmarking has become more formalized and open. No longer regarded as spying, **benchmarking** is now a systematic approach to identifying the best practices to help an organization take action to improve performance.

The formalization of benchmarking is largely attributed to a book written in the 1980s by Robert Camp of Xerox. Since then, many managers have come to believe that benchmarking is a requirement for success. Although benchmarking can focus on anything of interest, it typically deals with target costs for a product, service, or operation, customer satisfaction, quality, inventory levels, inventory turnover, cycle time, and productivity. Benchmarking initially focused on studying competitors, but benchmarking efforts have changed dramatically in recent years to include competitors, as well as companies in very different industries. For example, an electronics company like Samsung may benchmark its order fulfillment processes against Amazon, or a grocery company like the Kroger Company may benchmark its inventory management processes against an apparel company like Gap.

In considering how to go about benchmarking, an organization must be careful because it must consider nonfinancial limitations. No single numerical measurement can completely describe the performance of a complex device such as a microprocessor or a television camera, but benchmarks can be useful tools for comparing different products, components, and systems. The only totally accurate way to measure the performance of a given product is to test it against other products while performing the exact same activity. The following Business Insight box describes how Intel Corporation makes benchmarks available with some information on how to use them.

Business Insight ■ Intel Benchmarks Performance

Intel Corporation divides its benchmarks into two types, component and system. *Component benchmarks* measure the performance of specific parts of a computer system, such as a microprocessor or hard disk drive. *System benchmarks* typically measure the performance of the entire computer system. The performance obtained will almost certainly vary from benchmark performance for a number of reasons. First, individual components must usually be tested in a complete computer system, and it is not always possible to eliminate the considerable effects that differences in system design and configuration have on benchmark results. For instance, vendors sell systems with a wide variety of disk capabilities and speeds, system memory, and video and graphics capabilities, all of which influence how the system components perform in actual use. Differences in software, including operating systems and compilers, also affect component and system performance. Finally, benchmark tests are typically written to be exemplary for only a certain type of computer application, which might or might not be similar to what is being compared.

A benchmark is, at most, only one type of information that an organization might use during the purchasing or manufacturing process. To get a true picture of the performance of a component or system being considered, the organization should consult industry sources, publicly available research reports, and even government publications of related information.

Source: As described on the Intel website at: http://www.intel.com/content/www/us/en/benchmarks/resources-benchmark-limitations.html

Benchmarking provides measurements that are useful in setting goals. It can lead to dramatic innovations, and it can help overcome resistance to change. When presented with a major cost reduction target, employees often believe they are being asked to do the impossible. Benchmarking can be a psychological tool that helps overcome resistance to change by showing how others have already met the target.

Although each organization has its own approach to benchmarking, the following six steps are typical:

1. Decide what to benchmark.
2. Plan the benchmark project.
3. Understand your own performance.
4. Study others.
5. Learn from the data.
6. Take action.

In recent years, professional organizations, such as the Institute of Management Accountants, have set up clearinghouses for benchmark information or have performed benchmarking studies of interest to members as have certain corporations such as Intel.

Distinguishing Between Benchmarking and Competitor Research LO5 **Review 8-5**

Visit the website iSixSigma.com. iSixSigma provides information on the Lean Six Sigma process and training and tools for Six Sigma certifications. The website dedicates a page to understanding the purpose and use of benchmarking.

Required

Visit: https://www.isixsigma.com/methodology/benchmarking/understanding-purpose-and-use-benchmarking/. Identify a few differences between benchmarking and competitor research.

Solution on p. 307.

Guidance Answers

You Are the Vice President of Product Development

Pg. 294 You should consider adopting target costing methods for new product development. Great product research ideas are successful only when they translate into products that can be produced and sold for an acceptable profit. Creating and producing new products before determining what the customer wants and is willing to pay often leads to failure. Target costing methods reverse this process by applying value chain concepts to bring customers and suppliers along the value chain together to produce a product only if it has features and a selling price that are acceptable to potential customers, and if its production costs allow the seller to make an acceptable profit.

Key Ratios

$$\text{Markup on cost base} = \frac{\text{Costs not included in the base + Desired profit}}{\text{Costs included in the base}}$$

Key Terms

activity, 281
benchmarking, 296
chained target costing, 292
continuous improvement (Kaizen) costing, 294
design for manufacture, 291
life-cycle costs, 293
marginal cost, 284
marginal revenue, 284
processes, 281
target costing, 289
value chain, 280
virtual integration, 283

Multiple Choice

1. In a value chain analysis:
   a. The links of the chain are the various entities beginning with the producers of raw materials and ending with the final customer
   b. Processes are collections of related activities intended to achieve a common purpose, such as procurement or production
   c. Activities are the units of work that take place within the various processes, such as moving products from one workstation to another
   d. All of the above
2. In a cost-based pricing model, the markup percentage is determined by an equation that
   a. Has the cost base in the denominator and any remaining costs plus the desired profit in the numerator
   b. Has variable costs plus fixed costs in the denominator and total profit in the numerator
   c. Always has only variable costs in the numerator
   d. Always has desired profit as part of the denominator

Multiple Choice Answers
1. d 2. a 3. b 4. c 5. b 6. c

3. Brown Company makes profits with varying pricing structures, but it wants to determine the minimum markup percentage for all products based on manufacturing costs that will ensure that it does not fall below break-even point. It has estimated the following costs for the coming year for its planned production of all products.

Variable manufacturing costs	$600,000
Fixed manufacturing costs	200,000
Selling expenses	100,000
Administrative expenses	150,000

The markup percentage required for Brown Company to break even is
a. 320%
b. 31.25%
c. 75%
d. Cannot be determined unless desired profit is known

4. Electronics Inc. is considering producing a new MP3 player that will offer several new features, including wireless earphones and wireless download of music and videos from any computer to the device. After much market research, it has determined that the appropriate target price for the new product is $90. To achieve its normal minimum profit margin of 20%, Electronics must be able to produce the product at a maximum total cost of
a. $108
b. $70
c. $72
d. $18

5. Orange Inc. produces electronic devices such as computers and cell phones. It has recently introduced a digital reader, called the e-pad, but realizes that to compete effectively in the future, it must be able to lower the cost of production and the selling price. The current cost per unit for producing the e-pad is $138, and Orange is estimating inflation on e-pad components and supplies purchased externally to be 1.5% in the coming year. In the most recent period, these items had a cost of $74. Despite these cost increases, Orange has adopted a Kaizen cost improvement model that targets a 5% cost decrease. Orange's Kaizen cost target (rounded to two decimal places) for the e-pad is
a. $131.11
b. $132.15
c. $133.07
d. $130.05

6. Typical characteristics of benchmarking include each of the following except
a. Planning the benchmarking project
b. Understanding your own performance
c. Focusing on performance measures
d. Studying others

Questions

Q8-1. What are the relationships among an organization's value chain, processes, and activities?

Q8-2. What should be the goal of every organization along the value chain?

Q8-3. Distinguish between the value-added perspective and the value chain perspective.

Q8-4. Why are economic models seldom used for day-to-day pricing decisions?

Q8-5. Identify three reasons that cost-based approaches to pricing have traditionally been important.

Q8-6. Identify four drawbacks to cost-based pricing.

Q8-7. How does target costing differ from cost-based pricing?

Q8-8. Why is cost-based pricing more a technique, and target costing is more a philosophy? Which approach takes a more proactive approach to cost management?

Q8-9. Distinguish between the marketing life cycles of products incorporating advanced technology (such as household electronic equipment) and those using more traditional technology (such as household paper products). Why would life-cycle costing be more important to a manufacturer of household electronic equipment than to a manufacturer of household paper products?

Q8-10. What is the relationship between target costing and continuous improvement (Kaizen) costing?

Q8-11. Distinguish between the seller's and the buyer's perspective of life-cycle costs.

Q8-12. What advantage is derived from benchmarking against firms other than competitors?

Assignments with the MBC logo in the margin are available in myBusinessCourse. See the Preface of the book for details.

Mini Exercises

M8-13. Developing a Value Chain from the Perspective of the Final Customer LO1

Prepare a value chain for bottled milk that was purchased for personal consumption at an on-campus cafeteria.

M8-14. Developing a Value Chain: Upstream and Downstream Entities LO1

Prepare a value chain for a company that manufactures furniture. Clearly identify upstream and downstream entities in the value chain.

M8-15. Classifying Activities Using the Generic Internal Value Chain: Aluminum Cable Manufacturer LO1

Using the generic internal value chain shown in **Exhibit 8.2**, classify each of the following activities of an aluminum cable manufacturer as inbound logistics, operations, outbound logistics, marketing and sales, service, or support.

a. Advertising in a construction magazine
b. Inspecting incoming aluminum ingots
c. Placing bar codes on coils of finished products
d. Borrowing money to finance a buildup of inventory
e. Hiring new employees
f. Heating aluminum ingots
g. Drawing wire from aluminum ingots
h. Coiling wire
i. Visiting a customer to determine the cause of cable breakage
j. Filing tax returns

M8-16. Classifying Activities Using the Generic Internal Value Chain: Cable TV Company LO1

Using the generic internal value chain shown in **Exhibit 8.2**, classify each of the following activities of a cable television company as inbound logistics, operations, outbound logistics, marketing and sales, service, or support.

a. Installing coaxial cable in the apartment of a new customer
b. Repairing coaxial cable after a windstorm
c. Mailing brochures to prospective customers
d. Discussing a rate increase with members of a regulatory agency
e. Selling shares of stock in the company
f. Monitoring the quality of reception at the company's satellite downlink
g. Preparing financial statements
h. Visiting a customer to determine the cause of poor-quality television reception
i. Traveling to a conference to learn about technological changes affecting the industry
j. Replacing old routers with updated technology

M8-17. Product Pricing: Single Product LO2 Sue Bee Honey

Sue Bee Honey is one of the largest processors of its product for the retail market. Assume that one of its plants has annual fixed costs totaling $16,317,500, of which $5,250,500 is for administrative and selling efforts. Sales are anticipated to be 950,000 cases a year. Variable costs for processing are $35 per case, and variable selling expenses are 10% of selling price. There are no variable administrative expenses.

Required

If the company desires a pretax profit of $9,000,000, what is the selling price per case?

LO2 Pinkberry

M8-18. Product Pricing: Single Product

Assume that you plan to open a Pinkberry franchise at a local shopping mall. Fixed operating costs for the year are projected to be \$144,500. Variable costs per serving include the cost of the ice cream and cone, \$1.50, and a franchise fee payable to Pinkberry, \$0.20. A market analysis prepared by Pinkberry indicates that annual sales should total 130,000 servings.

Required

Determine the price you should charge for each serving to achieve a \$125,000 pretax profit for the year.

LO2 **M8-19. Product Pricing**

A few years ago, Hotel Klingerhoffer, a large hotel chain, announced that because occupancy rates had declined during the previous quarter, it was raising room rates to cover the cost of its increase in vacant rooms. Although not referring to accounting or economics, several business journalists during the week following the announcement questioned the basis for the rate increases. One stated that "Hotel Klingerhoffer increases rates of vacant rooms."

Required

a. Did the journalist mean that vacant rooms would be more expensive? Explain.

b. Do you think Hotel Klingerhoffer's action to raise room rates was based on economics, accounting, or both?

LO5 **M8-20. Benchmarking**

Your company is developing a new product for the computer printer industry. You have talked to several material vendors about being able to supply quality components for the new product. The product designers are satisfied with the company's ability to make the product in the current facilities. Numerous potential customers also have been surveyed, and most have indicated a willingness to buy the product if the price is competitive.

Required

What are some means of benchmarking the development and production of your new product?

Exercises

LO2

E8-21. Product Pricing: Single Product

Presented is the current year contribution income statement of Grafton Products.

GRAFTON PRODUCTS Contribution Income Statement For Year Ended December		
Sales (15,000 units)		\$2,625,000
Less variable costs		
Cost of goods sold	\$1,275,000	
Selling and administrative	150,000	(1,425,000)
Contribution margin		1,200,000
Less fixed costs		
Manufacturing overhead	685,000	
Selling and administrative	330,000	(1,015,000)
Net income		\$ 185,000

Next year, Grafton expects an increase in variable manufacturing costs of \$10 per unit and in fixed manufacturing costs of \$30,000.

Required

a. If sales for next year remain at 15,000 units, what price should Grafton charge to obtain the same profit as last year?

b. Management believes that sales can be increased to 18,000 units if the selling price is lowered to \$165. Is this action desirable? (Use the cost data from part *a.*)

c. After considering the expected increases in costs, what sales volume is needed to earn a pretax profit of \$200,000 with a unit selling price of \$165?

E8-22. Cost-Based Pricing and Markups with Variable Costs LO2

Computer Consultants provides computerized inventory consulting. The office and computer expenses are $830,000 annually and are not assigned to specific jobs. The consulting hours available for the year total 18,000, and the average consulting hour has $40 of variable costs.

Required

a. If the company desires a profit of $250,000, what should it charge per hour?

b. What is the markup on variable costs if the desired profit is $322,000?

c. If the desired profit is $100,000, what is the markup on variable costs to cover (1) unassigned costs and (2) desired profit?

E8-23. Computing Markups LO2

The predicted annual costs for Mighty Motors are as follows:

Manufacturing Costs		Selling and Administrative Costs	
Variable	$250,000	Variable	$250,000
Fixed	350,000	Fixed	550,000

Average total assets for the year are predicted to be $7,500,000.

Required

a. If management desires a 10% rate of return on total assets, what are the markup percentages based on total variable costs and based on total manufacturing costs?

b. If the company desires an 8% rate of return on total assets, what is the markup percentage on total manufacturing costs for (1) unassigned costs and (2) desired profit?

E8-24. Product Pricing: Two Products LO2 Verbatim CMC Magnetics

Assume Verbatim, a subsidiary of CMC Magnetics, manufactures two products, CDs and DVDs, both on the same assembly lines and packaged 30 disks per pack. The predicted sales are 150,000 packs of CDs and 500,000 packs of DVDs. The predicted costs for the year are as follows:

	Variable Costs	Fixed Costs
Materials	$4,000,000	$1,560,000
Other	2,000,000	2,052,500

CDs use 25% of the materials costs and 10% of the other costs. DVDs use 75% of the materials costs and 90% of the other costs. The management of Verbatim desires an annual profit of $450,000.

Required

a. What price should Verbatim charge for each disk pack if management believes the DVDs sell for twice the price of the CDs?

b. What is the total profit per product using the selling prices determined in part *a*?

E8-25. Product Pricing: Two Products LO2

Refer to the previous exercise, E8-24. Based on your calculations of the selling price and profit for CDs and DVDs, how should Verbatim evaluate the status of these two products? Should either CDs or DVDs be discontinued? What additional information does the management of Verbatim need in order to make an appropriate judgment on the future status of these two products?

E8-26. Target Costing LO3 Champion Power Equipment

Assume Champion Power Equipment wants to develop a new log-splitting machine for rural homeowners. Market research has determined that the company could sell 7,500 log-splitting machines per year at a retail price of $1,200 each. An independent catalog company would handle sales for an annual fee of $12,000 plus $75 per unit sold. The cost of the raw materials required to produce the log-splitting machines amounts to $200 per unit.

Required

If company management desires a return equal to 30% of the final selling price, what is the target conversion and administrative cost per unit? *Hint*: The target unit cost will only or should only include conversion costs and remaining or additional sales and administrative costs.

Problems

LO2 Macquarium Inc.

P8-27. Product Pricing: Two Products

Macquarium Inc. provides computer-related services to its clients. Its two primary services are Web page design (WPD) and Internet consulting services (ICS). Assume that Macquarium's management expects to earn a 35% annual return on the assets invested. Macquarium has invested $6 million since its opening. The annual costs for the coming year are expected to be as follows:

	Variable Costs	Fixed Costs
Consulting support	$250,000	$1,750,000
Sales and administration	150,000	850,000

The two services expend about equal costs per hour, and the predicted hours for the coming year are 15,000 for WPD and 25,000 for ICS.

Required

a. If markup is based on variable costs, how much revenue must each service generate to provide the profit expected by corporate headquarters? What is the anticipated revenue per hour for each service? *Hint*: Start by determining the markup rate.

b. If the markup is based on total costs, how much revenue must each service generate to provide the expected profit?

c. Explain why answers in requirements (*a*) and (*b*) are either the same or different.

d. Comment on the advantages and disadvantages of using a cost-based pricing model.

LO3 Ericsson (ERIC)

P8-28. Target Costing

Ericsson is a large global company providing hardware, software, and related services for radio-access networks within mobile telecommunication systems. Assume that it is developing a new networking system for smaller, private telephone companies. To attract small companies, Ericsson must keep the price low without giving up too many of the features of larger networking systems. A marketing research study conducted on the company's behalf found that the price range must be $50,000 to $75,000. Management has determined a target price to be $65,000. The company's minimum profit percentage of sales is normally 15%, but the company is willing to reduce it to 12% to get the new product on the market. The fixed costs for the first year are anticipated to be $8,000,000. If sales reach 400 installed networks, the company needs to know how much it can spend on variable costs, which are primarily related to installation.

Required

a. What is the amount of total cost allowed if the 12% profit target is allowed and the 400 installations sales target is met? Show the amount for fixed and for variable costs.

b. What is the amount of total costs allowed if the 15% normal profit target is desired at the 400 installations sales target? Show the amount for fixed and for variable costs.

c. Discuss the advantages of using a target costing model versus using cost-based pricing.

LO4 **P8-29. Continuous Improvement (Kaizen) Costing**

Samira Company does contract manufacturing of compact video cameras. At its Pacific plant, cost control has become a concern of management. The actual costs per unit for the previous two years were as follows:

	Year 1		Year 2	
Direct materials				
Plastic case.	$ 5.10		$ 4.75	
Lens set	12.00		10.90	
Electrical component set.	8.30		7.00	
Film track	10.50		10.05	
Direct labor.	48.00	(1.6 hours)	45.00	(1.5 hours)
Indirect manufacturing costs				
Variable.	5.60		5.00	
Fixed.	16.00	(100,000 unit base)	12.75	(120,000 unit base)

The company manufactures all of the camera components except the lens sets, which it purchases from several vendors. The company has used target costing in the past but has not been able to meet the very competitive global pricing. Beginning in Year 2, the company implemented a continuous improvement program that requires cost reduction targets.

Required

a. If continuous improvement (Kaizen) costing sets a target of a 10% reduction of the first year cost base, how successful was the company in meeting the per unit cost reduction targets in the second year? Support your answer with appropriate computations.

b. Evaluate and discuss Samira's use of Kaizen costing.

P8-30. Continuous Improvement (Kaizen) Costing

LO4 General Electric (GE)

Assume that GE Capital, a division of General Electric, has been displeased with the costs of servicing its consumer loans. Assume that it has decided to implement a Kaizen-based cost improvement program. For the current year, GE Capital incurred the following costs ($ millions):

Loan processing	$12,500
Customer relations	2,800
Printing, mailing, and postage	550

For the next two years, GE Capital expects an increase in consumer loans of 8% annually with related increases in costs.

Required

a. If the company has a continuous improvement goal of 4% each year, develop a budget for the next two years for the consumer loan department.

b. Identify some possible ways that GE Capital can achieve the Kaizen costing goal.

c. Discuss the potential benefits and limitations of GE's Kaizen costing model.

P8-31. Price Setting: Multiple Products

LO2

Tech Com's predicted variable and fixed costs for next year are as follows:

	Variable Costs	Fixed Costs
Manufacturing	$405,000	$ 424,200
Selling and administrative	102,000	594,000
Total	$507,000	$1,018,200

Tech Com is a small company producing a wide variety of computer interface devices. Per-unit manufacturing cost information about one of these products, a high-capacity flash drive, is as follows:

Direct materials	$8
Direct labor	4
Manufacturing overhead	
Variable	3
Fixed	6
Total manufacturing costs	$21

Variable selling and administrative costs for the flash drive are $4 per unit. Management has set a target profit for next year of $300,000 on the sale of the flash drive.

Required

a. Determine the markup percentage on variable costs required to earn the desired profit.

b. Use variable cost markup to determine a suggested selling price for the flash drive.

c. For the flash drive, break the markup on variable costs into separate parts for fixed costs and profit. Explain the significance of each part.

d. Determine the markup percentage on manufacturing costs required to earn the desired profit.

e. Use the manufacturing costs markup to determine a suggested selling price for the flash drive.

f. Evaluate the variable and the manufacturing cost approaches to determine the markup percentage.

LO2 P8-32. Price Setting: Multiple Products

Pipestem Golf produces a wide variety of golfing equipment. In the past, product managers set prices using their professional judgment. Samuel Snead, the new controller, believes this practice has led to the significant underpricing of some products (with lost profits) and the significant overpricing of other products (with lost sales volume). You have been asked to assist Snead in developing a corporate approach to pricing. The output of your work should be a cost-based formula that can be used to develop initial selling prices for each product. Although product managers are allowed to adjust these prices to meet competition and to take advantage of market opportunities, they must explain such deviations in writing. The following cost information from the current year accounting records is available:

	Manufacturing Costs	Selling and Administrative Costs
Variable	$335,000	$ 55,000
Fixed	245,000	365,000

During the year, Pipestem Golf reported earnings of $200,000. However, the controller believes that proper pricing should produce earnings of at least $250,000 on the same sales mix and unit volume. Accordingly, you are to use the preceding cost information and a target profit of $250,000 in developing a cost-based pricing formula. Selling and administrative expenses are not currently associated with individual products. However, you have obtained the following unit production cost information for the TW Irons:

Variable manufacturing costs	$145
Fixed manufacturing costs	105
Total	$250

Required

a. Determine the standard markup percentage for each of the following cost bases. Round answers to two decimal places.
1. Full costs, including fixed and variable manufacturing costs, and fixed and variable selling and administrative costs.
2. Manufacturing costs plus variable selling and administrative costs.
3. Manufacturing costs.
4. Variable costs.
5. Variable manufacturing costs.

b. Explain why the markup percentages become progressively larger from requirement (*a*), parts (1) through (5).

c. Determine the initial price of a set of TW Irons using the manufacturing cost markup and the variable manufacturing cost markup.

d. Do you believe the controller's approach to product pricing is reasonable? Why or why not?

Cases and Projects

LO2 C8-33. Pricing Decision

Most utility poles carry electric and telephone lines. In areas served by cable television, they also carry television cables. However, cable television companies rarely own any utility poles. Instead, they pay utility companies a rental fee for the use of each pole on a yearly basis. The determination of the rental fee is a source of frequent disagreement between the pole owners and the cable television companies. In one situation, pole owners were arguing for a $10 annual rental fee per pole; this was the standard rate the electric and telephone companies charged each other for the use of poles.

"We object to that," stated the representative of the cable television company. "With two users, the $10 fee represents a rental fee for one-half the pole. This fee is too high because we only use about six inches of each 40-foot pole."

"You are forgetting federal safety regulations," responded a representative of the electric company. "They specify certain distances between different types of lines on a utility pole. Television cables must be a minimum of 40 inches below power lines and 12 inches above telephone lines. If your cable is added to the pole, the total capacity is reduced because this space cannot be used for anything else. Besides, we have an investment in the poles; you don't. We should be entitled to a fair return on this investment. Furthermore, speaking of fair, your company should pay the same rental fee that the telephone company pays us and we pay them. We do not intend to change this fee."

In response, the cable television company representative made two points. First, any fee represents incremental income to the pole owners because the cable company would pay all costs of moving existing lines. Second, because the electric and telephone companies both strive to own the same number of poles in a service area, their pole rental fees cancel themselves. Hence, the fee they charge each other is not relevant.

Required

Evaluate the arguments presented by the cable television and electric company representatives. What factors should be considered in determining a pole rental fee?

C8-34. Target Costing LO3

The president of Houston Electronics was pleased with the company's newest product, the HE Versatile CVD. The product is portable and can be attached to a computer to play or record computer programs or sound, attached to an amplifier to play or record music, or attached to a television to play or record TV programs. It can even be attached to a camcorder to record videos directly on compact disks rather than on tape. It also can be used with a headset to play or record sound. The proud president announced that this unique and innovative product would be an important factor in reestablishing the North American consumer electronics industry.

Based on development costs and predictions of sales volume, manufacturing costs, and distribution costs, the cost-based price of the HE Versatile CVD was determined to be $425. Following a market-skimming strategy, management set the initial selling price at $525. The marketing plan was to reduce the selling price by $50 during each of the first two years of the product's life to obtain the highest contribution possible from each market segment.

The initial sales of the HE Versatile CVD were strong, and Houston Electronics found itself adding second and third production shifts. Although these shifts were expensive, at a selling price of $525, the product had ample contribution margin to remain highly profitable. The president was talking with the company's major investors about the desirability of obtaining financing for a major plant expansion when the bad news arrived. A foreign company had announced that it would shortly introduce a similar product that would incorporate new design features and sell for only $350. The president was shocked. "Why," she remarked, "it costs us $375 to put a complete unit in the hands of customers."

Required

How could the foreign competitor profitably sell a similar product for less than the manufacturing costs to Houston Electronics? What advice do you have for the president concerning the HE Versatile CVD? What advice would you have to help the company avoid similar problems in the future?

Solutions to Review Problems

Review 8-1—Solution

e 1. Remaking any food or beverage item that a customer is not satisfied with at no additional cost to the customer
b 2. Managing stores owned and operated by the company
c 3. Offering online sales for limited products
a 4. Sourcing unroasted coffee beans from growers in farming communities in key coffee-growing regions
d 5. Increasing the company budget for promotions, advertising, and public relations activities
a 6. Maintaining storage sites and regional distribution centers
c 7. Offering a limited selection of products for sale in leading supermarket chains
b 8. Investing in innovative equipment that quickly brews high-quality coffee

Review 8-2—Solution

a.

Desired annual profit ($2,000,000 × 0.10)	$200,000
Actual profit	(150,000)
Amount actual profit fell short of achieving the desired return	$ 50,000

b.

Predicted costs		
Variable	$450,000	
Fixed	600,000	$1,050,000
Desired profit		250,000
Required revenue		$1,300,000
Unit sales		÷ 100,000
Required unit selling price		$ 13

c.

Variable manufacturing costs per unit ($300,000/100,000 units)	= $3
Selling price as a percent of variable manufacturing costs	= $13/3
	= 433⅓%
Markup as a percent of variable manufacturing costs ($10/$3)	= 333⅓%

d. Detail of markup on variable manufacturing costs:

1. Unassigned costs		
Variable selling and administrative	$150,000	
Fixed costs	600,000	$750,000
Variable manufacturing costs		÷300,000
Markup on variable manufacturing costs to cover unassigned costs		250%
2. Desired profit		$250,000
Variable manufacturing costs		÷300,000
Additional markup on variable manufacturing costs to achieve desired profit ($250,000)		83⅓%

Review 8-3—Solution

a.

Total revenue (150,000 × $35,000)	$5,250,000,000
Required profit margin (15%)	−787,500,000
Total cost	$4,462,500,000
Number of units	÷ 150,000
Target cost per unit	$ 29,750

b. A new product such as an automobile is an extremely complex product with hundreds, if not thousands, of different components, involving many different vendors. Once Chrysler has determined what product features potential customers want, a cross-functional team of employees is formed from diverse areas of the company including marketing, product design, manufacturing, and management accounting. The team may even include suppliers of raw materials. The team determines how best to provide those features through product design, manufacturing procedures, and the selection of necessary raw materials. The task is to determine how best to provide the final product that meets customer price, function, and quality requirements while providing the desired profit.

c. If the team's initial cost estimates are too high, they should explore every possibility, including redesign of the product, using components from existing products, developing new production systems, etc. to meet the target cost. If it is finally determined that the target cannot be reached, then management has to decide if it is willing to go forward with the product with a lower than desired initial profit margin. In some cases, managers will proceed with the idea that additional cost savings will be found (using Kaizen costing methods) after the product is in production. Other times, managers may decide not to pursue the new product.

Review 8-4—Solution

Item	Year 1	× Target %	Year 2 Target	Year 2 Actual	Variance
Direct materials (per unit):					
Plastic case	$ 4.50	0.95	$ 4.275	$ 4.40	$ 0.125 U
Lens set	17.00	0.95	16.15	17.20	1.05 U
Electrical set	6.60	0.95	6.27	5.70	0.57 F
Film track	11.00	0.95	10.45	10.00	0.45 F
Direct labor (per unit)	32.00	0.95	30.40	30.00	0.40 F
Indirect mfg (per unit):					
Variable costs	7.50	0.95	7.125	7.10	0.025 F
Indirect mfg (in total)					
Fixed costs	$300,000	1.00	$300,000	$342,000	$42,000 U

The company made progress during Year 2 with favorable variances for all components except cases and lens sets. The unfavorable lens items may require more consideration since they are vendor purchased. Maybe new vendors can be found, or current vendor contracts may be renegotiated.

The fixed manufacturing costs also need attention. The total fixed costs increased from $300,000 (100,000 × $3) to $342,000 (120,000 × $2.85). If they are fixed, why did they increase? Did increased production or other factors cause the increase? If it was volume driven, maybe some of the costs are not fixed.

Review 8-5—Solution

According to iSixSigma.com, neither approach is superior to the other. Which approach to use will depend on an organization's available time and resources. A few of the differences identified by iSixSigma.com include the following:

Differences Between Benchmarking and Competitor Research

Benchmarking	Competitor Research
Focuses on best practices	Focuses on performance measures
Strives for continuous improvement	Bandage or quick fix
Partnering to share information	Considered corporate spying by some
Needed to maintain a competitive edge	Simply a "nice to have"
Adapting based on customer needs after examination of the best	Attempting to mirror another company/process

Source: https://www.isixsigma.com/methodology/benchmarking/understanding-purpose-and-use-benchmarking/

Chapter 9

Operational Budgeting and Profit Planning

Learning Objectives

LO1 Discuss the importance of budgets. (p. 310)

LO2 Describe basic approaches to budgeting. (p. 312)

LO3 Explain the relationship among elements of a master budget and develop a basic budget. (p. 314)

LO4 Explain and develop a basic manufacturing cost budget. (p. 323)

LO5 Analyze the relationship between budget development and manager behavior. (p. 327)

Every experienced executive knows that budgeting is the lifeblood of a business enterprise. It is the mechanism by which we plan the entity's operations for the upcoming year, or even decade. It's the way we quantitatively communicate those plans and coordinate the employees' efforts throughout the organization. The budget is unambiguous and unassailable; you either make your numbers or you don't, which makes the budget a valuable feedback loop by which to evaluate past operations. More importantly, preparing a budget alerts management ahead of time to the risks faced by the entity in the coming periods, whether those risks are a shortage of cash, too few or too many employees, or idle versus excess capacity.

Each period, most businesses prepare what is called a "master budget." The master budget covers every aspect of the financial (and often nonfinancial) operations. The first step in the master budget is to budget or forecast sales revenue. But how do you prepare a budget for a company that, until recently, generated zero revenue while experiencing explosive growth? Pinterest has over 320 million active users worldwide each month and has been valued at over $10 billion. Pinterest was founded in 2010 but didn't even have a revenue model until 2014. The company works with businesses to understand how Pinterest traffic can generate sales revenue for those businesses by advertising on Pinterest. The advertising fees paid by those companies exceeded $1 billion for the 12 months ended September 30, 2019.

From a budgeting perspective, Pinterest may need to prepare its sales budget using several what-if scenarios to help it determine the proper pricing for its advertisements. It will also need to develop expense budgets for everything from labor to selling to general and administrative expenses. At the time of this writing, the company had grown to over 2,000 employees, including new hires from Facebook, Google, and Amazon.

Clearly, Pinterest is an evolving, dynamic company, but it will have to pay close attention to its budgeting to manage its cash flow and capital investments. The budgeting techniques discussed in this chapter will aid the manager in planning and managing the organization's revenues, costs, and other quantitative variables in the face of constantly changing business conditions.

Road Map

LO	Learning Objective | Topics	Page	eLecture	Guided Example	Assignments
LO1	**Discuss the importance of budgets.** Compel Planning :: Promote Communication and Coordination :: Guide to Action and Evaluation :: Risk Management	310	e9–1	Review 9-1	23
LO2	**Describe basic approaches to budgeting.** Output/Input :: Activity Based :: Incremental :: Minimum Level	312	e9–2	Review 9-2	17, 18, 23, 24, 25
LO3	**Explain the relationships among elements of a master budget and develop a basic budget.** Master Budget :: Sales Budget :: Purchases Budget :: Selling Expense Budget :: General and Administrative Expenses Budget :: Cash Budget :: Budgeted Financial Statements	314	e9–3	Review 9-3	19, 20, 26, 27, 28, 29, 30, 31, 32, 33, 36, 37, 38, 39, 40, 41, 42
LO4	**Explain and develop a basic manufacturing cost budget.** Production Budget :: Manufacturing Cost Budget	323	e9–4	Review 9-4	21, 22, 34, 35, 38, 39, 40, 41, 42
LO5	**Analyze the relationship between budget development and manager behavior.** Imposed Budget :: Participative Budget :: Budget Periods :: Forecasts :: Ethics :: Open Book Management	327	e9–5	Review 9-5	43, 44, 45, 46

CHAPTER ORGANIZATION

Operational Budgeting and Profit Planning

Reasons for Budgeting	General Approaches to Budgeting	Master Budget	Budget Development in Manufacturing Organizations	Budget Development and Manager Behavior
• Compel Planning • Promote Communication and Coordination • Provide a Guide to Action and Basis of Evaluation • Aid in Risk Management	• Output/Input Approach • Activity-Based Approach • Incremental Approach • Minimum Level Approach	• Sales Budget • Purchases Budget • Selling Expense Budget • General and Administrative Expense Budget • Cash Budget • Budgeted Financial Statements • Finalizing the Budget	• Production Budget • Manufacturing Cost Budget	• Employee Participation • Budgeting Periods • Forecasts • Ethics • Open Book Management

A **budget** is a formal plan of action expressed in monetary terms. The purpose of this chapter is to examine the concepts, relationships, and procedures used in budgeting. Our emphasis is on **operating budgets**, which concern the development of detailed plans to guide operations throughout the budget period. We consider the reasons that organizations budget and alternative approaches to budget development. We also examine budget assembly and consider issues related to manager behavior and the budgeting process.

Reasons for Budgeting

LO1 Discuss the importance of budgets.

Operating managers frequently regard budgeting as a time-consuming task that diverts attention from current problems. Indeed, the development of an effective budget is a difficult job. It is also a necessary one. Organizations that do not plan are likely to wander aimlessly and ultimately succumb to the swirl of current events. The formal development of a budget helps to ensure both success and survival. As discussed below, budgeting compels planning; it improves communications and coordination among organizational elements; it provides a guide to action; and it provides a basis of performance evaluation. Budget models are also used to analyze and prepare for various business risks.

Compel Planning

Formal budgeting procedures require people to think about the future. Without the discipline of formal planning procedures, busy operating managers would not find time to plan. Immediate needs would consume all available time. Formal budgeting procedures, with specified deadlines, force managers to plan for the future by making the completion of the budget another immediate need. Budgeting moves an organization from an informal "reactive" style to a formal "proactive" style of management. As a result, management and other employees spend less time solving unanticipated problems and more time on positive measures and preventative actions.

Promote Communication and Coordination

When operating responsibilities are divided, it is difficult to synchronize activities. Production must know what marketing intends to sell. Purchasing and personnel must know the factory's material and labor requirements. The treasurer must plan to ensure the availability of the cash to support receivables, inventories, and capital expenditures. Budgeting forces the managers of these diverse functions to communicate their plans and coordinate their activities. It helps ensure that plans are feasible (Can purchasing obtain adequate inventories to support projected sales?) and that they are synchronized

(Will inventory be available in advance of an advertising campaign?). The final version of the budget emerges after an extensive (often lengthy) process of communication and coordination.

Provide a Guide to Action and Basis of Evaluation

Once the budget has been finalized, the various operating managers know what is expected of them, and they can set about doing it. If employees do not have a guide to action, their efforts could be wasted on unproductive or even counterproductive activities.

After employees accept the budget as a guide to action, they can be held responsible for their portion of the budget. When results do not agree with plans, managers attempt to determine the cause of the divergence. This information is then used to adjust operations or to modify plans. More generally, budgeting is an important part of **management by exception**, whereby management directs attention only to those activities not proceeding according to plan. Without the budget, management might spend an inordinate amount of time seeking explanation of past activities and not enough time planning future activities.

Aid in Risk Management

The models used for budgeting are also used in managing risk. **Risk** is the danger that things will not go according to plan. Although some risk results from anticipated events having a positive impact, such as an increase in sales volume or selling prices, risk is more typically associated with events that have a negative impact, like a work stoppage at a key supplier, a fire, or hackers shutting down a retail website for an extended period of time.

Risk management (also called enterprise risk management) is the process of identifying, evaluating, and planning possible responses to risks that could impede an organization from achieving its plans. It also involves monitoring the sources of risk. An organization's budget model can be used to evaluate the financial impact of a risk and to determine, from a financial perspective, the best response to a risk. The following Research Insight summarizes a proposed approach to risk management. The performance evaluation procedures considered in Chapter 10, if completed on a timely basis, assist in monitoring risk.

Research Insight ■ A Systematic Approach to Risk Management

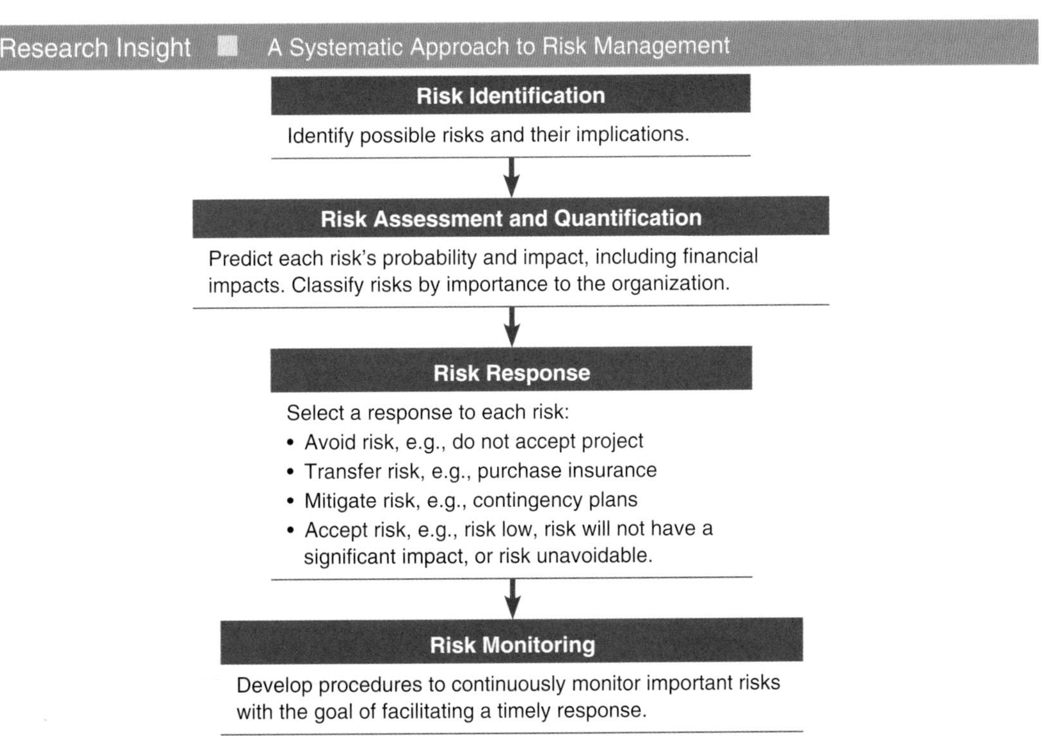

Risk Identification
Identify possible risks and their implications.
Risk Assessment and Quantification
Predict each risk's probability and impact, including financial impacts. Classify risks by importance to the organization.
Risk Response
Select a response to each risk:
• Avoid risk, e.g., do not accept project
• Transfer risk, e.g., purchase insurance
• Mitigate risk, e.g., contingency plans
• Accept risk, e.g., risk low, risk will not have a significant impact, or risk unavoidable.
Risk Monitoring
Develop procedures to continuously monitor important risks with the goal of facilitating a timely response.

Source: Alan J. Chilcott, "Risk Management—A Developing Field of Study and Application," *Cost Engineering*, September 9, 2010, pp. 21–26; Neville Turbit, "Basics of Managing Risk," The Project Perfect White Paper Collection, www.projectperfect.com.au.

Review 9-1 LO1 Discussing the Benefits of Budgeting

Mark Fisher was recently hired as an intern at Mobile Innovations, a small manufacturer and seller of conveyer systems, which are used by other businesses in their manufacturing processes. After recently finishing a course in management accounting, Mark asks his manager if he can see a copy of the current year's operating budget. His manager replies that as a small business, they are too busy focusing on day-to-day operations to take the time to create a budget.

Required

Solution on p. 346.

Discuss some ways that an operating budget might benefit Mobile Innovations.

General Approaches to Budgeting

LO2 Describe basic approaches to budgeting.

Before an organization can develop operating budgets, management must decide which approaches to budget planning will be used for the various revenue and expenditure activities and organizational units. Widely used planning approaches to budgeting include the output/input, activity-based, incremental, and minimum level approaches.

Output/Input Approach

The **output/input approach** budgets physical inputs and costs as a function of planned unit-level activities. This approach is often used for service, merchandising, manufacturing, and distribution activities that have defined relationships between effort and accomplishment. If each unit produced requires 2 pounds of direct materials that cost $5 each, and the planned production volume is 25 units, the budgeted inputs and costs for direct materials are 50 pounds (25 units × 2 pounds per unit) and $250 (50 pounds × $5 per pound).

The budgeted inputs are a function of the planned outputs. The output/input approach starts with the planned outputs and works backward to budget the inputs. It is difficult to use this approach for costs that do not respond to changes in unit-level cost drivers.

Activity-Based Approach

The **activity-based approach** is a type of output/input method, but it reduces the distortions in the transformation through emphasis on the expected cost of the planned activities that will be consumed for a process, department, service, product, or other budget objective. Overhead costs are budgeted on the basis of the cost objective's anticipated consumption of activities, not based only on some broad-based cost driver such as direct labor hours or machine hours.

The amount of each activity cost driver used by each budget objective (for example, product or service) is determined and multiplied by the cost per unit of the activity cost driver. The result is an estimate of the costs of each product or service based on cost drivers such as assembly-line setup or inspections, as well as the traditional volume-based drivers such as direct labor hours or units of direct materials consumed. Activity-based budgeting predicts costs of budget objectives by adding all costs of the activity cost drivers that each product or service is budgeted to consume. In evaluating the proposed budget, management would focus their attention on identifying the optimal set of activities rather than just the output/input relationships.

Incremental Approach

The **incremental approach** budgets costs for a coming period as a dollar or percentage change from the amount budgeted for (or spent during) some previous period. This approach is often used when the relationships between inputs and outputs are weak or nonexistent. For example, it is difficult to establish a clear relationship between sales volume and advertising expenditures. Consequently, the budgeted amount of advertising for a future period is often based on the budgeted or actual advertising expenditures in a previous period. If budgeted advertising expenditures for last year were $200,000, the budgeted expenditures for this year would be some increment, say 5%, above $200,000.

In evaluating the proposed current year budget, management would accept the $200,000 base and focus attention on justifying the increment.

The incremental approach is widely used in government and not-for-profit organizations. In seeking a budget appropriation, a manager using the incremental approach need only justify proposed expenditures in excess of the previous budget. The primary advantage of the incremental approach is that it simplifies the budget process by considering only the increments in the various budget items. A major disadvantage is that existing waste and inefficiencies could escalate year after year.

Minimum Level Approach

Using the **minimum level approach**, an organization establishes a base amount for budget items and requires explanation or justification for any budgeted amount above the minimum (base). This base is usually significantly less than the base used in the incremental approach. It likely is the minimum amount necessary to keep a program or organizational unit viable. For example, the corporate director of product development would need some basic amount to avoid canceling ongoing projects. Additional increments might also be included, first to support the current level of product development and second to undertake desirable new projects.

Some organizations, especially units of government, employ a variation of the minimum level approach, identified as zero-based budgeting. Under **zero-based budgeting** every dollar of expenditure must be justified. The essence of zero-based budgeting is breaking an organizational unit's total budget into program packages with related costs. Management then ranks all program packages on the basis of the perceived benefits in relation to their costs. Program packages are then funded for the budget period using this ranking. High-ranking packages are most likely to be funded and low-ranking packages are least likely to be funded.

Business Insight ■ Budgeting for Uncertainty

As a firm builds its master budget, budgeting for uncertainty is essential. The financial struggles of Kodak can be seen as a cautionary tale for mature firms dealing with technological uncertainty. Kodak was decidedly ahead of the digital camera trend, creating its first prototype in the 1970s. Kodak's technology was foiled by its approach to uncertainty. Traditional approaches to long-term strategy and budgeting focus on forecasting trends and committing to the best single strategy. Kodak knew that the future of photography was digital but chose to bet on its core business rather than making risky investments in new products that would undermine its core.

Analysts at Bain and Company argue that firms should budget for a "range of futures," by

1. Deciding what uncertainties could affect the company. (The potential of digital photography is just such an uncertainty.)
2. Develop probable scenarios for the future. Consider the upsides and downsides of each scenario. (Kodak clearly knew that digital photography was a potential scenario.)
3. Match strategic plans to scenarios, balancing investment with flexibility to adjust to various states of the world.
4. Establish signals that trigger adoption of scenarios.

Though Kodak had the technology to adapt to the new market, the company was unable, or unwilling, to restructure its business accordingly. If the management team had agreed that they would shift toward digital cameras when digital had 15% market share, it would have been positioned to switch. By preparing for multiple uncertain futures and setting triggers, managers pre-commit to difficult decisions, and are prepared to be flexible.

General Electric's $200 million "multimodal" factory in Pune, India, is an example of this flexible scenario-based approach. Leadership was confident that four different businesses would need capacity in India, but the mix was uncertain. Rather than commit to a mix, GE built flexibility into the factory. The advanced facility they built is designed to switch between production of jet engines, locomotives, wind turbines, and water treatment equipment. Rather than committing to one business model, GE prepared for several possible scenarios. GE has since gone on to open other multimodal factories, including one in Vietnam in 2018.

Source: Martin Toner, Nikhil Ojha, Piet de Paepe, and Miguel Simoes de Melo, "A Strategy for Thriving in Uncertainty," *Bain Brief*, Bain & Company, August 12, 2015.

Budgeting for objectives is a variation on the minimum level approach that combines elements of activity-based and zero-based budgeting with a need to live within fixed financial constraints. The minimum level approach improves on the incremental approach by questioning the necessity for costs included in the base of the incremental approach, but it is very time-consuming. All three approaches are often used within the same organization. A pharmaceutical company might use the output/input or the activity-based approach to budget distribution expenditures, the incremental approach to budget administrative salaries, and the minimum level approach to budget research and development.

Review 9-2 LO2 Applying the Output/Input Approach and Activity-Based Approach to Budgeting

To illustrate the various approaches to budgeting discussed above, assume that McNeil, a division of Johnson & Johnson, manufactures two products in institutional quantities, Regular Strength Tylenol and Tylenol Extra Strength. Suppose last period, McNeil produced 18,000 units of Regular and 45,000 units of Extra Strength at a total unit cost of $38 for Regular and $32 for Extra Strength. Assume estimated overhead costs of $408,500 for the next period include the cost of assembly-line setups, engineering and maintenance, and inspections. Total estimated assembly hours are 50,000 hours; therefore, the estimated overhead cost per assembly hour is $8.17. Other predicted data for the next period follow:

	Regular	Extra Strength
Direct materials (per unit)	$20.00	$14.50
Direct labor hours of assembly time (per unit)	0.5	0.8
Assembly labor cost (per hour)	$18	$18
Total estimated production (in units)	20,000	50,000
Total setup hours	1,000	1,500
Total engineering and maintenance hours	500	600
Total inspections	650	580
Setup cost (per setup hour)	$25	$25
Engineering and maintenance (per hour)	$35	$35
Inspection cost (per inspection)	$250	$250

Required

a. Calculate McNeil's budgeted cost per unit to produce Regular and Extra Strength Tylenol during the next period, assuming it uses an output/input approach and budgets overhead cost based only on assembly hours.

b. Repeat *a*, assuming McNeil uses an activity-based approach and budgets overhead cost based on budgeted activity costs.

Solution on p. 347.

Master Budget

LO3 Explain the relationships among elements of a master budget and develop a basic budget.

The culmination of the budgeting process is the preparation of a **master budget** for the entire organization that considers all interrelationships among organization units. The master budget groups together all budgets and supporting schedules and coordinates all financial and operational activities, placing them into an organization-wide set of budgets for a given time period.

Because it explicitly considers organizational interrelationships, the master budget is more complex than budgets developed for products, services, organization units, or specific processes. The elements of the master budget depend on the nature of the business, its products or services, processes and organization, and management needs.

A major goal of developing a master budget is to ensure the smooth functioning of a business throughout the budget period and the organization's operating cycle. As shown in **Exhibit 9.1**, the operating cycle involves the conversion of cash into other assets, which are intended to produce revenues in excess of their costs. The cycle generally follows a path from cash, to inventories, to receivables (via sales or services), and back to cash. There are, of course, intermediate processes such as the purchase or manufacture of inventories, payments of accounts payable, and the collection of receivables. The master budget is merely a detailed model of the firm's operating cycle that includes all internal processes.

Exhibit 9.1 Operating Cycle of a Manufacturer or Merchandiser

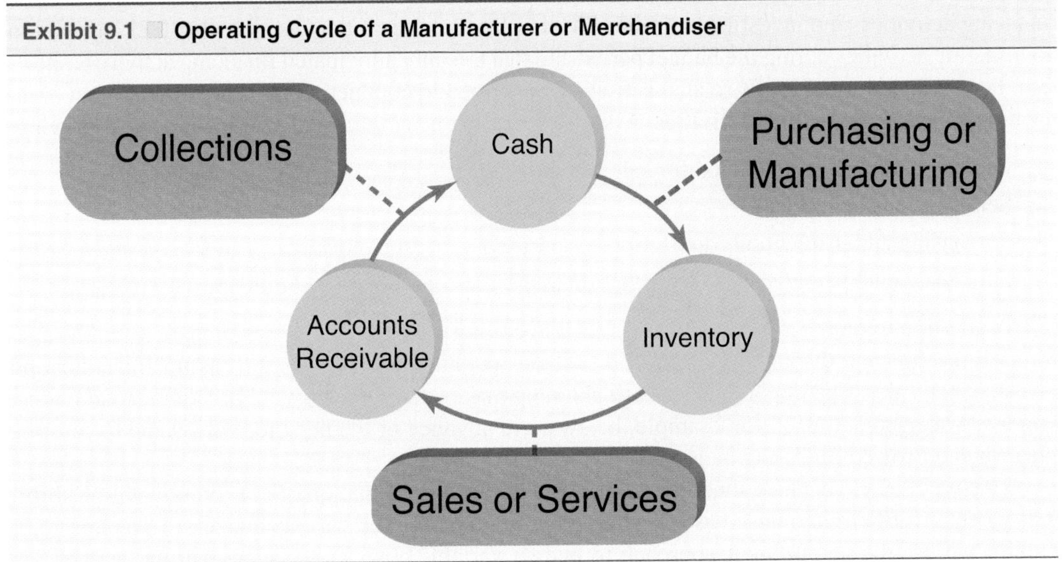

Most for-profit organizations begin the budgeting process with the development of the sales budget and conclude with the development of budgeted financial statements. **Exhibit 9.2** depicts the annual budget assembly process in a retail merchandising organization. Most of the budget data flow from sales toward cash and then toward the budgeted financial statements.

To illustrate the procedures involved in budget assembly, a hypothetical monthly budget for the second quarter of the year is developed for REI, a retail organization specializing in gear and apparel for outdoor and fitness activities. The assembly sequence follows the overview illustrated in **Exhibit 9.2**. Each element of the budget process in **Exhibit 9.2** is illustrated in a separate exhibit. Because of the numerous elements in the budget process illustrated for REI, you will find it useful to refer to **Exhibit 9.2** often.

Exhibit 9.2 Budget Assembly for a Merchandiser

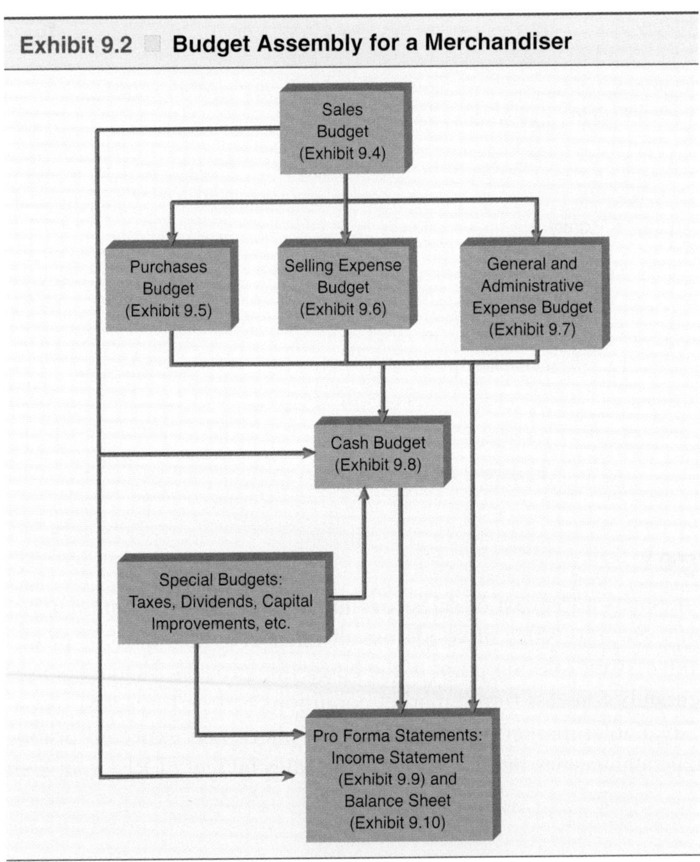

Operating activities

Activities related to generating business income.

Financing activities

Activities related to funding operations or expansion.

Investing activities

Activities related to buying and selling long-term assets and investments.

The activities of a business can be summarized under three broad categories: operating activities, financing activities, and investing activities. To simplify the illustration, assume that REI engaged in no investing activities during the budget period and that the only anticipated financing activity is short-term borrowing. Normal profit-related activities performed in conducting the daily affairs of an organization are called **operating activities**. Assume the operating activities of REI include the following:

1. Purchasing inventory intended for sale.
2. Selling goods or services.
3. Purchasing and using goods and services classified as selling expenses.
4. Purchasing and using goods and services classified as general and administrative expenses.

In addition to preparing the budget for each operating activity, companies prepare a cash budget for cash receipts and disbursements related to their operating activities as well as for financing and investing activities. The importance of cash planning makes this budget a vital part of the total budget process. Management must, for example, be aware in advance of the need to borrow and have some idea when borrowed funds can be repaid.

The hypothetical balance sheet for April 1, the start of the second quarter, is presented in **Exhibit 9.3**. It contains information used as a starting point in preparing the various budgets. To reduce complexity, we use the output/input approach to budget variable costs and assume that the budgets for other costs were previously developed using the incremental approach. Budgets to be prepared include those for sales, purchases, selling expense, general and administrative expense, and cash.

Beginning of the period balance sheet

The balance sheet at the beginning of the budgeted period contains information used as a starting point in preparing the various budgets.

Exhibit 9.3 Initial Balance Sheet

REI Balance Sheet April 1			
Assets			
Current assets			
Cash		$ 15,000	
Accounts receivable, net		59,200	
Merchandise inventory		157,000	$231,200
Fixed assets			
Buildings and equipment	$460,000		
Less accumulated depreciation	(124,800)	335,200	
Land		60,000	395,200
Total assets			$626,400
Liabilities and Stockholders' Equity			
Current liabilities			
Accounts payable		$ 84,000	
Taxes payable*		35,000	$119,000
Stockholders' equity			
Capital stock		350,000	
Retained earnings		157,400	507,400
Total liabilities and stockholders' equity			$626,400

*Quarterly income taxes are paid within 30 days of the end of each quarter.

Sales Budget

The **sales budget** includes a forecast of sales revenue, and it can also contain a forecast of unit sales and sales collections. Because sales drive almost all other activities in a for-profit organization, developing a sales budget is the starting point in the budgeting process. Managers use the best available information to accurately forecast future market conditions. These forecasts, when considered along with merchandise available, marketing and promotion plans, and expected pricing policies, should lead to the most dependable sales budget. Assume the sales budget of REI is in **Exhibit 9.4**.

Exhibit 9.4 **Sales Budget**

REI
Sales Budget
For the Second Quarter Ending June 30

	April	May	June	Quarter Total	July
Sales.	$190,000	$228,000	$250,000	$668,000	$309,000

Sales budget

Developing a sales budget is the starting point in the budgeting process.

The information in the sales budget along with predictions of the expected portion of cash sales and the timing of collections from credit sales are used to calculate cash receipts. In the event of a projected cash shortfall, management could consider ways to increase cash sales or to accelerate the collection of receipts from credit sales.

Purchases Budget

The **purchases budget** indicates the materials that must be acquired to meet sales needs and ending inventory requirements. It can be referred to as a merchandise budget if it contains only purchases of merchandise for sale. (For a manufacturer, the purchases budget would include raw materials costs.) The purchases budget, shown in **Exhibit 9.5**, includes only purchases of merchandise.

Exhibit 9.5 **Purchases Budget**

REI
Purchases Budget
For the Second Quarter Ending June 30

	April	May	June	Quarter Total	July
Budgeted sales (**Exhibit 9.4**)	$190,000	$228,000	$250,000	$668,000	$309,000
Current cost of goods sold*	$114,000	$136,800	$150,000	$400,800	
Desired ending inventory**	168,400	175,000	192,700	192,700	
Total needs.	282,400	311,800	342,700	593,500	
Less beginning inventory***	(157,000)	(168,400)	(175,000)	(157,000)	
Purchases.	$125,400	$143,400	$167,700	$436,500	

*Cost of goods sold is 60% of selling price
**Fifty percent of inventory required for next month's budgeted sales plus base inventory of $100,000.
April: ($228,000 May sales x 0.60 cost x 0.50 desired ending inventory) + $100,000
May: ($250,000 June sales x 0.60 cost x 0.50 desired ending inventory) + $100,000
June :($309,000 July sales x 0.60 cost x 0.50 desired ending inventory) + $100,000
***Fifty percent of current month sales x 0.60 cost plus base inventory of $100,000. Note monthly beginning inventory. Same as previous month's ending inventory.

Purchases budget

The purchases budget indicates the merchandise that must be acquired to meet sales needs and ending inventory requirements.

In reviewing REI's purchases budget, note the following:

- Because REI sells a wide variety of items, the purchases budget is expressed in terms of sales dollars, with the assumed cost of merchandise averaging 60% of the selling price. Management also keeps detailed records for budgeting the number of units of items carried. An organization that only sold a small number of items might present the sales budget in units as well as dollars.
- The budget assumes management desires to have 50% of the inventory needed to fill the following month's sales in stock at the end of the previous month.
- To provide for a possible delay in the receipt of inventory and to meet variations in customer demand, the budget assumes that REI maintains an additional base inventory of $100,000.
- The total inventory needs equal current sales plus desired ending inventory, including the base inventory.
- Budgeted purchases are computed as total inventory needs less the beginning inventory.

The information in the purchases budget and the information on expected timing of payments for purchases are used to budget cash disbursements for purchases. In the event of a projected cash shortfall, management can consider ways to delay the purchase of inventory or the payment for inventory purchases.

Selling Expense Budget

The **selling expense budget** presents the expenses the organization plans to incur in connection with sales and distribution. In the selling expense budget, **Exhibit 9.6**, the budgeted variable selling expenses are determined as a percentage of budgeted sales dollars. The budgeted fixed selling expenses are based on amounts obtained from the manager of the sales department. To simplify the presentation of the cash budget, the budget assumes REI pays its selling expenses in the month they are incurred.

Selling expense budget

The selling expense budget presents the expenses the organization plans to incur in connection with sales and distribution.

Exhibit 9.6 Selling Expense Budget

REI
Selling Expense Budget
For the Second Quarter Ending June 30

	April	May	June	Quarter Total
Budgeted sales (**Exhibit 9.4**)	$190,000	$228,000	$250,000	$668,000
Variable selling expenses				
Setup/Display (1% sales)	$ 1,900	$ 2,280	$ 2,500	$ 6,680
Commissions (2% sales)	3,800	4,560	5,000	13,360
Miscellaneous (1% sales)	1,900	2,280	2,500	6,680
Total	7,600	9,120	10,000	26,720
Fixed selling expenses				
Advertising	2,250	2,250	2,250	6,750
Office	1,250	1,250	1,250	3,750
Miscellaneous	1,000	1,000	1,000	3,000
Total	4,500	4,500	4,500	13,500
Total selling expenses	$ 12,100	$ 13,620	$ 14,500	$ 40,220

General and Administrative Expense Budget

The **general and administrative expense budget** presents the expenses the organization plans to incur in connection with the general administration of the organization. Included are expenses for the accounting department, the computer center, and the president's office, for example. REI's assumed general and administrative expense budget is presented in **Exhibit 9.7**.

General and administrative expense budget

The general and administrative expense budget presents the expenses the organization plans to incur in connection with the general administration of the organization.

Exhibit 9.7 General and Administrative Expense Budget

REI
General and Administrative Expense Budget
For the Second Quarter Ending June 30

	April	May	June	Quarter Total
General and administrative expenses				
Compensation	$25,000	$25,000	$25,000	$75,000
Insurance	2,000	2,000	2,000	6,000
Depreciation	2,000	2,000	2,000	6,000
Utilities	3,000	3,000	3,000	9,000
Miscellaneous	1,000	1,000	1,000	3,000
Total general and administrative expenses	$33,000	$33,000	$33,000	$99,000

The depreciation of $2,000 per month is a noncash item and is not carried forward to the cash budget. No variable general and administrative costs are included because most expenditures categorized as general and administrative are related to top-management operations that do not vary with unit-level cost drivers. To simplify the presentation of the cash budget, the budget assumes that general and administrative expenses, except depreciation, are paid in the month they are incurred.

Cash Budget

The **cash budget** summarizes all cash receipts and disbursements expected to occur during the budget period. Cash is critical to survival. Income is like food and cash is like water. Food is necessary to survive and prosper over time, but you can get along without food for a short period of time. You cannot survive very long without water. Hence, cash budgeting is very important, especially in a small business where cash receipts from sales lag purchases of inventory. As pointed out in the following Business Insight, cash budgets are also critical for managing the impact of changing customer preferences.

Business Insight ■ Budgeting within a Consumer Products Giant

Budgeting within a large diversified multinational corporation is challenging when the business spans many markets and countries. Unilever operates segments across the globe with product lines from dairy to skin care, so the company must make sure it has the ability to invest in new products in these areas while insulating its performance from exchange rate fluctuations. In the first quarter of 2016, Unilever PCL posted an increase in both volume and price of sales but a 2% decrease in revenue. To limit its exposure to exchange rates, Unilever adopted strict cost controls and restructured its portfolio of brands to keep up with shifting demand.

Unilever's food business has been lagging behind other areas, especially personal care. Originally a Dutch margarine producer, Unilever is considering dropping the butter substitute altogether. Unilever is shifting resources to focus on men's skin and hair care as men are spending more time and money on their appearance and customers are returning to real butter. Rob Candelino, VP of hair care marketing at Unilever, says that "This generation of man—on all aspects of how they are taking care of themselves—is caring much more than previous generations." Therefore, the company is developing new products and has acquired the Dollar Shave Club, a low-cost direct provider of shaving supplies for men.

Careful cash budgeting is essential for Unilever in managing the impact of changing customer preferences and global economic fluctuations while still investing in continued growth.

Sources: Saabira Chaudhuri, "Unilever Sales Fall on Currencies, Offsetting Better Volume, Prices," *Wall Street Journal*, April 14, 2016.
Sharon Terlep, "Dollar Shave Club's $1 Billion Deal: A Victory for Simplicity over Technology," *Wall Street Journal*, July 20, 2016.
Elizabeth Holmes, "Young Men Are Obsessed with Their Hair" *Wall Street Journal*, March 1, 2016.
Saabira Chaudhuri, "Will Margarine Become Toast at Unilever?" *Wall Street Journal*, January 19, 2016.

After it makes sales predictions, an organization uses information regarding credit terms, collections policy, and prior collection experience to develop a cash collections budget. Collections on sales normally include receipts from the current period's sales and collections from sales of prior periods. An allowance for bad debts, which reduces each period's collections, is also predicted. Other items often included are cash sales, sales discounts, allowances for volume discounts, and seasonal changes of sales prices and collections. REI's assumed cash budget is in **Exhibit 9.8**. Note the following important points:

- Management estimates that one-half of all sales are for cash and the other half are on the company's credit card. (When sales are on bank credit cards, the collection is immediate, less any bank user fee; however, the budget assumes charges using REI's credit card are collected by the company from the customer.) Twenty-five percent of the credit card sales are collected in the month of sale, and 74% are collected in the following month. Bad debts are budgeted at 1% of credit sales. This resource flow is graphically illustrated as follows:

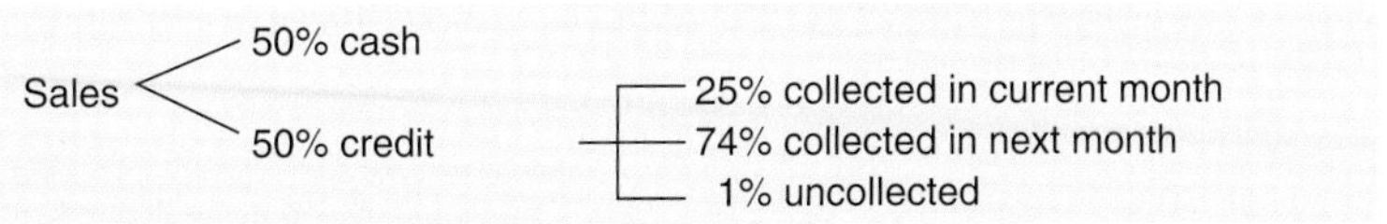

- The budget assumes payments for purchases are made 20% in the month purchased and 80% in the next month.

Cash budget

The cash budget summarizes all cash receipts and disbursements expected to occur during the budget period.

Exhibit 9.8 Cash Budget

REI Cash Budget For the Second Quarter Ending June 30	April	May	June	Quarter Total
Budgeted sales (**Exhibit 9.4**)	$190,000	$228,000	$250,000	$668,000
Cash balance, beginning	$ 15,000	$ 15,770	$ 44,850	$ 15,000
Collections on sales				
Cash sales (50% sales)	95,000	114,000	125,000	
Credit sales				
Current month (25% credit sales)	23,750	28,500	31,250	
Prior month (74% credit sales)	59,200*	70,300	84,360	
Total	177,950	212,800	240,610	631,360
Cash available for operations	192,950	228,570	285,460	646,360
Disbursements				
Purchases (**Exhibit 9.5**)				
Current month (20% purchases)	25,080	28,680	33,540	
Prior month (80% purchases)	84,000**	100,320	114,720	
Total	109,080	129,000	148,260	386,340
Selling expenses (**Exhibit 9.6**)	12,100	13,620	14,500	40,220
General & Administrative Expenses (**Exhibit 9.7**, excluding depreciation)	31,000	31,000	31,000	93,000
Taxes (**Exhibit 9.3**)	35,000			35,000
Total	(187,180)	(173,620)	(193,760)	(554,560)
Excess (deficiency) cash available over disbursements	5,770	54,950	91,700	91,800
Short-term financing***				
New loans	10,000			10,000
Repayments		(10,000)		(10,000)
Interest	—	(100)	—	(100)
Net cash from financing	10,000	(10,100)	—	(100)
Cash balance, ending	$ 15,770	$ 44,850	$ 91,700	$ 91,700

*April 1 accounts receivable.
**April 1 accounts payable.
***Loans are obtained in $1,000 increments at the start of the month to maintain a minimum balance of $15,000 at all times. Repayments are made at the end of the month, as soon as adequate cash is available. Assume interest of 12% per year (1% per month) is paid when the loan is repaid.

- Information on cash expenditures for selling expenses and for general and administrative expenses is based on budgets for these items. The monthly cash expenditures for general and administrative expenses are $31,000 rather than $33,000. The $2,000 difference relates to depreciation, which does not require use of cash.
- The budget assumes REI's income taxes are determined on the basis of predicted taxable income following IRS rules. Estimated tax payments are made during the month following the end of each quarter. Hence, the taxes payable on April 1 are paid during April.
- The cash budget shows cash operating deficiencies and surpluses expected to occur at the end of each month; this is used to plan for borrowing and loan payment.
- The budget assumes the cash maintenance policy for REI specifies that a minimum balance of $15,000 is to be maintained.

- The budget assumes REI has a line of credit with a bank, with any interest on borrowed funds computed at the simple interest rate of 12.0% per year, or 1.0% per month. All necessary borrowing is assumed to occur at the start of each month in increments of $1,000. Repayments including interest are assumed to occur at the end of the month.
- The cash budget indicates REI needs to borrow $10,000 in April. The $10,000 plus interest is repaid in May.

If REI had any cash disbursements for dividends or capital expenditures, they would be included in the cash budget. These items, along with information on income taxes, would be shown in special budgets.

Budgeted Financial Statements

The preparation of the master budget culminates in the preparation of budgeted financial statements. **Budgeted financial statements** are pro forma statements that reflect the "as-if" effects of the budgeted activities on the actual financial position of the organization. That is, the statements reflect the results of operations assuming all budget predictions are correct. Spreadsheets that permit the user to immediately determine the impact of any assumed changes facilitate developing budgeted financial statements. The budgeted income statement can follow the functional format traditionally used for financial accounting or the contribution format introduced in Chapter 3. In either case, the balance sheet amounts reflect the corresponding budgeted entries.

Exhibit 9.9 presents the budgeted income statement for the quarter ending June 30. If all predictions made in the operating budget are correct, REI will produce a net income of $51,540 for the quarter. Almost every item on the budgeted income statement comes from one of the budget schedules.

Exhibit 9.9 Budgeted Income Statement

REI Budgeted Income Statement For the Second Quarter Ending June 30		
Sales (**Exhibit 9.4**)		$668,000
Cost of goods sold*		
Beginning inventory (**Exhibit 9.3**)	$157,000	
Purchases (**Exhibit 9.5**)	436,500	
Cost of merchandise available	593,500	
Ending inventory (**Exhibit 9.5**)	(192,700)	(400,800)
Gross profit		267,200
Other expenses		
Bad debt (1% of credit sales)**	3,340	
Selling (**Exhibit 9.6**)	40,220	
General and administrative (**Exhibit 9.7**)	99,000	(142,560)
Income from operations		124,640
Interest expense (**Exhibit 9.8**)		(100)
Net income from operations		124,540
Allowance for income taxes***		(73,000)
Net income		$ 51,540

*Also computed at sales × 0.6
**$668,000 × 0.5 credit sales × 0.01 bad debts
***Provided by accounting

The budgeted balance sheet, presented in **Exhibit 9.10**, shows REI's financial position as of June 30, assuming that all budget predictions are correct. Sources of the budgeted balance sheet data are included as part of the exhibit.

Exhibit 9.10 Budgeted Balance Sheet

REI Balance Sheet June 30			
Assets			
Current assets			
Cash (**Exhibit 9.8**)		$ 91,700	
Accounts receivable, net*		92,500	
Merchandise inventory (Exhibits 9.5 and 9.9)		192,700	$376,900
Fixed assets			
Buildings and equipment (**Exhibit 9.3**)	$460,000		
Less accumulated depreciation (**Exhibit 9.3** plus depreciation **Exhibit 9.7**)	(130,800)	329,200	
Land (**Exhibit 9.3**)		60,000	389,200
Total assets			$766,100
Liabilities and Stockholders' Equity			
Current liabilities			
Accounts payable**		$134,160	
Taxes payable (**Exhibit 9.9**)		73,000	$207,160
Stockholders' equity			
Capital stock (**Exhibit 9.3**)		350,000	
Retained earnings (**Exhibit 9.3** plus net income **Exhibit 9.9**)		208,940	558,940
Total liabilities and stockholders' equity			$766,100

*June credit sales collected in July, $250,000 × 0.50 × 0.74.
**June purchases paid in July, $167,700 × 0.80.

Finalizing the Budget

After studying the REI example, you might conclude that developing the master budget is a mechanical process. That is not the case. Understanding the basics of budget assembly is not the end; it is a tool to assist in efficient and effective budgeting. Before finalizing the budget, the following two questions must be addressed:

- Is the proposed budget feasible?
- Is the proposed budget acceptable?

To be feasible, the organization must be able to actually implement the proposed budget. Without the assumed line of credit, REI's budget is not feasible because the company would run out of cash sometime in April. Knowing this, management can take timely corrective action. Possible actions include obtaining equity financing, issuing long-term debt, reducing the amount of inventory on hand at the end of each quarter, or obtaining a line of credit. Other constraints that would make the budget infeasible include the availability of merchandise and, in the case of a manufacturing organization, production capacity.

Once management determines that the budget is feasible, they still need to determine if it is acceptable. To evaluate acceptability, management might consider various financial ratios, such as return on assets. They might compare the return provided by the proposed budget with past returns, industry averages, or some organizational goal.

Preparing a Budget for a Merchandising Organization

LO3 Review 9-3

Bleu Mont Dairy is a wholesale distributor of artisan cheese and ice cream. Suppose the following information is available for April.

Estimated sales	
Cheese	160,000 hoops at $10 each
Ice cream	240,000 gallons at $5 each

Estimated costs	
Cheese	$8 per hoop
Ice cream	$2 per gallon

	Beginning	Ending
Desired inventories (in units)		
Cheese	10,000	12,000
Ice cream	4,000	5,000

Assumed financial information follows:

- Beginning cash balance is $400,000.
- Purchases of merchandise are paid 60% in the month of purchase and 40% in the following month. Purchases totaled $1,800,000 in March and are estimated to be $2,000,000 in May.
- Employee wages and salaries are paid for in the current month. Employee expenses for April totaled $156,000.
- Overhead expenses are paid in the next month. The accounts payable amount for these expenses from March is $80,000 and for May will be $90,000. April's overhead expenses total $80,000.
- Sales are on credit and are collected 70% in the current period and the remainder in the next period. March's sales were $3,000,000, and May's sales are estimated to be $3,200,000. Bad debts average 1% of sales.
- Selling and administrative expenses are paid monthly and total $450,000, including $40,000 of depreciation.
- All unit costs for April are the same as they were in March.

Required

Prepare the following for April:

a. Sales budget in dollars.
b. Purchases budget.
c. Cash budget.
d. Budgeted income statement.

Solution on p. 347.

Budget Development in Manufacturing Organizations

LO4 Explain and develop a basic manufacturing cost budget.

The importance of inventory in various organizations was introduced in Chapter 5 where **Exhibit 5.1** (page 155) summarized inventory and related expense accounts for service, merchandising, and manufacturing organizations. Recall that service organizations usually have a low percentage of their assets invested in inventory, usually consisting of the supplies needed to facilitate operations. In contrast, merchandising organizations usually have a high percentage of their total assets invested in inventory, with the largest inventory investment in merchandise purchased for resale. The preceding illustration of the development of a master budget was for a merchandising organization. In this section, we will illustrate the the development of a master budget for a manufacturing organization. We will contrast the assembly of a budget for a merchandiser in **Exhibit 9.2** with the assembly of a budget for a manufacturer in **Exhibit 9.11**.

Exhibit 9.11 Budget Assembly for a Manufacturer

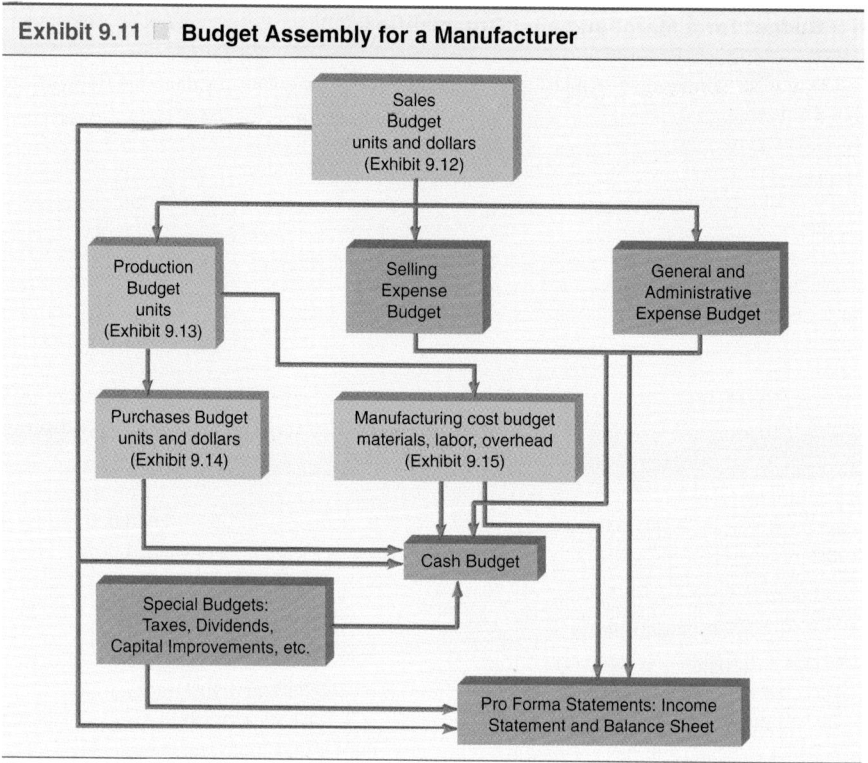

Production Budget

Because manufacturing organizations convert raw materials into finished goods that are sold to customers, there are additional steps in developing their master budget. The management of a manufacturing organization must determine the production volume required to support sales and finished goods ending inventory requirements (production budget). Then, based on available inventories or raw materials and the raw materials required for production, management develops a purchases budget.

Manufacturing Cost Budget

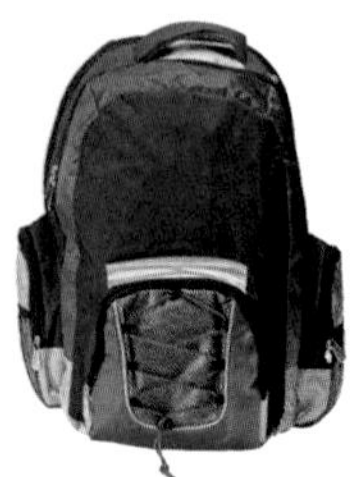

In addition to a selling expense budget and a general and administrative expense budget, management needs also to develop a manufacturing cost budget, which is similar in design to a statement of cost of goods manufactured (see **Exhibit 5.6**, page 168) except that it is prepared in advance of production rather than after production. Reflecting these additional steps, the cash budget includes payments for direct labor and manufacturing overhead, based on information in the manufacturing cost budget, and payments for purchases of raw materials based on the purchases budget. Note cash disbursements are for materials purchased rather than materials used in production.

Continuing our REI example, assume that management is considering the option of manufacturing a high-quality backpack, tentatively named the "Trekpack" as an alternative to purchasing a similar item from an outside vendor. Unit variable and monthly fixed cost estimates associated with the manufacture of Trekpacks follow:

Unit costs		
Direct materials		
Fabric: 2 square yards at $10 per yard	$20	
Hardware kits (buckles, straps, etc.)	5	$ 25
Direct labor 0.5 hours at $30 per hour		15
Variable overhead, per unit		8
Total variable costs per unit		$ 48
Fixed costs per month (rent, utilities, supervision)		$6,000

Because management anticipates an average monthly production volume of 500 Trekpacks, the average fixed cost per unit, a predetermined overhead rate, is $12 ($6,000/500).

For budgeting purposes, management uses a standard cost, a budget per unit of product, for valuing inventories and forecasting the cost of goods sold. The standard cost of a Trekpack is $60:

Direct materials	$25
Direct labor	15
Variable overhead	8
Fixed overhead	12
Standard cost	$60

Management, planning to introduce this new product in May, developed the sales budget shown in **Exhibit 9.12**. In this case, because unit information is necessary to determine production requirements, the sales budget is expressed in units as well as dollars.

Introducing Trekpacks in May requires some April production. To meet the initial sales requirement for the start of each month, management desires end-of-month inventories equal to 40% of the following month's budgeted sales. The sales budget and ending inventory plans, along with information on beginning inventories, are used to develop the production budget in **Exhibit 9.13**.

The production budget, along with information on beginning inventories of raw materials and planned ending inventory levels (500 square yards of fabric and 200 kits), is then used to budget the purchases in **Exhibit 9.14** for raw materials in units and dollars. The production budget, along with standard variable and predicted fixed cost information, is also used to develop the manufacturing cost budget in **Exhibit 9.15**.

Because it does not require the introduction of new concepts, the cash budget and the pro forma financial statements for REI with the manufacturing of Trekpacks are not presented. Keep in mind that the cash budget will include disbursements for purchases shown in **Exhibit 9.14** and for direct labor, variable overhead, and fixed overhead shown in **Exhibit 9.15**. A pro forma functional income statement using absorption costing will include the predicted cost of goods sold for Trekpacks at a $60 standard cost per unit. A contribution income statement using variable costing would include the cost of goods sold for Trekpacks at a $48 standard cost per unit with all fixed manufacturing costs expensed

Manufacturing sales budget

Because unit information is necessary to determine production requirements, the sales budget is expressed in units as well as dollars.

Exhibit 9.12 Sales Budget

REI
Sales Budget (Trekpacks)
For the Second Quarter Ending June 30

	April	May	June	Quarter Total	July
Sales—Units	0	400	500	900	600
Sales—Dollars ($100 each)	0	$40,000	$50,000	$90,000	$60,000

Production budget

The sales budget and ending inventory plans, along with information on beginning inventories, are used to develop the production budget.

Exhibit 9.13 Production Budget

REI
Production Budget (Trekpacks)
For the Second Quarter Ending June 30

	April	May	June	Quarter Total
Budgeted sales	0	400	500	900
Desired ending inventory 40% following month sales	160	200	240	240
Total requirements	160	600	740	1,140
Less beginning inventory	0	(160)	(200)	0
Budgeted production	160	440	540	1,140

in the period incurred. Finally, the pro forma balance sheet will include standard costs of any June raw materials (500 square yards at $10 per yard and 200 kits at $5 each), work in process (none), and finished goods. Any unpaid liabilities for purchases of raw materials, direct labor, and manufacturing overhead would also be shown under current liabilities. Note that completing the cash budget and the pro forma statements requires information on the timing of payments for the purchases of raw materials, direct labor, and manufacturing overhead.

Purchases budget

The production budget, along with information on beginning inventories of raw materials and planned ending inventory levels, is then used to budget the purchases for raw materials in units and dollars.

Exhibit 9.14 Purchase Budget

REI
Purchases Budget
For the Second Quarter Ending June 30

	April	May	June	Quarter Total
Fabric				
Current needs (2 yards per unit)	320	880	1,080	2,280
Desired ending inventory (500 yards)	500	500	500	500
Total requirements	820	1,380	1,580	2,780
Less beginning inventory	(0)	(500)	(500)	(0)
Fabric purchases in yards	820	880	1,080	2,780
Assembly kits				
Current needs (1 per unit)	160	440	540	1,140
Desired ending inventory (200 kits)	200	200	200	200
Total requirements	360	640	740	1,340
Less beginning inventory	(0)	(200)	(200)	(0)
Kit purchases in units	360	440	540	1,340
Purchases (Dollars)				
Fabric at $10 per yard	$ 8,200	$ 8,800	$10,800	$27,800
Kits at $5 each	1,800	2,200	2,700	6,700
Total purchases in dollars	$10,000	$11,000	$13,500	$34,500

Manufacturing cost budget

The production budget, along with standard variable and predicted fixed cost information, is also used to develop the manufacturing cost budget.

Exhibit 9.15 Manufacturing Cost Budget

REI
Manufacturing Cost Budget
For the Second Quarter Ending June 30

	April	May	June	Quarter Total
Direct materials				
Fabric used in production (production × 2 yards × $10)	$ 3,200	$ 8,800	$10,800	$22,800
Kits used in production (production × 1 kit × $5)	800	2,200	2,700	5,700
Total	4,000	11,000	13,500	28,500
Direct labor (production × 1/2 hour × $30)	2,400	6,600	8,100	17,100
Manufacturing overhead				
Variable ($8 per unit)	1,280	3,520	4,320	9,120
Fixed	6,000	6,000	6,000	18,000
Total	7,280	9,520	10,320	27,120
Total manufacturing costs	$13,680	$27,120	$31,920	$72,720

Preparing a Budget for a Manufacturer LO4 **Review 9-4**

Assume DeWalt, a subsidiary of Stanley Black and Decker, manufactures and sells two industrial products in a single plant. Suppose a new manager wants to have quarterly budgets and has prepared the following information for the first quarter of the year:

Budgeted sales		
Drills	60,000 at $100 each	
Saws	40,000 at $125 each	
Budgeted inventories	**Beginning**	**Ending**
Drills, finished	20,000 units	25,000 units
Saws, finished	8,000 units	10,000 units
Metal, direct materials	32,000 pounds	36,000 pounds
Plastic, direct materials	29,000 pounds	32,000 pounds
Handles, direct materials	6,000 each	7,000 each

Standard variable costs per unit

	Drills		**Saws**	
Direct materials				
Metal	5 pounds × $8.00	$40.00	4 pounds × $8.00	$32.00
Plastic	3 pounds × $5.00	15.00	3 pounds × $5.00	15.00
Handles	1 handle × $3.00	3.00		
Total		58.00		47.00
Direct labor	2 labor hours × $12.00	24.00	3 labor hours × $16.00	48.00
Variable manufacturing Overhead	2 hours × $1.50	3.00	3 hours × $1.50	4.50
Total		$85.00		$99.50

Assume fixed manufacturing overhead is $214,000 per quarter (including noncash expenditures of $156,000) and is allocated on total units produced. Financial information follows:

- Beginning cash balance is $1,800,000.
- Sales are on credit and are collected 50% in the current period and the remainder in the next period. Last quarter's sales were $8,400,000. There are no bad debts.
- Purchases of direct materials and labor costs are paid for in the quarter acquired.
- Manufacturing overhead expenses are paid in the quarter incurred.
- Selling and administrative expenses are all fixed and are paid in the quarter incurred. They are budgeted at $340,000 per quarter, including $90,000 of depreciation.

Required

For the first quarter of the year, prepare the following:

a. Sales budget in dollars.
b. Production budget in units.
c. Purchases budget.
d. Manufacturing cost budget.
e. Cash budget.
f. Budgeted contribution income statement. (*Hint:* See Chapter 3.)

Solution on p. 349.

Budget Development and Manager Behavior

LO5 Analyze the relationship between budget development and manager behavior.

Organizations are composed of individuals who perform a wide variety of activities in pursuit of the organization's goals. To accomplish these goals, management must recognize the effects that budgeting and performance evaluation methods have on the behavior of the organization's employees.

Employee Participation

Budgeting should be used to promote productive employee behavior directed toward meeting the organization's goals. While no two organizations use exactly the same budgeting procedures, two approaches to employee involvement in budgeting represent possible end points on a continuum. These approaches are sometimes referred to as top-down and bottom-up methods.

With a **top-down** or **imposed budget**, top management identifies the primary goals and objectives for the organization and communicates them to lower management levels. Because relatively few people are involved in top-down budgeting, an imposed budget saves time. It also minimizes the slack that managers at lower organizational levels are sometimes prone to build into their budgets. However, this nonparticipative approach to budgeting can have undesirable motivational consequences. Personnel who do not participate in budget preparation might lack a commitment to achieve their part of the budget.

With a **bottom-up** or **participative budget**, managers at all levels—and in some cases, even nonmanagers—are involved in budget preparation. Budget proposals originate at the lowest level of management possible and are then integrated into the proposals for the next level, and so on, until the proposals reach the top level of management, which completes the budget.

Participation helps ensure that important issues are considered and that employees understand the importance of their roles in meeting the organization's goals. It also provides opportunities for problem solving and fosters employee commitment to agreed-upon goals. Hence, budget predictions are likely to be more accurate, and the people responsible for the budget are more likely to strive to accomplish its objectives. These self-imposed budgets reinforce the concept of participative management and should strengthen the overall budgeting process.

Budgetary slack

Cushion created in a budget to minimize risk that managers might fail to meet budgeted results.

Participative approaches to budgeting have a few disadvantages. Because they require the involvement of many people, the preparation period is longer than that for an imposed budget. Another disadvantage is the tendency of some managers to intentionally understate revenues or overstate expenses to provide **budgetary slack**. A manager might do this to reduce his or her concern regarding unfavorable performance reviews or to make it easier to obtain favorable performance reviews. If a department consistently produces favorable variances (actual results versus budget) with little apparent effort, this might be a symptom of budgetary slack.

Managerial Decision ■ You Are the Chief Financial Officer

As the CFO of a relatively new and fast-growing entrepreneurial enterprise, you and the other top managers have previously emphasized technical and marketing innovation and creativity over planning and budgeting. But now with growing competition and the maturing of the company's products, you recognized that a culture of better financial planning must be established if the company is to succeed in the long run. You feel that the financial staff has the best expertise and understanding of the business to prepare effective budgets, but you are concerned about the motivational effects of excluding the lower-level managers from the process and are seeking advice. [Answer, p. 331.]

Budgeting Periods

Although most organizations use a one-year budget period, some organizations budget for shorter or longer periods. In addition to fixed-length budget periods, two other types of budget periods commonly used are life-cycle budgeting and continuous budgeting.

When a fixed time period is not particularly relevant to planning, an organization can use **life-cycle budgeting**, which involves developing a budget for a project's entire life. An ice cream vendor at the beach might develop a budget for the season. A general contractor might budget costs for the entire (multiple-year) time required to construct a building.

Under **continuous budgeting**, the budget (sometimes called a **rolling budget**) is based on a moving time frame. For example, an organization on a continuous four-quarter budget system adds a quarter to the budget at the end of each quarter of operations, thereby always maintaining a budget for four quarters into the future. Under this system, plans for a full year into the future are always available, whereas under a fixed annual budget, operating plans for a full year ahead are available only at the beginning of the budget year. Because managers are constantly involved in this type of budgeting, the budget process becomes an active and integral part of the management process. Managers are forced to be future oriented throughout the year rather than just once each year.

Forecasts

Budget preparation requires the development of a variety of forecasts. The sales forecast is based on a variety of interrelated factors such as historical trends, product innovation, general economic conditions, industry conditions, and the organization's strategic position for competing on the basis of price, product differentiation, or market niche. Many organizations first determine the industry forecast for a given product or service and then extract from it their sales estimations.

Although the sales forecast is primary to most organizations, there are many other forecasts of varying importance that must be made, including (a) the collection period for sales on account, (b) percent of uncollectable sales on account, (c) cost of materials, supplies, utilities, and so forth, (d) employee turnover, (e) time required to perform activities, (f) interest rates, and (g) development time for new products or services.

Business Insight ■ Developing Honesty in Budgeting

Often the budgeting process involves soliciting information from mid-level managers, and honesty in this participative process is essential. Lower-level managers often have much better information about their sphere of the company's operations, but often these managers have financial incentives to misreport.

Experiments by researchers at the University of Indiana and the University of Kentucky suggest that publishing rankings of division performance can eliminate these incentives. When mid-level managers are ranked by their department's contribution to firm performance, their budget reports become quite accurate. This result is independent of the manager's compensation structure. Firms who rely heavily on information from mid-level managers should be careful to construct incentive and recognition structures that encourage honest reporting.

Source: Jason L. Brown, Joseph G. Fisher, Matthew Sooy, and Geoffrey B. Sprinkle, "The Effect of Rankings on Honesty in Budget Reporting," *Accounting, Organizations and Society*, 39, no. 4 (May 2014): 237–246. http://dx.doi.org/10.1016/j.aos.2014.03.001.

Ethics

Because most wrongful activities related to budgeting are unethical, rather than illegal, organizations often have difficulty dealing with them. However, when managers' actions cross the gray area between ethical and fraudulent behavior, organizations are not reluctant to dismiss employees or even pursue legal actions against them.

Although most managers have a natural inclination to be conservative in developing their budgets, at some level the blatant padding or building slack into the budget becomes unethical. In an extreme case, it might even be considered theft if an inordinate level of budgetary slack creates favorable performance variances that lead to significant bonuses or other financial gain for the manager. Another form of falsifying budgets occurs when managers include expense categories in their budgets that are not needed in their operations and subsequently use the funds to pad other budget categories. The deliberate falsification of budgets is unethical behavior and is grounds for dismissal in most organizations.

Ethical issues might also arise in the reporting of performance results, which usually compares actual data with budgeted data. Examples of unethical reporting of actual performance data include misclassification of expenses, overstating revenues or understating expenses, postponing or accelerating the recording of activities at the end of the accounting period, or creating fictitious activities.

Open Book Management

If an organization is to obtain the full benefit of budgeting, support for the budget must be obtained from employees at all levels. Many organizations, especially smaller ones, have used open book management to obtain employee support for the budget. **Open book management** involves sharing financial and related information with employees, teaching employees to understand financial numbers, encouraging employees to use the information in their work, and sharing financial results with employees, perhaps through a bonus program. The following Research Insight examines the success of open book management in small companies.

Properly used, an operating budget is an effective mechanism for motivating employees to higher levels of performance and productivity. Improperly developed and administered, budgets can foster feelings of animosity toward management and the budget process. Behavioral research has generally concluded that when employees participate in the preparation of budgets and believe that the budgets represent fair standards for evaluating their performance, they receive personal satisfaction from accomplishing the goals set in the budgets.

Research Insight ■ Open Book Management Opens the Door to Profits

Open book management has its roots at Springfield Remanufacturing Corp. (SRC). In the late 1970s, SRC was a subsidiary of International Harvester and was losing money. International Harvester sent a new plant manager, Jack Stack, to turn SRC around. Stack made SRC profitable by sharing information and using gamification techniques to improve firm performance. Stack's performance game is based on three principles:

1. Transparency: Make the business's goals and planning transparent; then continually educate employees about the plan.
2. Involvement: Involve employees in both planning and ownership.
3. Measurement: Create a "Critical Number," a measure of performance that the whole organization is invested in working toward.

The key to this approach is that all employees understand how their work fits into the larger success of the organization, and share the proceeds from success. In this context, sharing financial information with employees empowers them to find solutions to problems and inefficiencies throughout the organization.

This approach was so successful that in 1983 Stack and 12 employees bought SRC from International Harvester and have since grown the business to 1,200 employee-owners and 31 businesses, including a corporate training and education practice. The success of these practices extends far beyond SRC. Research by the McGill University Institute for Health and Social Policy finds that firms large and small are able to improve efficiency and profitability by following SRC's model.

Sources: Neil Amato, "Opening the Books, Growing the Business," *CGMA Magazine*, June 1, 2016.
Jody Heymann, with Magda Berrerra, "Profit at the Bottom of the Ladder," *Harvard Business School Press*, 2010.

Review 9-5 LO5 Identifying Manager Behaviors Related to Operational Budgeting

Items 1 though 4 represent manager behaviors related to operational budgeting.

1. Budgetary Slack
2. Participative Budget
3. Open Book Management
4. Life-Cycle Budgeting

Required

Identify the above term that most appropriately describes the scenarios below:

_____ *a.* The marketing department is asked to provide an estimate as to how much it will spend on print ads during the next fiscal year.

_____ *b.* The marketing department provides a budget amount for print ads for the next fiscal year that includes the expected expenditures plus 10% to account for uncertainty.

_____ *c.* Tristan Renken owns and operates a food truck that sells Mexican food along the beaches in Chicago. Tristan only operates the food truck during the summer and developed a budget to estimate how much he will make during the upcoming summer season.

_____ *d.* Top management hosts semi-annual meetings to discuss the budget and current performance vs. the budget. Management provides employees with tools to help gauge their own performance against the budgeted expectations.

Solution on p. 351.

Guidance Answers

You Are the Chief Financial Officer

Pg. 328 You seem to be leaning toward using a top-down approach to budgeting. While this method may produce an effective set of benchmarks for planning and evaluation, it does not maximize the benefits of budgeting. A key element in any effective budgeting system is that it must be embraced by the managers whose performance will be evaluated by it. If the budget is imposed from the top down, it is far less likely to be embraced by managers than if they have participated from the beginning of the budget development process. The most effective budgeting systems are those that are strongly embraced by managers at all levels, which is most readily achieved through a participative (bottom-up) approach.

Key Terms

activity-based approach, 312
bottom-up budget, 328
budget, 310
budgetary slack, 328
budgeted financial statements, 321
cash budget, 319
continuous budgeting, 328
general and administrative expense budget, 318
imposed budget, 328
incremental approach, 312
life-cycle budgeting, 328
management by exception, 311
master budget, 314
minimum level approach, 313
open book management, 329
operating activities, 316
operating budgets, 310
output/input approach, 312
participative budget, 328
purchases budget, 317
risk, 311
risk management, 311
rolling budget, 328
sales budget, 316
selling expense budget, 318
top-down budget, 328
zero-based budgeting, 313

Multiple Choice

1. Each of the following is a true statement regarding the budgeting process, except
a. The budget is the basis for evaluating performance.
b. Budgets represent a guide for accomplishing goals and objectives.
c. The budget is developed by the finance team and its primary purpose is to predict costs.
d. An organization's budget model can be used to evaluate the financial impact of a risk.

2. Budgeted sales of the East End Burger Joint for the first quarter of the year are as follows:

January	$50,000
February	60,000
March	68,000

The cost of sales averages 40% of sales revenue and management desires ending inventories equal to 25% of the following month's sales. Assuming the January 1 inventory is $5,000, the January purchases budget is
a. $19,000
b. $21,000
c. $31,000
d. $69,000

3. Syracuse Distribution's sales budget for the first quarter follows:

January	$250,000
February	300,000
March	290,000

Multiple Choice Answers
1. c 2. b 3. c 4. b 5. b 6. c

All sales are on account (credit) with 50% collected in the month of sale, 30% collected in the month after sale, and 20% collected in the second month after sale. There are no uncollectable accounts. The March cash receipts are

a. $140,000
b. $235,000
c. $285,000
d. None of the above

4. Refer to question 2 and determine the accounts receivable at the end of March:

a. $147,000
b. $205,000
c. $235,000
d. $285,000

5. Presented is selected second quarter budget data for the Arnold Company.

	Sales
April	20,000 units
May	30,000 units
June	36,000 units

Additional information:

- Each unit of finished product requires three pounds of raw materials.
- Arnold maintains ending finished goods inventories equal to 20% of the following month's budgeted sales.
- Arnold maintains raw materials inventories equal to 25% of the following month's budgeted production.
- April 1 inventories are in line with Arnold's inventory policy.

Arnold's budgeted purchases (in pounds) for April are

a. 66,000 pounds
b. 72,900 pounds
c. 89,400 pounds
d. None of the above

6. Presented is additional information for the Arnold Company (refer to question 4):

- Price per pound of raw materials — $20
- Direct labor per unit of finished product — 0.40 hours at $25 per hour
- Total monthly factory overhead — $200,000 + $10 per direct labor hour

Arnold's total manufacturing cost budget for April is

a. $880,000
b. $1,680,000
c. $1,828,000
d. $1,966,000

Questions

Q9-1. What are the primary phases in the planning and control cycle?

Q9-2. Does budgeting require formal or informal planning? What are some advantages of this style of management?

Q9-3. Identify the advantages and disadvantages of the incremental approach to budgeting.

Q9-4. Explain the minimum level approach to budgeting.

Q9-5. How does activity-based budgeting predict a cost objective's budget?

Q9-6. Explain the continuous improvement concept of budgeting.

Q9-7. Which budget brings together all other budgets? How is this accomplished?

Q9-8. What budgets are normally used to support the cash budget? What is the net result of cash budget preparations?

Q9-9. Define *budgeted financial statements.*

Q9-10. Identify the two budgets that are part of the master budget of a manufacturing organization but not part of the master budget of a merchandising organization.

Q9-11. Contrast the top-down and bottom-up approaches to budget preparation.

Q9-12. Is budgetary slack a desirable feature? Can it be prevented? Why or why not?

Q9-13. Why are annual budgets not always desirable? What are some alternative budget periods?

Q9-14. Explain how continuous budgeting works.

Q9-15. In addition to the sales forecast, what forecasts are used in budgeting?

Q9-16. Why should motivational considerations be a part of budget planning and utilization? List several ways to motivate employees with budgets.

Assignments with the logo in the margin are available in myBusinessCourse. See the Preface of the book for details.

Mini Exercises

M9-17. Output/Input Budget LO2

Vinyard Clinic has the following resource input information available for a routine physical examination.

- Each exam normally requires 0.75 hours of examining room time, including
  - 30 minutes of nursing services,
  - 15 minutes of physician services.
- Each exam also utilizes one package of examination supplies costing $50 each.
- Including benefits, physicians earn $90/hour and nurses earn $35/hour.
- Variable overhead is budgeted at $15 per examining room hour and fixed overhead is budgeted at $8,000 per month.

Required

Prepare an output/input budget for October when 500 routine examinations are planned. Discuss some of the likely benefits to Vinyard Clinic of dedicating time to go through the budgeting process.

M9-18. Incremental Budget LO2

Wood County uses an incremental approach to budgeting. The current year cash budget for the Wood County Department of Motor Vehicles is presented as follows:

Supplies	$ 12,000
Temporary and seasonal wages	32,000
Wages of full-time employees	200,000
Supervisor salaries	60,000
Rent	48,000
Insurance	16,000
Utilities	10,000
Miscellaneous	9,600
Contingencies and equipment	25,000
Total	$412,600

Required

Prepare an incremental cash budget for next year, assuming the planned total budget increase is 3%. Budget details include a budget increment for salaries and wages of 3%, no change in rent, and 2.5% increases in the budget for supplies and miscellaneous. Utility companies have received approvals for rate increases amounting to 2% and insurance companies have announced an increase in premiums of 4%. (*Hint:* The Contingencies and equipment budget is a plug.)

M9-19. Purchases Budget in Units and Dollars LO3 Thunder Road Guitars

Thunder Road Guitars specializes in vintage, used, and rare guitars. Assume budgeted sales for the first six months of the year are as follows:

Month	Unit Sales	Month	Unit Sales
January	15	April	18
February	12	May	22
March	16	June	20

Beginning inventory for the year is 7 units. The budgeted inventory at the end of a month is 50% of units to be sold the following month. Purchase price per unit is $800.

Required

Prepare a purchases budget in units and dollars for each month, January through May.

LO3 **M9-20. Cash Budget**

Patrick's Retail Company is planning a cash budget for the next three months. Estimated sales revenue is as follows:

Month	Sales Revenue	Month	Sales Revenue
January	$250,000	March	$400,000
February	350,000	April	375,000

All sales are on credit; 75% is collected during the month of sale, and 25% is collected during the next month. Cost of goods sold is 70% of sales. Payments for merchandise sold are made in the month following the month of sale. Operating expenses total $125,000 per month and are paid during the month incurred. The cash balance on February 1 is estimated to be $55,000.

Required

Prepare monthly cash budgets for February, March, and April.

LO4 **M9-21. Production and Purchases Budgets in Units**

At the end of business on June 30, the PE Rug Company had 35,000 square yards of rugs and 100,000 pounds of raw materials on hand. Budgeted sales for the third quarter are

Month	Sales
July	50,000 sq. yards
August	35,000 sq. yards
September	42,000 sq. yards
October	48,000 sq. yards

The PE Rug Company wants to have sufficient square yards of finished product on hand at the end of each month to meet 60% of the following month's budgeted sales and sufficient pounds of raw materials to meet 40% of the following month's production requirements. Seven pounds of raw materials are required to produce one square yard of carpeting.

Required

Prepare a production budget for the months of July, August, and September and a purchases budget in units for the months of July and August.

LO4 **M9-22. Manufacturing Cost Budget**

Assume Carolina Table, a furniture manufacturer located in South Carolina, produces a conference table with the following standard costs:

Unit costs		
Direct materials		
Wood: 24 square feet at $35	$840	
Hardware kits (screws, etc.)	20	$ 860
Direct labor 0.75 hours at $40 per hour		30
Variable overhead, per unit		25
Total variable costs per unit		$ 915
Fixed costs per month (rent, utilities, supervision)		$91,250

Management plans to produce 250 units in April.

Required

Prepare a manufacturing cost budget for April.

Exercises

E9-23. Activity-Based Budget LO1, 2

Highland Industries has the following budget information available for February:

Units manufactured	25,000
Factory administration	$145,000
Assembly	¼ hour per unit × $20
Direct materials	3 pounds per unit × $6
Inspection	$40 per batch of 1,000 units
Manufacturing overhead	$8 per unit
Product development	$50,000
Setup cost	$100 per batch of 1,000 units

Required

a. Use activity-based costing to prepare a manufacturing cost budget for February. Clearly distinguish between unit, batch, product, and facility-level costs.

b. The operating managers at Highland Industries are concerned that the budgeting process is too time-consuming and diverts attention from their current day-to-day responsibilities. Discuss the reasons that Highland should continue budgeting.

E9-24. Product and Department Budgets Using Activity-Based Approach LO2

The following data are from the general records of the Loading Department of Jonah Freight Company for November.

- Cleaning incoming trucks, 30 minutes.
- Obtaining and reviewing shipping documents for loading truck and instructing loaders, 15 minutes.
- Loading truck, 1 hour.
- Cleaning shipping dock and storage area after each loading, 15 minutes.
- Employees perform both cleaning and loading tasks and are currently averaging $25 per hour in wages and benefits.
- The supervisor spends 15% of her time overseeing the cleaning activities; 35% overseeing various loading activities; and the remainder of her time making general plans and managing the department. Her current salary is $6,000 per month.
- Other overhead of the department amounts to $12,000 per month, 30% for cleaning, 65% for loading, and 5% for adminstration.

Required

Prepare an activities budget for cleaning and loading in the Loading Department for November, assuming 20 working days and the loading of an average of 25 trucks per day.

E9-25. Activity-Based Budgeting LO2 Mountain View Hospital

Assume Mountain View Hospital uses an activity-based budgeting approach for all costs except physician care. Some of the patients are treated in the emergency room as outpatients. Others are admitted to the hospital for additional tests and treatments. Its emergency room has three activity areas with cost drivers as follows:

1. *Reception*—paperwork of incoming patients. Cost driver is the number of forms completed.
2. *Treatment*—initial diagnosis and treatment of patients. Cost driver is the number of diagnoses treated.
3. *Cleaning*—general cleaning plus preparing treatment facilities for next patient. Cost driver is the number of people visiting the emergency room.

		Budgeted Amount of Cost Driver	
Activity Area	**Cost Driver Rates**	**Outpatients**	**Admitted Patients**
Reception	$ 20	9,200 forms	8,800 forms
Treatment	175	4,600 diagnoses	2,200 diagnoses
Cleaning	30	4,500 people	3,000 people

Required

a. Prepare the total budgeted cost for each activity.

b. How might you adjust the budget approach if you found that outpatients were kept in the emergency room for one hour on average while admitted patients remained for two hours?

c. What advantage does an activity-based approach have over the hospital's former budgeting method of basing the next year's budget on the last year's actual amount plus a percentage increase?

LO3 Honolulu Shirt Shop

E9-26. Sales Budget

Honolulu Shirt Shop has very seasonal sales. Assume that for next year management is trying to decide whether to establish a sales budget based on average sales or on sales estimated by quarter. The unit sales for next year are expected to be 5% higher than current year sales. Unit shirt sales by quarter for this year were as follows:

	Children's	Women's	Men's	Total
Winter quarter	80	80	140	300
Spring quarter	180	120	160	460
Summer quarter	500	600	260	1,360
Fall quarter	120	160	160	440
Total	880	960	720	2,560

Children's T-shirts sell for $10 each, women's sell for $15, and men's sell for $18.

Required

Assuming a 5% increase in sales, prepare a sales budget for each quarter of the year using the following:

a. Average quarterly sales. (*Hint:* Winter quarter children's shirts are 231 [880 × 1.05 ÷ 4].)

b. Actual quarterly sales. (*Hint:* Winter quarter children's shirts are 84 [80 × 1.05].)

c. Suggest advantages of each method.

LO3

E9-27. Cash Budget & Short-Term Financing

Presented are partial October, November, and December cash budgets for Holiday Events:

HOLIDAY EVENTS
Partial Cash Budgets

	October	November	December	Total
Cash balance, beginning	$ 25,000	$?	$?	$?
Collections on sales	100,000	90,000	140,000	?
Cash available for operations	?	?	?	?
Disbursements for operations	(115,000)	(110,000)	(115,000)	?
Ending cash before borrowings or replacements	?	?	?	?
Short-term finance	?	?	?	?
New loans	?	?	?	?
Repayments	?	?	?	?
Interest	?	?	?	?
Cash balance, ending	$?	$?	$?	$?

Loans are obtained in increments of $1,000 at the start of each month to maintain a minimum end-of-month balance of $12,000. Interest is 1% simple interest (no compounding) per month, payable when a loan payment is made. Repayments are made as soon as possible, subject to the minimum end-of-month balance.

Required

Complete the short-term financing section of the cash budget.

LO3

E9-28. Purchases and Cash Budgets

On July 1, MTC Wholesalers had a cash balance of $125,000 and accounts payable of $160,000, and Inventory of $78,000. Actual sales for May and June, and budgeted sales for July, August, September, and October are

Month	Actual Sales	Month	Budgeted Sales
May	$250,000	July	$260,000
June	225,000	August	240,000
		September	270,000
		October	275,000

All sales are on credit with 60% collected during the month of sale, 30% collected during the next month, and 10% collected during the second month following the month of sale. Cost of goods sold averages 60% of sales revenue. Ending inventory is one-half of the next month's predicted cost of sales. The other half of the merchandise is acquired during the month of sale. All purchases are paid for in the month after purchase. Operating costs are estimated at $95,000 each month and are paid during the month incurred.

Required
Prepare purchases and cash budgets for July, August, and September.

E9-29. Cash Receipts

The sales budget for Andrew Inc. is forecasted as follows:

Month	Sales Revenue
May	$150,000
June	175,000
July	160,000
August	200,000

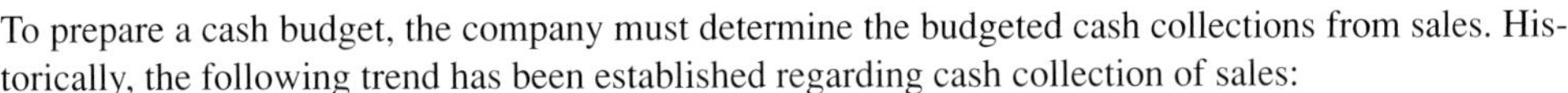

To prepare a cash budget, the company must determine the budgeted cash collections from sales. Historically, the following trend has been established regarding cash collection of sales:

- 60% in the month of sale.
- 20% in the month following sale.
- 15% in the second month following sale.
- 5% uncollectible.

The company gives a 2% cash discount for payments made by customers during the month of sale. The accounts receivable balance on April 30 is $85,000, of which $25,000 represents uncollected March sales and $60,000 represents uncollected April sales. (*Hint:* For collections of March and April receivables, start by determining total sales for the month. Assume the normal sales pattern.)

Required
Prepare a schedule of budgeted cash collections from sales for May, June, and July. Include a three-month summary of estimated cash collections.

E9-30. Cash Disbursements

Assume Stimson Lumber, headquartered in Portland, Oregon, is in the process of preparing its budget for next year. Cost of goods sold has been estimated at 60% of sales. Lumber purchases and payments are to be made during the month preceding the month of sale. Wages are estimated at 20% of sales and are paid during the month of sale. Other operating costs amounting to 5% of sales are to be paid in the month following the month of sale. Additionally, a monthly lease payment of $10,000 is paid for computer services. Sales revenue is forecast as follows:

Month	Sales Revenue
February	$340,000
March	420,000
April	440,000
May	520,000
June	480,000
July	560,000

Required
Prepare a schedule of cash disbursements for April, May, and June.

E9-31. Cash Disbursements

Assume that Ringwood Manufacturing manages its cash flow from its home office. Ringwood controls cash disbursements by category and month. In setting its budget for the next six months, beginning in July, it used the following managerial guidelines:

Category	Guidelines
Purchases	Pay 60% in current month and 40% in following month.
Payroll	Pay half in current and half in following month.
Loan payments	Pay total amount due each month.

Predicted activity for selected months follow:

Category	May	June	July	August
Purchases	$75,000	$80,000	$70,000	$85,000
Payroll	45,000	40,000	50,000	45,000
Loan payments	15,000	15,000	15,000	15,000

Required

Prepare a schedule showing cash disbursements by account for July and August.

LO3 **E9-32. Budgeted Income Statement**

Quality Wool Company, a merchandising company, is developing its master budget for next year. The income statement for the current year is as follows:

QUALITY WOOL COMPANY Income Statement For Year Ending December 31	
Gross sales	$1,200,000
Less uncollectible accounts	(26,000)
Collected sales	1,174,000
Cost of goods sold	(780,000)
Profit before operating expense	394,000
Operating expenses (including $15,000 depreciation)	(206,000)
Income before tax	$ 188,000

The following are management's goals and forecasts for next year:

1. Selling prices will increase by 3%, and sales volume will increase by 5%.
2. The cost of merchandise will increase by 2%.
3. All operating expenses are fixed. Price increases for operating expenses will be 4%. The company uses straight-line depreciation.
4. The estimated uncollectibles are 2% of budgeted sales.

Required

Prepare a budgeted functional income statement for next year.

LO3 **E9-33. Budgeted Income Statement with CVP**

Barnes & Noble, Inc.

Assume Barnes & Noble is planning a budget for one of its stores. The estimate of sales revenue is $2,000,000 and of cost of goods sold is 70% of sales revenue. Depreciation on the office building and fixtures is budgeted at $36,000. Salaries and wages are budgeted at $375,000. Advertising has been budgeted at $12,000, and other operating costs should amount to $15,000. Income tax is estimated at 20% of operating income.

Required

a. Prepare a budgeted income statement for next year.

b. Assuming management desired an after-tax income of $150,000, determine the necessary sales volume.

LO4 **E9-34. Production and Purchases Budgets**

At the beginning of October, Comfy Cushions had 3,400 cushions and 8,500 pounds of raw materials on hand. Budgeted sales for the next three months are

Month	Sales
October	11,000 cushions
November	12,000 cushions
December	10,000 cushions

Comfy Cushions wants to have sufficient raw materials on hand at the end of each month to meet 20% of the following month's production requirements and sufficient cushions on hand at the end of each month to meet 30% of the following month's budgeted sales. Four pounds of raw materials, at a standard cost of $1.10 per pound, are required to produce each cushion.

Required

a. Prepare a production budget for October and November.
b. Prepare a purchases budget in units and dollars for October.

E9-35. Production and Purchases Budgets

LO4 Advance Drainage Systems, Inc. (WMS)

Advance Drainage Systems produces thermoplastic corrugated pipe. Assume budgeted unit sales for one of its products (a 12" by 20-ft pipe) over the next several months are

Month	Sales
September	3,000
October	2,500
November	1,500
December	500

At the beginning of September, 850 units of finished goods were in inventory. During the final third of the year, as road construction declines, plans are to have an inventory of finished goods equal to 30% of the following month's sales. Each unit of finished goods requires 70 pounds of raw materials at a cost of $1.50 per pound. Management wishes to maintain month-end inventories of raw materials equal to 40% of the following month's needs. Sixty thousand pounds of raw materials were on hand at the start of September.

Required

a. Prepare a production budget for September, October, and November.
b. Prepare a purchases budget in units and dollars for September and October.

Problems

P9-36. Cash Budget

LO3 Office Depot, Inc. (ODP)

Assume all Office Depot stores do cash budgeting every quarter. One store is planning its cash needs for the third quarter of the year, and the following information is available to assist in preparing a cash budget. Budgeted income statements for July through October are as follows:

	July	August	September	October
Sales	$45,000	$52,000	$60,000	$75,000
Cost of goods sold	23,500	25,500	30,500	35,000
Gross profit	21,500	26,500	29,500	40,000
Less other expenses				
Selling	6,000	8,000	8,500	10,500
Administrative	9,100	10,500	8,500	9,400
Total	(15,100)	(18,500)	(17,000)	(19,900)
Net income	$ 6,400	$ 8,000	$12,500	$20,100

Additional information follows:

1. Other expenses, which are paid monthly, include $3,500 of depreciation per month.
2. Sales are 44% for cash and 56% on credit.
3. Credit sales are collected 50% in the month of sale, 35% one month after sale, and 15% two months after sale. May sales were $40,000, and June sales were $42,000.

4. Merchandise is paid for 50% in the month of purchase; the remaining 50% is paid in the following month. Accounts payable for merchandise at June 30 totaled $12,000.
5. The store maintains its ending inventory levels at 30% of the cost of goods to be sold in the following month. The inventory at June 30 is $7,600.
6. An equipment note of $10,000 per month is being paid through August.
7. The store must maintain a cash balance of at least $10,000 at the end of each month. The cash balance on June 30 is $10,000.
8. The store can borrow from its bank as needed. Borrowings and repayments must be in multiples of $100. All borrowings take place at the beginning of a month, and all repayments are made at the end of a month. When the principal is repaid, interest on the repayment is also paid. The interest rate is 6% per year.

Required

a. Prepare a monthly schedule of budgeted operating cash receipts for July, August, and September.
b. Prepare a monthly purchases budget and a schedule of budgeted cash payments for purchases for July, August, and September.
c. Prepare a monthly cash budget for July, August, and September. Show borrowings from the store's bank and repayments to the bank as needed to maintain the minimum cash balance.

LO3 **P9-37. Cash Budget**

The Williams Supply Company sells for $50 one product that it purchases for $20. Budgeted sales in total dollars for the year are $3,000,000. The sales information needed for preparing the July budget follows:

Month	Sales Revenue
May	$175,000
June	240,000
July	295,000
August	320,000

Account balances at July 1 include these:

Cash	$125,000
Merchandise inventory	47,200
Accounts receivable (sales)	84,530
Accounts payable (purchases)	47,200

The company pays for one-half of its purchases in the month of purchase and the remainder in the following month. End-of-month inventory must be 40% of the budgeted sales in units for the next month. A 2% cash discount on sales is allowed if payment is made during the month of sale. Experience indicates that 60% of the billings will be collected during the month of sale, 25% in the following month, 12% in the second following month, and 3% will be uncollectible. Total budgeted selling and administrative expenses (excluding bad debts) for the fiscal year are estimated at $1,200,000, of which three-fourths is fixed expense (inclusive of a $36,000 annual depreciation charge). Fixed expenses are incurred evenly during the year. The other selling and administrative expenses vary with sales. Expenses are paid during the month incurred.

Required

a. Prepare a schedule of estimated cash collections for July.
b. Prepare a schedule of estimated July cash payments for purchases. *Hint:* Start by doing a purchase budget.
c. Prepare schedules of July selling and administrative expenses, separately identifying those requiring cash disbursements.
d. Prepare a schedule of cash receipts over disbursements assuming no equipment purchases or loan payments.

LO3, 4 **P9-38. Budgeting Purchases, Revenues, Expenses, and Cash in a Service Organization**

Wauconda Medical Center is located in a summer resort community. During the summer months (June through August), the center operates an outpatient clinic for the treatment of minor injuries and illnesses. The clinic is administered as a separate department within the hospital. It has its own staff and maintains its own financial records. All patients requiring extensive or intensive care are referred to other hospital departments.

An analysis of past operating data for the outpatient clinic reveals the following:

- Staff: Seven full-time employees with total monthly salaries of $42,000. On a monthly basis, one additional staff member is hired for every 500 budgeted patient visits in excess of 3,000, at a cost of $7,000 per month.
- Facilities: Monthly facility costs, including depreciation of $2,500, total $15,000.
- Supplies: The supplies expense averages $20 per patient visit. The center maintains an end-of-month supplies inventory equal to 10% of the predicted needs of the following month, with a minimum ending inventory of $4,000, which is also the desired inventory at the end of August.
- Additional variable patient costs, such as medications, are charged directly to the patient by the hospital pharmacy.
- Payments: All staff and maintenance expenses are paid in the month the cost is incurred. Supplies are purchased at cost directly from the hospital with an immediate transfer of cash from the clinic cash account to the hospital cash account.
- Collections: The average bill for services rendered is $75. Of the total bills, 40% are paid in cash at the time the service is rendered, 10% are never paid, and the remaining 50% are covered by insurance. In the past, insurance companies have disallowed 30% of the claims filed and paid the balance two months after services are rendered.
- May 30 status: At the end of May, the clinic had $15,000 in cash and supplies costing $5,000.

Budgeted patient visits for next summer are as follows:

Month	Patient Visits
June	3,000
July	3,500
August	4,500

Required

For the Wauconda Outpatient Clinic:

a. Prepare a supplies purchases budget for June, July, and August with a total column.
b. Prepare a revenue and expense budget for June, July, and August with a total column.
c. Prepare a cash budget for June, July, and August with a total column. (*Hint:* See requirement *d.*)
d. Is the cash budget for the annual summer outpatient clinic feasible? If not, make appropriate recommendations for management's consideration.

P9-39. Developing a Master Budget for a Merchandising Organization

LO3, 4
Nordstrom, Inc.
(JWN)

Assume Nordstrom prepares budgets quarterly. The following information is available for use in planning the second quarter budgets for one of its stores.

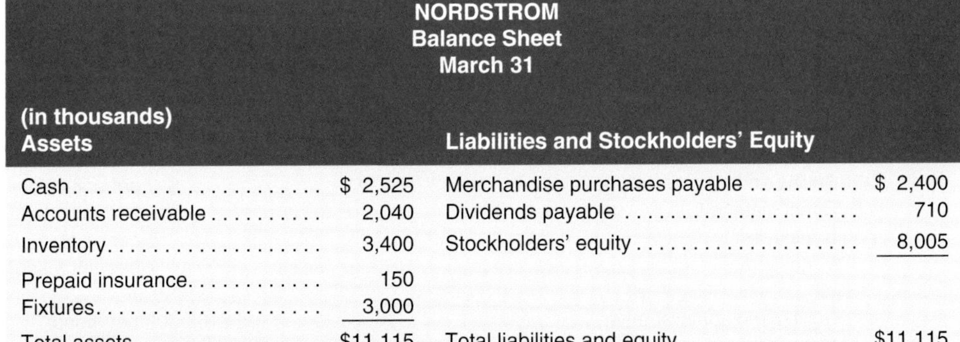

NORDSTROM Balance Sheet March 31			
(in thousands) **Assets**		**Liabilities and Stockholders' Equity**	
Cash	$ 2,525	Merchandise purchases payable	$ 2,400
Accounts receivable	2,040	Dividends payable	710
Inventory	3,400	Stockholders' equity	8,005
Prepaid insurance	150		
Fixtures	3,000		
Total assets	$11,115	Total liabilities and equity	$11,115

Actual and forecasted sales for selected months in the upcoming year are as follows:

Month (in thousands)	Sales Revenue
January	$2,600
February	2,700
March	3,000
April	3,600
May	3,800
June	3,500
July	3,200
August	4,000

Monthly operating expenses (in thousands) are as follows:

Wages and salaries	$750
Depreciation	75
Advertising	55
Other costs	350

Cash dividends for the store of $710 thousand are declared during the third month of each quarter and are paid during the first month of the following quarter. Operating expenses, except insurance, rent, and depreciation are paid as incurred. The prepaid insurance is for five more months. Cost of goods sold is equal to 60% of sales. Ending inventories are sufficient for 150% of the next month's cost of sales. Purchases during any given month are paid in full during the following month. Cash sales account for 50% of the revenue. Of the credit sales, 60% are collected in the next month and 40% are collected in the month after. Money can be borrowed and repaid in multiples of $100 thousand at an interest rate of 12% per year. The company desires a minimum cash balance of $2 million on the first of each month. At the time the principal is repaid, interest is paid on the portion of principal that is repaid. All borrowing is at the beginning of the month, and all repayment is at the end of the month. Money is never repaid at the end of the month it is borrowed.

Required

a. Prepare a purchases budget for each month of the second quarter ending June 30.
b. Prepare a cash receipts schedule for each month of the second quarter ending June 30. Do not include borrowings.
c. Prepare a cash disbursements schedule for each month of the second quarter ending June 30. Do not include repayments of borrowings.
d. Prepare a cash budget for each month of the second quarter ending June 30. Include budgeted borrowings and repayments.
e. Prepare an income statement for each month of the second quarter ending June 30.
f. Prepare a budgeted balance sheet as of June 30.

LO3, 4 **P9-40. Developing a Master Budget for a Manufacturing Organization**

Cubs Incorporated manufactures a product with a selling price of $75 per unit. Units and monthly cost data follow:

Variable	
Selling and administrative	$ 3 per unit sold
Direct materials	15 per unit manufactured
Direct labor	5 per unit manufactured
Variable manufacturing overhead	7 per unit manufactured
Fixed	
Selling and administrative	$160,000 per month
Manufacturing (including depreciation of $15,000)	150,000 per month

Cubs Inc. pays all bills in the month incurred. All sales are on account with 50% collected the month of sale and the balance collected the following month. There are no sales discounts or bad debts.

Cubs Inc. desires to maintain an ending finished goods inventory equal to 40% of the following month's sales and a raw materials inventory equal to 20% of the following month's production. January 1 inventories are in line with these policies.

Actual unit sales for December and budgeted unit sales for January, February, and March are as follows:

CUBS INCORPORATED Sales Budget For the Months of January, February, and March				
Month	December	January	February	March
Sales—Units	10,000	12,000	11,500	12,500
Sales—Dollars	$750,000	$900,000	$862,500	$937,500

Additional information:

- The January 1 beginning cash is projected as $10,000.
- For the purpose of operational budgeting, units in the January 1 inventory of finished goods are valued at variable manufacturing cost.
- Each unit of finished product requires one unit of raw materials.
- Cubs Inc. intends to pay a cash dividend of $15,000 in January

Required

a. A production budget for January and February.
b. A purchases budget in units for January.
c. A manufacturing cost budget for January.
d. A cash budget for January.
e. A budgeted contribution income statement for January.

P9-41. Risk Management in a Manufacturing Organization **LO3, 4**

Required

Continuing problem P9-40, management is concerned that their supplier of raw materials will have a strike. Determine the budget implications if management plans to increase the January-end raw materials inventory to 150% of February's production needs. Offer any recommendations you believe appropriate.

P9-42. Developing a Master Budget for a Manufacturing Organization: Challenge Problem **LO3, 4**

Electric Monkey Computer Accessories assembles a computer networking device from kits of imported components. You have been asked to develop a quarterly and annual operating budget and pro forma income statements for next year. You have obtained the following information:

Beginning-of-year balances			
Cash	$ 75,000		
Accounts receivable (previous quarter's sales)	$245,000		
Raw materials	950 kits		
Finished goods	1,500 kits		
Accounts payable (materials)	$125,000		
Borrowed funds	$ 30,000		
Desired end-of-year inventory balances			
Raw materials	1,000 kits		
Finished goods	1,600 kits		
Desired end-of-quarter balances			
Cash	$ 30,000		
Raw materials as a portion of the following quarter's production	0.20		
Finished goods as a portion of the following quarter's sales	0.30		
Manufacturing costs			
Standard cost per unit	Units	Unit price	Total
Raw materials	1 kit	$75.00	$75.00
Direct labor hours at rate	0.50 hour	$30.00	15.00
Variable overhead/labor hour	0.50 hour	$ 5.00	2.50
Total standard variable cost			$92.50

continued

continued from previous page

Fixed cost per quarter				
Cash		$110,000		
Depreciation		15,000		
Total		$125,000		
Selling and administrative costs				
Variable cost per unit		$8.00		
Fixed costs per quarter				
Cash		$150,000		
Depreciation		7,500		
Total		$157,500		
Interest rate per quarter		0.015		
Portion of sales collected				
Quarter of sale		0.70		
Subsequent quarter		0.29		
Bad debts		0.01		
Portion of purchases paid				
Quarter of purchase		0.60		
Subsequent quarter		0.40		
Unit selling price		$225.00		
Sales forecast				
Quarter	First	Second	Third	Fourth
Unit sales	4,400	4,600	4,500	4,800

Additional information

- All cash payments except purchases are made quarterly as incurred.
- All borrowings occur at the start of a quarter.
- All repayments on borrowings occur at the end of a quarter.
- At the time the principal is repaid, interest is paid on the portion of principal that is repaid.
- Borrowings and repayments may be made in any amount.

Required

a. A sales budget for each quarter and the year. (*Hint:* Use of spreadsheet software strongly recommended for this problem.)
b. A production budget for each quarter and the year.
c. A purchases budget for each quarter and the year.
d. A manufacturing cost budget for each quarter and the year.
e. A selling and administrative expense budget for each quarter and the year.
f. A cash budget for each quarter and the year.
g. A pro forma contribution income statement for each quarter and the year.

Cases and Projects

LO5 **C9-43. Behavioral Implications of Budgeting**

Cindy Jones, controller of Systematic Designs, believes that effective budgeting greatly assists in meeting the organization's goals and objectives. She argues that the budget serves as a blueprint for the operating activities during each reporting period, making it an important control device. She believes that sound management evaluations can be based on the comparisons of performance and budgetary schedules and that employees respond more favorably when they participate in the budgetary process. Kevin Dobbs, treasurer of Systematic Designs, agrees that budgeting is essential for overall organization success, but he argues that human resources are too valuable to spend much time planning and preparing the budgetary process. He thinks that the roles people play in budgetary preparation are not important in the final analysis of a budget's effectiveness.

Required

Contrast the participative versus imposed budgeting concepts and indicate how the ideas of Jones and Dobbs fit the two categories.

C9-44. Behavioral Considerations and Budgeting LO5

Anthony Wagner, the controller in the Division of Transportation for the state, recognizes the importance of the budgetary process for planning, control, and motivation purposes. He believes that a properly implemented participative budgeting process for planning purposes and a management by exception reporting procedure based on that budget will motivate his subordinates to improve productivity within their particular departments. Based on this philosophy, Wagner has implemented the following budget procedures.

- An appropriation target figure is given to each department manager. This amount is the maximum funding that each department can expect to receive in the next fiscal year.
- Department managers develop their individual budgets within the following spending constraints as directed by the controller's staff.
    1. Expenditure requests cannot exceed the appropriation target.
    2. All fixed expenditures should be included in the budget; these should include items such as contracts and salaries at current levels.
    3. All government projects directed by higher authority should be included in the budget in their entirety.
- The controller consolidates the departmental budget requests from the various departments into one budget that is to be submitted for the entire division.
- Upon final budget approval by the legislature, the controller's staff allocates the appropriation to the various departments on instructions from the division manager. However, a specified percentage of each department's appropriation is held back in anticipation of potential budget cuts and special funding needs. The amount and use of this contingency fund are left to the discretion of the division manager.
- Each department is allowed to adjust its budget when necessary to operate within the reduced appropriation level. However, as stated in the original directive, specific projects authorized by higher authority must remain intact.
- The final budget is used as the basis of control for a management by exception form of reporting. Excessive expenditures by account for each department are highlighted on a monthly basis. Department managers are expected to account for all expenditures over budget. Fiscal responsibility is an important factor in the overall performance evaluation of department managers.

Wagner believes that his policy of allowing the department managers to participate in the budget process and then holding them accountable for their performance is essential, especially during these times of limited resources. He also believes that department managers will be positively motivated to increase the efficiency and effectiveness of their departments because they have provided input into the initial budgetary process and are required to justify any unfavorable performances.

Required

a. Explain the operational and behavioral benefits that generally are attributed to a participative budgeting process.

b. Identify deficiencies in Wagner's participative budgetary policy for planning and performance evaluation purposes. For each deficiency identified, recommend how the deficiency can be corrected.

(CMA Adapted)

C9-45. Budgetary Slack with Ethical Considerations LO5

Karen Bailey was promoted to department manager of a production unit in Parkway Industries three years ago. She enjoys her job except for the evaluation measures that are based on the department's budget. After three years of consistently poor annual evaluations based on a set annual budget, she has decided to improve the evaluation situation. At a recent budget meeting of junior-level managers, the topic of budgetary slack was discussed as a means to maintain some consistency in budgeting matters. As a result of this meeting, Bailey decided to take the following steps in preparing the upcoming year's budget:

1. Use the top quartile for all wage and salary categories.
2. Select the optimistic values for the estimated production ranges for the coming year. These are provided by the marketing department.
3. Use the average of the three months in the current year with poorest production efficiency as benchmarks of success for the coming year.
4. Base equipment charges (primarily depreciation) on replacement values furnished by the purchasing department.
5. Base other fixed costs on current cost plus an inflation rate estimated for the coming year.

6. Use the average of the 10 newly hired employees' performance as a basis of labor efficiency for the coming year.

Required

a. For each item on Bailey's list, explain whether it will create budgetary slack. Use numerical examples as necessary to illustrate.

b. Given the company's use of static budgets as one of the performance evaluation measures of its managers, can the managers justify the use of built-in budgetary slack?

c. What would you recommend as a means for Bailey to improve the budgeting situation in the company? Provide some specific examples of how the budgeting process might be improved.

LO5 **C9-46. Budgetary Slack with Ethical Considerations**

Norton Company, a manufacturer of infant furniture and carriages, is in the initial stages of preparing the annual budget for next year. Scott Ford recently joined Norton's accounting staff and is interested to learn as much as possible about the company's budgeting process. During a recent lunch with Marge Atkins, sales manager, and Pete Granger, production manager, Ford initiated the following conversation:

Ford: Since I'm new around here and am going to be involved with the preparation of the annual budget, I'd be interested to learn how the two of you estimate sales and production numbers.

Atkins: We start out very methodically by looking at recent history, discussing what we know about current accounts, potential customers, and the general state of consumer spending. Then we add that usual dose of intuition to come up with the best forecast we can.

Granger: I usually take the sales projections as the basis for my projections. Of course, we have to make an estimate of what this year's closing inventories will be, which is sometimes difficult.

Ford: Why does that present a problem? There must have been an estimate of closing inventories in the budget for the current year.

Granger: Those numbers aren't always reliable since Marge makes some adjustments to the sales numbers before passing them on to me.

Ford: What kind of adjustments?

Atkins: Well, we don't want to fall short of the sales projections, so we generally give ourselves a little breathing room by lowering the initial sales projection anywhere from 5% to 10%.

Granger: So, you can see why this year's budget is not a very reliable starting point. We always have to adjust the projected production rates as the year progresses; of course, this changes the ending inventory estimates. By the way, we make similar adjustments to expenses by adding at least 10% to the estimates; I think everyone around here does the same thing.

Required

a. Marge Atkins and Pete Granger have described the use of budgetary slack.

1. Explain why Atkins and Granger behave in this manner, and describe the benefits they expect to realize from the use of budgetary slack.
2. Explain how the use of budgetary slack can adversely affect Atkins and Granger.

b. As a management accountant, Scott Ford believes that the behavior described by Marge Atkins and Pete Granger could be unethical and that he might have an obligation not to support this behavior. Explain why the use of budgetary slack could be unethical.

(CMA Adapted)

Solutions to Review Problems

Review 9-1—Solution

Operating managers frequently regard budgeting as a time-consuming task that diverts attention from current problems. The development of a budget can be difficult and time-consuming, although it is a necessary process. Organizations that plan will have a focus and their work and tasks will better support the organization's goals and objectives. Without a plan, although managers and employees might be busy, they may not be working on tasks that move their companies forward in a thoughtful way. The plan will allow them to more efficiently focus efforts on tasks that are productive toward the organization's goals.

The use of a budgeting model (a) compels planning by forcing managers to be more proactive in planning for the future and focusing on work and tasks that better support the organization's goals and objectives; (b) promotes communication and coordination by forcing managers of diverse functions to communicate and coordinate activities; (c) provides a guide to action and a basis of evaluation by directing managers' attention to areas where results do not agree with the plan (management by exception); and (d) acts as an aid in risk management through the evaluation of the financial impact of risk and the determination of the best response from a financial perspective.

Review 9-2—Solution

a. Under the output/input approach, the output of units dictates the expected cost inputs. Here budgeted overhead costs are based on the number of budgeted assembly hours.

	Regular	Extra Strength
Direct materials (20,000 × $20)	$400,000	
(50,000 × $14.50)		$ 725,000
Direct assembly labor (20,000 × 0.5 × $18)	180,000	
(50,000 × 0.8 × $18)		720,000
Overhead (20,000 × 0.5 × $8.17)	81,700	
(50,000 × 0.8 × $8.17)		326,800
Total budgeted cost	$661,700	$1,771,800
Unit Cost	$33.085	$35.436

b. Under the activity-based approach, budgeted overhead costs are based on expected activities to produce the products, not only on assembly hours.

	Regular	Extra Strength
Direct materials (20,000 × $20)	$400,000	
(50,000 × $14.50)		$ 725,000
Direct assembly labor (20,000 × 0.5 × $18)	180,000	
(50,000 × 0.8 × $18)		720,000
Setup (1,000 hours × $25)	25,000	
(1,500 hours × $25)		37,500
Engineering and Maintenance (500 hours × $35)	17,500	
(600 hours × $35)		21,000
Inspections (650 inspections × $250)	162,500	
(580 inspections × $250)		145,000
Total budgeted cost	$785,000	$1,648,500
Unit cost	$39.25	$32.97

Review 9-3—Solution

a.

BLEU MONT DAIRY
Sales Budget
For Month of April

	Units	Price	Sales
Cheese	160,000	$10	$1,600,000
Ice cream	240,000	5	1,200,000
Total			$2,800,000

b.

BLEU MONT DAIRY
Purchases Budget
For Month of April

	Cheese	Ice Cream	Total
Units			
Sales needs	160,000	240,000	
Desired ending inventory	12,000	5,000	
Total	172,000	245,000	
Less beginning inventory	(10,000)	(4,000)	
Purchases (in units)	162,000	241,000	
Purchases (in dollars)	$1,296,000	$482,000	$1,778,000

c.

BLEU MONT DAIRY
Cash Budget
For Month of April

Cash balance, beginning		$ 400,000
Collections on sales		
Current month's sales ($2,800,000 × 0.70)	$1,960,000	
Previous month's sales ($3,000,000 × 0.29)	870,000	2,830,000
Cash available from operations		3,230,000
Less budgeted disbursements		
March purchases ($1,800,000 × 0.40)	720,000	
April purchases ($1,778,000 × 0.60)	1,066,800	
Wages and salaries	156,000	
Overhead (March)	80,000	
Selling and administrative ($450,000 – $40,000 depreciation)	410,000	(2,432,800)
Cash balance, ending		$ 797,200

d.

BLEU MONT DAIRY
Budgeted Income Statement
For Month of April

Sales (sales budget)			$2,800,000
Costs of merchandise sold			
Cheese (160,000 × $8)	$1,280,000		
Ice cream (240,000 × $2)	480,000	$1,760,000	
Wages and salaries	156,000		
Overhead	80,000		
Selling and administrative ($450,000 + $28,000)	478,000	714,000	(2,474,000)
Net income			$ 326,000

Review 9-4—Solution

a.

DEWALT
Sales Budget
For First Quarter

	Units	Price	Sales
Drills	60,000	$100	$ 6,000,000
Saws	40,000	125	5,000,000
Total			$11,000,000

b.

DEWALT
Production Budget
For First Quarter

	Drills	Saws
Budget sales	60,000	40,000
Plus desired ending inventory	25,000	10,000
Total inventory requirements	85,000	50,000
Less beginning inventory	(20,000)	(8,000)
Budgeted production	65,000	42,000

c.

DEWALT
Purchases Budget
For First Quarter

	Drills	Saws	Total
Metal purchases			
Production units (production budget)	65,000	42,000	
Metal (pounds)	× 5	× 4	
Production needs (pounds)	325,000	168,000	493,000
Desired ending inventory (pounds)			36,000
Total metal needs (pounds)			529,000
Less beginning inventory (pounds)			(32,000)
Purchases needed (pounds)			497,000
Cost per pound			× $8
Total metal purchases			$3,976,000
Plastic purchases			
Production units (production budget)	65,000	42,000	107,000
Plastic (pounds)			× 3
Production needs (pounds)			321,000
Desired ending inventory (pounds)			32,000
Total plastic needs (pounds)			353,000
Less beginning inventory (pounds)			(29,000)
Purchases needed (pounds)			324,000
Cost per pound			× $5
Total plastic purchases			$1,620,000

continued

continued from previous page

DEWALT
Purchases Budget
For First Quarter

	Drills	Saws	Total
Handle purchases			
Production units (production budget)	65,000		65,000
Handles			× 1
Production needs			65,000
Desired ending inventory			7,000
Total handle needs			72,000
Less beginning inventory			(6,000)
Purchases needed			66,000
Cost per handle			× $3
Total handle purchases			$ 198,000
Total purchases			
Metal			$3,976,000
Plastic			1,620,000
Handles			198,000
Total purchases			$5,794,000

d.

DEWALT
Manufacturing Cost Budget
For First Quarter

	Drills	Saws	Total
Direct materials			
Metal			
Production units (production budget)	65,000	42,000	
Metal per unit of product (pounds)	× 5	× 4	
Production needs for metal (pounds)	325,000	168,000	
Unit cost	× $8	× $8	
Cost of metal issued to production	$2,600,000	$1,344,000	$3,944,000
Plastic			
Production units (production budget)	65,000	42,000	
Plastic (pounds)	× 3	× 3	
Production needs for plastic (pounds)	195,000	126,000	
Unit cost	× $5	× $5	
Cost of plastic issued to production	$ 975,000	$ 630,000	1,605,000
Handles			
Production units (production budget)	65,000		
Handles	× 1		
Production needs for handles	65,000		
Unit cost	× $3		
Cost of handles issued to production	$ 195,000		195,000
Total			5,744,000
Direct labor			
Budgeted production	65,000	42,000	
Direct labor hours per unit	× 2	× 3	
Total direct labor hours	130,000	126,000	
Labor rate	× $12	× $16	
Labor expenditures	$1,560,000	$2,016,000	3,576,000

continued

continued from previous page

DEWALT Manufacturing Cost Budget For First Quarter	Drills	Saws	Total
Variable manufacturing overhead			
Direct labor hours	130,000	126,000	
Variable manufacturing overhead rate	× $1.50	× $1.50	
Total variable overhead	$ 195,000	$ 189,000	384,000
Fixed manufacturing overhead			214,000
Total			$9,918,000

e.

DEWALT Cash Budget For First Quarter		
Cash balance, beginning		$ 1,800,000
Collections on sales		
Current quarter's sales ($11,000,000 × 0.50)	$5,500,000	
Previous quarter's sales ($8,400,000 × 0.50)	4,200,000	9,700,000
Cash available from operations		11,500,000
Less budgeted disbursements		
Materials (purchases budget)	5,794,000	
Labor (manufacturing cost budget)	3,576,000	
Manufacturing overhead (manufacturing cost budget) ([$384,000 + $214,000] – $156,000 noncash)	442,000	
Selling and administrative ($340,000 – $90,000 depreciation)	250,000	(10,062,000)
Cash balance, ending		$ 1,438,000

f.

DEWALT Contribution Income Statement For First Quarter		
Sales (sales budget)		$11,000,000
Less variable costs of goods sold		
Drills (60,000 × $85.00)	$5,100,000	
Saws (40,000 × $99.50)	3,980,000	(9,080,000)
Gross profit		1,920,000
Less fixed costs		
Manufacturing overhead	214,000	
Selling and administrative expenses	340,000	(554,000)
Net income		$ 1,366,000

Review 9-5—Solution

__2__ *a.* The marketing department is asked to provide an estimate as to how much it will spend on print ads during the next fiscal year.

__1__ *b.* The marketing department provides a budget amount for print ads for the next fiscal year that includes the expected expenditures plus 10% to account for uncertainty.

__4__ *c.* Tristan Renken owns and operates a food truck that sells Mexican food along the beaches in Chicago. Tristan only operates the food truck during the summer and developed a budget to estimate how much he will make during the upcoming summer season.

__3__ *d.* Top management hosts semi-annual meetings to discuss the budget and current performance vs. the budget. Management provides employees with tools to help gauge their own performance against the budgeted expectations.

Chapter 10

Standard Costs and Performance Reports

Learning Objectives

LO1 Explain responsibility accounting. (p. 354)

LO2 Differentiate between static and flexible budgets for performance reporting. Prepare a flexible budget. (p. 357)

LO3 Determine the components of standard cost variance analysis. Formulate and interpret direct materials cost variances. (p. 360)

LO4 Formulate and interpret direct labor cost variances. (p. 364)

LO5 Formulate and interpret overhead cost variances. (p. 366)

LO6 Calculate revenue variances and prepare a performance report for a revenue center. (p. 369)

LO7 Formulate and interpret fixed overhead cost variances (Appendix 10A). (p. 373)

LO8 Reconcile budgeted and actual income (Appendix 10B). (p. 374)

Southwest Airlines

www.southwest.com

In the last chapter, we discussed how budgeting was critical to planning within a business. But planning is only half of the story; at the end of the period, the operating results are compared to the budget. By evaluating the differences between the budgeted and the actual results, a manager can identify areas of the business that need attention. We call these differences *budget variances*, and a thorough analysis of these variances aids the manager in controlling the human and physical resources of the business.

To effectively control the business through variance analysis, it is important that the lines of responsibility are clearly defined among the managers. Managers (and the people who evaluate their results) need to understand who is responsible for revenues, costs, profits, capital investments, or some combination of those elements. This assignment of responsibility prevents managers from "passing the buck" when something goes wrong. Consider the case of Southwest Airlines, the Dallas, Texas–based airline, which completed a merger with Air Tran. When a structural shift such as a merger takes place, the lines of responsibility may be temporarily blurred. This can impede not only variance analysis, but also the integration of the merged entities.

While other airlines have bolstered revenue by charging fees for baggage, additional legroom, Wi-Fi, and changed flights, Southwest's strategy has been to offer passengers inexpensive and flexible flight arrangements with no hidden fees for baggage or other basic services. Inconsistencies between Southwest and Air Tran were prevalent in the merged business. Southwest permits customers to buy early boarding privileges, but Air Tran did not. Bags fly free on Southwest, but not on Air Tran. There is no business class on Southwest, whereas Air Tran passengers frequently received complementary upgrades to business class. The two reservation systems could not easily rebook passengers across the two airlines, and their frequent flier miles were not transferrable between the two airlines.

Even today, the merged airline is likely to encounter differences between expected and actual operating results. Some of the variances may relate to usage or efficiency, whereas others may relate to the dollar amount spent on a resource. For example, the airline could use more or less fuel than is expected and the price paid per gallon of fuel could differ from expectations. Flight personnel may work more or fewer hours than expected and scheduling issues may result in paying higher- or lower-than-average wages than expected for the number of hours worked. Variance analysis can be extended to issues such as bag handling, overbooking, and number of passenger complaints.

Even though mergers can decrease the level of competition within an industry, customers still have some choice of airlines available to them. Managers prefer timely notification of potential variances so they still have time to "right the ship" before the end of the reporting period. In this chapter, we focus on performance assessment and variance analysis.

Road Map

LO	Learning Objective | Topics	Page	eLecture	Guided Example	Assignments
LO1	**Explain responsibility accounting.** Management by Exception :: Performance Reporting :: Cost Center :: Profit Center :: Investment Center :: Financial and Nonfinancial Performance Measures	354	e10–1	Review 10-1	42, 44
LO2	**Differentiate between static and flexible budgets for performance reporting. Prepare a flexible budget.** Static Budget :: Flexible Budget :: Flexible Budget Variance :: Standard Cost	357	e10–2	Review 10-2	16, 25, 30, 35, 36, 40, 41, 43, 44
LO3	**Determine the components of standard cost variance analysis. Formulate and interpret direct materials cost variances.** Components of Standard Cost Analysis :: Direct Materials Price Variance :: Direct Materials Quantity Variance :: Interpreting Material Variances	360	e10–3	Review 10-3	17, 18, 27, 31, 32, 33, 34, 35, 36. 37. 40, 41, 44
LO4	**Formulate and interpret direct labor cost variances.** Direct Labor Rate Variance :: Direct Labor Efficiency Variance :: Interpreting Labor Variances	364	e10–4	Review 10-4	19, 20, 26, 27, 31, 32, 33, 34, 35, 36, 37, 40, 41, 44
LO5	**Formulate and interpret overhead cost variances.** Variable Overhead Spending Variance :: Variable Overhead Efficiency Variance :: Interpreting Variable Overhead Variances	366	e10–5	Review 10-5	21, 26, 27, 33, 34, 35, 36, 37, 40, 41, 44
LO6	**Calculate revenue variances and prepare a performance report for a revenue center.** Revenue Variance :: Sales Price Variance :: Sales Volume Variance :: Controllable Costs :: Net Sales Volume Variance	369	e10–6	Review 10-6	22, 28, 39, 40, 41
LO7	**Formulate and interpret fixed overhead cost variances (Appendix 10A).** Fixed Overhead Budget Variance :: Standard Fixed Overhead Rate	373	e10–7	Review 10-7	23, 29, 38, 40, 41
LO8	**Reconcile budgeted and actual income (Appendix 10B).** Contribution Format :: Assigning Variances to Responsibility Centers	374	e10–8	Review 10-8	24, 39, 40, 41, 45

CHAPTER ORGANIZATION

Standard Costs and Performance Reports

Responsibility Accounting	Performance Reporting for Cost Centers	Variance Analysis for Costs	Performance Reports for Revenue Centers	Additional Topics in Standard Costing (Appendices 10A and 10B)
• Performance Reporting and Organization Structures • Types of Responsibility Centers • Financial and Nonfinancial Performance Measures	• Development of Flexible Budgets • Flexible Budgets Emphasize Performance • Standard Costs and Performance Reports	• Components of Standard Cost Analysis • Establishing and Using Standards for Direct Materials • Establishing and Using Standards for Direct Labor • Establishing and Using Standards for Variable Overhead • Fixed Overhead Variances	• Inclusion of Controllable Costs • Revenue Centers as Profit Centers	• Establishing and Using Fixed Overhead Variances • Reconciling Budgeted and Actual Income

Management accounting tools aid in the assessment of the performance of the firm as a whole and all of its various components. Feedback in the form of performance reports is essential if the benefits of budgeting and other types of planning are to be fully realized. To control current operations and to improve future operations, managers must know how actual results compare with the current budget. These performance reports should be prepared in accordance with the concept of **responsibility accounting**, which is the structuring of performance reports addressed to individual (or group) members of an organization to emphasize the factors they control.

This chapter focuses on responsibility accounting and performance assessment. We examine responsibility accounting and identify various types of responsibility centers. We then take a close look at performance assessment for cost centers and conclude by considering performance reports for revenue centers. Responsibility accounting for major business segments is considered in Chapter 11.

Responsibility Accounting

LO1 Explain responsibility accounting.

Performance reports that include comparisons of actual results with plans or budgets serve as assessment tools and attention-directors to help managers control activities. According to the concept of *management by exception*, the absence of significant differences indicates that activities are proceeding as planned, whereas the presence of significant differences indicates a need to either take corrective action or revise plans. These evaluations and actions are made within the framework of an organization's overall mission, goals, and strategies.

Responsibility accounting reports are customized to emphasize the activities of specific organizational units. For example, a performance report addressed to the head of a production department contains manufacturing costs controllable by the department head; it should not contain costs (such as advertising, sales commissions, or the president's salary) that the head of the production department cannot control. Including noncontrollable costs in the report distracts the manager's attention from the controllable costs, thereby diluting a manager's efforts to deal with controllable items.

If too much pressure is placed on managers to meet performance targets, they may take actions that are not in the best interest of the organization. The Business Insight that follows presents a classic example of such actions referred to as channel stuffing. The designers of an organization's responsibility accounting system need to be aware of the potential pressures that such a system can place on managers. The decision-making model of the organization should be such that managers are not influenced to make undesirable decisions just to receive bonuses or promotions.

Business Insight ■ Meeting Targets by Channel Stuffing

Good business requires good measurement, and GAAP requires measurement too. Financial accountants measure performance and communicate it to capital markets. Management accountants do the same for internal decision-making and stewardship. Bonuses are tied to these numbers, as are stock market performance and promotions. Where there are incentives for performance, there are incentives for unethical practices. Channel stuffing, as *Business Insider*'s Jim Edwards says, is the "oldest—and worst—trick in the book."

Channel stuffing occurs when a company ships more product to retailers than they need, and then books these increased shipments as sales. The immediate effect is that revenue goes up, but this technique almost always backfires. In the following period, the retailers have more than enough inventory, and revenues fall again. At this point the game is up, unless the company turns to more fraudulent methods. Often, firms will take the excess inventory back as sales returns and maintain the overshipping, thus increasing sales but also increasing return expense. This is a red flag for the SEC. Diageo, maker of Johnny Walker and Smirnoff, is being investigated by the SEC for just this impropriety. While it remains to be seen what action the SEC will take in this case, as not all channel stuffing amounts to fraud, it is important for firms to monitor this sort of behavior.

Source: "What Is Channel Stuffing and How Might It Affect Your Business?" PwC Fraud Academy Blog, May 12, 2016; Jim Edwards, "The SEC Wants to Know If Diageo Used the Oldest — and Worst — Trick in the Book to Fudge Its Numbers," *Business Insider*, July 24, 2015.

Performance Reporting and Organization Structures

Before implementing a responsibility accounting system, all areas of authority and responsibility within an organization must be clearly defined. Organization charts and other documents should be examined to determine an organization's authority and responsibility structure. **Organization structure** is the arrangement of lines of authority and responsibility within an organization. These structures vary widely. Some companies have functional-based structures along the lines of marketing, production, research, and so forth; others use products, services, customers, or geography as the basis of organization. When an attempt is made to implement a responsibility accounting system, management could find instances of overlapping duties, authority not commensurate with responsibility, and expenditures for which no one appears responsible. The identification and resolution of these problems can be a major benefit of implementing a responsibility accounting system.

Although performance reports can be developed for areas of responsibility as narrow as a single worker, the basic responsibility unit in most organizations begins with the department and progresses to division and corporate levels. In manufacturing plants, separate performance reports may be prepared for each production and service department, and then summarized into a performance report for all manufacturing activities. In large universities, reports may be prepared for individual departments such as history, philosophy, and English, and then summarized into a performance report of a college, such as Liberal Arts.

Types of Responsibility Centers

Based on the nature of their responsibility, responsibility centers can be classified as cost centers, revenue centers, profit centers, or investment centers.

Cost Center

A **cost center** manager is only responsible for costs; there is no revenue responsibility. A cost center can be as small as a segment of a department or large enough to include a major aspect of the organization, such as all manufacturing activities. Typical examples of cost centers include the following:

Organization	Cost Center
Manufacturing plant	Tooling department
	Assembly activities
Retail store	Inventory control function
	Maintenance department
Hospital	Radiology
	Emergency room
College	History department
	Registrar's office
City government	Public safety (police and fire)
	Road maintenance

Revenue Center

A **revenue center** manager is responsible for the generation of sales revenues. Even though the basic performance report of a revenue center emphasizes sales, revenue centers are likely to be assigned responsibility for the controllable costs they incur in generating revenues. If revenues and costs are evaluated separately, the center has dual responsibility as a revenue center and as a cost center. If controllable costs are deducted from revenues to obtain some bottom-line contribution, the center is, in fact, being treated more like a profit center than a revenue center.

Profit Center

A **profit center** manager is responsible for revenues, costs, and the resulting profits. A profit center could be an entire organization, but it is more frequently a segment of an organization such as a product line, marketing territory, or store. In the context of performance evaluation, the word "profit" does not necessarily refer to the bottom line of an income statement; instead, it likely refers to the profit center's contribution to common corporate costs and profit. Profit is computed as the center's revenues less all costs directly associated with operating the center. Having limited authority regarding the size of total assets, the profit center manager is not held responsible for the relationship between profits and assets. In recent years many hospitals have been treating critical care and clinical service departments as profit centers to encourage physician chiefs to manage their departments as small businesses. The following Research Insight examines some of the issues associated with this movement.

Research Insight ■ When Profit Centers Break Down

Profit centers may be a poor fit for health care. In a 2008 article, Dr. David Young contends that there are four central problems with profit-based performance evaluation in hospitals:

1. Departments vary in their profitability for fundamental reasons unrelated to performance. Cardiovascular surgery will be more profitable than pediatrics due to the fundamental structure of health care rather than through performance.
2. Both transfer pricing and use of outside services are complicated, and in some cases impossible. It is impossible for the orthopedic surgery department to use outside radiology in some procedures, as that would require leaving the hospital.
3. The trend in health care is to integrate care across departments. For example, a trend in women's health is to integrate clinical and critical care seamlessly. This makes financially separating clinical and critical care both difficult and possibly counterproductive.
4. A focus on operating profit creates incentives for critical care departments not to treat low-income or uninsured patients.

Dr. Young's arguments are supported by a recent study of hospital profitability, which shows that hospital profitability is strongly determined by the market in which the hospital functions. Factors such as market power and the socioeconomic status of patients are important determinants of profitability and are clearly out of the control of individual departments within the hospital.

Sources: David W. Young, "Profit Centers in Clinical Care Departments an Idea Whose Time Has Gone: A Case Can Be Made for Converting a Hospital's Clinical Care Departments from Profit Centers into Standard Expense Centers," *Healthcare Financial Management* (March 2008): 66+. Academic OneFile. Web. July 25, 2016. G. Bai and G. F. Anderson, "A More Detailed Understanding of Factors Associated with Hospital Profitability," *Health Affairs*, Vol. 35, No. 5 (2016): pp. 889–897. DOI: 10.1377/hlthaff.2015.1193. Harris Meyer, "Not-for-Profits Dominate Top-10 List of Hospitals with Biggest Surpluses," *Modern Healthcare*, May 2, 2016.

Investment Center

An **investment center** manager is responsible for the relationship between its profits and the total assets invested in the center. Investment center managers have a high degree of organization autonomy. In general, the management of an investment center is expected to earn a target profit per dollar invested. Investment center managers are evaluated on the basis of how well they use the total resources entrusted to their care to earn a profit. An investment center is the broadest and most inclusive type of responsibility center. Managers of these centers have more authority and responsibility than other managers and are primarily responsible for planning, organizing, and controlling firm activities. Because of their authority regarding the size of corporate assets, they are held responsible for the relationship between profits and assets. Investment centers are discussed further in Chapter 11.

Financial and Nonfinancial Performance Measures

This chapter's emphasis is on financial performance reports. Dollar-based financial reports have several advantages over other financial measures. Their "bottom line" impact is readily apparent. If actual fixed costs exceed budgeted fixed costs by $10,000, the before-tax income of an organization is $10,000 less than it would be without the extra fixed costs. Additionally, because dollars are additive and applicable to all organizational units, financial measures are easily summarized and reported up the organization chart.

It is important to keep in mind that although financial measures may indicate results are not in accordance with the budget, they do not indicate the root cause of financial deviations. The identification and analysis of the root cause of financial variances require asking questions and, frequently, the use of nonfinancial data. Managers and employees at lower levels of the organization are often better served by performance reports focusing on data directly related to their job, such as units processed or customers served per hour. Although financial performance is still critical to Southwest Airline's top management and still used to evaluate managers, aircraft, and routes, the focus for the evaluation should include customer satisfaction. Other examples of nonfinancial performance measures include defects per thousand units in a manufacturing plant, average and longest waiting time in a restaurant, nursing staff hours per patient day in a hospital, response time for a fire department, and customer satisfaction at a retail store or bank.

When organizations seek to improve financial performance beyond what is possible with current products, procedures, or services, the initial focus is most often on nonfinancial measures. Trader Joe's grocery stores might benchmark the length of their cash-register waiting times against Whole Foods'.

Identifying Responsibility Centers **LO1 Review 10-1**

Eli's Cheesecake is a family-owned business based out of Chicago, IL. Eli's operates its corporate office, bakery, retail store, and café from one location on the west side of the city and recently opened a Cheesecake Café at Chicago's O'Hare Airport.

Required

Peruse Eli's website at http://www.elicheesecake.com to become more familiar with the company. Listed below are likely reporting centers for Eli's. Identify the type of responsibility center that would most likely be assigned to each reporting center: (1) Cost Center, (2) Revenue Center, (3) Profit Center, or (4) Investment Center.

_____ Bakery
_____ Accounting department
_____ Product line—Original Plain Cheesecake
_____ Human resources department
_____ Cheesecake Café at O'Hare Airport

Solution on p. 391.

Performance Reporting for Cost Centers

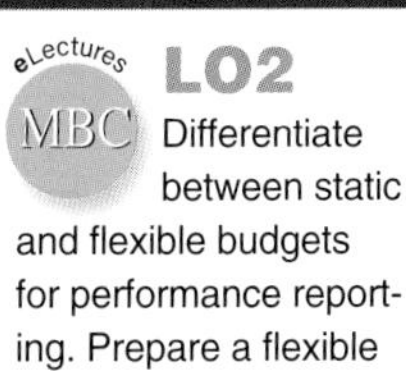

LO2 Differentiate between static and flexible budgets for performance reporting. Prepare a flexible budget.

Financial performance reports for cost centers include a comparison of actual and budgeted (or allowed) costs and identify the difference as a **variance**. *Allowed costs* in performance reports are the flexible budget amounts for the actual level of activity. The variance is favorable if actual costs are less than budgeted (or allowed) costs and unfavorable if actual costs are more than budgeted (or allowed) costs. These comparisons are made in total and individually for each type of controllable cost assigned to the cost center.

Development of Flexible Budgets

A budget that is based on a prediction of sales and production is called a **static budget**. The operating budget explained in Chapter 9 is a static budget. Budgets can also be set for a series of possible production and sales volumes, or budgets can be adjusted to a particular level of production after the fact. These budgets, based on cost-volume relationships, are called **flexible budgets**; they are used to determine what costs should be for a level of activity. For example, if the college cafeteria budgets $15,000 for food during April for 5,000 meals but provides 6,000 meals, the budget needs to be adjusted by the original food budget rate of $3 ($15,000/5,000 meals). If $17,500 was spent on food during the month, the analysis might appear as follows:

Budget Item	Actual	Budget	Difference
Static analysis			
Food	$17,500	5,000 meals × $3 = $15,000	$2,500 over budget
Flexible analysis			
Food	$17,500	6,000 meals × $3 = $18,000	$500 under budget

The cafeteria manager is better evaluated based on what actually happened with the flexible budget than with the static budget, especially if the manager had no control over how many student meals were requested.

For a complete example of a flexible budget, assume that Tumi, which produces high-quality bags, luggage, and accessories, produces only one product, a computer bag. Also assume Tumi has only three departments: production, sales, and administration. Focusing on the production department, the flexible budget cost-estimating equations for total monthly production costs of computer bags are based on the production standards for variable and fixed costs. The standards follow:

Variable costs
- Direct materials—2 pounds per bag at $5 per pound, or $10 per bag
- Direct labor—0.25 hour per bag at $24 per hour, or $6 per bag
- Variable overhead—2 pounds of direct material per bag at $4 per pound, or $8 per bag

Fixed costs—$52,000

If management plans to produce 10,000 computer bags in July, the budgeted manufacturing costs are $292,000:

TUMI Manufacturing Cost Budget For Month of July	
Manufacturing costs	
Variable costs	
Direct materials (10,000 bags × 2 pounds × $5)	$100,000
Direct labor (10,000 bags × 0.25 hours × $24)	60,000
Variable overhead (10,000 bags × 2 pounds × $4)	80,000
Fixed costs	52,000
Total	$292,000

Flexible Budgets Emphasize Performance

If actual production happened to equal budgeted production, the production department is evaluated by comparing the actual and budgeted costs. If production needs change, perhaps due to an unexpected increase or decrease in sales volume, the production department should attempt to make appropriate changes.

When the actual production volume is anything other than the originally budgeted amount, the production department's financial responsibility for costs should be based on the actual level of production.

For the purpose of evaluating the financial performance of cost centers, a flexible budget is tailored, after the fact, to the actual level of activity. A **flexible budget variance** is computed for each cost as the difference between the actual cost and the flexible budget cost. Assume actual production for July totaled 11,000 bags rather than 10,000 bags. Examples of a performance report for July manufacturing costs based on static and flexible budgets are presented in **Exhibit 10.1**. When the production department's financial performance is evaluated using the static budget, the actual cost of producing 11,000 bags is compared to the budgeted cost of producing 10,000 bags. The result is a series of unfavorable static budget variances totaling $20,000.

Exhibit 10.1 Flexible Budgets and Performance Evaluation

TUMI
Production Department Performance Report
For Month of July

	Based on Static Budget			Based on Flexible Budget		
	Actual	Original Budget	Static Budget Variance	Actual	Flexible Budget*	Flexible Budget Variance
Volume	11,000	10,000		11,000	11,000	
Variable costs						
Direct materials	$108,000	$100,000	$ 8,000 U	$108,000	$110,000	$2,000 F
Direct labor	70,000	60,000	10,000 U	70,000	66,000	4,000 U
Variable overhead	81,000	80,000	1,000 U	81,000	88,000	7,000 F
Fixed costs	53,000	52,000	1,000 U	53,000	52,000	1,000 U
Totals	$312,000	$292,000	$20,000 U	$312,000	$316,000	$4,000 F

* Flexible budget manufacturing costs: (Actual level × Budgeted per bag cost)
Direct materials (11,000 bags × 2 pounds × $5)
Direct labor (11,000 bags × 0.25 labor hour × $24)
Variable overhead (11,000 bags × 2 pounds × $4)

When the production department's financial performance is evaluated by comparing actual costs with costs allowed in a flexible budget drawn up for the actual production volume, the results are mixed. Direct materials have a $2,000 favorable variance. Direct labor has a $4,000 unfavorable variance. The variable overhead variance is $7,000 favorable. The fixed overhead variance remains $1,000 unfavorable since the static and flexible fixed budgets stay the same. The net flexible budget variance is $4,000 favorable, a substantial change from the static variance of $20,000 unfavorable.

Flexible budget variances provide a much better indicator of performance than static budget variances that do not consider the increased level of production (11,000 bags rather than 10,000 bags). When production exceeds the planned level, the static budget variances are usually unfavorable. Likewise, when actual production is substantially below the planned level of activity, the static variances are usually favorable. While it is important to isolate and determine the cause of any variation between planned and actual production, the financial-based performance report is not the appropriate place to mix volume-created variances with those related to the actual production levels.

Standard Costs and Performance Reports

A **standard cost** indicates what it should cost to provide an activity or produce one batch or unit of product under planned and efficient operating conditions. In a standard costing environment, the flexible budget is based on standard unit costs. Traditionally, standard costs have been developed from an engineering analysis or from an analysis of historical data adjusted for expected changes in the product, production technology, or costs. When standards are developed using historical data, management must be careful to ensure that past inefficiencies are excluded from current standards.

To obtain the full benefit of standard costs, the standards must be based on realistic expectations. Suppose the standard cost for direct labor for Tumi is $6.00 per bag (computed as 0.25 direct labor hours × $24 per hour). Some organizations intentionally set "tight" standards to motivate employees toward higher levels of production. The management of Tumi might set their standards for direct labor at 0.22 hours per bag rather than at the expected 0.25 hours per bag, hoping that employees will strive toward the lower time and, consequently, the lower cost of $5.28 ($24 × 0.22). The use of tight standards often causes planning and behavioral problems. Management expects them to result in unfavorable variances. Accordingly, tight standards should not be used to budget input requirements and cash flows because management expects to incur more labor costs than the standards allow. The use of tight standards can have undesirable behavioral effects if employees find that a second set of standards is used in the "real" budget or if they are constantly subject to unfavorable performance reports. These employees could come to distrust the entire budgeting and performance evaluation system, or they may quit trying to achieve any of the organization's standards.

Tight standards are more likely to occur in an imposed budget than in a participation budget. In a participation budget, the problem may be to avoid overstating the costs required to produce a product. Loose standards may fail to properly motivate employees and can make the company uncompetitive due to costs that are higher than competitors'.

Review 10-2 LO2 — Preparing a Flexible Budget for Performance Reporting

Suppose you receive the following performance report from the accounting department for your first month as plant manager for a new company. Your supervisor, the vice president of manufacturing, has concerns that the report does not provide an accurate picture of your performance in the area of cost control.

	Actual	Budgeted	Variance
Units	10,000	12,000	2,000 U
Costs			
Direct materials	$ 299,000	$ 360,000	$ 61,000 F
Direct labor	345,500	432,000	86,500 F
Variable factory overhead	180,000	216,000	36,000 F
Fixed factory overhead	375,000	360,000	15,000 U
Total costs	$1,199,500	$1,368,000	$168,500 F

Required

Solution on p. 391.

Prepare a revised budget that better reflects your performance.

Variance Analysis for Costs

Components of Standard Cost Analysis

LO3 Determine the components of standard cost variance analysis. Formulate and interpret direct materials cost variances.

To use and interpret standard cost variances properly, managers must understand the processes and activities that drive costs. Cost variances are merely signals. They do not explain why costs differ from expectations. Underlying causes of variances must be investigated before final judgment is passed on the effectiveness and efficiency of an operation or activity.

Standard cost variance analysis is a systematic approach to examining flexible budget variances. Actual costs are determined from the organization's financial transactions. Flexible budget costs are determined by multiplying standard quantities allowed for the output times the standard price per unit. For a company using activity-based costing, each manufacturing activity could have its own standard costs that focus on underlying concepts and cost drivers, and companies even develop their own set of variances.

Standard cost variance analysis identifies the general causes of the total flexible budget variance by breaking it into separate price and quantity variances for each production component. Two possible reasons that actual cost could differ from flexible budget cost for a given amount of output produced are (1) a difference between actual and standard prices paid for the production components—the price variance—and (2) a difference between the actual quantity and the standard quantity allowed for the production components—the quantity variance. Variances have different names for different cost categories as follows:

Cost Category	Price Variance Name	Quantity Variance Name
Direct materials	Materials price variance	Materials quantity variance
Direct labor	Labor rate variance	Labor efficiency variance
Variable overhead	Variable overhead spending variance	Variable overhead efficiency variance

Fixed overhead is excluded from the unit standard costs because, within the relevant range of normal activity, it does not vary with the volume of production. To facilitate product costing, however, many organizations develop a standard fixed overhead cost per unit.

In the following sections, we analyze the flexible budget cost variances for materials, labor and variable overhead. Our illustration is based on the following hypothetical July activity and costs of Tumi's production department.

TUMI Actual Manufacturing Costs For Month of July	
Actual bags completed	11,000
Manufacturing costs	
Unit level costs	
Direct materials (24,000 pounds × $4.50)	$108,000
Direct labor (2,800 hours × $25.00)	70,000
Variable overhead	81,000
Fixed overhead costs	53,000
Total	$312,000

Research Insight ■ When Are Variances Evidence of Fraud?

Standard cost variances can help firms hold managers and employees accountable for their work. Dr. Cecily Raiborn and her coauthors argue that variance analysis can also help strengthen internal controls, ultimately detecting fraud early and pointing to areas of the company that are weak. If purchasing managers are receiving kickbacks from suppliers, the behavior may show up in frequent, slightly unfavorable price variances. If employees are stealing materials for resale or personal use, the firm may see unfavorable materials variances.

This sort of data analysis for indicators of fraud is important enough for auditors that the Big Four auditing firms are developing tools to automate this process. KPMG recently partnered with IBM to use Watson's artificial intelligence engine to comb through financial data for just the sort of behaviors that will show up in the variances discussed here. EY (formerly Ernst & Young) has poured $400 million into its own tools for this analysis. Automating the data analysis allows all of the client's transactions to be considered, not just the top-level numbers that come out in variance analysis.

Such tools find patterns that raise suspicion, which can be variances or issues as simple as sales clustered just before the quarter end and expenses clustered just after. These tools do the work of combing through the firm's data for suspicious patterns, but it remains the job of management accountants and auditors to determine whether the patterns are operational or fraudulent.

Sources: Cecily Raiborn, Janet Butler, and Lucian Zelazny, "Standard Costing Variances: Potential Red Flags of Fraud?" *Cost Management*, 2013.
Michael Rapoport, "Auditing Firms Count on Technology for Backup," *Wall Street Journal*, March 7, 2016.

Note that detailed information on actual pounds and an actual rate is not provided for variable overhead. That is because variable overhead represents a pool of related costs driven by a number of factors rather than a single cost with a single driver. Although the basis used in budgeting variable overhead may, and should, have a high correlation with actual variable overhead, it is a surrogate for the multiple cost elements that comprise variable overhead. Issues related to variable overhead are discussed in greater detail later in this chapter.

Establishing and Using Standards for Direct Materials

The two basic elements contained in the standards for direct materials are the *standard price* and the *standard quantity*. Materials standards indicate how much an organization should pay for each input unit of direct materials and the quantity of direct materials it should use to produce one unit of output. The standard price per unit of direct materials should include all reasonable costs necessary to acquire the materials. These costs include the invoice price of materials, less planned discounts plus freight, insurance, special handling, and any other costs related to the acquisition of the materials. The standard quantity represents the number of units of raw materials allowed for the production of one unit of finished product. This amount should include the amount dictated by the physical characteristics of the process and the product, plus a reasonable allowance for normal spoilage, waste, and other inefficiencies. The quantity standard can be determined by engineering analysis, professional judgment, or by averaging the actual amount used for several periods. An average of actual past materials usage may not be a good standard because it could include excessive wastes and inefficiencies in the standard quantity.

Direct Materials Variances

The **materials price variance** is the difference between the actual materials cost and the standard cost of actual materials inputs. The **materials quantity variance** is the difference between the standard cost of actual materials inputs and the flexible budget cost for materials. The direct materials variances for Tumi follow.

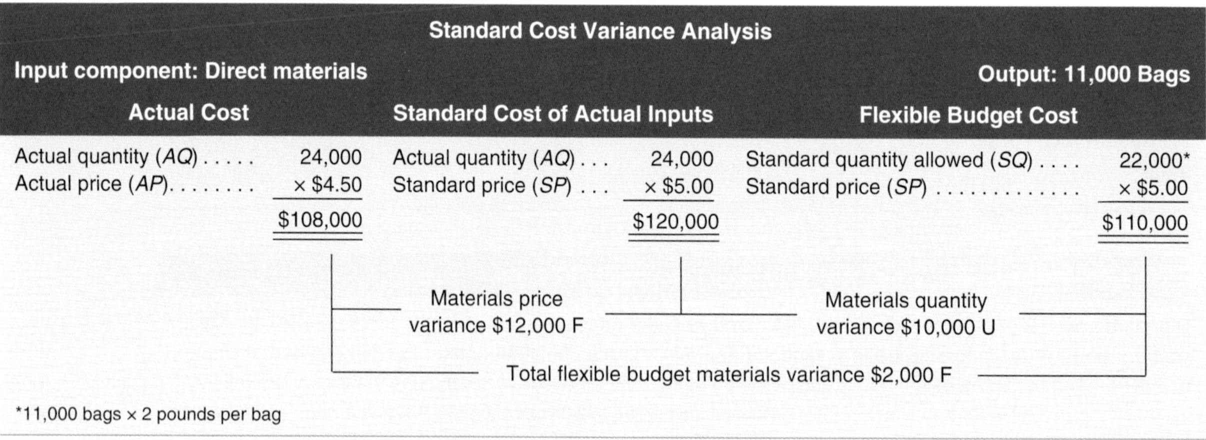

Standard Cost Variance Analysis

Input component: Direct materials — Output: 11,000 Bags

Actual Cost		Standard Cost of Actual Inputs		Flexible Budget Cost	
Actual quantity (*AQ*)	24,000	Actual quantity (*AQ*) . . .	24,000	Standard quantity allowed (*SQ*)	22,000*
Actual price (*AP*).	× $4.50	Standard price (*SP*) . . .	× $5.00	Standard price (*SP*)	× $5.00
	$108,000		$120,000		$110,000

Materials price variance $12,000 F

Materials quantity variance $10,000 U

Total flexible budget materials variance $2,000 F

*11,000 bags × 2 pounds per bag

Tumi had a favorable materials price variance of $12,000 because the actual cost of materials used ($108,000) was less than the standard cost of actual materials used ($120,000). The price variance can also be computed using a formula approach as the actual quantity (*AQ*) used times the difference between the actual price (*AP*) and the standard price (*SP*). Tumi paid $0.50 per pound below the standard price for 24,000 pounds for a total savings of $12,000:

Materials price variance = AQ(AP – SP)
= 24,000($4.50 – $5.00)
= 24,000 × $0.50
= $12,000 F

The unfavorable quantity variance of $10,000 occurred because the standard cost of actual materials used, $120,000 (24,000 × $5), was higher than the cost of materials allowed by the flexible budget, $110,000 (22,000 × $5). A total of 22,000 pounds of materials is allowed to produce 11,000 units of finished outputs. This is computed as 11,000 finished bags times 2.0 pounds of direct materials per bag. The materials quantity variance can also be computed using a formula approach as the standard price (*SP*) per pound times the difference between the number of pounds actually used (*AQ*) and the number of pounds allowed (*SQ*):

$$\textbf{Materials quantity variance} = \text{SP(AQ} - \text{SQ)}$$
$$= \$5(24{,}000 - 22{,}000)$$
$$= \$5 \times 2{,}000$$
$$= \$10{,}000\ \text{U}$$

Interpreting Materials Variances

As highlighted in the following two Business Insights, after computing variances, managers are in a better position to analyze their business's results and to make better and more relevant decisions. A *favorable materials price variance* indicates that the employee responsible for materials purchases paid less per unit than the price allowed by the standards. This could result from receiving discounts for purchasing more than the normal quantities, effective bargaining by the employee, purchasing substandard-quality materials, purchasing from a distress seller, or other factors. Ordinarily, when a favorable price variance is reported, the employee's performance is interpreted as favorable. However, if the favorable price variance results from the purchase of materials of lower than standard quality or from a purchase in more than desirable quantities, the employee's performance would be questionable. All large variances, including favorable variances, should be thoroughly investigated for causes and corrections.

Business Insight ■ Variance Analysis Helps Hospitals Understand Impact of Policy

To understand the impact of California's Hospital Fair Pricing Act (CHFPA), Professor Ge Bai of Washington and Lee University applied variance analysis to California hospitals' expense recovery data. Expense recovery is simply the rate at which the hospital is able to recover the costs of serving a patient by collecting from insurers.

The CHFPA stipulates that hospitals can only charge low-income, uninsured patients Medicare rates for services. The act also makes it more difficult to collect payment from these patients. Dr. Bai's study shows that the CHFPA decreases the rate of expense recovery from low-income patients and increases the share of these patients in the health-care system, consistent with the aims of the CHFPA. His study also shows that hospitals appear to be offsetting the cost of treating more low-income patients at lower rates by collecting more aggressively from both public programs and from private insurance companies.

Source: Ge Bai, "Applying Variance Analysis to Understand California Hospitals' Expense Recovery Status by Patient Groups," *Accounting Horizons* Vol. 30, No. 2 (June 2016): pp. 211–223.

An *unfavorable materials price variance* means that the purchasing employee paid more per unit for materials than the price allowed by the standards. This could be caused by failure to buy in sufficient quantities to receive normal discounts; purchase of higher-quality materials than called for in the product specifications; failure to place materials orders on a timely basis; failure to bargain for the best available prices; or other factors. An unfavorable variance does not always mean that the employee performed unfavorably. Many noncontrollable factors surround the purchasing function, including unanticipated price increases, the need to increase production to meet unanticipated sales, and supply chain problems such as a work stoppage at a vendor.

A *favorable materials quantity variance* means that the actual quantity of raw materials used was less than the quantity allowed for the units produced. This could result from factors such as less materials waste than allowed by the standards, better than expected machine efficiency, direct materials of higher quality than required by the standards, and more efficient use of direct materials by employees. An *unfavorable materials quantity variance* occurs when the quantity of raw materials used exceeds the quantity allowed for the units produced. This could result from incurring more waste than provided for in the standards, poorly maintained machinery requiring larger amounts of raw materials, raw materials of lower quality than required by the standards, or poorly trained employees who were unable to use the materials at the level of efficiency required by the standards.

Business Insight ■ Unfavorable Price Variance? Buy a Farm

Demand for organic ingredients is outpacing supply. Sales of organic food tripled from 2003 to 2013, and supply of some products is not keeping up. Not only are prices rising (unfavorable rate variance) but shortages are also interrupting supply chains for large food companies (unfavorable efficiency variance). In 2015, Nature's Path Foods Inc. decided that it had had enough. So it bought a 2,800-acre farm in Montana. Nature's Path had been dealing with supply shortages and unpredictable prices, once even importing ingredients from Sweden on very short notice. The company plans to invest $2 million each year in purchasing and converting farmland.

It turns out that changing a farm from conventional to organic requires a transition period that is tough for farmers. It takes between one and three years to transition a farm. During transition, the farm is using more costly organic practices, but farmers cannot sell their products as organic. Chipotle Mexican Grill Inc. and Pacific Foods of Oregon Inc. are trying to help farmers switch by offering financing and training. The maker of Garden of Eatin' corn chips, Hain Celestial Group Inc., is offering farmers long-term contracts to lock in corn supply and to help offset some of the risks farmers face.

When supply is erratic, companies may find that capital budgeting choices that include purchasing their suppliers make sense.

Source: Ilan Brat, "Hunger for Organic Foods Stretches Supply Chain," *Wall Street Journal*, April 3, 2015.

Review 10-3 LO3 — Calculating Standard Cost Variances for Direct Materials

Suppose the flexible budget performance report for REI's camping chair product for March follows.

	Actual Costs	Flexible Budget Cost	Flexible Budget Variances
Output units	5,000	5,000	
Direct materials	$104,125	$100,000	$ 4,125 U
Direct labor	82,400	75,000	7,400 U
Variable manufacturing overhead			
Category 1	31,000	30,000	1,000 U
Category 2	18,000	20,000	2,000 F
Fixed manufacturing overhead	42,000	40,000	2,000 U
Total	$277,525	$265,000	$12,525 U

The standard unit cost for folding chairs follows:

Direct materials (4 pounds × $5.00 per pound)	$20
Direct labor (1.25 hours × $12.00 per hour)	15
Variable overhead, Category 1 (1.25 hours × $4.80)	6
Variable overhead, Category 2 ($4 per finished unit)	4
Total standard variable cost per unit	$45

Actual cost of materials is based on 21,250 pounds of direct materials purchased and used at $4.90 per pound; actual cost of assembly is based on 7,000 labor hours. Variable overhead is applied on labor hours for Category 1 and finished units for Category 2.

Required

Calculate all standard cost variances for direct materials.

Solution on p. 392.

LO4 Formulate and interpret direct labor cost variances.

Establishing and Using Standards for Direct Labor

To evaluate management performance in controlling labor costs, it is necessary to determine the *standard labor rate* for each hour allowed and the *standard time allowed* to produce a unit. Setting labor rate standards can be quite simple or extremely complex. If all employees have the same wage rate, determining the standard cost is relatively easy: Simply adopt the normal wage rate as the standard labor rate. If there are variations in employee wage rates, the standard labor rate should be based on the expected mix of employee wage rates.

The standard labor time per unit can be determined by an engineering approach or an empirical observation approach. When using an engineering approach, industrial engineers ascertain the amount of time required to produce a unit of finished product by applying time and motion methods or other available techniques. Normal operating conditions are assumed in arriving at the labor standard. Therefore, allowances must be made for normal machine downtime, employee personal breaks, and so forth. Under the empirical approach, the average time required to produce a unit under normal operating conditions is used as a basis for the standard.

Direct Labor Variances

Using the general variance model that was used for materials, we can compute the labor rate and efficiency variances. The **labor rate variance** is the difference between the actual cost and the standard cost of actual labor inputs. The **labor efficiency variance** is the difference between the standard cost of actual inputs and the flexible budget cost for labor.

Tumi's labor standards provide for 0.25 hour of labor per bag produced at $24 per hour. During July, 2,800 hours were used at a cost of $25 per hour. Using these data, the labor rate (price) variance and labor efficiency (quantity) variance can be computed as shown in the following illustration.

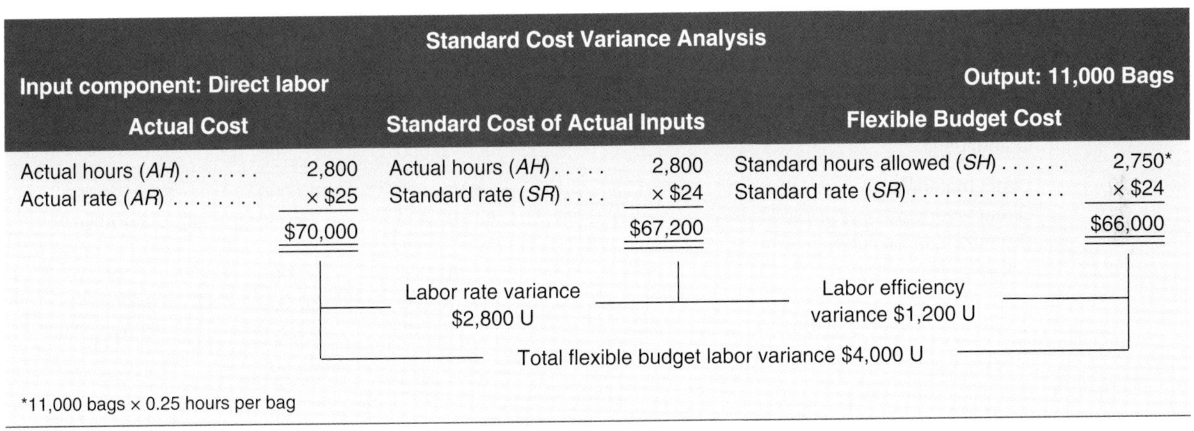

Standard Cost Variance Analysis

Input component: Direct labor | Output: 11,000 Bags

Actual Cost		Standard Cost of Actual Inputs		Flexible Budget Cost	
Actual hours (*AH*)	2,800	Actual hours (*AH*)	2,800	Standard hours allowed (*SH*)	2,750*
Actual rate (*AR*)	× $25	Standard rate (*SR*)	× $24	Standard rate (*SR*)	× $24
	$70,000		$67,200		$66,000

Labor rate variance $2,800 U

Labor efficiency variance $1,200 U

Total flexible budget labor variance $4,000 U

*11,000 bags × 0.25 hours per bag

The labor rate variance can also be computed in formula form as the actual number of hours used times the difference between the actual rate and the standard rate.

$$\textbf{Labor rate variance} = \text{AH(AR} - \text{SR)}$$
$$= 2{,}800(\$25 - \$24)$$
$$= 2{,}800 \times \$1$$
$$= \$2{,}800 \text{ U}$$

This computation of the labor rate variance shows that the company paid $1 more than the standard rate for each of the 2,800 hours worked.

Since 11,000 units of product were finished during the period and 0.25 hour of labor was allowed for each bag, the total number of standard hours allowed was 2,750 (11,000 bags × 0.25 hour). The labor efficiency variance can also be computed as the standard rate times the difference between the actual labor hours and the standard hours allowed:

$$\textbf{Labor efficiency variance} = \text{SR(AH} - \text{SH)}$$
$$= \$24(2{,}800 - 2{,}750)$$
$$= \$24 \times 50$$
$$= \$1{,}200 \text{ U}$$

Tumi's labor efficiency variance indicates that the company used 50 more labor hours than allowed. By itself, this inefficiency caused an unfavorable variance of $1,200.

Interpreting Labor Variances

The possible explanations for labor rate variances are rather limited. An *unfavorable labor rate variance* can be caused by the use of higher-paid laborers than the standards provided. An increase in wage rates not reflected in the standards can also cause an unfavorable labor rate variance. A *favorable labor rate variance* occurs if lower-paid workers were used or if actual wage rates declined.

Unfavorable labor efficiency variances occur when the actual labor hours exceed the number of hours allowed for the actual output. This could be caused by using poorly trained workers or poorly maintained machinery or by the use of low-quality materials. Low employee morale and generally poor working conditions could also adversely affect the efficiency.

Favorable labor efficiency variances occur when the actual labor hours are less than the number of hours allowed for the actual output. This above-normal efficiency can be caused by the company's use of higher-skilled (and higher-paid) workers, better machinery, or higher-quality raw materials than the standards require. High employee morale, improved job satisfaction, or generally improved working conditions could also account for the above-normal efficiency of the workers.

Review 10-4 LO4 Calculating Standard Cost Variances for Direct Labor

Suppose the flexible budget performance report for REI's camping chair product for March follows.

	Actual Costs	Flexible Budget Cost	Flexible Budget Variances
Output units	5,000	5,000	
Direct materials	$104,125	$100,000	$ 4,125 U
Direct labor	82,400	75,000	7,400 U
Variable manufacturing overhead			
Category 1	31,000	30,000	1,000 U
Category 2	18,000	20,000	2,000 F
Fixed manufacturing overhead	42,000	40,000	2,000 U
Total	$277,525	$265,000	$12,525 U

The standard unit cost for folding chairs follows:

Direct materials (4 pounds × $5.00 per pound)	$20
Direct labor (1.25 hours × $12.00 per hour)	15
Variable overhead, Category 1 (1.25 hours × $4.80)	6
Variable overhead, Category 2 ($4 per finished unit)	4
Total standard variable cost per unit	$45

Actual cost of materials is based on 21,250 pounds of direct materials purchased and used at $4.90 per pound; actual cost of assembly is based on 7,000 labor hours. Variable overhead is applied on labor hours for Category 1 and finished units for Category 2.

Required

Calculate all standard cost variances for direct labor.

Solution on p. 392.

Establishing and Using Standards for Variable Overhead

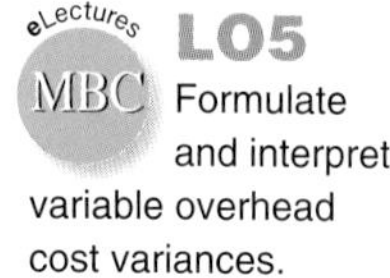

LO5 Formulate and interpret variable overhead cost variances.

The traditional unit-level approach to cost estimation, budgeting, and variance analysis separates overhead costs into fixed and variable elements. This separation is necessary because fixed costs are primarily driven by factors related to capacity and variable costs are primarily driven by factors related to volume.

Because it includes many heterogeneous costs, manufacturing overhead poses a unique problem in establishing standards for the standard quantity and the standard price of inputs. Direct materials have a natural physical measure of quantity such as tons, barrels, pounds, and liters. Similarly, labor or assembly is measurable in hours or minutes. However, no single quantity measure is common to all overhead items. Overhead is a cost group that can simultaneously include costs measurable in hours, pounds, liters, and kilowatts.

The most frequent approach to dealing with the problem of multiple quantity measures in variable manufacturing overhead is to use a single surrogate (or substitute) measure to represent the quantity of all items in a given group. Typical substitute measures include machine hours, units of finished product, direct labor hours, and direct labor dollars. The variable overhead standard is then stated in terms of this surrogate measure.

Variable Overhead Variances

The **variable overhead spending variance** is the difference between the actual variable overhead cost and the standard variable overhead cost for the actual inputs of the surrogate measure. The **variable overhead efficiency variance** is the difference between the standard variable overhead cost for the actual inputs of the surrogate measure and the flexible budget cost allowed for variable overhead based on outputs.

Assume for Tumi, the actual variable overhead in July was $81,000. This represents the actual cost of overhead items such as indirect materials and indirect labor. Pounds of materials is Tumi's surrogate measure for quantity for variable overhead allowed and used. This means that the standard costs allowed for variable overhead varies with the pounds of direct materials allowed. Hence the standard cost of actual inputs is calculated as actual pounds of direct materials (*AQ*) times the standard variable overhead rate per pound (*SR*):

Standard cost of actual inputs = (AQ × SR)
= 24,000 × $4
= $96,000

The flexible budget cost for variable overhead allowed for the actual outputs is based on the 22,000 pounds of direct materials allowed (*SQ*) for the bags produced during the period (11,000 bags × 2 pounds). The allowed quantities are multiplied by the standard variable overhead rate (*SR*). The resulting variable overhead flexible budget cost is $88,000:

Flexible budget cost = (SQ × SR)
= 22,000 × $4
= $88,000

Using these data, the variable overhead spending (price) variance and the variable overhead efficiency (quantity) variance follow.

Standard Cost Variance Analysis				
Input component: Variable overhead				**Output: 11,000 Bags**
Actual Cost	**Standard Cost of Actual Inputs**		**Flexible Budget Cost**	
$81,000	Actual pounds (*AQ*)	24,000	Pounds allowed (*SQ*)	22,000*
	Standard rate (*SR*)	× $4	Standard rate (*SR*)	× $4
	Total	$96,000	Total	$88,000
	Variable overhead spending variance $15,000 F		Variable overhead efficiency variance $8,000 U	
	Total flexible budget variable overhead variance $7,000 F			

*11,000 bags × 2 lbs.

An alternative to the computation of the variable overhead effectiveness variance follows:

Variable overhead efficiency variance = SR(AQ – SQ)
= $4(24,000 – 22,000)
= $8,000 U

This approach emphasizes that the 2,000 extra pounds used should have increased variable overhead by $8,000 at the standard rate of $4 per pound.

Interpreting Variable Overhead Variances

A *favorable spending variance* encompasses all factors that cause actual expenditures to be less than the amount expected for the actual inputs of the measurement base, including consumption and payment. Conversely, an *unfavorable spending variance* results when the actual expenditures are more than expected for the inputs of the measurement base. This is caused by consuming more overhead items than expected, or by paying more than the expected amount for overhead items consumed, or by both. Thus, the term *spending variance* is used instead of *price variance*.

The key to understanding the variable overhead spending variance is recognizing that the amount of variable overhead cost allowed is determined by the level of the surrogate measurement base used. Any deviation from this spending budget causes a spending variance to occur.

The variable overhead efficiency variance measures the difference between the standard variable overhead cost for the actual quantity of the surrogate measurement base and the standard variable overhead cost for the allowed quantity of the surrogate measurement base. This variance measures the amount of variable overhead that should have been saved (or incurred) because of the efficient (or inefficient) use of the surrogate measurement base. It provides no information about the degree of efficiency in using variable overhead items such as indirect materials and indirect labor. This information is reflected in the spending variance.

Managerial Decision ■ You Are the Vice President of Manufacturing

Your company has had a practice for many years of budgeting variable overhead costs based on direct labor hours. The managerial accountants have argued that if direct labor hours are controlled, variable overhead costs will take care of themselves since direct labor hours drive variable overhead costs. You (and your plant managers) have become very skeptical of this policy because in recent years variable overhead variances have been very erratic—sometimes being large favorable amounts and other times being large unfavorable amounts. You are beginning to plan for the coming budget year. How do you think you should budget variable overhead and evaluate managers who control these costs? [Answer, p. 376]

Fixed Overhead Variances

By definition, the quantity of goods and services purchased by fixed expenditures is not expected to change in proportion to short-run changes in the level of production. For example, in the short run, the production level does not affect the amount of depreciation on buildings, the number of fixed salaried employees, or the amount of real property subject to property taxes. Whether the organization produces 10,000 or 15,000 cases, the same quantity of fixed overhead is expected to be incurred, as long as the production level is within the relevant range of activity provided by the current fixed overhead items. Therefore, an efficiency variance is not computed for fixed overhead costs.

Even though the components of fixed overhead are not expected to be affected by the production activity level in the short run, the actual amount spent for fixed overhead items can differ from the amount budgeted. For example, higher than budgeted supervisors' salaries could be paid, there may be unanticipated increases in property taxes or insurance premiums, and the cost of leased facilities may increase. Fixed overhead costs in excess of the amount budgeted are reflected in the fixed overhead budget variance. The **fixed overhead budget variance** is, simply, the difference between budgeted and actual fixed overhead. Using the assumed fixed costs of Tumi as an example:

Fixed overhead budget variance = Actual fixed overhead − Budgeted fixed overhead
= $53,000 − $52,000
= $1,000 U

The fixed overhead budget variance is always the same as the total fixed overhead flexible budget variance. Because budgeted fixed overhead is the same for all outputs within the relevant range, the budget variance explains the total flexible budget variance between actual and allowed fixed overhead.

Similar to variable overhead, fixed overhead variances can be caused by a combination of price and quantity factors. Fixed overhead variances are examined further in Appendix 10A.

Business Insight ■ The Correct Diagnosis Is the Efficient Diagnosis

Misdiagnosis in the medical field is rampant. At its core, misdiagnosis is simply misidentifying a problem—a pathologist doesn't identify cancerous cells that exist, or a doctor may diagnose a patient as having cancer when, in fact, the patient does not. Second opinions of diagnoses raise questions in 25% of cases and prevent procedures that are costly for both the health-care system and the patient. On the other hand, second opinions can also catch missed diagnoses and help patients avoid costly convalescence. But getting a second opinion isn't always easy, especially in rural areas. Currently, lab samples must be physically transported across the country for diagnosis. GE is working with the US FDA to introduce a digital diagnosis system that allows samples to move more easily across the country for primary and secondary diagnoses. Getting the diagnosis right will have positive effects on both the patient's quality of life and medical bills and will yield better information for the hospital's budgeting process.

Sources: Laura Landro, "New Ways Doctors Reach Agreement on Patient Diagnoses," *Wall Street Journal*, June 9, 2015.

Calculating Standard Cost Variances for Variable Manufacturing Overhead — LO5 Review 10-5

Suppose the flexible budget performance report for REI's camping chair product for March follows.

	Actual Costs	Flexible Budget Cost	Flexible Budget Variances
Output units	5,000	5,000	
Direct materials	$104,125	$100,000	$ 4,125 U
Direct labor	82,400	75,000	7,400 U
Variable manufacturing overhead			
Category 1	31,000	30,000	1,000 U
Category 2	18,000	20,000	2,000 F
Fixed manufacturing overhead	42,000	40,000	2,000 U
Total	$277,525	$265,000	$12,525 U

The standard unit cost for folding chairs follows:

Direct materials (4 pounds × $5.00 per pound)	$20
Direct labor (1.25 hours × $12.00 per hour)	15
Variable overhead, Category 1 (1.25 hours × $4.80)	6
Variable overhead, Category 2 ($4 per finished unit)	4
Total standard variable cost per unit	$45

Actual cost of materials is based on 21,250 pounds of direct materials purchased and used at $4.90 per pound; actual cost of assembly is based on 7,000 labor hours. Variable overhead is applied on labor hours for Category 1 and finished units for Category 2.

Required
Calculate all standard cost variances for variable manufacturing overhead.

Solution on p. 392.

Performance Reports for Revenue Centers

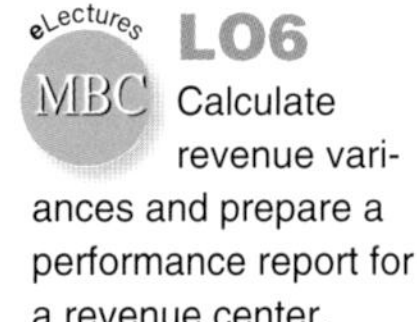

LO6 Calculate revenue variances and prepare a performance report for a revenue center.

The financial performance reports for revenue centers include a comparison of actual and budgeted revenues. Controllable costs can be deducted from revenues to obtain some bottom-line contribution margin. If the center is then evaluated on the basis of this contribution, it is being treated as a profit center.

If the organization is to meet its budgeted profit goal for a period, with its budgeted fixed and variable costs, the organization's revenue centers must meet their original revenue budgets. Consequently, the original budget (a static budget) rather than a flexible budget is used to evaluate the financial performance of revenue centers.

Assume that Tumi's July sales budget called for the sale of 10,000 bags at $40.00 each. If Tumi actually sold 11,000 bags at $38.50 each, the total revenue variance is $23,500 favorable:

Actual revenues (11,000 × $38.50)	$423,500
Budgeted revenues (10,000 × $40)	(400,000)
Revenue variance	$ 23,500 F

The **revenue variance** is the difference between the budgeted sales volume at the budgeted selling price and the actual sales volume at the actual selling price. Because Tumi's actual revenues exceeded budgeted revenues, the revenue variance is favorable. It can be presented as follows:

Revenue variance = (Actual volume × Actual price) – (Budgeted volume × Budgeted price)

The separate impact of changing prices and volume on revenue is analyzed with the sales price and sales volume variances. The **sales price variance** is computed as the change in selling price times the actual sales volume:

Sales price variance = (Actual selling price – Budgeted selling price) × Actual sales volume

For Tumi, the sales price variance for July follows:

Sales price variance = ($38.50 – $40.00) × 11,000 bags
= $16,500 U

The **sales volume variance** indicates the impact of the change in sales volume on revenues, assuming there was no change in selling price. The sales volume variance is computed as the difference between the actual and the budgeted sales volumes times the budgeted selling price:

Sales volume variance = (Actual sales volume – Budgeted sales volume) × Budgeted selling price

For Tumi, the sales volume variance for July follows:

Sales volume variance = (11,000 bags – 10,000 bags) × $40
= $40,000 F

The net of the sales price and the sales volume variances is equal to the revenue variance:

Sales price variance	$16,500 U
Sales volume variance	40,000 F
Revenue variance	$23,500 F

Interpretation of these variances is subjective. In this case, we could say that if the increase in sales volume had not been accompanied by a decline in selling price, revenues would have increased $40,000 instead of $23,500. The $1.50 per unit decline in selling price cost the company $16,500 in revenues. Alternatively, we might note that a $1.50 reduction in the unit selling price was more than offset by an increase in sales volume. An economic analysis could explain the relationship as volume being sensitive to price (price elasticity).

In any case, variances are merely signals that actual results are not proceeding according to plan. They help managers identify potential problems and opportunities. An investigation into their cause(s) could even indicate that a manager who received a favorable variance was doing a poor job, whereas a manager who received an unfavorable variance was doing an outstanding job. Consider Tumi's favorable revenue variance. This occurred because actual sales exceeded budgeted sales by 1,000 bags (10%), which on the surface indicates good performance. But what if the total market for the company's products exceeded the company's forecast by 15%? In this hypothetical case, Tumi's sales volume falls below its expected percentage share of the market; the favorable variance could occur (despite a poor marketing effort) because of strong customer demand that competitors could not fill.

Inclusion of Controllable Costs

Controllable costs should also be considered when evaluating the overall performance of revenue centers. A failure to consider costs could encourage uneconomic selling practices, such as excessive advertising and entertaining, and spending too much time on small accounts. The controllable costs of revenue centers include variable and fixed selling costs. These costs are sometimes further classified into order-getting and order-filling costs. **Order-getting costs** are incurred to obtain customers' orders (for example, advertising, salespersons' salaries and commissions, travel, telephone, and entertainment). **Order-filling costs** are distribution costs incurred to place finished goods in the hands of purchasers (for example, storing, packaging, and transportation).

The performance of a revenue center in controlling costs can be evaluated with the aid of a flexible budget drawn up for the actual level of activity. Assume that Tumi's July budget for the sales department calls for fixed costs of $10,000 and variable costs of $5 per bag sold. If the actual fixed and variable selling expenses for July are $9,500 and $65,000, respectively, the total cost variances assigned to the sales department, detailed in **Exhibit 10.2**, are $9,500 unfavorable. In evaluating the sales department's performance as both a cost center and a revenue center, management should consider these cost variances as well as the revenue variances. Although the revenue variances are based on the original budget, the cost variances are based on the flexible budget.

Exhibit 10.2 Sales Department Performance Report for Controllable Costs

TUMI
Sales Department Performance Report for Controllable Costs
For Month of July

	Based on Flexible Budget		
	Actual	Flexible Budget*	Flexible Budget Variance
Bags	11,000	11,000	
Selling expenses			
Variable	$65,000	$55,000	$10,000 U
Fixed	9,500	10,000	500 F
Total	$74,500	$65,000	$ 9,500 U

* Flexible budget formulas:
Variable selling expenses ($5 per bag)
Fixed selling expenses($10,000 per month)

Revenue Centers as Profit Centers

Even though we have computed revenue and cost variances for Tumi's sales department, we are still left with an incomplete picture of this revenue center's performance. Is the sales department's performance best represented by the $23,500 favorable revenue variance, by the $9,500 unfavorable cost variance, or by the net favorable variance of $14,000 ($23,500 F – $9,500 U)? Actually, it is inappropriate to attempt to obtain an overall measure of the sales department's performance by combining these separate revenue and selling cost variances. The combination of revenue and cost variances is appropriate only for a profit center; so far, we have left out one important cost that must be assigned to the sales department before it can be treated as a profit center. That cost is the *standard variable cost of goods sold.*

As a profit center, the sales department acquires units from the production department and sells them outside the firm. Its total responsibilities include revenues, the standard variable cost of goods sold, and actual selling expenses. The sales department is assigned the *standard,* rather than the *actual, variable cost of goods sold.* Because the sales department does not control production activities, it should not be assigned actual production costs. Doing so results in passing the production department's variances on to the sales department. Fixed manufacturing costs are not assigned to the sales department because short-run variations in sales volume do not normally affect the total amount of these costs.

To evaluate the sales department as a profit center, the net sales volume variance must be computed. The **net sales volume variance** indicates the impact of a change in sales volume on the contribution margin given the budgeted selling price *and* the standard variable costs. It is computed as the difference between the actual and the budgeted sales volumes times the budgeted unit contribution margin.

Net sales volume variance = (Actual volume − Budgeted volume) × Budgeted contribution margin

Using the $40 budgeted selling price, the standard variable manufacturing costs, and the standard variable selling expenses, the budgeted contribution margin is $11.00:

Sales		$40.00
Direct materials	$10.00	
Direct labor	6.00	
Variable manufacturing overhead	8.00	
Selling	5.00	(29.00)
Contribution margin		$11.00

The net sales volume variance is computed as follows:

Net sales volume variance = (11,000 − 10,000) × $11.00
= $11,000 F

As a profit center, the sales department has responsibility for the sales price variance, the net sales volume variance, and any cost variances associated with its operations. As shown in **Exhibit 10.3**, the sales department variances, as a profit center, net to $15,000 unfavorable:

Exhibit 10.3 Sales Department Profit Center Performance Report

TUMI Sales Department Profit Center Performance Report For Month of July	
Sales price variance	$16,500 U
Net sales volume variance	11,000 F
Selling expense variance	9,500 U
Sales Department variances, net	$15,000 U

In an attempt to improve their overall performance, managers often commit themselves to unfavorable variances in some areas, believing that these variances will be more than offset by favorable variances in other areas. When the sales department is evaluated as a revenue center, the favorable sales volume variance more than offsets the price reductions and the higher selling expenses. The more complete evaluation of the sales department as a profit center (with a $15,000 unfavorable variance) gives a very different impression than the evaluation of the sales department as a pure revenue center (with a $23,500 favorable variance) or as a revenue center responsible only for its own direct costs with net favorable variances of $14,000, computed as $23,500 F minus $9,500 U. The performance reports of all the organization's responsibility centers are summarized to reconcile budgeted and actual income in Appendix 10B.

Review 10-6 LO6 Calculating Revenue Variances

Sales Variances Presented is information pertaining to an item sold by Winding Creek General Store:

	Actual	Budget
Unit sales	150	125
Unit selling price	$26	$25
Unit standard variable costs	(20)	(20)
Unit contribution margin	$ 6	$ 5
Revenues	$3,900	$3,125
Standard variable costs	(3,000)	(2,500)
Contribution margin at standard costs	$ 900	$ 625

Required

Solution on p. 393. Compute the revenue, sales price, and the sales volume variances.

Appendix 10A: Fixed Overhead Variances

eLectures MBC **LO7** Formulate and interpret fixed overhead cost variances.

By definition, the quantity of goods and services purchased by fixed expenditures is not expected to change in proportion to short-run changes in the level of production. For example, in the short run, the production level does not affect the amount of depreciation on buildings, the number of fixed salaried employees, or the amount of real property subject to property taxes.

Even though the components of fixed overhead are not expected to be affected by the production activity level in the short run, the actual amount spent for fixed overhead items can differ from the amount budgeted. For example, higher than budgeted supervisors' salaries could be paid, insurance premiums may increase unexpectedly, and price increases could cause the amounts paid for equipment to be higher than expected. Fixed overhead costs in excess of the amount budgeted are reflected in the fixed overhead budget variance. Tumi's fixed overhead budget variance was previously determined as

Fixed overhead budget variance = Actual fixed overhead − Budgeted fixed overhead
= \$53,000 − \$52,000
= \$1,000 U

The fixed overhead budget variance is always the same as the total fixed overhead flexible budget variance. Because budgeted fixed overhead is the same for all outputs within the relevant range, the budget variance explains the total flexible budget variance between actual and allowed fixed overhead.

Recall that predetermined overhead rates are computed by dividing the predicted overhead costs for the period by the predicted activity of the period. The motivation for using a standard fixed overhead rate is the same as the motivation for using a predetermined overhead rate; namely, quicker product costing and assigning identical fixed costs to identical products, regardless of when they are produced during the year.

When a standard fixed overhead rate is used, total fixed overhead costs assigned to production behave as variable costs. As production increases, the total fixed overhead assigned to production increases. Because total budgeted fixed overhead does not vary, differences arise between budgeted and assigned fixed overhead, and managers often inquire about the cause of the differences.

The standard fixed overhead rate is computed as the budgeted fixed costs divided by some budgeted standard level of activity. Assume Tumi applies fixed manufacturing overhead on the basis of machine hours and that 0.40 machine hours are allowed to produce one computer bag. Further assume that the budgeted production is 10,000 computer bags per month, a level that allows 4,000 (10,000 × 0.40) machine hours. The standard fixed overhead rate per machine hour is \$13.

Standard fixed overhead rate = Budgeted total fixed overhead ÷ Budgeted activity level
= \$52,000 ÷ 4,000 hours
= \$13 per machine hour

The total fixed overhead assigned to production is computed as the standard rate of \$13 multiplied by the standard hours allowed for the units produced. Note that assigned fixed overhead cost equals budgeted fixed overhead only if the allowed activity equals the budgeted activity of 4,000 hours. If less than 4,000 hours are allowed, the fixed overhead assigned to production is less than the \$52,000 budgeted; if more than 4,000 hours are allowed, the fixed overhead assigned to production is more than the amount budgeted.

Even though budgeted fixed overhead is not affected by production below or above 4,000 hours, the fixed overhead assigned to production increases at the rate of \$13 per allowed machine hour. The difference between budgeted fixed overhead and fixed overhead assigned to production is called the **fixed overhead volume variance**. This variance is sometimes referred to as the **capacity variance**, a term that emphasizes the maximum output of an operation. The fixed overhead volume variance indicates neither good nor poor performance. Instead, it indicates the difference between the activity allowed for the actual output and the budget level used as the denominator in computing the standard fixed overhead rate.

To explain the difference between actual fixed overhead and fixed overhead assigned to production, two fixed overhead variances are computed: the fixed overhead budget variance and the fixed overhead volume variance. As previously explained, the fixed overhead budget variance represents the difference between actual fixed overhead and budgeted fixed overhead. The fixed overhead budget variance is caused by a combination of price and quantity factors related to the use of fixed overhead goods and services (e.g., depreciation, insurance, supervisors' salaries). The \$1,000 unfavorable budget variance for Tumi was caused either by using higher quantities of fixed overhead goods and services, or by paying higher prices than expected for those items, or both.

The fixed overhead volume variance represents the difference between budgeted and assigned fixed overhead and is caused by a difference between the activity level allowed for the actual output and the budgeted activity used in computing the fixed overhead rate. Suppose for Tumi, actual July output of 11,000 bags resulted in 4,400 allowed machine hours and applied fixed overhead of $57,200 (11,000 bags × 0.40 hours × $13). The $5,200 favorable fixed overhead volume variance (budgeted costs of $52,000 minus applied costs of $57,200) indicates that the activity level allowed for the actual output was more than the budgeted activity level. As previously stated, this variance ordinarily cannot be used to control costs. If the budgeted activity is based on production capacity, an unfavorable variance alerts management that facilities are underutilized, and a favorable variance alerts management that facilities are utilized above their expectations. A summary standard cost variance analysis for fixed costs is shown on the following page.

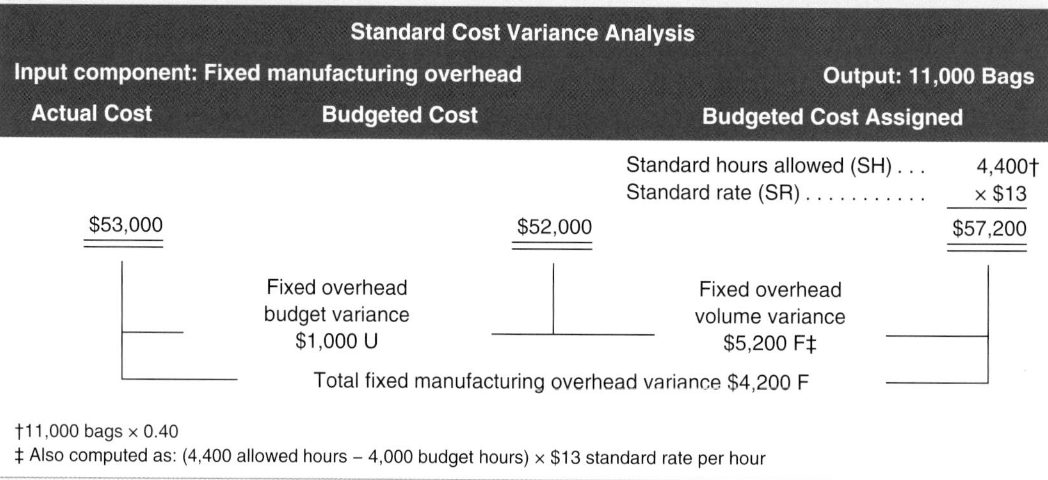

Review 10-7 LO7 Calculating Fixed Overhead Budget Variance

Assume that Marathon Oil uses a standard cost system for each of its refineries. For the Texas City refinery, the monthly fixed overhead budget is $6,000,000 for a planned output of 2,000,000 barrels. For September, the actual fixed cost was $6,250,000 for 2,100,000 barrels.

Required

a. Determine the fixed overhead budget variance.

b. If fixed overhead is applied on a per-barrel basis, determine the volume variance.

Solution on p. 393.

Appendix 10B: Reconciling Budgeted and Actual Income

LO8 Reconcile budgeted and actual income.

Using a contribution format, it is possible to reconcile the difference between budgeted and actual net income for an entire organization. This is done by assigning all costs and revenues to responsibility centers and summarizing the financial performance of each responsibility center. Tumi's budgeted and actual income statements, in a contribution format, for July are presented in Exhibit 10B.1.

Exhibit 10B.1 Budgeted and Actual Income Statements: Contribution Format

TUMI Budgeted Income Statement For Month of July			
Sales (10,000 bags × $40)			$400,000
Less variable costs			
Variable cost of goods sold			
Direct materials (10,000 bags × $10)	$100,000		
Direct labor (10,000 bags × $6)	60,000		
Manufacturing overhead (10,000 bags × $8)	80,000	$240,000	
Selling (10,000 bags × $5)		50,000	(290,000)
Contribution margin			110,000
Less fixed costs			
Manufacturing overhead		52,000	
Selling		10,000	
Administrative		4,000	(66,000)
Budgeted net income			$ 44,000

Actual Income Statement For the Month of July			
Sales (11,000 bags × $38.50)			$423,500
Less variable costs			
Variable cost of goods sold			
Direct materials	$108,000		
Direct labor	70,000		
Manufacturing overhead	81,000	$259,000	
Selling		65,000	(324,000)
Contribution margin			99,500
Less fixed costs			
Manufacturing overhead		53,000	
Selling		9,500	
Administrative		3,800	(66,300)
Net income			$ 33,200

We've assumed Tumi contains three responsibility centers: a production department, a sales department, and an administration department. Earlier in the chapter, we discussed both the production and the sales department variances. The sales department's variances in **Exhibit 10.3** net to $15,000 U and the production department's variances in **Exhibit 10.1** net to $4,000 F. Next, we assume that the administration department had a budgeted amount of $4,000 while the actual amount spent was $3,800. Because the administration department is a discretionary cost center, this variance of $200 ($3,800 actual – $4,000 budget) is best identified as being under budget. For consistency in the performance reports, however, it is labeled favorable. By assigning all variances to these three responsibility centers, the reconciliation of budgeted and actual income is as shown in Exhibit 10B.2.

Exhibit 10B.2 Reconciliation of Budgeted and Actual Income

TUMI Reconciliation of Budgeted and Actual Income For Month of July	
Budgeted net income	$44,000
Sales department variances (**Exhibit 10.3**)	15,000 U
Production department variances (**Exhibit 10.1**)	4,000 F
Administration department variances ($3,800 actual – $4,000 budgeted)	200 F
Actual net income	$33,200

Review 10-8 LO8 Reconciling Budgeted and Actual Contribution Margin

The following information pertains to Midstate Supply Company for the month of November:

Static Budget	Units	Unit Price	Total
Sales	1,000	$300	$300,000
Variable manufacturing costs	1,000	$100	100,000
Variable selling costs	1,000	$50	50,000
Contribution margin			$150,000
Actual Results	**Units**	**Unit Price**	**Total**
Sales	1,400	$275	$385,000
Variable manufacturing costs	1,400	$110	154,000
Variable selling expense	1,400	$45	63,000
Contribution margin			$168,000
Variance between static budget and actual results:			$ 18,000 F

Required

a. Prepare a schedule for November showing actual results, a flexible budget, and the static budget.

b. Calculate the following variances for the month of November using information from part (a) where applicable and reconcile to the total variance of $18,000. Which variance(s) are due to differences in units from budget and which variance(s) are due to differences of unit dollar amounts from budget?

1. Sales price variance
2. Net sales volume variance
3. Variable manufacturing cost flexible budget variance
4. Variable selling expense flexible budget variance

c. If the company had two responsibility centers, sales and production, how would the variances be allocated to the centers?

Solution on p. 393.

Guidance Answers

You Are the Vice President of Manufacturing

Pg. 368 It appears that direct labor hours may no longer be a reliable basis for budgeting variable overhead in your company. If actual variable overhead costs do not appear to correlate closely with direct labor hours, this could be an indication that the components of variable overhead have changed since direct labor hours was selected as the cost driver. Your cost accountants should consider other unit-level cost drivers for budgeting variable overhead costs. However, an activity-based costing method using multiple overhead cost pools with separate cost drivers might provide a more reliable basis for budgeting and controlling variable overhead costs.

Key Ratios

Materials price variance = Actual quantity (Actual price − Standard price)

Materials quantity variance = Standard price (Actual quantity − Standard quantity)

Labor rate variance = Actual hours (Actual rate − Standard rate)

Labor efficiency variance = Standard rate (Actual hours − Standard hours)

Standard variable overhead cost of actual inputs = (Actual quantity × Standard variable overhead rate)

Flexible variable overhead budget cost = (Standard quantity × Standard variable overhead rate)

Variable overhead efficiency variance = Standard rate (Actual quantity − Standard quantity)

Fixed overhead budget variance = Actual fixed overhead − Budgeted fixed overhead

Revenue variance = (Actual volume × Actual price) − (Budgeted volume × Budgeted price)

Sales price variance = (Actual selling price − Budgeted selling price) × Actual sales volume

Sales volume variance = (Actual sales volume − Budgeted sales volume) × Budgeted selling price

Net sales volume variance = (Actual volume − Budgeted volume) × Budgeted contribution margin

Standard fixed overhead rate = Budgeted total fixed overhead ÷ Budgeted activity level

Key Terms

capacity variance, 373
cost center, 355
fixed overhead budget variance, 368
fixed overhead volume variance, 373
flexible budgets, 358
flexible budget variance, 359
investment center, 357
labor efficiency variance, 365
labor rate variance, 365
materials price variance, 362
materials quantity variance, 362
net sales volume variance, 371
order-filling costs, 371
order-getting costs, 371
organization structure, 355
profit center, 356
responsibility accounting, 354
revenue center, 356
revenue variance, 370
sales price variance, 370
sales volume variance, 370
standard cost, 359
standard cost variance analysis, 360
variable overhead efficiency variance, 367
variable overhead spending variance, 367
variance, 357

Multiple Choice

1. Which of the following statements least describes characteristics of an investment center?
a. It is responsible for the relationship between its profits and the total assets invested in the center.
b. It is most frequently a segment of an organization such as a product line, marketing territory, or store.
c. It is expected to earn a target profit per dollar invested.
d. It is the broadest and most inclusive type of responsibility center.

2. Presented is an abbreviated performance report for the month of July:

	Actual	Budget	Variance
Units	5,500	5,000	
Costs:			
Direct materials	$ 45,500	$ 40,000	$ 5,500 U
Direct labor	181,500	150,000	31,500 U
Variable factory overhead	208,000	160,000	48,000 U
Fixed factory overhead	125,000	120,000	5,000 U
Total costs	$560,000	$470,000	$90,000 U

The total flexible budget variance is
a. $55,000 Unfavorable
b. $90,000 Unfavorable
c. $50,000 Favorable
d. $55,000 Favorable

Note: Questions 3, 4, and 5 analyze the flexible budget cost variances from question 2.

3. The following additional information is available for the materials costs in question 2:
- Standard cost per unit produced: 2 liters @ $4.00 per liter
- Actual use of raw materials 13,000 liters @ $3.50 per liter

The materials price and materials quantify variances are
a. $5,500 F materials price variance and $8,000 U materials quantity variance
b. $6,500 F materials price variance and $8,000 U materials quantity variance
c. $6,500 F materials price variance and $12,000 U materials quantity variance
d. None of the above

4. The following additional information is available for the labor costs in question 2.
- Standard cost per unit of product 1.5 direct labor hours @ $20 per labor hour
- Actual use of direct labor is 8,250 hours @ $22 per hour

The labor rate and the labor efficiency variances are
a. $16,500 U labor rate variance and $0 labor efficiency variance
b. $16,500 F labor rate variance and $0 labor efficiency variance
c. $16,500 U labor rate variance and $15,000 U labor efficiency variance
d. None of the above

Multiple Choice Answers
1. b 2. a 3. b 4. a 5. d 6. b

5. The following additional information is available for the variable overhead costs in question 2:
   - Standard cost per unit of product 2 liters of raw materials @ $16 per liter
   - Actual use of raw materials was 13,000 liters and actual variable overhead was $208,000

   The variable overhead spending and variable overhead efficiency variances are
   a. $32,000 U spending and $0 efficiency
   b. $32,000 U spending and $16,000 U efficiency
   c. $16,000 U spending and $32,000 U efficiency
   d. $0 spending and $32,000 U efficiency

6. Budgeted June sales of the Tack Shop include 100 western saddles at $650 each. Actual sales were 90 saddles at $725 each. The June sales price and sales volume variances for western saddles are
   a. $250 F sales price variance and $10 U sales volume variance
   b. $6,750 F sales price variance and $6,500 U sales volume variance
   c. $7,500 F sales price variance and $6,500 U sales volume variance
   d. None of the above

Questions

Q10-1. What is responsibility accounting? Why should noncontrollable costs be excluded from performance reports prepared in accordance with responsibility accounting?

Q10-2. How can responsibility accounting lead to unethical practices?

Q10-3. Responsibility accounting reports must be expanded to include what nonfinancial areas? Give some examples of nonfinancial measures.

Q10-4. What is a cost center? Give some examples.

Q10-5. How is a cost center different from either an investment or a profit center?

Q10-6. What problems can result from the use of tight standards?

Q10-7. What is a standard cost variance, and what is the objective of variance analysis?

Q10-8. Standard cost variances can usually be broken down into two basic types of variances. Identify and describe these two types of variances.

Q10-9. Identify possible causes for (1) a favorable materials price variance; (2) an unfavorable materials price variance; (3) a favorable materials quantity variance; and (4) an unfavorable materials quantity variance.

Q10-10. How is standard labor time determined? Explain the two ways.

Q10-11. In the standard cost system, what is the appropriate treatment of a change in wage rates (per new labor union contract) that dominate the cost of labor?

Q10-12. Explain the difference between the revenue variance and the sales price variance.

Q10-13. Explain the net sales volume variance and list its components.

Q10-14. Explain the difference between how the *actual costs* and the *standard cost of actual inputs* are computed in variable overhead analysis.

Q10-15. Explain what the net sales volume variance measures.

Assignments with the MBC logo in the margin are available in myBusinessCourse. See the Preface of the book for details.

Mini Exercises

LO2 **M10-16. Flexible Budgets and Performance Evaluation**

Presented is the January performance report for the Production Department of Nowwhat Company.

NOWWHAT COMPANY Production Department Performance Report For Month of January	Actual	Budget
Volume	50,000	46,000
Manufacturing costs		
Direct materials	$130,500	$124,200
Direct labor	118,000	105,800
Variable overhead	72,000	69,000
Fixed overhead	252,000	250,000
Total	$572,500	$549,000

Required

a. Evaluate the performance report.

b. Prepare a more appropriate performance report. *Hint:* Start by determining the standard unit costs.

M10-17. Materials Variances LO3

Dark Wind manufactures decorative weather vanes that have a standard materials cost of three pounds of raw materials at $4.00 per pound. During September 17,500 pounds of raw materials costing $4.25 per pound were used in making 6,000 weather vanes.

Required

Determine the materials price and quantity variances.

M10-18. Materials Variances LO3 Pearle Vision

Assume that Pearle Vision uses standard costs to control the materials in its made-to-order sunglasses. The standards call for 3 ounces of material for each pair of lenses. The standard cost per ounce of material is $12. During July, the Santa Clara location produced 6,000 pairs of sunglasses and used 17,750 ounces of materials. The cost of the materials during July was $12.25 per ounce, and there were no beginning or ending inventories.

Required

a. Determine the flexible budget materials cost for the completion of the 6,000 pairs of glasses.

b. Determine the actual materials cost incurred for the completion of the 6,000 pairs of glasses and compute the total materials variance.

c. How much of the total variance was related to the price paid to purchase the materials?

d. How much of the difference between the answers to requirements (a) and (b) was related to the quantity of materials used?

M10-19. Direct Labor Variances LO4 Advanced Micro Devices (AMD)

Advanced Micro Devices develops high-performing computing products. Assume one of its processors, Ryzen 7 Pro, has a standard labor time of 0.25 hours and a standard labor rate of $20 per hour. During February, the following activities pertaining to direct labor for Ryzen 7 Pro were recorded:

Direct labor hours used	64,000
Direct labor cost	$1,248,000
Units of Ryzen 7 Pro manufactured	250,000

Required

a. Determine the labor rate variance.

b. Determine the labor efficiency variance.

c. Determine the total flexible budget labor cost variance.

M10-20. Significance of Direct Labor Variances LO4

The Tomorrow Company's April budget called for labor costs of $192,000. Because the actual labor costs were exactly $192,000, management concluded there were no labor variances.

Required

Comment on management's conclusion.

LO5 Sony (SNE)

M10-21. Variable Overhead Variances

Assume that the best cost driver that Sony has for variable factory overhead in the assembly department is machine hours. During April, the company budgeted 585,000 machine hours and $4,972,500 for its Texas plant's assembly department. The actual variable overhead incurred was $5,002,500, which was related to 575,000 machine hours.

Required

a. Determine the variable overhead spending variance.
b. Determine the variable overhead efficiency variance.

LO6

M10-22. Sales Variances

Presented is information pertaining to an item sold by Wheeping Creek General Store:

	Actual	Budget
Unit sales	650	600
Unit selling price	$38	$40
Unit variable costs	31	32
Unit contribution margin	$7	$8
Revenues	$24,700	$24,000
Variable costs	20,150	19,200
Contribution margin at standard costs	$ 4,550	$ 4,800

Required

Compute the revenue, sales price, and the sales volume variances.

LO7 ExxonMobil (XOM)

M10-23. Fixed Overhead Variances

Assume that ExxonMobil uses a standard cost system for each of its refineries. For the Houston refinery, the monthly fixed overhead budget is $9,900,000 for a planned output of 6,000,000 barrels. For September, the actual fixed cost was $10,115,000 for 5,950,000 barrels.

Required

a. Determine the fixed overhead budget variance.
b. If fixed overhead is applied on a per-barrel basis, determine the volume variance.

LO7

M10-24. Fixed Overhead Variances

Tazer Inc. summarized the following production information for the most recent year.

Budgeted fixed overhead costs in total	$62,400	Actual fixed overhead costs in total	$68,900
Budgeted direct labor hours	5,200	Actual output of final units	9,900
Budgeted direct labor hours per unit	0.50		

Required

If fixed manufacturing overhead is applied on the basis of direct labor hours, compute (a) the fixed overhead budget variance and (b) the fixed overhead volume variance. Indicate whether each variance is favorable or unfavorable.

Exercises

LO2

E10-25. Elements of a Flexible Budget

Presented are partial flexible cost budgets for various levels of output.

	Rate per Unit	Units		
		5,000	7,500	10,000
Direct materials	a.	$20,000	b.	c.
Direct labor	d.	e.	11,250	f.
Variable overhead	$2	g.	h.	i.
Fixed overhead		j.	k.	l.
Total		m.	n.	$140,000

Required
Solve for items "a" though "n."

E10-26. Elements of Labor and Variable Overhead Variances LO4, 5

Chelsea Fabricating applies variable overhead to products on the basis of standard direct labor hours. Presented is selected information for last month when 25,000 units were produced.

	Direct Labor	Variable Overhead
Actual cost	a.	f.
Standard hours/unit	b.	b.
Actual hours (total)	12,000	12,000
Standard rate/hour	$25.00	$15.00
Actual rate	$25.50	
Flexible budget	$312,500	$187,500
Labor rate or variable overhead spending variance . .	c.	g.
Efficiency variances	d.	h.
Total flexible budget variance	e.	$5,000 U

Required
Solve for items "a" through" h."

E10-27. Causes of Standard Cost Variances (Comprehensive) LO3, 4, 5

Following are 10 unrelated situations that would ordinarily be expected to affect one or more standard cost variances:

1. A salaried production supervisor is given a raise, but no adjustment is made in the labor cost standards.
2. The materials purchasing manager gets a special reduced price on raw materials by purchasing a train carload. A warehouse had to be rented to accommodate the unusually large amount of raw materials. The rental fee was charged to Rent Expense, a fixed overhead item.
3. An unusually hot August caused the company to use 30,000 kilowatts more electricity than provided for in the variable overhead standards.
4. The local electric utility company raised the charge per kilowatt-hour. No adjustment was made in the variable overhead standards.
5. The plant manager traded in his leased company car for a new one in July, increasing the monthly lease payment by $85.
6. A machine malfunction on the assembly line (caused by using cheap and inferior raw materials) resulted in decreased output by the machine operator and higher than normal machine repair costs. Repairs are treated as variable overhead costs.
7. Two assembly workers retired after 20 years on the job. They were replaced by two young apprentices.
8. An announcement that vacation benefits had been increased resulted in improved employee morale. Consequently, raw materials pilferage and waste declined, and production efficiency increased. Employee benefits are charged to overhead.
9. The plant manager reclassified her secretary to administrative assistant and gave him an increase in salary.
10. A union contract agreement calling for an immediate 4% increase in production worker wages was signed. No changes were made in the standards.

Required
For each of these situations, indicate by letter which of the following standard cost variances would be affected. More than one variance will be affected in some cases.

a. Materials price variance.
b. Materials quantity variance.
c. Labor rate variance.
d. Labor efficiency variance.
e. Variable overhead spending variance.
f. Variable overhead efficiency variance.
g. Fixed overhead budget variance.

LO6 Casio Computer Company, LTD.

E10-28. Sales Variances

Assume that Casio Computer Company, LTD. sells G-Shock for $50 during August as a back-to-school special. The normal selling price is $100. The standard variable cost for each device is $35. Sales for August had been budgeted for 500,000 units nationwide; however, due to the uptick in the economy, sales came in at 525,000.

Required

Compute the revenue, sales price, sales volume, and net sales volume variances. *Hint:* Compute the variances using the normal selling price as the standard.

LO7

E10-29. Fixed Overhead Variances

Petra Company uses standard costs for cost control and internal reporting. Fixed costs are budgeted at $125,000 per month at a normal operating level of 25,000 units of production output. During October, actual fixed costs were $122,000, and actual production output was 24,000 units.

Required

a. Determine the fixed overhead budget variance.

b. Assume that the company applied fixed overhead to production on a per-unit basis. Determine the fixed overhead volume variance.

c. Was the fixed overhead budget variance from requirement (*a*) affected because the company operated below the normal activity level of 25,000 units? Explain.

d. Explain the possible causes for the volume variance computed in requirement (*b*). How is reporting of the volume variance useful to management?

Problems

LO2

P10-30. Multiple Product Performance Report

Case Products manufactures two models of DVD storage cases: regular and deluxe. Presented is standard cost information for each model:

Cost Components			Regular			Deluxe
Direct materials						
Acrylic sheets	3 sheets × $12	=	$36.00	5 sheets × $12	=	$60.00
Assembly kit		=	5.00		=	5.00
Direct labor.	0.5 hour × $20	=	10.00	0.75 hours × $20	=	15.00
Variable overhead . . .	0.5 labor hr. × $5	=	2.50	0.75 labor hrs. × $5	=	3.75
Total			$53.50			$83.75

Budgeted fixed manufacturing overhead is $46,000 per month. During July, the company produced 8,000 regular and 3,500 deluxe storage cases while incurring the following manufacturing costs:

Direct materials.	$561,300
Direct labor.	130,800
Variable overhead	34,625
Fixed overhead.	48,150
Total	$774,875

Required

Prepare a flexible budget performance report for the July manufacturing activities.

LO3, 4

P10-31. Computation of Variable Cost Variances

The following information pertains to the standard costs and actual activity for Repine Company for September:

Standard cost per unit	
Direct materials	3 units of material A × \$8.00 per unit
	2 units of material B × \$4.00 per unit
Direct labor	2 hours × \$15.00 per hour
Activity for September	
Materials purchased	
Material A	7,000 units × \$7.80 per unit
Material B	4,800 units × \$4.50 per unit
Materials used	
Material A	6,430 units
Material B	3,950 units
Direct labor used	4,100 hours × \$15.50 per hour
Production output	2,000 units

There were no beginning direct materials inventories.

Required

a. Determine the materials price and quantity variances.

b. Determine the labor rate and efficiency variances.

P10-32. Variance Computations and Explanations LO3, 4 Tarptent

Tarptent manufactures camping tents from a lightweight synthetic fabric. Assume the company's two-person tent has a standard materials cost of \$60, consisting of 4 yards of fabric at \$15 per yard. The standards call for 1.5 hours of assembly at \$20 per hour. The following data were recorded for October, the first month of operations:

Fabric purchased	6,500 yards × \$14.50 per yard
Fabric used in production of 1,200 tents	4,850 yards
Direct labor used	1,850 hours × \$19.50 per hour

Required

a. Compute all standard cost variances for materials and labor.

b. Give one possible reason for each of the preceding variances.

c. Determine the standard variable cost of the 1,200 tents produced, separated into direct materials and labor.

P10-33. Determining Unit Costs, Variance Analysis, and Interpretation LO3, 4, 5 Nestlé (NESN)

Nestlé, manufacturer of Purina Dog Chow, produces its product in 500-bag batches. Assume the standard batch consists of 10,000 pounds of direct materials at \$0.25 per pound, 16 direct labor hours at \$15 per hour, and variable overhead cost (based on machine hours) at the rate of \$20 per hour with 10 machine hours per batch. The following variable costs were incurred for the last 500-bag batch produced:

Direct materials	10,250 pounds costing \$2,255 were purchased and used
Direct labor	15 hours costing \$231
Variable overhead	\$215
Machine hours used	9.5 hours

Required

a. Determine the actual and standard variable costs per bag of dog food produced, separated into direct materials, direct labor, and variable overhead.

b. For the last 500-bag batch, determine the standard cost variances for direct materials, direct labor, and variable overhead.

c. Explain the possible causes for each of the variances determined in requirement (*b*).

P10-34. Computation of Variances and Other Missing Data LO3, 4, 5

The following data for Bernie Company pertain to the production of 1,000 units of Product X during December. Selected data items are omitted.

Direct materials (all materials purchased were used during period)
  Standard cost per unit: (a) pounds at $3.20 per pound
  Total actual cost: (b) pounds costing $10,626
  Standard cost allowed for units produced: $9,600
  Materials price variance: (c)
  Materials quantity variance: $704 U
Direct labor
  Standard cost: 2.5 hours at $12.00
  Actual cost per hour: $12.25
  Total actual cost: (d)
  Labor rate variance: (e)
  Labor efficiency variance: $144 F
Variable overhead
  Standard costs: (f) hours at $4.00 per direct labor hour
  Actual cost: $10,600
  Variable overhead spending variance: (g)
  Variable overhead efficiency variance: (h)

Required

Complete the missing amounts lettered (a) through (h).

LO2, 3, 4, 5 **P10-35. Flexible Budgets and Performance Evaluation**

Kathy Vanderbosch, supervisor of housecleaning for Hotel Valhalla, was surprised by her summary performance report for March given below.

HOTEL VALHALLA
Housekeeping Performance Report
For the Month of March

Actual	Budget	Variance	%Variance
$260,708	$252,000	$8,708 U	3.456% U

Kathy was disappointed. She thought she had done a good job controlling housekeeping labor and towel usage, but her performance report revealed an unfavorable variance of $8,708. She had been hoping for a bonus for her good work, but now expected a series of questions from her manager.

The cost budget for housekeeping is based on standard costs. At the beginning of a month, Kathy receives a report from Hotel Valhalla's Sales Department outlining the planned room activity for the month. Kathy then schedules labor and purchases using this information. The budget for the housekeeping was based on 8,000 room nights. Each room night is budgeted based on the following standards for various materials, labor, and overhead:

Shower supplies	4 bottles @ $0.50 each
Towels*	1 @ $4.00
Laundry	8 lbs. @ $0.25 a lb.
Labor	¾ hour @ $15.00 an hour
VOH	$3.00 per labor hour
FOH	$10 a room night (based on 8,000 room nights)

*Replacements for towels evaluated by housekeeping as inappropriate for cleaning and reuse.

With 8,600 room nights sold, actual costs and usage for housekeeping during April were

$14,620 for 36,550 bottles of shower supplies.
$32,121 for 7,740 towels.
$20,898 for 69,660 lbs. of laundry.
$91,504 for 6,020 labor hours.
$19,565 in total VOH.
$82,000 in FOH.

Required

a. Develop a complete budget column for the above performance report presented to Kathy. Break it down by expense category. The following format, with additional lines for expense categories, is suggested:

Account	Actual	Budget	Variance
Shower Supplies.	$ 14,620	?	?
⋮	⋮	⋮	⋮
Total	$260,708	$252,000	$8,708 U

b. Evaluate the usefulness of the cost center performance report presented to Kathy.

c. Prepare a more logical performance report where standard allowed is based on actual output. Also, split each variance into its price/rate/spending and quantity/efficiency components (except fixed of course). The following format, with additional lines for expense categories, is suggested:

Account	Actual	Flexible Budget	Total Variance	Price/Rate/ Spending Variance	Quantity/ Efficiency Variance
Shower Supplies.	$ 14,620	?	?	?	?
⋮	⋮	⋮	⋮		
Total	$260,708	?	?		

d. Explain to Kathy's boss what your report suggests about Kathy's department performance.

e. Identify additional nonfinancial performance measures management might consider when evaluating the performance of the housekeeping department and Kathy as a manager.

P10-36. Flexible Budget Performance Evaluation with Process Costing **LO2, 3, 4, 5**

The Evanston Company produces a single product on a continuous basis. During January, 2,000 units were completed. The July 31 ending work-in-process inventory contained 500 units, 50% complete as to materials and 25% complete as to conversion.

Evanston uses standard costs for planning and control. The following standard costs are based on a monthly volume of 2,000 equivalent units with fixed manufacturing overhead budgeted at $80,450 per month.

Direct materials [(3 square meters per unit × $12.00 per meter) × 2,000]	$72,000
Direct labor [(2 hours per unit × $22.00 per hour) × 2,000]	88,000
Variable overhead [(2 hours per unit × $5.00 per hour) × 2,000]	20,000
Fixed manufacturing overhead.	80,450

Actual July production costs were

Direct materials.	$ 80,525
Direct labor	95,250
Manufacturing overhead.	101,165

Required

a. Determine the equivalent units of materials and conversion manufactured during July using the weighted average method.

b. Based on the July equivalent units of materials and conversion, prepare a July performance report for the Evanston Company. *Hint:* Combine variable and fixed manufacturing overhead data in the report.

c. Explain the treatment of overhead in the July performance report.

P10-37. Measuring the Effects of Decisions on Standard Cost Variances (Comprehensive) **LO3, 4, 5**

The following five unrelated situations affect one or more standard cost variances for materials, labor (assembly), and overhead:

1. Sally Smith, a production worker, announced her intent to resign to accept another job paying $1.75 more per hour. To keep Sally, the production manager agreed to raise her salary from $12 to $14 per hour. Sally works an average of 175 regular hours per month.

2. At the beginning of the month, a supplier of a component used in our product notified us that, because of a minor design improvement, the price will be increased by 10% above the current standard price of $125 per unit. As a result of the improved design, we expect the number of defective components to decrease by 50 units per month. On average, 1,200 units of the component are purchased each month. Defective units are identified prior to use and are not returnable.
3. In an effort to meet a deadline on a rush order in Department A, the plant manager reassigned several higher-skilled workers from Department B, for a total of 360 labor hours. The average salary of the Department B workers was $2.15 more than the standard $11.00 per hour rate of the Department A workers. Since they were not accustomed to the work, the average Department B worker was able to produce only 24 units per hour instead of the standard 36 units per hour. (Consider only the effect on Department A labor variances.)
4. Robbie Wallace is an inspector who earns a base salary of $2,000 per month plus a piece rate of 40 cents per bundle inspected. His company accounts for inspection costs as manufacturing overhead. Because of a payroll department error in June, Robbie was paid $1,500 plus a piece rate of 60 cents per bundle. He received gross wages totaling $2,100. *Hints:* Robbie's compensation has both fixed and variable components.
5. The materials purchasing manager purchased 5,000 units of component K2X from a new source at a price $20 below the standard unit price of $200. These components turned out to be of extremely poor quality with defects occurring at three times the standard rate of 6%. The higher rate of defects reduced the output of workers (who earn $12 per hour) from 20 units per hour to 16 units per hour on the units containing the discount components. Each finished unit contains one K2X component. To appease the workers (who were irate at having to work with inferior components), the production manager agreed to pay the workers an additional $0.50 for each of the components (good and bad) in the discount batch. Variable manufacturing overhead is applied at the rate of $6.00 per direct labor hour. The defective units also caused a 25-hour increase in total machine hours. The actual cost of electricity to run the machines is $2.00 per hour.

Required

For each of the preceding situations, determine which standard cost variance(s) will be affected, and compute the amount of the effect for one month on each variance. Indicate whether the effect is favorable or unfavorable. Assume that the standards are not changed in response to these situations. (Round calculations to two decimal places.)

LO7 P10-38. Fixed Overhead Budget and Volume Variance

Four-Leaf Clover Company assigns fixed overhead costs to inventory for external reporting purposes by using a predetermined standard overhead rate based on direct labor hours. The standard rate is based on a normal activity level of 30,000 standard allowed direct labor hours per year. There are five standard allowed hours for each unit of output. Budgeted fixed overhead costs are $420,000 per year. During the prior year, the company produced 5,800 units of output, and actual fixed costs were $425,000.

Required

a. Determine the standard fixed overhead rate used to assign fixed costs to inventory.
b. Determine the amount of fixed overhead assigned to inventory during the year.
c. Determine the fixed overhead budget variance.

LO6, 8 P10-39. Profit Center Performance Report

Bach Tunes is a classical music retailer specializing in the Internet sale of MP3 albums of the works of J. S. Bach. Although prices vary with album popularity and file sizes, the albums sell for an average of $12 each and Bach Tunes pays a fixed royalty of $5.75 per MP3 album. With the exception of royalty fees, the operating costs of Bach Tunes are fixed. Presented are budgeted and actual income statements for the month of September.

BACH TUNES Budgeted and Actual Contribution Statements For Month of September	Actual	Budget
Unit sales	7,500	8,000
Unit selling price	$12.50	$12.00
Sales revenue	$93,750	$96,000
Cost of goods sold	(43,125)	(46,000)
Gross profit	50,625	50,000
Operating costs	(34,700)	(35,000)
Contribution to corporate costs and profits	$15,925	$15,000

Required

Compute variances to assist in evaluating the performance of Bach Tunes as a profit center. What was the likely cause of the shortfall in sales revenue?

P10-40. Profit Center Performance Report LO2, 3, 4, 5, 6, 7, 8 Falafel, Inc.

Falafel, Inc. operates fast-food restaurants in Washington, DC. Its main product is a serving of falafel that requires ground chick peas (direct material) and food preparation (direct labor). Assume the April budget for Falafel Inc.'s Georgetown restaurant was

- Sales 24,000 servings at $4.25 each
- Standard food cost of $0.50 per serving (1/4 pound @ $2.00 per pound)
- Standard direct labor of $0.60 per serving (1/25th hour @ $15.00 per hour)
- Fixed occupancy expenses (equipment and rent) of $7,500

Actual April performance of the Georgetown restaurant was

- Sales 26,000 servings at $4.50 each
- Food cost of $14,820 for 7,800 pounds
- Direct labor cost of $19,240 for 1,300 hours
- Fixed occupancy expenses of $7,200

In early May, the manager received the following financial performance report:

FALAFEL, INC.—GEORGETOWN Performance Report For the Month of April	Actual	Budgeted	Variance
Revenues	$117,000	$102,000	$15,000 F
Food Cost	(14,820)	(12,000)	2,820 U
Labor Cost	(19,240)	(14,400)	4,840 U
Occupancy	(7,200)	(7,500)	300 F
Profit	$ 75,740	$ 68,100	$ 7,640 F

Required

a. Partition variance into variances for 1) selling price and net sales volume, 2) food variances for price and quantity, and 3) labor variances for rate and efficiency.

b. Using the results of your analysis, prepare an alternative reconciliation of budgeted and actual profit. Be sure to include the occupancy variance. *Hint:* The net variance in your revised reconciliation will still be $7,640 F.

c. Explain why the total variances for sales, food, and labor in your reconciliation differ from those originally presented to the restaurant manager.

P10-41. Comprehensive Performance Report LO2, 3, 4, 5, 6, 7, 8

Instant Computing is a contract manufacturer of laptop computers sold under brand named companies. Presented are Instant's budgeted and actual contribution income statements for October. The company has three responsibility centers: Production, Selling and Distribution, and Administration. Production and Administration are cost centers while Selling and Distribution is a profit center.

INSTANT COMPUTING
Budgeted Contribution Income Statement
For Month of October

Sales (2,000 × $400)			$800,000
Less variable costs			
Variable cost of goods sold			
Direct materials (2,000 × $60)	$120,000		
Direct labor (2,000 × $40)	80,000		
Manufacturing overhead (2,000 × $20)	40,000	$240,000	
Selling and Distribution (2,000 × $45)		90,000	(330,000)
Contribution margin			470,000
Less fixed costs			
Manufacturing overhead		160,000	
Administrative		125,000	
Selling and Distribution		75,000	(360,000)
Net income			$110,000

INSTANT COMPUTING
Actual Contribution Income Statement
For Month of October

Sales (2,250 × $385)			$866,250
Less variable costs			
Cost of goods sold			
Direct materials	$139,500		
Direct labor	85,500		
Manufacturing overhead	43,875	$268,875	
Selling and Distribution		105,750	(374,625)
Contribution margin			491,625
Less fixed costs			
Manufacturing overhead		168,000	
Administrative		135,000	
Selling and Distribution		74,600	(377,600)
Net income (loss)			$114,025

Required

a. Prepare a performance report for Production that compares actual and allowed costs.
b. Prepare a performance report for Selling and Distribution that compares actual and allowed costs.
c. Determine the sales price and the net sales volume variances.
d. Prepare a report that summarizes the performance of Selling and Distribution.
e. Determine the amount by which Administration was over or under budget.
f. Prepare a report reconciling budgeted and actual net income. Your report should focus on the performance of each responsibility center.

Cases and Projects

LO1 C10-42. Discretionary Cost Center Performance Reports

TruckMax had been extremely profitable, but the company has been hurt in recent years by competition and a failure to introduce new consumer products. Three years ago, Tom Lopez became head of Consumer Products Research (CPR) and began a number of product development projects. Under his leadership the group had good ideas that led to the introduction of several promising products. Nevertheless, when financial results for Lopez's second year were reviewed, CPR's report revealed large unfavorable variances leading management to criticize Lopez for poor cost control. Management was quite concerned about cost control because profits were low, and the company's cash budget indicated that additional borrowing would be required to cover out-of-pocket costs. Because of his inability to exert proper cost control, Lopez was relieved of his responsibilities last year, and Gabriella Garcia became head of Consumer Products Research. Garcia vowed to improve the performance of CPR and scaled back CPR's development activities to obtain favorable financial performance reports.

By the end of this year, the company had improved its market position, profitability, and cash position. At this time, the board of directors promoted Garcia to president, congratulating her for the contribution CPR made to the revitalization of the company, as well as her success in improving the financial performance of CPR. Garcia assured the board that the company's financial performance would improve even more in the future as she applied the same cost-reducing measures that had worked so well in CPR to the company as a whole.

Required

a. For the purpose of evaluating financial performance, what responsibility center classification should be given to the Consumer Products Research Department? What unique problems are associated with evaluating the financial performance of this type of responsibility center?

b. Compare the performances of Lopez and Garcia in the role as head of Consumer Products Research. Did Garcia do a much better job, thereby making her deserving of the promotion? Why or why not?

C10-43. Developing Cost Standards for Materials and Labor **LO2**

After several years of operating without a formal system of cost control, DeWalt Company, a tools manufacturer, has decided to implement a standard cost system. The system will first be established for the department that makes lug wrenches for automobile mechanics. The standard production batch size is 100 wrenches. The actual materials and labor required for eight randomly selected batches from last year's production are as follows:

Batch	Materials Used (in pounds)	Labor Used (in hours)
1	504.0	10.00
2	508.0	9.00
3	506.0	9.00
4	521.0	5.00
5	516.0	8.00
6	518.0	7.00
7	520.0	6.00
8	515.0	8.00
Average	513.5	7.75

Management has obtained the following recommendations concerning what the materials and labor quantity standards should be:

- The manufacturer of the equipment used in making the wrenches advertises in the toolmakers' trade journal that the machine the company uses can produce 100 wrenches with 500 pounds of direct materials and 5 labor hours. Company engineers believe the standards should be based on these facts.
- The accounting department believes more realistic standards would be 505 pounds and 5 hours.
- The production supervisor believes the standards should be 512 pounds and 7.75 hours.
- The production workers argue for standards of 522 pounds and 8 hours.

Required

a. State the arguments for and against each of the recommendations, as well as the probable effects of each recommendation on the quantity variance for materials and labor.

b. Which recommendation provides the best combination of cost control and motivation to the production workers? Explain.

C10-44. Behavioral Effect of Standard Costs **LO1, 2, 3, 4, 5**

Merit Inc. has used a standard cost system for evaluating the performance of its responsibility center managers for three years. Top management believes that standard costing has not produced the cost savings or increases in productivity and profits promised by the accounting department. Large unfavorable variances are consistently reported for most cost categories, and employee morale has fallen since the system was installed. To help pinpoint the problem with the system, top management asked for separate evaluations of the system by the plant manager, the controller, and the human resources director. Their responses are summarized here.

Plant Manager—The standards are unrealistic. They assume an ideal work environment that does not allow materials defects or errors by the workers or machines. Consequently, morale has gone down and productivity has declined. Standards should be based on expected actual prices and recent past averages for efficiency. Thus, if we improve over the past, we receive a favorable variance.

Controller—The goal of accounting reports is to measure performance against an absolute standard and the best approximation of that standard is ideal conditions. Cost standards should be comparable to "par" on a golf course. Just as the game of golf uses a handicap system to allow for differences in individual players' skills and scores, it could be necessary for management to interpret variances based on the circumstances that produced the variances. Accordingly, in one case, a given unfavorable variance could represent poor performance; in another case, it could represent good performance. The managers are just going to have to recognize these subtleties in standard cost systems and depend on upper management to be fair.

Human Resources Director—The key to employee productivity is employee satisfaction and a sense of accomplishment. A set of standards that can never be met denies managers of this vital motivator. The current standards would be appropriate in a laboratory with a controlled environment but not in the factory with its many variables. If we are to recapture our old "team spirit," we must give the managers a goal that they can achieve through hard work.

Required

Discuss the behavioral issues involved in Merit Inc.'s standard cost dilemma. Evaluate each of the three responses (pros and cons) and recommend a course of action.

LO8 **C10-45. Evaluating a Companywide Performance Report**

Mr. Chandler, the production supervisor, bursts into your office, carrying the company's prior year performance report and thundering, "There is villainy here, sir! And I shall get to the bottom of it. I will not stop searching until I have found the answer! Why is Mr. Richards so down on my department? I thought we did a good job last year. But Richards claims my production people and I cost the company $31,500! I plead with you, sir, explain this performance report to me." Trying to calm Chandler, you take the report from him and ask to be left alone for 15 minutes. The report is as follows:

DICKENS COMPANY, LIMITED
Performance Report
For the Prior Year

	Actual	Budget	Variance
Unit sales	9,000	7,500	
Sales	$526,500	$450,000	$ 76,500 F
Less manufacturing costs			
Direct materials	42,750	37,500	5,250 U
Direct labor	19,350	15,000	4,350 U
Manufacturing overhead	192,100	190,000*	2,100 U
Total	(254,200)	(242,500)	(11,700) U
Gross profit	272,300	207,500	64,800 F
Less selling and administrative expenses			
Selling (all fixed)	52,750	50,000	2,750 U
Administrative (all fixed)	54,785	50,000	4,785 U
Total	(107,535)	(100,000)	(7,535) U
Net income	$164,765	$107,500	$ 57,265 F
Performance summary			
Budgeted net income			$107,500
Sales department variances			
Sales revenue	$ 76,500 F		
Selling expenses	2,750 U	$ 73,750 F	
Administration department variances		4,785 U	
Production department variances		11,700 U	57,265 F
Actual net income			$164,765

*Includes fixed manufacturing overhead of $160,000.

Required

a. Evaluate the performance report. Is Mr. Richards correct, or is there "villainy here"?

b. Assume that the sales department is a profit center and that the production and administration departments are cost centers. Determine the responsibility of each for cost, revenue, and income variances, and prepare a report reconciling budgeted and actual net income. Your report should focus on the performance of each responsibility center.

Solutions to Review Problems

Review 10-1—Solution

There is some discretion as to how each of the reporting units below would be classified by Eli's. However, likely classifications would be as follows:

Bakery—Cost Center: In this case, the bakery is the "manufacturing facility." Typically, a manufacturing facility is a cost center. The bakery is responsible for producing high-quality products in the most cost-effective way possible.

Accounting—Cost Center

Product line/Original Plain Cheesecake—Profit Center: Typically, a product line is a profit center. The product manager of the Original Plain Cheesecake is likely responsible for the revenues, costs, and resulting profits of his or her product line. A product line is not typically an investment center as many of the production assets are shared with other products; therefore, any decisions regarding the overall bakery assets will be made at a higher level in the organization.

Human resources—Cost Center

Cheesecake Café at O'Hare Airport—Investment Center: The Café at O'Hare will have separate assets such as a display case, cash register, and refrigerators. It will be responsible for attractive displays and customer service. So it is likely that the Café will be evaluated based on its target profit per dollar invested.

Review 10-2—Solution

The performance report prepared by the accounting department was based on a "static" budget. A better basis for evaluating your performance is to compare actual performance with a flexible budget. By dividing the budgeted variable costs amounts by 12,000 units, the budgeted unit variable costs amounts can be determined as follows:

Direct materials cost	\$360,000 ÷ 12,000 units = \$30 per unit
Direct labor	\$432,000 ÷ 12,000 units = \$36 per unit
Variable factory overhead	\$216,000 ÷ 12,000 units = \$18 per unit

Using these budgeted unit values, a flexible budget can be prepared as follows:

	Actual	Flexible Budget	Variance
Units	10,000	10,000	
Costs			
Direct materials	\$ 299,000	\$ 300,000	\$ 1,000 F
Direct labor	345,500	360,000	14,500 F
Variable factory overhead	180,000	180,000	
Fixed factory overhead	375,000	360,000	15,000 U
Total plant costs	\$1,199,500	\$1,200,000	\$ 500 F

The plant did not produce the number of units originally budgeted. Therefore, from a cost control standpoint, a flexible budget is a better basis for evaluating performance because it compares the actual cost of producing 10,000 units with a budget also based on 10,000 units. Based on the flexible budget, your performance is still quite good; however, it is much less favorable than it appeared using a static budget.

Review 10-3—Solution

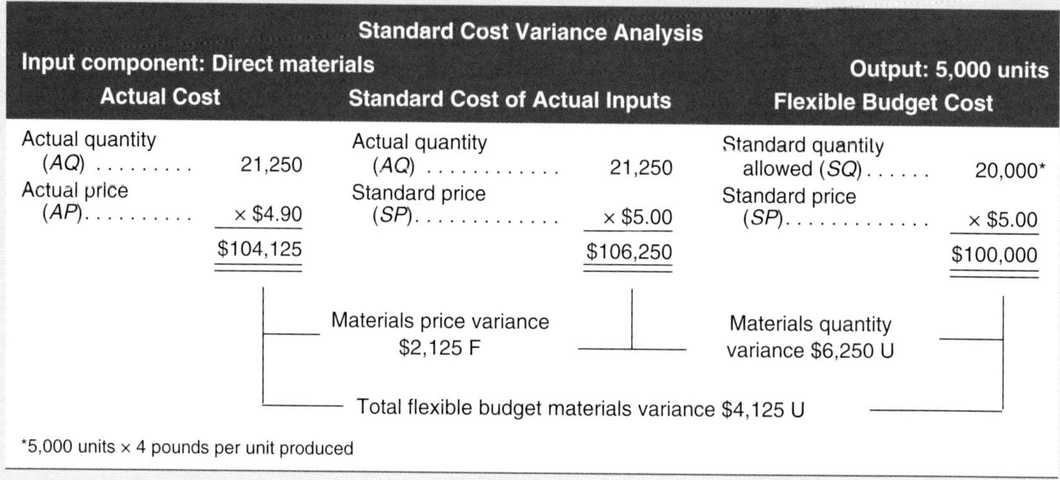

Standard Cost Variance Analysis

Input component: Direct materials — **Output: 5,000 units**

Actual Cost		Standard Cost of Actual Inputs		Flexible Budget Cost	
Actual quantity (*AQ*)	21,250	Actual quantity (*AQ*)	21,250	Standard quantity allowed (*SQ*)	20,000*
Actual price (*AP*)	× $4.90	Standard price (*SP*)	× $5.00	Standard price (*SP*)	× $5.00
	$104,125		$106,250		$100,000

Materials price variance $2,125 F

Materials quantity variance $6,250 U

Total flexible budget materials variance $4,125 U

*5,000 units × 4 pounds per unit produced

Review 10-4—Solution

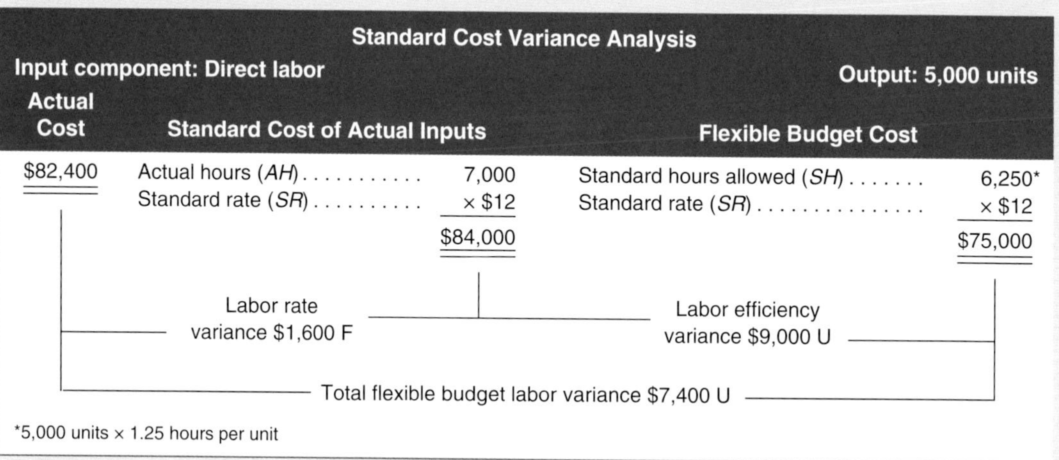

Standard Cost Variance Analysis

Input component: Direct labor — **Output: 5,000 units**

Actual Cost	Standard Cost of Actual Inputs		Flexible Budget Cost	
$82,400	Actual hours (*AH*)	7,000	Standard hours allowed (*SH*)	6,250*
	Standard rate (*SR*)	× $12	Standard rate (*SR*)	× $12
		$84,000		$75,000

Labor rate variance $1,600 F

Labor efficiency variance $9,000 U

Total flexible budget labor variance $7,400 U

*5,000 units × 1.25 hours per unit

Review 10-5—Solution

Standard Cost Variance Analysis

Input component: Variable overhead — **Output: 5,000 units**

Actual Costs		Standard Cost of Actual Inputs		Flexible Budget Cost	
Category 1	$31,000	Actual labor hours	7,000	Standard hours allowed	6,250
Category 2	18,000	Standard rate	× $4.80	Standard rate	× $4.80
Total	$49,000	Driver total	$33,600	Driver total	$30,000
		Finished units	5,000	Finished units	5,000
		Standard rate	× $4.00	Standard rate	× $4.00
		Driver total	$20,000	Driver total	$20,000
		Total	$53,600	Total	$50,000

Variable overhead spending variance $4,600 F

Variable overhead efficiency variance $3,600 U

Total flexible budget variable overhead variance $1,000 F

Review 10-6—Solution

Revenue variance	=	(AQ × AP) − (BQ × BP)
	=	(150 × \$26) − (125 × \$25)
	=	\$775 F
Sales price variance	=	(AP − BP) × AQ
	=	(\$26 − \$25) × 150
	=	\$150 F
Sales volume variance	=	(AQ − BQ) × BP
	=	(150 − 125) × \$25
	=	\$625 F

Review 10-7—Solution

a.

Actual fixed overhead cost	\$6,250,000
Budgeted fixed overhead cost	(6,000,000)
Fixed overhead budget variance	\$ 250,000 U

b.

Fixed overhead rate = \$6,000,000/2,000,000 = \$3.00/barrel

Budgeted fixed overhead cost	\$6,000,000
Applied fixed overhead (2,100,000 barrels × \$3.00)	(6,300,000)
Volume variance	\$ 300,000 F

Review 10-8—Solution

a.

	Actual Results	Flexible Budget	Static Budget
Sales	\$385,000	\$420,000	\$300,000
Variable manufacturing costs	154,000	140,000	100,000
Variable selling costs	63,000	70,000	50,000
Contribution margin	\$168,000	\$210,000	\$150,000

b.

Variance	Amount
Sales price variance	\$ 35,000 U
Net sales volume variance	(60,000) F
Variable manufacturing cost flexible budget variance	14,000 U
Variable selling cost flexible budget variance	(7,000) F
Net variances	\$(18,000) F

The sales volume variance results from difference in units from budget while the remaining variances result from differences of unit dollar amounts.

c.

	Variance
Sales department	\$(32,000) F
Production department	14,000 F
Net variances	\$(18,000) F

Chapter 11

Segment Reporting, Transfer Pricing, and Balanced Scorecard

Learning Objectives

LO1 Define a strategic business segment and prepare and use segment reports. (p. 396)

LO2 Explain transfer pricing and assess alternative transfer-pricing methods. (p. 401)

LO3 Determine and contrast return on investment and residual income. (p. 406)

LO4 Describe the balanced scorecard as a comprehensive performance measurement system. (p. 413)

On the shores of the Mittelland Canal, in the shadow of Wolfsburg Castle, stands the 70 million square-foot factory of Volkswagen (VW). Along with employing 60,500 workers, VW's presence is felt throughout the region from the Volkswagen Arena to the VW-owned Ritz Carlton to Autostadt, VW's sprawling theme park housing the most popular car museum in the world, the ZeitHaus. But VW's products go beyond its flagship brand to include Audi, Porsche, Lamborghini, Bentley, Bugatti, Ducati, SEAT, Skoda, MAN, Scania, and Volkswagen Commercial Vehicles, encompassing a total of 365 different vehicle models. VW also has manufacturing or assembly plants in 31 different countries in Europe, the Americas, Africa, and Asia.

Given the company's diversity by product line and geographic region, preparing the VW's financial and operating reports by segment assists VW managers in determining where the company should expand or contract its operations. However, the sheer complexity and volume of the company's business make the allocation of common costs across segments a difficult proposition.

One of VW's initiatives to manage the business across product and geographic lines is the introduction of modular tool-kit assemblies. This system allows the company to build all of its vehicles using four basic setups: a different tool kit for small, midsize, sports, or large/SUV vehicles. Doing this allows VW to standardize its engineering platforms and reduce inventory costs by using shared components wherever possible. With standardization comes an increase in transfers of components across product line and geographic divisions. However, what is the correct "price" to charge between internal divisions? The "selling" division would like to maximize its divisional performance by charging the highest price possible on the transfer, while the "buying" division would prefer to minimize its costs by paying the lowest price possible to the selling division. And each country in which VW manufactures and assembles its vehicles resides in a different tax jurisdiction such that the choice of a transfer price has real economic consequences for the overall corporate entity.

In this chapter, we will discuss performance measures that overcome the weaknesses of traditional performance ratios by taking into account leverage, taxation, level of investment, and the cost of accessing financial capital to make those investments.

Road Map

LO	Learning Objective | Topics	Page	eLecture	Guided Example	Assignments
LO1	**Define a strategic business segment and prepare and use segment reports.** Strategic Business Segment :: Segment Reports :: Segment Margin	396	e11–1	Review 11-1	15, 16, 17, 31, 32, 33, 34
LO2	**Explain transfer pricing and assess alternative transfer-pricing methods.** Management Considerations :: Market Price :: Variable Costs :: Variable Costs Plus Opportunity Costs :: Absorption Cost Plus Markup :: Negotiated Prices :: Dual Prices	401	e11–2	Review 11-2	18, 19, 20, 24, 25, 26, 37, 38, 40, 41, 42
LO3	**Determine and contrast return on investment and residual income.** ROI :: Investment Center Income :: Investment Center Asset Base :: Valuation Issues :: Residual Income :: Economic Value Added	406	e11–3	Review 11-3	21, 22, 27, 28, 29, 35, 36, 37
LO4	**Describe the balanced scorecard as a comprehensive performance measurement system.** Balanced Scorecard Framework :: Balanced Scorecard Strategy	413	e11–4	Review 11-4	23, 30, 39

CHAPTER ORGANIZATION

Segment Reporting, Transfer Pricing, and Balanced Scorecard

Strategic Business Segments and Segment Reporting	Transfer Pricing	Investment Center Evaluation Measures	Balanced Scorecard
• Multilevel Segment Income Statements • Interpreting Segment Reports	• Management Considerations • Determining Transfer Prices	• Return on Investment • Investment Center Income • Investment Center Asset Base • Other Valuation Issues • Residual Income • Economic Value Added	• Balanced Scorecard Framework • Balanced Scorecard and Strategy

Organizations that maintain multiple product lines or that operate in several industries or in multiple markets often adopt a decentralized organization structure in which managers of major business units or strategic segments enjoy a high degree of autonomy. Examples of strategic business segments include the Porsche division of Volkswagen and the Asia Pacific Group of The Coca-Cola Company. Sometimes companies establish segments within segments such as at Coca-Cola, whose Asia Pacific Group has separate business units for individual countries (Japan, Korea, etc.). In organizations such as Volkswagen and Coca-Cola, upper management typically sets specific performance and profitability objectives for each segment and allows the manager of the segment the decision-making freedom to achieve those objectives.

This chapter explains the ways that an organization evaluates strategic business segments. It also considers transfer pricing and some of the problems that occur when one segment provides goods or services to another segment in the same organization.

Strategic Business Segments and Segment Reporting

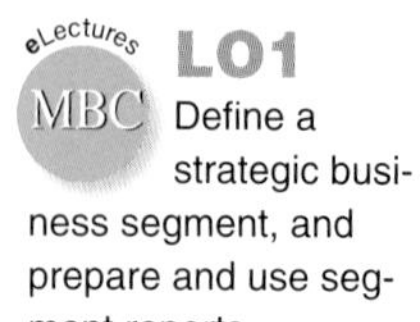

LO1 Define a strategic business segment, and prepare and use segment reports.

A **strategic business segment** has its own mission and set of goals. Its mission influences the decisions that top managers make in both short-run and long-run situations. The organization structure dictates to a large extent the type of financial segment reporting and other measures used to evaluate the segment and its managers. In decentralized organizations, for example, the reporting units (typically called *divisions*) normally are quasi-independent companies, often having their own computer system, cost accounting system, and administrative and marketing staffs. With this type structure, top management monitors the segments to ensure that these independent units are functioning for the benefit of the entire organization.

Although segment reports are normally produced to coincide with managerial lines of responsibility, some companies also produce segment reports for smaller slices of the business that do not represent separate responsibility centers. These parts of the business are not significant enough to be identified as "strategic" business units as defined, but management could want information about them on a continuing basis.

For example, AT&T has four strategic business units: Communication, WarnerMedia, Latin America, and Xandr. Financial reports are prepared for each of these units. Within the WarnerMedia segment, AT&T can also prepare segment reports on a more detailed basis to determine the profitability of its smaller segments, such as Turner, Home Box Office, and Warner Bros. Most public companies are required to provide some segment information in their annual reports.

The point is that segment reporting is not constrained by lines of responsibility. A segment report can be prepared for any part of the business for which management believes more detailed information is useful in managing that portion of the business.

Business Insight ■ Strategic Segment Organization

Very few automakers have sold 10 million vehicles in a year. The first two were General Motors and Volkswagen, and both companies famously struggled after hitting the 10 million mark. Toyota's sales have been above 10 million vehicles for two years running, and the firm has had its struggles. Senior executives at Toyota have expressed concern that this scale of production, sales, and distribution is difficult to manage.

In order to remain nimble and competitive, Toyota has reorganized operations, shifting from a geographic organization to one based on product lines. Toyota President Akio Toyoda has said that as companies reach the 10 million milestone, reorganization is inevitable at all levels. "We can't talk about our future without finding new ways to do our jobs," Toyoda said. Analysts who cover the auto industry feel that this attitude is key to Toyota's ability to adjust more swiftly to challenges such as recalls and natural disasters.

One of the key ways that this new structure can help is by streamlining Toyota's product lines. Previously, Toyota modified the marketing and design of its vehicles to the target geography. The Vitz compact, sold in Japan, has a closely related model, the Yaris, sold only in Europe and the United States, while India has the Etios. What Japanese and American customers recognize as the Prius C is marketed in Europe as the Aqua. This geographical focus served Toyota well as it grew to its current size. Now there are gains to be had by simplifying the product lines, partially due to the size of the company, but also due to the global familiarity with Toyota vehicles. All companies should be prepared to modify internal structures as the firm evolves.

Sources: Naomi Tajitsu, "Toyota Shakes Up Corporate Structure to Focus on Product Lines," *Reuters*, March 2, 2016. Yoko Kubota, "Toyota Plans Organizational Shake-Up," *Wall Street Journal*, February 29, 2016.

Segment reports are income statements for portions or segments of a business. Segment reporting is used primarily for internal purposes, although generally accepted accounting principles also require some disclosure of segment information for public corporations. Even though there are many different types of segment reports, at least three steps are basic to the preparation of all segment reports:

1. Identify the segments.
2. Assign direct costs to segments.
3. Allocate indirect costs to segments.

The format of segment income statements varies depending on the approach adopted by a company for reporting income statements internally. The income statement formats illustrated earlier in this text, including the functional format and the contribution format, can be used for segment reporting. Data availability can, however, dictate the format used. Regardless of the format adopted, it is essential that costs be separable into those directly traceable to the segments and those not directly traceable to segments. See **Exhibit 11.1**, below, for how the three steps above can be incorporated in the development of segment income.

Exhibit 11.1 ■ **Preparation of Segment Reports**

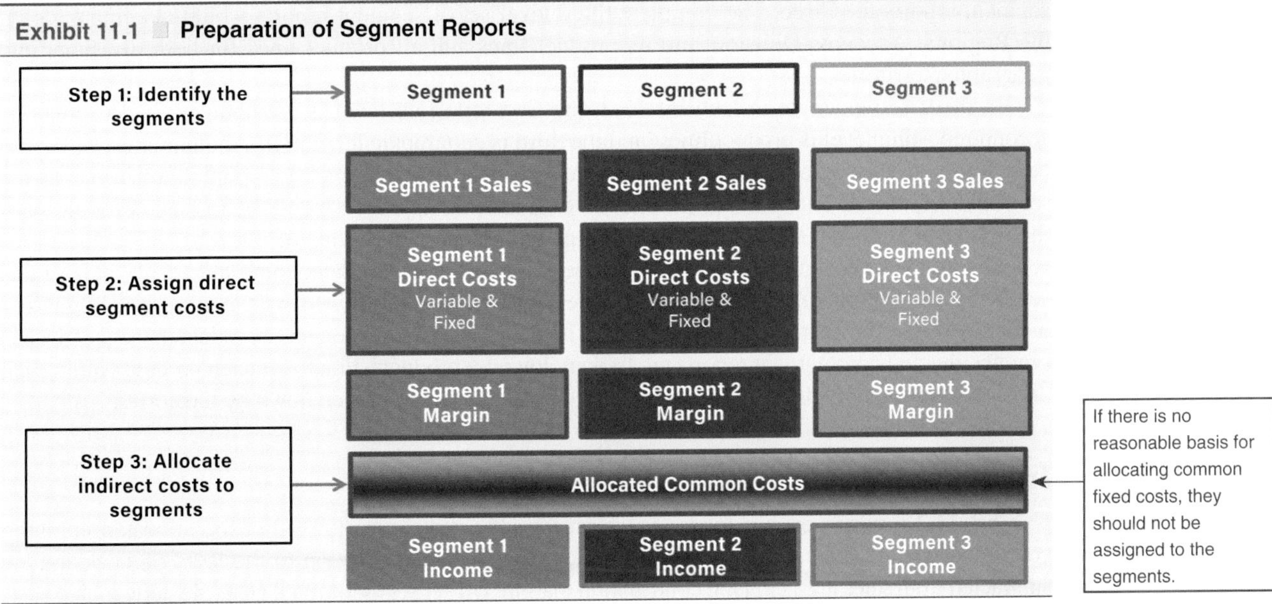

Determining the segment reporting structure is often a more difficult decision than choosing the format for the segment income statements. Companies must decide whether to structure segment reporting along the lines of responsibility reporting, and whether segment reports will be prepared only on one level or on several levels.

For example, assume Cisco has two market divisions, three products, and two geographic territories. Suppose Cisco's two divisions include the National Division (serving large national accounts) and the Regional Division (serving smaller regional and local accounts). Further assume Cisco's three main product lines are switching, routing, and wireless. The company is organized into two geographic territories, United States and International. If Cisco were using only a single-level segment reporting approach for all three groupings, one report would show the total company income statement broken down into the two divisions, a second report would show the total company income statement broken down into the three products, and a third report would show the total company income statement broken down into the two geographic territories.

Multilevel Segment Income Statements

If top management of Cisco wants to know how much a particular product is contributing to the income of one of the two divisions or how much income a particular product in one of its two geographic territories contributes, it is necessary to prepare multilevel segment income statements. Since Cisco sells three products and operates through two divisions in two territories, many combinations of divisions, products, and territories could be used in structuring the company's multilevel segment reporting. The goal is not to slice and dice the revenue and cost data in as many ways as possible but to provide useful and meaningful information to management. Therefore, deciding what type of reporting structure is most useful in managing the company is important.

This decision will be constrained to a great extent by data availability and cost. If there were no data constraints, Cisco could look at the company's net income for every possible combination of division, product, and territory. The more data required to support a reporting system, however, the more costly it is to maintain the system, so management must determine the value and the cost of the additional information and make an appropriate cost-benefit judgment.

Panel A of **Exhibit 11.2** illustrates hypothetical multilevel segment reporting for Cisco in which the first level shows the total company income statement segmented into the two market divisions, National Accounts and Regional Accounts. Panel B of **Exhibit 11.2** shows a second-level report for Cisco in which the National Division's segment income statement is broken down into its three product lines, switching, routing, and wireless. Panel C then provides a third-level income statement for the National Division's switching product line sales in each of the company's two geographic territories, the U.S. and International territories. The example in **Exhibit 11.2** shows only part of the segment reports for Cisco. The complete three-level set of segment reports would also break down the Regional Accounts Division into its product lines and all product lines for both divisions into geographic territories.

In the Cisco example in **Exhibit 11.2**, the first reporting level is the company's divisions, its second reporting level is product lines, and the third is geographic territories. Another approach could be to structure the segment reports with product lines as the first level, geographic territories as the second level, and divisions as the third level. Still another approach would be to make product lines the first level, divisions the second level, and geographic territories the third level.

Regardless of how many different ways the company segments the income statements, at least one set of segment reports follows the company's responsibility reporting system; therefore, one of the segment reports has the operating divisions as the first level. If each division has a product manager for each product, the division segment reports are broken down by products. Finally, if each product within each division has a territory manager, the product segment reports are broken down by territories.

Interpreting Segment Reports

Exhibit 11.2 reports costs in four categories: variable costs, direct fixed costs, allocated common costs, and unallocated common costs. Variable costs vary in proportion to the level of sales and are subtracted from sales in calculating contribution margin. **Direct segment fixed costs** are nonvariable costs

Exhibit 11.2 Multilevel Segment Reports

Panel A: First-Level Segment Report of Cisco—For Divisions

(in thousands)	Segments (Divisions) National Accounts	Regional Accounts	Company Total
Sales	$100,000	$ 200,000	$300,000
Less variable costs	(55,000)	(95,000)	(150,000)
Contribution margin	45,000	105,000	150,000
Less direct fixed costs	(20,000)	(60,000)	(80,000)
Division margin	25,000	45,000	70,000
Less allocated segment costs	(10,000)	(25,000)	(35,000)
Division income	$ 15,000	$ 20,000	35,000
Less unallocated common costs			(12,000)
Net income			$ 23,000

Panel B: Second-Level Segment Report of the National Division—For Products

(in thousands)	Segments (Products) Switching	Routing	Wireless	National Accounts Total
Sales	$30,000	$40,000	$30,000	$100,000
Less variable costs	(15,000)	(19,000)	(21,000)	(55,000)
Contribution margin	15,000	21,000	9,000	45,000
Less direct fixed costs	(9,000)	(4,000)	(2,000)	(15,000)
Product margin	6,000	17,000	7,000	30,000
Less allocated segment costs	(5,000)	(4,000)	(1,000)	(10,000)
Product income	$ 1,000	$13,000	$ 6,000	20,000
Less unallocated common costs				(5,000)
National Division income				$ 15,000

Panel C: Third-Level Segment Report of the Switching Product Line in the National Division—For Geographic Territories

(in thousands)	Segments (Territories) U.S.	International	Switching Total
Sales	$20,000	$10,000	$30,000
Less variable costs	(11,000)	(4,000)	(15,000)
Contribution margin	9,000	6,000	15,000
Less direct fixed costs	(3,000)	(4,000)	(7,000)
Territory margin	6,000	2,000	8,000
Less allocated segment costs	(2,000)	(3,000)	(5,000)
Territory income	$ 4,000	$(1,000)	3,000
Less unallocated common costs			(2,000)
Switching income			$ 1,000

Common segment costs that are incurred for the common benefit of all related segments.

directly traceable to the segments incurred for the specific benefit of the respective segments. **Segment margin** equals the contribution margin minus the direct segment fixed costs. For Cisco, segment margins are referred to as *division margins, product margins,* and *territory margins*. Segment margins represent the amount that a segment contributes directly to the company's profitability in the short run.

Common segment costs are incurred for the common benefit of all related segments shown on a segment income statement. In some cases, allocating some common costs is reasonable even though they cannot be directly traced to the various segments based on benefits received. For example, if segments share common space, allocating all space-related costs to the segments based on building space occupied could be appropriate. If there is no reasonable basis for allocating common costs, they should not be allocated to the segments. In Panel C of **Exhibit 11.2**, if advertising costs to promote the company's switching products on national television could not be reasonably allocated to the two geographic territories, they would be charged to the switching product line as an unallocated common cost, not to the individual territories.

If some portion of common costs can be reasonably allocated to the segments, those allocated costs are subtracted from the segment margins to determine segment income. Hence, **segment income** represents all revenues of the segment minus all costs directly or indirectly charged to it.

To properly interpret segment income, we should ask whether segment income represents the amount by which net income of the company will change if that segment is discontinued. For example, if Cisco discontinues the wireless product line in the National Division, does this mean that Cisco's net income will decrease by $6 million? Also, does it mean that if the National Division stops selling switching products in the International territory, Cisco's net income will increase by $1 million?

The answer to these questions depends on whether the costs allocated to the segments are avoidable. **Avoidable common costs** are allocated common costs that eventually can be avoided (that is, can be eliminated) if a segment is discontinued. If all allocated common costs are avoidable, the effect of discontinuing the segment on corporate profitability equals the amount of segment income. In most cases, the short-term impact of discontinuing a segment equals the segment margin because allocated costs are capacity costs that cannot be adjusted in the short run. Over time, the company should be able to adjust capacity and eliminate some, or possibly all, of the allocated common costs or find productive uses for that capacity in other segments of the business. The unallocated common costs cannot be changed readily in the short term or the long term without causing major disruptions to the company and its strategy. Therefore, over the long term, the impact of discontinuing a segment should be, approximately, its segment income.

If Cisco discontinues selling switching products in the International territory (see **Exhibit 11.2**, Panel C), the short-term effect on the company's profits will probably be a $2 million reduction of profits, which equals the International territory's margin. The revenues and costs that make up the International territory margin would all be lost if switching sales were discontinued in the International territory, but the $3 million of common costs allocated to the International territory would continue, at least in the short term. Over the long term, however, after adjusting the capacity for selling this product in the International territory and eliminating the $3 million of allocated common costs, the effect of discontinuing switching products in the International territory on profits should be an increase of about $1 million, which is the amount of the segment loss for switching products in the International territory.

To summarize, generally, segment margin is relevant for measuring the short-term effects of decisions to continue or discontinue a segment; however, segment income is relevant for measuring the long-term effects of decisions to continue or discontinue.

Review 11-1 LO1 Reporting by Segment

Refer to the Cisco example in **Exhibit 11.2**, Panel B. The following additional information is provided for the wireless product line in the National Division (in thousands):

Sales—U.S. territory	$12,000
Sales—International territory	18,000
Direct fixed cost—U.S. territory	500
Direct fixed cost—International territory	800
Allocated segment costs—U.S. territory	200
Allocated segment costs—International territory	600

Required

a. If the wireless product line is dropped, in the short run, what is the impact on National Division Income?

b. Prepare a geographic territory segment report of the wireless product line in the National division. Assume variable costs are always the same percent of sales for wireless products.

c. Explain why the total of the Territory Margins for geographic segments of the wireless product line does not equal the product margin of the wireless product segment in Panel B of **Exhibit 11.2**.

Solution on p. 433.

Transfer Pricing

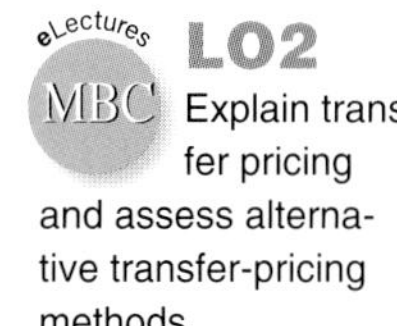

LO2 Explain transfer pricing and assess alternative transfer-pricing methods.

To determine whether each division is achieving its organizational objectives, managers must be accountable for the goods and services they acquire, both externally and internally. When goods or services are exchanged internally between segments of a decentralized organization, the way that the transferor and the transferee will report the transfer must be determined, either by negotiations between the two segments or by corporate policy. A **transfer price** is the internal value assigned a product or service that one division provides to another. The transfer price is recognized as revenue by the division providing goods or services and as expense (or cost) by the division receiving them. Transfer-pricing transactions normally occur between profit or investment centers rather than between cost centers of an organization; however, managers often consider cost allocations between cost centers as a type of transfer price. The focus in this section is on transfers between responsibility centers that are evaluated based on profits.

Management Considerations

The desire of the selling and buying divisions of the same company to maximize their individual performance measures often creates transfer-pricing conflicts within an organization. Acting as independent units, divisions could take actions that are not in the best interest(s) of the organization as a whole. The three examples that follow illustrate the need for organizations to maintain a *corporate* profit-maximizing viewpoint while attempting to allow *divisional* autonomy and responsibility.

Suppose Sony Corporation has five divisions, some of which transfer products and product components to other Sony divisions. Suppose the Monitors and Displays (M&D) Division manufactures two products, Yokia Mount and PVMA. It sells Yokia Mount externally for $50 per unit and transfers PVMA to the Television Division for $60 per unit. The costs associated with the two products follow:

Monitors and Displays Division	Product	
	Yokia Mount	PVMA
Variable costs		
Direct materials	$15	$14
Direct labor	5	10
Variable manufacturing overhead	5	16
Selling	4	0
Fixed costs		
Fixed manufacturing overhead	6	15
Total	$35	$55

An external company has just proposed to supply a PVMA substitute product to the Television Division at a price of $52. From the company's viewpoint, this is merely a make or buy decision. The relevant costs are the differential outlay costs of the alternative actions. Assuming that the fixed manufacturing costs of the M&D Division are unavoidable, the relevant costs of this proposal from the company's perspective are as follows:

Buy		$52
Make		
Direct materials	$14	
Direct labor	10	
Variable manufacturing overhead	16	(40)
Difference		$12

From the corporate viewpoint, the best decision is for the product to be transferred since the relevant cost is $40 rather than to buy it from an external source for $52. The decision for the Television Division management is basically one of cost minimization: Buy from the source that charges the lowest price. If the M&D Division is not willing to transfer PVMA at a price of $52 or less, the Television Division management could go to the external supplier to maximize the division's profits. (Although the Television Division's managers are concerned about the cost of PVMA, they are also concerned about the quality of the goods. If the $52 product does not meet its quality standards, the Television Division could decide to buy from the M&D Division at the higher price. For this discussion, assume that the internal and external products are identical; therefore, acting in its best interest, the Television Division purchases PVMA for $52 from the external source unless the M&D Division can match the price.)

Prior to Television's receipt of the external offer, the M&D Division had been transferring PVMA to the Television Division's for $60. The M&D Division must decide whether to reduce the contribution margin on its transfers of PVMA to the Television Division and, therefore, lower divisional profits or to try to find an alternative use for its resources. Of course, corporate management could intervene and require the internal transfer even though it would hurt M&D Division's profits.

As the second example, assume that the M&D Division has the option to sell an equivalent amount of PVMA externally for $60 per unit if the Television Division discontinues its transfers from the M&D Division. Now the decision for M&D's management is simple: Sell to the buyer willing to pay the most. From the corporate viewpoint, it is best for the M&D Division to sell to the external buyer for $60 and for Television to purchase from the external provider for $52.

To examine a slightly different transfer-pricing conflict, assume that the M&D Division can sell all the Yokia that it can produce (it is operating at capacity). Also assume that there is no external market for PVMA, but there is a one-to-one trade-off between the production of Yokia and PVMA, which use equal amounts of the M&D Division's limited capacity. (In other words, another Yokia can be made for every PVMA not made by the M&D Division.)

The corporation still regards this as a make or buy decision, but the costs of producing PVMA have changed. The cost of PVMA now includes an outlay cost and an opportunity cost. PVMA's opportunity cost is the net benefit foregone if the M&D Division's limited capacity is used to produce PVMA rather than Yokia:

Selling price of Yokia		$50
Outlay costs of Yokia		
Direct materials	$15	
Direct labor	5	
Variable manufacturing overhead	5	
Variable selling	4	(29)
Opportunity cost of making PVMA		$21

The outlay cost of PVMA is its variable cost of $40 ($14 + $10 + $16), as previously computed. Accordingly, the relevant costs in the make or buy decision are as follows.

Make		
Outlay cost of PVMA	$40	
Opportunity cost of PVMA	21	$61
Buy		$52

From the corporate viewpoint, the Television Division should purchase PVMA from the outside supplier for $52 because in this case it costs $61 to make the product. If there were no outside suppliers, the corporation's relevant cost of manufacturing PVMA would be $61. This is another way of saying that the Television Division should not acquire PVMA internally unless its revenues cover all outlay costs (including the $40 in the M&D Division) and provide a contribution of at least $21 ($61 – $40). From the corporate viewpoint, the relevant costs in make or buy decisions are the external price, the outlay costs to manufacture, and the opportunity cost to manufacture. The opportunity cost is zero if there is excess capacity.

The transfer of goods and services between divisions of a company located in different countries that have unequal tax structures often attracts the attention of the taxing authorities. Companies are sometimes accused of trying to minimize their total tax costs by setting transfer prices that shift profits from the division in the higher-tax-rate country to the division in the lower-tax-rate country. For example, assume that IBM has a division in Denmark that produces software that it sells to its systems division in the U.S. Denmark's corporate tax rate is about 50%; whereas, the U.S. rate is about 20%. By setting a transfer price at the lowest possible level, the profits of the Danish division will be less, and those of the American division will be higher, resulting in lower overall taxes for the company. The taxing authorities in the high-tax-rate country always insist that the transfer price for goods and services sold to divisions in other countries be at least as high as fair market value of the goods or services transferred out. The following Business Insight discusses a recent attempt by the IRS to collect taxes of more than $521 million from Guidant Corp. related to improper transfer prices.

Business Insight ■ Transfer Pricing and the IRS

In late 2010, Boston Scientific Corp. reported that the IRS had ruled that its Guidant Corp. division owed $521.1 million in taxes plus interest as a result of an audit of Guidant's prior year's tax returns. The company indicated that the IRS was "assessing additional taxes related to transfer prices on technology license agreements between some of Guidant's U.S. and foreign businesses."

Boston Scientific asked the U.S. Tax court to throw out the case based on two complaints about the methodology the IRS used. First, Boston Scientific argued that the IRS should have determined the separate taxable income for each Guidant business involved in the complaint. Second, Boston Scientific argued that the IRS failed to make the appropriate adjustments to the transactions in question. In early 2016 the court ruled that the case should go forward. Boston Scientific ultimately settled with the IRS in July 2016 for $275 million in taxes plus interest.

Sources: "IRS Wins on Question of Aggregation in 'Guidant' Case," *Bloomberg BNA*, March 1, 2016.
"Boston Scientific Owes Half Billion in Taxes, IRS Says; Company to Fight Ruling on Guidant Division," *Boston Globe*, December 22, 2010.

Determining Transfer Prices

As illustrated, the transfer price of goods or services can be subject to much controversy. The most widely used and discussed transfer prices are covered in this section. Although a price must be agreed upon for each item or service transferred between divisions, the selection of the pricing method depends on many factors. The conditions surrounding the transfer determine which of the alternative methods discussed subsequently is selected.

Although no method is likely to be ideal, one must be selected if the profit or investment center concept is used. In considering each method, observe that each transfer results in a revenue entry on the supplier's books and a cost entry on the receiver's books. Transfers can be considered as sales by the supplier and as purchases by the receiver.

Market Price

When there is an existing market with established prices for an intermediate product and the transfer actions of the company will not affect prices, market prices are ideal transfer prices. If divisions are free to buy and sell outside the firm, the use of market prices preserves divisional autonomy and leads divisions to act in a manner that maximizes corporate goal congruence. Unfortunately, not all product transfers have equivalent external markets. Furthermore, the divisions should carefully evaluate whether the market price is competitive or controlled by one or two large companies. When substantial selling expenses are associated with outside sales, many firms specify the transfer price as market price less selling expenses. The internal sale may not require the incurrence of costs to get and fill the order.

To illustrate using the hypothetical Sony example, assume that product Yokia of the M&D Division can be sold competitively at $50 per unit or transferred to a third division, the Medical Equipment Division, for additional processing. Under most situations, the M&D Division will never sell Yokia for less than $50, and the Medical Equipment Division will likewise never pay more than $50 for it. However, if any variable expenses related to marketing and shipping can be eliminated by divisional transfers, these costs are generally subtracted from the competitive market price. In our illustration in which variable selling expenses are $4 for Yokia, the transfer price could be reduced to $46 ($50 – $4). A price between $46 and $50 would probably be better than either extreme price. To the extent that these transfer prices represent a nearly competitive situation, the profitability of each division can then be fairly evaluated.

Variable Costs

If excess capacity exists in the supplying division, establishing a transfer price equal to variable costs leads the purchasing division to act in a manner that is optimal from the corporation's viewpoint. The buying division has the corporation's variable cost as its own variable cost as it enters the external market. Unfortunately, establishing the transfer price at variable cost causes the supplying division to report zero profits or a loss equal to any fixed costs. If excess capacity does not exist, establishing a transfer price at variable cost would not lead to optimal action because the supplying division would have to forgo external sales that include a markup for fixed costs and profits. If PVMA could be sold externally for $60, the M&D Division would not want to transfer PVMA to the Television Division for a $40 transfer price based on the following variable costs:

Direct materials	$14
Direct labor	10
Variable manufacturing overhead	16
Total variable costs	$40

The M&D Division would much rather sell outside the company for $60, which covers variable costs and provides a profit contribution margin of $20:

Selling price of PVMA	$60
Variable costs	(40)
Contribution margin	$20

Variable Costs Plus Opportunity Costs

From the organization's viewpoint, this is the optimal transfer price. Because all relevant costs are included in the transfer price, the purchasing division is led to act in a manner optimal for the overall company, whether or not excess capacity exists.

With excess capacity in the supplying division, the transfer price is the variable cost per unit. Without excess capacity, the transfer price is the sum of the variable and opportunity costs. Following this rule in the previous example, if the M&D Division had excess capacity, the transfer price of PVMA would be set at PVMA's variable costs of $40 per unit. At this transfer price, the Television Division would buy PVMA internally, rather than externally at $52 per unit. If the M&D Division cannot sell PVMA externally but can sell all the Yokia it can produce and is operating at capacity, the transfer price per unit would be set at $61, the sum of PVMA's variable and opportunity costs ($40 + $21). (Refer back two pages.) At this transfer price, the Television Division would buy PVMA externally for $52. In both situations, the management of the Television Division has acted in accordance with the organization's profit-maximizing goal.

There are two problems with this method. First, when the supplying division has excess capacity, establishing the transfer price at variable cost causes the supplying division to report zero profits or a loss equal to any fixed costs. Second, determining opportunity costs when the supplying division produces several products is difficult. If the problems with the previously mentioned transfer-pricing methods are too great, three other methods can be used: absorption cost plus markup, negotiated prices, and dual prices.

Absorption Cost Plus Markup

According to absorption costing, all variable and fixed manufacturing costs are product costs. Pricing internal transfers at absorption cost eliminates the supplying division's reported loss on each product that can occur using a variable cost transfer price. Absorption cost plus markup provides the supplying division a contribution toward unallocated costs. In "cost-plus" transfer pricing, "cost" should be defined as standard cost rather than as actual cost. This prevents the supplying division from passing on the cost of inefficient operations to other divisions, and it allows the buying division to know its cost in advance of purchase. Even though cost-plus transfer prices may not maximize company profits, they are widely used. Their popularity stems from several factors, including ease of implementation, justifiability, and perceived fairness. Once everyone agrees on absorption cost plus markup pricing rules, internal disputes are minimized.

Negotiated Prices

Negotiated transfer prices are used when the supplying and buying divisions independently agree on a price. As with market-based transfer prices, negotiated transfer prices are believed to preserve divisional autonomy. Negotiated transfer prices can lead to some suboptimal decisions, but this is regarded as a small price to pay for other benefits of decentralization. When they use negotiated transfer prices, some corporations establish arbitration procedures to help settle disputes between divisions. However, the existence of an arbitrator with any real or perceived authority reduces divisional autonomy.

Negotiated prices should have market prices as their ceiling and variable costs as their floor. Although frequently used when an external market for the product or component exists, the most common use of negotiated prices occurs when no identical-product external market exists. Negotiations could start with a floor price plus add-ons such as overhead and profit markups or with a ceiling price less adjustments for selling and administrative expenses and allowances for quantity discounts. When no identical-product external market exists, the market price for a similar completed product can be used, less the estimated cost of completing the product from the transfer stage to the completed stage.

Dual Prices

Dual prices exist when a company allows a difference in the supplier's and receiver's transfer prices for the same product. This method should minimize internal squabbles of division managers and problems of conflicting divisional and corporate goals. The supplier's transfer price normally approximates market price, which allows the selling division to show a "normal" profit on items that it transfers internally. The receiver's price is usually the internal cost of the product or service, calculated as variable cost plus opportunity cost. This ensures that the buying division will make an internal transfer when it is in the best interest of the company to do so.

In most cases, a market-based transfer price achieves the optimal outcome for both the divisions and the company as a whole. As discussed earlier, an exception occurs when a division is operating below full capacity and has no alternative use for its excess capacity. In this case, it is best for the company to have an internal transfer; therefore, to ensure that the receiving division makes an internal transfer, the company must require the internal transfer as long as its price does not exceed the established market rate. The only time an external price is more attractive when excess capacity exists is when the external price is below the variable cost of the providing internal division, and that scenario is highly unlikely.

A potential transfer-pricing problem exists when divisions exchange goods or services for which no established market exists. For example, suppose that a company is operating its information technology (IT) service department as a profit center that transfers services to other profit center departments using a cost-plus transfer price. If the departments using IT services can choose to use those services or to replicate them inside their departments, users might not make a decision that is best for the company. It could be best for the company to have all IT services come from the IT department, but other profit centers could believe that they can provide those services for themselves at lower cost. In this case, the company must decide how important it is to maintain the independence of its profit center. In the interest of maintaining a strong profit center philosophy, top management can decide that it is acceptable to suboptimize by allowing profit centers to provide IT services for themselves.

The ideal transfer-pricing arrangement is seldom the same for both the providing and receiving divisions for every situation. In these cases, what is good for one division is likely not to be good for the other division, resulting in no transfer, even though a transfer could achieve corporate goals. These conflicts are sometimes overcome by having a higher-ranking manager impose a transfer price and insist that a transfer be made. Managers in organizations that have a policy of decentralization, however, often regard these orders as undermining their autonomy. Therefore, the imposition of a price could solve the corporate profit optimization problem but create other problems regarding the company's organization strategy. Transfer pricing thus becomes a problem with no ideal solutions.

The previous discussion has focused on the challenges of establishing transfer prices that motivate managers to make decisions that are beneficial to their divisions as well as the overall company. However, research, discussed in the following Research Insight box, concluded that there are often price benefits when dealing with outside vendors, if the company has the option of acquiring the goods or services internally.

Research Insight ■ Transfer Pricing and External Competition

Researchers found that a firm can glean benefits from discussing transfer-pricing problems with external suppliers. Though transfer prices above marginal cost introduce interdivision coordination problems, they also reduce a firm's willingness to pay outside suppliers. Knowing that costly internal transfers will eat into demand, the supplier is more willing to set lower prices. Such supplier discounts can make decentralization worthwhile for the firm. The benefit of decentralization is shown to be robust in both downstream and upstream competition.

Source: Anil Arya and Brian Mittendorf, "Interacting Supply Chain Distortions: The Pricing of Internal Transfers and External Procurement," *The Accounting Review*, May 2007.

Review 11-2 LO2 — Analyzing Purchase Decisions with Transfer Pricing

University Poster Company has a Publication Division that is currently producing and selling 200,000 posters per year but has a capacity of 300,000 posters. The variable costs of each poster are $16, and the annual fixed costs are $1,350,000. The posters sell for $24 on the open market. The company's Retail Division wants to buy 100,000 posters at $13.50 each. The Publication Division manager refuses the order because the price is below variable cost. The Retail Division manager argues that the order should be accepted because it will lower the fixed cost per poster from $6.75 to $4.50.

Required

a. Should the Retail Division order be accepted? Why or why not?

b. From the viewpoints of the Publication Division and the company, should the order be accepted if the manager of the Retail Division intends to sell each print on the outside market for $44 after incurring additional costs of $10 per print?

c. What action should the company take, assuming it believes in divisional autonomy?

Solution on p. 433.

Investment Center Evaluation Measures

LO3 Determine and contrast return on investment and residual income.

Two of the most common measures of investment center performance, return on investment and residual income, are discussed in the following sections. Several supporting components of these measures that help clarify the applications are also presented. (Earlier in the book, we explained the advantages of separating operating and nonoperating items to compute sales, assets, income, and so forth. We can similarly separate operating and nonoperating items for performance measurement. In this case, all measures would be adjusted to yield operating sales, operating assets, operating income, and so forth. Then, the following analysis would apply to those operating metrics and would reflect the operating performance of each center.)

Return on Investment

Return on investment (ROI) is a measure of the earnings per dollar of investment. This assumes that financing decisions are made at the corporate level rather than the division level. Hence, the corporation's investment in the division equals the division's asset base. The return on investment of an investment center is computed by dividing the income of the center by its asset base (usually total assets):

$$\textbf{ROI} = \frac{\textbf{Investment center income}}{\textbf{Investment center asset base}}$$

ROI can be disaggregated into investment turnover times the return-on-sales ratio:

$$\textbf{ROI = Investment turnover} \times \textbf{Return-on-sales}$$

where

$$\textbf{Investment turnover} = \frac{\textbf{Sales}}{\textbf{Investment center asset base}}$$

and

$$\textbf{Return-on-sales} = \frac{\textbf{Investment center income}}{\textbf{Sales}}$$

When investment turnover is multiplied by return-on-sales, the product is the same as investment center income divided by investment center asset base:

$$\textbf{ROI} = \frac{\textbf{Sales}}{\textbf{Investment center base}} \times \frac{\textbf{Investment center income}}{\textbf{Sales}} = \frac{\textbf{Investment center income}}{\textbf{Investment center asset base}}$$

Once ROI has been computed, it is compared to some previously identified performance criteria. These include the investment center's previous ROI, overall company ROI, the ROI of similar divisions, or the ROI of nonaffiliated companies that operate in similar markets. The breakdown of ROI into investment turnover and return-on-sales is useful in determining the source of variance in overall performance.

To illustrate the computation and use of ROI, suppose the following information is available concerning the operations of Procter & Gamble Co. (P&G) (in thousands) for a single year:

Division	Asset Base	Sales	Divisional Income
Beauty	$8,000,000	$12,000,000	$1,440,000
Healthcare	4,000,000	8,000,000	960,000
Grooming	7,500,000	5,000,000	1,650,000
Fabric & Homecare	3,800,000	5,700,000	1,026,000

Using this information and the preceding equations, a set of performance measures is shown in **Exhibit 11.3**. To illustrate, the Beauty Division earned a return on its investment base of 18% ($1,440,000 ÷ $8,000,000), consisting of an investment turnover of 1.50 ($12,000,000 ÷ $8,000,000) and a return-on-sales of 0.12 ($1,440,000 ÷ $12,000,000). Using such an analysis, the company has three measurement criteria with which to evaluate the performance of the Beauty Division: (1) ROI, (2) investment turnover, and (3) return-on-sales.

Exhibit 11.3 Performance Evaluation Data

PROCTER & GAMBLE CO.
Performance Measures
For Year Ending June 30

	Performance Measures		
	Investment Turnover ×	Return-on-Sales =	ROI
Operating unit			
Beauty	1.50	0.12	0.18
Healthcare	2.00	0.12	0.24
Grooming	0.67	0.33	0.22
Fabric & Homecare	1.50	0.18	0.27
Company performance criteria			
Projected minimums	1.20	0.15	0.18

For the year, P&G chose to evaluate its divisions based on company ROI and its interrelated components of investment turnover and return-on-sales. Because each division is different in size, the company evaluation standard is not a simple average of the divisions but is based on desired relationships between assets, sales, and income.

Based on ROI, the Fabric & Homecare Division had the best performance, the Healthcare Division excelled in investment turnover, and the Grooming Division had the highest return-on-sales. From **Exhibit 11.3**, the Fabric & Homecare Division had the best year because it was the only division that exceeded each of the company's performance criteria. Each division equaled or exceeded the minimum ROI established by the company for the year, even though the component criteria of ROI were not always achieved.

To properly evaluate each division, the company should study the underlying components of ROI. For the Beauty Division, management would want to know why the minimum investment turnover was exceeded while the return-on-sales minimum was not. The Beauty Division could have incurred higher unit costs by producing inefficiently. As a result of inefficient production, the return-on-sales declined to a point below the minimum desired level. Evaluating a large operating division based on one financial indicator is difficult. Management should select several key indicators of performance when conducting periodic reviews of its operating segments.

A similar analysis of ROI and its components is useful for planning. In developing plans for the next year, management wants to know the possible effect of changes in the major elements of ROI for the Beauty Division. Sensitivity analysis can be used to predict the impact of changes in sales, the investment center asset base, or the investment center income.

Assuming the investment asset base is unchanged, a projected ROI can be determined for the Beauty Division for a sales goal of \$16,000,000 and an income goal of \$1,600,000:

$$\textbf{ROI} = \frac{\textbf{Sales}}{\textbf{Investment center asset base}} \times \frac{\textbf{Investment center income}}{\textbf{Sales}}$$

$$= \frac{\$16{,}000{,}000}{\$8{,}000{,}000} \times \frac{\$1{,}600{,}000}{\$16{,}000{,}000}$$

$$= 2.0 \times 0.10$$

$$= 0.20 \text{ or } 20\%$$

ROI increased from 18% to 20%, even though the return-on-sales decreased from 12% to 10%. The change in turnover from 1.5 to 2.0 more than offset the reduced return-on-sales.

Sensitivity analysis can involve changing only one factor or a combination of factors in the ROI model. When more than one factor is changed, it is important to analyze exactly how much change is caused by each factor.

Research Insight ■ Nonprofit Donations Decrease When Donors Believe Managers Are Overpaid

Over 1.4 million nonprofit organizations across the United States received more than \$260 billion in donations during the year 2009. Yet with the weakening economy, contributors to nonprofit organizations are less willing to tolerate inflated salaries of the charity's executives. Specifically, donors decrease their contributions to the organization when the media reports an increase in executive compensation. On average, organizations that draw media coverage over executive compensation increases grow 15% less over the two years surrounding the media mention than their peer organizations. However, when this increase is reported on Form 990 for the Internal Revenue Service (IRS), only sophisticated donors reduce their contributions. Small donors may not know where to seek the compensation information out on their own, and larger donors have a greater stake in the stewardship of their donated funds. Among these larger donors, the study reports that contributions decrease by 3% for every \$100,000 increase in executive compensation.

Source: Steven Balsam and Erica E. Harris, "The Impact of CEO Compensation on Nonprofit Donations," *The Accounting Review* 89, no. 2 (March 2014): 425–450.

Statistics such as ROI, investment turnover, and return-on-sales mean little by themselves. They take on meaning only when compared with an objective, a trend, another division, a competitor, or an industry average. Many businesses establish minimum ROIs for each of their divisions, expecting them to attain or exceed this minimum return. The salaries, bonuses, and promotions of division managers can be tied directly to their division's ROI. Without other evaluation techniques, managers often strive for ROI maximization, sometimes to the long-run detriment of the entire organization.

Investment Center Income

Despite the relevance and conceptual simplicity of ROI, a division's ROI cannot be determined until management decides how to measure divisional income and investment. Divisional income equals divisional revenues less divisional operating expenses. Determining divisional revenues is usually a relatively easy task since revenues are typically generated and recorded at the division level, but determining total operating expenses for divisions is more complicated. Because many expenses are incurred at the corporate level for the common benefit of the various operating divisions and to support corporate headquarters operations, the cost assignment issues discussed early in this chapter affect investment center income.

Direct division expenses are always included in division operating expenses, but there are conflicting viewpoints about how to deal with common corporate expenses. As stated earlier in this chapter, in corporate annual reports, many companies are required to provide segment revenues and expenses segmented by product lines, geographic territories, customer markets, and so on. Companies also show operating income for their various segments in their annual reports, but they include a category called *corporate* or *unallocated* for company expenses that cannot be reasonably allocated to the various segments. ("Unallocated" typically includes costs for corporate staffs, certain goodwill write-offs, and nonoperational gains and losses.) For example, the Toyota Motor Corporation's 2019 annual report includes the following breakdown of its operating income by segments (stated in millions of yen):

Japan	1,691,675 Yen
North America	114,515
Europe	124,868
Asia	457,489
Other (Central and South America, Oceania, Africa, and the Middle East)	91,110
Unallocated	(12,112)
Total operating income	2,467,545 Yen

For internal segment reporting, some companies do not allocate corporate costs that cannot be associated closely with individual segments. Other companies insist on allocating all common corporate costs to the operating divisions to emphasize that the company does not earn a profit until revenues have covered all costs. Some top managers believe that since only operating divisions produce revenues, they should also bear all costs, including corporate costs. These managers want to ensure that the sum of the division income for the various segments equals the total income for the company.

Division managers do not control corporate costs; therefore, these costs are seldom relevant in evaluating a division manager's performance. To deal with this conflict, some companies allocate some, or possibly all, common corporate costs in reporting segment operating income, but for ROI calculation purposes exclude allocated corporate costs that are not closely associated with the divisions. These companies include in the ROI calculation costs that represent an identifiable benefit to the divisions but not general corporate costs that provide no identifiable benefits to the divisions. In practice, the treatment of corporate costs for division performance evaluation varies widely.

Investment Center Asset Base

Because the primary purpose for computing ROI is to evaluate the effectiveness of a division's operating management in using the assets entrusted to them, most organizations define *investment* as the average total assets of a division during the evaluation period. For most companies, the *investment base* is defined as each division's operating assets. These normally include those assets held for productive use, such as accounts receivable, inventory, and plant and equipment. Nonproductive assets, such as land for a future plant site, are not included in the investment base of a division but in the investment base for the company.

General corporate assets allocated to divisions should not be included in their bases. Although the divisions might need additional administrative facilities if they were truly independent, they have no control over the headquarters' facilities. The joint nature and use of corporate facility-level expenses make any allocation arbitrary.

The investment base can also be measured as operating assets less current operating liabilities (net operating assets). Operating liabilities are obligations directly related to normal business operations, such as accounts payable and accrued liabilities.

Other Valuation Issues

Once divisional investment and income have been operationally defined and ROI computations have been made, the significance of the resulting ratios can still be questioned. Return on investment can be overstated in terms of constant dollars because inflation and arbitrary inventory and depreciation procedures cause an undervaluation of the inventory and fixed assets included in the investment center asset base. Asset measurement is particularly troublesome if inventories are valued at last-in, first-out (LIFO) cost or if fixed assets were acquired many years ago. For example, a division manager could hesitate to replace an old, inefficient asset with a new, efficient one because the replacement could lower income and ROI through an increased investment base and increased depreciation.

To improve the comparability between divisions with old and new assets when computing ROI, some firms value assets at original cost rather than at net book value (cost less accumulated depreciation). This procedure does not reflect inflation, however. An old asset that cost $120,000 ten years ago is still being compared with an asset that costs $200,000 today. A better solution could be to value old assets at their replacement cost, although replacement costs are often difficult to determine.

Managerial Decision ■ You Are the Division Vice President

Division managers in your company are evaluated primarily based on division return on investment, and you recently received financial reports for your division for the most recent period and discovered that the ROI for your division was 14.5%; whereas, the target ROI for your division set by the CFO and the CEO was 15%. What action can you take to try to avoid missing your performance target for the next period? [Answer, p. 417]

Residual Income

Residual income is an often-mentioned alternative to ROI for measuring investment center performance. **Residual income** is the excess of investment center income over the minimum rate or dollar of return. The *minimum rate of return* represents the rate that can be earned on alternative investments of similar risks, which is the opportunity cost of the investment. The *minimum dollar return* is computed as a percentage of the investment center's asset base. When residual income is the primary basis of evaluation, the management of each investment center is encouraged to maximize residual income rather than ROI. (We can again measure assets, sales, income, and so forth, as excluding all nonoperating components; similarly, the investment base can be measured as operating assets less operating liabilities.)

To illustrate the computation, assume that a company requires a minimum return of 12% on each division's investment base. The residual income of a division with an annual net operating income of $2,000,000 and an investment base of $15,000,000 is $200,000 as computed here:

Division income	$2,000,000
Minimum return ($15,000,000 × 0.12)	(1,800,000)
Residual income	$ 200,000

Economic Value Added

A variation of residual income, referred to as **economic value added** or **EVA®**, is also often used as a basis for evaluating investment center performance. (The term EVA is a registered trademark of the financial consulting firm of Stern Stewart and Company.) EVA measures residual income earned on all funds committed long term to the organization by lenders (debt) or shareholders (equity). The key differences from the residual income approach, as discussed in the previous section, are the use of after-tax income and an organization's weighted average cost of capital. EVA can be calculated as follows:

Income after taxes − [(Total assets − Current liabilities) × Weighted average cost of capital]

Weighted average cost of capital is an average of the after-tax cost of all long-term borrowing and the cost of equity.[1] Economic value is added only if a division's taxable income exceeds its net cost

[1] Weighted average cost of capital computations is covered in introductory corporate finance textbooks.

of investing. (We can again measure assets, sales, income, and so forth, as excluding all nonoperating components; similarly, the net asset base can be measured as operating assets less operating liabilities.)

Using the preceding situation, assume that the company has a cost of capital of 10%, $1,800,000 in current liabilities, and a 30% tax rate. The economic value added is $80,000, computed as follows:

Division income after taxes ($2,000,000 × 0.70)	$1,400,000
Cost of capital employed [($15,000,000 – $1,800,000) × 0.10]	(1,320,000)
Economic value added	$ 80,000

In calculating EVA, users often ignore any accounting principles that are viewed as distorting the measurement of wealth creation. In practice, EVA consultants have identified up to 150 different adjustments to GAAP income and equity that could be made to restore equity and income to their true economic values. Most companies use no more than about five adjustments (such as the capitalization of research and development cost, recognition of the market value of certain assets, and the elimination of goodwill write-offs).

EVA provides a good operational metric for assessing managers' performance in terms of maximizing the market value of the company over time. It is a model that can be used to guide managerial action. Companies that use EVA for evaluating performance use it in making a broad range of decisions such as evaluating capital expenditure proposals, adding or dropping a product line, or acquiring another company. Only alternatives that provide economic value are accepted. The following Business Insight box discusses how Whole Foods uses EVA to guide decisions about store locations.

Business Insight ■ Economic Value Added

One of the major puzzles facing the grocery industry is investing in new stores. Organic grocer Whole Foods Market uses economic value added (EVA) to guide its decisions about store locations. Whole Foods analyzes potential sites based on population density, income levels, and education levels. A prospective site is then studied in depth, considering sales projections and estimates of construction and operating costs. Before the company commits capital to a new store, the project must meet an EVA hurdle based on the company's cost of capital. This hurdle is generally positive EVA in under five years.

According to Joel Stern, CEO of Stern Stewart and Company (a consulting company), the EVA ethos pervades the entire Whole Foods Organization. Stern says that Whole Foods employees are trained to add value to every customer interaction. The practice is for employees to take customers to the items that they are looking for and to point out relevant specials on the way rather than simply giving directions.

Sources: "SEC Form 10-K, Whole Foods Market, Inc.," The Securities and Exchange Commission EDGAR SYSTEM, November 13, 2015, 6.
Joel Stern and Joseph Willett, "A Look Back at the Beginnings of EVA and Value-Based Management," *Journal of Applied Corporate Finance* 26, no. 1 (Winter 2014): 39–46.

Which Measure Is Best?

Many executives view residual income or EVA as a better measure of managers' performance than ROI. They believe that residual income and EVA encourage managers to make profitable investments that managers might reject if being measured exclusively by ROI.

To illustrate, assume that three divisions of Monsanto have an opportunity to make an investment of $100,000 that requires $10,000 of additional current liabilities and that will generate a return of 20%. The manager of the Chemical Division is evaluated using ROI, the manager of the Agriculture Division is evaluated using residual income, and the manager of the Nutrition Division is evaluated using economic value added. The current ROI of each division is 24%. Each division has a current income of $120,000, a minimum return of 18% on invested capital, and a cost of capital of 14%. If each division has a current investment base of $500,000, current liabilities of $40,000, and a tax rate of 30%, the effect of the proposed investment on each division's performance is as follows:

	Current	+	Proposed	=	Total
Chemical Division					
Investment center income/Asset base	$120,000 / $500,000		$ 20,000 / $100,000		$140,000 / $600,000
ROI	24%		20%		23.3%
Agriculture Division					
Asset base	$500,000		$100,000		$600,000
Investment center income	$120,000		$ 20,000		$140,000
Minimum return (0.18 × base)	(90,000)		(18,000)		(108,000)
Residual income	$ 30,000		$ 2,000		$ 32,000
Nutrition Division					
Assets	$500,000		$100,000		$600,000
Current liabilities	(40,000)		(10,000)		(50,000)
Evaluation base	$460,000		$ 90,000		$550,000
Investment center income	$120,000		$ 20,000		$140,000
Income taxes (30%)	(36,000)		(6,000)		(42,000)
Income after taxes	84,000		14,000		98,000
Cost of capital (0.14 × base)	(64,400)		(12,600)		(77,000)
Economic value added	$ 19,600		$ 1,400		$ 21,000

The Chemical Division manager will not want to make the new investment because it reduces the current ROI from 24% to 23.3%. This is true, even though the company's minimum return is only 18%. Not wanting to explain a decline in the division's ROI, the manager will probably reject the opportunity even though it could have benefited the company as a whole.

The Agriculture Division manager will probably be happy to accept the new project because it increases residual income by $2,000. Any investment that provides a return more than the required minimum of 18% will be acceptable to the Agriculture Division manager. Given a profit maximization goal for the organization, the residual income method is preferred over ROI evaluations because it encourages division managers to accept all projects with returns above the 18% cutoff. The same is true for the Nutrition Division manager, although the EVA increase is not as high as that of the residual income because it has a different base.

The primary disadvantage of the residual income and EVA methods as comparative evaluation tools is that they measure performance in absolute dollars rather than percentages. Although they can be used to compare period-to-period results of the same division or with similar-size divisions, they cannot be used effectively to compare the performance of divisions of substantially different sizes. For example, the residual income of a multimillion dollar sales division should be higher than that of a half-million-dollar sales division. Because most performance evaluations and comparisons are made between units or alternative investments of different sizes, ROI continues to be extensively used. The following Business Insight box discusses the changing role of IT as the need for data management and analysis grows.

Business Insight ■ Measuring the Value of an IT Project

Historically, a company's IT department has been a support department for the core business. According to research by The Hackett Group, the modern IT group has the opportunity to redefine its role as the need for data management and analysis grows. The issue facing leaders of IT departments is that traditional metrics for IT departments focus on minimizing costs. To redefine the role of the IT department, managers need to redefine the way department performance is measured. The Hackett Group recommends the use of key performance indicators (KPIs), developed with input from stakeholders across the organization, that focus on the transformative contribution of the IT department. In the past, IT supported the software and hardware that employees used to do their jobs. Now the IT group can support managers with information they can use to implement their strategic decisions.

Source: "IT Strives to Reinvent Itself Despite Budget Restrictions While Delivering Improved Information and Analytics," *The Hackett Group*, April 1, 2014.

Computing Return on Investment and Residual Income

LO3 Review 11-3

KBR Inc., a decentralized engineering and construction organization, has three divisions, Engineering, Construction, and Military. Assume corporate management desires a minimum return of 15% on its investments and has a 20% tax rate. Suppose the divisions' current results follow (in thousands):

Division	Income	Investment
Engineering	$30,000	$200,000
Construction	50,000	250,000
Military	22,000	100,000

The company is planning an expansion project next year that will cost $50,000,000 and return $9,000,000 per year.

Required

a. Compute the ROI for each division for the current year.
b. Compute the residual income for each division for the current year.
c. Rank the divisions according to their ROI and residual income.
d. Assuming that other income and investments will remain unchanged, determine the ROI of the project by itself. What is the effect on ROI and residual income, if the new project is added to each division?

Solution on p. 434.

Balanced Scorecard

eLectures MBC **LO4** Describe the balanced scorecard as a comprehensive performance measurement system.

Although financial measures have been emphasized throughout this text, several sections stress that other measures, specifically qualitative measures, are important in evaluating managerial performance. This section examines one popular method of performance evaluation using *both* financial and nonfinancial information.

We might ask: why not use just financial measures? First, no single financial measure captures all performance aspects of an organization. More than one measure must be used. Second, financial measures have reporting time lags that could hinder timely decision making. Third, financial measures might not accurately capture the information needed for current decision making because of the delay that sometimes occurs between making financial investments and receiving their results. For example, building a new nuclear power plant can take several years with the investment in total assets increasing the entire time without generating any revenues.

Balanced Scorecard Framework

Comprehensive performance measurement systems are one suggested solution. The basic premise is to establish a set of diverse key performance indicators to monitor performance. The **balanced scorecard** is a performance measurement system that includes financial and operational measures related to a firm's goals and strategies. The balanced scorecard comprises several categories of measurements, the most common of which include the following:

- Financial: Measures the company's financial performance
- Customer: Reflects the customer's view of the company
- Internal processes: Measures the effectiveness of the company's operations
- Innovation and learning: Reflects the willingness of employees to improve and create company value

A balanced scorecard is usually a set of reports required of all common operating units in an organization. To facilitate the periodic evaluation of performance, a cover sheet (or sheets for a large operation) can be used to summarize the performance of each area using the established criteria for each category.

For example, Einstein Brothers might have a balanced scorecard that looks something like the one in **Exhibit 11.4**. This balanced scorecard uses four categories for evaluation and includes financial and nonfinancial information. Each category being monitored has information from the previous period and the standard related to the category. The report should always include the current period, at least one previous period, and some standard. Each store manager should attach documentation and an appropriate explanation as to the change in the measurements during the reporting period.

Exhibit 11.4 Balanced Scorecard Illustration

	Standard	Prior Period	Current Period
Financial			
Cash flow	$ 25,000	$ 28,000	$ 21,000
Return on investment (ROI)	0.18	0.22	0.19
Sales	$4,400,000	$4,494,000	$4,342,000
Customer			
Average customers per hour	75	80	71
Number of customer complaints per period	22	21	17
Number of sales returns per period	10	8	5
Internal Processes			
Bagels sold/produced per day ratio	0.96	0.93	0.91
Daily units lost (burned, dropped, etc.)	25	32	34
Employee turnover per period	0.10	0.07	0.00
Innovation and Learning			
New products introduced during period	1	1	0
Products discontinued during period	1	1	1
Number of sales promotions	3	3	2
Special offers, discounts, etc.	4	5	3

In making assessments with the evaluation categories, it is important to consider both trailing and leading performance measures. *Trailing measures* look backward at historical data while *leading measures* provide some idea of what to expect currently or in the near future. For example, in the financial category, ROI is a trailing indicator while a budget of production units and costs for the next period is a leading indicator. In the customer category, the number of sales invoices per store might tell us whether each store is maintaining its customer base (a trailing indicator) while the number of product complaints per 1,000 invoices might be a leading indicator of customer satisfaction, quality control problems, and future sales.

The use of balanced scorecard systems to monitor and assess managerial and organizational performance is increasing worldwide. The following Business Insight discusses some of the complexities involved in the Department of Education's implementation of the College Scorecard.

Business Insight ■ Understanding Your Strategy: The First Step to a Balanced Scorecard

Since 2013, the Department of Education has been applying a modified version of the balanced scorecard to universities. The College Scorecard was developed to help prospective students evaluate universities before applying. Like all balanced scorecard approaches, the efficacy of the College Scorecard depends on how well what is measured reflects the underlying economics of the business or organization, which is reflected in both the praise and criticism of the College Scorecard. Proponents of the scorecard point to measurement of alumni debt and salaries as powerful reflections of important economic realities that prospective students should consider. Critics of the College Scorecard note that the data in the Scorecard does not allow students to compare themselves by major. A history major considering two schools can only compare average students at the two schools, not history majors at the two schools. Critics also point to the fact that the scorecard only considers full-time students who start and finish at the same school.

With all balanced scorecard approaches to performance evaluation, two essential considerations underpin success. First, the scorecard must be based on a clear understanding of the business activity. Second, the limitations of what can be measured should be carefully considered. Users of the scorecard approach must be careful to craft measurements that accurately reflect the underlying value creation process.

Sources: Peter McPherson and Andrew Kelly, "The College Scorecard Strikes Out," *Wall Street Journal*, March 16, 2015. Jonathan Rothwell, "Understanding the College Scorecard," *Brookings*, September 28, 2015.

A balanced scorecard gives management a perspective of the organization's performance on a recurring set of criteria. Since each reporting unit knows what reports are expected, no one is surprised by changing monthly requests for data. Because the multiple perspectives provide management a broad analysis of the organization's performance, it allows them to determine how and where the goals and objectives are either being achieved or not achieved.

For most management teams, the balanced scorecard highlights trade-offs between measures. For example, a substantial increase in customer satisfaction can result in a short-run decrease in ROI because the extra effort to please customers is expensive, thereby reducing ROI. A balanced scorecard can be filtered down the organization with successively lower-level operating units having their own scorecards that mimic those of the higher-level units. This provides all levels of management an opportunity to evaluate operations from more than just a financial perspective.

Research Insight ■ A Picture May Be Worth a Higher Stock Price

In his book *The Winter of Our Discontent*, John Steinbeck wrote, "For the most part people are not curious except about themselves." Psychologists define narcissism as a sense of self-importance, uniqueness, entitlement, self-absorption, arrogance, and vanity. However, some of these same traits are correlated with leadership qualities. In a recent study, researchers investigate the link between CEO narcissism and financial performance, specifically, earnings per share (EPS) and stock price.

They measure CEO narcissism by examining the size and composition of the CEO's photograph in the annual report and components of the CEO's compensation package. They find that narcissistic managers are more likely to take actions that increase sales and production levels, such as extending lenient credit terms, offering sales discounts, and overproducing. There is no evidence that these same managers attempt to manage earnings through accrual-related actions.

Source: Kari Joseph Olsen, Kelsey Kay Dworkis, and S. Mark Young, "CEO Narcissism and Accounting: A Picture of Profits," *Journal of Management Accounting Research* 26, no. 2 (Fall 2014): 243–267.

As with all management tools and techniques, the use of the balanced scorecard must be incorporated with the other information sources within the organization. Just as the accounting information system cannot stand alone in managing a business, neither can the balanced scorecard. Some areas could need extensive accounting information in great detail to make the best possible decision while other areas need great detail in production or service integration to be at the right place at the right time. By using a multifaceted approach to managing, the organization should be able to better establish an operating strategy that coincides with its overall goals and objectives.

Balanced Scorecard and Strategy

When a balanced scorecard system is fully utilized to monitor and evaluate an organization's progress, it becomes a system for operationalizing the organization's strategy. Having a goal to maximize shareholder value or generate a certain income does not constitute a strategy. Maximizing shareholder value can be an overarching corporate goal, but it will not likely be realized without a well-developed strategy that identifies and establishes a balanced set of goals on various dimensions of performance.

A balanced scorecard can be the primary vehicle for translating strategy into action and establishing accountability for performance. The balanced scorecard identifies the areas of managerial action that are believed to be the drivers of corporate achievement. If the corporate goal is to increase ROI or residual income, the balanced scorecard should include key performance indicators that drive these measures.

An interesting parallel to the successful management of a company can be drawn by considering the key performance indicators the manager of a professional baseball team uses in setting goals and evaluating progress. The manager of the New York Yankees does not just tell his players and managers at the beginning of the baseball season that the team's goal is to win the World Series or even a certain number of ball games. The win-loss record is only one metric used to set goals and evaluate performance for a baseball team. The manager looks at many different drivers of success related to hitting, pitching, and fielding, including the earned-run averages of the pitchers, the batting and on-base averages of hitters, the number of errors per game by fielders, and the number of bases stolen by base runners. At the end of the season, the manager measures success not just by whether the Yankees won the World Series, but also by the batting average, number of home runs, and number of bases stolen by individual players, and whether or not a team member won a Golden Glove award or the Cy Young award. These are all measures by which to evaluate achievement and strategic accomplishment. By achieving the goals for each of these areas of the game, the win-loss ratio will take care of itself. If the win-loss results are not acceptable, then the manager adjusts his strategic goals with respect to the key performance indicators (or the manager is dismissed).

Like a baseball team, a company can use a balanced scorecard to develop performance metrics for managers from the top of the company to the lowest-level department. The scorecard becomes a vehicle for communicating the factors that are key to the success of managers, factors that upper management will monitor in evaluating the success of lower managers in carrying out the corporate strategy. To make balanced scorecards more user friendly, several companies use performance monitoring **dashboards**, which are computer-generated graphics that present scorecard results using graphics, some of which mimic the instrument displays on an automobile dashboard.

The following Business Insight provides an illustration of dashboard graphics.

Business Insight ■ Balanced Scorecard Dashboard

Balanced scorecard dashboards provide information about an organization in an "at-a-glance" format. Many software companies now provide utilities for generating dashboards from SAP, Excel, QuickBooks, and other databases. The following is an example of a dashboard for Sonatica, a fictional company, designed by Dundas Dashboard for assessment of financial performance. The shaded tabs present financial information graphics for Sales and Support. Additional screens would provide performance data on other scorecard dimensions such as internal processes, customers, and innovation and growth.

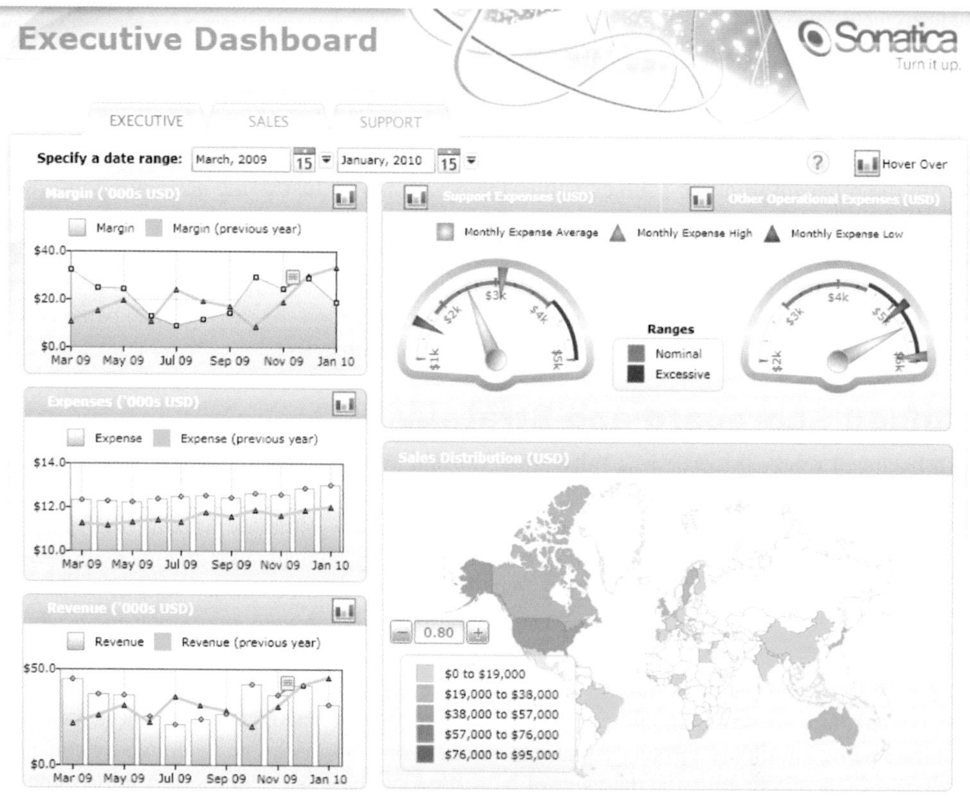

Source: http://www.dashboardinsight.com/dashboards/live-dashboards/dundas-dashboard-v-2-0-demo.aspx

Assigning Metrics to the Balanced Scorecard Categories

LO4 Review 11-4

Balanced Scorecard The following alphabetically ordered list of financial and nonfinancial performance metrics is provided for Northeast Inc.

Average call wait	Job offer acceptance rate	Net profit margin
Average customer survey rating	Market share	Number of complaints
Employee turnover ratio	New customer count	Number of defects reported
Expense as a % of revenue	New customer sales value	Service error rate
Expense variance %	New product acceptance rate	Time to market on new products
Fulfillment %	New product revenue	Unique repeat customer count
Headcount growth	New product ROI	Year-over-year revenue growth
Industry quality rating	Net profit	

Required

a. Assign the above metrics to the four balanced scorecard categories of (1) Financial Success, (2) Customer Satisfaction and Brand Improvement, (3) Business Process Improvement, (4) Learning and Growth of Motivated Workforce.

b. Comment on the use of balanced scorecard versus a single financial measure such as ROI or EVA.

Solution on p. 435.

Guidance Answers

You Are the Division Vice President

Pg. 410 ROI is primarily a measure of the profitability of a division's assets, which is in turn a measure of how effectively the investment in assets was used to generate sales, and how profitable those sales were. ROI is driven by investment (or asset) turnover (which is division sales divided by assets) and return on sales (which is division net income divided by division sales). Therefore, increasing ROI is similar to a simultaneous balancing act involving controlling sales, expenses, and asset investment. You can increase ROI by increasing sales more than expenses, while holding asset investment constant, or by other combinations of these three variables that ultimately increase ROI. If you adjust one of these variables, at the same time you must keep your eye on the other two variables or you may not achieve your goal of increasing ROI.

Key Ratios

$$\text{Return on investment} = \frac{\text{Investment center income}}{\text{Investment center asset base}}$$

Return on investment = Investment turnover × Return-on-sales

$$\text{Investment turnover} = \frac{\text{Sales}}{\text{Investment center asset base}}$$

$$\text{Return-on-sales} = \frac{\text{Investment center income}}{\text{Sales}}$$

$$\text{Return on investment} = \frac{\text{Sales}}{\text{Investment center base}} \times \frac{\text{Investment center income}}{\text{Sales}} = \frac{\text{Investment center income}}{\text{Investment center asset base}}$$

Key Terms

avoidable common costs, 400
balanced scorecard, 413
common segment costs, 399
dashboards, 416
direct segment fixed costs, 398
economic value added or EVA®, 410
residual income, 410
return on investment (ROI), 406
segment income, 400
segment margin, 399
segment reports, 397
strategic business segment, 396
transfer price, 401
weighted average cost of capital, 410

Multiple Choice

Multiple Choice Answers
1. c 2. d 3. a 4. c 5. a 6. d

1. Northern Communications Inc. has two divisions (Individual and Business) and has the following information available for the current year:

Sales revenue—Individual	$3,000,000
Sales revenue—Business	5,000,000
Variable costs—Individual	1,200,000
Variable costs—Business	2,250,000
Direct fixed costs—Individual	400,000
Direct fixed costs—Business	550,000
Allocated fixed costs—Individual	250,000
Allocated fixed costs—Business	350,000
Unallocated common fixed costs	150,000

Northern Communications Inc.'s Business segment income is
a. $2,400,000
b. $2,200,000
c. $1,850,000
d. $1,765,250

2. Refer to the previous question. The following information is available for the Individual Division, which has two product lines (Land and Mobile):

Sales revenue—Land	$1,200,000
Sales revenue—Mobile	1,800,000
Variable costs—Land	680,000
Variable costs—Mobile	520,000
Direct fixed costs—Land	150,000
Direct fixed costs—Mobile	250,000
Allocated fixed costs—Land	100,000
Allocated fixed costs—Mobile	150,000
Unallocated common fixed costs	125,000

The product margin for Land is
a. $270,000
b. $170,000
c. $520,000
d. $370,000

3. Varcore Inc. is currently acquiring a key component from its sister company, Farcore Inc., at a transfer price of $10 per unit. Farcore's variable cost of purchasing the unit is $4, and its fixed cost per unit is $3 per unit. Farcore does not have any excess capacity and can sell all it makes to external customers at $10 per unit. Varcore has been offered a price of $9 per unit for the component from another vendor and is insisting that Farcore reduce its price to $9. Which of the following statements below is false regarding this scenario?
a. Varcore should not accept the outside offer because the variable cost of purchasing it inside is only $4 per unit.
b. Varcore should purchase the unit externally because the internal cost of purchasing the unit internally is a variable cost of $4 per unit plus an opportunity cost of $6 per unit, or $10.
c. The company will be better off if Farcore rejects Varcore's demand and instead sells the units that Varcore would buy to outside customers.
d. Since Farcore is operating at full capacity and has other external customers ready to purchase additional units, the best transfer price is its regular market price.

4. Shealy's Lawn and Garden Supply Company has recently acquired a lawn sod company that grows turf grasses for lawns. Previously, Shealy's was purchasing sod from other suppliers at 50 cents per square foot. The new sod division, which has substantial excess capacity, is able to produce grass sod at a cost of 35 cents per square foot, including direct materials and direct labor cost of 25 cents, variable overhead of 5 cents, and fixed overhead of 5 cents per square foot. The supply division manager argues that the transfer price should be no more than 35 cents per square foot. What transfer price between the sod and the supply divisions will lead the manager of the supply division to act in a manner that will maximize company profits?

a. 50 cents
b. 25 cents
c. 30 cents
d. 35 cents

5. SGA Inc., a division of AGS Inc., had sales of $4,000,000, total assets of $2,000,000, and net income of $400,000. Senior management of AGS Inc. has set a target minimum rate of return for SGA Inc. of 18%. Calculate SGA's residual income.

a. $40,000
b. $36,000
c. $72,000
d. None of the above

6. Which of the following is not one of the four most common categories of measurement presented in a balanced scorecard?

a. Financial
b. Internal processes
c. Innovation and learning
d. External processes

Questions

Q11-1. What is the relationship between segment reports and reports of operating results by product?

Q11-2. What is a business segment? How is it determined?

Q11-3. Can a company have more than one type of first-level statement in segment reporting?

Q11-4. Explain the relationships between any two levels of statements in segment reporting.

Q11-5. Distinguish between direct and indirect segment costs.

Q11-6. What types of information are needed before management should decide to drop a segment?

Q11-7. In what types of organizations and for what purpose are transfer prices used?

Q11-8. What problems arise when transfer pricing is used?

Q11-9. When do transfer prices lead to suboptimization? How can suboptimization be minimized? Can it be eliminated? Why or why not?

Q11-10. For what purpose do organizations use return on investment? Why is this measure preferred to net income?

Q11-11. What advantages do residual income and EVA have over ROI for segment evaluations?

Q11-12. Contrast the difference between residual income and EVA.

Q11-13. Explain how a balanced scorecard helps with the evaluation process of internal operations.

Q11-14. How can a balanced scorecard be used as a strategy implementation tool?

Assignments with the MBC logo in the margin are available in myBusinessCourse. See the Preface of the book for details.

Mini Exercises

M11-15. Multiple Levels of Segment Reporting LO1

Connect Inc. manufactures four different lines of computer devices: modems, routers, servers, and drives. Each of the product lines is produced in all of the company's three plants: Beckley, Huntington, and Charleston. Marketing efforts of the company are divided into five regions: East, West, South, North, and Central.

Required

a. Develop a reporting schematic that illustrates how the company might prepare single-level reports segmented on three different bases.

b. Develop a segment reporting schematic that has three different levels. Be sure to identify each segment's level. Briefly explain why you chose the primary-level segment.

LO1 Pentel of America, LTD

M11-16. Income Statements Segmented by Territory

Assume Pentel has two product lines. The September income statements of each product line and the company are as follows:

PENTEL OF AMERICA, LTD Product Line and Company Income Statements For Month of September (in thousands)	Pens	Pencils	Total
Sales	$60,000	$60,000	$120,000
Less variable expenses	(27,000)	(27,000)	(54,000)
Contribution margin	33,000	33,000	66,000
Less direct fixed expenses	(16,000)	(14,000)	(30,000)
Product margin	$17,000	$19,000	36,000
Less common fixed expenses			(15,500)
Net income			$20,500

Pens and pencils are sold in two sales regions, West and East, as follows:

(in thousands)	West	East
Pen sales	$35,000	$25,000
Pencil sales	20,000	40,000
Total sales	$55,000	$65,000

The common fixed expenses (in thousands) are traceable to each territory as follows:

West fixed expenses	$5,500
East fixed expenses	6,500
Home office administration fixed expenses	3,500
Total common fixed expenses	$15,500

The direct fixed expenses of pens, $16,000, and of pencils, $14,000, cannot be identified with either territory. The company's accountants were unable to allocate any of the common fixed expenses to the various segments.

Required

Prepare income statements segmented by territory for September, including a column for the entire firm.

LO1

M11-17. Income Statements Segmented by Products

Francisco Consulting Firm provides three types of client services in three health-care-related industries. The income statement for July is as follows:

FRANCISCO CONSULTING FIRM Income Statement For Month of July		
Sales		$820,000
Less variable costs		(580,750)
Contribution margin		239,250
Less fixed expenses		
Service	$85,600	
Selling and administrative	70,400	(156,000)
Net income		$ 83,250

The sales, contribution margin ratios, and direct fixed expenses for the three types of services are as follows:

	Hospitals	Physicians	Nursing Care
Sales	$340,000	$205,000	$275,000
Contribution margin ratio	25%	35%	30%
Direct fixed expenses of services	$ 36,500	$ 8,500	$ 18,750
Allocated common fixed services expense	$ 8,500	$ 2,500	$ 4,000

Required

Prepare income statements segmented by client categories. Include a column for the entire firm in the statement.

M11-18. Internal or External Acquisitions: No Opportunity Costs LO2

The Van Division of Travel Vans Corporation has offered to purchase 48,000 wheels from the Wheel Division for $80 per wheel. At a normal volume of 320,000 wheels per year, production costs per wheel for the Wheel Division are as follows:

Direct materials	$20
Direct labor	12
Variable overhead	8
Fixed overhead	25
Total	$65

The Wheel Division has been selling 320,000 wheels per year to outside buyers at $100 each. Capacity is 400,000 wheels per year. The Van Division has been buying wheels from outside suppliers at $95 per wheel.

Required

a. Should the Wheel Division manager accept the offer? Show computations.

b. From the standpoint of the company, will the internal sale be beneficial?

M11-19. Transfer Prices at Full Cost with Excess Capacity: Divisional Viewpoint LO2

Karakomi Cameras Inc. has a Disposables Division that produces a camera that sells for $10 per unit in the open market. The cost of the product is $5.50 (variable manufacturing of $3.00, and fixed manufacturing of $2.50). Total fixed manufacturing costs are $100,000 at the normal annual production volume of 40,000 units. The Overseas Division has offered to buy 10,000 units at the full cost of $5.50. The Disposables Division has excess capacity, and the 10,000 units can be produced without interfering with the current outside sales of 40,000 units. The total fixed cost of the Disposables Division will not change.

Required

Explain whether the Disposables Division should accept or reject the offer. Show calculations.

M11-20. Transfer Pricing with Excess Capacity: Divisional and Corporate Viewpoints LO2 Art.com

Assume Art.com has a Print Division that is currently producing 150,000 prints per year but has a capacity of 200,000 prints. The variable costs of each print are $30, and the annual fixed costs are $1,650,000. The prints sell for $44 in the open market. The company's Retail Division wants to buy 50,000 prints at $20 each. The Print Division manager refuses the order because the price is below variable cost. The Retail Division manager argues that the order should be accepted because it will lower the fixed cost per print from $11 to $8.25.

Required

a. Should the Retail Division order be accepted? Why or why not?

b. From the viewpoints of the Print Division and the company, should the order be accepted if the manager of the Retail Division intends to sell each print in the outside market for $40 after incurring additional costs of $5 per print?

c. What action should the company take, assuming it believes in divisional autonomy?

M11-21. ROI and Residual Income: Impact of a New Investment LO3

The Stallion Division of Motortown Motors had an operating income of $805,000 and net assets of $3,500,000. Motortown Motors has a target rate of return of 20%.

Required

a. Compute the return on investment.

b. Compute the residual income.

c. The Stallion Division has an opportunity to increase operating income by $165,000 with an $800,000 investment in assets.

1. Compute the Stallion Division's return on investment if the project is undertaken. (Round your answer to three decimal places.)
2. Compute the Stallion Division's residual income if the project is undertaken.

LO3 **M11-22. ROI: Fill in the Unknowns**

Provide the missing data in the following situations:

	Eastern Division	Western Division	Southern Division
Sales	?	$8,000,000	?
Net operating income	$250,000	$ 600,000	$1,080,000
Operating assets	?	?	$3,000,000
Return on investment	20%	15%	?
Return on sales	5%	?	6%
Investment turnover	?	?	6

LO4 **M11-23. Selection of Balanced Scorecard Items**

The Worldwide Auditors' Association is a professional association. Its current membership totals 65,400 worldwide. The association operates from a central headquarters in New Zealand but has local membership units throughout the world. The local units hold monthly meetings to discuss recent developments in accounting and to hear professional speakers on topics of interest. The association's journal, *Worldwide Auditor,* is published monthly with feature articles and topical interest areas. The association publishes books and reports and sponsors continuing education courses. A statement of revenues and expenses follows:

WORLDWIDE AUDITORS' ASSOCIATION
Statement of Revenues and Expenses
For Year Ending November 30

($ in thousands)		
Revenues		$50,702
Expenses		
Salaries	$28,050	
Other personnel costs	5,872	
Occupancy costs	5,545	
Reimbursement to local units	2,536	
Other membership services	1,200	
Printing and paper	383	
Postage and shipping	165	
General and administrative	845	44,596
Excess of revenues over expenses		$ 6,106

Additional information follows:

- Membership dues are $480 per year, of which $100 is considered to cover a one-year subscription to the association's journal. Other benefits include membership in the association and unit affiliation.
- One-year subscriptions to *Worldwide Auditor* are sold to nonmembers for $120 each. A total of 10,000 of these subscriptions was sold. In addition to subscriptions, the journal generated $500,000 in advertising revenue. The cost per magazine was $50.
- A total of 30,000 technical reports was sold by the Books and Reports Department at an average unit selling price of $110. Average costs per publication were $36.
- The association offers a variety of continuing education courses to both members and nonmembers. During the year, the one-day course, which cost participants an average of $600 each, was attended by 25,600 people. A total of 3,800 people took two-day courses at a cost of $1,000 per person.

- General and administrative expenses include all other costs incurred by the corporate staff to operate the association.
- The organization has net capital assets of $87,230,000 and had an actual cost of capital of 6%.

Required

a. Give some examples of key financial performance indicators (no computations needed) that could be part of a balanced scorecard for the IAA.

b. Give some examples of key customer and operating performance indicators (no computations needed) that could be part of a balanced scorecard for IAA.

Exercises

E11-24. Appropriate Transfer Prices: Opportunity Costs

LO2 Olam International Limited

Olam International Limited sources and processes agricultural products including edible nuts and spices. Assume the company recently acquired a peanut-processing company that has a normal annual capacity of 180,000 bushels and that sold 125,000 bushels last year at a price of $35 per bushel. The purpose of the acquisition is to furnish peanuts for a new peanut butter plant, which needs 75,000 bushels of peanuts per year. It has been purchasing peanuts from suppliers at the market price. Production costs per bushel of the peanut-processing company are as follows:

Direct materials	$9
Direct labor	4
Variable overhead	2
Fixed overhead at normal capacity	10
Total	$25

Management is trying to decide what transfer price to use for sales from the newly acquired Peanut Division to the Peanut Butter Division. The manager of the Peanut Division argues that $35, the market price, is appropriate. The manager of the Peanut Butter Division argues that the cost price of $25 (or perhaps even less) should be used since fixed overhead costs should be recomputed. Any output of the Peanut Division up to 180,000 bushels that is not sold to the Peanut Butter Division could be sold to regular customers at $35 per bushel.

Required

a. Compute the annual gross profit for the Peanut Division using a transfer price of $35.

b. Compute the annual gross profit for the Peanut Division using a transfer price of $25.

c. What transfer price(s) will lead the manager of the Peanut Butter Division to act in a manner that will maximize company profits?

E11-25. Negotiating a Transfer Price with Excess Capacity

LO2

The Foundry Division of Findlay Pumps Inc. produces metal parts that are sold to the company's Assembly Division and to outside customers. Operating data for the Foundry Division for the current year are as follows:

	To the Assembly Division	To Outside Customers	Total
Sales			
600,000 parts × $8.00	$4,800,000		
400,000 parts × $9.00		$3,600,000	$8,400,000
Variable expenses at $3.75	(2,250,000)	(1,500,000)	(3,750,000)
Contribution margin	2,550,000	2,100,000	4,650,000
Fixed expenses*	(1,350,000)	(900,000)	(2,250,000)
Net income	$1,200,000	$1,200,000	$2,400,000

*Allocated on the basis of unit sales.

The Assembly Division has just received an offer from an outside supplier to supply parts at $5.50 each. The Foundry Division manager is not willing to meet the $5.50 price. She argues that it costs her $6.00 per part to produce and sell to the Assembly Division, so she would show no profit on the Assembly Division sales. Sales to outside customers are at a maximum, 400,000 parts.

Required

a. Verify the Foundry Division's $6 unit cost figure.

b. Should the Foundry Division meet the outside price of $5.50 for Assembly Division sales? Explain.

c. Could the Foundry Division meet the $5.50 price and still show a net profit for sales to the Assembly Division? Show computations.

LO2 **E11-26. Dual Transfer Pricing**

The Athens Company has two divisions, Alpha and Delta. Delta Division produces a product at a variable cost of $12 per unit, and sells 200,000 units to outside customers at $20 per unit and 60,000 units to Alpha Division at variable cost plus 50%. Under the dual transfer price system, Alpha Division pays only the variable cost per unit. Delta Division's fixed costs are $575,000 per year. After further processing, Alpha sells the 60,000 units to outside customers at $40 per unit. Alpha has variable costs of $11 per unit, in addition to the costs from Delta Division. Alpha Division's annual fixed costs are $380,000. There are no beginning or ending inventories.

Required

a. Prepare the income statements for the two divisions and the company as a whole.

b. Why is the income for the company less than the sum of the profit figures shown on the income statements for the two divisions? Explain.

LO3 **E11-27. ROI and Residual Income: Basic Computations**

Watkins Associated Industries

Watkins Associated Industries is a privately held conglomerate. Assume that the company uses return on investment and residual income as two of the evaluation tools for division managers. The company has a minimum desired rate of return on investment of 15%. Selected operating data for three of the divisions of the company follow.

	Trucking Division	Seafood Division	Construction Division
Sales	$6,450,000	$1,845,000	$5,200,000
Operating assets	3,750,000	580,000	1,750,000
Net operating income	525,000	116,000	385,000

Required

a. Compute the return on investment for each division. (Round answers to three decimal places.)

b. Compute the residual income for each division.

LO3 **E11-28. ROI and Residual Income: Assessing Performance**

Refer to the computations in the previous exercise E11-27. Assess the performance of the division managers, basing your conclusions on ROI. Assess the performance of the division managers, basing your conclusions on residual income. Which manager is doing the best job?

LO3 **E11-29. ROI, Residual Income, and EVA with Different Bases**

Envision Company has a target return on capital of 10%. In evaluating operations, management looks at book values (GAAP compliant) and current values. Current values reflect management's estimates of asset values. The following financial information is available for October ($ thousands):

	Software Division (Value Base)		Consulting Division (Value Base)		Venture Capital Division (Value Base)	
	Book	Current	Book	Current	Book	Current
Sales	$200,000	$200,000	$450,000	$450,000	$625,000	$625,000
Pretax income	35,000	37,200	37,000	38,500	63,000	43,200
Operating assets	250,000	310,000	185,000	175,000	700,000	720,000
Current liabilities	30,000	30,000	20,000	20,000	65,000	65,000

Required

a. Compute the return on investment using both book and current values for each division. (Round answers to three decimal places.) For ROI calculations, Envision uses operating assets as the investment base.

b. Compute the residual income for both book and current values for each division.

c. Compute the economic value-added income for both book and current values for each division if the tax rate is 20% and the weighted average cost of capital is 8%.

d. Does book value or current value provide a better basis for performance evaluation? Which division do you consider the most successful?

E11-30. Balanced Scorecard Preparation LO4

The following information is in addition to that presented in exercise M11-23 for the Worldwide Auditors' Association. In the budget for the current year, the organization had set a membership goal of 75,000 members with the following anticipated results:

Worldwide Auditors' Association Planned Revenues and Expenses For Year Ending November 30 ($ in thousands)		
Revenues		$54,436
Expenses		
Salaries	28,000	
Other personnel costs	7,000	
Occupancy costs	6,000	
Reimbursement to local units	2,500	
Other membership services	1,500	
Printing and paper	500	
Postage and shipping	300	
General and administrative	1,000	46,800
Excess of revenues over expenses		$ 7,636

Additional information follows:

- One-year subscriptions to *Worldwide Auditor* were anticipated to be 8,000 units.
- Advertising revenue was budgeted at $450,000. Each magazine was budgeted at a cost of $48.
- A total of 25,000 technical reports was anticipated at an average price of $100 with average costs of $36.
- The budgeted one-day courses had an anticipated attendance of 25,000 with an average fee of $600. The two-day courses had an anticipated attendance of 5,000 with an average fee of $1,000 per person.
- The organization began the year with net capital assets of $84,100,000 with a planned cost of capital of 6%.

Required

a. Prepare a balanced scorecard for IAA for November with calculated key performance indicators presented in two columns for planned performance and actual performance—include key financial, customer, and operating performance indicators.

b. Which of the evaluation areas you selected indicated success and which indicated failure?

c. Give some explanations of the successes and failures.

Problems

P11-31. Multiple Segment Reports LO1

Worldwide Communications, Incorporated, sells telecommunication products throughout the world in three sales territories: Europe, Asia, and the Americas. For July, all $945,000 of administrative expense is traceable to the territories, except $200,000, which is common to all units and cannot be traced or allocated to the sales territories. The percentage of product line sales made in each of the sales territories and the assignment of traceable fixed expenses follow:

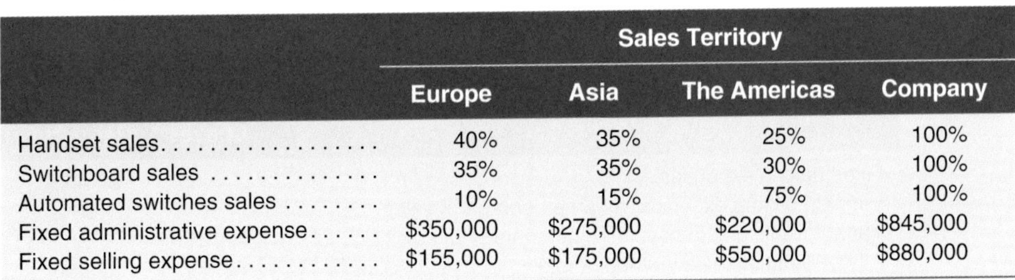

	Sales Territory			
	Europe	Asia	The Americas	Company
Handset sales	40%	35%	25%	100%
Switchboard sales	35%	35%	30%	100%
Automated switches sales	10%	15%	75%	100%
Fixed administrative expense	$350,000	$275,000	$220,000	$845,000
Fixed selling expense	$155,000	$175,000	$550,000	$880,000

The manufacturing takes place in one large facility with three distinct manufacturing operations. Selected product-line cost data follow.

	Handset	Switchboard	Automated Switches	Company
Variable costs	$ 15	$ 850	$ 1,950	
Depreciation and supervision	60,000	175,000	275,000	$ 585,000*
Other mfg. overhead (common)				650,000
Fixed administrative expense (common)				1,045,000
Fixed selling expense (common)				880,000

*Includes common costs of $75,000

The unit sales and selling prices for each product follow.

	Unit Sales	Selling Price
Handset	6,500	$ 25
Switchboard	1,500	1,900
Automated	2,500	3,500

Required

a. Prepare an income statement for July segmented by product line. Include a column for the entire firm.

b. Prepare an income statement for July segmented by sales territory. Include a column for the entire firm.

c. Prepare an income statement for July by product line for The Americas sales territory. Include a column for the territory as a whole. Products are manufactured in a single facility. Although depreciation and supervision are allocated by product line, those costs are not allocated by territory.

d. Discuss the value of multilevel segment reporting as a managerial tool. Compare and contrast the benefits of the reports generated in parts *a*, *b*, and *c*.

The Essential Baking Company

P11-32. Segment Reporting and Analysis

The Essential Baking Company bakes artisan loaves, baguettes, and rolls and sells them in cities throughout the Northwest. Assume the following March income statement was prepared for the stores located in Seattle and Portland:

THE ESSENTIAL BAKING COMPANY
Territory Income Statements
For Month of March

(in thousands)	Seattle	Portland	Total
Sales	$8,400	$6,800	$15,200
Cost of goods sold	(4,796)	(3,894)	(8,690)
Gross profit	3,604	2,906	6,510
Selling and administrative expenses	(2,755)	(2,155)	(4,910)
Net income	$ 849	$ 751	$ 1,600

Sales and selected variable expense data are as follows:

	Products		
	Loaves	Baguettes	Rolls
Fixed baking expenses	$ 565	$ 450	$410
Variable baking expenses as a percentage of sales	50%	50%	40%
Variable selling expenses as a percentage of sales	10%	20%	20%
City of Seattle, sales (in thousands)	$3,800	$2,650	$1,950
City of Portland, sales (in thousands)	$3,250	$2,150	$1,400

The fixed selling expenses were $1,440 for March, of which $860 was a direct expense of the Seattle market and $580 was a direct expense of the Portland market. Fixed administrative expenses were $1,135, which management has decided not to allocate when using the contribution approach.

Required

a. Prepare a segment income statement showing the margin for each territory (city) for March. Include a column combining the two territories.

b. Prepare segment income statements showing the product margin for each product. Include a column for the combined products.

c. If the rolls line is dropped and fixed baking expenses do not change, what is the product margin for loaves and baguettes?

d. What other type of segmentation might be useful to The Essential Baking Company. Explain.

P11-33. Segment Reporting and Analysis LO1

Business Book Publishers, Inc. has prepared income statements segmented by divisions, but management is still uncertain about actual performance. Financial information for May is given as follows:

	Textbook Division	Professional Division	Company Total
Sales	$150,000	$307,500	$457,500
Less variable expenses			
Manufacturing	24,000	153,750	177,750
Selling and administrative	7,500	15,375	22,875
Total	(31,500)	(169,125)	(200,625)
Contribution margin	118,500	138,375	256,875
Less direct fixed expenses	(15,000)	(150,000)	(165,000)
Net income	$103,500	$ (11,625)	$ 91,875

Management is concerned about the Professional Division and requests additional analysis. Additional information regarding May operations of the Professional Division is as follows:

	Professional Division		
	Accounting Books Segment	Executive Books Segment	Management Books Segment
Sales	$105,000	$105,000	$97,500
Variable manufacturing expenses as a percentage of sales	60%	40%	50%
Other variable expenses as a percentage of sales	5%	5%	5%
Direct fixed expenses	$37,500	$55,100	$37,500
Allocated common fixed expenses	$ 3,000	$ 1,500	$ 4,500

The professional accounting books are sold to auditors and controllers. The current information on these markets is as follows:

	Accounting Books Segment		
	Auditors Market	Controllers Market	Total
Sales	$22,500	$82,500	$105,000
Variable manufacturing expenses as a percentage of sales	60%	60%	—
Other variable expenses as a percentage of sales	6%	6%	—
Direct fixed expenses	$11,250	$22,500	$33,750
Allocated common fixed expenses	$ 1,125	$ 1,500	$ 2,625

Required

a. Prepare an income statement segmented by product for the Professional Division. Include a column for the division as a whole.

b. Prepare an income statement segmented by market for the Accounting Books Segment of the Professional Division.

c. Evaluate which Accounting Books Segment the Professional Division should keep or discontinue in the short run.

d. What is the correct long-run decision? Explain fully, including any possible risks associated with your recommendation.

LO1 **P11-34. Segment Reports and Cost Allocations**

All Things Greek Inc. has three sales divisions. One of the key evaluation inputs for each division manager is the performance of his or her division based on division income. The division statements for August are as follows:

	Alpha	Beta	Gamma	Total
Sales	$250,000	$300,000	$275,000	$825,000
Cost of sales	139,500	165,000	158,250	462,750
Division overhead	39,000	45,000	41,250	125,250
Division expenses	(178,500)	(210,000)	(199,500)	(588,000)
Division contribution	71,500	90,000	75,500	237,000
Corporate overhead	(41,000)	(49,000)	(45,000)	(135,000)
Division income	$ 30,500	$ 41,000	$ 30,500	$102,000

The Gamma manager is unhappy that his profitability is the same as that of the Alpha Division and 74% that of the Beta Division when his sales are halfway between these two divisions. The manager knows that his division must carry more product lines because of customer demands, and many of these additional product lines are not very profitable. He has not dropped these marginal product lines because of idle capacity; all of the products cover their own variable costs. After analyzing the product lines with the lowest profit margins, the divisional controller for Gamma provided the following to the manager:

Sales of marginal products		$55,000
Cost of sales	$34,100	
Avoidable fixed costs	13,500	47,600
Product margin		$ 7,400

Although these products were 20% of Gamma's total sales, they contributed only about 10% of the division's profits. The controller also noted that the corporate overhead allocation was based on relative sales proportions and the allocation would decrease if the weak product line was dropped.

Required

a. Prepare a set of segment statements for August assuming that all facts remain the same except that Gamma's weak product lines are dropped and corporate overhead is allocated as follows: Alpha, $43,800; Beta, $52,600; and Gamma, $38,600. Does the Gamma Division appear better after this action? What will be the responses of the other two division managers?

b. Suggest improvements for All Things Greek's reporting process that will better reflect the actual operations of the divisions. Keep in mind the utilization of the reporting process to assist in the evaluation of the managers. What other changes could be made to improve the manager evaluation process?

LO3 **P11-35. ROI, Residual Income, and EVA: Impact of a New Investment**

EEG Inc. is a decentralized organization with four autonomous divisions. The divisions are evaluated on the basis of the change in their return on invested assets. Operating results in the Commercial Division for the year follow:

EEG INC.—COMMERCIAL DIVISION Income Statement For Year Ending December 31	
Sales	$3,000,000
Less variable expenses	(1,550,000)
Contribution margin	1,450,000
Less fixed expenses	(1,200,000)
Net operating income	$ 250,000

Operating assets for the Commercial Division currently average $2,500,000. The Commercial Division can add a new product line for an investment of $400,000. Relevant data for the new product line are as follows:

Sales	$625,000
Variable expenses (% of sales)	60%
Fixed expenses	$220,000
Increase in current liabilities	$ 18,000

Required

a. Determine the effect on ROI of accepting the new product line. (Round calculations to three decimal places.)

b. If a return of 6% is the minimum that any division should earn and residual income is used to evaluate managers, would this encourage the division to accept the new product line? Explain and show computations.

c. If EVA is used to evaluate managers, should the new product line be accepted if the weighted average cost of capital is 6% and the income tax rate is 20%?

P11-36. Valuing Investment Center Assets **LO3**

Six Flags Entertainment Corp (SIX)

Six Flags Entertainment Corp operates theme parks in the United States, Mexico, and Europe. One of its first theme parks, Six Flags over Georgia, was built in the 1960s in Atlanta on a large tract of land that has appreciated enormously over the years. Although most of the rides and other attractions have a fairly short life, some of the major buildings that are still in use on the property have been fully depreciated since they were built. Assume that Six Flags over Georgia operates as an investment center with total assets that have a book value of $75 million and current liabilities of $5 million. Assume also that in the current year, this particular theme park had sales of $65 million and pretax division income of $12 million. The replacement cost of all the assets in this park is estimated to be $115 million. The company has a 20% tax rate and a target return of 10% and a cost of capital of 6%.

Required

a. Calculate the ROI, residual income, and EVA for Six Flags over Georgia using asset book value in the valuation basis for the investment center asset base.

b. Repeat requirement (*a*) using replacement cost as the investment center asset value.

c. Which valuation, accounting book value, or replacement cost do you think the company uses to evaluate the managers of its various theme parks? Discuss.

P11-37. Transfer Pricing with and without Capacity Constraints **LO2, 3**

Elise Carpets Inc. has just acquired a new backing division that produces a rubber backing, which it sells for $3.75 per square yard. Sales are about 1 million square yards per year. Since the Backing Division has a capacity of 1.5 million square yards per year, top management is thinking that it might be wise for the company's Tufting Division to start purchasing from the newly acquired Backing Division. The Tufting Division now purchases 350,000 square yards per year from an outside supplier at a price of $3.50 per square yard. The current price is lower than the Backing division's $3.75 price as a result of the large quantity discounts. The Backing Division's cost per square yard follows.

Direct materials	$1.25
Direct labor	0.50
Variable overhead	0.15
Fixed overhead (1,000,000 level)	0.85
Total cost	$2.75

Required

a. If both divisions are to be treated as investment centers and their performance evaluated by the ROI formula, what transfer price would you recommend? Why?

b. If fixed costs are assumed not to change, determine the effect on corporate profits of making the backing.

c. Based on your transfer price, would you expect the ROI in the Backing Division to increase, decrease, or remain unchanged? Explain.

d. What would be the effect on the ROI of the Tufting Division using your transfer price? Explain.

e. Assume that the Backing Division is now selling 1.5 million square yards per year to retail outlets. What transfer price would you recommend? What will be the effect on corporate profits?

f. If the Backing Division is at capacity and decides to sell to the Tufting Division for $3.50 per square yard, what will be the effect on the company's profits?

LO2 **P11-38. Transfer Pricing and Special Orders**

Washington State Products has several manufacturing divisions. The Seattle Division produces a component part that is used in the manufacture of electronic equipment. The cost per part for July is as follows:

Variable cost	$150
Fixed cost (at 3,000 units per month capacity)	90
Total cost per part	$240

Some of Seattle Division's output is sold to outside manufacturers, and some is sold internally to the Redmond Division. The price per part is $375. The Redmond Division's cost and revenue structure follow.

Selling price per unit		$1,500
Less variable costs per unit		
Cost of parts from the Seattle Division	$375	
Other variable costs	550	(925)
Contribution margin per unit		575
Less fixed costs per unit (at 2,000 units per month)		(175)
Net income per unit		$ 400

The Redmond Division received a one-time order for 500 units. The buyer wants to pay only $750 per unit.

Required

a. From the perspective of the Redmond Division, should the $750 price be accepted? Explain.

b. If both divisions have excess capacity, would the Redmond Division's action benefit the company as a whole? Explain.

c. If the Redmond Division has excess capacity but the Seattle Division does not and can sell all of its parts to outside manufacturers, what would be the advantage or disadvantage of accepting the 500 unit order at the $750 price to the Redmond Division?

d. To make a decision that is in the best interest of the company, what transfer-pricing information does the Redmond Division need?

LO4 **P11-39. Balanced Scorecard**

JPMorgan Chase & Co. (JPM)

Assume Chase Bank recently decided to adopt a balanced scorecard system of performance evaluation. Below is a list of primary performance goals for four major performance categories that have been identified by corporate management and the board of directors.

1. Financial Perspective—Maintain and grow the bank financially
   a. Increase customer deposits
   b. Manage financial risk
   c. Provide profits for the stockholders
2. Customer Perspective—Maintain and grow the customer base
   a. Increase customer satisfaction
   b. Increase number of depositors and customer retention
   c. Increase quality of deposits

3. Internal Perspective—Improve internal processes
   a. Achieve best practices for processing transactions
   b. Improve employee satisfaction
   c. Improve employee promotion opportunities
4. Learning and Innovation—Improve market differentiation
   a. Beat competitors in introducing new products
   b. Become first mover in establishing customer benefit for customers
   c. Become recognized as an innovator in the industry

Required

a. For each of the 12 goals above, suggest at least one measure of performance to measure the achievement of the goal.

b. At what level of the organization should the balanced scorecard be implemented as a means of evaluating performance? Explain.

Cases and Projects

C11-40. Transfer Price Decisions LO2 IBM Corporation (IBM)

The Consulting Division of IBM Corporation is often involved in assignments for which IBM computer equipment is sold as part of a systems installation. The Computer Equipment Division is frequently a vendor of the Consulting Division in cases for which the Consulting Division purchases the equipment from the Computer Equipment Division. The Consulting Division does not view itself as a sales arm of the Computer Equipment Division but as a strong competitor to the major consulting firms of information systems. The Consulting Division's goal is to maximize its profit contribution to the company, not necessarily to see how much IBM equipment it can sell. If the Consulting Division is truly an autonomous investment center, it has the freedom to purchase equipment from competing vendors if the consultants believe that a competitor's products serve the needs of a client better than the comparable IBM product in a particular situation.

Required

a. In this situation, should corporate management be concerned about whether the Consulting Division sells IBM products or those of other computer companies? Should the Consulting Division be required to sell only IBM products?

b. Discuss the transfer-pricing issues that both the Computer Equipment Division manager and the Consulting Division manager should consider. If top management does not have a policy on pricing transfers between these two divisions, what alternative transfer prices should the division managers consider?

c. What is your recommendation regarding how the managers of the Consulting and Computer Equipment Divisions can work together in a way that will benefit each of them individually and the company as a whole?

C11-41. Transfer Pricing at Absorption Cost LO2

The Injection Molding Division of Universal Sign Company produces molded parts that are sold to the Sign Division. This division uses the parts in constructing signs that are sold to various businesses. The Molding Division contains two operations, injection and finishing. The unit variable cost of materials and labor used in the injection operation is $150. The fixed injection overhead is $1,200,000 per year. Current production (20,000 units) is at full capacity. The variable cost of labor used in the finishing operation is $24 per part. The fixed overhead in this operation is $600,000 per year. The company uses an absorption-cost transfer price. The price data for each operation presented to the Sign Division by the Molding Division follow.

Injection		
Variable cost per unit	$150	
Fixed overhead cost per unit ($1,200,000 ÷ 40,000 units)	30	$180
Finishing		
Labor cost per unit	24	
Fixed overhead cost per unit ($600,000 ÷ 40,000 units)	15	39
Total cost per unit		$219

An outside company has offered to lease machinery to the Sign Division that would perform the finishing portion of the parts manufacturing for $400,000 per year. With the new machinery, the labor cost per part would remain at $24. If the Molding Division transfers the units for $180, the following analysis can be made:

Current process		
Finishing process costs (40,000 × $39)		$1,560,000
New process		
Machine rental cost per year	$400,000	
Labor cost ($24 × 40,000 units)	960,000	1,360,000
Savings		$ 200,000

The manager of the Sign Division wants approval to acquire the new machinery.

Required

a. How would you advise the company concerning the proposed lease?

b. How could the transfer-pricing system be modified or the transfer-pricing problem eliminated?

LO2 C11-42. **Transfer Pricing Dispute**

MBR Inc. consists of three divisions that were formerly three independent manufacturing companies. Bader Corporation and Roper Company merged several years ago, and the merged corporation acquired Mitchell Company a year later. The name of the corporation was subsequently changed to MBR Inc., and each company became a separate division retaining the name of its former company.

The three divisions have operated as if they were still independent companies. Each division has its own sales force and production facilities. Each division management is responsible for sales, cost of operations, acquisition and financing of divisional assets, and working capital management. The corporate management of MBR evaluates the performance of the divisions and division management on the basis of return on investment.

Mitchell Division has just been awarded a contract for a product that uses a component manufactured by the Roper Division and also by outside suppliers. Mitchell used a cost figure of $3.80 for the component manufactured by Roper in preparing its bid for the new product. Roper supplied this cost figure in response to Mitchell's request for the average variable cost of the component; it represents the standard variable manufacturing cost and variable selling and distribution expenses.

Roper has an active sales force that is continually soliciting new prospects. Roper's regular selling price for the component Mitchell needs for the new product is $6.50. Sales of this component are expected to increase. The Roper management has indicated, however, that it could supply Mitchell the required quantities of the component at the regular selling price less variable selling and distribution expenses. Mitchell's management has responded by offering to pay standard variable manufacturing cost plus 20%.

The two divisions have been unable to agree on a transfer price. Corporate management has never established a transfer-pricing policy because interdivisional transactions have never occurred. As a compromise, the corporate vice president of finance suggested a price equal to the standard full manufacturing cost (i.e., no selling and distribution expenses) plus a 15% markup. The two division managers have also rejected this price because each considered it grossly unfair.

The unit cost structure for the Roper component and the three suggested prices follow.

Standard variable manufacturing cost	$3.20
Standard fixed manufacturing cost	1.20
Variable selling and distribution expenses	0.60
	$5.00
Regular selling price less variable selling and distribution expenses ($6.50 – $0.60)	$5.90
Standard full manufacturing cost plus 15% ($4.40 × 1.15)	$5.06
Variable manufacturing plus 20% ($3.20 × 1.20)	$3.84

Required

a. What should be the attitude of the Roper Division's management toward the three proposed prices?

b. Is the negotiation of a price between the Mitchell and Roper Divisions a satisfactory method of solving the transfer-pricing problem? Explain your answer.

c. Should the corporate management of MBR Inc. become involved in this transfer-price controversy? Explain your answer.

(CMA Adapted)

Solutions to Review Problems

Review 11-1—Solution

a. In the short run, the National Division income would decrease by the product margin of wireless or $7 million.

b.

(in thousands)	Segments (Territories) U.S.	International	Wireless Total
Sales	$12,000	$18,000	$30,000
Less variable costs	(8,400)	(12,600)	(21,000)
Contribution margin	3,600	5,400	9,000
Less direct fixed costs	(500)	(800)	(1,300)
Territory margin	3,100	4,600	7,700
Less allocated segment costs	(200)	(600)	(800)
Territory income	$ 2,900	$ 4,000	6,900
Less unallocated common costs			(900)
Wireless income			$ 6,000

c. The Product Margin for the wireless product line in Panel B was $7 million and reflected $2 million of direct fixed costs that were attributable to that product line in the National Division. However, when the wireless product segment income statement is further segmented into geographic segments, only $1.3 million of the $2 million could be directly traced to the two geographic territories. Therefore, $700,000 of costs that were direct costs at the product segment level became common costs (either allocated or unallocated) at the territory segment level. This reflects the general notion that as segmentation is extended down to lower and lower levels, the total amount of common costs increases and direct costs decrease. Hence, segmentation rarely is extended to more than three levels.

Review 11-2—Solution

a. No.

	Current Sales	Proposed Sales
Selling price	$ 24.00	$ 13.50
Variable costs	(16.00)	(16.00)
Unit contribution margin	$ 8.00	$ (2.50)
Unit sales	× 200,000	× 100,000
Contribution margin	$1,600,000	$(250,000)

Currently, the division is making $250,000 on 100,000 posters ($1,600,000 – $1,350,000 fixed costs); but under the proposal, with a $250,000 negative contribution, it would revert to a break-even situation:

Current contribution margin		$1,600,000
Fixed costs	$1,350,000	
Loss on special order	250,000	(1,600,000)
Net income		$ 0

As a general rule, a project should never be undertaken if the contribution margin is negative.

b. What the Retail Division does with the posters after receiving them is of no concern to the Publication Division. Hence, the Publication Division would still object to a transfer price of $13.50. However, for the company, the proposal does have a contribution of $18 per unit ($44 – $16 – $10). Consequently, the order is desirable from the viewpoint of the company.

c. If the company believes in autonomous divisions, it should not require the Publication Division to sell, nor should it dictate a higher transfer price. On the other hand, the company may want to create incentives to encourage (but not require) the two division managers to reach some compromise transfer price that would increase the contribution and profits of both divisions, and the company as a whole.

Review 11-3—Solution

(in thousands)

a.

$$\text{Return on investment} = \frac{\text{Investment center income}}{\text{Investment center asset base}}$$

Engineering Division = $30,000 ÷ $200,000
= 0.15 or 15%

Construction Division = $50,000 ÷ $250,000
= 0.20 or 20%

Military Division = $22,000 ÷ $100,000
= 0.22 or 22%

b. **Residual income = Investment center income − (Minimum return × Investment center asset base)**

Engineering Division = $30,000 − (0.15 × $200,000)
= $0.00

Construction Division = $50,000 − (0.15 × $250,000)
= $12,500

Military Division = $22,000 − (0.15 × $100,000)
= $7,000

c. ROI ranks the Military Division first, the Construction Division second, and the Engineering Division third. Residual income ranks the Construction Division first, the Military Division second, and the Engineering Division third. Because the investments for each division are different, it is somewhat misleading to rank the divisions according to residual income. The Construction Division had the highest residual income, but it also had the largest investment. The Military Division's residual income was 56% of the Construction Division's income but only 40% of the investment of the Construction Division. This fact, along with the best ROI ranking, probably justifies the Military Division being evaluated as the best division of KBR.

d. Return on investment:

Investment = $9,000 ÷ $50,000
= 0.18 or 18%

Engineering Division = ($30,000 + $9,000) ÷ ($200,000 + $50,000)
= 0.156 or 15.6%

Construction Division = ($50,000 + $9,000) ÷ ($250,000 + $50,000)
= 0.1967 or 19.67%

Military Division = ($22,000 + $9,000) ÷ ($100,000 + $50,000)
= 0.2067 or 20.67%

ROI will increase for the Engineering Division but decrease for the Construction and Military Divisions, even though the project's ROI of 18% exceeds the company's minimum return of 15%.

Residual income:

Engineering Division = ($30,000 + $9,000) − [0.15 × ($200,000 + $50,000)]
= $1,500

Construction Division = ($50,000 + $9,000) − [0.15 × ($250,000 + $50,000)]
= $14,000

Military Division = ($22,000 + $9,000) − [0.15 × ($100,000 + $50,000)]
= $8,500

Because the project's ROI exceeds the company's minimum return, the residual income of all divisions will increase.

Review 11-4—Solution

a. Financial Success
- Expense as a % of revenue
- Expense variance %
- New product ROI
- Net profit
- Net profit margin
- Year-over-year revenue growth
- New product revenue

Customer Satisfaction and Brand Improvement
- Number of complaints
- Market share
- Average customer survey rating
- New customer count
- New customer sales value
- Unique repeat customer count

Business Process Improvement
- Average call wait
- Service error rate
- Fulfillment %
- Industry quality rating
- New product acceptance rate
- Number of defects reported
- Time to market on new products

Learning and Growth of Motivated Workforce
- Employee turnover ratio
- Headcount growth
- Job offer acceptance rate

Note that some of the key performance indicators could be included in more than one category. For example New Product ROI is an indicator of the success of introducing new products, but it is also an indicator of financial success.

b. The balanced scorecard has been quite successful in helping companies to better focus managers' attention on the factors that drive ultimate success. If only a general performance metric such as ROI or EVA is used to evaluate performance, managers are left on their own to figure out for themselves the components of managerial performance that drive improvements in the overall indicator. Balanced scorecard provides a framework and structure for carefully thinking about the key performance indicators that drive ultimate success. Once top management has identified the key performance indicators with input from all levels, some or all of the indicators can be used to evaluate managers and employees throughout the organization.

Chapter 12

Capital Budgeting Decisions

Learning Objectives

LO1 Explain the role of capital budgeting in long-range planning. (p. 438)

LO2 Analyze capital budgeting decisions, using models such as net present value and internal rate of return, that consider the time value of money. (p. 442)

LO3 Analyze capital budgeting decisions, using models such as payback period and accounting rate of return, that do not consider the time value of money. (p. 447)

LO4 Evaluate the strengths and weaknesses of alternative capital budgeting models. (p. 449)

LO5 Examine the impact of judgment, attitudes toward risk, and relevant cash flow information on capital budgeting decisions. (p. 452)

LO6 Determine the net present value of investment proposals with consideration of taxes. (p. 456)

LO7 Compute basic present value cash flow amounts (Appendix 12A). (p. 459)

LO8 Determine internal rate of return using present value tables (Appendix 12B). (p. 464)

Seattle-based Amazon.com Inc. started out as an online bookseller in 1995 and quickly expanded its product offerings to DVDs, electronics, jewelry, apparel, and now a full spectrum of consumer goods. Amazon sells more goods online than all other Internet retailers, including Staples, Apple, Walmart, and Best Buy. Amazon's meteoric rise was no doubt fueled by well-chosen capital investments, including its website infrastructure that highlighted customer-centric features such as the first shopping carts, one-click buying, email purchase confirmations, and post-shipping follow-ups. Over the years Amazon has kept its prices low by leveraging its purchasing volume, thereby staving off its competition. To maintain its position, Amazon has forgone profits in favor of continual improvement of its business model. In an effort to gain more control over its fulfillment process, Amazon has invested billions of dollars in warehouses and inventory management information systems. As a result, Amazon has been able to offer expedited shipping on its orders since 2005. This program, called Amazon Prime, offers customers two-day shipping for an annual fee of $119.

Amazon is also beginning to open brick-and-mortar bookstore locations, including stores in Oregon, Washington, California, and New York. In 2017, Amazon made its first Prime Air drone delivery, testing its ability to make deliveries using drones. Amazon's management team needs to tread carefully in evaluating these new investments. Amazon's managers should be asking themselves these questions: How will these investments be financed, and at what cost can we raise the needed funds? What tax deductions or incentives might defray some of the costs of this investment? How long before the investment has been recouped through increased revenues? Does this estimate consider increases in operating costs? In other words, Amazon needs to determine which capital investments will have a positive effect on operating results.

This chapter will detail important tools that Amazon and managers can use to increase the probability that their capital investments will be sound.

Road Map

LO	Learning Objective | Topics	Page	eLecture	Guided Example	Assignments
LO1	Explain the role of capital budgeting in long-range planning. **Capital Expenditures :: Capital Budgeting :: Long-Range Planning**	438	e12–1	Review 12-1	41, 42
LO2	Analyze capital budgeting decisions, using models such as net present value and internal rate of return, that consider the time value of money. **Expected Cash Flows :: Net Present Value :: Table Approach :: Spreadsheet Approach :: Internal Rate of Return :: Cost of Capital**	442	e12–2	Review 12-2	13, 14, 15, 16, 20, 21, 22, 23, 25, 26, 27, 28, 29, 30, 31, 33, 34, 35, 36, 37, 39, 40, 41, 42
LO3	Analyze capital budgeting decisions, using models such as payback period and accounting rate of return, that do not consider the time value of money. **Payback Period :: Accounting Rate of Return**	447	e12–3	Review 12-3	17, 18, 19, 22, 23, 25, 26, 27, 28, 29, 31, 36, 38
LO4	Evaluate the strengths and weaknesses of alternative capital budgeting models. **Strength and Weaknesses of Each Approach**	449	e12–4	Review 12-4	28, 39
LO5	Examine the impact of judgment, attitudes toward risk, and relevant cash flow information on capital budgeting decisions. **Evaluating Risk :: Differential Analysis :: High-Tech Investments**	452	e12–5	Review 12-5	26, 27, 35, 36, 37, 38, 39, 40, 41, 42
LO6	Determine the net present value of investment proposals with consideration of taxes. **Depreciation Tax Shield :: Investment Tax Credit**	456	e12–6	Review 12-6	24, 30, 31, 32, 40
LO7	Compute basic present value cash flow amounts (Appendix 12A). **Future Value :: Present Value :: Annuities :: Unequal Cash Flows :: Deferred Returns**	459	e12–7	Review 12-7	13, 14
LO8	Determine internal rate of return using present value tables (Appendix 12B). **Equal Cash Flows :: Unequal Cash Flows**	464	e12–8	Review 12-8	15, 16, 20, 21, 22, 29, 39

CHAPTER ORGANIZATION

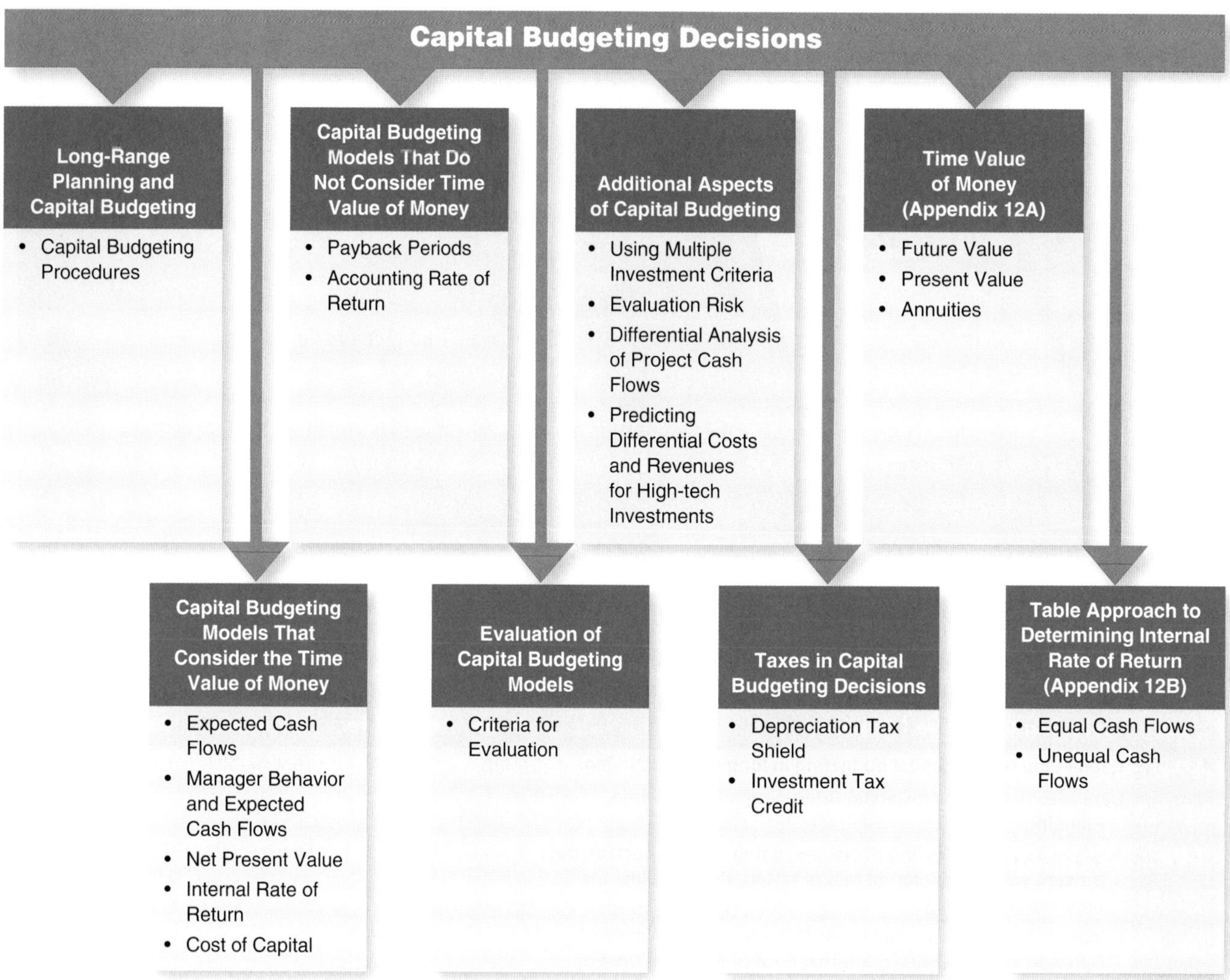

eLectures MBC **LO1** Explain the role of capital budgeting in long-range planning.

Capital expenditures are investments of financial resources in projects to develop or introduce new products or services, to expand current production or service capacity, or to change current production or service facilities. Capital expenditures are made with the expectation that the new product, process, or service will generate future financial inflows that exceed the initial costs. Capital expenditure decisions affect structural cost drivers. They are made infrequently but once made are difficult to change. They commit the organization to the use of certain facilities and activities to satisfy customer needs. In making large capital expenditure decisions, such as for Amazon's warehouse facilities, management is risking the future existence of the company.

Although capital expenditure decisions are fraught with risk, management accounting provides the concepts and tools needed to organize information and evaluate the alternatives. This systematic organization and analysis is the essence of capital budgeting. This chapter introduces important capital budgeting concepts and models, and it explains the proper use of accounting data in these models.

Capital budgeting is a process that involves identifying potentially desirable projects for capital expenditures, evaluating capital expenditure proposals, and selecting proposals that meet minimum criteria. A number of quantitative models are available to assist managers in evaluating capital expenditure proposals.

The best capital budgeting models are conceptually similar to the short-range planning models used in Chapters 3 and 4. They all emphasize cash flows and focus on future costs (and revenues) that differ among decision alternatives. The major difference is that capital budgeting models involve cash flows over several years, whereas short-range planning models involve cash flows for a year or less. When the cash flows associated with a proposed activity extend over several years, an adjustment is necessary to make the cash flows comparable when they are expected to occur at different points in time.

The *time value of money concept* explains why monies received or paid at different points in time must be adjusted to comparable values. The time value of money is introduced in Appendix 12A at the end of this chapter.

Long-Range Planning and Capital Budgeting

Most organizations plan not only for operations in the current period but also for the longer term, perhaps 5, 10, or even 20 years in the future. Most planning beyond the next budget year is called *long-range planning*.

Increased uncertainty and business alternatives add to the difficulty of planning as the horizon lengthens. Even though long-range planning is difficult and involves uncertainties, management must make long-range planning and capital expenditure decisions. Capital expenditure decisions will be made. The question is: How will they be made? Will they be made on the basis of the best information available? Will care be taken to ensure that capital expenditure decisions are in line with the organization's long-range goals? Will the potential consequences, both positive and negative, of capital expenditures be considered? Will important alternative uses of the organization's limited financial resources be considered in a systematic manner? Will managers be held accountable for the capital expenditure programs they initiate? The alternative to a systematic approach to capital budgeting is the haphazard expenditure of resources on the basis of a hunch, immediate need, or persuasion—without accountability by the person(s) making the decisions.

The steps of an effective capital budgeting process are outlined in **Exhibit 12.1**. A basic requirement for a systematic approach to capital budgeting is a defined mission, a set of long-range goals, and a business strategy. These elements provide focus and boundaries that reduce the types of capital expenditure decisions management considers. If, for example, Dunkin' Donuts's goal is to become the largest fast-food restaurant chain in North America, its management should not consider a proposal to purchase and operate a bus line.

A well-defined business strategy will likewise guide capital expenditure decisions. If Cisco Systems is following a strategy to obtain technological leadership, it might seriously consider a proposal to meet customer needs by investing in innovative production facilities but would not consider a proposal to purchase and refurbish used (but seemingly cost-efficient) equipment. The following Business Insight box identifies companies that focus capital budgeting decisions on the strategic goal of energy efficiency, and therefore, reducing expenses.

Business Insight ■ Using the Capital Budget to Save Money

Consumers Energy, a public utility in Michigan serving 6.7 million people, has plans to spend $25 billion before 2030 to replace aging gas and electric equipment with solar panels, wind turbines, and large-scale battery storage units. When Consumers first started looking at renewable energy sources in 2016, its analysts forecasted decreases in solar prices of 30% over the next 20 years. But in the 18 months it took the company to complete the study, prices had already fallen 30%. The initial costs of solar and wind technologies were now competitive with the costs of natural gas plants. Because wind and sunlight are free, Consumers will be able to save hundreds of millions of dollars each year on fuel costs while reducing its carbon output by 90% over the levels in 2005. The company is also working to help customers reduce their consumption of electricity through the use of smart thermostats and smart meters. The focus on reducing consumption of Consumers' primary source of revenue may seem counterintuitive, but the company believes that the switch to renewable energy sources, along with better management of energy demand, will ultimately result in higher profits. Most capital budget decisions are about deciding to spend money to make money. The decision by Consumers to budget for energy efficiency was about spending money to save money and reduce its carbon emissions.

Source: Katherine Blunt, "How A Utility's Counterintuitive Strategy Might Fuel A Greener Future," *Wall Street Journal*, February 8, 2020.

Exhibit 12.1 Capital Budgeting Procedures

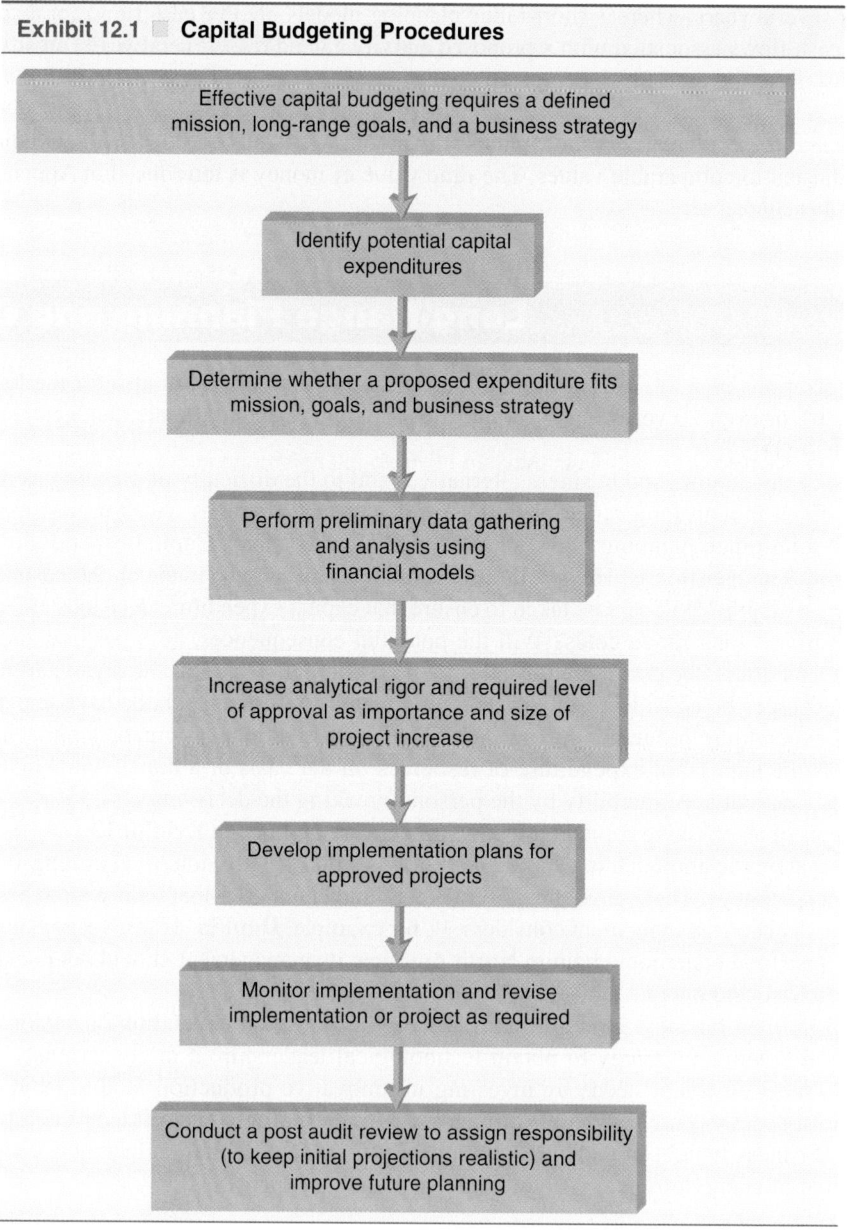

Management should also develop procedures for the review, evaluation, approval, and post-audit of capital expenditure proposals. In a large organization, a capital budgeting committee that provides guidance to managers in the formulation of capital expenditure proposals is key to these procedures. This committee also reviews, analyzes, and approves or rejects major capital expenditure proposals. Major projects often require the approval of top management and even the board of directors. The capital budgeting committee should include persons knowledgeable in capital budgeting models; financing alternatives and costs; operating procedures; cost estimation and prediction methods; research and development efforts; the organization's goals and basic strategy; and the expectations of the organization's stockholders or owners. A management accountant who is generally expert in data collection, retrieval, and analysis is normally part of the capital budgeting committee.

Not all capital expenditure proposals require committee approval or are subject to formal evaluation. With the approval of top management, the committee might provide guidelines indicating the type and dollar amount of capital expenditures that managers at each level of the organization can make without formal evaluation or committee approval, or both. The guidelines might state that expenditures of less than $20,000 do not require committee approval and that only expenditures of more than $100,000 must be evaluated using capital budgeting models.

Typically, managers at higher levels have greater discretion in making capital expenditures. In a college or university, a department chairperson could have authority to purchase office and instructional equipment with a maximum limit of $10,000 per year. A dean may have authority to renovate offices or classrooms with a maximum limit of $50,000 per year, but the conversion of the power plant from one fuel source to another at a cost of $400,000 could require the formal review of a capital budgeting committee and final approval of the board of trustees.

The post-audit of approved capital expenditure proposals is an important part of a well-formulated approach to capital budgeting. A *post-audit* involves the development of project performance reports comparing planned and actual results. Project performance reports should be provided to the manager who initiated the capital expenditure proposal, the manager assigned responsibility for the project (if a different person), the project manager's supervisor, and the capital budgeting committee. These reports help keep the project on target (especially during the initial investment phase), identify the need to reevaluate the project if the initial analysis was in error or significant environmental changes occur, and improve the quality of investment proposals. When managers know they will be held accountable for the results of projects they initiate, they are likely to put more care into the development of capital expenditure proposals and take a greater interest in approved projects. Problems can occur when decision makers are rewarded for undertaking major projects but are not held responsible for the consequences that occur several years later.

A post-audit review of approved projects also helps the capital budgeting committee do a better job in evaluating new proposals. The committee might learn how to adjust proposals for the biases of individual managers, learn of new factors that should be considered in evaluating proposals, and avoid the routine approval of projects that appear desirable by themselves but are related to larger projects that are not meeting management's expectations. As summarized in the following Business Insight, capital budgeting models play an important role in strategic decision making.

Business Insight ■ SodaStream and Pepsi, Partners Not Competitors

Consumer health concerns contributed to the steady decrease in sales of carbonated soft drinks over the last 20 years. Companies like PepsiCo, Coca-Cola, and Nestlé successfully responded by adding bottled water products to their product lines. Now, that business is threatened by consumer environmental concerns and soda makers are again looking for product alternatives. In 2015, PepsiCo partnered with SodaStream, an Israeli company that makes a countertop soda maker with a dizzying array of flavorings. Pepsi later purchased SodaStream in 2018. Pepsi also launched Drinkafinity in the United States in 2018. With Drinkafinity, consumers can infuse tap water with caffeine, vitamins, electrolytes, and flavors contained in pods that attach to a specially designed, reusable bottle. Pepsi's decision makers likely depend on net present value analysis in making decisions to add new products.

Source: Thomas Mulier and Corinne Gretler, "Coke, Pepsi, and Nestle Plan to Profit From Your Tap Water," *Bloomberg*, October 31, 2019.

Managerial Decision ■ You Are the Vice President of Finance

You have recently accepted the position of VP of finance for a rapidly growing biotech company. Last year the company made capital expenditures of $10 million and you anticipate that annual capital expenditures will exceed $30 million in a couple of years. You believe it is time to develop a more formal approach to making capital expenditure decisions. Where do you begin? [Answer p. 466]

Explaining Terms Relevant to Capital Budgeting Decisions — LO1 Review 12-1

Below is a list of terms relevant to capital budgeting decisions.

1. Capital budgeting
2. Capital expenditures
3. Time value of money concept
4. Long-range planning
5. Post audit

continued

continued from previous page

Required

For each of the statements below, select the most relevant term from the above list. Each term above may be used more than once.

____ *a.* Investment of financial resources with the expectation it will generate future financial inflows that exceed the initial cost.

____ *b.* Process that involves identifying desirable projects, evaluating proposals, and selecting proposals that meet minimum criteria.

____ *c.* Involves the development of project performance reports comparing planned and actual results.

____ *d.* Concepts and tools that organize information and evaluate alternatives.

____ *e.* Explains why monies received or paid at different points in time must be adjusted to comparable values.

____ *f.* Requires an adjustment to make cash flows comparable when they are expected to occur at different points in time.

____ *g.* Planning beyond the next budget year.

Solution on p. 480. ____ *h.* Helps the capital budgeting committee do a better job in evaluating new proposals.

Capital Budgeting Models That Consider Time Value of Money

LO2 Analyze capital budgeting decisions, using models such as net present value and internal rate of return, that consider the time value of money.

The capital budgeting models in this chapter have gained wide acceptance by for-profit and not-for-profit organizations. Our primary focus is on the *net present value* and the *internal rate of return models*, which are superior because they consider the time value of money. Later discussions will consider more traditional capital budgeting models, such as the payback period and the accounting rate of return that, while useful under certain circumstances, do not consider the time value of money. Although we briefly consider the cost of financing capital expenditures, we leave a detailed treatment of this topic, as well as a detailed examination of the sources of funds for financing investments, to books on financial management.

Expected Cash Flows

The focus of capital budgeting models that consider the time value of money is on future cash receipts and future cash disbursements that differ under decision alternatives. It is often convenient to distinguish between the following three phases of a project's cash flows:

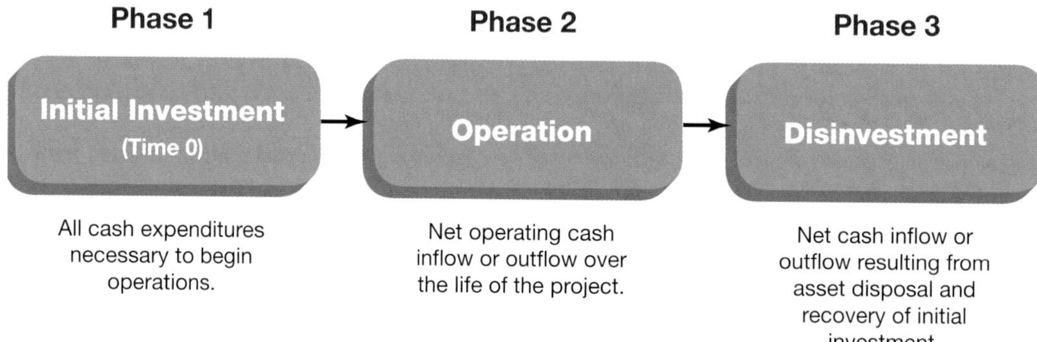

All cash expenditures necessary to begin operations are classified as part of the project's *initial investment phase*. Expenditures to acquire property, plant, and equipment are part of the initial investment. Less obvious, but equally important, are expenditures to acquire working capital to purchase inventories and recruit and train employees. Although the initial investment phase often extends over many years, in our examples, we assume that the initial investment takes place at a single point in time.

Cash receipts from sales of goods or services, as well as normal cash expenditures for materials, labor, and other operating expenses, occur during the operation phase. The *operation phase* is typically broken down into one-year periods; for each period, operating cash expenditures are subtracted from operating cash receipts to determine the net operating cash inflow or outflow for the period.

The *disinvestment phase* occurs at the end of the project's life when assets are disposed of for their salvage value and any initial investment of working capital is recovered. Also included are any expenditures to dismantle facilities and dispose of waste. Although this phase might extend over many years, in our examples, we assume disinvestment takes place at a single point in time.

To illustrate the analysis of a project's cash flows, assume the management of Mobile Taqueria is considering a capital expenditure proposal to operate a new shop in a resort community. Each Mobile Taqueria is located in a specially constructed motor vehicle that moves on a regular schedule throughout the community it serves. The predicted cash flows associated with the project, which has an expected life of five years, are presented in **Exhibit 12.2**.

Exhibit 12.2 Analysis of a Project's Predicted Cash Flows

Initial investment (at time 0)			
Vehicle and equipment		$ (90,554)	Phase 1
Inventories and other working capital		(4,000)	
Total investment cash outflow		$ (94,554)	
Operation (per year for 5 years)			
Sales		$ 175,000	Phase 2
Cash expenditures			
Food	$47,000		
Labor	65,000		
Supplies	9,000		
Fuel and utilities	8,000		
Advertising	4,000		
Miscellaneous	12,000	(145,000)	
Net annual cash inflow		$ 30,000	
Disinvestment (at the end of 5 years)			
Sale of vehicle and equipment		$ 8,000	Phase 3
Recovery of investment in inventories and other working capital		4,000	
Total disinvestment cash inflow		$ 12,000	

Manager Behavior and Expected Cash Flows

Accurately predicting the cash flows associated with a capital expenditure proposal is critical to properly evaluating the proposal. Managers might be overly optimistic with their predictions, and they are sometimes tempted to modify predictions to justify capital expenditures. Perhaps they are interested in personal rewards. They might also want to avoid a loss of prestige or employment for themselves or to keep a local facility operating for the benefit of current employees and the local economy. Unfortunately, if a major expenditure does not work out, not only the local plant but also the entire company could be forced out of business. For example, under pressure to increase current sales, automobile leasing companies could be tempted to overstate cash receipts during the disinvestment phase of a lease.

Net Present Value

A project's **net present value**, usually computed as of the time of the initial investment, is the present value of the project's net cash inflows from operations and disinvestment less the amount of the initial investment. Appendix 12A contains an introduction to the time value of money, including net present value fundamentals. In computing a project's net present value, the cash flows occurring at different points in time are adjusted for the time value of money using a **discount rate** that is the minimum rate of return required for the project to be acceptable. Projects with positive net present values (or values at least equal to zero) are acceptable, and projects with negative net present values are unacceptable. Two methods to compute net present value follow.

Table Approach

Assuming that management uses a 12% discount rate, the net present value of the proposed investment in a Mobile Taqueria is shown in **Exhibit 12.3** (a) to be $20,398. Since the net present value is more than zero, the investment in the Mobile Taqueria is expected to be profitable, even when adjusted for the time value of money.

We can verify the amounts and computations in **Exhibit 12.3**. Start by tracing the cash flows back to **Exhibit 12.2**. Next, determine the 12% present value factors by referring to Exhibits 12A.1 and 12A.2 in Appendix 12A. The initial investment is assumed to occur at a single point in time (identified as time 0), the start of the project. In net present value computations, all cash flows are restated in terms of their value at time 0. Hence, time 0 cash flows have a present value factor of 1. To simplify computations, all other cash flows are assumed to occur at the end of years 1 through 5, even if they occurred during the year. Although further refinements could be made to adjust for cash flows occuring throughout each year, such adjustments are seldom necessary. Observe that net operating cash inflows are treated as an *annuity*, whereas cash flows for the initial investment and disinvestment are treated as *lump-sum amounts*. If net operating cash flows varied from year to year, we would treat each year's cash flow as a separate amount.

Spreadsheet Approach

Spreadsheet software contains functions that compute the present value of a series of cash flows. With this software, simply enter a column or row containing the net cash flows for each period and the appropriate formula. The discount rate of 0.12 is entered as part of the formula. Sample spreadsheet input to determine the net present value of the proposed investment in a Mobile Taqueria is shown on the left in **Exhibit 12.3** (b). The spreadsheet output is shown on the right, in **Exhibit 12.3** (b).

Exhibit 12.3 Net Present Value of a Project's Predicted Cash Flows

(a) Table approach:

	Predicted Cash Inflows (outflows) (A)	Year(s) of Cash Flows (B)	12% Present Value Factor (C)	Present Value of Cash Flows (A) × (C)
Initial investment	$(94,554)	0	1.00000	$ (94,554)
Operation	30,000	1–5	3.60478	108,143
Disinvestment	12,000	5	0.56743	6,809
Net present value of all cash flows				$ 20,398

(b) Spreadsheet approach:

Input:

	A	B
1	Year of cash flow	Cash flow
2	1	$30,000
3	2	30,000
4	3	30,000
5	4	30,000
6	5	42,000
7	Present value	=NPV(0.12,B2:B6)
8	Initial investment at time 0	(94,554)
9	Net present value	=B7+B8

Output:

	A	B
1	Year of cash flow	Cash flow
2	1	$ 30,000
3	2	30,000
4	3	30,000
5	4	30,000
6	5	42,000
7	Present value	$114,952.41
8	Initial investment at time 0	(94,554.00)
9	Net present value	$ 20,398.41

Two cautionary notes follow:

1. The spreadsheet formula for the net present value assumes that the first cash flow occurs at time "1," rather than at time "0." Hence, we cannot include the initial investment in the data set analyzed by the spreadsheet formula when computing the net present value. Instead, the initial investment is subtracted from the present value of future cash flows.
2. Arrange the cash flows subsequent to the initial investment from *top* to bottom in a column, or *left* to right in a row.

Internal Rate of Return

The **internal rate of return (IRR)**, often called the **time-adjusted rate of return**, is the discount rate that equates the present value of a project's cash inflows with the present value of the project's cash outflows. Other ways to describe IRR include (1) the minimum rate that could be paid for the money invested in a project without losing money, and (2) the discount rate that results in a project's net present value equaling zero.

All practical applications of the IRR model use a calculator or spreadsheet. Thus, we illustrate determining an IRR with a spreadsheet. A table approach to determining a project's internal rate of return is illustrated in Appendix 12B of this chapter.

With spreadsheet software, simply enter a column or row containing the net cash flows for each period and the appropriate formula. Spreadsheet input for Mobile Taqueria's investment proposal is shown in **Exhibit 12.4**. The spreadsheet formula for the IRR assumes that the first cash flow occurs at time "0."

The spreadsheet approach requires an initial prediction or guess of the project's internal rate of return. Although the closeness of the prediction to the final solution affects computational speed, for textbook examples almost any number can be used. We use an initial estimate of 0.08 in all illustrations. Because the IRR formula assumes that the first cash flow occurs at time 0, the initial investment is included in the data analyzed by the IRR formula. Again, we must order the cash flows from top to bottom in a column or left to right in a row. As shown on the right column in **Exhibit 12.4**, the spreadsheet software computes the IRR as 20%.

Exhibit 12.4 Spreadsheet Approach to Determining Internal Rate of Return

Input:

	A	B
1	Year of cash flow	Cash flow
2	0	$(94,554)
3	1	30,000
4	2	30,000
5	3	30,000
6	4	30,000
7	5	42,000
8	IRR	=IRR(B2:B7,0.08)*

Output:

	A	B
1	Year of cash flow	Cash flow
2	0	$(94,554)
3	1	30,000
4	2	30,000
5	3	30,000
6	4	30,000
7	5	42,000
8	IRR	0.20

**The formula is "=IRR(Input data range, guess)." The guess, which is any likely rate of return, is used as an initial starting point in determining the solution. We use 0.08 in all illustrations.*

The calculated internal rate of return is compared to the discount rate established by management to evaluate investment proposals. If the proposal's IRR is greater than or equal to the discount rate, the project is acceptable; if it is less than the discount rate, the project is unacceptable. Because Mobile Taqueria has a 12% discount rate, the project is acceptable using the IRR model.

Although a project's IRR should be compared to the discount rate established by management, such a discount rate is often unknown. In these situations, computing the IRR still provides insights into a project's profitability.

Although a computer and appropriate software quickly and accurately perform tedious computations, computational ease increases the opportunity for inappropriate use. The ability to plug numbers into a computer or calculator and obtain an output labeled NPV or IRR could mislead the unwary into believing that capital budgeting models are easy to use. This is not true. Training and professional judgment are required to identify relevant costs, to implement procedures to obtain relevant cost information, and to make a good decision once results are available. Capital budgeting models are merely decision aids. Managers, not models, make the decisions. To better illustrate underlying concepts, all subsequent textbook illustrations use a table approach.

Cost of Capital

When discounting models are used to evaluate capital expenditure proposals, management must determine the discount rate (1) used to compute a proposal's net present value or (2) used as the standard for evaluating a proposal's IRR. An organization's cost of capital is often used as this discount rate.

The **cost of capital** is the average cost an organization pays to obtain the resources necessary to make investments. This average rate considers items such as the following:

- Effective interest rate on debt (notes or bonds).
- Effective dividend rate on preferred stock.
- Discount rate that equates the present value of all dividends expected on common stock over the life of the organization to the current market value of the organization's common stock.

The cost of capital for a company that has no debt or preferred stock equals the cost of equity capital, computed as follows:

$$\textbf{Cost of equity capital} = \frac{\textbf{Current annual dividend per common share}}{\textbf{Current market price per common share}} + \textbf{Expected dividend growth rate}$$

Procedures for determining the cost of capital for more complex capital structures are covered in finance books. Investing in a project that has an internal rate of return equal to the cost of capital should not affect the market value of the firm's securities. Investing in a project that has a return higher than the cost of capital should increase the market value of a firm's securities. If, however, a firm invests in a project that has a return less than the cost of capital, the market value of the firm's securities should fall.

The cost of capital is the minimum return acceptable for investment purposes. Any investment proposal not expected to yield this minimum rate should normally be rejected. Because of difficulties encountered in determining the cost of capital, many organizations adopt a discount rate or a target rate of return without complicated mathematical analysis.

Review 12-2 LO2 Calculating Net Present Value and Internal Rate of Return

Consider the following investment proposal:

Initial investment	
Depreciable assets	$27,740
Working capital	3,000
Operations (per year for 4 years)	
Cash receipts	25,000
Cash expenditures	15,000
Disinvestment	
Salvage value of plant and equipment	2,000
Recovery of working capital	3,000

Required

Determine each of the following:

a. Net present value at a 10% discount rate.

b. Internal rate of return. (Refer to Appendix 12B if using the table approach.)

Solution on p. 480.

Capital Budgeting Models That Do Not Consider Time Value of Money

eLectures MBC

LO3 Analyze capital budgeting decisions, using models such as payback period and accounting rate of return, that do not consider the time value of money.

Years ago, capital budgeting models that do not consider the time value of money were more widely used than discounting models. Although most large organizations use net present value or internal rate of return as their primary evaluation tool, currently they often use nondiscounting models as an initial screening device. Further, as discussed in the following Research Insight, nondiscounting models remain entrenched in small businesses. We consider two nondiscounting models, the *payback period* and the *accounting rate of return*.

Research Insight ■ Size and Education Matter in Capital Budgeting

A survey of small businesses (with an average of 10 employees) by Danielson and Scott shows that owners make capital expenditure decisions based on "gut feel" much more often than on other methods predicted by theory. Owners' gut feelings were followed by a payback period, then accounting rate of return—only a few firms reported using discounted cash flows. Danielson and Scott emphasize the following points:

1. Capital investments by small businesses tend not to be discretionary. The firm often either invests or goes out of business.
2. Use of a payback period increases with the formal education of the owner, and owners with advanced degrees are most likely to have a formal business plan and use discounted future cash flows.
3. Accounting rate of return is most common for firms that are planning to expand, or are required to provide financial information to banks.

Graham and Harvey surveyed Fortune 500 CFOs and CFOs of smaller members of the Financial Executives Institute. CFOs generally have advanced degrees in business, and 46% of these firms have sales over $1 billion. In this group most firms use multiple models for budgeting, and their use fits much more with the theory:

1. 76% use internal rate of return.
2. 75% use net present value.
3. More than 50% use a payback period.
4. About 20% use accounting rate of return.

Even in this sample, the smaller firms (sales under $100 million) are less likely to use net present value than larger firms. Follow-up research in Canada and Europe has confirmed that these results generalize beyond the United States and the Fortune 500, with two additional insights. First, there is a long-term trend toward use of discounted cash flows in all firms, and second, the wealth of the firm's home nation also affects the sophistication of modeling.

Sources: Morris Danielson and Johnathan Scott, "The Capital Budgeting Decisions of Small Businesses," *Journal of Applied Finance* (Fall/Winter 2006): 46–56.
John Graham and Campbell Harvey, "The Theory and Practice of Corporate Finance: Evidence from the Field," *Journal of Financial Economics* (May–June 2001): 187–243.
Karim Bennouna, Geoffrey G. Meredith, and Teresa Marchant, "Improved Capital Budgeting Decision Making: Evidence from Canada," *Management Decision* 48, no. 2 (2010): 225–247.
Gyorgy Andor, Sunil K. Mohanty, and Tamas Toth, "Capital Budgeting Practices: A Survey of Central and Eastern European Firms," *Emerging Markets Review* 23 (June 2015): 148–172, http://dx.doi.org/10.1016/j.ememar.2015.04.002.

Payback Period

The **payback period** is the time required to recover the initial investment in a project from operations. The payback decision rule states that acceptable projects must have less than some maximum payback period designated by management. Payback emphasizes management's concern with liquidity and the need to minimize risk through a rapid recovery of the initial investment. It is frequently used for small expenditures having such obvious benefits that the use of more sophisticated capital budgeting models is not required or justified.

When a project is expected to have equal annual operating cash inflows, its payback period is computed as follows:

$$\textbf{Payback period} = \frac{\textbf{Initial investment}}{\textbf{Annual operating cash inflows}}$$

For Mobile Taqueria's investment proposal, outlined in **Exhibit 12.2**, the payback period is 3.15 years:

$$\textbf{Payback period} = \frac{\$94{,}554}{\$30{,}000}$$
$$= 3.15$$

Determining the payback period for a project having unequal cash flows is slightly more complicated. Assume that Costco Wholesale is evaluating a capital expenditure proposal that requires an initial investment of $50,000,000 and has the following expected net cash inflows:

Year	Net Cash Inflow
1	$15,000,000
2	25,000,000
3	40,000,000
4	20,000,000
5	10,000,000

To compute the payback period, we must determine the net unrecovered amount at the end of each year. In the year of full recovery, the net cash inflows are assumed to occur evenly and are prorated based on the unrecovered investment at the start of the year. Full recovery of Costco's investment proposal is expected to occur in Year 3:

Year	Net Cash Inflow	Unrecovered Investment
0	$ 0	$50,000,000
1	15,000,000	35,000,000
2	25,000,000	10,000,000
3	40,000,000	0

Therefore, $10,000,000 of $40,000,000 is needed in Year 3 to complete the recovery of the initial investment. This provides a proportion of 0.25 ($10,000,000 ÷ $40,000,000) and a payback period of 2.25 years (2 years plus 0.25 of Year 3). This project is acceptable if management specified a maximum payback period of three years. Because they occur after the payback period, the net cash inflows of Years 4 and 5 are ignored.

Accounting Rate of Return

The **accounting rate of return** is the average annual increase in net income that results from the acceptance of a capital expenditure proposal divided by either the initial investment or the average investment in the project. This method differs from other capital budgeting models in that it focuses on accounting income rather than on cash flow. In most capital budgeting applications, accounting net income is approximated as net cash inflow from operations minus expenses not requiring the use of cash, such as depreciation.

Consider Mobile Taqueria's capital expenditure proposal whose cash flows were outlined in **Exhibit 12.2**. The vehicle and equipment costs are $90,554 and have a disposal value of $8,000 at the end of five years, resulting in an average annual increase in net income of $13,489:

Annual net cash inflow from operations	$30,000
Less average annual depreciation [($90,554 – $8,000) ÷ 5]	(16,511)
Average annual increase in net income	$13,489

Considering the investment in inventories and other working capital, the initial investment is $94,554 ($90,554 + $4,000), and the *accounting rate of return on initial investment* is 14.27%:

$$\textbf{Accounting rate of return on initial investment} = \frac{\textbf{Average annual increase in net income}}{\textbf{Initial investment}} = \frac{\$13{,}489}{\$94{,}554} = 0.1427$$

The average investment, computed as the initial investment plus the expected value of any disinvestment, all divided by 2, is $53,277 [($94,554 + $12,000) ÷ 2]. The *accounting rate of return on average investment* is 25.32%:

$$\textbf{Accounting rate of return on average investment} = \frac{\textbf{Average annual increase in net income}}{\textbf{Average investment}} = \frac{\$13{,}489}{\$53{,}277} = 0.2532$$

When using the accounting rate of return, management specifies either the initial investment or average investment plus some minimum acceptable rate. Management rejects capital expenditure proposals with a lower accounting rate of return but accepts proposals with an accounting rate of return higher than or equal to the minimum.

Computing the Payback Period and the Accounting Rate of Return — LO3 Review 12-3

Consider the following investment proposal:

Initial investment	
Depreciable assets	$27,740
Working capital	3,000
Operations (per year for 4 years)	
Cash receipts	25,000
Cash expenditures	15,000
Disinvestment	
Salvage value of plant and equipment	2,000
Recovery of working capital	3,000

Required

Determine each of the following:

a. Payback period.
b. Accounting rate of return on initial investment and on average investment.

Solution on p. 481.

Evaluation of Capital Budgeting Models

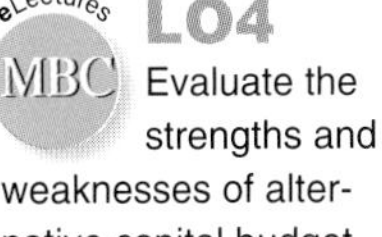

LO4 Evaluate the strengths and weaknesses of alternative capital budgeting models.

As a single criterion for evaluating capital expenditure proposals, capital budgeting models that consider the time value of money are superior to models that do not consider it. The payback model concerns merely how long it takes to recover the initial investment from a project, yet investments are not made with the objective of merely getting the money back. Indeed, not investing has a payback period of 0. Investments are made to earn a profit. Hence, what happens after the payback period is more important than is the payback period itself. The payback period model, when used as the sole investment criterion, has a fatal flaw in that it fails to consider cash flows after the payback period. Despite this flaw, payback is a rough-and-ready approach to getting a handle on investment proposals. Sometimes a project is so attractive using payback that, when its life is considered, no further analysis is necessary.

For total life evaluations, the accounting rate of return is superior to the payback period because it does consider a capital expenditure proposal's profitability. Using the accounting rate of return, a project that merely returns the initial investment will have an average annual increase in net income of 0 and an accounting rate of return of 0. The problem with the accounting rate of return is that it fails to consider the timing of cash flows. It treats all cash flows within the life of an investment proposal equally despite the fact that cash flows occurring early in a project's life are more valuable than cash flows occurring late in a project's life. Early period cash flows can earn additional profits by being invested elsewhere. Consider the two investment proposals summarized in **Exhibit 12.5**. Both have an accounting rate of return of 5%, but Project A is superior to Project B because most of its cash flows occur in the first two years. Because of the timing of the cash flows when discounted at an annual rate of 10%, Project A has a net present value of $1,120 while Project B has a negative net present value of $(10,928).

Exhibit 12.5 Evaluating Capital Budgeting Models with Differences in Cash Flow Timing

Accounting rate of return analysis of Projects A and B

	Project A	Project B
Predicted net cash inflow from operations		
Year 1	$ 50,000	$ 10,000
Year 2	50,000	10,000
Year 3	10,000	50,000
Year 4	10,000	50,000
Total	120,000	120,000
Total depreciation	(100,000)	(100,000)
Total net income	$ 20,000	$ 20,000
Project life	÷ 4 years	÷ 4 years
Average annual increase in net income	$ 5,000	$ 5,000
Initial investment	÷ 100,000	÷ 100,000
Accounting rate of return on initial investment	0.05	0.05

Net present value analysis of Project A

	Predicted Cash Inflows (outflows)	Year(s) of Cash Flows	10% Present Value Factor	Present Value of Cash Flows
Initial investment	$(100,000)	0	1.00000	$(100,000)
Operation	50,000	1–2	1.73554	86,777
Operation	10,000	3–4	3.16987 − 1.73554	14,343
Net present value of all cash flows				$ 1,120

Net present value analysis of Project B

	Predicted Cash Inflows (outflows)	Year(s) of Cash Flows	10% Present Value Factor	Present Value of Cash Flows
Initial investment	$(100,000)	0	1.00000	$(100,000)
Operation	10,000	1–2	1.73554	17,355
Operation	50,000	3–4	3.16987 − 1.73554	71,717
Net present value of all cash flows				$ (10,928)

The net present value and the internal rate of return models both consider the time value of money and project profitability. They almost always provide the same evaluation of individual projects whose acceptance or rejection will not affect other projects. An exception can occur when periods of net cash outflows are mixed with periods of net cash inflows. Under these circumstances, an investment proposal could have multiple internal rates of return. The net present value and the internal rate of return models, however, have two basic differences that often lead to differences in the evaluation of competing investment proposals:

1. The net present value model gives explicit consideration to investment size. The internal rate of return model does not.
2. The net present value model assumes that all net cash inflows are reinvested at the discount rate; the internal rate of return model assumes that all net cash inflows are reinvested at the project's internal rate of return.

When there is a difference in the size of competing investment proposals, and funds not invested in the accepted proposal can only be invested at the cost of capital, the net present value method is superior.

Business Insight ■ Patient Capital

In the UK, "patient capital" is outpacing traditional venture capital investment. Where venture capital (VC) groups expect returns after a fixed period, usually around 10 years, patient capital is characterized by willingness to wait and see. Of investments in new UK tech firms, 36% came from patient capital investors, while 34% came from traditional VCs. These two sources combined total just shy of $2 billion of funding.

Firms also use the patient capital principle to budget capital for activities such as research and development (R&D). The success of Corning's Gorilla Glass highlights what can go right with patient capital. Corning saw revenue from sales of Gorilla Glass, which was originally developed in the 1960s, go from $0 to $1 billion in 2007 when the glass was selected as the surface of the iPhone.

Because patient capital requires patient investors or owners, less established firms need to be creative to allow time for their investments to make good. Drugmaker Celator used a combination of quick returns from improving the delivery of existing leukemia drugs and funding from the Leukemia and Lymphoma Society to buy time while its revolutionary treatment for acute myeloid leukemia went through clinical trials. Now that the drug is widely used, investors' patience is being rewarded.

Sources: Muran Ahmed, "Patient Capital Overtakes VC for UK Tech Groups," *Financial Times*, November 1, 2015.
Martin Tillier, "Corning (GLW) and Coherent (COHR): Old Tech Companies Still Worth Investing In," *Nasdaq News*, January 8, 2014.
Brian Gormley, "Venture Investors in Celator Pharma Rewarded for Taking the Long View," *Wall Street Journal*, June 1, 2016.

Evaluating Investment Proposals — LO4 Review 12-4

Olive Theory Pizzeria is considering three different unrelated capital investments. Presented is information pertaining to each investment proposal.

	Proposal A	Proposal B	Proposal C
Initial investment.	$45,000	$45,000	$45,000
Cash flow from operations			
Year 1	40,000	22,500	45,000
Year 2	5,000	22,500	
Year 3	22,500	22,500	
Investment life (years)	3 years	3 years	1 year

Required

Determine each of the following:

a. Rank these investment proposals using the payback period, the accounting rate of return on initial investment, and the net present value criteria. Assume that the organization's cost of capital is 10%. Round all calculations to two decimal places.

b. Explain the difference in rankings. Which investment would you recommend?

Solution on p. 481.

Additional Aspects of Capital Budgeting

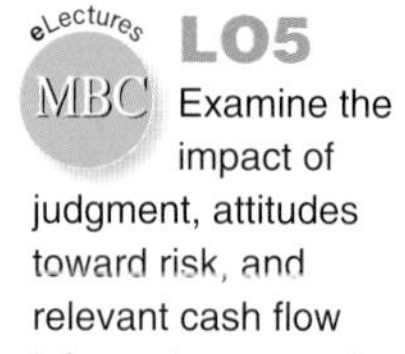

LO5 Examine the impact of judgment, attitudes toward risk, and relevant cash flow information on capital budgeting decisions.

The capital budgeting models discussed do not make investment decisions. Rather, they help managers separate capital expenditure proposals that meet certain criteria from those that do not. Managers can then focus on those proposals that pass the initial screening.

Using Multiple Investment Criteria

In performing this initial screening, management can use a single capital budgeting model or multiple models, including some we have not discussed. Management might specify that proposals must be in line with the organization's long-range goals and business strategy, have a maximum payback period of three years, have a positive net present value when discounted at 14%, and have an initial investment of less than $500,000. The maximum payback period might be intended to reduce risk, the present value criterion might be to ensure an adequate return to investors, and the maximum investment size might reflect the resources available for investment.

Nonquantitative factors such as market position, operational performance improvement, and strategy implementation often play a decisive role in management's final decision to accept or reject a capital expenditure proposal that has passed the initial screening. Also important at this point are top management's attitudes toward risk and financing alternatives, their confidence in the professional judgment of other managers making investment proposals, their beliefs about the future direction of the economy, and their evaluation of alternative investments. In the following sections, we will focus on evaluating risk, differential analysis of project cash flows, predicting differential costs and revenues for high-tech investments, and evaluating mutually exclusive investments.

Evaluating Risk

All capital expenditure proposals involve risk, including risk related to the following:

- Cost of the initial investment.
- Time required to complete the initial investment and begin operations.
- Whether the new facilities will operate as planned.
- Life of the facilities.
- Customers' demand for the product or service.
- Final selling price.
- Operating costs.
- Disposal values.

Projected cash flows (such as those summarized for the Mobile Taqueria proposal in **Exhibit 12.2**) are based on management's best predictions. Although these predictions are likely to reflect the professional judgment of economists, marketing personnel, engineers, and accountants, they are far from certain.

Many techniques have been developed to assist in the analysis of the risks inherent in capital budgeting. Suggested approaches include the following:

- *Adjust the discount rate for individual projects based on management's perception of the risks associated with a project.* A project perceived as being almost risk free might be evaluated using a discount rate of 12%; a project perceived as having moderate risk may be evaluated using a discount rate of 16%; and a project perceived as having high risk might be evaluated using a discount rate of 20%.
- *Compute several internal rates of return and/or net present values for a project.* For example, a project's net present value might be computed three times: first assuming the most optimistic projections of cash flows; second assuming the most likely projections of cash flows; and third assuming the most pessimistic projections of cash flows. The final decision is then based on

management's attitudes toward risk. A project whose most likely outcome is highly profitable would probably be rejected if its pessimistic outcome might lead to bankruptcy.

- *Subject a capital expenditure proposal to sensitivity analysis*, a study of the responsiveness of a model's dependent variable(s) to changes in one or more of its independent variables. Management might want to know, for example, the minimum annual net cash inflows that will provide an internal rate of return of 12% with other cost and revenue projections being as expected.

Research Insight ■ Global Economic Changes Can Drive Capital Budgets

Global investment can shift due to factors far beyond the control of investors. The impact of the UK's decision to leave the European Union hit capital investment long before it officially hit the EU parliament. Investors, worried that their capital would be stuck in UK funds, pulled out quickly. This, coupled with a weakening British pound, slowed investment by domestic funds. Merger and acquisition (M&A) activity within the UK slowed, along with acquisition of foreign firms by UK firms. However, with the pound down and UK funds off the market, foreign firms found a window of relative affordability in the wake of the vote.

In the month following the vote, foreign companies closed 60 deals totaling $35 billion, compared to only $30 billion in the previous quarter. It is important to remember that capital budgeting decisions may depend directly on outside factors such as exchange rates and political processes around the globe.

Sources: Attracta Mooney, "Brexit 'Stampede' Out of UK Funds," *Financial Times*, July 24, 2016.
Pamela Barbaglia and Freya Berry, "Corporate Raiders Seek Brexit Bargains in Britain," *Reuters*, July 24, 2016.
Iain Macmillan, Siram Prakash, and Ian Stewart, "Impact of the EU Referendum on M&A Activity in the UK," *Deloitte*, June 2016.

Differential Analysis of Project Cash Flows

All previous examples assume that capital expenditure proposals produce additional net cash inflows, but this is not always the case. Units of government and not-for-profit organizations might provide services that do not produce any cash inflows. For-profit organizations might be required to make capital expenditures to maintain product quality or to bring facilities up to environmental or safety standards. In these situations, it is impossible to compute a project's payback period, accounting rate of return, or internal rate of return. It is possible, however, to compute the present value of all life-cycle costs associated with alternative ways of providing the service or meeting the environmental or safety standard. Here, the alternative with the smallest negative net present value is preferred.

Capital expenditure proposals to reduce operating costs by upgrading facilities might not provide any incremental cash inflows. Again, we can use a total cost approach and calculate the present value of the costs associated with each alternative, with the low-cost alternative being preferred. Alternatively, we can perform a differential analysis of cash flows and, treating any reduced operating costs as if they were cash inflows, compute the net present value or the internal rate of return of the cost reduction proposal. Recall from Chapter 4 that a relevant cost analysis focuses on the costs that differ under alternative actions. Once the differential amounts have been determined, they can be adjusted for the time value of money. To illustrate the differential approach, we consider an example introduced in Chapter 4.

Let's again assume Beats produces a variety of electronic components, including 10,000 units per year of a component used in wireless headsets. Further assume the machine currently used in manufacturing the headset components is two years old and has a remaining useful life of four years. It cost $90,000 and has an estimated salvage value of zero dollars at the end of its useful life. Its current book value (original cost less accumulated depreciation) is $60,000, but its current disposal value (resale value) is only $35,000.

Management is evaluating the desirability of replacing the machine with a new machine. The new machine costs $80,000, has a useful life of four years, and a predicted salvage value of zero dollars at the end of its useful life. Although the new machine has the same productive capacity as the old machine, its predicted operating costs are lower because it requires less electricity. Furthermore, because of a computer control system, the new machine will require less frequent and less expensive inspections and adjustments. Finally, the new machine requires less maintenance.

An analysis of the cash flows associated with this cost reduction proposal, separated into the three phases of the project's life, are presented in **Exhibit 12.6**. Because the proposal does not have a disposal value, this portion of the analysis could have been omitted. (A detailed explanation of the relevant costs included in this analysis is in **Exhibit 4.1** and the accompanying Chapter 4 discussion of relevant costs.) Assuming that Beats has a discount rate of 12%, the proposal's net present value (computed in **Exhibit 12.7**) is $2,686, and the proposal is acceptable.

Exhibit 12.6 Differential Analysis of Predicted Cash Flows

	One Year Totals		
	Keep Old Machine (A)	Replace with New Machine (B)	Difference (income effect of replacement) (A) – (B)
Initial investment			
Cost of new machine		$80,000	$(80,000)
Disposal value of old machine		(35,000)	35,000
Net initial investment			$(45,000)
Annual operating cash savings			
Conversion			
Old machine (10,000 units × $5)	$50,000		
New machine (10,000 units × $4)		$40,000	$10,000
Inspection and adjustment			
Old machine (10 setups × $500 per setup)	5,000		
New machine (5 setups × $300 per setup)		1,500	3,500
Machine maintenance			
Old machine ($200 per month × 12 months)	2,400		
New machine ($200 per year)		200	2,200
Net annual cost savings			$15,700
Disinvestment at end of life			
Old machine	$ 0		
New machine		$ 0	

Exhibit 12.7 Differential Analysis of Predicted Cash Flows

	Predicted Cash Inflows (outflows) (A)	Year(s) of Cash Flows (B)	12% Present Value Factor (C)	Present Value of Cash Flows (A) × (C)
Initial investment	$(45,000)	0	1.00000	$(45,000)
Operation	15,700	1–4	3.03735	47,686
Disinvestment	0	4	0.63552	0
Net present value of all cash flows				$ 2,686

Predicting Differential Costs and Revenues for High-Tech Investments

Care must be taken when evaluating proposals for investments in technological innovations such as flexible manufacturing systems and computer integrated manufacturing. The three types of errors to consider are (1) investing in unnecessary or overly complex equipment, (2) overestimating cost saving, and (3) underestimating incremental sales.

Investing in Unnecessary or Overly Complex Equipment

A common error is to simply compare the cost associated with the current inefficient way of doing things with the predicted cost of performing the identical operations with more modern equipment. Although capital budgeting models might suggest that such investments are justifiable, the result could be the costly and rapid completion of non-value-added activities. Consider the following examples.

- A company invests in an automated system to speed the movement of work in process between workstations without first evaluating the plant layout. The firm is still unable to compete with other companies having better organized plants that allow lower cycle times, lower work-in-process inventories, and lower manufacturing costs. Management should have evaluated the plant layout before investing in new equipment. They may have found that rearranging the factory floor would have reduced materials movement and eliminated the need for the investment.
- A company invests in an automated warehouse to permit the rapid storage and retrieval of goods while competitors work to eliminate excess inventory. The firm is left with large inventories and a large investment in the automated warehouse while competitors, not having to earn a return on similar investments, are able to charge lower prices. Management should have evaluated the need for current inventory levels and perhaps shifted to a just-in-time approach to inventory management before considering the investment in an automated warehouse.
- A company hires staff to perform quality inspections while competitors implement total quality management and seek to eliminate the need for quality inspections. While defective products or services are now identified before they affect customers, they still exist. Furthermore, the company has higher expenditures than competitors, resulting in a less competitive cost structure. The inspections might not have been needed if management had shifted from inspecting for conformance to an emphasis on "doing it right the first time."
- A company invests in automated welding equipment to more efficiently produce printer casings while competitors simplify the product design and shift from welded to molded plastic casings. Although the cost of producing the welded casings might be lower, the company's cost structure is still not competitive.

All of these examples illustrate the limitations of capital budgeting models and the need for good judgment. *In the final analysis, managers, not models, make decisions.* Management must carefully evaluate the situations and determine whether they have considered the proper alternatives and all important cash flows.

Overestimating Cost Savings

When a number of activities drive manufacturing overhead costs, estimates of overhead cost savings based on a single activity cost driver can significantly overestimate cost savings. Assume, for example, that a company containing both machine-intensive and labor-intensive operations develops a cost-estimating equation for overhead with labor as the only independent variable. Because of this, all overhead costs are associated with labor. The predicted cost savings can be computed as the sum of predicted reductions in labor plus predicted reductions in overhead; the predicted reductions in overhead are computed as the overhead per direct labor dollar or labor hour multiplied by the predicted reduction in direct labor dollars or labor hours. Because a major portion of the overhead is driven by factors other than direct labor, reducing direct labor will not provide the predicted savings. Capital budgeting models might suggest that the investment is acceptable, but the models are based on inaccurate cost data.

Management should beware of overly simplistic computations of cost savings. This is an area in which management needs the assistance of well-trained management accountants and engineers.

Underestimating Incremental Sales or Cost Savings

In evaluating proposals for investments in new equipment, management often assumes that the baseline for comparison is the current sales level, but this might not be the case. If competitors are investing in equipment to better meet customer needs and to reduce costs, a failure to make similar investments might result in uncompetitive prices and declining, rather than steady, sales. Hence, the baseline for sales without the investment is overstated, and the incremental sales of the investment is understated. Not considering the likely decline in sales understates the incremental sales associated with the investment and biases the results against the proposed investment.

Investments in manufacturing technologies, such as flexible manufacturing systems (FMS) and computer integrated manufacturing (CIM), do more than simply allow the efficient production of current products. Flexible manufacturing systems are designed to easily adapt to changes in the type and quantity of the product being manufactured. In computer integrated manufacturing, companies can use computers to not only manage what equipment does but also manage the flow of materials and inventory levels. Such investments also make possible the rapid, low-cost switching to new products. The result is expanded sales opportunities.

Such investments might also produce cost savings further down the value chain, either within or outside the company. Beats' decision to acquire a new machine might have the unanticipated consequence of reducing customer warranty claims or increasing sales because customers are attracted to a higher-quality product.

Unfortunately, because such opportunities are difficult to quantify, they are often ignored in the evaluation of capital expenditure proposals. The solution to this dilemma involves the application of management's professional judgment, a willingness to take risks based on this professional judgment, and recognition that certain investments transcend capital budgeting models in that they involve strategic as well as long-range planning. At this level of planning, qualitative decisions concerning the nature of the organization are at least as important as quantified factors.

Review 12-5 LO5 Considering Nonquantitative Factors in Capital Budgeting Decisions

Hilltop Ski Resort is considering making a capital investment in a new ski lift. Hilltop's finance team assessed the investment using the net present value model and predicts the ski lift will generate a positive net present value cash flow over the life of the asset.

Required

Identify and discuss additional factors that Hilltop's management should consider after the initial screening of the capital investment in the ski lift, before making a final evaluation of the investment.

Solution on p. 482.

Taxes in Capital Budgeting Decisions

eLectures MBC **LO6** Determine the net present value of investment proposals with consideration of taxes.

To focus on capital budgeting concepts, we deferred consideration of the impact of taxes. Because income taxes affect cash flows and income, their consideration is important in evaluating investment proposals in for-profit organizations.

The cost of investments in plant and equipment is not deducted from taxable revenues in determining taxable income and income taxes at the time of the initial investment. Instead, the amount of the initial investment is deducted as depreciation over the operating life of an asset. To illustrate the impact of taxes on cash flows, assume the following:

- Revenues and operating cash receipts are the same each year.
- Depreciation is the only noncash expense of an organization.

Depreciation Tax Shield

Depreciation does not require the use of cash (the funds were spent at the initial investment), but depreciation is said to provide a "tax shield" because it reduces cash payments for income taxes. The **depreciation tax shield** (the reduction in taxes due to the deductibility of depreciation from taxable revenues) is computed as follows:

Depreciation tax shield = Depreciation × Tax rate

The value of the depreciation tax shield is illustrated using Mobile Taqueria's capital expenditure proposal summarized in **Exhibit 12.2**. Mobile Taqueria's annual straight-line depreciation of $16,511 is computed as the initial investment of $90,554 minus the predicted disposal value of $8,000, all divided by the predicted five-year life $16,511 [($90,554 – $8,000)/5]. With an assumed tax rate of 34%, the annual depreciation tax shield is $5,614 ($16,511 depreciation × 0.34 tax rate). The increase in annual cash flows provided by the depreciation tax shield is illustrated in **Exhibit 12.8**. Examine this exhibit, paying particular attention to the lines for depreciation, income taxes, and net annual cash flow.

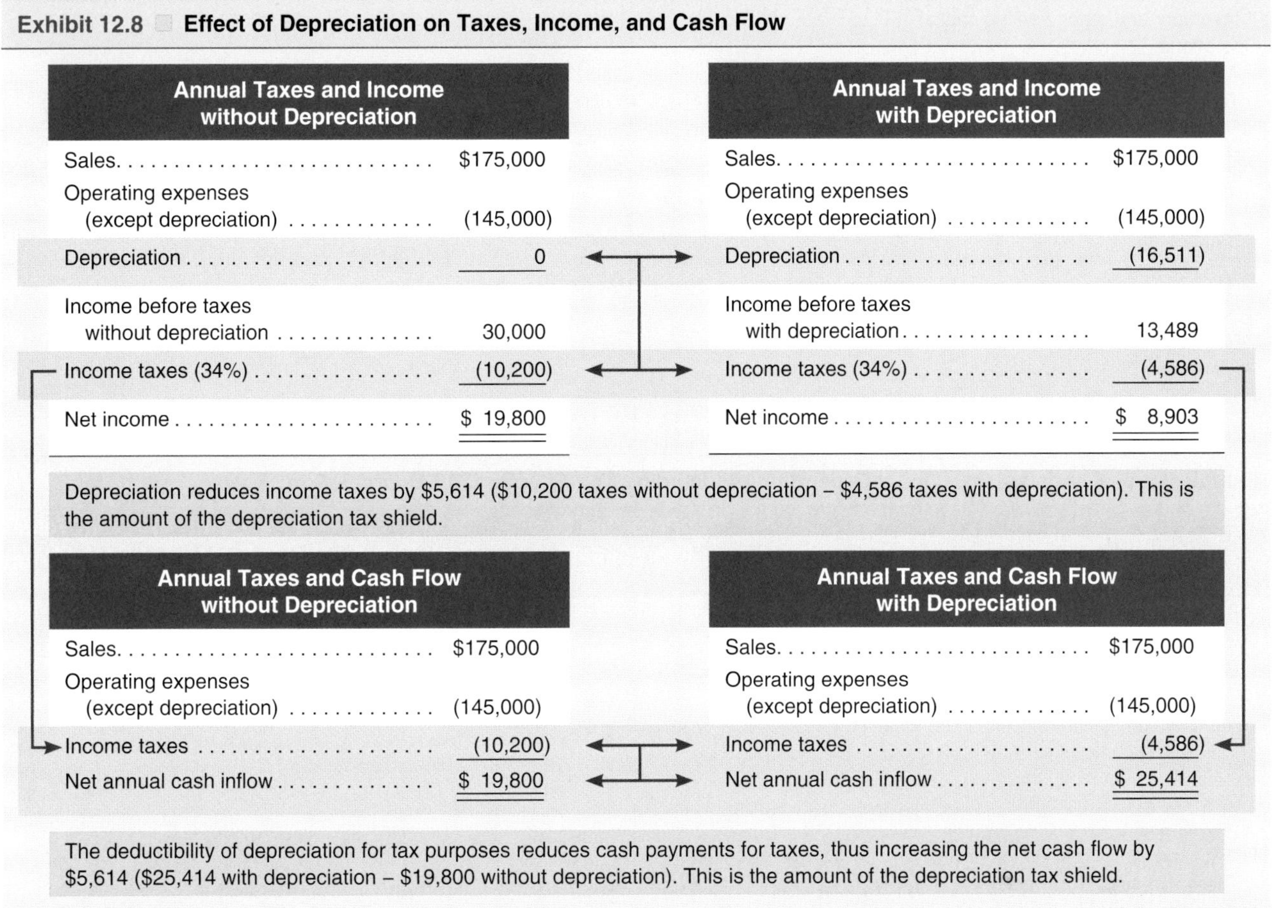

Exhibit 12.8 Effect of Depreciation on Taxes, Income, and Cash Flow

Annual Taxes and Income without Depreciation		Annual Taxes and Income with Depreciation	
Sales	$175,000	Sales	$175,000
Operating expenses (except depreciation)	(145,000)	Operating expenses (except depreciation)	(145,000)
Depreciation	0	Depreciation	(16,511)
Income before taxes without depreciation	30,000	Income before taxes with depreciation	13,489
Income taxes (34%)	(10,200)	Income taxes (34%)	(4,586)
Net income	$ 19,800	Net income	$ 8,903

Depreciation reduces income taxes by $5,614 ($10,200 taxes without depreciation – $4,586 taxes with depreciation). This is the amount of the depreciation tax shield.

Annual Taxes and Cash Flow without Depreciation		Annual Taxes and Cash Flow with Depreciation	
Sales	$175,000	Sales	$175,000
Operating expenses (except depreciation)	(145,000)	Operating expenses (except depreciation)	(145,000)
Income taxes	(10,200)	Income taxes	(4,586)
Net annual cash inflow	$ 19,800	Net annual cash inflow	$ 25,414

The deductibility of depreciation for tax purposes reduces cash payments for taxes, thus increasing the net cash flow by $5,614 ($25,414 with depreciation – $19,800 without depreciation). This is the amount of the depreciation tax shield.

The U.S. Tax Code contains guidelines concerning the depreciation of various types of assets. (Analysis of these guidelines is beyond the scope of this text.) Tax guidelines allow organizations a choice in tax depreciation procedures between straight-line depreciation and an accelerated depreciation method detailed in the Tax Code. Because of the time value of money, profitable businesses should usually select the tax depreciation procedure that provides the earliest depreciation. To illustrate the effect of accelerated depreciation on taxes and capital budgeting, we use double-declining balance depreciation rather than the accelerated method detailed in the Code. When making capital expenditure decisions, managers should, of course, refer to the most current version of the Tax Code to determine the specific depreciation guidelines in effect at that time.

Exhibits 12.9 and 12.10 illustrate the effect of two alternative depreciation procedures, straight-line and double-declining balance, on the net present value of Mobile Taqueria's proposed investment. The cash flows for this investment were presented in **Exhibit 12.2**, and the effect of taxes on the investment's annual cash flows were examined in **Exhibit 12.8**. Ignoring taxes, the investment was shown (in **Exhibit 12.3**) to have a positive net present value of $20,398 at a discount rate of 12%. With taxes, the investment has a positive net present value of $3,866 using straight-line depreciation and $6,082 using double-declining balance depreciation. Although taxes and cash flows are identical over the entire life of the project, the use of double-declining balance depreciation for taxes results in a higher net present value because it results in lower cash expenditures for taxes in the earlier years of an asset's life.

Exhibit 12.9 Analysis of Capital Expenditures Including Tax Effects: Straight-Line Depreciation

	Predicted Cash Inflows (outflows) (A)	Year(s) of Cash Flows (B)	12% Present Value Factor (C)	Present Value of Cash Flows (A) × (C)
Initial investment				
Vehicle and equipment	$(90,554)	0	1.00000	$ (90,554)
Inventory and other working capital	(4,000)	0	1.00000	(4,000)
Operations				
Annual taxable income without depreciation	30,000	1–5	3.60478	108,143
Taxes on income ($30,000 × 0.34)	(10,200)	1–5	3.60478	(36,769)
Depreciation tax shield*	5,614	1–5	3.60478	20,237
Disinvestment				
Sale of vehicle and equipment	8,000	5	0.56743	4,539
Inventory and other working capital	4,000	5	0.56743	2,270
Net present value of all cash flows				$ 3,866

*Computation of depreciation tax shield:

Annual straight-line depreciation	$16,511
Tax rate	× 0.34
Depreciation tax shield	$ 5,614

Exhibit 12.10 Analysis of Capital Expenditures Including Tax Effects: DDB Depreciation

	Predicted Cash Inflows (outflows) (A)	Year(s) of Cash Flows (B)	12% Present Value Factor (C)	Present Value of Cash Flows (A) × (C)
Initial investment				
Vehicle and equipment	$(90,554)	0	1.00000	$ (90,554)
Inventory and other working capital	4,000	0	1.00000	(4,000)
Operations				
Annual taxable income without depreciation	30,000	1–5	3.60478	108,143
Taxes on income ($30,000 × 0.34)	(10,200)	1–5	3.60478	(36,769)
Depreciation tax shield*				
Year 1	12,315	1	0.89286	10,996
Year 2	7,389	2	0.79719	5,890
Year 3	4,434	3	0.71178	3,156
Year 4	2,660	4	0.63552	1,690
Year 5	1,270	5	0.56743	721
Disinvestment				
Sale of vehicle and equipment	8,000	5	0.56743	4,539
Inventory and other working capital	4,000	5	0.56743	2,270
Net present value of all cash flows				$ 6,082

*Computation of depreciation tax shield:

Year	Depreciation Base† (A)	Annual Rate (B)	Annual Depreciation (C) = (A) × (B)	Tax Rate (D)	Tax Shield (E) = (C) × (D)
1	$90,554	2/5	$36,222	0.34	$12,315
2	54,332	2/5	21,733	0.34	7,389
3	32,599	2/5	13,040	0.34	4,434
4	19,559	2/5	7,824	0.34	2,660
5	11,735	balance	3,735	0.34	1,270

†The depreciation base is reduced by the amount of all previous depreciation. The annual rate is twice the straight-line rate. For simplicity, we depreciated the remaining balance in the fifth year and did not switch to straight-line depreciation when the straight-line amount exceeds the double-declining balance amount. This would happen in the fourth year, when $19,559 ÷ 2 = $9,780. Although the depreciable base excludes the predicted disposal value of $8,000, under double-declining balance depreciation, an asset is only depreciated down to its disposal value. Hence, Year 5 depreciation is computed as the $11,735 depreciable base minus the $8,000 disposal value.

Investment Tax Credit

From time to time, for the purpose of stimulating investment and economic growth, the U.S. federal government has implemented an investment tax credit. An **investment tax credit** reduces taxes in the year a new asset is placed in service by some stated percentage of the cost of the asset. In recent years tax credits, such as the credits for purchasing hybrid automobiles, have been used to stimulate investments that reduce the emission of greenhouses gases. Typically, this is done without reducing the depreciation base of the asset for tax purposes. An investment tax credit reduces cash payments for taxes and, hence, is treated as a cash inflow for capital budgeting purposes. This additional cash inflow increases the probability that a new asset will meet a taxpayer's capital expenditure criteria.

Calculating Net Present Value with the Consideration of Income Taxes **LO6 Review 12-6**

Assume that Architecture Design is considering a proposal to change the company's manual design system to a computer-aided design system. The new system is expected to save 9,000 design hours per year; an operating cost savings of $45 per hour. The annual cash expenditures of operating the new system are estimated to be $200,000. The new system would require an initial investment of $550,000. The estimated life of this system is five years with no salvage value. The tax rate is 35%, and Architecture Design uses straight-line depreciation for tax purposes. Architecture Design has a cost of capital of 14%.

Required

a. Compute the annual after-tax cash flows related to the new design system.
b. Determine the project's net present value.

Solution on p. 483.

Appendix 12A: Time Value of Money

LO7 Compute basic present value cash flow amounts.

When asked to choose between $500 today or an IOU for $500 to be paid one year later, rational decision makers choose the $500 today. Two reasons for this involve the *time value of money* and the *risk*. A dollar today is worth more than a dollar tomorrow or at some future time. Having a dollar provides flexibility. It can be spent, buried, or invested in a number of projects. If invested in a savings account, it will amount to more than one dollar at some future time because of the effect of interest. The interest paid by a bank (or borrower) for the use of money is analogous to the rent paid for the use of land, buildings, or equipment. Furthermore, we live in an uncertain world, and, for a variety of reasons, the possibility exists that an IOU might not be paid.

Future Value

Future value is the amount that a current sum of money earning a stated rate of interest will accumulate to at the end of a future period. Suppose we deposit $500 in a savings account at a financial institution that pays interest at the rate of 10% per year. At the end of the first year, the original deposit of $500 will total $550 ($500 × 1.10). If we leave the $550 for another year, the amount will increase to $605 ($550 × 1.10). It can be stated that $500 today has a future value in one year of $550, or conversely, that $550 one year from today has a present value of $500. Interest of $55 ($605 – $550) was earned in the second year, whereas interest of only $50 was earned in the first year. This happened because interest during the second year was earned on the principal plus interest from the first year ($550). When periodic interest is computed on principal plus prior periods' accumulated interest, the interest is said to be *compounded*. Compound interest is used throughout this text.

To determine future values at the end of one period (usually a year), multiply the beginning amount (present value) by 1 plus the interest rate. When multiple periods are involved, the future value is determined by repeatedly multiplying the beginning amount by 1 plus the interest rate for each period. When $500 is invested for two years at an interest rate of 10% per year, its future value is computed as $500 × 1.10 × 1.10. The following equation is used to figure future value:

$$\mathbf{fv = pv(1 + i)^n}$$

where:

fv = future value amount
pv = present value amount
i = interest rate per period
n = number of periods

For our $500 deposit, the equation becomes:

$$\begin{aligned} \textbf{fv of \$500} &= \textbf{pv}(1 + i)^n \\ &= \$500(1 + 0.10)^2 \\ &= \$605 \end{aligned}$$

In a similar manner, once the interest rate and number of periods are known, the future value amount of any present value amount is easily determined.

Present Value

Present value is the current worth of a specified amount of money to be received at some future date at some interest rate. Solving for *pv* in the future value equation, the new present value equation is determined as follows:

$$pv = \frac{fv}{(1+i)^n}$$

Using this equation, the present value of $8,800 to be received in one year, discounted at 10%, is computed as follows:

$$\begin{aligned} \text{pv of \$8,800} &= \frac{\$8,800}{(1+0.10)^1} \\ &= \frac{\$8,800}{(1.10)} \\ &= \$8,000 \end{aligned}$$

Thus, when the discount rate is 10%, the present value of $8,800 to be received in one year is $8,000. The present value equation is often expressed as the future value amount times the present value of $1:

$$pv = fvn\frac{\$1}{(1+i)^n}$$

Using the equation for the present value of $1, the present value of $8,800 to be received in one year, discounted at 10%, is computed as follows:

$$\begin{aligned} \text{pv of \$8,800} &= \$8,800 \times \frac{\$1}{(1+0.10)^1} \\ &= \$8,800 \times 0.90909 \\ &= \$8,000 \end{aligned}$$

The present value of $8,800 two periods from now is $7,273, computed as [$8,800 ÷ $(1.10)^2$] or [$8,800 × $1 ÷ $(1.10)^2$].

If a calculator or computer with spreadsheet software is not available, present value computations can be done by hand. Tables, such as Exhibit 12A.1 for the present value of $1 at various interest rates and time periods, can be used to simplify hand computations. Using the factors in Exhibit 12A.1, the present value of any future amount can be determined. For example, with an interest rate of 10%, the present value of the following future amounts to be received in one period are as follows:

Future Value Amount		Present Value Factor of $1		Present Value
$ 100	×	0.90909	=	$ 90.91
628	×	0.90909	=	570.91
4,285	×	0.90909	=	3,895.45
9,900	×	0.90909	=	8,999.99

To further illustrate the use of Exhibit 12A.1, consider the following application. Suppose Beats wants to invest its surplus cash at 12% to have $10,000 to pay off a long-term note due at the end of five years. Exhibit 12A.1 shows that the present value factor of $1, discounted at 12% per year for five years, is 0.56743. Multiplying $10,000 by 0.56743, the present value is determined to be $5,674:

$$\begin{aligned}\textbf{pv of \$10,000} &= \textbf{\$10,000} \times \textbf{Present value factor for \$1}\\ &= \textbf{\$10,000} \times \textbf{0.56743}\\ &= \textbf{\$5,674}\end{aligned}$$

Therefore, if Beats invests $5,674 today, it will have $10,000 available to pay off its note in five years.

Managers also use present value tables to make investment decisions. Assume that Monroe Company can make an investment that will provide a cash flow of $12,000 at the end of eight years. If the company demands a rate of return of 14% per year, what is the most it will be willing to pay for this investment? From Exhibit 12A.1, we find that the present value factor for $1, discounted at 14% per year for eight years, is 0.35056:

$$\begin{aligned}\textbf{pv of \$12,000} &= \textbf{\$12,000} \times \textbf{Present value factor for \$1}\\ &= \textbf{\$12,000} \times \textbf{0.35056}\\ &= \textbf{\$4,207}\end{aligned}$$

If the company demands an annual return of 14%, the most it would be willing to invest today is $4,207.

Annuities

Not all investments provide a single sum of money. Many investments provide periodic cash flows called *annuities*. An **annuity** is a series of equal cash flows received or paid over equal intervals of time. Suppose that $100 will be received at the end of each of the next three years. If the discount rate is 10%, the present value of this annuity can be determined by summing the present value of each receipt:

Year 1 $100 × $1 ÷ $(1 + 0.10)^1$ =	**$ 90.90**
Year 2 $100 × $1 ÷ $(1 + 0.10)^2$ =	**82.65**
Year 3 $100 × $1 ÷ $(1 + 0.10)^3$ =	**75.13**
Total	**$248.68**

Alternatively, the following equation can be used to compute the present value of an annuity with cash flows at the end of each period:

$$\text{pva} = \frac{a}{i} \times \left[1 - \frac{1}{(1+i)^n}\right]$$

where:

pva = present value of an annuity (also called the annuity factor)
i = prevailing rate per period
n = number of periods
a = annuity amount

This equation was used to compute the factors presented in Exhibit 12A.2 for an annuity amount of $1. The present value of an annuity of $1 per period for three periods discounted at 10% per period is as follows:

$$\begin{aligned}\textbf{pva of \$1} &= \frac{1}{0.10} + \left[1 - \frac{1}{(1+0.10)^3}\right]\\ &= 2.48685\end{aligned}$$

Using this factor, the present value of a $100 annuity can be computed as $100 × 2.48685, which yields $248.689. To determine the present value of an annuity of any amount, the annuity factor for $1 can be multiplied by the annuity amount.

To further illustrate the use of Exhibit 12A.2, assume that Red Kite Company is considering an investment in a piece of equipment that will produce net cash inflows of $2,000 at the end of each year for five years. If the company's desired rate of return is 12%, an investment of $7,210 will provide such a return:

$$\begin{aligned}\textbf{pva of \$2,000} &= \textbf{\$2,000} \times \begin{array}{l}\textbf{Present value for an annuity of \$1}\\ \textbf{for five periods discounted at 12\%}\end{array}\\ &= \textbf{\$2,000} \times \textbf{3.60478}\\ &= \textbf{\$7,210}\end{aligned}$$

Exhibit 12A.1 Present Value of $1

Present value of $1 = $\frac{1}{(1+i)^n}$

Discount rate (i)

Periods (n)	4%	6%	8%	10%	12%	14%	16%	18%	20%	22%	24%	26%	28%
1	0.96154	0.94340	0.92593	0.90909	0.89286	0.87719	0.86207	0.84746	0.83333	0.81967	0.80645	0.79365	0.78125
2	0.92456	0.89000	0.85734	0.82645	0.79719	0.76947	0.74316	0.71818	0.69444	0.67186	0.65036	0.62988	0.61035
3	0.88900	0.83962	0.79383	0.75131	0.71178	0.67497	0.64066	0.60863	0.57870	0.55071	0.52449	0.49991	0.47684
4	0.85480	0.79209	0.73503	0.68301	0.63552	0.59208	0.55229	0.51579	0.48225	0.45140	0.42297	0.39675	0.37253
5	0.82193	0.74726	0.68058	0.62092	0.56743	0.51937	0.47611	0.43711	0.40188	0.37000	0.34111	0.31488	0.29104
6	0.79031	0.70496	0.63017	0.56447	0.50663	0.45559	0.41044	0.37043	0.33490	0.30328	0.27509	0.24991	0.22737
7	0.75992	0.66506	0.58349	0.51316	0.45235	0.39964	0.35383	0.31393	0.27908	0.24859	0.22184	0.19834	0.17764
8	0.73069	0.62741	0.54027	0.46651	0.40388	0.35056	0.30503	0.26604	0.23257	0.20376	0.17891	0.15741	0.13878
9	0.70259	0.59190	0.50025	0.42410	0.36061	0.30751	0.26295	0.22546	0.19381	0.16702	0.14428	0.12493	0.10842
10	0.67556	0.55839	0.46319	0.38554	0.32197	0.26974	0.22668	0.19106	0.16151	0.13690	0.11635	0.09915	0.08470
11	0.64958	0.52679	0.42888	0.35049	0.28748	0.23662	0.19542	0.16192	0.13459	0.11221	0.09383	0.07869	0.06617
12	0.62460	0.49697	0.39711	0.31863	0.25668	0.20756	0.16846	0.13722	0.11216	0.09198	0.07567	0.06245	0.05170
13	0.60057	0.46884	0.36770	0.28966	0.22917	0.18207	0.14523	0.11629	0.09346	0.07539	0.06103	0.04957	0.04039
14	0.57748	0.44230	0.34046	0.26333	0.20462	0.15971	0.12520	0.09855	0.07789	0.06180	0.04921	0.03934	0.03155
15	0.55526	0.41727	0.31524	0.23939	0.18270	0.14010	0.10793	0.08352	0.06491	0.05065	0.03969	0.03122	0.02465
16	0.53391	0.39365	0.29189	0.21763	0.16312	0.12289	0.09304	0.07078	0.05409	0.04152	0.03201	0.02478	0.01926
17	0.51337	0.37136	0.27027	0.19784	0.14564	0.10780	0.08021	0.05998	0.04507	0.03403	0.02581	0.01967	0.01505
18	0.49363	0.35034	0.25025	0.17986	0.13004	0.09456	0.06914	0.05083	0.03756	0.02789	0.02082	0.01561	0.01175
19	0.47464	0.33051	0.23171	0.16351	0.11611	0.08295	0.05961	0.04308	0.03130	0.02286	0.01679	0.01239	0.00918
20	0.45639	0.31180	0.21455	0.14864	0.10367	0.07276	0.05139	0.03651	0.02608	0.01874	0.01354	0.00983	0.00717

Exhibit 12A.2 Present Value of an Annuity of $1

Present value of an annuity of $1 = $\frac{1}{i} \times \left[1 - \frac{1}{(1+i)^n}\right]$

Discount rate (i)

Periods (n)	4%	6%	8%	10%	12%	14%	16%	18%	20%	22%	24%	26%	28%
1	0.96154	0.94340	0.92593	0.90909	0.89286	0.87719	0.86207	0.84746	0.83333	0.81967	0.80645	0.79365	0.78125
2	1.88609	1.83339	1.78326	1.73554	1.69005	1.64666	1.60523	1.56564	1.52778	1.49153	1.45682	1.42353	1.39160
3	2.77509	2.67301	2.57710	2.48685	2.40183	2.32163	2.24589	2.17427	2.10648	2.04224	1.98130	1.92344	1.86844
4	3.62990	3.46511	3.31213	3.16987	3.03735	2.91371	2.79818	2.69006	2.58873	2.49364	2.40428	2.32019	2.24097
5	4.45182	4.21236	3.99271	3.79079	3.60478	3.43308	3.27429	3.12717	2.99061	2.86364	2.74538	2.63507	2.53201
6	5.24214	4.91732	4.62288	4.35526	4.11141	3.88867	3.68474	3.49760	3.32551	3.16692	3.02047	2.88498	2.75938
7	6.00205	5.58238	5.20637	4.86842	4.56376	4.28830	4.03857	3.81153	3.60459	3.41551	3.24232	3.08331	2.93702
8	6.73274	6.20979	5.74664	5.33493	4.96764	4.63886	4.34359	4.07757	3.83716	3.61927	3.42122	3.24073	3.07579
9	7.43533	6.80169	6.24689	5.75902	5.32825	4.94637	4.60654	4.30302	4.03097	3.78628	3.56550	3.36566	3.18421
10	8.11090	7.36009	6.71008	6.14457	5.65022	5.21612	4.83323	4.49409	4.19247	3.92318	3.68186	3.46481	3.26892
11	8.76048	7.88687	7.13896	6.49506	5.93770	5.45273	5.02864	4.65601	4.32706	4.03540	3.77569	3.54350	3.33509
12	9.38507	8.38384	7.53608	6.81369	6.19437	5.66029	5.19711	4.79322	4.43922	4.12737	3.85136	3.60595	3.38679
13	9.98565	8.85268	7.90378	7.10336	6.42355	5.84236	5.34233	4.90951	4.53268	4.20277	3.91239	3.65552	3.42718
14	10.56312	9.29498	8.24424	7.36669	6.62817	6.00207	5.46753	5.00806	4.61057	4.26456	3.96160	3.69485	3.45873
15	11.11839	9.71225	8.55948	7.60608	6.81086	6.14217	5.57546	5.09158	4.67547	4.31522	4.00129	3.72607	3.48339
16	11.65230	10.10590	8.85137	7.82371	6.97399	6.26506	5.66850	5.16235	4.72956	4.35673	4.03330	3.75085	3.50265
17	12.16567	10.47726	9.12164	8.02155	7.11963	6.37286	5.74870	5.22233	4.77463	4.39077	4.05911	3.77052	3.51769
18	12.65930	10.82760	9.37189	8.20141	7.24967	6.46742	5.81785	5.27316	4.81219	4.41866	4.07993	3.78613	3.52945
19	13.13394	11.15812	9.60360	8.36492	7.36578	6.55037	5.87746	5.31624	4.84350	4.44152	4.09672	3.79851	3.53863
20	13.59033	11.46992	9.81815	8.51356	7.46944	6.62313	5.92884	5.35275	4.86958	4.46027	4.11026	3.80834	3.54580

Here, the $2,000 annuity is multiplied by 3.60478, the factor for an annuity of $1 for five periods found in Exhibit 12A.2, discounted at 12% per period.

Another use of Exhibit 12A.2 is to determine the amount that must be received annually to provide a desired rate of return on an investment. Assume that Corning invests $33,550 in a piece of machinery and desires a return of the investment plus interest of 8% in equal year-end payments for 10 years. The minimum amount that must be received each year is determined by solving the equation for the present value of an annuity:

$$\text{pva} = \text{a} \times (\text{pva of \$1})$$

$$\text{a} = \frac{\text{pva}}{\text{pva of \$1}}$$

From Exhibit 12A.2, we see that the 8% factor for 10 periods is 6.71008. Dividing the $33,550 investment by 6.71008, the required annuity is computed to be $5,000:

$$\text{a} = \frac{\$33{,}550}{6.71008}$$

$$= \$5{,}000$$

Unequal Cash Flows

Many investment situations do not produce equal periodic cash flows. When this occurs, the present value for each cash flow must be determined independently because the annuity table can be used only for equal periodic cash flows. Exhibit 12A.1 is used to determine the present value of each future amount separately. To illustrate, assume that the Atlanta Braves wish to acquire the contract of a popular baseball player who is known to attract large crowds. Management believes this player will return incremental cash flows to the team at the end of each of the next three years in the amounts of $2,500,000, $4,000,000, and $1,500,000. After three years, the player anticipates retiring. If the team's owners require a minimum return of 14% on their investment, how much would they be willing to pay for the player's contract?

To solve this problem, it is necessary to determine the present value of the expected future cash flows. Here we use Exhibit 12A.1 to find the $1 present value factors at 14% for Periods 1, 2, and 3. The cash flows are then multiplied by these factors:

Year	Annual Cash Flow		Present Value of $1 at 14%		Present Value Amount
1	$2,500,000	×	0.87719	=	$2,192,975
2	4,000,000	×	0.76947	=	3,077,880
3	1,500,000	×	0.67497	=	1,012,455
Total					$6,283,310

The total present value of the cash flows for the three years, $6,283,310, represents the maximum amount the team would be willing to pay for the player's contract.

Deferred Returns

Many times, organizations make investments for which they receive no cash until several periods have passed. The present value of an investment discounted at 12% per year, which has a $2,000 return only at the end of Years 4, 5, and 6, can be determined as follows:

Year	Amount		Present Value of $1 at 12%		Present Value Amount
1	$ 0	×	0.89286	=	$ 0
2	0	×	0.79719	=	0
3	0	×	0.71178	=	0
4	2,000	×	0.63552	=	1,271
5	2,000	×	0.56743	=	1,135
6	2,000	×	0.50663	=	1,013
Total					$3,419

Computation of the present value of the deferred annuity can also be performed using the annuity tables if the cash flow amounts are equal for each period. The present value of an annuity for six years minus the present value of an annuity for three years yields the present value of an annuity for Years 4 through 6.

Present value of an annuity for 6 years at 12%: $2,000 × 4.11141 =	$8,223
Present value of an annuity for 3 years at 12%: 2,000 × 2.40183 =	(4,804)
Present value of the deferred annuity	$3,419

Review 12-7 LO7 Performing Present Value Calculations Using the Table Approach

Using the equations and tables in Appendix 12A of this chapter, determine the answers to each of the following independent situations:

a. The future value in two years of $2,000 deposited today in a savings account with interest compounded annually at 6%.

b. The present value of $8,000 to be received in four years, discounted at 12%.

c. The present value of an annuity of $2,000 per year for five years discounted at 14%.

d. An initial investment of $32,010 is to be returned in eight equal annual payments. Determine the amount of each payment if the interest rate is 12%.

e. A proposed investment will provide cash flows of $20,000, $8,000, and $6,000 at the end of Years 1, 2, and 3, respectively. Using a discount rate of 20%, determine the present value of these cash flows.

f. Find the present value of an investment that will pay $5,000 at the end of Years 10, 11, and 12. Use a discount rate of 14%.

Solution on p. 483.

Appendix 12B: Table Approach to Determining Internal Rate of Return

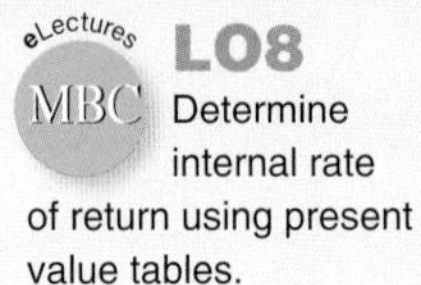

LO8 Determine internal rate of return using present value tables.

We consider the use of present value tables to determine the internal rate of return of a series of cash flows with (1) equal net cash flows after the initial investment and (2) unequal net cash flows after the initial investment.

Equal Cash Inflows

An investment proposal's internal rate of return is easily determined when a single investment is followed by a series of equal annual net cash flows. The general relationship between the initial investment and the equal annual cash inflows is expressed as follows:

$$\textbf{Initial investment} = \textbf{Present value factor for an annuity of \$1} \times \textbf{Annual net cash inflow}$$

Solve for the appropriate present value factor as follows:

$$\textbf{Present value factor for an annuity of \$1} = \frac{\textbf{Initial investment}}{\textbf{Annual net cash inflows}}$$

Once the present value factor is calculated, use Exhibit 12A.2 and go across the row corresponding to the expected life of the project until a table factor equal to or closest to the project's computed present value factor is found. The corresponding percentage for the present value factor is the proposal's internal rate of return. If a table factor does not exactly equal the proposal's present value factor, a more accurate answer can be obtained by interpolation (which is not discussed in this text).

To illustrate, assume that Mobile Taqueria's proposed investment has a zero disinvestment value. Using all information in **Exhibit 12.2** (except that for disinvestment), the proposal's present value factor is 3.15180:

$$\text{Present value factor for an annuity of \$1} = \frac{\text{Initial investment}}{\text{Annual net cash inflows}}$$

$$= \frac{\$94{,}554}{\$30{,}000}$$

$$= 3.15180$$

Using Exhibit 12A.2, go across the row for five periods; the closest table factor is 3.12717, which corresponds to an internal rate of return of 18%.

Unequal Cash Inflows

If periodic cash flows subsequent to the initial investment are unequal, the simple procedure of determining a present value factor and looking up the closest corresponding factor in Exhibit 12A.2 cannot be used. Instead, a trial-and-error approach must be used to determine the internal rate of return.

The first step is to select a discount rate estimated to be close to the proposal's IRR and to compute the proposal's net present value. If the resulting net present value is zero, the selected discount rate is the actual rate of return. However, it is unlikely that the first rate selected will be the proposal's IRR. If the computation results in a positive net present value, the actual IRR is higher than the initially selected rate. In this case, the next step is to compute the proposal's net present value using a higher rate. If the second computation produces a negative net present value, the actual IRR is less than the selected rate. Therefore, the actual IRR is between the first and the second rates. This trial-and-error approach continues until a discount rate is found that equates the proposal's cash inflows and outflows. For Mobile Taqueria's investment proposal outlined in **Exhibit 12.2**, the details of the trial-and-error approach are presented in Exhibit 12B.1.

In Exhibit 12B.1 the first rate produced a negative net present value, indicating that the proposal's IRR is less than 24%. To produce a positive net present value, a smaller rate was selected for the second trial. Since the second rate produced a positive net present value, the proposal's true IRR must be between 16% and 24%. The 20% rate selected for the third trial produced a net present value of $(13) which is approximately zero, indicating that this is the proposal's IRR.

Exhibit 12B.1 Internal Rate of Return with Unequal Cash Flows

First trial with a 24% discount rate

	Predicted Cash Inflows (outflows) (A)	Year(s) of Cash Flows (B)	24% Present Value Factor (C)	Present Value of Cash Flows (A) × (C)
Initial investment	$(94,554)	0	1.00000	$(94,554)
Operation	30,000	1–5	2.74538	82,361
Disinvestment	12,000	5	0.34111	4,093
Net present value of all cash flows				$ (8,100)

Second trial with a 16% discount rate

	Predicted Cash Inflows (outflows) (A)	Year(s) of Cash Flows (B)	16% Present Value Factor (C)	Present Value of Cash Flows (A) × (C)
Initial investment	$(94,554)	0	1.00000	$(94,554)
Operation	30,000	1–5	3.27429	98,229
Disinvestment	12,000	5	0.47611	5,713
Net present value of all cash flows				$ 9,388

Third trial with a 20% discount rate

	Predicted Cash Inflows (outflows) (A)	Year(s) of Cash Flows (B)	20% Present Value Factor (C)	Present Value of Cash Flows (A) × (C)
Initial investment	$(94,554)	0	1.00000	$(94,554)
Operation	30,000	1–5	2.99061	89,718
Disinvestment	12,000	5	0.40188	4,823
Net present value of all cash flows				$ (13)

Review 12-8 LO8 Determining the Internal Rate of Return Using the Table Approach

The internal rate of return is often referred to as the time-adjusted rate of return. It is the discount rate that equates the present value of a project's cash inflows with the present value of the project's cash outflows.

Required

Using the information provided in Review 12-2, determine the internal rate of return of the project using the table approach.

Solution on p. 484.

Guidance Answers

You Are the Vice President of Finance

Pg. 441 There is no single correct response to this question. It is useful to start by learning how other companies in similar circumstances handle capital expenditure decisions. This might be done through personal contacts or through professional organizations, such as the Financial Executives Institute. Another starting point might be the formation of a small capital budgeting committee, which could be expanded as necessary once formal procedures were in place. Early tasks of the committee might include developing guidelines for the size of expenditures at various organizational levels subject to committee review and developing guidelines for the criteria used in formal reviews. You would want to ensure that the CEO is in agreement with these proposals. If the company has a board of directors, you would also want some mutual understanding of the board's role in the approval of capital expenditures. Finally, you would want to make clear the importance of a post-audit review.

Key Ratios

$$\text{Cost of equity capital} = \frac{\text{Current annual dividend per common share}}{\text{Current market price per common share}} + \text{Expected dividend growth rate}$$

$$\text{Payback period} = \frac{\text{Initial investment}}{\text{Annual operating cash inflows}}$$

$$\text{Accounting rate of return on initial investment} = \frac{\text{Average annual increase in net income}}{\text{Initial investment}}$$

$$\text{Accounting rate of return on average investment} = \frac{\text{Average annual increase in net income}}{\text{Average investment}}$$

$$\text{Depreciation tax shield} = \text{Depreciation} \times \text{Tax rate}$$

$$fv = pv(1 + i)n$$

Where: fv = future value amount, pv = present value amount, i = interest rate per period, n = number of periods.

$$pv = \frac{fv}{(1+i)^n}$$

Where: fv = future value amount, pv = present value amount, i = interest rate per period, n = number of periods.

$$pva = \frac{a}{i} \times \left[1 - \frac{1}{(1+i)^n}\right]$$

Where: pva = present value of an annuity, i = prevailing rate per period, n = number of periods, a = annuity amount.

$$\text{Present value factor for an annuity of \$1} = \frac{\text{Initial investment}}{\text{Annual net cash flows}}$$

Key Terms

accounting rate of return 448
annuity 461
capital budgeting 438
capital expenditures 438
cost of capital 446
depreciation tax shield 456
discount rate 444
future value 459
internal rate of return (IRR) 444
investment tax credit 459
net present value 444
payback period 447
present value 460
time-adjusted rate of return 444

Multiple Choice

1. Which of the following statements is not a characteristic of an effective capital budgeting process?
   a. Requires an adjustment to make cash flows comparable when they are expected to occur at different points in time.
   b. Develops implementation plans for approved projects.
   c. All projects should be required to go through formal review of a capital budgeting committee.
   d. Conducts a post audit review to assign responsibility and improve future planning.

Use Exhibits 12A.1 and 12A.2 in Appendix 12A to answer questions 2, 3, and 4.

2. Max is considering an investment proposal that requires an initial investment of $91,100, has predicted cash inflows of $30,000 per year for four years and no salvage value. At a discount rate of 10% the projects net present value is
   a. $3,996
   b. $20,486
   c. $24,486
   d. $95,096

3. The internal rate of return of the investment proposal presented in question 2 is
   a. 8%
   b. 10%
   c. 12%
   d. Less than 8%

4. The Pepper Shop is evaluating a capital expenditure proposal with the following predicted cash flows:

Initial investment	$(40,000)
Operations, each year for four years	15,000
Salvage	5,000

At a discount rate of 12%, the project's net present value is
   a. $2,383
   b. $5,560
   c. $8,738
   d. $20,740

5. The payback period of the investment proposal presented in question 4 is
   a. 0.37 years
   b. 0.50 years
   c. 2.00 years
   d. 2.67 years

6. The accounting rate of return on the initial investment presented in question 4 is
   a. 0.125
   b. 0.156
   c. 0.219
   d. 0.375

Multiple Choice Answers
1. c **2.** a **3.** c **4.** c **5.** d **6.** b **7.** c **8.** c **9.** b **10.** c

7. Each of the following statements is true regarding capital budgeting decisions, except
   a. Capital expenditure proposals involve risk.
   b. A common error is to invest in unnecessary or overly complex equipment.
   c. Capital budgeting models cannot be relied on when a project is projected to have cash flows over a period of time greater than three years.
   d. When a number of activities drive manufacturing overhead costs, estimates of overhead cost based on a single activity driver can significantly overestimate cost savings.

8. For a typical $120,000 investment in equipment with a five-year life and no salvage value, determine the present value of the tax shield using straight-line depreciation. Assume an income tax rate of 21% and a discount rate of 16%.
   a. $24,000
   b. $8,400
   c. $16,502
   d. $30,511

9. Compute the present value of an investment at 10% per year, which has a $3,000 return only at the end of Years 3, 4, and 5.
   a. $11,372
   b. $6,166
   c. $16,579
   d. $13,066

10. Assume that the Yogurt Shoppe has a proposed investment of $68,500 with a zero disinvestment value. The life of the investment is expected to be five years and the annual net cash inflows are expected to be $20,000. Determine the investment proposal's IRR using the tables in Appendix 12A.
   a. 18%
   b. 16%
   c. 14%
   d. 12%

Questions

Q12-1. What is the relationship between long-range planning and capital budgeting?

Q12-2. What tasks are often assigned to the capital budgeting committee?

Q12-3. What purposes are served by a post-audit of approved capital expenditure proposals?

Q12-4. Into what three phases are a project's cash flows organized?

Q12-5. State three alternative definitions or descriptions of the internal rate of return.

Q12-6. Why is the cost of capital an important concept when discounting models are used for capital budgeting?

Q12-7. What weakness is inherent in the payback period when it is used as the sole investment criterion?

Q12-8. What weakness is inherent in the accounting rate of return when it is used as an investment criterion?

Q12-9. Why are the net present value and the internal rate of return models superior to the payback period and the accounting rate of return models?

Q12-10. State two basic differences between the net present value and the internal rate of return models that often lead to differences in the evaluation of competing investment proposals.

Q12-11. Identify several nonquantitative factors that are apt to play a decisive role in the final selection of projects for capital expenditures.

Q12-12. In what way does depreciation affect the analysis of cash flows for a proposed capital expenditure?

Assignments with the logo in the margin are available in myBusinessCourse.
See the Preface of the book for details.

Mini Exercises

M12-13. Time Value of Money: Basics

LO2, 7

Using the equations and tables in Appendix 12A of this chapter, determine the answers to each of the following independent situations:

a. The future value in two years of $5,000 deposited today in a savings account with interest compounded annually at 4%.
b. The present value of $15,000 to be received in four years, discounted at 10%.
c. The present value of an annuity of $2,500 per year for five years discounted at 12%.
d. An initial investment of $69,845 is to be returned in eight equal annual payments. Determine the amount of each payment if the interest rate is 8%.
e. A proposed investment will provide cash flows of $20,000, $25,000, and $30,000 at the end of Years 1, 2, and 3, respectively. Using a discount rate of 6%, determine the present value of these cash flows.
f. Find the present value of an investment that will pay $3,000 at the end of Years 10, 11, and 12. Use a discount rate of 8%.

M12-14. Time Value of Money: Basics

LO2, 7

Using the equations and tables in Appendix 12A of this chapter, determine the answers to each of the following independent situations:

a. The future value in three years of $8,900 invested today in a certificate of deposit with interest compounded annually at 6%.
b. The present value of $12,000 to be received in five years, discounted at 6%.
c. The present value of an annuity of $25,000 per year for four years discounted at 8%.
d. An initial investment of $66,200 is to be returned in six equal annual payments. Determine the amount of each payment if the interest rate is 10%.
e. A proposed investment will provide cash flows of $10,000, $7,500, and $5,000 at the end of Years 1, 2, and 3, respectively. Using a discount rate of 14%, determine the present value of these cash flows.
f. Find the present value of an investment that will pay $15,000 at the end of Years 8, 9, and 10. Use a discount rate of 16%.

M12-15. NPV and IRR: Equal Annual Net Cash Inflows

LO2, 8

Kailey James Company is evaluating a capital expenditure proposal that requires an initial investment of $30,723, has predicted cash inflows of $5,000 per year for 10 years, and has no salvage value.

Required

a. Using a discount rate of 8%, determine the net present value of the investment proposal.
b. Determine the proposal's internal rate of return. (Refer to Appendix 12B if you use the table approach.)
c. What discount rate would produce a net present value of zero?

M12-16. NPV and IRR: Equal Annual Net Cash Inflows

LO2, 8
Spotify Technology SA (SPOT)

Assume Spotify is evaluating a capital expenditure proposal that requires an initial investment of $294,800, has predicted cash inflows of $67,750 per year for six years, and has no salvage value.

Required

a. Using a discount rate of 12%, determine the net present value of the investment proposal.
b. Determine the proposal's internal rate of return. (Refer to Appendix 12B if you use the table approach.)
c. What discount rate would produce a net present value of zero?

LO3 **M12-17. Payback Period and Accounting Rate of Return: Equal Annual Operating Cash Flows without Disinvestment**

Juliana is considering an investment proposal with the following cash flows:

Initial investment—depreciable assets	$74,250
Net cash inflows from operations (per year for 5 years)	16,500
Disinvestment	0

Required

a. Determine the payback period.
b. Determine the accounting rate of return on initial investment.
c. Determine the accounting rate of return on average investment.

LO3 **M12-18. Payback Period and Accounting Rate of Return: Equal Annual Operating Cash Flows with Disinvestment**

Minn is considering an investment proposal with the following cash flows:

Initial investment—depreciable assets	$227,500
Net cash inflows from operations (per year for 10 years)	32,500
Disinvestment—depreciable assets	22,750

Required

a. Determine the payback period.
b. Determine the accounting rate of return on initial investment.
c. Determine the accounting rate of return on average investment.

LO3 **M12-19. Payback Period and Accounting Rate of Return: Equal Annual Operating Cash Flows with Disinvestment**

Roopali is considering an investment proposal with the following cash flows:

Initial investment—depreciable assets	$100,000
Initial investment—working capital	20,000
Net cash inflows from operations (per year for 5 years)	24,000
Disinvestment—depreciable assets	20,000
Disinvestment—working capital	20,000

Required

a. Determine the payback period.
b. Determine the accounting rate of return on initial investment.
c. Determine the accounting rate of return on average investment.

Exercises

LO2, 8 **E12-20. NPV and IRR: Unequal Annual Net Cash Inflows**

Goodrich Petroleum Corporation (GDP)

Assume that Goodrich Petroleum Corporation is evaluating a capital expenditure proposal that has the following predicted cash flows:

Initial investment	$(160,000)
Operation	
Year 1	42,000
Year 2	95,000
Year 3	65,000
Salvage	0

Required

a. Using a discount rate of 10%, determine the net present value of the investment proposal.

b. Determine the proposal's internal rate of return. (Refer to Appendix 12B if you use the table approach.) *Hint:* You will need to use a trial-and-error approach.

E12-21. NPV and IRR: Unequal Annual Net Cash Inflows LO2, 8

Rocky Road Company is evaluating a capital expenditure proposal that has the following predicted cash flows:

Initial investment	$(85,000)
Operation	
Year 1	30,500
Year 2	60,000
Year 3	31,000
Salvage	0

Required

a. Using a discount rate of 12%, determine the net present value of the investment proposal.

b. Determine the proposal's internal rate of return. (Refer to Appendix 12B if you use the table approach.) *Hint:* You will need to use a trial-and-error approach.

E12-22. Payback Period, IRR, and Minimum Cash Flows LO2, 3, 8

The management of Mohawk Limited is currently evaluating the following investment proposal:

	Time 0	Year 1	Year 2	Year 3	Year 4
Initial investment	$210,000	—	—	—	—
Net operating cash inflows	—	$70,000	$70,000	$70,000	$70,000

Required

a. Determine the proposal's payback period.

b. Determine the proposal's internal rate of return. (Refer to Appendix 12B if you use the table approach.)

c. Given the amount of the initial investment, determine the minimum annual net cash inflows required to obtain an internal rate of return of 14%.

E12-23. Time-Adjusted Cost-Volume-Profit Analysis LO2, 3 The Hershey Company (HSY)

Assume The Hershey Company is considering the desirability of producing a new chocolate candy called Pleasure Bombs. Before purchasing the new equipment required to manufacture Pleasure Bombs, the company performed the following analysis:

Unit selling price	$2.50
Variable manufacturing and selling costs	(1.85)
Unit contribution margin	$0.65
Annual fixed costs	
Depreciation (straight-line for 5 years)	$ 62,000
Other (all cash)	48,500
Total	$110,500
Annual break-even sales volume = $110,500 ÷ $0.65 = 170,000 units	

Because the expected annual sales volume is 200,000 units, Hershey decided to undertake the production of Pleasure Bombs. This required an immediate investment of $310,000 in equipment that has a life of four years and no salvage value. After four years, the production of Pleasure Bombs will be discontinued.

Required

a. Evaluate the analysis performed by the company.

b. If Hershey has a time value of money of 8%, should it make the investment with projected annual sales of 200,000 units?

c. Considering the time value of money, what annual unit sales volume is required to break even?

LO6 **E12-24. Time-Adjusted Cost-Volume-Profit Analysis with Income Taxes**

Assume the same facts as given in Exercise E12-23 for Hershey.

Required

With a 20% tax rate and a 8% time value of money, determine the annual unit sales required to break even on a time-adjusted basis. Assume straight-line depreciation is used to determine tax payments.

LO2, 3 **E12-25. Payback Period and IRR of a Cost Reduction Proposal—Differential Analysis**

A light-emitting diode (LED) is a semiconductor diode that emits narrow-spectrum light. Although relatively expensive when compared to incandescent bulbs, they use significantly less energy and last six to ten times longer, with a slow decline in performance rather than an abrupt failure.

Metropolitan City currently has 40,000 incandescent bulbs in traffic lights at approximately 6,000 intersections. It is estimated that replacing all the incandescent bulbs with LEDs will cost $17.7 million. However, the investment is also estimated to save the city $4.42 million per year in energy costs.

Required

a. Determine the payback period of converting Metropolitan City traffic lights to LEDs.
b. If the average life of an incandescent streetlight is one year and the average life of an LED street-light is seven years, should the city finance the investment in LEDs at an interest rate of 5% per year? Justify your answer.

LO2, 3, 5 **E12-26. Payback Period and NPV of a Cost Reduction Proposal—Differential Analysis**

Hermione decided to purchase a new automobile. Being concerned about environmental issues, she is leaning toward the hybrid rather than the gasoline only model. Nevertheless, as a new business school graduate, she wants to determine if there is an economic justification for purchasing the hybrid, which costs $2,200 more than the regular model. She has determined that city/highway combined gas mileage of the hybrid and regular models are 40 and 30 miles per gallon respectively. Hermione anticipates she will travel an average of 15,000 miles per year for the next several years.

Required

a. Determine the payback period of the incremental investment if gasoline costs $2.60 per gallon.
b. Assuming that Hermione plans to keep the car about six years and does not believe there will be a trade-in premium associated with the hybrid model, determine the net present value of the incremental investment at 6% time value of money.
c. Determine the cost of gasoline required for a payback period of four years.
d. At $4.00 per gallon, determine the gas mileage required for a payback period of four years.

LO2, 3, 5 **E12-27. Payback Period and NPV of Alternative Automobile Purchase**

Homework MBC

Wendy Li decided to purchase a new Honda Accord. Being concerned about environmental issues, she is leaning toward a Honda Accord Hybrid rather than the completely gasoline-powered LX model. Nevertheless, she wants to determine if there is an economic justification for purchasing the Hybrid, which costs $2,000 more than the LX. Based on a mix of city and highway driving, she predicts that the average gas mileage of each car is 48 MPG for the Hybrid and 30 MPG for the LX. Wendy also anticipates she will drive an average of 15,000 miles per year and that gasoline will cost an average of $2.50 per gallon over the next four years. She also plans to replace whichever car she purchases at the end of four years when the resale values of the Hybrid and the LX are predicted to be $12,500 and $9,000 respectively.

Required

a. Determine the payback period of the incremental investment associated with purchasing the Hybrid.
b. Determine the net present value of the incremental investment associated with purchasing the Hybrid at a 8% time value of money.
c. Determine the cost of gasoline required for a payback period of two and a half years on the incremental investment.
d. Identify other factors Wendy should consider before making her decision.

Problems

P12-28. Ranking Investment Proposals: Payback Period, Accounting Rate of Return, and Net Present Value LO2, 3, 4

Presented is information pertaining to the cash flows of three mutually exclusive investment proposals:

	Proposal A	Proposal B	Proposal C
Initial investment	$100,000	$100,000	$100,000
Cash flow from operations			
Year 1	60,000	25,000	110,000
Year 2	40,000	40,000	—
Year 3	35,000	70,000	—
Disinvestment	0	0	0
Life (years)	3 years	3 years	1 year

Required

a. Rank these investment proposals using the payback period, the accounting rate of return on initial investment, and the net present value criteria. Assume that the organization's cost of capital is 12% and that all investments are in depreciable assets. Round calculations to four decimal places.

b. Explain the difference in rankings. Which investment would you recommend?

P12-29. Cost Reduction Proposal: IRR, NPV, and Payback Period LO2, 3, 8

PA Chemical currently discharges liquid waste into Pittsburgh's municipal sewer system. However, the Pittsburgh municipal government has informed PA that a surcharge of $6 per thousand cubic liters will soon be imposed for the discharge of this waste. This has prompted management to evaluate the desirability of treating its own liquid waste.

A proposed system consists of three elements. The first is a retention basin, which would permit unusual discharges to be held and treated before entering the downstream system. The second is a continuous self-cleaning rotary filter required where solids are removed. The third is an automated neutralization process required where materials are added to control the alkalinity-acidity range.

The system is designed to process 700,000 liters a day. However, management anticipates that only about 350,000 liters of liquid waste would be processed in a normal workday. The company operates 300 days per year. The initial investment in the system would be $1,500,000, and annual operating costs are predicted to be $280,000. The system has a predicted useful life of 10 years and a salvage value of $100,000.

Required

a. Determine the project's net present value at a discount rate of 14%.

b. Determine the project's approximate internal rate of return. (Refer to Appendix 12B if you use the table approach.)

c. Determine the project's payback period.

P12-30. NPV with Income Taxes: Straight-Line versus Accelerated Depreciation LO2, 6

Carl William, Inc. is a conservatively managed boat company whose motto is, "The old ways are the good ways." Management has always used straight-line depreciation for tax and external reporting purposes. Although they are reluctant to change, they are aware of the impact of taxes on a project's profitability.

Required

For a typical $200,000 investment in equipment with a five-year life and no salvage value, determine the present value of the advantage resulting from the use of double-declining balance depreciation as opposed to straight-line depreciation. Assume an income tax rate of 21% and a discount rate of 20%. Also assume that there will be a switch from double-declining balance to straight-line depreciation in the fourth year.

LO2, 3, 6
United Technologies Corporation (UTX)

P12-31. Payback Period and NPV: Taxes and Straight-Line Depreciation

Assume that United Technologies Corporation is evaluating a proposal to change the company's manual design system to a computer-aided design (CAD) system. The proposed system is expected to save 12,000 design hours per year; an operating cost savings of $65 per hour. The annual cash expenditures of operating the CAD system are estimated to be $600,000. The CAD system requires an initial investment of $200,000. The estimated life of this system is five years with no salvage value. The tax rate is 21%, and United Technologies uses straight-line depreciation for tax purposes. United Technologies has a cost of capital of 14%.

Required

a. Compute the annual after-tax cash flows related to the CAD project.
b. Compute each of the following for the project:
1. Payback period.
2. Net present value.

LO6

P12-32. NPV: Taxes and Accelerated Depreciation

Assume the same facts as given in P12-31, except that management intends to use double-declining balance depreciation with a switch to straight-line depreciation (applied to any undepreciated balance) starting in Year 4.

Required

Determine the project's net present value.

LO2
Mitsubishi Chemical Holdings Corporation (MTLHY)

P12-33. NPV Total and Differential Analysis of Replacement Decision

Assume Mitsubishi Chemical is evaluating a proposal to purchase a new compressor that would cost $200,000 and have a salvage value of $20,000 in five years. Mitsubishi's cost of capital is 16%. It would provide annual operating cash savings of $22,500, as follows:

	Old Compressor	New Compressor
Salaries	$60,000	$75,000
Supplies	12,000	7,500
Utilities	23,000	15,000
Cleaning and maintenance	35,000	10,000
Total cash expenditures	$130,000	$107,500

If the new compressor is purchased, Mitsubishi will sell the old compressor for its current salvage value of $60,000. If the new compressor is not purchased, the old compressor will be disposed of in five years at a predicted scrap value of $6,000. The old compressor's present book value is $85,000. If kept, the old compressor will require repairs one year from now predicted to cost $75,000.

Required

a. Use the total cost approach to evaluate the alternatives of keeping the old compressor and purchasing the new compressor. Indicate which alternative is preferred.
b. Use the differential cost approach to evaluate the desirability of purchasing the new compressor.

LO2
Pinstripes Cleaning and Restoration

Homework MBC

P12-34. NPV Total and Differential Analysis of Replacement Decision

Assume Pinstripes Cleaning and Restoration, near Dallas, Texas, must either have a complete overhaul of its current dry-cleaning system or purchase a new one. Its cost of capital is 16%. The following cost projections have been developed:

	Old System	New System
Purchase cost (new)	$85,000	$90,000
Remaining book value	17,000	
Overhaul needed	25,000	
Annual cash operating costs	60,850	40,200
Current salvage value	12,000	
Salvage value in 5 years	4,500	10,000

If Pinstripes keeps the old system, it will have to be overhauled immediately. With the overhaul, the old system will have a useful life of five more years.

Required

a. Use the total cost approach to evaluate the alternatives of keeping the old system and purchasing the new system. Indicate which alternative is preferred.

b. Use the differential cost approach to evaluate the desirability of purchasing the new system.

P12-35. NPV Differential Analysis of Replacement Decision LO2, 5

The management of Dusseldorf Manufacturing Company is currently evaluating a proposal to purchase a new, innovative drill press as a replacement for a less efficient piece of similar equipment, which would then be sold. The cost of the equipment, including delivery and installation, is $320,000. If the equipment is purchased, Dusseldorf will incur a $10,000 cost in removing the present equipment and revamping service facilities. The present equipment has a book value of $150,000 and a remaining useful life of 10 years. Because of new technical improvements that have made the present equipment obsolete, it now has a disposal value of only $70,500. Management has provided the following comparison of manufacturing costs:

	Present Equipment	New Equipment
Annual production (units)	500,000	500,000
Annual costs		
Direct labor (per unit)	$0.15	$0.08
Overhead		
Depreciation (10% of asset's book value)	$15,000	$32,000
Other	$84,600	$42,500

Additional information follows:

- Management believes that if the current equipment is not replaced now, it will have to wait 10 years before replacement is justifiable.
- Both pieces of equipment are expected to have a negligible salvage value at the end of 10 years.
- Management expects to sell the entire annual production of 500,000 units.
- Dusseldorf's cost of capital is 14%.

Required

Evaluate the desirability of purchasing the new equipment.

Cases and Projects

C12-36. Payback, ARR, and IRR: Evaluating the Sale of Government Assets (Requires Spreadsheet) LO2, 3, 5 Morgan Stanley (MS)

In 2008 the City of Chicago agreed to lease 35,000 parking meters to a Morgan Stanley–led partnership for a one-time sum of $1.15 billion. The lease has been criticized as an example of "one-shot" deals arrived at behind closed doors to balance a current budget at the expense of future generations. Some have observed that deals such as this are akin to individuals using their retirement savings to meet current needs, instead of planning for the future. "These deals are rarely done under the light of public scrutiny," says Richard G. Little, director of the Keston Institute for Public Finance at the University of Southern California. "Often the facts come out long after the deal is done."

Since the lease was signed, helped by parking-fee hikes, the partnership has earned a profit before taxes and depreciation of $0.80 per dollar of revenue. In 2010, total revenues over the 75-year life of the lease were projected to be $11.6 billion.

Defending the city's action, Gene Saffold, Chicago's chief financial officer, stated that "The concession agreement was absolutely the best deal for Chicagoans. ... The net present value of $11.6 billion in revenue over the life of the 75-year agreement is consistent with $1.15 billion.[1]

Required

Evaluate the 75-year lease and determine if the projected revenues are consistent with the initial investment. To simplify your analysis, assume equal revenues and operating costs in all periods, no investment required in working capital, and no salvage value at the end of the lease. Use a corporate tax rate of 34% (in effect in 2008) in your calculations. Suggested elements of your solution include the following:

a. Determine the payback period in the absence of taxes.

b. Determine the accounting rate of return on the initial investment in the absence of taxes.

[1] "Windfall for Investors, A Loss for the Windy City," *Bloomberg Businessweek*, August 29, 2010, pp. 44-45; Ianthe Jeanne Dugan, "Facing Budget Gaps, Cities Sell Parking, Airports, Zoo," *Wall Street Journal*, August 23, 2010, pp. A1, A12.

c. Determine the accounting rate of return on the initial investment using 34% as the tax rate.
d. Determine the internal rate of return in the absence of taxes.
e. Determine the internal rate of return using 34% as the tax rate.
f. Summary of analysis and conclusions.

LO2, 5 C12-37. **Determining Terms of Automobile Leases (Requires Spreadsheet)**

Avant-Garde Motor Company has asked you to develop lease terms for the firm's popular Avant-Garde Challenger, which has an average selling price (new) of $25,000. You know that leasing is attractive because it assists consumers in obtaining new vehicles with a small down payment and "reasonable" monthly payments. Market analysts have told you that to attract the widest number of young professionals, the Challenger must have an initial down payment of no more than $500, monthly payments of no more than $400, and lease terms of no more than five years. When the lease expires, Avant-Garde will sell the used Challengers at the automobile's resale market price at that time. It is difficult to predict the future price of the increasingly popular Challenger, but you have obtained the following information on the average resale prices of used Challengers:

Age	Resale Price
1 year	$21,000
2 years	18,000
3 years	17,000
4 years	15,500
5 years	13,000

Avant-Garde's cost of capital is 12% per year, or 1% per month.

Required

a. With the aid of spreadsheet software, develop a competitive and profitable lease payment program. Assuming a $500 down payment, calculate the program's monthly payments for two-, three-, four-, and five-year leases. Assume the down payment and the first lease payment are made immediately and that all subsequent lease payments are made at the start of the month. [*Hint:* Most software packages include a function such as the following: PMT (rate,nper,pv,fv,type), where rate = the time value of money; nper = the number of periods; pv = the present value; fv = the future value; and type = 0 (when the payment is at the end of the period) or 1 (when the payment is at the beginning of the period). For monthly payments, rate should be set at the annual rate divided by 12, and npr should be set at the number of months in the lease. Here, fv is the residual value.]
b. Reevaluate the lease program assuming a down payment of $1,000.
c. Reevaluate the lease program assuming a down payment of $500 and a $1,000 increase in residual values.
d. Reevaluate the lease program assuming a down payment of $1,000 and a $1,000 increase in residual values.
e. What is your final recommendation? What risks are associated with your recommendation? Are there any other actions to consider?

LO3, 5 C12-38. **Evaluating Data and Using Payback Period for an Investment Proposal**

To determine the desirability of investing in a larger computer monitor (as opposed to the typical monitor that comes with a new personal computer), researchers developed an experiment testing the time required to perform a set of tasks. The tasks included the following:

- Setting up a meeting using electronic mail.
- Reviewing meeting requests.
- Checking an online schedule.
- Embedding a video file into a document.
- Searching a customer database to find a specific set of contracts.
- Copying a database into a spreadsheet.
- Modifying a slide presentation.

The researchers assumed this was a typical set of tasks performed by a manager. They determined that there was a 9% productivity gain using the larger monitor. One test manager commented that the largest productivity gain came from being able to have multiple applications open at the same time and from being able to view several files at once.

Required

Accepting the 9% productivity gain as accurate, what additional information is needed to determine the payback period of an investment in a larger monitor that is to be used by a manager? Make any necessary assumptions and obtain whatever data you can (perhaps from computer component advertisements) to determine the payback period for the proposed investment.

C12-39. IRR and NPV with Performance Evaluation Conflict **LO2, 4, 5, 8**

Pepperoni Pizza Company owns and operates fast-service pizza parlors throughout North America. The firm operates on a regional basis and provides almost complete autonomy to the manager of each region. Regional managers are responsible for long-range planning, capital expenditures, personnel policies, pricing, and so forth. Each year the performance of regional managers is evaluated by determining the accounting return on fixed assets in their regions; a return of 16% is expected. To determine this return, regional net income is divided by the book value of fixed assets at the start of the year. Managers of regions earning a return of more than 18% are identified for possible promotion, and managers of regions with a return of less than 14% are subject to replacement.

Mr. Light, with a degree in hotel and restaurant management, is the manager of the Northeast region. He is regarded as a "rising star" and will be considered for promotion during the next two years. Light has been with Pepperoni for a total of three years. During that period, the return on fixed assets in his region (the oldest in the firm) has increased dramatically. He is currently considering a proposal to open five new parlors in the Boston area. The total project involves an investment of $1,000,000 and will double the number of Pepperoni pizzas sold in the Northeast region to a total of 600,000 per year. At an average price of $9 each, total sales revenue will be $5,400,000.

The expenses of operating each of the new parlors include variable costs of $5 per pizza and fixed costs (excluding depreciation) of $175,000 per year. Because each of the new parlors has only a five-year life and no salvage value, yearly straight-line depreciation will be $40,000 [($1,000,000 ÷ 5 parlors) ÷ 5 years].

Required

a. Evaluate the desirability of the $1,000,000 investment in new pizza parlors by computing the internal rate of return and the net present value. Assume a time value of money of 16%. (Refer to Appendix 12B if you use the table approach.)

b. If Light is shrewd, will he approve the expansion? Why or why not? (Additional computations are suggested.)

C12-40. NPV and Project Reevaluation with Taxes, Straight-Line Depreciation **LO2, 5, 6**

Last year, the Bayside Chemical Company prepared the following analysis of an investment proposal for a new manufacturing facility:

	Predicted Cash Inflows (outflows) (A)	Year(s) of Cash Flows (B)	12% Present Value Factor (C)	Present Value of Cash Flows (A) × (C)
Initial investment				
Fixed assets	$(810,000)	0	1.00000	$ (810,000)
Working capital	(100,000)	0	1.00000	(100,000)
Operations				
Annual taxable income without depreciation	310,000	1–5	3.60478	1,117,482
Taxes on income ($310,000 × 0.21)	(65,100)	1–5	3.60478	(234,671)
Depreciation tax shield	34,020*	1–5	3.60478	122,635
Disinvestment				
Site restoration	80,000	5	0.56743	(45,394)
Tax shield of restoration ($80,000 × 0.21)	16,800	5	0.56743	9,533
Working capital	100,000	5	0.56743	56,743
Net present value of all cash flows				$ 116,328

*Computation of depreciation tax shield:

Annual straight-line depreciation ($810,000 ÷ 5)	*$162,000*
Tax rate	*× 0.21*
Depreciation tax shield	*$ 34,020*

Because the proposal had a positive net present value when discounted at Bayside's cost of capital of 12%, the project was approved; all investments were made at the end of the year. Shortly after production began this year, a government agency notified Bayside of required additional expenditures totaling

$300,000 to bring the plant into compliance with new federal emission regulations. Bayside has the option either to comply with the regulations by the end of the year, or to sell the entire operation (fixed assets and working capital) for $350,000. The improvements will be depreciated over the remaining four-year life of the plant using straight-line depreciation. The cost of site restoration will not be affected by the improvements. If Bayside elects to sell the plant, any book loss can be treated as an offset against taxable income on other operations. This tax reduction is an additional cash benefit of selling.

Required

a. Should Bayside sell the plant or comply with the new federal regulations? To simplify calculations, assume that any additional improvements are paid for on the last day of the current year.

b. Would Bayside have accepted the proposal at the beginning of the year if it had been aware of the forthcoming federal regulations?

c. Do you have any suggestions that might increase the project's net present value? (No calculations are required.)

LO1, 2, 5 **C12-41. Post-Audit and Reevaluation of Investment Proposal: NPV**

Anthony Company's capital budgeting committee is evaluating a capital expenditure proposal for the production of a high-definition television receiver to be sold as an add-on feature for personal computers. The proposal calls for an independent contractor to construct the necessary facilities by December 31 of the current year at a total cost of $350,000. Payment for all construction costs will be made on that date. An additional $75,000 in cash will also be made available on December 31of the current year, for working capital to support sales and production activities.

Management anticipates that the receiver has a limited market life; there is a high probability that within six years all new PCs will have built-in high-definition receivers. Accordingly, the proposal specifies that production will cease after six years. The investment in working capital will be recovered on that date, and the production facilities will be sold for $80,000. Predicted net cash inflows from operations for the next six years are as follows:

20X1	$125,000
20X2	125,000
20X3	125,000
20X4	60,000
20X5	60,000
20X6	60,000

Anthony Company has a time value of money of 14%. For capital budgeting purposes, all cash flows are assumed to occur at the end of each year.

Required

a. Evaluate the capital expenditure proposal using the net present value method. Should Anthony accept the proposal?

b. Assume that the capital expenditure proposal is accepted, but construction delays caused by labor problems and difficulties in obtaining the necessary construction permits delay the completion of the project. Payments totaling $250,000 were made to the construction company on December 31 of the current year. However, completion is now scheduled for December 31, 20X1, and an additional $150,000 will be required to complete construction. If the project is continued, the additional $150,000 will be paid at the end of 20X1, and the plant will begin operations on January 1, 20X2.

Because of the cost overruns, the capital budgeting committee requests a reevaluation of the project, before agreeing to any additional expenditures. After much effort, the following revised predictions of net operating cash inflows are developed:

20X2	$150,000
20X3	125,000
20X4	60,000
20X5	60,000
20X6	60,000

The working capital investment and disinvestment and the plant salvage values have not changed, except that the cash for working capital would now be made available on December 31, 20X1. Use the net present value method to reevaluate the initial decision to accept the proposal. Given the information currently available about the project, should it have been accepted? (*Hint:* Determine the net present value as of December 31 of the current year assuming management has not committed Anthony to the proposal.)

c. Given the situation that exists in early 20X1, should management continue or cancel the project? Assume that the facilities have a current salvage value of $95,000. (*Hint:* Assume that the decision is being made on January 1, 20X1.)

C12-42. Post-Audit and Reevaluation of Investment Proposal: IRR **LO1, 2, 5**

Throughout his four years in college, Ronald King worked at the local Beef Burger Restaurant in College City. Although the working conditions were good and the pay was not bad, Ron believed he could do a much better job of managing the restaurant than the current owner-manager. In particular, Ron believed that the proper use of marketing campaigns and sales incentives, such as selling a second burger for a 25% discount, could increase annual sales by 40%.

Just before graduation Ron inherited $600,000 from his great uncle. He seriously considered buying the restaurant. It seemed like a good idea because he liked the town and its college atmosphere, knew the business, and always wanted to work for himself. He also knew that the current owner wanted to sell the restaurant and retire to Florida. As part of a small business management course, Ron developed the following income statement for the restaurant's prior year operations:

BEEF BURGER RESTAURANT: COLLEGE CITY Income Statement For Prior Year Ended December 31		
Sales		$495,000
Expenses		
Cost of food	$165,000	
Supplies	22,000	
Employee expenses	154,000	
Utilities	30,800	
Property taxes	22,000	
Insurance	11,000	
Advertising	8,800	
Depreciation	66,000	479,600
Net income		$ 15,400

Ron believed that the cost of food and supplies were all variable, the employee expenses and utilities were one-half variable and one-half fixed last year, and all other expenses were fixed. If Ron purchased the restaurant and followed through on his plans, he believed there would be a 40% increase in unit sales volume and all variable costs. Of the fixed costs, only advertising would increase by $10,000. The use of discounts and special promotions would, however, limit the increase in sales revenue to only 30% even though sales volume increased 40%.

Required

a. Determine
   1. The current annual net cash inflow.
   2. The predicted annual net cash inflow if Ron executes his plans and his assumptions are correct.

b. Ron believes his plan would produce equal net cash inflows during each of the next 15 years, the period remaining on a long-term lease for the land on which the restaurant is built. At the end of that time, the restaurant would have to be demolished at a predicted net cost of $88,000. Assuming Ron would otherwise invest the money in stock expected to yield 12%, determine the maximum amount he should pay for the restaurant.

c. Assume that Ron accepts an offer from the current owner to buy the restaurant for $450,000. Unfortunately, although the expected increase in sales volume does occur, customers make much more extensive use of the promotions than Ron had anticipated. As a result, total sales revenues are 8% below projections. Furthermore, to improve employee attitudes, Ron gave a 10% raise immediately after purchasing the restaurant. Reevaluate the initial decision using the actual sales revenue and the increase in labor costs, assuming conditions will remain unchanged over the remaining life of the project. Was the investment decision a wise one?

d. Ron can sell the restaurant to a large franchise operator for $350,000. Alternatively, he believes that additional annual marketing expenditures and changes in promotions costing $25,000 per year could bring the sales revenues up to their original projections, with no other changes in costs. Should Ron sell the restaurant or keep it and make the additional expenditures? Assume that Ron has just purchased the restaurant and his original assumptions remain unchanged; however, he immediately gave his employees a 10% raise.

Solutions to Review Problems

Review 12-1—Solution

a. **Capital expenditures**—Investment of financial resources with the expectation it will generate future financial inflows that exceed the initial cost.
b. **Capital budgeting**—Process that involves identifying desirable projects, evaluating proposals, and selecting proposals that meet minimum criteria.
c. **Post audit**—Involves the development of project performance reports comparing planned and actual results.
d. **Capital budgeting**—Concepts and tools that organize information and evaluate alternatives.
e. **Time value of money concept**—Explains why monies received or paid at different points in time must be adjusted to comparable values.
f. **Capital budgeting**—Requires an adjustment to make cash flows comparable when they are expected to occur at different points in time.
g. **Long-Range Planning**—Planning beyond the next budget year.
h. **Post Audit**—Helps the capital budgeting committee do a better job in evaluating new proposals.

Review 12-2—Solution

Basic computations:

Initial investment	
Depreciable assets	$(27,740)
Working capital	(3,000)
Total cash outflow	$(30,740)
Operation	
Cash receipts	$ 25,000
Cash expenditures	(15,000)
Net cash inflow	$ 10,000
Disinvestment	
Sale of depreciable assets	$ 2,000
Recovery of working capital	3,000
Total cash inflow	$ 5,000

a. Net present value at a 10% discount rate:

	Predicted Cash Inflows (outflows) (A)	Year(s) of Cash Flows (B)	10% Present Value Factor (C)	Present Value of Cash Flows (A) × (C)
Initial investment	$(30,740)	0	1.00000	$(30,740)
Operation	10,000	1–4	3.16987	31,699
Disinvestment	5,000	4	0.68301	3,415
Net present value of all cash flows				$ 4,374

b. Internal rate of return:
Using a spreadsheet, the proposal's internal rate of return is readily determined to be 16%:

	A	B
1	Year of cash flow	Cash flow
2	0	$(30,740)
3	1	10,000
4	2	10,000
5	3	10,000
6	4	15,000
7	IRR	0.16

Review 12-3—Solution

Basic computations:

Initial investment	
Depreciable assets	$27,740
Working capital	3,000
Total	$30,740
Operation	
Cash receipts	$25,000
Cash expenditures	(15,000)
Net cash inflow	$10,000
Disinvestment	
Sale of depreciable assets	$ 2,000
Recovery of working capital	3,000
Total	$ 5,000

a. Payback period = $30,740 ÷ $10,000
= 3.074 years

b. Accounting rate of return on initial and average investments:

Annual net cash inflow from operations	$10,000
Less average annual depreciation [($27,740 – $2,000) ÷ 4]	(6,435)
Average annual increase in net income	$ 3,565

Average investment = ($30,740 + $5,000) ÷ 2
= $17,870

Accounting rate of return on initial investment = $\frac{\$\ 3{,}565}{\$30{,}740}$

= 0.1160 or 11.6%

Accounting rate of return on average investment = $\frac{\$\ 3{,}565}{\$17{,}870}$

= 0.1995 or 19.95%

Review 12-4—Solution

a.

	Proposal A	Proposal B	Proposal C
Payback period	2 years	2 years	1 year
Accounting rate of return			
Total increase in income before depreciation	$67,500	$67,500	$45,000
Total depreciation	(45,000)	(45,000)	(45,000)
Total increase in income	$22,500	$22,500	$0
Life in years	÷ 3	÷ 3	÷ 1
Average annual increase in net income	$7,500	$7,500	$0
Initial investment	÷45,000	÷45,000	÷45,000
Accounting rate of return	0.1667	0.1667	0.0

Net present value at 10%:

Year	Factor	Present Values		
		Proposal A	Proposal B	Proposal C
1	0.90909	$36,363.60	$20,454.53	$40,909.05
2	0.82645	4,132.25	18,595.13	
3	0.75131	16,904.48	16,904.48	
Total		57,400.33	55,954.14	40,909.05
Initial investment		(45,000.00)	(45,000.00)	(45,000.00)
Net present value		$12,400.33	$10,954.14	$ (4,090.95)

Rankings:

	Proposal A	Proposal B	Proposal C
Payback	2–3	2–3	1
Accounting rate of return	1–2	1–2	3
Net present value	1	2	3

b. While the accounting rate of return and the net present value criteria consider profitability, payback considers only the time required to recover the investment. Proposal C provides for the shortest payback; hence, it ranks first using the payback criterion even though Proposal C does not provide a profit.

Proposals A and B have identical total cash flows over their lives; hence, they have identical accounting rates of return. However, the timing of their cash flows differs. Because Proposal A has higher early-period cash flows, its net present value is higher than that of Proposal B. Of the three criteria used, only net present value considers both profitability and the timing of cash flows; thus, we would recommend Proposal A.

Review 12-5—Solution

In making the final decision to accept or reject a capital expenditure proposal that has passed the initial screening, nonquantitative factors should also be considered. Very important at this point are management's attitudes toward risk and financing alternatives, their confidence in the professional judgment of managers making investment proposals, their beliefs about the future direction of the economy, and their evaluation of alternative investments.

Specific to Hilltop's investment decision, their management might consider factors such as the following:

- Will new models of the ski lift be available in the next few years that will be more efficient and/or safer?
- How is the economy and do they expect to be able to sustain the number of skiers that they have had in recent years?
- How likely is it that they will see a decline in customers?
- Are there any other revenue-generating uses for the space, such as snowmobile rentals, that might be a better alternative to skiing?

Review 12-6—Solution

a.

Operating cost savings (9,000 hours × $45)	$405,000
Operating costs of CAD/CAM system	(200,000)
Before-tax cash savings	205,000
Income taxes without tax shield at 35%	(71,750)
Depreciation tax shield [($550,000/5 years) × 0.35]	38,500
Relevant annual after-tax cash flow	$171,750

b.

	Design System
Relevant annual after-tax cash flow	$171,750
Present value of annuity (PV(0.14,5,–171750))	589,632
Initial investment	(550,000)
Net present value	$ 39,632

Review 12-7—Solution

a. $fv = pv(1 + r)^n$
$= \$2,000\ (1 + 0.06)^2$
$= \$2,247$

or

$2,000/0.89000 = $2,247

b. pv = $8,000 × 0.63552
= $5,084

c. pva = $2,000 × 3.43308
= $6,866

d. a = $32,010/4.96764
= $ 6,444

e.

Year	Cash Flow		Present Value at 20%		Present Value Amount
1	$20,000	×	0.83333	=	$16,667
2	8,000	×	0.69444	=	5,556
3	6,000	×	0.57870	=	3,472
Total					$25,695

f.

Present value of an annuity for 12 years at 14% ($5,000 × 5.66029)	$28,301
Present value of an annuity for 9 years at 14% ($5,000 × 4.94637)	(24,732)
Present value of the deferred annuity	$ 3,569

or

$5,000 × (5.66029 – 4.94637) = $3,570

Review 12-8—Solution

Based on the solution of Review 12-2, the net present value of this project using a discount rate of 10% is $4,374. Because the proposal has a positive net present value when discounted at 10%, its internal rate of return must be higher than 10%. Through a trial-and-error approach, the internal rate of return is determined to be 16%.

	Predicted Cash Inflows (outflows) (A)	Year(s) of Cash Flows (B)	16% Present Value Factor (C)	Present Value of Cash Flows (A) × (C)
Initial investment.	$(30,740)	0	1.00000	$(30,740)
Operation	10,000	1–4	2.79818	27,982
Disinvestment.	5,000	4	0.55229	2,761
Net present value of all cash flows.				$ 3

Managerial Analysis of Financial Statements

Learning Objectives

LO1 Describe the importance of analyzing financial statements for managers. (p. 488)

LO2 Evaluate factors that influence financial statements and their analysis. (p. 489)

LO3 Specify alternative standards useful in financial statement analysis. Perform vertical and horizontal analysis. (p. 490)

LO4 Explain the analysis of a firm's solvency. (p. 495)

LO5 Explain the analysis of a firm's performance. (p. 498)

General-purpose financial statements are designed to provide information to a large and diverse group of users, including stockholders, creditors, and managers. The objectives of financial statements are broad and, as such, they do not include certain financial measures that specific user groups often need. Through financial statement analysis, however, individual users are able to generate additional useful information and metrics from the statements.

Financial statement analysis is the process of interpreting and evaluating financial statements by using data and disclosures contained in them to produce additional financial measures. Financial statement analysis involves comparing financial statements for the current period with those of previous periods and/or other companies, assessing the internal composition of the financial statements, and measuring relations within and among the financial statements.

The purpose of this appendix is to describe basic measures of financial statement analysis and to consider how managers and others use these measures. For purposes of presentation, assume that the chief financial officer (CFO) of Columbia Corporation is reviewing the publicly available financial statements of Berkeley Inc., a partially-owned subsidiary whose controlling interest is being considered for sale to another conglomerate. The CFO has read several newspaper and magazine articles critical of Berkeley's current operations and its position in the furniture industry. Although Berkeley's sales continue to increase, its profits are relatively flat. This concerns the CFO and she is in the process of gathering additional information about the company and the industry. Her final report will go to the board of directors of Columbia for a decision on the continuation of Berkeley as part of the conglomerate.

Financial statement analysis taps a large amount of useful information that otherwise is not immediately obvious. Credit analysts must evaluate the likelihood that a loan client will make its interest and principal payments on time, stockholders must evaluate the profitability of a firm's assets and the return on investment to various equity holders, and managers must evaluate their overall effectiveness in using the resources entrusted to them by creditors and stockholders.

Two measures often used in financial statement analysis, return on investment (ROI) and residual income, are common to profitability analysis, which was the theme of Chapter 11. Refer to that chapter for a detailed discussion of these measures and how they can also be used for evaluation purposes.

Road Map

LO	Learning Objective I Topics	Page	eLecture	Guided Example	Assignments
LO1	**Describe the importance of analyzing financial statements for managers.** Overall Measure of Performance :: Identify Potential Weaknesses :: Compliance with Lending Agreements :: Outsiders' Perspective	488	eApp A–1	Review App A-1	25
LO2	**Evaluate factors that influence financial statements and their analysis.** Relevant Evaluation Measures :: Alternative Accounting Procedures :: Inflation and Deflation :: Changes in Product Mix	489	eApp A–2	Review App A-2	20, 23, 24
LO3	**Specify alternative standards useful in financial statement analysis. Perform vertical and horizontal analysis.** Financial Measures for a Single Firm :: Comparable Measures for Other Firms :: Budgeted Performance :: Vertical Analysis :: Horizontal Analysis	490	eApp A–3	Review App A-3	21, 26, 27, 28, 29, 30
LO4	**Explain the analysis of a firm's solvency.** Current Ratio :: Working Capital :: Acid Test Ratio :: Inventory Turnover :: Days Sales in Receivables :: Debt-to-Equity Ratio :: Times-Interest-Earned	495	eApp A–4	Review App A-4	15, 16, 19, 20, 22, 23, 25, 27, 28, 29, 30, 31
LO5	**Explain the analysis of a firm's performance.** Asset Turnover :: Return on Sales :: Return on Assets :: Return on Equity :: Earnings per Share	498	eApp A–5	Review App A-5	17, 18, 23, 24, 25, 27, 28, 29, 30, 31

CHAPTER ORGANIZATION

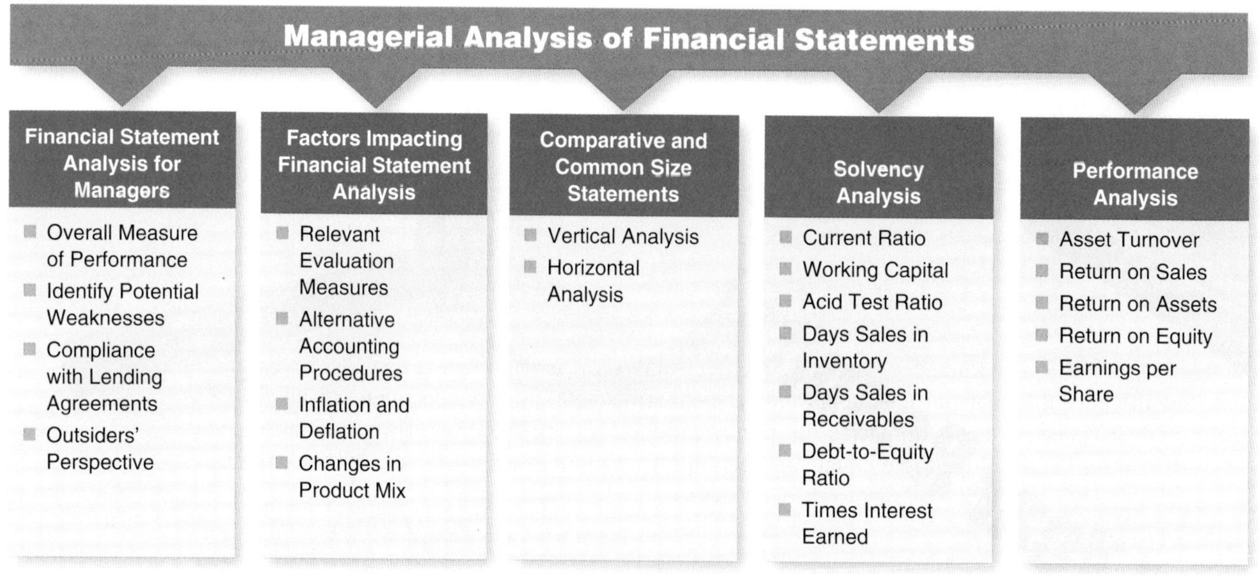

Financial Statement Analysis for Managers

eLectures MBC **LO1** Describe the importance of analyzing financial statements for managers.

One of the most important reasons for managers to analyze their firm's financial statements is to evaluate the overall performance of the firm, especially as seen by those external to the firm. Managers should be aware of total company performance, not just the performance of their particular areas of responsibility. By analyzing the financial statements for the company as a whole, managers gain a perspective on how the organization is performing *and* how it is perceived.

General-purpose financial statements provide the only overall measure of an organization's performance to some managers. The internal reporting system is often limited to reporting component performance, with no report of overall performance provided to managers below the executive level. This reporting limitation excludes many of the financial and nonfinancial sources of information discussed in this book. There is frequently no overall reporting of quality measures, value-added analysis, or activity-based costing between the component level and that of top management.

By evaluating the overall performance of the organization, managers are able to compare their firm with similar firms and to identify potential weaknesses that are worthy of management attention. For example, should managers be alarmed if their firm had a return on equity of 8%, while the industry norm is 15%? There can be good reasons for the below industry-average return; without financial analysis, however, management may not even be aware of the deficiency or the conditions causing it. Since internal reports of other companies are not available, the only basis for making comparisons with those companies is through their external financial statements and other published materials.

Financial analysis is also necessary for managers whose firms have lending agreements that impose financial restrictions on the organization. Analysis of financial statements is often necessary to determine if restrictions are being met. For example, an agreement may require the debt-to-equity ratio to be maintained below a specified level. Failure to comply could result in a call for immediate liquidation of the debt and could damage the firm's credit rating and its ability to obtain borrowed capital in the future.

A more subtle, but no less important, reason for managers to analyze financial statements is to see their firm as outsiders see it. The financial statements are, in effect, the only window through which many outsiders view the firm. By evaluating the firm's financial statements, managers can better understand outsiders' behavior and attitudes toward the firm and thereby develop a more realistic view of the firm.

Explaining the Importance of Financial Statement Analysis by Internal Managers LO1 **Review Appendix A-1**

Financial statement analysis is not only important to stakeholders outside of an organization but also to a company's internal management.

Required

Discuss some of the key reasons why it is important for a company's management to perform financial statement analysis on their own organization.

Solution on p. 513.

Factors Impacting Financial Statement Analysis

eLectures MBC

LO2 Evaluate factors that influence financial statements and their analysis.

Before learning the procedures for financial statement analysis, it is important to consider several factors that influence the financial statements and the evaluation methods. First, no single financial statement analysis measure can summarize the performance of an organization. This is because each analysis measure is developed to evaluate an operating procedure or a specific area of the organization's performance. For example, sales ratios are used to measure various characteristics or conditions of sales. Although sales ratios help evaluate sales, they do not contribute to the analysis of operating expenses. Before drawing conclusions about the financial condition of an organization, the manager should select several evaluation measures that are germane to the organization being evaluated.

Second, the manager must know which alternative accounting procedures the firm uses. Also, if comparing the results with other companies or with industry standards, the manager must know the accounting procedures each uses. Alternative accounting procedures critical for financial statement analysis include methods of depreciation, inventory valuation (cost or lower of cost or market), and inventory cost flow method (FIFO, LIFO, or average costing). Each of these has an impact on various income statement, cash flow statement, and balance sheet amounts.

Third, inflation, or deflation, can distort the comparisons of financial statements between periods because the statements are based on historical dollars, not on dollars of the same value. Allowances must be made for these effects, or the analysis is distorted. To illustrate, assume that Etson Company has 20X2 sales of $100,000 and cost of sales totaling $40,000. During 20X3, when inflation is 5%, the company's selling prices increase by 5%, while its costs have a net increase of only 3% due to inventory available at 20X2 prices. In 20X4, both selling prices and costs go up by 5%. Therefore, the company has an increase in 20X3 gross profit due primarily to inflation of $3,800 and an increase in 20X4 gross profit of $3,190 due solely to inflation.

	20X2	20X3	20X4
Sales	$100,000	$105,000	$110,250
Cost of sales	40,000	41,200	43,260
Gross profit	$ 60,000	$ 63,800	$ 66,990

A manager must be careful to avoid stating that the company has increased operating efficiency when all it did was keep pace with inflation. As a general rule, ignoring inflation produces favorable results when other things remain equal. Inflation can even produce favorable results when actual, constant dollar results are unfavorable. We must remember that external financial statements are presented in historical dollars that have not been adjusted for inflation.

Fourth, changes in the product mix can distort a comparison of financial statements because most products have unique profit margins and their mix influences the firm's profit margin. Assume Blackstar Amplifier sells two types of guitar amplifiers, the Artist and the Core. During 20X4, Blackstar sold 1,000 units of each product; and in 20X5, it sold 850 units of Artist and 1,250 units of Core. The gross profit for Artist is $100 per unit; for Core, it is $70 per unit. Total gross profit for 20X4 and 20X5 follows.

	20X4			20X5		
	Artist	Core	Company	Artist	Core	Company
Gross profit.	$100,000	$70,000	$170,000	$85,000	$87,500	$172,500

Without looking past the total numbers on the financial statements, the analyst might conclude that the company performed better in 20X5 than it did in 20X4. Total sales units went up from 2,000 to 2,100, and profit increased by $2,500. However, when the individual products are analyzed, another opinion might emerge. Although Core had increased unit sales of 25%, Artist, the product with the higher profit per unit, declined 15%. This could signal problems if Artist unit sales continue to decline. For companies with large numbers of products, the changing product mix generally does not have a strong impact. However, companies with only a few products, or with some products that have large profit margins, can have financial results that are difficult to interpret unless the underlying facts are analyzed.

Fifth, changes in organizational structure should be reviewed as part of financial analysis. Today's business environment of mergers, acquisitions, and other changes creates many variations in the financial statements. As organizations are restructured, their accounting procedures change, new information systems are implemented, and many other changes take place that complicate financial analysis.

Review Appendix A-2 LO2 Identifying Factors that Influence Financial Statement Analysis

Patricia Adams was recently hired as a managerial accountant by Blackstar Amplification. Patricia was asked to perform a financial statement analysis of Blackstar and report her results to her manager. Patricia is excited to do the project as she knows how important it is to understand how the organization is performing and how it is perceived.

Required

Review some of the factors that might influence Patricia's evaluation of Blackstar's financial statements.

Solution on p. 513.

Application of Financial Statement Analysis

Evaluative Standards and Benchmarks

eLectures MBC **LO3** Specify alternative standards useful in financial statement analysis. Perform vertical and horizontal analysis.

Information obtained directly from financial statements and analytical measures derived from statements have little usefulness alone. To be interpreted effectively, this information must be evaluated against some standard. Depending on their objectives, managers can use several different standards. The most common financial analysis standards are (1) **vertical analysis**, the restatement of amounts in the current financial statements as a percentage of some base measure such as sales; (2) **horizontal analysis**, the comparison of a firm's current financial measures to those of previous periods; (3) **competitor analysis**, the comparison of a firm's financial measures to similar measures for other firms in the industry or to industry averages; and (4) the comparison of a firm's financial measures to its budgeted measures.

Financial statement analysis often begins with an examination of the relations among various accounts. This is normally performed through vertical analysis, where one account, the base account, is set at 100%, and all other accounts are presented as a percentage of the base account. In an income statement, sales is typically the base account. After all accounts of a given financial statement are converted into percentages, the statement is known as a **common size statement**. Analysis of common size statements is useful for detecting items that are out of line, that deviate from some preset amount, or that are indicative of other problems. Vertical analysis can be improved by combining it with horizontal analysis and reviewing the common size statements of more than one year. Vertical and horizontal analyses are limited in that they involve comparisons of financial measures only for a single firm. If the firm's performance has been poor or mediocre in the past, these standards do not alert management or the analyst to the need for improvements.

Evaluating financial measures against comparable measures for other firms in the same industry is also beneficial to managers, especially to those in competitive industries. Several financial information services (including Dun and Bradstreet, Standard & Poor's, and Moody's) publish averages for commonly used financial measures for all major industries. Failure to perform close to industry norms can signal difficulties in competing with other firms in the future.

When comparing a firm's financial measures with those of other firms, it is necessary to consider any significant differences that might exist among the firms. For example, if one firm is located farther from major suppliers than are other firms in the industry, higher freight costs and possibly lower profits can occur. Differences in accounting practices must also be taken into account in comparing firms; for example, allowances must be made in comparing two firms that use different methods of inventory valuation. Although there are limitations in making intercompany comparisons, looking at other firms' performances is a useful indicator of relative performance.

From management's perspective, the most realistic standard of performance is probably the firm's budgeted performance. Chapter 9 discussed operating budgets and pro forma financial statements, which represent management's most realistic expectations for the period. Managers should compare the analytical measures taken from these statements with the same measures derived from the actual financial statements for the period. For performance evaluation purposes, this comparison is likely to provide managers a useful evaluation of current financial statements.

In addition to the computation of common size statements for vertical and horizontal analysis, financial statement analysis measures include computations that measure the firm's solvency and performance. For a comprehensive analysis of a firm, these measures should be compared to industry norms if available. All of these concepts are illustrated using the 20X2, 20X3, and 20X4 balance sheets and income statements for Berkeley Inc., which are in Exhibit A.1. The only major economic change in Berkeley's operations during this period occurred in 20X4 when it added a new product line. Financial statements for three successive periods are presented because several of the measures require multiple periods or averages. To obtain average information for a period, the beginning and ending balances are summed and divided by 2. Averages computed from values for only two points during the year (beginning and ending) should be used only if monthly or quarterly data are not available. In the following discussions, each analytical measure is presented in general form, along with the measure for Berkeley Inc. All examples use Berkeley 20X4 data unless otherwise noted.

Comparative and Common Size Statements

Converting balance sheets and income statements to common size statements is one of the most direct ways to analyze changes over time. Before the various ratios and account analyses are performed, the manager generally evaluates the income statement and balance sheet using common size statement measures such as sales and total assets. The percentages can also be related to some base period, a month or year, for example. The evaluation of trends in terms of financial statement percentages over time allows for analysis of the underlying movements and shifts in the firm's financial composition.

The percent columns of Exhibit A.1 provide the data needed for this initial evaluation for Berkeley Inc. for 20X4. The computation of common size statements for three to five years allows the manager or analyst to evaluate the activities of the company based on trends of prior periods.

Vertical Analysis

The vertical analysis of the common size statements for Berkeley uses sales from the income statement and total assets from the balance sheet as the bases; these are set at 100%. This analysis helps to identify significant changes that have taken place during the period and to determine whether the changes have favorable or unfavorable impacts on solvency and performance.

For example, in evaluating Berkeley's cash needs, the CFO might not be as concerned with the amount of cash as with the percentage of cash to total assets. For Berkeley, the relation of cash to total assets is approximately 17% in 20X2 and 20X3. The decline to 15.3% in 20X4 could indicate a need to examine the status of cash flows. Before becoming overly concerned with the situation, the CFO would want to compare the status of the 20X4 account balances with the company's guidelines or standards and available industry norms. Just because these items deviate from expectations does not indicate a problem. The deviation might indicate improved cash management or changes in credit sales or credit collection policies. The deviation should not be ignored, however, because it might indicate an undesirable trend leading to future difficulties.

Another useful application of common size balance sheet statements is the determination of where shifts occur within major categories. In current assets, for example, the decline in the percentage of

Exhibit A.1 Comparative Financial Statements

BERKELEY INC.
Comparative Balance Sheets with Common Size Statements
December 31, 20X4, 20X3, and 20X2

$ thousands, except par value	20X4		20X3		20X2	
Assets						
Current assets						
Cash	$1,335	15.3%	$1,341	17.7%	$1,295	17.0%
Marketable securities	250	2.9	200	2.6	228	3.0
Accounts receivable	1,678	19.2	1,386	18.3	1,371	18.0
Inventories	1,703	19.5	1,439	19.0	1,437	18.9
Prepaid items	280	3.2	156	2.1	150	2.0
Total current assets	5,246	60.0	4,522	59.9	4,481	58.8
Property, plant, and equipment	6,934	79.2	6,113	80.9	6,090	80.0
Less accumulated depreciation	3,426	39.1	3,080	40.8	2,955	38.8
Net property, plant and equipment	3,508	40.0	3,033	40.1	3,135	41.2
Total assets	$8,754	100.0%	$7,555	100.0%	$7,616	100.0%
Liabilities and stockholders' equity						
Current liabilities						
Accounts payable	$1,564	17.9%	$1,228	16.3%	$1,243	16.3%
Taxes payable	482	5.5	336	4.4	380	5.0
Accrued expenses payable	202	2.3	178	2.4	152	2.0
Total current liabilities	2,248	25.7	1,742	23.1	1,775	23.3
Long-term debt	1,208	13.8	1,422	18.8	1,976	25.9
Total liabilities	3,456	39.5	3,164	41.9	3,751	49.3
Stockholders' equity						
Common stock ($1 par)	414	4.7	404	5.3	404	5.3
Additional paid-in capital	531	6.1	270	3.6	270	3.5
Retained earnings	4,353	49.7	3,717	49.2	3,191	41.9
Total stockholders' equity	5,298	60.5	4,391	58.1	3,865	50.7
Total liabilities and equity	$8,754	100.0%	$7,555	100.0%	$7,616	100.0%

BERKELEY INC.
Comparative Income Statements with Common Size Statements
For Years Ended December 31, 20X4, 20X3, and 20X2

$ thousands, except per share	20X4		20X3		20X2	
Sales	$9,734	100.0%	$8,028	100.0%	$7,841	100.0%
Cost of goods sold	6,085	62.5	4,843	60.3	4,648	59.3
Gross profit	3,649	37.5	3,185	39.7	3,193	40.7
Operating expenses						
Expenses, excluding depreciation	1,030	10.6	891	11.1	868	11.1
Depreciation	602	6.2	527	6.6	500	6.4
Total operating expenses	1,632	16.8	1,418	17.7	1,368	17.4
Operating income	2,017	20.7	1,767	22.0	1,825	23.3
Other expenses (revenues)						
Dividend and interest revenue	(80)	(0.8)	(84)	(1.0)	(86)	(1.1)
Interest expense	345	3.5	314	3.9	342	4.4
Gain on sale of investments	(45)	(0.5)	—	—	—	—
Loss on sale of PP&E	35	0.4	—	—	—	—
Total other expenses (revenues)	255	2.6	230	2.9	256	3.3
Income before income taxes	1,762	18.1	1,537	19.1	1,569	20.0
Provision for income taxes	599	6.2	523	6.5	533	6.8
Net income	$1,163	11.9%	$1,014	12.6%	$1,036	13.2%
Earnings per share	$2.81		$2.51		$2.56	

Some percentage totals may not sum due to rounding.

cash is offset by increases in accounts receivable and inventories as a percent of total assets. Since the company experienced an increase in sales, it is logical for accounts receivable and inventories to increase. However, if these two accounts had increased and cash had decreased with no corresponding increases in sales, management should be concerned. The latter situation suggests excessive inventory investments and problems collecting accounts receivable.

Vertical analysis is also used with common size income statements. When evaluating the income statement, the manager can use common size measurements to determine quickly whether the company's operating goals are met. If Berkeley's target gross profit margin is 40%, attained in 20X3 (39.7%), the manager can readily see that 20X4 fell short of the goal by 2.5 percentage points (40% – 37.5%). This suggests that lower prices or items within cost of goods sold were not kept in control. Although the income statement alone cannot provide the answer, it has helped identify the problem and given management a starting point in looking for the cause. Comparable evaluations can be performed on any of the income statement items and, as such, provide a different perspective of evaluation rather than simple reliance on dollar amounts.

Horizontal Analysis

Horizontal analysis is used to evaluate trends in the financial condition of an organization. This analysis allows current year common size statements to be compared to those of prior years and to the organization's goals and objectives. For companies that have few organizational changes and little growth, dollar amounts can be of use for horizontal analysis. However, for companies experiencing major economic changes during the period under evaluation (for example, new product lines, dropping product lines, new sales territories, mergers, or acquisitions), comparisons of dollar amounts are not meaningful. This is true for Berkeley when comparing dollar amounts for 20X3 and 20X4. Because sales increased substantially when Berkeley added a new product line, it is difficult to evaluate what the dollar amounts should be for most of the other income statement items. In this case, percentages are a better means for comparison.

Using inventories as an item for analysis, we examine how horizontal analysis helps in the evaluation process. From 20X2 to 20X3, inventories increased by $2,000 ($1,439,000 – $1,437,000), an acceptable change for such a large dollar amount and given that sales increased also. From 20X3 to 20X4, inventories increased $264,000 ($1,703,000 – $1,439,000), an increase of 18% over 20X3, which can be alarming without further analysis. However, because the company added a new product line, some increase is expected—but how much of an increase? The current dollar amount seems large. Before rendering judgment, are the percentages from the common size statements just as large? From Exhibit A.1, we see that the percentages for inventory are 18.9%, 19.1%, and 19.5%, respectively, for 20X2, 20X3, and 20X4. Although inventory as a percent of assets has increased, it does not appear unreasonable given the new product line and the overall increase in assets.

After the vertical and horizontal analyses are completed for the common size statements, the manager then begins to make computations concerning other relations within the company's financial reporting system. The most common financial analysis procedures used for financial statement evaluation are considered in the remainder of this appendix.

Performing Vertical and Horizontal Analyses **LO3 Review Appendix A-3**

Comparative 20X4 and 20X3 income statements and balance sheets for Oxford Inc. follow.

OXFORD INC.
Comparative Income Statements
For Years Ended December 31, 20X4 and 20X3

$ 000s	20X4	20X3
Sales	$3,000	$2,500
Cost of goods sold	2,600	2,300
Gross profit	400	200
Operating expenses		
Selling	125	105
General and administrative	70	60
Total operating expenses	195	165
Operating income	205	35

continued

continued from previous page

OXFORD INC.
Comparative Income Statements
For Years Ended December 31, 20X4 and 20X3

$ 000s	20X4	20X3
Other expenses (revenues)		
Interest income	(10)	(5)
Interest expense	40	20
Total other expenses	30	15
Income before income taxes	175	20
Provision for income taxes	60	7
Net income	$ 115	$ 13
Earnings per share	$ 1.28	$ 0.19

OXFORD INC.
Comparative Balance Sheets
December 31, 20X4 and 20X3

$ 000s, except par value	20X4	20X3
Assets		
Current assets		
Cash and cash equivalents	$ 375	$ 315
Accounts receivable	325	280
Inventories	400	350
Interest receivable	60	55
Total current assets	1,160	1,000
Property, plant, and equipment	1,500	1,300
Less accumulated depreciation	800	750
Property, plant, and equipment, net	700	550
Other assets	15	12
Total assets	$1,875	$1,562
Liabilities and stockholders' equity		
Current liabilities		
Accounts payable	$ 435	$ 330
Income taxes payable	45	5
Interest payable	50	45
Total current liabilities	530	380
Long-term debt	300	250
Total liabilities	830	630
Stockholders' equity		
Common stock ($1 par)	90	70
Additional paid-in capital	15	10
Retained earnings	940	852
Total stockholders' equity	1,045	932
Total liabilities and equity	$1,875	$1,562

Additional information

- During 20X4, operating expenses included $50,000 in depreciation expense.
- Cash dividends of $27,000 are declared and paid during 20X4.
- Common stock of $15,000 is issued at par for cash in 20X4.
- Equipment costing $200,000 is acquired during 20X4 by paying cash of $190,000 and issuing 5,000 shares of common stock worth $10,000.
- During 20X4, long-term debt of $20,000 is paid off with cash and new long-term debt of $70,000 is issued for cash.
- The company extended a $3,000 loan to the company president in 20X4.

continued

continued from previous page

Required

a. Prepare common size statements and perform a vertical analysis of the financial statements for 20X4 and 20X3. Use sales as the base for the income statements and total assets as the base for the balance sheets. Summarize your findings.

b. Prepare a horizontal analysis of the financial statements for 20X4 and 20X3. Summarize your findings. **Solution on p. 514.**

Solvency Analysis

LO4 Explain the analysis of a firm's solvency.

Solvency refers to the firm's ability to pay its debts as they come due. Primary measures of short-term solvency are the current ratio, acid test ratio, inventory turnover, and days sales in receivables. The debt-to-equity ratio and the times-interest-earned measures are useful in assessing long-term solvency. Information to compute these measures is available in corporate annual reports.

Current Ratio

The **current ratio** measures the relation between current assets and current liabilities. The general equation for the current ratio and the computation for Berkeley, as of December 31, 20X4, follow:

$$\textbf{Current ratio} = \frac{\textbf{Current assets}}{\textbf{Current liabilities}}$$

$$\textbf{For Berkeley:} = \frac{\$5{,}246{,}000}{\$2{,}248{,}000}$$

$$= \underline{\underline{2.33}}$$

Current assets represent cash and other assets that will be converted into cash (either directly or indirectly) through operations within a reasonably short period of time. Under normal operating conditions, cash is generated by sales of inventory and collection of accounts receivable. Current liabilities are financial obligations that will become due within a relatively short period of time and will be paid from cash currently available and from the pool of cash generated from current assets. Therefore, comparing current assets to current liabilities indicates the extent to which current assets are available to cover current liabilities. Berkeley's current ratio of 2.33 implies that it has $2.33 of current assets for each $1 of current liabilities.

There is no universal guideline for evaluating the current ratio. Although a current ratio of 1.5 is often considered to be the norm, using such an artificial guideline can lead to erroneous conclusions. For example, a current ratio of 1.5 is inadequate for a firm that has 90% of its current assets tied up in obsolete or slow-moving inventory, while most of its current liabilities are due in the near-term. The adequacy of a particular current ratio depends on (1) the composition of the current assets and how quickly they will convert to cash, and (2) how soon current liabilities must be paid.

Working Capital

The current asset and current liability accounts are often referred to as current operating, or current working, accounts because assets and liabilities related to operating revenues and expenses normally flow in and out of the balance sheet through these accounts. The difference between current assets and current liabilities is viewed as the net amount of working funds available in the short run. This fund is referred to as **working capital**. Berkeley's December 31, 20X4, working capital follows.

$$\textbf{Working capital} = \textbf{Current assets} - \textbf{Current liabilities}$$

$$= \$5{,}246{,}000 - \$2{,}248{,}000$$

$$= \underline{\underline{\$2{,}998{,}000}}$$

This means that Berkeley has $2,998,000 that it can use as operating funds in the near future. This working capital may be needed if accounts payable continues to increase as a result of the new product line started in 20X4.

For a basic illustration as to how working capital is used, consider the following transaction. Assume that during January 20X5, Berkeley needs to purchase equipment for $50,000 but does not want to incur a liability. The impact of this transaction is shown as follows.

$$\begin{aligned} \textbf{Working capital} &= \textbf{Current assets} - \textbf{Current liabilities} \\ &= \$(50{,}000) - \$0 \\ &= \$(50{,}000) \end{aligned}$$

This leaves a net result of

$$\begin{aligned} \textbf{Working capital} &= \textbf{Current assets} - \textbf{Current liabilities} \\ &= \$5{,}196{,}000 - \$2{,}248{,}000 \\ &= \underline{\underline{\$2{,}948{,}000}} \end{aligned}$$

Some transactions affect only current liabilities; others affect both current assets and current liabilities, but by different amounts; others affect both by the same amounts, resulting in no change in working capital; and some transactions have no effect on either. All of an organization's economic transactions—except those that deal solely with the long-term accounts; that is, property, plant and equipment, long-term liabilities, and equity—affect some aspect of the working capital equation.

Acid Test Ratio

Current liabilities are usually paid with cash, not with other current assets. The **acid test ratio** is more specific than the current ratio as a test of short-term solvency. It measures the availability of cash and other current monetary assets that can be quickly converted into cash to pay current liabilities. Current monetary assets include cash, marketable securities, and current receivables. The general equation for the acid test ratio and the computation for Berkeley, as of December 31, 20X4, follow.

$$\textbf{Acid test ratio} = \frac{\textbf{Cash} + \textbf{Marketable securities} + \textbf{Current accounts receivable}}{\textbf{Current liabilities}}$$

$$\textbf{For Berkeley:} = \frac{\$1{,}335{,}000 + \$250{,}000 + \$1{,}678{,}000}{\$2{,}248{,}000}$$

$$= \underline{\underline{1.45}}$$

Berkeley's acid test ratio indicates that it has $1.45 of current monetary assets for each $1 of current liabilities. (This ratio is also referred to as the **quick ratio** because it shows the amount of cash that can be obtained relatively quickly for each $1 of current liabilities outstanding.) Many analysts consider an acid test ratio of near 1.0 to be adequate for most businesses. However, as stated earlier in discussing the current ratio, the composition of the ratio components must be considered before deciding what an adequate ratio is. When evaluating the current and acid test ratios, the manager must consider other factors such as seasonal characteristics of the business, the availability of short-term credit lines, the collection terms for accounts receivable, and the payment terms of accounts payable.

As a follow-up to the current and acid test ratios, most analysts evaluate the liquidity of the primary assets in the cash flow stream—namely, inventory and accounts receivable. The inventory turnover and days sales in receivables are the measures ordinarily used for that purpose.

Inventory Turnover

Inventory turnover indicates the approximate number of times the average stock of inventory is sold and replenished during the year. Inventory turnover is often regarded as both a measure of solvency and a measure of performance. As a solvency measure, inventory turnover reveals how long it takes to convert inventory into current monetary assets. As a performance measure, inventory turnover reveals how well the firm is managing investments in inventory. Inventory turnover is computed as the total cost of the inventory sold during the year divided by the average inventory on hand during the year.

$$\textbf{Inventory turnover} = \frac{\textbf{Cost of goods sold}}{\textbf{Average inventory}}$$

$$\textbf{For Berkeley:} = \frac{\$6{,}085{,}000}{(\$1{,}703{,}000 + \$1{,}439{,}000)/2}$$

$$= \underline{\underline{3.87}} \textbf{ times}$$

During 20X4, Berkeley sold inventory costing $6,085,000, and the average inventory for the year was $1,571,000 ([$1,703,000 + $1,439,000]/2). Therefore, the average stock of inventory was sold and replenished 3.87 times during the year. Assuming a 365-day year, the **days sales in inventory** was 94.3 days (365 days/3.87). That is, during the year, the average inventory available was sufficient to meet the average sales needs for 94.3 days. Since ending inventory is somewhat higher than is the average inventory for the year, inventory at year-end is sufficient to supply somewhat more than 94.3 days' average sales.

What constitutes an appropriate inventory turnover ratio varies from industry to industry and over time. Obviously, a fast-food restaurant should have a high inventory turnover, whereas a jewelry store typically has a low inventory turnover. Firms adopting just-in-time approaches to inventory management should have an increase in their inventory turnovers. If a firm's competitors' inventory turnovers are increasing, this could indicate that competitors changed their approach to inventory management. The nature of the firm's supply sources, the use of inventory display in selling merchandise, the quickness with which inventory is delivered to customers, and information on the industry should all be considered in interpreting the inventory turnover ratio.

Days Sales in Receivables

Next to cash and marketable securities, receivables are the most liquid assets. They are converted directly into cash in the normal course of business. **Days sales in receivables** measures the average number of days it takes to generate the value of uncollected credit sales at a point in time. Days sales in receivables is a measure of both solvency and performance. As a measure of solvency, it reveals how many days on average it takes to convert accounts receivable into cash. As a performance measure, days sales in receivables reveals how well the firm is managing the credit extended to customers. The longer the collection period, the less cash is available for daily operations. Days sales in receivables is computed as receivables divided by average daily sales.

$$\textbf{Days sales in receivables} = \frac{\textbf{Accounts receivable}}{\textbf{Average daily credit sales}}$$

$$\textbf{For Berkeley:} = \frac{\$1{,}678{,}000}{\$9{,}734{,}000/365}$$

$$= \underline{\underline{62.9}} \textbf{ days}$$

At year-end 20X4, Berkeley had receivables equal to the average sales for 62.9 days (assuming all sales are on credit). In evaluating this measure, management should consider the terms under which credit sales are made. For example, if Berkeley sells goods and services on 30-day credit terms, a ratio of 62.9 days probably indicates serious receivables collection problems. This ratio, which is a broad average, is a reliable indicator only if the amount of daily sales was fairly even throughout the year. For more precise information, management should conduct a detailed analysis of year-end receivables to determine their ages and probable collection periods.

Debt-to-Equity Ratio

Most businesses have two basic sources of capital: debt and equity. The balance between the amounts of capital provided by creditors and owners is important in evaluating a business's long-term solvency. Creditors regard equity as a cushion against future operating losses and bankruptcy. The larger the percentage of total assets financed by equity capital, the more secure are the creditors. Aggressive, growth-oriented organizations tend to rely more heavily on debt than on equity, whereas stable, conservative organizations tend to have a larger proportion of equity. The **debt-to-equity ratio** is computed as total liabilities divided by total stockholders' equity.

$$\textbf{Debt-to-equity ratio} = \frac{\textbf{Total liabilities}}{\textbf{Total stockholders' equity}}$$

$$\textbf{For Berkeley:} \quad = \frac{\$3{,}456{,}000}{\$5{,}298{,}000}$$

$$= \underline{\underline{0.65}}$$

Berkeley's December 31, 20X4, debt-to-equity ratio of 0.65 indicates that its creditors have provided $0.65 of capital for each $1 that stockholders provided. Stated another way, for each $1.65 of asset book values, the company could suffer a $1 loss and still have total reported assets equal to total liabilities. Although the debt-to-equity ratio is useful as a general indicator of the adequacy of long-term solvency, the amount of long-term debt that a company can justify is primarily related to its ability to repay the funds plus interest.

Times-Interest-Earned

A financially sound business normally pays interest obligations out of current earnings. Accordingly, creditors are interested in the adequacy of earnings to provide payment of interest charges. **Times-interest-earned**, a measure of interest-paying ability, shows the relation between earnings available to pay interest and total interest expense.

$$\textbf{Times-interest-earned} = \frac{\textbf{Net income} + \textbf{Interest expense} + \textbf{Income taxes}}{\textbf{Interest expense}}$$

$$\textbf{For Berkeley:} \quad = \frac{\$1{,}163{,}000 + \$345{,}000 + \$599{,}000}{\$345{,}000}$$

$$= \underline{\underline{6.11}} \text{ times}$$

In the numerator, interest expense and income taxes are added to net income to determine the pool of earnings from which interest expense is paid. Since interest expense is deducted in computing taxable income, the earnings pool from which interest is paid is income before deductions for interest and taxes. For Berkeley, this pool of earnings for 20X4 is 6.11 times the amount of the current year's interest charge on debt.

See Exhibit A.3 on page 504 for a summary of the primary measures of solvency.

Review Appendix A-4 LO4 — Performing a Ratio Analysis to Evaluate Solvency

Solution on p. 516.

Refer to the data in Review Appendix A-3 on pages 493–494.

Required

Prepare a ratio analysis evaluating Oxford's 20X4 short-term and long-term solvency.

Performance Analysis

eLectures MBC **LO5** Explain the analysis of a firm's performance.

Operating performance is related to the broad objective of profitability. The basic activities that characterize a typical for-profit organization follow.

- Generating capital—equity and debt.
- Acquiring assets with capital.

- Using assets to generate sales and profits.
- Using profits to pay the cost of capital.

Primary measures of performance are asset turnover, return on sales, return on assets, return on equity, and earnings per share. Care must be taken when using ratios for performance evaluation. Several of the measures of solvency discussed previously are also used to assist in the evaluation of these activities. It is quite common to find inventory turnover and days sales in receivables as part of performance evaluation. Common measures of performance are discussed in this section.

Asset Turnover

The **asset turnover** ratio measures the firm's ability to use its assets to generate sales. Asset turnover is computed as sales divided by average total assets.

$$\textbf{Asset turnover} = \frac{\textbf{Sales}}{\textbf{Average total assets}}$$

$$\textbf{For Berkeley:} = \frac{\$9{,}734{,}000}{(\$8{,}754{,}000 + \$7{,}555{,}000)/2}$$

$$= \underline{\underline{1.19}} \textbf{ times}$$

For Berkeley, the asset turnover of 1.19 times indicates that, on the average, each \$1 of assets generated \$1.19 of sales during 20X4. The interpretation of this measure depends largely on the nature of the business. Organizations that are capital-intensive, such as utilities or heavily automated manufacturers, typically have a lower asset turnover than do organizations that are labor-intensive, such as garment manufacturers. Also, firms that generate a small amount of sales with each dollar of assets usually must earn a higher percentage of profit on each sales dollar than do firms that produce a high amount of sales with each invested asset dollar.

Return on Sales

The ability of a firm to generate sales with available assets is important. To be profitable, however, these sales must exceed the cost of generating them. **Return on sales** is a measure of the firm's ability to generate profits from sales produced by the firm's assets. Return on sales is computed by dividing the sum of net income and net-of-tax interest expense by sales.

$$\textbf{Return on sales} = \frac{\textbf{Net income + Net-of-tax interest expense}}{\textbf{Sales}}$$

$$\textbf{For Berkeley:} = \frac{\$1{,}163{,}000 + \$345{,}000 \times (1 - 0.34)}{\$9{,}734{,}000}$$

$$= \underline{\underline{0.143}}, \text{ or } \underline{\underline{14.3\%}}$$

Interest expense is added to net income because it is not considered an expense of using assets, but rather a cost of providing the capital invested in assets. Since interest expense reduces taxes, it is adjusted for taxes at the company's current effective tax rate of approximately 34%. This reveals that, on average, 14.3% of each \$1 of Berkeley 20X4 sales remained as profit after covering all expenses other than interest.

Return on Assets

The **return on assets** ratio combines asset turnover and return on sales to measure directly the firm's ability to use its assets to generate profits. The return on assets computation is derived from the asset turnover and return on sales ratios as follows.

Ratio derivation: $$\text{Return on assets} = \text{Asset turnover} \times \text{Return on sales}$$

$$= \frac{\text{Sales}}{\text{Average total assets}} \times \frac{\text{Net income} + \text{Net-of-tax interest expense}}{\text{Sales}}$$

$$\text{Return on assets} = \frac{\text{Net income} + \text{Net-of-tax interest expense}}{\text{Average total assets}}$$

For Berkeley:

$$= \frac{\$1{,}163{,}000 + \$345{,}000 \times (1 - 0.34)}{(\$8{,}754{,}000 + \$7{,}555{,}000)/2}$$

$$= \underline{\underline{0.171}}, \text{ or } \underline{\underline{17.1\%}}$$

Berkeley's 20X4 return on assets is also approximated by multiplying the asset turnover of 1.19 times the return on sales of 14.3%. From the previous analyses, we conclude that, on average, each dollar of assets generates $1.19 of sales and $0.171 of income and that each dollar of sales results in $0.143 of income. Return on assets is an important indicator of management's overall performance because it measures management's effectiveness in using the total capital entrusted to them by both creditors and stockholders. A variation of this ratio (return on investment), discussed in Chapter 11, is commonly used for evaluating the performance of divisions in decentralized organizations.

The return on assets ratio measures profitability before deducting capital costs (interest and dividends). Thus, the adequacy of the profitability indicated by this ratio depends on the cost of debt and the return stockholders expect on their investments.

Return on Equity

Return on equity measures the profits attributable to shareholders as a percentage of their equity in the firm. This measure is more specific than the return on assets ratio in measuring performance because return on equity focuses only on stockholders' profits and investment. The profits available to stockholders consist of net income after deducting all costs and expenses, including interest expense. Return on equity is computed as net income divided by average stockholders' equity.

$$\text{Return on equity} = \frac{\text{Net income}}{\text{Average stockholders' equity}}$$

For Berkeley:

$$= \frac{\$1{,}163{,}000}{(\$5{,}298{,}000 + \$4{,}391{,}000)/2}$$

$$= \underline{\underline{0.240}}, \text{ or } \underline{\underline{24.0\%}}$$

(If the company also has preferred stock outstanding, then return on equity is computed as the return on *common* equity; where net income is reduced by the amount of annual dividends on preferred stock, and stockholders' equity is reduced by the book value of preferred stock.)

The 20X4 return attributable to Berkeley's shareholders was 24%, compared to a return on assets of 17.1%. The return to shareholders is higher than is its return on assets as a result of financial leverage. **Financial leverage** refers to the use of capital that has a fixed interest or dividend rate. Any time capital can be acquired at a fixed rate, and the return on assets is higher than that fixed rate, the return to the common shareholders is increased through favorable financial leverage. (The interest rate on a variable rate loan can change from period to period as the prime rate changes; however, even in this case, the interest is fixed for a short period of time, and management's ability to generate favorable leverage varies inversely with interest rate changes.) Conversely, if the fixed cost of capital is greater than the return it generates, the shareholders are subsidizing the cost of debt or other fixed rate capital, which reflects unfavorable financial leverage. Berkeley's favorable financial leverage occurred because the return on assets was 17.1%, whereas the interest rate as a percent of average total liabilities was 10.4%, computed as follows.

$$\textbf{Average interest rate} = \frac{\textbf{Interest expense}}{\textbf{Average total liabilities}}$$

$$\textbf{For Berkeley} = \frac{\$345{,}000}{(\$3{,}456{,}000 + \$3{,}164{,}000)/2}$$

$$= \underline{\underline{0.104}}, \text{ or } \underline{\underline{10.4\%}}$$

Berkeley's total debt required a return of only $345,000 (or 10.4%). Therefore, the return above 10.4% on the assets acquired with debt increased the return to the shareholders to 24.0%.

Earnings per Share

For external reporting purposes, earnings per share amounts are disclosed on the face of the income statement. Berkeley's income statement in Exhibit A.1 reported earnings per share of $2.84 in 20X4 and $2.51 in 20X3. **Earnings per share** is defined as follows.

$$\textbf{Earnings per share} = \frac{\textbf{Net income}}{\textbf{Average number of common shares outstanding}}$$

$$\textbf{For Berkeley:} = \frac{\$1{,}163{,}000}{(414{,}000 + 404{,}000)/2}$$

$$= \underline{\underline{\$2.84}}$$

Earnings per share for companies with simple capital structures is computed as net income divided by the average number of shares outstanding for the period. A *simple capital structure* is one consisting only of common stock. The computations are more difficult for a company with a *complex capital structure* that includes preferred stock, convertible bonds, or other types of equity securities. Also, changes in a company's capital structure during the year and over time make it more difficult to compare earnings per share from year to year.

Investors use earnings per share measures as a basis in evaluating the firm's overall profitability. The advantage of the earnings per share measure is that it is reported on the same basis as stock prices—that is, on an individual share basis. Investors often use the **price earnings ratio**, which is the ratio of the current market price per share divided by the earnings per share of the stock, to arrive at a multiple of earnings.

$$\textbf{Price earnings ratio} = \frac{\textbf{Market price per share}}{\textbf{Earnings per share}}$$

Some managers use earnings per share as a broad measure of overall performance. However, earnings per share should not be relied on too heavily, nor should it be substituted for other, more detailed profitability ratios that managers can obtain. Other profitability measures are often more useful to managers in evaluating overall management performance. Another reason why managers must monitor earnings per share is to better understand a measure that investors use in making decisions about buying or selling a company's capital stock.

Finally, some managers compute the *dividend payout ratio*, defined as cash dividends per common share divided by earnings per common share. Companies that have high reinvestment of their earnings would have low dividend payout ratios. Similarly, companies that have few investment opportunities and shareholders that seek dividends would have high dividend payout ratios. Another measure known as the *dividend yield ratio*, defined as cash dividends per common share divided by market price per common share, reflects the percent of the share market price paid out in cash. A complete summary of the ratios discussed in this appendix is provided at the end of the appendix in Exhibit A.3.

Horizontal Analysis of Solvency and Performance

Horizontal analysis, as already illustrated, provides good measures of performance over time. This analysis can be readily extended to the financial ratios of solvency and performance measures. The annual reports of most companies include several years' data for key items such as gross sales, operating profit margin, net income, earnings per share, dividends paid, and net changes to retained earnings. However, annual reports rarely include financial ratios that are important for evaluation purposes.

Horizontal analysis requires little additional computations because many of the items that provide input for other financial analysis techniques are already computed. A typical analysis often includes the current ratio. Although a measure of solvency in the short run, the current ratio can be a measure of performance when compared over a period of years. For example, if the information for Berkeley is extended back to 20X0, a horizontal analysis of the current ratio reveals the following:

	20X4	20X3	20X2	20X1	20X0
Current ratio	2.33	2.60	2.52	2.56	2.61

It appears that the ratio of current assets to current liabilities has been slowly declining, with the exception of an increase in 20X3. Such an analysis might alert the manager to take investigative action before the current ratio becomes undesirable. If creditors are using similar analysis, the decline might alert them to be cautious in extending credit to Berkeley.

Horizontal analysis can be performed using both dollars and common size units. However, care must be used when horizontal analysis is based only on dollar amounts. To illustrate, if we refer to Exhibit A.1 and use dollars, horizontal analysis of the income statement reveals that cost of goods sold in 20X4 increased substantially over that of 20X3 whereas in 20X3 and 20X2 cost of goods sold were about the same. Is this good or bad, considering 20X4 sales also increased substantially? On the other hand, horizontal analysis with common size units reveals another picture—the increase is only 2.2% (62.5% − 60.3%).

Some types of analysis combine both dollars and common size units with two or more sets of data to make performance evaluations using horizontal analysis. Suppose the income statements for Berkeley appeared as follows:

	20X4	20X3	20X2	20X1	20X0
Sales.	$9,734,000	$8,028,000	$7,841,000	$7,260,000	$7,000,000
Operating income	2,017,000	1,767,000	1,825,000	1,670,000	1,610,000
Operating income as percent of sales	20.7%	22.0%	23.3%	23.0%	23.0%

If only the dollars are considered, the trend for Berkeley appears favorable, with sales increasing each year, including substantial growth in 20X4. Dollars of operating income are also increasing, except for 20X3, with 20X4 again showing a substantial increase. However, after adding the common size data to the analysis, the company's performance appears less favorable. After several years of operating with a 23% margin, performance slipped to 20.7%, even with the large 20X4 sales increase.

Another type of horizontal analysis is frequently used when a given point in time has been established as the base year or benchmark for comparison. Using the data above with 20X0 as the base year (100%), a horizontal analysis using common size units follows.

	20X4	20X3	20X2	20X1	20X0
Sales.	139%	115%	112%	104%	100%
Operating income	125	110	113	104	100

When we add this information to the previous analysis, it appears that the first sign of declining profit was in 20X3, when operating income increased much less than did sales. In fact, 20X3 operating income was less than that of 20X2 by 3 percentage points.

This application is frequently extended by converting an entire financial statement to a base period and computing the change in each account for several financial statements. This allows the manager to examine the movement of all items in relation to a single starting point. Exhibit A.2 reveals the results of holding 20X2 as the base year for Berkeley and adjusting all subsequent income statement accounts against those of 20X2. To illustrate this application, cost of goods sold showed an increase of 30.9%, whereas sales went up only 24.1% over the two-year period. Although gross profit increased 14.3% over the 20X3 base, it did not improve at the same level as sales improved. Therefore, the manager might conclude that the increased sales attributable to the new product do not provide the same profit margin as the other products, or maybe the new product hindered the efficiency of producing existing products. This type of analysis is also applied to base-year comparisons of balance sheets.

Exhibit A.2 Base-Year Common Size Statements

BERKELEY INC.
Common Size Comparative Income Statements
For Years Ended December 31, 20X4, 20X3, and 20X2

	20X4	20X3	20X2
Sales	124.1%	102.4%	100.0%
Cost of goods sold	130.9	104.2	100.0
Gross profit	114.3	99.7	100.0
Operating expenses			
Expenses, excluding depreciation	118.7	102.6	100.0
Depreciation	120.4	105.4	100.0
Total operating expenses	119.3	103.7	100.0
Operating income	110.5	96.8	100.0
Other expenses and revenues			
Interest and dividend revenue	93.0	97.7	100.0
Interest expense	100.9	91.8	100.0
Gain on sale of investments*	—	—	—
Loss on sale of PP&E*	—	—	—
Total other expenses and revenues	99.6	89.8	100.0
Income before income taxes	112.3	98.0	100.0
Provision for income taxes	112.4	98.1	100.0
Net income	112.3	97.9	100.0

*These items are reported only in 20X4 and, thus, have no base in 20X2.

Industry Benchmarking of Analysis Measures

Evaluation of a firm's financial condition and performance is incomplete without comparisons to, and benchmarking against, its industry (competitors) during the same operating period(s). Industry comparisons provide insight into the firm's relative financial condition and performance and show whether the firm is keeping pace, moving ahead, or lagging behind competitors. There are several sources, such as Moody's and Standard & Poor's, that provide industry benchmarks on key financial analysis ratios and indexes.

Comparative evaluations must be made cautiously. First, avoid generalizations, such as every company should have a current ratio of 2 to 1. This caution was expressed in the section on current ratios. Second, avoid using industry averages or medians as absolute guidelines for performance measurement. Although industry benchmarks are better than rule-of-thumb generalizations, they do not apply equally to all firms within an industry. The industry benchmark is likely comprised of data from large firms, new firms, growing firms, diversified firms, and numerous other firms that do not match the case of the firm being evaluated. It is helpful if a distribution of the data statistics is provided within industry. (This is provided for many industries in the aforementioned publications.) For example, if the firm being evaluated has a current ratio of 1.6 and the industry average is 2.2, there may be cause for concern. However, if it is known that the firm fits into a category of similar firms within the industry that have an average current ratio of 1.5, cause for concern is lessened.

A third caution relates to the overall industry performance. A firm that is slightly below average in a financially strong industry can be better than one at the top of a financially weak industry. Again, there are business publications that give periodic ratings by industry—for example, the *Wall Street Journal*.

Exhibit A.3 Summary of Financial Analysis Ratios

Ratio		Formula	Reflects
Solvency			
Working capital	=	Current assets − Current liabilities	Near-term debt-paying ability
Current ratio	=	$\frac{\text{Current assets}}{\text{Current liabilities}}$	Near-term debt-paying ability
Acid test ratio	=	$\frac{\text{Cash} + \text{Marketable securities} + \text{Current accounts receivable}}{\text{Current liabilities}}$	Near-term debt-paying ability
Inventory turnover	=	$\frac{\text{Cost of goods sold}}{\text{Average inventory}}$	Efficiency of inventory management
Days sales in receivables*	=	$\frac{\text{Average accounts receivable}}{\text{Average daily credit sales}}$	Liquidity of receivables
Days sales in inventory**	=	$\frac{\text{Average inventory}}{\text{Average daily cost of goods sold}}$	Liquidity of inventory
Debt-to-equity ratio	=	$\frac{\text{Total liabilities}}{\text{Total stockholders' equity}}$	Creditor versus owner financing
Times-interest-earned	=	$\frac{\text{Net income} + \text{Interest expense} + \text{Income taxes}}{\text{Interest expense}}$	Interest-paying ability
Performance			
Asset turnover	=	$\frac{\text{Net sales}}{\text{Average total assets}}$	Efficiency of total assets
Return on sales	=	$\frac{\text{Net income} + \text{Net-of-tax interest expense}}{\text{Sales}}$	Profitability of sales given assets
Return on assets	=	$\frac{\text{Net income} + \text{Net-of-tax interest expense}}{\text{Average total assets}}$	Profitability of assets
Return on equity	=	$\frac{\text{Net income}}{\text{Average stockholders' equity}}$	Profitability of shareholder investment
Average interest rate	=	$\frac{\text{Interest expense}}{\text{Average total liabilities}}$	Interest rate paid on debt
Earnings per share	=	$\frac{\text{Net income}}{\text{Average number of common shares outstanding}}$	Income per common share
Price earnings ratio	=	$\frac{\text{Market price per share}}{\text{Earnings per share}}$	Market value multiple of earnings
Dividend yield	=	$\frac{\text{Cash dividends per common share}}{\text{Market price per common share}}$	Cash return of market price
Dividend payout	=	$\frac{\text{Cash dividends per common share}}{\text{Earnings per common share}}$	Payout percent of earnings

* This ratio can also be calculated as = 365/Accounts receivable turnover
** This ratio can also be calculated as = 365/Inventory turnover

Fourth, a firm must be analyzed as to its diversity or homogeneity. A firm with diversified product lines will often not fit into any group or industry. Various reporting requirements (via government agencies) force companies to classify themselves under some predefined industry classification whether they are diversified or not. Also, diversified firms tend to distort industry benchmarks of firms that have homogeneous product lines and that fit nicely into that particular industry category.

Fifth, size influences how a firm compares to industry benchmarks. Larger firms within an industry should probably be compared to industry benchmarks in a different way than are smaller firms. This is not to imply that large firms are better—in many industries, large firms are the weaker performers.

Each of these cautions should be considered as appropriate when analyzing a firm's financial condition and comparing that analysis to industry benchmarks. Comparing incompatible sets of data can result in managers making incorrect decisions, causing future performance to deteriorate.

Returning to the CFO's analysis of Berkeley, she must render a decision to the board of directors concerning the status of this subsidiary. Assuming her evaluation of Berkeley's position as related to the furniture industry is compatible with the newspaper and magazine articles she read before beginning her analysis, she is left with drawing conclusions about future trends of the company. While the existing current ratio, asset turnover ratio, return on sales, and most other measures are acceptable, the CFO is concerned about the trend evident from the horizontal analysis. That is, the current ratio has been declining, operating income as a percentage of sales has been declining, and the growth of operating income has not kept pace with the growth of sales. It is when faced with such decisions that executives such as this CFO demand timely and relevant information to recommend what is best for the long-run benefits of the company.

Performing a Ratio Analysis to Evaluate Performance and Profitability LO5 **Review Appendix A-5**

Refer to the data in Review Appendix A-3 on pages 493–494.

Required

Prepare a ratio analysis evaluating Oxford's 20X4 performance and profitability.

Solution on p. 517.

Key Terms

acid test ratio, 496
asset turnover, 499
common size statement, 490
competitor analysis, 490
current ratio, 495
days sales in inventory, 497
days sales in receivables, 497
debt-to-equity ratio, 498
earnings per share, 501
financial leverage, 500
financial statement analysis, 486
horizontal analysis, 490
inventory turnover, 496
price earnings ratio, 501
quick ratio, 496
return on assets, 499
return on equity, 500
return on sales, 499
solvency, 495
times-interest-earned, 498
vertical analysis, 490
working capital, 495

Questions

QA-1. What is the general purpose for conducting ratio analysis of financial statements?

QA-2. Name three reasons why managers should analyze their firm's financial statements.

QA-3. What is the purpose of evaluation standards (benchmarks) in financial analysis?

QA-4. What types of standards (benchmarks) are probably most relevant for financial analysis by managers?

QA-5. Explain how managers use vertical and horizontal analysis when evaluating financial statements. What changes are usually made in the statements before managers use these techniques?

QA-6. Explain and differentiate the terms *solvency evaluation* and *performance evaluation*.

QA-7. Explain the difference between the current ratio and the acid test ratio.

QA-8. Why is it useful to compute inventory turnover and the days sales in receivables? How is each of these measures computed?

QA-9. What are the primary measures of long-term solvency? How are they computed?

QA-10. Which financial statement analysis measure provides information concerning the sales output that a firm's assets produce?

QA-11. Why is interest expense added in the numerator in computing return on assets?

QA-12. Explain the concept of financial leverage. What causes financial leverage to be favorable? Unfavorable?

QA-13. Explain why comparisons to industry norms or averages are important when analyzing financial statements.

QA-14. What cautions should the manager take when using industry norms or benchmarks for comparison?

Assignments with the MBC logo in the margin are available in myBusinessCourse. See the Preface of the book for details.

Mini Exercises

LO4 **MA-15. Short-Term Solvency Ratios**

Following are financial data from year-end financial statements of Portland Company for the last three years.

	20X3	20X2	20X1
Accounts receivable	$ 149,700	$ 159,100	$ 145,200
Cost of goods sold	1,072,875	914,595	1,056,000
Current assets	495,000	396,000	445,500
Current liabilities	300,000	247,500	341,000
Inventory	246,000	183,150	214,500
Sales	1,761,125	1,633,375	1,320,000

Required

a. Compute the following financial ratios for the most recent two years (20X3 and 20X2). (Assume Portland Company's current assets include cash, accounts receivable, marketable securities, and inventory.)
1. Current ratio
2. Acid test ratio
3. Inventory turnover
4. Days sales in receivables

b. Comment on the short-term solvency of Portland Company for 20X3 and 20X2. Did the company's short-term solvency improve or deteriorate during 20X3? Explain.

LO4 **MA-16. Long-Term Solvency Ratios**

Summary data from year-end financial statements of Palm Springs Company for the current year follow.

Summary Income Statement Data		
Sales		$10,500,600
Cost of goods sold	$6,050,000	
Selling expenses	685,000	
Administrative expenses	945,000	
Interest expense	783,500	
Income tax expense	427,791	8,891,291
Net income		$ 1,609,309

Summary Balance Sheet Data			
Cash	$ 84,700	Total liabilities	$749,700
Noncash assets	885,500	Stockholders' equity	220,500
Total assets	$970,200	Total liabilities and equity	$970,200

Required

a. Compute the ratio of times-interest-earned.
b. Compute the debt-to-equity ratio.

MA-17. Measures of Performance and Financial Leverage LO5

Following are selected data from year-end financial statements of Lima Corporation for its first two years of operations.

	Year 2	Year 1
Total assets	$3,895,000	$3,260,000
Interest expense.	47,500	42,000
Long-term liabilities.	625,000	680,000
Net income	532,055	486,500
Sales.	4,829,625	3,940,000
Stockholders' equity	2,766,686	2,553,864

Required

a. Compute the following performance measurement ratios for the second year of operations. (Ignore income taxes.)
   1. Asset turnover
   2. Return on sales
   3. Return on assets
   4. Return on equity

b. Is Lima Company using financial leverage? If so, is the leverage favorable or unfavorable? Explain.

MA-18. Financial Leverage LO5

Following are data from Nicole Company and Dana Company for the current year:

	Nicole	Dana
Net income	$ 93,500	$ 185,000
Interest expense.	20,000	22,600
Total assets, beginning of year.	817,200	1,992,960
Total assets, end of year	998,800	2,159,040
Stockholders' equity, beginning of year	561,000	1,271,875
Stockholders' equity, end of year	607,750	1,618,750

Required

a. Compute the following ratios for Nicole and Dana Companies at the end of the year. (Ignore income taxes.)
   1. Return on assets
   2. Return on equity

b. Comment on the use of financial leverage by these two companies. Which company is the more highly leveraged? Which company's stockholders are benefiting more from the use of leverage?

MA-19. Changes in Working Capital

Following is a list of typical financial, investing, and operating transactions. For each transaction indicate whether current assets, current liabilities, and working capital either increased, decreased, or are unchanged. Use the following column headings and relation: **Current assets − Current liabilities = Working capital**.

a. Sold capital stock for cash.
b. Purchased a building with a 10% cash payment and the balance financed with note due in five years.
c. Paid current liabilities with cash.
d. Issued long-term bonds payable for cash.
e. Collected cash due on prior month's sales.
f. Purchased a building site by issuing long-term bonds.
g. Sold equipment for a cash amount equal to book value.
h. Purchased treasury stock for cash.
i. A long-term note maturing next year is reclassified as a current liability at year-end.

Exercises

LO2, 4 Masimo Corporation (MASI)

EA-20. Effects of Financing Decisions

Assume Masimo Corporation, a medical technology company, has total assets of $3,500,000 and total liabilities of $3,000,000. Masimo is considering two alternatives for acquiring additional warehouse space. Under the first alternative, the building would be purchased for $200,000 and financed by issuing long-term bonds. Under the second alternative, the building would be rented with an annual lease cost of $20,000 per year.

Required

a. Compute the company's current debt-to-equity ratio.

b. Just after the agreements are signed, what effect would the addition of warehouse space have on its debt-to-equity ratio

1. Assuming the building is purchased by issuing bonds?
2. Assuming the building is rented on an annual lease basis?

LO3

EA-21. Common Size Statements

Comparative balance sheets for Ithaca Inc. follow for year-end 20X4 and 20X3. Its president is concerned about the decline in total assets and wants to know where most of the decline took place.

	20X4	20X3
Cash	$160,000	$150,000
Accounts receivable	225,000	200,000
Inventory	200,000	275,000
Property, plant, and equipment	650,000	650,000
Less accumulated depreciation	312,500	287,500
Total assets	$922,500	$987,500
Accounts payable	$180,000	$179,500
Long-term note payable	172,000	240,000
Common stock	250,000	250,000
Retained earnings	320,500	318,000
Total liabilities and equity	$922,500	$987,500

Required

Convert these comparative balance sheets to common size statements. Using the common size statements, explain to the president where the greatest changes occurred.

LO4

EA-22. Changes in Working Capital

Heller Industries had a July 31 current asset balance of $145,800 and a current liability balance of $116,300. The following transactions took place in August:

- Sold land for $125,000 cash.
- Collected $55,000 cash on a long-term note receivable.
- Paid $22,000 cash toward outstanding accounts payable.
- Financed $28,000 purchase of equipment with a note due in two years.
- Paid $25,000 cash to settle long-term bonds payable two years prior to maturity.

Required

Determine the effects on working capital for each of those transactions and then compute ending working capital. Use the following format (the beginning balances are listed):

	Current assets	–	Current liabilities	=	Working capital
Beginning balance	$145,800		$116,300		$29,500

LO2, 4, 5

EA-23. Assessing Inflationary Effects

The president of Office Products Inc. is pleased with the progress her company has made in recent years, but she cannot understand why the company is always having to borrow funds when sales continually increase. Her office staff is small, and the largest cost outside of merchandise inventory is sales commissions, which are 10% of sales. As the cost of merchandise changes, she continually changes retail prices. Thus, she believes the profit margin should remain near the same percentage level for each period. However, even with her best efforts, the company continues to experience cash shortages. After gathering financial data, you prepare the following set of information for the past four years:

	Year 1	Year 2	Year 3	Year 4
Sales	$220,000	$228,800	$238,638	$246,500
Cost of goods sold	$121,000	$127,000	$133,500	$140,000
Current ratio	1.60	1.55	1.43	1.35
Inventory turnover	6.20	6.21	6.19	6.22
Inflation rate	5.0%	5.0%	5.0%	5.0%

Required

What conclusions can be drawn about the operating condition of Office Products Inc.? Explain. *Hint:* Consider analyzing trends.

EA-24. Assessing Inflationary Effects LO2, 5

The Innovation Products Company wants to launch a new product to replace a current product that is technologically inferior. First-year sales for the replacement product are expected to be 50,000 units at a unit selling price of $12. The initial cost of the product is $9 per unit variable and $125,000 fixed. The expected sales growth is 1,000 units per year, and the expected inflation rate is in a range of 3% to 4% for both sales and variable costs.

Required

a. Determine the anticipated profit margin for the new product for the first four years assuming
   1. No inflation
   2. Inflation at 4%

b. Compute the profit margin difference between no inflation and 4% inflation. Would this information make a difference in your evaluation of the new product? Explain.

Problems

PA-25. Comprehensive Financial Analysis LO1, 4, 5

Comparative income statements and balance sheets for Blackwater Falls Company follow for 20X4 and 20X3.

BLACKWATER FALLS COMPANY
Comparative Income Statements
For Years Ended December 31, 20X4 and 20X3

$ thousands	20X4	20X3
Sales	$10,500	$10,240
Cost of goods sold	6,300	6,205
Gross profit	4,200	4,035
Selling and administrative expenses	3,374	3,271
Operating income	826	764
Other expenses (revenues)		
Interest revenue	(22)	(28)
Interest expense	34	37
Total other expenses (revenues)	12	9
Income before income taxes	814	755
Income taxes	171	159
Net income	$ 643	$ 596

BLACKWATER FALLS COMPANY
Comparative Balance Sheets
December 31, 20X4 and 20X3

$ thousands	20X4	20X3
Assets		
Cash	$ 102	$ 105
Marketable securities	46	45
Accounts receivable	915	880
Inventory	1,719	1,465
Prepaid expenses	80	75
Total current assets	2,862	2,570
Investments and other assets	270	265
Property, plant, and equipment, net	1,727	1,492
Trademarks and other intangibles	200	200
Total assets	$5,059	$4,527
Liabilities and stockholders' equity		
Notes payable	$ 108	$ 120
Current maturities of long-term debt	61	54
Accounts payable and accrued expenses	905	925
Total current liabilities	1,074	1,099
Long-term debt	505	528
Total liabilities	1,579	1,627
Common stock	100	100
Additional paid-in capital	235	235
Retained earnings	3,145	2,565
Total stockholders' equity	3,480	2,900
Total liabilities and equity	$5,059	$4,527

Required

a. Why is it important for the managers of Blackwater Falls to analyze their own firm's financial statements?

b. Prepare a comprehensive financial analysis of Blackwater Falls for 20X4, including the following measures.

1. Short-term solvency ratios
2. Long-term solvency ratios
3. Performance measurement ratios

c. Comment on the financial condition of Blackwater Falls with respect to short-term solvency, long-term solvency, and performance.

LO3 **PA-26. Comprehensive Common Size Statement Analysis**

After reviewing the financial analyses conducted in PA-25, the managers of Blackwater Falls Company are still uncertain about the performance of the company during 20X4. They believe that common size statements might provide additional insights as to the company's performance.

Required

a. Using the data pertaining to Blackwater Falls Company from PA-25, prepare common size statements and evaluate the company's performance in 20X4 as compared to 20X3. For the balance sheets, use total assets as the base; for the income statements, make one set using sales of each year as the base for that year and another set using the year 20X3 as the base for both years.

b. Comment on the condition of Blackwater Falls drawing on the common size statements.

LO3, 4, 5 **PA-27. Comprehensive Financial Statement Analysis**

Macy's, Inc.
(M)

Assume you are part of the acquisitions committee of Macy's and are asked to examine the potential acquisition of American Blues, a small retailer. Selected financial statement data from the past two years follow.

AMERICAN BLUES Comparative Balance Sheets December 31, 20X2 and 20X1	20X2	20X1
Cash	$ 35,000	$ 32,000
Accounts receivable	180,000	165,000
Inventory	210,000	205,000
Property, plant, and equipment	405,000	387,000
Less accumulated depreciation	(146,000)	(117,000)
Total assets	$684,000	$672,000
Accounts payable	$171,330	$177,000
Long-term note payable	105,000	145,000
Common stock	225,000	225,000
Retained earnings	182,670	125,000
Total liabilities and equity	$684,000	$672,000

AMERICAN BLUES Income Statement For Year Ended December 31, 20X2	
Sales	$1,275,000
Cost of goods sold	765,000
Wages expense	175,000
Facilities expense	140,000
Supplies expense	54,000
Depreciation expense	35,000
Interest expense	15,000
Loss on sale of fixed assets	18,000
Net income before taxes	73,000
Income taxes	15,330
Net income	$ 57,670

Required

a. Compute the following ratios for 20X2.

1. Current ratio
2. Acid test ratio
3. Inventory turnover
4. Days sales in receivables
5. Debt-to-equity ratio
6. Times-interest-earned
7. Asset turnover
8. Return on sales
9. Return on assets
10. Return on equity

b. Prepare common size statements for each of the statements.

c. What is your recommendation regarding the acquisition of American Blue?

Cases and Projects

CA-28. Financial Statement Analysis with Actual Annual Report **LO3, 4, 5**

Select a recent annual report or 10-K filing (or use one provided by your instructor) of a publicly held company and perform all of the financial analysis measures discussed in this appendix. Include vertical and horizontal analyses with common size statements. List any of the measures discussed in this appendix that you were unable to perform and state the reasons. Give your evaluation of the company's financial performance and trend, citing financial analysis measures to support your interpretation. If industry data are available, make a comparison of the company under analysis with its industry norms and benchmarks. Evaluate the position the company holds within its industry.

LO3, 4, 5 Levi Strauss & Co. (LEVI) **CA-29. Horizontal Analysis and Interpretation**

Assume the following represents financial data for Levi Strauss & Co. during a five-year period.

(in millions)	20X1	20X2	20X3	20X4	20X5
Average cash balance . .	$ 394	$ 308	$ 347	$ 505	$ 673
Sales.	$4,754	$4,494	$4,553	$4,904	$5,575
Operating income.	$ 314	$ 431	$ 462	$ 467	$ 537
Current ratio	1.88	1.81	2.21	2.27	2.17
Asset turnover	1.63	1.56	1.52	1.46	1.57

Required

What assessments can be made about this company's performance and operating performance for this five-year period? Explain.

LO3, 4, 5 **CA-30. Horizontal Analysis and Interpretation**

El Paso Investment Brokers is considering purchasing Rio Valley. The following data are from recent financial statements of Rio Valley ($ thousands):

	20X1	20X2	20X3	20X4	20X5
Sales.	$2,100	$2,160	$2,550	$2,475	$2,600
Operating income.	$ 540	$ 560	$ 675	$ 620	$ 650
Net income	$ 245	$ 258	$ 248	$ 240	$ 245
Current ratio	2.40	2.20	2.65	1.80	2.28
Asset turnover	1.03	1.38	1.72	1.78	2.08

Required

Determine the company's strengths and weaknesses as evident from the information provided. Identify one type of common size application for assessing the dollar amounts for your analysis. What do you recommend regarding the purchase of Rio Valley? Explain.

LO4, 5 **CA-31. Interpreting Financial Analysis Ratios**

Thorpe Company is a wholesale distributor of professional equipment and supplies. The company's sales averaged about $1.5 million annually over the last three years. Its total assets at the end of the most recent year (20X3) were $1.25 million. The president of Thorpe Company asked the controller to prepare a report summarizing the financial aspects of the company's operations for the past three years. This report is to be presented to its Board of Directors at its next meeting. In addition to comparative financial statements, the controller decides to report a number of relevant financial ratios to assist in the identification and interpretation of trends. The controller computes the following ratios for the recent three-year period.

	20X3	20X2	20X1
Current ratio	1.90	1.75	1.50
Acid test ratio	0.98	1.05	1.25
Days sales in receivables.	48.20	42.60	38.50
Inventory turnover.	3.90	4.65	5.30
Debt-to-equity ratio.	0.63	0.68	0.73
Asset turnover	2.04	1.95	1.86
Sales as a percentage of 20X1 sales.	104%	102%	100%
Gross profit percent	38.8%	39.4%	41.0%
Return on sales	7.9%	7.8%	7.9%
Return on assets	8.6%	8.5%	8.7%
Return on equity.	12.6%	13.2%	13.7%

In preparation of the report, the controller decides first to examine the financial ratios independently of any other data to determine if the ratios themselves reveal any significant trends over this three-year period.

Required

Answer the following questions. Indicate in each case which ratio(s) you used to arrive at your conclusion.

a. The current ratio is increasing, whereas the acid test ratio is decreasing. Using the ratios provided, identify and explain the contributing factor(s) for this apparently divergent trend.

b. In terms of the ratios provided, what conclusion(s) is drawn regarding the company's use of financial leverage during the three-year period? Explain.

c. Using the ratios provided, what conclusions are drawn regarding the company's ability to generate sales and profits from the assets available to management?

(CMA Adapted)

Solutions to Review Problems

Review Appendix A-1—Solution

One of the most important reasons for managers to analyze their firm's financial statements is to evaluate the overall performance of the firm, especially as seen by those external to the firm. Managers should be aware of total company performance, not just the performance of their particular areas of responsibility. By analyzing the financial statements for the company as a whole, managers gain a perspective on how the organization is performing *and* how it is perceived.

By evaluating the overall performance of the organization, managers are able to compare their firm with similar firms and to identify potential weaknesses that are worthy of management's attention. Financial analysis is also necessary for managers whose firms have lending agreements that impose financial restrictions on the organization. Analysis of financial statements is often necessary to determine if restrictions are being met.

A more subtle but no less important reason for managers to analyze financial statements is to see their firm as outsiders see it. The financial statements are, in effect, the only window through which many outsiders view the firm. By evaluating the firm's financial statements, managers can better understand outsiders' behavior and attitudes toward the firm and thereby develop a more realistic view of the firm.

Review Appendix A-2—Solution

- No single financial statement analysis measure can summarize the performance of an organization. This is because each analysis measure is developed to evaluate an operating procedure or a specific area of the organization's performance. Patricia will need to identify the most significant operating procedures and related accounts for the company, and make sure that she performs a thorough evaluation that includes these significant elements. For example, if Blackstar carries significant inventory and accounts receivables, she will want to include evaluation of the company's performance specific to these areas and how well they do relative to their competitors.
- Next, Patricia will need to understand which alternative accounting procedures Blackstar uses along with understanding which alternative accounting procedures its competitors use. In order to compare the companies' results, she may need to adjust for the fact that they use different accounting treatments. For example, Blackstar might report inventory using the FIFO method of inventory valuation while its competitors might use LIFO.
- Third, inflation, or deflation, can distort the comparisons of financial statements between periods because the statements are based on historical dollars, not on dollars of the same value. Allowances must be made for these effects, or the analysis is distorted. Patricia will want to research recent economic inflation/deflation activity and back its related impact out of any trending analysis to better isolate actual changes in operating performance over time.
- Fourth, changes in the product mix can distort a comparison of financial statements because most products have unique profit margins and their mix influences the firm's profit margin. Patricia will want to review Blackstar's recent sales mix and if it has changed in recent years. If it has changed, how does this change impact the financial statement evaluation?

Review Appendix A-3—Solution

a.

OXFORD INC.
Common Size Income Statements
For Years Ended December 31, 20X4 and 20X3

	20X4	20X3
Sales	100.0%	100.0%
Cost of goods sold	86.7	92.0
Gross profit	13.3	8.0
Operating expenses		
Selling	4.2	4.2
General and administrative	2.3	2.4
Total operating expenses	6.5	6.6
Operating income	6.8	1.4
Other expenses (revenues)		
Interest income	(0.3)	(0.2)
Interest expense	1.3	0.8
Total other expenses	1.0	0.6
Income before income taxes	5.8	0.8
Provision for income taxes	2.0	0.3
Net income	3.8%	0.5%

OXFORD INC.
Common Size Balance Sheets
December 31, 20X4 and 20X3

	20X4	20X3
Assets		
Current assets		
Cash and cash equivalents	20.0%	20.2%
Accounts receivable	17.3	17.9
Inventories	21.3	22.4
Interest receivable	3.2	3.5
Total current assets	61.9	64.0
Property, plant, and equipment:	80.0	83.2
Less accumulated depreciation	42.7	48.0
Net property, plant, and equipment	37.3	35.2
Other assets	0.8	0.8
Total assets	100.0%	100.0%
Liabilities and stockholders' equity		
Current liabilities		
Accounts payable	23.2%	21.1%
Income taxes payable	2.4	0.3
Interest payable	2.7	2.9
Total current liabilities	28.3	24.3
Long-term debt	16.0	16.0
Total liabilities	44.3	40.3
Stockholders' equity		
Common stock ($1 par)	4.8	4.5
Additional paid-in capital	0.8	0.6
Retained earnings	50.1	54.5
Total stockholders' equity	55.7	59.7
Total liabilities and equity	100.0%	100.0%

Some percentage totals may not sum due to rounding.

Vertical analysis:

- The common size statements reveal that current assets declined as a percentage of total assets, with the largest decline being inventories.
- The largest change as a percentage of total assets within assets occurred with net property, plant, and equipment.
- Total liabilities as a group increased by 4.0% as a percentage of total assets; accounts payable and taxes payable were the main drivers.
- The primary change in stockholders' equity is retained earnings, which decreased as a percentage of total assets from 54.5% to 50.1%.
- Cost of goods sold declined as a percentage of total sales from 92% to 86.7%.
- The only items that increased as a percentage of sales were interest income and expense and provisions for taxes.

(in thousands)	20X4	20X3	$ Change	% Change
Sales	$3,000	$2,500	$500	20%
Cost of goods sold	2,600	2,300	300	13%
Gross profit	400	200	200	100%
Operating expenses				
Selling	125	105	20	19%
General and administrative	70	60	10	17%
Total operating expenses	195	165	30	18%
Operating income	205	35	170	486%
Other expenses (revenues)				
Interest income	(10)	(5)	(5)	100%
Interest expense	40	20	20	100%
Total other expenses	30	15	15	100%
Income before income taxes	175	20	155	775%
Provision for income taxes	60	7	53	757%
Net income	$ 115	$ 13	$102	785%

(in thousands)	20X4	20X3	$ Change	% Change
Assets				
Current assets				
Cash and cash equivalents	$ 375	$ 315	$ 60	19%
Accounts receivable	325	280	45	16%
Inventories	400	350	50	14%
Interest receivable	60	55	5	9%
Total current assets	1,160	1,000	160	16%
Property, plant, and equipment	1,500	1,300	200	15%
Less accumulated depreciation	800	750	50	7%
Property, plant, and equipment, net	700	550	150	27%
Other assets	15	12	3	25%
Total assets	$1,875	$1,562	313	20%
Liabilities and stockholders' equity				
Current liabilities				
Accounts payable	$ 435	$ 330	$105	32%
Income taxes payable	45	5	40	800%
Interest payable	50	45	5	11%
Total current liabilities	530	380	150	39%
Long-term debt	300	250	50	20%
Total liabilities	830	630	200	32%
Stockholders' equity				
Common stock ($1 par)	90	70	20	29%
Additional paid-in capital	15	10	5	50%
Retained earnings	940	852	88	10%
Total stockholders' equity	1,045	932	113	12%
Total liabilities and equity	$1,875	$1,562	313	20%

b. Horizontal Analysis

- Total assets on the balance sheet increased over the prior year by 20%. Net property, plant and equipment showed a significant change over the prior year at 27%.
- Total liabilities increased over the prior year by 32% with increases in every category.
- Stockholders' equity increased by 12% with common stock increasing by 29%.
- On the income statement, sales increased by 20% and gross profit increased by 100%. We know from the common size analysis that this change is driven by the decrease in cost of goods sold as a percentage of sales. With such a large change in sales, it's important to combine the common size analysis with the horizontal analysis.
- Operating expenses increased by 18%, operating income increased by 486%, and net income increased by 785%.

Review Appendix A-4—Solution

Solvency measures ($ 000s):

Current ratio $= \dfrac{\text{Current assets}}{\text{Current liabilities}} = \dfrac{\$1,160}{\$530} = \underline{\underline{2.19}}$

Acid test ratio $= \dfrac{\text{Cash + Marketable securities + Current accounts receivable}}{\text{Current liabilities}} = \dfrac{\$375 + \$0 + \$325}{\$530} = \underline{\underline{1.32}}$

Inventory turnover $= \dfrac{\text{Cost of goods sold}}{\text{Average inventory}} = \dfrac{\$2,600}{(\$350 + \$400)/2} = \underline{\underline{6.93}}$ times

Days sales in receivables $= \dfrac{\text{Accounts receivable}}{\text{Average daily credit sales}} = \dfrac{\$325}{\$3,000/365} = 39.54$ days

Debt-to-equity ratio $= \dfrac{\text{Total liabilities}}{\text{Total stockholders' equity}} = \dfrac{\$830}{\$1,045} = \underline{\underline{0.79}}$

Times-interest-earned $= \dfrac{\text{Net income + Interest expense + Income taxes}}{\text{Interest expense}} = \dfrac{\$115 + \$40 + \$60}{\$40} = \underline{\underline{5.38}}$ times

Review Appendix A-5—Solution

Performance measures ($ 000):

Asset turnover $= \dfrac{\text{Sales}}{\text{Average total assets}}$

$= \dfrac{\$3{,}000}{(\$1{,}562 + \$1{,}875)/2}$

$= \underline{\underline{1.75}}$ times

Return on sales $= \dfrac{\text{Net income} + \text{Net-of-tax interest expense}}{\text{Sales}}$

$= \dfrac{\$115 + \$40(1 - 0.34)}{\$3{,}000}$

$= \underline{\underline{0.047}}$, or $\underline{\underline{4.7\%}}$

Return on assets $= \dfrac{\text{Net income} + \text{Net-of-tax interest expense}}{\text{Average total assets}}$

$= \dfrac{\$115 + \$40(1 - 0.34)}{(\$1{,}562 + \$1{,}875)/2}$

$= \underline{\underline{0.082}}$, or $\underline{\underline{8.2\%}}$

Return on equity $= \dfrac{\text{Net income}}{\text{Average stockholders' equity}}$

$= \dfrac{\$115}{(\$932 + \$1{,}045)/2}$

$= \underline{\underline{0.116}}$, or $\underline{\underline{11.6\%}}$

Appendix B
Data Analytics

Road Map

	Learning Objectives	Page	eLecture	Assignments
1	Identify and define the four types of data analytics.	519	eF.1	1, 6, 7, 8,
2	Describe the use of data analytics within the accounting profession.	520	eF.2	1, 6, 7, 8, 13, 18,
3	Describe the analytics mindset.	521	eF.3	2, 3, 10, 11, 12, 13, 14, 15, 16, 17, 18, 19, 20, 21, 22, 23, 24, 25
4	Describe data visualization best practices.	523	eF.4	4, 5, 10, 11, 12, 14, 15, 16, 17, 19, 20, 21, 22, 24

Data Analytics

Data analytics can broadly be defined as the process of examining sets of data with the goal of discovering useful information from patterns found in the data. Increasingly, this process is aided by computers running programs ranging from basic spreadsheet software, such as Microsoft Excel and Google Sheets, to specialized software, such as Tableau or Power BI. This technology can reveal trends and insights that would otherwise be lost in the overwhelming amount of data.

Big Data

The concept of data analytics is intertwined with the concept of **big data**. While no precise definition exists for big data, a commonly accepted definition is that big data is a collection of data that is both extremely large and also extremely complex, thus making its analysis beyond the scope of traditional tools. Important attributes of big data, commonly referred to as the four V's, are Volume, Variety, Velocity, and Veracity. **Volume** refers to the amount of data. According to IDC (a market intelligence company), there were 33 available zettabytes of data globally in 2018. IDC predicted that the amount of data would increase to 175 zettabytes by 2025. (Just so you know, there are 21 zeros in one zettabyte.) Total amounts of data are growing because we are creating more data (through new technologies) and because we are able to store more data (using cloud storage services like Amazon Web services [AWS] and Microsoft Azure). Massive data sets can't be managed on a single machine. They must be stored in clusters over multiple physical or virtual machines.

Variety refers to the source of data. Data can be structured, semi-structured, or unstructured. Structured data can be contained in rows and columns and stored in spreadsheets or relational databases. Although most accounting data is structured, it is estimated that less than 20 percent of all data is structured.

Unstructured data cannot be easily contained in rows and columns and is therefore difficult to search and analyze. Photos, video and audio files, and social media content are examples of unstructured data.

Semi-structured data has characteristics of both structured and unstructured data. It may include some defining details but doesn't completely conform to a rigid structure. For example, the words in an email are unstructured data. The email date and the addresses of the sender and the recipient are structured data. Artificial intelligence algorithms are used to process unstructured and semi-structured data in a way that makes the information useable.

Velocity refers to the speed at which the data is being produced. The amount of data is not only growing; it's growing exponentially as more people gain internet access, and more technology is created that connects humans to machines and machines to machines. Collecting and translating data (especially unstructured data) into usable information is complicated by how quickly new data is generated.

Veracity refers to the quality of the data. Data quality can be negatively affected by untrustworthy data sources, inconsistent or missing data, statistical biases, and human error. The veracity of unstructured data is especially difficult to determine. Machine learning, a type of artificial intelligence based on the idea that systems can learn from data and can identify patterns, is often used to assess data quality.

In summary, a set of data would be considered "big data" if:

- The data set is too large to be managed by traditional methods.
- The data set includes a variety of types of data (structured, semi-structured, and unstructured).
- The amount of data in the data set is expanding rapidly.
- The accuracy and reliability of the data may be uncertain.

Types of Data Analytics

LO1 Identify and define the four types of data analytics.

Data analytics can be categorized into four main types, ranging in sophistication from relatively straightforward to very complex. The first category is **descriptive analytics**, which describes what has happened over a given period of time. Simple examples include determining sales trends over a period of time and the relative effectiveness of various social media promotions based on click-through rates. Microsoft Excel and other spreadsheet programs include built-in functions that greatly simplify performing descriptive analytics.

Diagnostic analytics focuses more on why something occurred. This data analytics technique is used to monitor changes in data and often includes a certain amount of hypothesizing: Did the marketing campaign lead to the increase in sales? Did changing the beverage items affect food choices? Did the opening of competing restaurants negatively impact sales growth? Diagnostic analytics is useful because past performance is often a reliable predictor of future outcomes and can greatly aid in planning and forecasting.

Whereas descriptive and diagnostic analytics use data to try to understand what happened and why, **predictive analytics** uses data to try to determine what *will* happen. The movie *Moneyball* made the general manager of the Oakland Athletics, Billy Beane, famous for using predictive analytics to make personnel decisions in professional baseball. In his evaluation of baseball players, Beane used data to predict player performance so he could assemble the team with the greatest likelihood of winning the World Series. Banks also use predictive analytics to identify and prevent fraudulent transactions by monitoring customer credit card transactions and red flagging those that deviate from a customer behavior profile that was developed from previous transaction and geographic data.

Prescriptive analytics moves beyond what is going to happen to suggesting a course of action for what *should* happen to optimize outcomes. The forecasts created using predictive analytics can be used to make recommendations for future courses of action. For example, if we own a sports bar and determine there is a high likelihood of our local sports team winning the championship this year, we should expand the bar area and add more big-screen televisions to maximize revenues. **Exhibit B.1** summarizes the four types of data analytics.

Exhibit B.1 The Four Types of Data Analytics

Type of Data Analytics	Purpose	Example
Descriptive	To explain what happened	What were sales by month last year?
Diagnostic	To understand why it happened	Did the new advertising campaign cause sales to increase last quarter?
Predictive	To predict what will happen	Does this credit card charge deviate (amount, location, etc.) from past purchases by this credit card holder?
Prescriptive	To determine what should happen	How many servers should be on the schedule for game nights?

Data Analytics in the Accounting Profession

LO2 Describe the use of data analytics within the accounting profession.

Accountants are already preparing descriptive analytic reports regularly. Comparative income statements, sales reports by location, inventory valuation reports, and ratio calculations (average collection periods, days' sales in inventory, etc.) are all examples of descriptive analytics.

Budget variance reports and segment reports by region or product line prepared by accountants can be used for diagnostic analytics. Accountants may also work with sales and production managers to analyze the reasons behind changes in operating results. A distributor might want to know how much of the increase in overall sales last year was caused by the transfer of two of its representatives to other sales regions. A grocery store manager might want to know if the winter storm last month impacted sales in all or just some of the various departments. A production manager might work with the accounting department to determine any correlation between equipment repair costs and the number of units produced over the last two years.

Data analytics should not be limited to only descriptive and diagnostic analysis. Accountants can provide even more value by employing predictive and prescriptive analytics. Accountants can obtain data from a variety of company sources, including enterprise resource planning systems, customer relationship management systems, and point-of-sale systems, to aid them in obtaining insight into future outcomes and providing guidance for future actions. The area of credit granting provides an example. Predictive analytics can help compute credit scores to predict the likelihood of future payments. As a result, prescriptive analytics can aid in suggesting terms for granting credit. Predictive analytics can also be used to help analyze outstanding accounts receivables and determine estimated credit losses based on how much time has elapsed since the credit sale took place.

Many other opportunities exist for accountants to utilize data analytics. Tax accountants can apply data analysis to unique tax issues to suggest optimal tax strategies. Accountants serving as investment advisors can use big data to find patterns in consumer behavior that others can use to build analytic models for identifying investment opportunities.

Perhaps no area of accounting can benefit more from an understanding of data analytics than auditing. Auditors employ data analytics to shift from the sample-based audit model to one based on continuous modeling of much larger data sets. This allows auditors to identify the riskiest areas of an audit by focusing on outliers and exceptions.

The major accounting firms have fully embraced the power of data analytics. PricewaterhouseCoopers (PWC), Deloitte, Ernst & Young (EY), and KPMG all devote significant staffing resources to provide data analytics services to their clients. These firms claim they can help their clients optimize their data assets to aid in faster and better decisions. For example, PWC provides a flowchart starting with the building of a data foundation and applies advanced analytics to improving business performance, ultimately leading to opportunities for innovation.

While computers and software are instrumental in the entire process, the human element is the most critical factor in the success of any data analytics program. One commonality among surveys of top company managers is the value placed on data analytics for the company's future. Another commonality is the need for professionals trained in data analytics to help the company attain its goals.

Data Analytics in Accounting

Benford's Law provides an example of how data analytics has been used to uncover fraud in a national call center. Forensic accountants utilized their knowledge of Benford's Law to form evidence of a problem by observing patterns in the data. According to Benford's Law, in any list of financial transactions, the number one should occur as the first digit 30.1 percent of the time, with each successive number occurring as the first digit in lesser percentages, with the number nine occurring less than 5 percent of the time. Forensic accountants examined issued refunds and noticed an excessively high occurrence of the number four. The forensic accountants learned that the company had a policy that required supervisor approval of refunds that exceeded $50. The accountants were able to identify a small group of operators who had been issuing fraudulent refunds to family, friends, and themselves. These fraudulent $40 refunds totaled several hundred thousand dollars.

In order to be useful, data needs to be analyzed. Technology has provided the analyst with powerful tools that allow big data to provide insights that would not have been possible in the past. Still, the most important tool in the analytics toolkit comes from the analyst. Without critical thinking and good judgement, the value would remain locked within the data.

The Analytics Mindset[1]

eLectures
MBC
LO3
Describe the analytics mindset.

The analytics mindset consists of a four-step process of (1) asking the right questions; (2) extracting, transforming, and loading the necessary data; (3) applying appropriate data analytics techniques; and (4) interpreting and presenting the results. **Exhibit B.2** summarizes the steps and requirements of an analytics mindset.

[1] The analytics mindset discussed here is an approach developed by the Ernst & Young Foundation.

Exhibit B.2 Steps of an Analytics Mindset

Steps in the Analytics Mindset	Requirements
Ask the right questions	Understand the objectives of the end user Understand the underlying business processes
Extract, transform, and load the data	Know what to ask for Manage the data security Transform the data into the required format Cleanse the data for completeness and accuracy
Apply the appropriate analytics techniques	Determine if the need is for a confirmatory or an exploratory approach
Interpret and present the results	Use appropriate critical judgement regarding what you see Visually display the results in a format that is easy to understand without unnecessary clutter

Note that while technology is imbedded in this process, the process still begins and ends with the human element of asking the right questions and interpreting the results. Nothing is more critical than the first step of knowing what to ask. The right questions guide the process to find the right data to analyze and interpret.

Asking the right questions requires a few prerequisites. First, you need to know the audience that the analysis is for and what their objectives are. Next, you need to understand the context underlying the problem. For example, to analyze a marketing question you should understand the industry characteristics and the consumer demographics. Without this knowledge you may not select the correct indicators to analyze.

Along with knowing the right questions to ask, an analytical mindset requires you to form an idea of what to expect from the data. For example, when analyzing inventory salability, you would expect to see certain associated movements in sales and receivables.

After your questions are formed, you need to determine the data needed to aid in finding answers to those questions. This requires a knowledge of the data characteristics of the four V's previously mentioned. With this knowledge you can begin the data extraction process. Here you will need to know what data to ask for, how to manage data security, and what form the data will take.

Once you have the data, you will need to transform it into a format suitable for analysis. This is often referred to as data cleaning. Data is rarely found in the form of a nicely organized Excel spreadsheet. Rather, the data will often need to be converted into a proper format and tested for completeness and accuracy. Further, unnecessary data should be removed from the data set.

The data should then be loaded into the proper analysis tool, such as **Tableau** or Microsoft's **Power BI**. Once loaded, the data should again be cleansed to be sure it is ready for analysis in the chosen software.

It is necessary to determine the appropriate technique to analyze the data within the analysis tool. There are a multitude of ways that the data can be analyzed. Possible choices include computing ratios between associated measures, identifying trends among various measures, creating comparisons between dates, and sorting measures. The proper technique to use will be guided by the questions being asked.

In your interpretation of the data, you should ask yourself what do you see and is this what you expected? In other words, do these results make sense or did the results create new questions that require further analysis?

Eventually, the results must be packaged into a presentation that can be shared with the intended audience. Software such as Tableau, Power BI, or Excel can greatly enhance these presentations through their ability to create **visualizations** and **dashboards**. These visualizations can take many forms, from simple tables to bar or pie charts, to more sophisticated scatter plots, map charts, heat maps and more. Dashboards are created by combining multiple visualizations. Interactive dashboards allow users to filter out or drill down on content included in the charts and tables, on demand.

Data Analytic Tools

Technologies used by organizations to analyze data and communicate information to users are known as Business Intelligence (BI) tools. Data warehousing (data storage), data mining (extracting usable insights from data), and reporting and querying software are all BI tools.

Excel and Tableau are two popular BI tools that you will be using in the exercises and problems at the end of this Appendix.

Although Excel and Tableau can be used in similar ways, there are some important differences. Excel is a software application that is used for creating, organizing, and analyzing data. Tableau is a data visualization tool. Although calculations can be performed in Tableau, those calculations are made to create new fields for use in visualizations, not as support for accounting transactions. For example, Excel might be used to calculate sales commission amounts, which are then inputted into the accounting system. Tableau would not be used for that purpose.

Users in both Excel[2] and Tableau can

- Connect with different data sources
- Create visualizations and dashboards
- Work with big data sets

Tableau has much stronger interactivity tools and a more comprehensive selection of chart options. Excel generally has more flexibility and more extensive analytics tools.[3]

Accessing Excel and Tableau

Excel, if not available to you through your school, can be accessed for free by creating a Microsoft account at https://office.live.com/start/Excel.aspx. A free version of Tableau (Tableau Public) is available to you at https://public.tableau.com/en-us/s/. Tableau Public has most of the functions of Tableau Desktop (the full version). However, you can't save your workbooks locally if you're using Tableau Public. Instead, all workbooks are saved online and are accessible to any Tableau user unless you elect to hide your visualizations. Hiding visualizations is done in Settings once you've registered for Tableau on the Tableau website. Walk-through videos are available for every exercise and problem at cambridgepub.com. Tableau tutorial videos are available at https://www.tableau.com/learn/training/.

Data Visualization

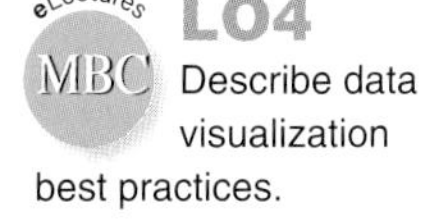

LO4 Describe data visualization best practices.

As noted above, the final step in the analytics mindset is to present your results. This is often done in the form of a visualization. While it is possible to present results as a bunch of tables full of numbers, visualizations with imagery are often a far better means to convey the raw numbers. Visualizations can be thought of as a blending of the art of design with the science of data.

There is an unlimited number of ways that data can be presented; however, certain best practices exist that can serve as a guide when building a visualization. For example, the exact same data on GDP levels are shown in the three charts in **Exhibit B.3**, but each displays the data differently. The table presents the raw data; however, the reader cannot easily rank the different economies. The two bar charts both show the same data, however the one all in blue makes it far easier to compare economies by showing the data in sorted order. Also, note that adding multiple colors to the other bar chart does nothing to aid the reader, rather it just adds confusion.

Visualizations can be divided into two primary categories, exploratory and explanatory. **Exploratory visualizations** are meant to allow the reader to explore the data presented in order to do additional analysis. Exploratory visualizations would normally include interactive tools like filters that allow the user to change the level of data displayed. This can be useful when the problem is not clearly defined, and the reader wishes to gain a further understanding of the data.

[2] Full functionality in Excel is only available if you have Excel 2010 or newer and you are running a 64-bit version of Windows. To determine the version of Windows on your computer, go to Settings>System>About. The version will be listed in the Device specifications section.

[3] Pan and Blankley, Excel vs. Tableau: See your data differently, *Journal of Accountancy*, February 29, 2020.

Exhibit B.3 ■ Different Displays of the Same Data

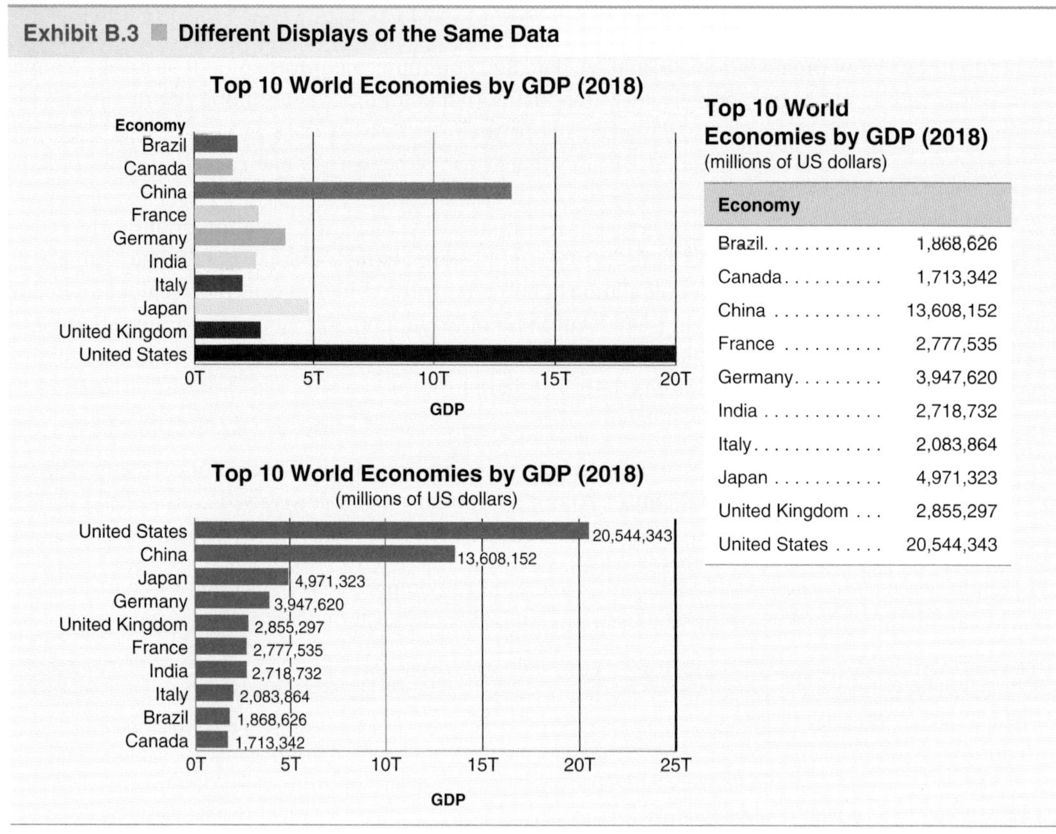

Top 10 World Economies by GDP (2018)
(millions of US dollars)

Economy	
Brazil.	1,868,626
Canada.	1,713,342
China	13,608,152
France	2,777,535
Germany.	3,947,620
India	2,718,732
Italy.	2,083,864
Japan	4,971,323
United Kingdom . . .	2,855,297
United States	20,544,343

In contrast to exploratory visualizations, **explanatory visualizations** are used to convey information to the audience. A classic example of such a visualization was prepared in 1854 by the British physician Dr. John Snow. Dr. Snow plotted cholera deaths in central London on a map that also showed the location of water pumps. The visualization identified the relationship between these deaths and the Broad Street water pump and lead to a change in the water and waste systems. Dr. Snow's visualization is shown in **Exhibit B.4**.

Exhibit B.4 ■ Cholera Deaths in London in 1854

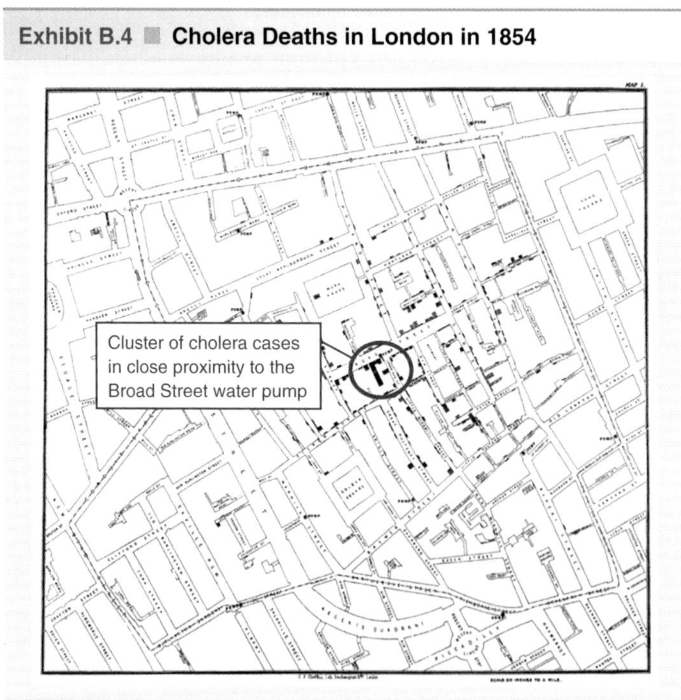

Good visualization design can be enhanced by considering how our brains process visual details such as form, position, and color.

For example, items that are different from the rest become the focus of attention as shown in **Exhibit B.5**. An item that is longer, wider, or in a different orientation will stand out, as will an item that is of a different size, shape, in a different position, or has a different hue or intensity of color.

Exhibit B.5 Displays that Emphasize How Differences Focus Our Attention

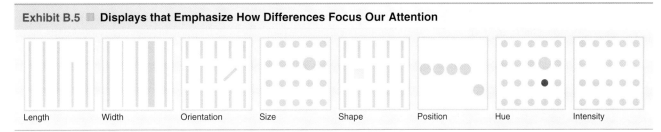

Length | Width | Orientation | Size | Shape | Position | Hue | Intensity

While the use of color can help an item to stand out, it is important to use color correctly. The use of too much color can add to visual clutter. And it's important that color is used consistently, such as always representing a certain year or category. The choice of color is also important since color can convey meanings that differ from one culture to another. For example, red may mean good luck and green may mean jealousy.

Good visualization design requires the removal of items that detract from the message that we are trying to communicate. **Visual clutter** confuses the audience and lessens the chance that they will be able to easily understand the information that is being conveyed. The concept that less is more is the essence of the visualization design principles developed by Edward Tufte, a statistician and professor emeritus at Yale University. Tufte uses the term chart-junk to refer to any unnecessary or confusing elements included in information displays. His principles show that "excellence in statistical graphics consists of ideas communicated with clarity, precision and efficiency."[4]

Exhibit B.6 illustrates **Tufte's principles**. Note in the first visualization all of the visual clutter only serves to distract the audience from seeing the main point that the U.S. is the largest economy based on its GDP. Now notice how much cleaner the second visualization is after removing the distracting yellow background, the color coding of each economy, the redundant labeling, and the unnecessary grid lines.

Exhibit B.6 Illustration of Tufte's Principles

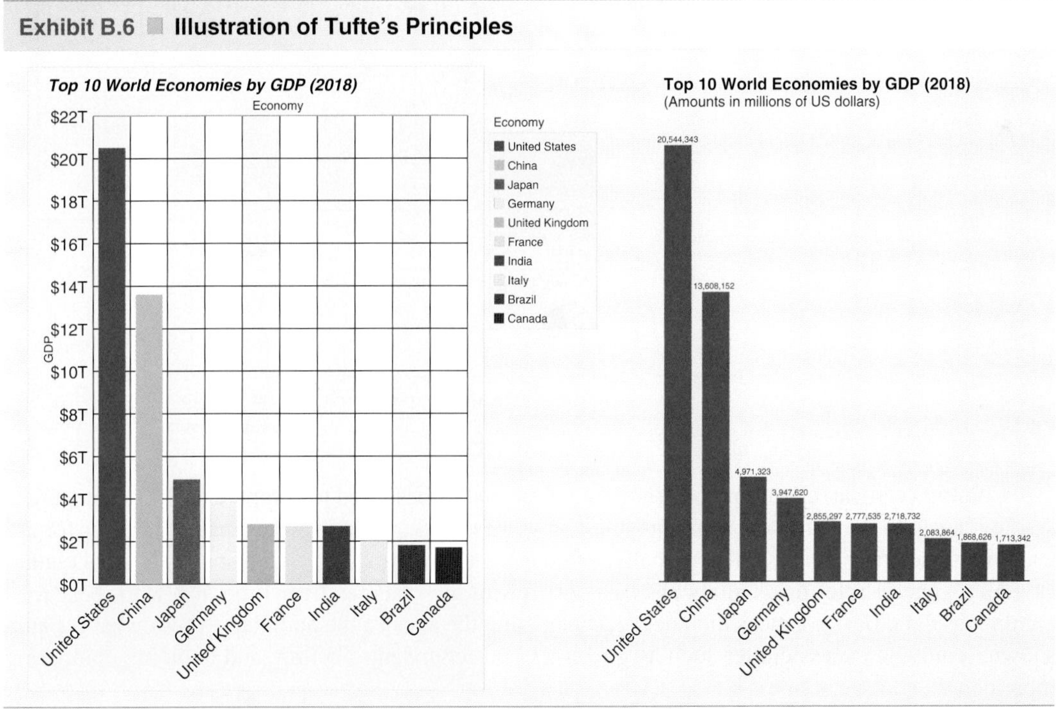

[4] E.R. Tufte, *The Visual Display of Quantitative Information* (Graphics Press, Cheshire, CT 2001).

Good visualization construction also involves choosing the most effective chart type depending on what information is being presented.

The starting point for all of the visualizations we will be discussing is a simple table of data. While the table is excellent for looking up values and can precisely communicate numerical values, visualizations in the form of charts provide the audience an easier method to see what the analyst is attempting to convey.

Among the most used chart types, column and bar charts are best for showing comparisons, line charts are useful for showing trends, pie charts are typically used for showing how individual parts make up a whole, and scatter plots are best for showing relationships and distributions. **Exhibit B.7**, reprinted with permission from the author, provides an excellent tool to help in choosing the correct chart type.[5]

Exhibit B.7 Chart Types

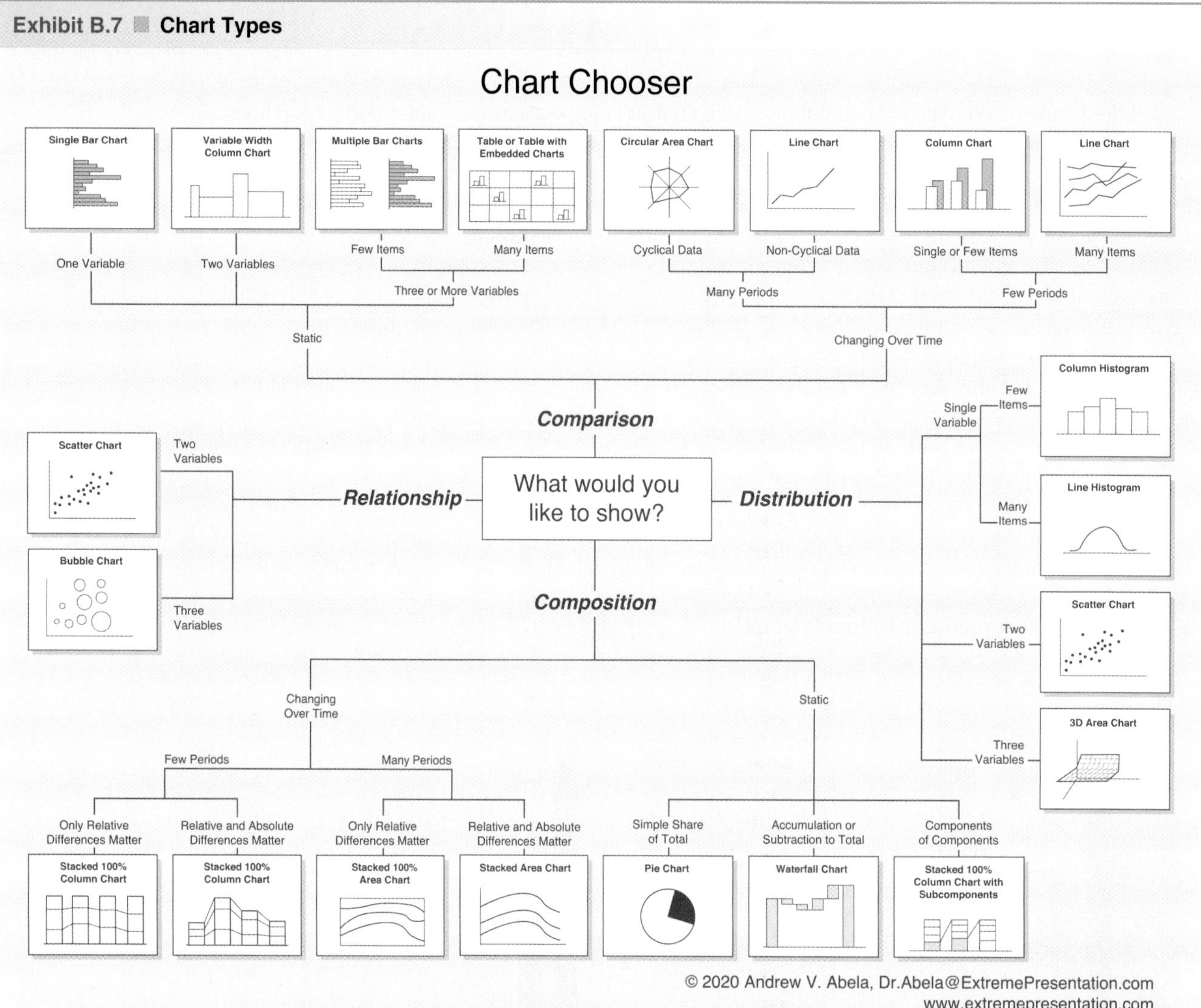

Column (vertical) charts and **bar** (horizontal) charts are best used to compare different categories. Adding labels to the bars rather than just having values showing on the axes makes it easier for the audience to determine these values. Finally, avoid using too many colors that just add to visual clutter.

As a general rule, **line charts** are best for illustrating changes over time and work best with continuous data. Best practices include clearly labeling the axes so the audience knows what is being shown, removing excess clutter such as grid lines and redundant labeling, and avoiding comparing more than five to seven lines.

[5] Abela, Andrew V. (2013). *Advanced Presentations by Design: Creating Communication that Drives Action*. John Wiley & Sons.

Pie charts are best used to show parts of a whole. Be sure the parts add up to 100 percent. Pie charts work best when there are just a few categories. If there are many categories of similar size, consider using a bar or column chart instead. Finally, avoid the temptation to get "fancy" with 3-D imagery and tilting the pie chart.

Scatter plots are useful if the goal is to show correlations between two variables. They are also useful for showing data distributions and clustering, which can identify anomalies and outliers. A **bubble chart** can extend the capability of a scatter plot by adding an additional dimension through changing the size of each bubble in the scatter plot. The more data that is included in a scatter plot or bubble chart, the better are the comparisons that can be made. If the elements being graphed are distributed over a very wide range, the horizontal axis can be converted from a linear to a logarithmic scale (where the numbers on the horizontal axis increase by multiples of a number). Bubble charts should use only circles rather than other shapes. Bubble charts should be scaled based on the area of the circle and not the diameter.

A **map chart** is a good choice if the data being conveyed in the visualization includes geographic locations. Map charts are best at showing relative differences in numerical values among geographic locations rather than precise differences since the values are usually portrayed as differences in a color gradient.

There are several general rules to follow regardless of the chart type. The following list was found from a search of best practices for data visualization charts.[6]

- Time axis. When using time in charts, set it on the horizontal axis. Time should run from left to right. Do not skip values (time periods), even if there are no values.
- Proportional values. The numbers in a chart (displayed as bar, area, bubble, or other physically measured element in the chart) should be directly proportional to the numerical quantities presented.
- Visual clutter. Remove any excess information, lines, colors, and text from a chart that do not add value.
- Sorting. For column and bar charts, to enable easier comparison, sort your data in ascending or descending order by the value, not alphabetically. This applies also to pie charts.
- Legend. You don't need a legend if you have only one data category.
- Labels. Use labels directly on the line, column, bar, pie, etc., whenever possible, to avoid indirect look-up.
- Colors. In any chart, don't use more than six colors.
- Colors. For comparing the same value at different time periods, use the same color in a different intensity (from light to dark).
- Colors. For different categories, use different colors. The most widely used colors are black, white, red, green, blue, and yellow.
- Colors. Keep the same color palette or style for all charts in the series and the same axes and labels for similar charts to make your charts consistent and easy to compare.

Summary of Learning Objectives

Identify and define the four types of data analytics. LO1

- Data analytics can broadly be defined as the process of examining sets of data with the goal of discovering useful information from patterns found in the data.
- Data analytics can be categorized into four types: descriptive, diagnostic, predictive, and prescriptive.

Describe the use of data analytics within the accounting profession. LO2

- Many accountants are already performing descriptive and diagnosite data analytics.
- Accountants can add value by performing predictive and prescriptive data analytics.
- The large accounting firms have devoted large resources to data analytics.
- Being well trained in data analytics is important for future accountants.

[6] https://eazybi.com/blog/data_visualization_and_chart_types/

LO3 **Describe the analytics mindset.**

- Big data has the characteristics of volume, variety, velocity, and veracity.
- Analytics is the process of deriving value from the data.
- An analytics mindset requires critical thinking and judgement.
- The four steps of the analytics mindset include (1) asking the right questions; (2) extracting, transforming, and loading the data; (3) applying the proper analytics techniques; and (4) interpreting and presenting the results.

LO4 **Describe data visualization best practices.**

- Form, position, and color can be used to have elements stand out without any conscious effort by the audience.
- Tufte's principles of design emphasize the elimination of visual clutter that serves to distract from the ability of a visualization to convey its message.
- Use of the proper chart type can help the intended audience to visualize comparisons, compositions, distributions, and relationships in the data.

Key Concepts and Terms

Bar (p. 526)
Benford's Law (p. 521)
Big data (p. 519)
Bubble chart (p. 527)
Column chart (p. 526)
Dashboards (p. 522)
Data analytics (p. 519)
Descriptive analytics (p. 520)
Diagnostic analytics (p. 520)
Explanatory visualizations (p. 524)
Exploratory visualizations (p. 523)
Line charts (p. 526)
Map chart (p. 527)
Pie chart (p. 527)
Predictive analytics (p. 520)
Prescriptive analytics (p. 520)
Scatter plot (p. 527)
Tufte's principles (p. 525)
Variety (p. 519)
Velocity (p. 519)
Veracity (p. 519)
Visual clutter (p. 525)
Visualizations (p. 522)
Volume (p. 519)

Questions

LO1, 2 **QB-1.** Which of the following are the four categories of data analytics?

a. Descriptive, diagnostic, predictive, prescriptive
b. Expressive, diagnostic, predictive, prescriptive
c. Descriptive, analytical, predictive, prescriptive
d. Descriptive, diagnostic, prognostic, prescriptive

LO3 **QB-2.** Which of the following are four characteristics of big data?

a. Volume, variety, vagueness, veracity
b. Volume, variety, velocity, veracity
c. Volume, validate, velocity, veracity
d. Volume, variety, velocity, vulnerability

LO3 **QB-3.** What is the correct order of the steps in the analytics mindset?

a. Extract, transform, and load the data; ask the right questions; apply the proper analytics techniques; interpret and present the results.
b. Ask the right questions; extract, transform, and load the data; apply the proper analytics techniques; interpret and present the results.
c. Ask the right questions; extract, transform, and load the data; interpret and present the results; apply the proper analytics techniques.
d. Ask the right questions; apply the proper analytics techniques; extract, transform, and load the data; interpret and present the results.

QB-4. Charts are used in visualizations to convey the following primary types of information: **LO4**

a. comparisons, compositions, distributions, and relationships.

b. comparisons, historical, distributions, and relationships.

c. comparisons, compositions, forecasts, and relationships.

d. geographical, compositions, distributions, and relationships.

QB-5. Which of the following statements is not true regarding the use of color in a chart? **LO4**

a. Use at most six different colors in a chart.

b. To show changes in an item over time use a color gradient rather than different colors.

c. Always use color in a chart to differentiate items.

d. Use the same color palette in a chart series.

Assignments with the logo in the margin are available in myBusinessCourse. See the Preface of the book for details.

Exercises

EB-6. Public Accounting Firms and Data Analytics **LO1, 2**
Go to PWC.com and select "Services" and then "Data and Analytics." Choose a topic and write about how PWC is using data analytics to help its clients.

EB-7. Public Accounting Firms and Data Analytics **LO1, 2**
Go to KPMG.com and select "Insights." Under "Areas of interest," select "Special Attention" and then "Data and Analytics." Choose a topic and write about how KPMG is using data analytics to help its clients.

EB-8. Public Accounting Firms and Data Analytics **LO1, 2**
Go to Deloitte.com and select "Services" and then "Analytics." Choose a topic and write about how Deloitte is using data analytics to help its clients.

EB-9. Public Accounting Firms and Data Analytics **LO1, 2**
Go to EY.com and enter Big data and analytics in the search bar. Choose a topic and write about how Ernst & Young is using data analytics to help its clients.

Problems

Problems PB-10 through PB-12 use financial statement data for S&P 500 companies for the years 2015 through 2019. The Excel file Compustat_SP500_2015_2019.xlsx is accessible on the textbook's website. A video demonstrating Tableau tools used to answer the questions in the next two problems is also available on the website.

PB-10. Building Basic Tableau Visualizations **LO3, 4**

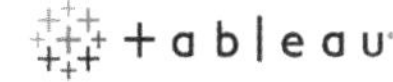

a. Connect the Tableau software to the Excel file Compustat_SP500_2015_2019.xlsx. This file consists of four workbooks. First bring in the Balance sheet workbook and then join both the cash flow statement and the income statement workbook to the balance sheet workbook using both of the fields company name and year.

b. What is the sum of net income for all firms in the database for all years combined? One way to determine this is to drag the measure Net income to the canvas.

c. How many unique companies are included in the database? One way to determine this is to drag the dimension Company name to the rows shelf and then select Measure Count(Distinct) from the pull down menu on the Company name pill.

d. How many distinct firms are there in each segment? One way to determine this is to drag the dimension Segment to the Columns shelf in the visualization created in part *c*. The totals for each segment will appear if the Show marks label is checked in the Label card.

e. What is the sum of total assets for all companies in each segment for the year 2018? One way to determine this is to drag the dimension Segment to the Columns shelf and then drag the Total Assets measure to the Rows shelf. Next drag the Year dimension to the filters shelf, select year as the filter, click next and then check 2018. Totals for total assets can be seen in the tool tip by hovering over any bar or by checking Show marks label in the Label card.

f. What firm had the most sales in 2018? What segment was this firm in? One way to determine this is to drag the dimension Company name to the rows shelf and drag the measure Sales to the columns shelf. Next drag the Year dimension to the filters shelf, select year as the filter, click next and then check 2018. Segments can be highlighted by dragging the dimension Segment over the color card. Finally sort the Company names by Sales by clicking the sort icon in the tool bar.

g. Save the file for future use.

LO3, 4

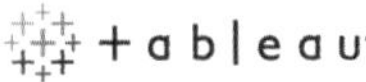

PB-11. Tableau Visualizations to Analyze Accounting Performance Measures

You recently joined a firm as a junior financial analyst, and you would like to make a good impression by showing your manager the power of visualizations for analyzing data. In order to get a feel for the Tableau software and the dataset you created of financial statement data for S&P 500 firms, you decided to create a few very basic visualizations. Two widely used ratios to analyze company performance are gross profit percentage and return on sales. You decide to create a visualization that compares these two ratios by segment and further compares segment performance to the median values of these ratios for the entire database of companies.

a. Because of the way cost of goods sold is reported for companies in the real estate segment you decide to exclude this segment from the visualization. After excluding real estate, for the year 2017, which segment reported the highest median value for gross profit percentage and for return on sales?

b. Did any segment report a higher median return on sales than the upper band of the 95 percent confidence interval of overall median return on sales in 2015?

c. What company had the highest gross profit percentage in 2018 for the segment with the highest median gross profit percentage?

LO3, 4

PB-12. Using Tableau to Analyze Inventory

You have learned of the importance of a company being able to sell its products in a timely fashion, and that the ratio of days sales in inventory provides this useful information. You decide a dashboard would be helpful in seeing if this ratio is improving or declining in the consumer discretionary and the consumer staples segments between 2017 and 2018. You build two sheets that are included in the dashboard. The first sheet shows the level of the ratio for each segment for the two years in question. The second sheet shows the change in the ratio between the two years.

Has the ratio days sales in inventory improved or declined in the consumer discretionary and the consumer staples segments between 2017 and 2018. By how much?

LO2, 3

+tableau

PB-13. Using Tableau for Fraud Detection

Benford's Law represents a powerful tool in the forensic accountant's toolkit to aid in the detection of fraud. Benford's Law is a mathematical law that recognizes the leading (first) digit in many real-life number sets is distributed in a certain manner, and often not in the manner that a fraudster would expect. Specifically the number 1 occurs as the first digit approximately 30 percent of the time, with each succeeding digit appearing less often as follows: 1–30%, 2–18%, 3–12%, 4–10%, 5–8%, 6–7%, 7–6%, 8–5%, and 9–5%. Fraudsters who are unaware of this natural ordering will often arrange digits in a random order that deviates from Benford's Law.

In Part A of this problem you will use Tableau to show how a natural data set of GDP by country conforms to Benford's Law and how a random set of numbers does not. In Part B you will use the same data used in an actual court case to convict a fraudster of embezzlement. Finally, in Part C you will use Benford's Law to test a new reimbursement procedure for possible fraud. A video demonstrating the Tableau tools used in this problem is available on this textbook's website.

Part A Use Tableau to show how a natural data set of GDP by country conforms to Benford's Law and how a random set of numbers does not.

- Download the file **GDP Tableau.xlsx** from the textbook website. The file contains World Bank GDP data by country for 2018, along with a separate column of random numbers that was generated in Excel using the command =RAND()*1000.

- After you have uploaded the workbook to Tableau, create two calculated fields.
- The first calculated field will pull the first digit from each country's GDP amount. Choose Analysis > Create Calculated Field and name the calculation First Integer. Then either type or paste the following formula in the formula area: LEFT(STR([GDP]),1)
- Next create a second calculated field named Benfords Law by typing or pasting the following in the formula area: LOG(INT([First Integer])+1)- LOG(INT([First Integer]))
- To create the visualization, drag First Integer from the Dimensions area to Columns and drag Number of Records from the Measures area to Rows. Click Sum(Number of Records) on Rows to show the pull-down menu and choose Quick Table Calculation > Percent of Total. The visualization should now show a bar chart with the bars conforming to Benford's Law.
- While it is relatively easy to see that the data conforms to Benford's Law, with a little more work the visualization can be significantly enhanced. To do this, drag Benfords Law from the Measures area of the Data pane to Detail on the Marks card, and then click Benfords Law on the Marks card and choose Measure > Minimum.
- Next switch from the current Data pane to the Analytics pane and then drag Distribution Band over the chart and drop it on the cell icon in the pop-up. A dialog box will appear. Under computation change the value to percentages of 90,100,110 and select Percent of to be Min(Benfords Law). Choose a fill line as the thick black line and then click OK.
- Finally click on the Label icon in the Marks section and select the Show marks labels box.

a. Does the GDP data appear to conform to Benford's Law?

Now return to the Data pane and create a new calculated field for the random numbers by naming the calculation Random Values and typing or pasting the following formula in the formula area: LEFT(STR([Random]),1)

- Drag the Min(Benfords Law) pill out of the Marks area to remove the bands and drag Random Values from the Dimensions area on top of First Integer to replace it in the visualization. If both pills remain in the columns section, simply drag First Integer away.

b. Do the random values appear to conform with Benford's Law?

Part B Use the same data used in an actual court case to convict a fraudster of embezzlement.

In the 1993 court case *State of Arizona v. Wayne James Nelson* Benford's Law was used to convict the defendant of defrauding the state of nearly $2 million by diverting money to a nonexistent vendor. Nelson tried to make the checks appear random; however, he was unaware that these check amounts should actually follow Benford's Law much closer than the random distribution he created. Download the file **Arizona fraud.xlsx** from the textbook website and follow the same procedure as you did in Part A above.

a. From a casual observation of the checks, can you detect anything suspect?
b. After using Benford's Law, does the list of checks appear suspect?

Part C Use Benford's Law to test a new reimbursement procedure for possible fraud.

Wally's Enterprises has been reimbursing its employees for business expenses after the employee submits detailed evidence of the expense, such as paid receipts. Management has recently changed the reimbursement policy because of the time spent checking all the submitted evidence, with an especially high volume of smaller reimbursement requests. The new policy only requires evidence be submitted if the reimbursement request exceeds $50. As the company's internal auditor, you are concerned that this policy change may result in fraudulent reimbursement requests. In order to test the new policy, you have gathered a random sample of 100 reimbursement requests from both before and after the policy change. This data is located in the file **Expense Reimbursement.xlsx** on the textbook's web page. Download this file and use Benford's Law to test whether the new policy appears to have resulted in any fraud.

a. Do the reimbursement requests prior to the policy change appear to follow Benford's Law?
b. Do the reimbursement requests occurring after the policy change appear to follow Benford's Law?
c. What, if anything, leads you to believe that fraud may be occurring?

LO3, 4

PB-14. Segment Reports Using Tableau (Descriptive and Diagnostic Analytics)
Southern Comforts, Inc. is a department store chain with stores in North Carolina, Tennessee, Kentucky, and West Virginia. Its corporate headquarters are located in Charlotte, North Carolina.

In the past, the store owners only received financial reports for the company operations overall. They have recently asked for reports of costs and profitability by segment (Location and department). Southern Comforts' locations include the four stores (Charlotte, Nashville, Virginia Beach, and Louisville) and the corporate office (Charlotte HQ). Departments include the product lines (Mens, Womens, Kids, Shoes, and Home) and the overhead expense types (Facilities, Labor, and Other).

They have provided you with an Excel workbook that includes Southern Comfort transactions for 2020. (The workbook, **Segment Report Data Set Tableau.xlsx**, is accessible on the textbook's website. A video demonstrating Tableau tools used to answer the questions in this problem is also available on the website.)

The first step is to make sure the data is in the form needed.

- Convert the data to a table.
- Check each column to make sure there is no missing or inconsistent data. Make any corrections necessary. *HINT:* There are two errors. One error is in the Month column. The other is in the State column.
- All transactions are included in the Transactions column. You will need to separate revenue transactions from expense transactions. Use the IF function to create a Revenues column and an Expenses column. (All positive numbers in the Transactions columns are Revenues; all negative numbers are expenses. You may want to change the sign of the amounts in the Expense column to positives.)
- Add a column after Month and call it Month Name. Use the TEXT function to convert the date format to a text format (name of the month).

Save the file with a new name. Open Tableau and import the workbook.

1. Create Sheets in Tableau to answer the following questions:
   a. Which store was the most profitable (in dollars)? What was that store's profit? Which store had the most revenue? How much?
   b. Which month had the highest revenue? How much? What percentage of total sales occurred during that month? (Round % to two decimals.) Which month was the least **profitable** (in dollars)? What was the net profit that month? *HINT:* You will need to include the corporate costs to determine net profit.
   c. What was the total gross margin (in dollars) for 2020? Which store had the highest gross margin? How much? *HINT:* You will need to filter out the overhead expense categories (Facilities, Labor, and Other).
   d. What was the total gross profit ratio for 2020? (Round % to two decimals.) Which store had the lowest gross profit ratio? Which product line (department) had the highest gross profit ratio?
2. The store with the highest sales (b.) and the highest gross margin (d.) was not the most profitable (a.). Why? Look at the revenues, gross profit margins and ratios, and the overhead expenses for both stores.
3. Create charts on your Sheets and use them to create an interactive dashboard. Include filters to allow users to look at selected data.

LO3, 4

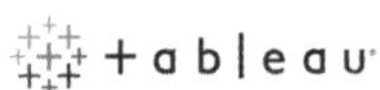

PB-15. Job Profitability Using Tableau (Descriptive and Diagnostic Analytics)
Harvard Products is a job shop (a company that manufactures custom products in small batches). Each batch is managed by one of Harvard's four project managers. Manufacturing facilities are located in Illinois, Wisconsin, Michigan, and Indiana.

The President of Harvard Products has asked for information about costs and profits by job, Location, customer, and project manager. A summary of costs (by job) is included in the **Job Order Data Set-Tableau.xlsx** file available on the textbook's website. A video demonstrating Tableau tools used to answer the questions in this problem is also available on the website.

Before uploading the workbook to Tableau, add columns to the Data sheet to separate out account amounts (revenue, direct material, etc.). The IF function is useful here.

Once you've uploaded the workbook to Tableau, change the data type for Job # to text. (It should be a Dimension, not a Measure.) Give Location a geographic role.

Create sheets in Tableau to answer the following questions:

1. Which customer was the most profitable for Harvard? What was the job number for the most profitable job for that customer? What was the average revenue on jobs for that customer ? What was the average revenue for all jobs?
2. Which Location was the least profitable (in dollars) for Harvard? What appears to have contributed more to the lower profits at that Location—size of jobs (average revenue) or profit margin ratios? Which Location had the highest average revenue per job?

HINT: To answer the next three questions, you will need to create four new fields. One for the gross profit ratio and one for the three expense ratios.

3. Which Location had the highest gross profit ratio? Which cost element had the highest expense ratio in that Location? What Location had the lowest gross profit ratio? Which cost element had the highest expense ratio in that Location? Which cost element had the largest expense ratio difference between Locations? What factors might be causing those differences?
4. The President of Harvard Products has decided to give performance bonuses to project managers. Determine which project manager will receive the highest bonus if performance is based on:
   a. Average revenue per job?
   b. Number of jobs? *HINT:* You'll need to duplicate Job # to get a count. (Counts would be Measures.)
   c. Total profit?
   d. Profit margin ratios?
5. Create a Dashboard the president could use when evaluating different bonus calculation performance measures. Use a map for one of the sheets included in the dashboard.
6. Based solely on the information you have available, would you encourage management to close the facility with the lowest profit margin? Why or why not? Include in your answer the information you might need to have before making a final decision.

PB-16. Determining Fixed vs. Variable Cost Components Using Tableau (Diagnostic Analytics) LO3, 4

+ a b l e a u

Genessee Industries introduced a new product last year (6582-D). Although it was very popular, it wasn't very profitable. Management has asked you to provide them with information to help them set a new sales price.

You know that the direct costs per unit are $25 for direct materials and $5 for direct labor. You are given information about last year's monthly production levels and manufacturing overhead costs (indirect materials, indirect labor, and other). (That information is included in the **Fixed and Variable Data Set Tableau.xlsx** file available on the textbook's website. A video demonstrating Tableau tools used to answer the questions in this problem is also available on the website.)

1. Use the Trendline tool in Tableau to determine the fixed and variable components for each of the three manufacturing overhead components. Use the default model type (linear). (Round all amounts to two decimals.)
   a. What is the cost formula for indirect materials?
   b. What is the cost formula for indirect labor?
   c. What is the cost formula for other manufacturing overhead?
2. What is the cost formula for 6582-D (per month)?
3. Determine the minimum sales price Genessee could charge to achieve a monthly gross profit of $7,500 next year. Management expects unit sales will average 1,500 per month. *HINT:* You won't be able to use Tableau for this. Start by determining the CVP formula.

PB-17. Forecasting Using Tableau (Predictive Analytics) LO3, 4

+ a b l e a u

Melton Manufacturing opened in January 2019. Sales have increased significantly in the first two years of operations, and management is now looking to expand production capacity. To finance the purchase of a new factory, they would need to either raise capital or borrow funds.

They have asked you to make some projections for the next year of operations. They intend to share these with potential investors and lenders.

Information about unit sales, sales revenues, and net profits for the past two years is included in the **Forecasting Data Set Tableau.xlsx** file available on the textbook's website. (A video demonstrating Tableau tools used to answer the questions in this problem is also available on the website.)

1. Create a worksheet that shows revenues, net operating income, and units sold by month. Add a Forecast. *HINT:* There will be three graphs
   a. Extend the trendline out for one full year. Since you have complete data for each month, do not ignore the last month of 2020.
   b. Use a prediction interval of 95%

2. Use the forecasts to determine:
   a. Expected unit sales in October 2021
   b. Expected sales revenue in June 2021
   c. Expected net operating income in December 2021
3. Open the Describe Forecast screen. Use the Summary tab to determine:
   a. What percent of the forecast was attributed to seasonality for net operating income?
   b. What was the range given for number of units sold for January 2021?
5. Duplicate the worksheet as a cross-tab and swap the axes. Filter out details for net operating income and units sold. For December 2021, what is Tableau's:
   a. estimate?
   b. lower prediction interval?
   c. upper prediction interval?
6. How could Melton use forecasts to manage or expand the business?

A video demonstrating the use of Microsoft Excel to use Benford's Law in the detection of fraud is available on the textbook's website to assist in solving problem PB-18.

LO2, 3

PB-18. Using Excel for Fraud Detection

Benford's Law represents a powerful tool in the forensic accountant's toolkit to aid in the detection of fraud. Benford's Law is a mathematical law that recognizes the leading (first) digit in many real-life number sets is distributed in a certain manner, and often not in the manner that a fraudster would expect. Specifically the number 1 occurs as the first digit approximately 30 percent of the time, with each succeeding digit appearing less often as follows: 1–30%, 2–18%, 3–12%, 4–10%, 5–8%, 6–7%, 7–6%, 8–5%, and 9–5%. Fraudsters who are unaware of this natural ordering will often arrange digits in a random order that deviates from Benford's Law.

In Part A of this problem you will use Microsoft Excel to show how a natural data set of GDP by country conforms to Benford's Law and how a random set of numbers does not. In Part B you will use the same data used in an actual court case to convict a fraudster of embezzlement. Finally, in Part C you will use Benford's Law to test a new reimbursement procedure for possible fraud. A video demonstrating the Excel tools used in this problem is available on the textbook's website.

Part A Use Microsoft Excel to show how a natural data set of GDP by country conforms to Benford's Law and how a random set of numbers does not.

- Download the file **GDP.xlsx** from the textbook website. The file contains World Bank GDP data by country for 2018.
- In order to use Benford's Law you need to first extract the leading digit from each country's GDP amount. To do this, place the cursor in cell C2 and input the formula =Left(B2,1). Copy this formula down column C for each country.
- Next in cells F2 through F10 input the numbers 1 through 9. In cell G2 input the formula =COUNTIF(c2:C205,F2) and copy the formula down for each number 1 through 9. This formula goes through the entire range of extracted first digits in column C and records the count of these digits in the cell if it matches the number in column F.
- Sum the column total in cell G11.
- Next determine the percentage that each leading digit appears by dividing the amount in column G by the total of these amounts in cell G11 and place this figure in column H.
- In column I, compute the predicted occurrences of each digit (given above) by placing the formula
  =Log10(1/F2+1) in cell I2 and copying the formula down the column.
- Finally create a Combo chart to visualize these results by highlighting cells H1:I10 and selecting Combo chart.

a. Do the naturally occurring GDP amounts appear to follow Benford's Law?

- Next replace the GDP amounts with random numbers to see if random numbers also obey Benford's Law.
- Input the formula =Rand()*1000 in cell B2 and copy this formula down the column.
- Observe the results in the table and the chart. Try to recalculate the spreadsheet several times to obtain different sets of random numbers.

b. Do random numbers appear to follow Benford's Law?

Part B Use the same data used in an actual court case to convict a fraudster of embezzlement.

In the 1993 court case *State of Arizona v. Wayne James Nelson* Benford's Law was used to convict the defendant of defrauding the state of nearly $2 million by diverting money to a nonexistent vendor. Nelson tried to make the checks appear random; however, he was unaware that these check amounts should actually follow Benford's Law much closer than the distribution he created. Download the file **Arizona fraud.xlsx** from the textbook website and follow the same procedure as you did in Part A above.

a. From a casual observation of the checks, can you detect anything suspect?
b. After using Benford's Law, does the list of checks appear suspect?

Part C Use Benford's Law to test a new reimbursement procedure for possible fraud.

Jimmy's Enterprises has been reimbursing its employees for business expenses after the employee submits detailed evidence of the expense, such as paid receipts. Management has recently changed the reimbursement policy because of the time spent checking all the submitted evidence, with an especially high volume of smaller reimbursement requests. The new policy requires evidence be submitted only if the reimbursement request exceeds $50. As the company's internal auditor, you are concerned that this policy change may result in fraudulent reimbursement requests. In order to test the new policy, you have gathered a random sample of 100 reimbursement requests from both before and after the policy change. This data is located in the file **Expense Reimbursement Excel.xlsx** on the textbook's web page. Download this file and use Benford's Law to test whether the new policy appears to have resulted in any fraud.

a. Do the reimbursement requests prior to the policy change appear to follow Benford's Law?
b. Do the reimbursement requests occurring after the policy change appear to follow Benford's Law?
c. What, if anything, leads you to believe that fraud may be occurring?

PB-19. Segment Reports Using Excel (Descriptive and Diagnostic Analytics) **LO3, 4**

Southern Comforts, Inc. is a department store chain with stores in North Carolina, Tennessee, Kentucky, and West Virginia. Its corporate headquarters are located in Charlotte, North Carolina.

In the past, the store owners only received financial reports for the company operations overall. They have recently asked for reports of costs and profitability by segment (location and department). Southern Comforts' locations include the four stores (Charlotte, Nashville, Virginia Beach, and Louisville) and the corporate office (Charlotte HQ). Departments include the product lines (Mens, Womens, Kids, Shoes, and Home) and the overhead expense types (Facilities, Labor, and Other).

They have provided you with an Excel workbook that includes Southern Comfort transactions for 2020. (The workbook, **Segment Report Data Set.xlsx**, is accessible on the textbook's website. A video demonstrating Excel tools used to answer the questions in this problem is also available on the website.).

The first step is to make sure the data is in the form needed.

- All transactions are included in the Transactions column. You will need to separate revenue transactions from expense transactions. Add two columns to the table. Use the IF function to create a Revenues column and an Expenses column. (All positive numbers in the Transactions columns are Revenues; all negative numbers are expenses.) *HINT:* To save some time, convert the data to a Table.
- Add a column after Month and call it Month Name. Use the TEXT function to convert the date format to a text format.

1. Use pivot tables to answer the following questions:
   a. Which store was the most profitable (in dollars)? What was the store's profit?
   b. Which store had the most revenue? How much? Which month had the highest revenue? How much? What percentage of total sales occurred during that month? (Round % to two decimals.)
   c. Which month was the least **profitable** (in dollars)? What was the net profit that month?
   d. What was the total gross margin (in dollars) for 2020? Which store had the highest gross margin? How much? *HINT:* Consider creating a calculated field using the Revenues and Expenses columns in the data sheet. Slicers can be used to filter out the overhead expense categories (Facilities, Labor, and Other).
   e. What was the total gross profit ratio for 2020? (Round % to two decimals.) *HINT:* You can create another calculated field using the gross margin field from d. Which store had the lowest gross profit ratio? What was it? Which product line (department) had the highest gross profit ratio? What was it?

2. The store with the highest sales (b.) and the highest gross margin (d.) was not the most profitable (a.). Why? Look at the revenues, gross profit margins and ratios, and the overhead expenses for both stores.
3. Create pivot charts from some of your pivot tables and use them to create an interactive dashboard. Include slicers on the dashboard that allow management to filter by location or month.

LO3, 4 **PB-20. Job Profitability Using Excel (Descriptive and Diagnostic Analytics)**

Harvard Products is a job shop (a company that manufactures custom products in small batches). Each batch is managed by one of Harvard's four project managers. Manufacturing facilities are located in Illinois, Wisconsin, Michigan, and Indiana.

The President of Harvard Products has asked for information about costs and profits by job, location, customer, and project manager. A summary of costs (by job) is included in the **Job Order Data Set.xlsx** file available on the textbook's website. A video demonstrating Excel tools used to answer the questions in this problem is also available on the website. *HINT:* Add columns to the Data sheet to separate out account amounts (revenue, direct material, etc.). The IF function is useful here.

Create PivotTables to answer the following questions:

1. Which customer was the most profitable for Harvard? What was the job number for the most profitable job for that customer? What was the average revenue on jobs for that customer? What was the average revenue for all jobs?
2. Which location was the least profitable (in dollars) for Harvard? What appears to have contributed more to the lower profits at that location – size of jobs (average revenue) or profit margin ratios? Which location had the highest average revenue per job?
3. The President of Harvard Products has decided to give performance bonuses to project managers. Determine which project manager will receive the highest bonus if performance is based on:
   a. Average revenue per job?
   b. Number of jobs?
   c. Total profit?
   d. Profit margin ratios?
4. Based solely on the information you have available, would you encourage management to close the facility with the lowest profit margin? Why or why not? Include in your answer the information you might need to have before making a final decision.

LO3, 4 **PB-21. Determining Fixed vs. Variable Cost Components Using Excel (Diagnostic Analytics)**

Genessee Industries introduced a new product last year (6582-D). Although it was very popular, it wasn't very profitable. Management has asked you to provide them with information to help them set a sales price that will provide them with a monthly gross profit of $7,500. (Last year's sales price was $75 per unit.)

You know that the direct costs per unit are $25 for direct materials and $5 for direct labor. You are given information about last year's monthly production levels and manufacturing overhead costs (indirect materials, indirect labor, and other). (That information is included in the **Fixed and Variable Data Set.xlsx** file available on the textbook's website. A video demonstrating Excel tools used to answer the questions in this problem is also available on the website.)

1. Determine the cost formula for 6582-D. Use Excel's regression analysis tool to calculate the fixed and variable manufacturing overhead costs. Round elements to two decimal places.
   a. Check the 95% confidence level. Consider checking the box to add a line fit plot for each indirect cost element to show the relationship in chart form. (You may need to change the minimum bound on the horizontal axis to 700 to see the line clearly.)
2. Use the prior year data to create a graph of the various overhead costs by month.
   a. Create a combo chart as follows:
      i. The primary vertical axis in dollars, and the secondary vertical axis is units of production.
      ii. The horizontal axis is Months.
      iii. Units produced should be a clustered column type; the overhead cost elements should be line type. (Units produced would be linked to the secondary vertical axis.
3. Use Excel's Goal Seek tool to determine the sales price required to meet the $7,500 gross profit goal. Management believes monthly sales will average 1,500 next year. Assume the company will not maintain any inventory of finished goods.
4. Discuss how Goal Seek (or any other Excel tool) might help management with CVP Analysis.

PB-22. Forecasting Using Excel (Predictive Analytics) **LO3, 4**

Melton Manufacturing opened in January 2019. Sales have increased significantly in the first two years of operations, and management is now looking to expand production capacity. To finance the purchase of a new factory, they would need to either raise capital or borrow funds.

They have asked you to make some projections for the next year of operations. They intend to share these with potential investors and lenders.

Information about unit sales, sales revenues, and net profits for the past two years is included in the **Forecasting Data Set.xlsx** file available on the textbook's website. A video demonstrating Excel tools used to answer the questions in this problem is also available on the website.

1. Create three line graphs in Excel (one for units sold, one for sales revenue, and one for net operating income). Add trendlines to all graphs.
   a. Extend the trendline out for 12 months.
   b. Use the Polynomial (Order 2) trendline option for all charts
   c. To see how closely the trendline matches the data, check the *Display R-squared value on chart* box. The closer the R-square value is to 1, the better the match.
2. Create the same three graphs using the Forecast Sheet tool (line charts) in Excel.
   a. Set the *Forecast End* to 12/1/2021.
   b. Use an 85% *Confidence Interval.*
   c. Check the *Include forecast statistics* box.
   d. Leave remaining defaults as is.
3. Use the trendline graphs to determine: (*HINT:* To help identify the answers, display gridlines. Consider changing vertical axis bounds.)
   a. Expected unit sales in October 2021
   b. Expected sales revenue in June 2021
   c. Expected net profits in December 2021
4. Use the Forecast sheets to determine:
   a. Range of expected unit sales in October 2021 (Upper to lower Confidence bounds)
   b. Expected sales revenue in June 2021 (Upper to lower Confidence bounds)
   c. Range of expected net profits in December 2021 (Upper to lower Confidence bounds)
5. To evaluate the Forecast sheets, rerun the forecasts. This time change the *Forecast Start* date to 1/1/2020 to see what the model would have predicted for 2020. (Leave all other options the same as B. above.) Were the predictions higher or lower than the actual results? What could have caused the differences?

PB-23. Utilization of Constrained Resources Using Excel (Prescriptive analytics) **LO3**

Backyard Helpers, Inc. is a small manufacturing company with 18 different gardening tools in its product line. All of the products are fabricated using the same equipment.

Recently, sales demand has increased. Unfortunately, Backyard Helpers cannot produce enough products with existing equipment to meet that demand. Facilities can be expanded, and new equipment purchased, but it will be at least two years before that happens. The production manager needs to make production scheduling decisions now.

The **Constrained Resource Data Set.xlsx** file available on the textbook's website includes information about demand, sales price, cost, and fabrication time on the shared equipment for each of Backyard Helpers' products. A video demonstrating Excel tools used to answer the questions in this problem is also available at cambridgepub.com.

Maximum machine time is 40,500 minutes per month. The demand for all products is spread equally throughout the month. Fixed costs (manufacturing, selling, and administrative) total $755,750 per month. Backyard Helpers maintains no inventory of finished goods. (All units produced are sold during the month.)

1. Ignore machine time limits in answering the following:
   a. Which product has the highest contribution margin per unit? How many units of that product should be produced each month?
   b. If Backyard could meet demand, what would be the total net operating income per month?
2. If demand was unlimited for all products, which products should Backyard Helpers produce?
3. Given the maximum number of machine minutes per month, use Solver in Excel to answer the following:
   a. How many of the following products should be produced each month?
      i. R25
      ii. JK369

b. Which products would be temporarily eliminated from Backyard Helpers product line under the Excel solution?

c. What is the total net operating income per month given the machine time constraints and the quantities determined by Solver?

d. What is the **maximum** amount Backyard Helpers should be willing to pay to rent fabrication time from another company? (Assume transportation and other costs would total $50,000.)

4. In Questions 3b, you identified products that would be temporarily eliminated if Backyard followed the Excel solution. What reasons, if any, might management have for continuing to produce some of those products even if it means reducing the supply of some of the other products?

LO3, 4 **PB-24. Budget Variance Analysis Using Excel (Descriptive and Diagnostic Analytics)**

Preston Township's City Council will be evaluating costs incurred in the various city departments at its next meeting. In total, costs exceeded budgeted amounts in the prior year by $576,277. The Council president has asked for information about actual vs. budgeted costs by department and by expense type to help in the evaluation process. Transaction and budget information is included in the **Budget Variance Data Set.xlsx** file available on the textbook's website. A video demonstrating Excel tools used to answer the questions in this problem is also available on the website.

1. Create two PivotTables.
   a. One for actual costs by department and expense type.
   b. One for budgeted costs by department and expense type.
2. Create two Budget Variance reports (one for variances by department and one for variances by expense type). Both reports should link actual and budget data from the PivotTables.
   a. The report should include columns for budgeted amounts, actual amounts, variance (in dollars), and variance (in percent). Show the unfavorable dollar variances as negative numbers, favorable variances as positive numbers. Show all percent variances as positive numbers. *HINT:* Use the ABS function in Excel in the formula to calculate percent variances.
3. Use the PivotTable and the variance reports to answer the following questions:
   a. Which department experienced the greatest variance between budgeted and actual cost (in dollars)? Which expense type in that department accounted for the largest share of the variance? *HINT:* Filter your PivotTables to update the variance reports.
   b. Which expense type had the highest unfavorable variance (in dollars)? Which department had the highest unfavorable variance in that expense type? Which expense type had the highest favorable variance (in dollars)? Which department had the highest favorable variance in that expense type?
   c. Which department had the highest percentage variance? Which type of expense was most over or under budget in that department? Which expense type had the highest percentage variance? Which department was most over or under budget in that expense type?
   d. Schools had the largest budget. Does it appear that the budget dollars were well managed? Explain your answer.
4. In general, should the council members be more concerned about the departments or expense types with the highest unfavorable dollar variances or the highest unfavorable percentage variances? Should the council members be concerned about departments or expense types with favorable variances? Explain your answers.

LO3 **PB-25. Activity-Based Costing Using Excel (Predictive Analytics)**

Kirkland Industries (a contract assembly manufacturer) has decided to adopt activity-based costing techniques to determine its manufacturing overhead rates. The production manager has identified three activities (materials movement, assembly, and packaging/shipping) and a number of possible activity measures (# of jobs, direct labor hours, machine hours, # of boxes shipped, and # of components used). Working together, the production and accounting managers have used historical data from 2014 to 2021 to determine total activity costs by month. Those results are included in the **ABC Cost Drivers Data Set.xlsx** file available on the textbook's website. The workbook also includes totals for the various activity measures from the same 2014-2021 period. (A video demonstrating Excel tools used to answer the questions in this problem is available on the website.)

Budgeted overhead dollars and activities are:

Budgeted Overhead		Budgeted Measures	
Materials movement	$1,080,000	# of jobs	480
Assembly	$1,950,000	Direct labor hours	16,000
Packaging/Shipping	$1,584,000	Machine hours	7,800
		# of boxes shipped	48,000
		# of components used	4,000,000

1. Use the correlation tool in Excel to determine which measure should be used for each activity. *HINT:* The correlation tool can be found on the *Analyze* menu on the Data tab in Excel. If the *Analyze* section does not appear, you will need to load the *Analysis ToolPak*. Click the *File* tab, click *Options*, and click *Add-Ins*. Make sure Excel *Add-ins* appears in the *Manage* field. Check the *Analysis ToolPak* option and click *OK*.
2. Using the measures identified in 1., determine the activity rates for allocating manufacturing overhead to jobs.
3. What would the predetermined rate be if direct labor hours were used to allocate all manufacturing overhead costs?
4. Assume Kirkland had a job that required 36 direct labor hours, 16 machine hours, 1,875 components, and 68 boxes. How much manufacturing overhead would be applied to that job under ABC? How does that compare to the amount applied if direct labor hours were used to allocate overhead? What might account for the difference?

Glossary

A

absorption costing An approach to product costing that treats both variable and fixed manufacturing costs as product costs.

accounting rate of return The average annual increase in net income that results from acceptance of a capital expenditure proposal divided by either the initial investment or the average investment in the project.

acid test ratio More specific than the current ratio as a test of short-term solvency, the acid test ratio (also known as the quick ratio) measures the availability of cash and other current monetary assets that can be quickly generated into cash to pay current liabilities. The general equation for the acid test ratio is: (Cash + Marketable securities + Current receivables)/Current liabilities.

activities list *See* operations list.

activity A unit of work.

activity cost drivers Specific units of work (activities) performed to serve customer needs that consume costly resources.

activity-based approach The activity-based approach to budgeting is an output/input approach that reduces the distortions in the transformation through emphasis on the expected cost of the planned activities that will be consumed for a process, department, service, product, or other budget objective.

activity-based budgeting An approach to budgeting that uses an activity cost hierarchy to budget physical inputs and costs as a function of planned activity. It is mechanically similar to the output/input approach to budgeting where physical inputs and costs are budgeted as a function of planned activity.

activity-based costing (ABC) Used to develop cost information by determining the cost of activities and tracing their costs to cost objectives on the basis of the cost objective's utilization of units of activity.

activity-based management (ABM) The identification and selection of activities to maximize the value of the activities while minimizing their cost from the perspective of the final consumer.

amortization The periodic writing off of an account balance to expense; similar to depreciation and usually refers to the periodic writing off of an intangible asset.

annuity A series of equal cash flows received or paid over equal intervals of time.

asset turnover A measure of performance, the asset turnover ratio measures the firm's ability to use its assets to generate sales. The general equation for asset turnover is: Net sales divided by Average total assets.

avoidable common costs Allocated common costs that eventually can be avoided (that is, can be eliminated) if a segment is discontinued.

B

backflush costing An inventory accounting system used in conjunction with JIT in which costs are assigned initially to cost of goods sold. At the end of the period, costs are backed out of cost of goods sold and assigned to appropriate inventory accounts for any inventories that may exist.

balance sheet A financial report based on the accounting equation that lists a company's assets, liabilities, and equity at a certain point in time.

balanced scorecard A performance measurement system that includes financial and operational measures which are related to the organizational goals. The basic premise is to establish a set of indicators that can be used to monitor performance progress and then compare the goals that are established with the results.

batch level activity An activity performed for each batch of product produced.

benchmarking A systematic approach to identifying the best practices to help an organization take action to improve performance.

big data The vast amount of data available to organizations, primarily driven by the advancement of technology. Big data is unique in that it is so large or complex that traditional analysis methods are often inadequate.

bill of materials A document that specifies the kinds and quantities of raw materials required to produce one unit of product.

bottom-up budget A budget where managers at all levels—and in some cases even non-managers—become involved in the budget preparation.

break-even point The unit or dollar sales volume where total revenues equal total costs.

budget A formal plan of action expressed in monetary terms.

budget committee A committee responsible for supervising budget preparation. It serves as a review board for evaluating requests for discretionary cost items and new projects.

budgetary slack Occurs when managers intentionally understate revenues or overstate expenses in order to produce favorable variances for the department.

budgeted financial statements Hypothetical statements that reflect the "as if" effects of the budgeted activities on the actual financial position of the organization. They reflect what the results of operations will be if all the predictions in the budget are correct.

budgeting Projecting the operations of an organization and their financial impact on the future.

C

capacity costs *See* committed fixed costs.

capacity variance *See* fixed overhead volume variance.

capital budgeting A process that involves the identification of potentially desirable projects for capital expenditures, the subsequent evaluation of capital expenditure proposals, and the selection of proposals that meet certain criteria.

capital expenditures Investments of significant financial resources in projects to develop or introduce new products or services, to expand current production or service capacity, or to change current production or service facilities. Expenditures that increase the book value of long-term assets; sometimes abbreviated as CAPEX.

cash budget Summarizes all cash receipts and disbursements expected to occur during the budget period.

chained target costing Bringing in suppliers as part of the coordination process to attain a competitively priced product that is delivered to the customer in a timely manner.

coefficient of determination (R2) A measure of the percent of variation in the dependent variable that is explained by variations in the independent variable when the least-squares estimation equation is used.

committed fixed costs (capacity costs) Costs required to maintain the current service or production capacity or to fill a previous legal commitment.

common cost A cost incurred for the benefit of two or more cost objectives—an indirect cost.

common segment costs Costs related to more than one segment and not directly traceable to a particular segment. These costs are referred to as common costs because they are incurred at one level for the benefit of two or more segments at a lower level.

common size statement A financial statement that has had all its accounts converted into percentages. As such, a common size statement is very useful for detecting items that are out of line, that deviate from some present amount, or that may be indications of other problems.

comparative financial statements A form of horizontal analysis involving comparison of two or more periods' financial statements showing dollar and/or percentage changes.

competitor analysis The comparison of a firm's financial measures to similar measures or other firms in the industry or to industry averages.

continuous budgeting Budgeting based on a moving time frame that extends over a fixed period. The budget system adds an identical time period to the budget at the end of each period of operations, thereby always maintaining a budget of exactly the same time length.

continuous improvement (Kaizen) budgeting An approach to budgeting that incorporates a targeted improvement (reduction) in costs; management requests that a given process will be improved during the budgeting process. This may be applied to every budget category or to specific areas selected by management. Kaizen budgeting is based upon prior performance and anticipated operating conditions during the upcoming period.

continuous improvement (Kaizen) costing Establishing cost reduction targets for products or services that an organization is currently providing to customers.

continuous improvement An approach to activity-based management where the employees constantly evaluate products, services, and processes, seeking ways to do better.

contribution income statement An income statement format in which variable costs are subtracted from revenues to figure contribution margin, and fixed costs are then subtracted from contribution margin to calculate net income.

contribution margin The difference between total revenues and total variable costs; this amount goes toward covering fixed costs and providing a profit.

contribution margin ratio The portion of each dollar of sales revenue contributed toward covering fixed costs and earning a profit.

controlling The process of ensuring that results agree with plans.

conversion cost The combined costs of direct labor and manufacturing overhead incurred to convert raw materials into finished goods.

corporate governance The system of policies, processes, laws, and regulations that affect the way a company is directed and controlled.

corporation A legal entity created by the granting of a charter from an appropriate governmental authority and owned by stockholders who have limited liability for corporate debt.

cost allocation base A measure of volume of activity, such as direct labor hours or machine hours, that determines how much of a cost pool is assigned to each cost objective.

cost behavior How costs respond to changes in an activity cost driver.

cost center A responsibility center whose manager is responsible only for managing costs.

cost driver A factor that causes or influences costs.

cost driver analysis The study of factors that influence costs.

cost estimation The determination of the relationship between activity and cost.

cost object An object to which costs are assigned. Examples include departments, products, and services.

cost of capital The average cost of obtaining the resources necessary to make investments.

cost of production report Used in a process costing system; summarizes unit and cost data for each department or process for each period.

cost pool A collection of related costs, such as departmental manufacturing overhead, that is assigned to one or more cost objectives, such as products.

cost prediction The forecasting of future costs.

cost prediction error The difference between a predicted future cost and the actual amount of the cost when, or if, it is incurred.

cost reduction proposal A proposed action or investment intended to reduce the cost of an activity that the organization is committed to keeping.

cost-volume-profit (CVP) analysis A technique used to examine the relationships among total volume of some independent variable, total costs, total revenues, and profits during a time period (typically a month or a year).

cost-volume-profit graph An illustration of the relationships among activity volume, total revenues, total costs, and profits.

current ratio A measure of solvency, the current ratio measures the relationship between current assets and current liabilities. The general equation for the current ratio is: Current assets divided by Current liabilities.

customer level activity An activity performed to obtain or maintain each customer.

customer profitability analysis A presentation showing the profits of individual or categories of customers net of the cost of serving and supporting those customers.

customer profitability profile A graphical presentation showing the cumulative profits from the most profitable to the least profitable customer.

cycle efficiency The ratio of value-added to nonvalue-added manufacturing activities.

cycle time The total time required to complete a process. It is composed of the times needed for setup, processing, movement, waiting, and inspection.

D

dashboards Software programs that tabulate and display scorecard results using graphics that mimic the instrument displays on an automobile dashboard.

days sales in receivables A measure of both solvency and performance, the days receivable outstanding tells how long it takes to convert accounts receivable into cash or how well the firm is managing the credit extended to customers. The general equation for days receivable outstanding is: Ending receivables/Average daily sales.

days sales in inventory Inventories divided by average daily cost of goods sold. The average number of days required for each turnover of inventory.

debt-to-equity ratio A measure of long-term solvency, the debt-to-equity ratio indicates the balance between the amounts of capital that creditors and owners provide. The general equation for the debt-to-equity ratio is: Total liabilities/Total stockholders' equity.

depreciation The decline in economic potential (using up) of plant assets originating from wear, deterioration, and obsolescence.

depreciation tax shield The reduction in taxes due to the deductibility of depreciation from taxable revenues.

design for manufacture Explicitly considering the costs of manufacturing and servicing a product while it is being designed.

differential cost analysis An approach to the analysis of relevant costs that focuses on the costs that differ under alternative actions.

direct costing *See* variable costing.

direct department cost A cost directly traceable to a department upon its incurrence.

direct labor Wages earned by production employees for the time they spend working on the conversion of raw materials into finished goods.

direct materials The costs of primary raw materials that are converted into finished goods.

direct method (for cost allocation) A method of allocating service department costs to producing departments based only on the amount of services provided to the producing departments; it does not recognize any interdepartmental services

direct segment fixed costs Costs that would not be incurred if the segment being evaluated were discontinued. They are specifically identifiable with a particular segment.

discount rate The minimum rate of return required for the project to be acceptable.

discretionary fixed costs Costs set at a fixed amount each period at the discretion of management.

dividend payout ratio Annual dividends per share divided by the earnings per share.

dividend yield Annual dividends per share divided by the market price per share.

division margin The amount each division contributes toward covering common corporate expenses and generating corporate profits. It is computed by subtracting all direct fixed expenses identifiable with each division from the contribution margin.

E

earnings per share A measure of performance, earnings per share are disclosed on the income statement. The general equation for basic earnings per share is: Net income less preferred stock dividends/ Weighted average number of common shares outstanding for the period.

earnings quality The degree to which reported earnings represent how well the firm has performed from an economic standpoint.

economic value-added (EVA) A variation of residual income calculated as income after taxes less the cost of capital employed; specifically, net operating profits after tax less a charge for the use of capital equal to beginning capital utilized in the business multiplied by the weighted average cost of capital.

enterprise risk management (ERM) A management process executed throughout an organization that is designed to identify potential risks, and to effectively manage those risks in order to achieve the organization's objectives.

equivalent completed units The number of completed units that is equal, in terms of production effort, to a given number of partially completed units.

ethics The moral quality, fitness, or propriety of a course of action that can injure or benefit people; also, the values, rules, and justifications that governs one's way of life.

external failure costs Quality costs incurred when nonconforming products or services are delivered to customers.

F

facility level activity An activity performed to maintain general manufacturing or marketing capabilities.

Financial Accounting Standards Board (FASB) The organization currently responsible for setting accounting standards for reporting financial information.

financial leverage The proportionate use of borrowed funds in the capital structure, computed as net financial obligations (NFO) divided by average equity; financial leverage is considered favorable if the return on assets is higher than the fixed rate on borrowed funds and unfavorable if the fixed rate is greater than the return it generates.

financial reporting The process of preparing financial statements (income statement, balance sheet, and statement of cash flows) for a firm in accordance with generally accepted accounting principles.

financial reporting objectives A component of the conceptual framework that specifies that financial statements should provide information (1) useful for investment and credit decisions, (2) helpful in assessing an entity's ability to generate future cash flows, and (3) about an entity's resources, claims to those resources, and the effects of events causing changes in these items.

financial statement analysis The process of interpreting and evaluating financial statements by using the data contained in them to produce additional financial measures. Financial statement analysis involves comparing financial statements for the current period with those of the previous periods, studying the internal composition of the financial statements, and studying relationships within and among the financial statements.

finished goods inventory The dollar amount of inventory that has completed the production process and is awaiting sale to customers.

first-in, first-out (FIFO) method (in process costing) A costing method that accounts for unit costs of beginning inventory units separately from those started during the current period. The first costs incurred each period are assumed to have been used to complete the unfinished units left over from the previous period.

fixed costs Costs that do not change with changes in sales volume (over a reasonable range); with a unit level cost driver as the independent variable, fixed costs are a constant amount per period of time.

fixed manufacturing overhead All fixed costs associated with converting raw materials into finished goods.

fixed overhead budget variance The difference between budgeted and actual fixed overhead.

fixed overhead volume variance The difference between total budgeted fixed overhead and total standard fixed overhead assigned to production.

fixed selling and administrative costs All fixed costs other than those directly associated with converting raw materials into finished goods.

flexible budget variance Computed for each cost as the difference between the actual cost and the flexible budget cost of producing a given quantity of product or service.

flexible budgets Budgets that are drawn up for a series of possible production and sales volumes or adjusted to a particular level of production after the fact. These budgets, based on cost-volume or cost-activity relationships, are used to determine what costs should have been for an attained level of activity.

forecast The projection of financial results over the forecast horizon and terminal periods.

for-profit organization An organization that has profit as a primary mission.

full absorption cost *See* absorption costing.

full costing *See* absorption costing.

full costs Include all costs, regardless of their behavior patterns (variable or fixed) or activity level.

functional income statement A type of income statement where costs are classified according to function, rather than behavior. It is typically included in external financial reports.

future value The amount a current sum of money (or series of monies) earning a stated rate of interest will accumulate to at the end of a future period.

G

general and administrative expense budget Presents the expenses the organization plans to incur in connection with the general administration of the organization. Included are expenses for such things as the accounting department, the computer center, and the president's office.

generally accepted accounting principles (GAAP) A set of standards and procedures that guide the preparation of financial statements.

goal A definable, measurable objective.

gross margin The difference between net sales and cost of goods sold: also called gross profit.

gross profit margin (GPM) (percentage) The ratio of gross profit on sales divided by net sales.

gross profit on sales The difference between net sales and cost of goods sold; also called gross margin.

H

high-low method of cost estimation Utilizes data from two time periods, a representative high activity period and a representative low activity period, to estimate fixed and variable costs.

horizontal analysis An evaluative standard, horizontal analysis is the comparison of a firm's current financial measures to those of previous periods. Horizontal analysis is used to evaluate trends in the firm's financial condition covering two or more years.

I

imposed budget *See* top-down budget.

income statement A financial report on operating activities that lists revenues less expenses over a period of time, yielding a company's net income.

incremental budgeting An approach to budgeting where costs for a coming period are budgeted as a dollar or percentage change from the amount budgeted for (or spent during) some previous period.

indirect department cost A cost reassigned, or allocated, to a department from another cost objective.

indirect segment costs *See* common segment costs.

inspection time The amount of time it takes units to be inspected.

interdepartmental services Services provided by one service department to other service departments.

internal controls The measures undertaken by a company to ensure the reliability of its accounting data, protect its assets from theft or unauthorized use, make sure that employees are following the company's policies and procedures, and evaluate the performance of employees, departments, divisions, and the company as a whole.

internal failure costs Quality costs incurred when materials, components, products, or services are identified as defective before delivery to customers.

internal rate of return (IRR) Often called the time-adjusted rate of return, the discount rate that equates the present value of a project's cash inflows with the present value of the project's cash outflows.

inventory carrying costs Costs of holding inventories, including warehousing, logistics, insurance, financing, and the risk of loss due to theft, damage, or technological or fashion change.

inventory turnover (in dollars) Often regarded as a measure of both solvency and performance, inventory turnover tells how long it takes to convert inventory into current monetary assets and how well the firm is managing investments in inventory. The general equation for inventory turnover is: Cost of goods sold/Average inventory cost.

investment center A responsibility center whose manager is responsible for the relationship between its profits and the total assets invested in the center. In general, the management of an investment center is expected to earn a target profit per dollar invested.

investment tax credit A reduction in income taxes of a percent of the cost of a new asset in the year the new asset is placed in service.

invoice A document that the seller sends to the purchaser to request payment for items that the seller shipped to the purchaser.

irrelevant costs Costs that do not differ among competing decision alternatives.

J

job cost sheet A document used to track the status of and accumulate the costs for a specific job in a job cost system.

job order production The manufacturing of products in single units or in batches of identical units.

job production *See* job order production.

joint costs All materials and conversion costs of joint products incurred prior to the split-off point.

joint products Two or more products simultaneously produced by a single process from a common set of inputs.

just-in-time (JIT) inventory management A comprehensive inventory management philosophy that stresses policies, procedures, and attitudes by managers and other workers that result in the efficient production of high-quality goods while maintaining the minimum level of inventories.

just-in-time (JIT) inventory philosophy Receive inventory from suppliers into the production process just at the point it is needed

K

Kaizen costing *See* continuous improvement costing.

Kanban system *See* materials pull system.

L

labor efficiency variance The difference between the standard cost of actual labor inputs and the flexible budget cost for labor.

labor rate (spending) variance The difference between the actual cost and the standard cost of actual labor inputs.

lean production A philosophy of inventory production and management that emphasizes increased coordination throughout the value chain, reduced inventory, reduced production times, increased product quality, and increased employee involvement and empowerment.

least-squares regression analysis Uses a mathematical technique to fit a cost estimating equation to the observed data in a manner that minimizes the sum of the vertical squared estimating errors between the estimated and actual costs at each observation.

leveraging The use of borrowed funds in the capital structure of a firm; the expectation is that the funds will earn a return higher than the rate of interest on the borrowed funds.

life-cycle budgeting An approach to budgeting when the entire life of the project represents a more useful planning horizon than an artificial period of one year.

life-cycle costs From the seller's perspective, all costs associated with a product or service ranging from those incurred with initial conception through design, pre-production, production, and after-production support. From the buyer's perspective, all costs associated with a purchased product or service, including initial acquisition costs and subsequent costs of operation, maintenance, repair, and disposal.

linear algebra method (reciprocal) method A method of allocating service department costs using a series of linear algebraic equations, which are solved simultaneously, to allocate service department costs both interdepartmentally among service departments and to the producing departments.

M

managed fixed costs *See* discretionary fixed costs.

management by exception An approach to performance assessment whereby management directs attention only to those activities not proceeding according to plan.

managerial accounting The activities carried out to provide managers and other employees with financial reporting information and control to assist management in the formulation and implementation of an organization's strategy.

manufacturers Companies that convert raw materials and components into finished products through the application of skilled labor and machine operations.

manufacturing cost budget A budget detailing the direct materials, direct labor, and manufacturing overhead costs that should be incurred by manufacturing operations to produce the number of units called for in the production budget.

manufacturing costs The costs of direct materials, direct labor, and manufacturing overhead incurred in the manufacture of a product.

manufacturing margin The result when direct manufacturing costs (variable costs) are deducted from product sales.

manufacturing overhead All manufacturing costs other than direct materials and direct labor.

margin of safety The amount by which actual or planned sales exceed the break-even point.

marginal cost The varying increment in total cost required to produce and sell an additional unit of product.

marginal revenue The varying increment in total revenue derived from the sale of an additional unit.

market segment level activity Performed to obtain or maintain operations in a market segment.

market value added (MVA) The increase in market value of the firm for the period.

master budget The grouping together of all budgets and supporting schedules. This budget coordinates all the financial and operational activities and places them into an organization wide set of budgets for a given time period.

materials inventory The physical component of inventory; the other components of manufactured inventory are labor costs and overhead costs.

materials price variance The difference between the actual materials cost and the standard cost of actual materials inputs.

materials pull system An inventory production flow system in which employees at each station work to replenish the inventory used by employees at subsequent stations. The building of excess inventories is strictly prohibited. When the number of units in inventory reaches a specified limit, work at the station stops until workers at a subsequent station pull a unit from the in-process storage area.

materials push system An inventory production flow system in which employees work to reduce the pile of inventory building up at their work stations. Workers at each station remove materials from an in-process storage area, complete their operation, and place the output in another in-process storage area. Hence, they push the work to the next work station.

materials quantity variance The difference between the standard cost of actual materials inputs and the flexible budget cost for materials.

materials requisition form A document used to record the type and quantity of each raw material issued to the factory.

merchandising organizations Organizations that buy and sell goods without performing manufacturing operations.

minimum level budgeting An approach to budgeting that establishes a base amount for all budget items and requires explanation or justification for any budgeted amount above the minimum (base).

mission The basic purpose toward which an organization's activities are directed.

mixed costs Costs that contain a fixed and a variable cost element.

movement time The time units spend moving between work or inspection stations.

N

net assets The difference between an entity's assets and liabilities; net assets are equal to stockholders' equity.

net income The excess of a firm's revenues over its expenses.

net loss The excess of a firm's expenses over its revenues.

net present value The present value of a project's net cash inflows from operations and disinvestment less the amount of the initial investment.

net sales volume variance Indicates the impact of a change in sales volume on the contribution margin, given the budgeted selling price and the standard variable costs. It is computed as the difference between the actual and the budgeted sales volumes times the budgeted unit contribution margin.

non-value-added activity An activity that does not add value to a product or service from the viewpoint of the customer.

not-for-profit organization An organization that does not have profit as a primary goal.

O

open book management An approach to management that includes sharing financial and related information with employees, teaching employees to understand financial numbers, encouraging employees to use the information in their work, and sharing financial results with employees, perhaps through a bonus program.

operating activities Business activities that involve transactions that are related to a company's normal income-earning activity (research, develop, produce, purchase, market, and distribute company products and services) and that enter into the calculation of net income on the income statement.

operating budget Detailed plans to guide operations throughout the budget period.

operating leverage A measure of the extent that an organization's costs are fixed.

operating leverage ratio Computed as the contribution margin divided by before-tax profit.

operations list A document that specifies the manufacturing operations and related times required to produce one unit or batch of product.

opportunity cost The net cash inflow that could be obtained if the resources committed to one action were used in the most desirable other alternative.

order level activity An activity performed for each sales order.

order-filling costs Costs incurred to place finished goods in the hands of purchasers (for example, storing, packaging, and transportation).

order-getting costs Costs incurred to obtain customers' orders (for example, advertising, salespersons' salaries and commissions, travel, telephone, and entertainment).

organization chart An illustration of the formal relationships existing between the elements of an organization.

organization structure The arrangement of lines of responsibility within the organization.

organizational cost drivers Choices concerning the organization of activities and the involvement of persons inside and outside the organization in decision making.

organizing The process of making the organization into a well-ordered whole.

outlay costs Costs that require future expenditures of cash or other resources.

output/input budgeting An approach to budgeting where physical inputs and costs are budgeted as a function of planned unit level activities. The budgeted inputs are a function of the planned outputs.

outsourcing The external acquisition of services or components.

P

participation budget *See* bottom-up budget.

payback period The time required to recover the initial investment in a project from operations.

period costs Expired costs not related to manufacturing inventory; they are recognized as expenses when incurred.

period statement A financial statement accumulating information for a specific period of time; examples are the income statement, the statement of stockholders' equity, and the statement of cash flows.

planning The process of selecting goals and strategies to achieve those goals.

practical capacity The maximum possible activity, allowing for normal repairs and maintenance.

predetermined manufacturing overhead rate An overhead rate established at the start of each year by dividing the predicted overhead costs for the year by the predicted volume of activity in the overhead base for the year.

present value The current worth of a specified amount of money to be received at some future date at some specified interest rate.

prevention costs Quality costs incurred to prevent nonconforming products from being produced or nonconforming services from being performed.

price earnings ratio A measure of performance, price earnings ratio compares the current market price with earnings per share of stock and arrives at a multiple of earnings represented by the selling price. Calculated as: Current market price per common share divided by Earnings per share.

process A collection of related activities intended to achieve a common purpose.

process manufacturing A manufacturing environment where production is on a continuous basis.

processing time The time spent working on units.

product costs All costs incurred in the manufacturing of products; they are carried in the accounts as an asset (inventory) until the product is sold, at which time they are recognized as an expense (cost of goods sold).

product level activity An activity performed to support the production of each different type of product.

production order A document that contains a job's unique identification number and specifies details for the job such as the quantity to be produced, the total raw materials requirements, the manufacturing operations and other activities to be performed, and perhaps even the time when each manufacturing operation should be performed.

profit center A responsibility center whose manager is responsible for revenues, costs, and resulting profits. It may be an entire organization, but it is more frequently a segment of an organization such as a product line, marketing territory, or store. profitability analysis An examination of the relationships between revenues, costs, and profits.

profitability analysis An examination of the relationships between revenues, costs, and profits.

profit-volume graph Illustrates the relationship between volume and profits; it does not show revenues and costs.

project-level activity An activity performed to support the completion of each project.

purchase order A document that formally requests a supplier to sell and deliver specific quantities of particular items of merchandise at specified prices.

purchase requisition An internal document that requests that the purchasing department order particular items of merchandise.

purchases budget Indicates the merchandise or materials that must be acquired to meet current needs and ending inventory requirements.

Q

quality Conformance to customer expectations.

quality circles Groups of employees involved in the production of products who have the authority, within certain parameters, to address and resolve quality problems as they occur, without seeking management approval.

quality costs Costs incurred because poor quality of conformance does (or may) exist.

quick ratio *See* acid test ratio; Defined as quick assets (cash and cash equivalents, short-term investments, and current receivables) divided by current liabilities.

R

raw materials inventories The physical ingredients and components that will be converted by machines and/or human labor into a finished product.

relevant costs Future costs that differ between competing decision alternatives.

relevant range The range of activity within which a linear cost function is valid.

residual income for investment center Excess of investment center income over the minimum rate of return set by top management. The minimum dollar return is computed as a percentage of the investment center's asset base.

responsibility accounting The structuring of performance reports addressed to individual (or group) members of an organization in a manner that emphasizes the factors they are able to control. The focus is on specific units within the organization that are responsible for the accomplishment of specific activities or objectives.

return on assets A financial ratio computed as net income divided by average total assets; sometimes referred to by the acronym ROA; as a measure of performance, return on assets combines the asset turnover and return on sales ratios to measure directly the firm's ability to use its assets to generate profits.

return on equity A measure of performance, the return on equity measures the profits attributable to the shareholders as a percentage of their equity in the firm. The general equation for return on equity is: Net income/Average shareholders' equity; sometimes referred to by the acronym ROE.

return on investment The ratio obtained by dividing income by average investment; sometimes referred to by the acronym ROI.

return on investment for investment center A measure of the earnings per dollar of investment. The return on investment of an investment center is computed by dividing the income of the center by its asset base (usually average total assets). It can also be computed as investment turnover times the return-on-sales ratio.

return on sales A measure of performance, the return on sales measures the firm's ability to generate profits from sales produced by the firm's assets. The general equation for return on sales is: net income divided by net sales; sometimes referred to by the acronym ROS.

revenue center A responsibility center whose manager is responsible for the generation of sales revenues.

revenue variance The difference between the budgeted sales volume at the budgeted selling price and the actual sales volume at the actual selling price.

revenues Inflows of earned resources from providing goods and services to customers; reflected as increases in stockholders' equity.

risk The danger that things will not go according to plan. Although some risk results from anticipated events having a positive impact, risk is more typically associated with events that have a negative impact.

risk management *See* enterprise risk management.

rolling budget *See* continuous budgeting.

S

sales budget A forecast of sales revenue for a future period. It may also contain a forecast of sales collections.

sales mix The relative portion of unit or dollar sales derived from each product or service.

sales price variance The impact on revenues of a change in selling price, given the actual sales volume. It is computed as the change in selling price times the actual sales volume.

sales volume variance Indicates the impact on revenues of change in sales volume, assuming there was no change in selling price. It is computed as the difference between the actual and the budgeted sales volumes times the budgeted selling price.

salvage value The expected net recovery when a plant asset is sold or removed from service; also called residual value.

scatter diagram A graph of past activity and cost data, with individual observations represented by dots.

Securities and Exchange Commission (SEC) The commission, created by the 1934 Securities Act, that has broad powers to regulate the issuance and trading of securities, and the financial reporting of companies issuing securities to the public.

segment income All revenues of a segment minus all costs directly or indirectly charged to it.

segment margin The amount that a segment contributes toward the common (indirect) costs of the organization and toward profits. It is computed as segment sales less direct segment costs.

segment reports Income statements that show operating results for portions or segments of a business. Segment reporting is used primarily for internal purposes, although generally accepted accounting principles also require disclosure of segment information for some public corporations.

segments Subdivisions of a firm for which supplemental financial information is disclosed.

selling expense budget Presents the expenses the organization plans to incur in connection with sales and distribution.

semi-variable costs *See* mixed costs.

sensitivity analysis The study of the responsiveness of a model to changes in one or more of its independent variables.

service costing The process of assigning costs to services performed.

service department A department that provides support services to production and/or other support departments.

service organizations Nonmanufacturing organizations that perform work for others, including banks, hospitals, and real estate agencies.

setup time The time required to prepare equipment to produce a specific product.

solvency Refers to the firm's ability to pay its debts as they become due.

split-off point The point in the process where joint products become separately identifiable.

standard cost variance analysis A system for examining the flexible budget variance, which is the difference between the actual cost and flexible budget cost of producing a given quantity of product or service.

standard cost A budget that indicates what it should cost to provide an activity or produce one batch or unit of product under efficient operating conditions.

statement of cash flows A financial statement that reports the major sources and uses of cash classified into operating, investing, and financing activities and that indicates the net increase or decrease in cash; the statement also includes a schedule of any significant noncash investing and financing activities that occur during the period.

statement of cost of goods manufactured A report that summarizes the cost of goods completed and transferred into finished goods inventory during the period.

statement of owner's equity A financial statement presenting information on the events causing a change in stockholders' equity during a period; the statement presents the beginning balance, additions to, deductions from, and the ending balance of stockholders' equity for the period.

static budget A budget based on a prior prediction of expected sales and production.

step costs Costs that are constant within a narrow range of activity but shift to a higher level with an increased range of activity. Total step costs increase in a step-like fashion as activity increases.

step method A method of allocating service department costs that gives partial recognition to interdepartmental services by using a methodology that allocates service department costs sequentially to both the remaining service departments and the producing departments.

strategic business segment A segment that has its own mission and set of goals to be achieved. The mission of the segment influences the decisions that its top managers make in both short-run and long-run situations.

strategic cost management Making decisions concerning specific cost drivers within the context of an organization's business strategy, its internal value chain, and its place in a larger value chain stretching from the development and use of resources to the final consumers.

strategic plan A guideline or framework for making specific medium-range or short-run decisions.

strategic position analysis An organization's basic way of competing to sell products or services.

strategic position How an organization wants to place itself in comparison to the competition.

strategy A course of action that will assist in achieving one or more goals.

structural cost drivers Fundamental choices about the size and scope of operations and technologies employed in delivering products or services to customers. These choices affect the types of activities and the costs of activities performed to satisfy customer needs.

sunk costs Costs resulting from past decisions that cannot be changed.

sustainability accounting Often used interchangeably with the term corporate social responsibility. Sustainability accounting incorporates the concept of the triple bottom-line which includes 1) economic performance, 2) social responsibility, and 3) environmental responsibility.

T

target costing Establishes the allowable cost of a product or service by starting with determining what customers are willing to pay for the product or service and then subtracting a desired profit on sales.

theory of constraints Every process has a bottleneck (constraining resource), and production cannot take place faster than it is processed through the bottleneck. The theory's goal is to maximize throughput in a constrained environment.

throughput Sales revenue minus direct materials costs; *see also* theory of constraints.

time-adjusted rate of return *See* internal rate of return.

times interest earned ratio A measure of long-term solvency and interest-paying ability; measured as income before interest expense and income taxes divided by interest expense.

top-down budget A budget where top management decides on the primary goals and objectives for the organization and communicates them to lower management levels.

transfer price The internal value assigned a product or service that one division provides to another.

U

unit contribution margin The difference between the unit selling price and the unit variable costs.

unit level activity An activity performed for each unit of product produced or sold.

unit level approach An approach to analyzing cost behavior that assumes changes in costs are best explained by changes in the number of units or sales dollars of products or services provided for customers.

V

value chain The set of value-producing activities stretching from basic raw materials to the final consumer.

value chain analysis The study of value-producing activities, stretching from basic raw materials to the final consumer of a product or service.

value-added activity An activity that adds value to a product or service from the viewpoint of the customer.

variable cost ratio Variable costs as a portion of sales revenue.

variable costing An approach to product costing that treats variable manufacturing costs as product costs and fixed manufacturing costs as period costs.

variable costs Those costs that change in proportion to changes in sales volume. Costs that are an identical amount for each incremental unit of activity. Their total amount increases as activity increases, equaling zero dollars when activity is zero and increasing at a constant amount per unit of activity.

variable manufacturing overhead All variable costs, except direct labor and direct materials, associated with converting raw materials into finished goods.

variable overhead efficiency variance The difference between the standard variable overhead cost for the actual inputs and the flexible budget cost for variable overhead based on outputs.

variable overhead spending variance The difference between the actual variable overhead cost and the standard variable overhead cost for the actual inputs.

variable selling and administrative costs All variable costs other than those directly associated with converting raw materials into finished goods.

variance A comparison of actual and budgeted (or allowed) costs or revenues which are usually identified in financial performance reports.

vertical analysis An evaluative standard that restates amounts in the current financial statements as a percentage of some base measure such as sales; focused on one period's statements.

virtual integration The use of information technology and partnership concepts to allow two or more entities along a value chain to act as if they were a single economic entity.

voucher Another name for the payment approval form.

W

waiting time The time units spend in temporary storage waiting to be processed, moved, or inspected.

weighted average cost of capital (WACC) The discount rate where the weights are the relative percentages of debt and equity in the capital structure and are applied to the expected returns on debt and equity respectively; an average of the after-tax cost of all long-term borrowings and the cost of equity.

weighted average method In process costing, a costing method that spreads the combined beginning inventory cost and current manufacturing costs (for materials, labor, and overhead) over the units completed and those in ending inventory on an average basis.

work in process inventory The cost of inventories that are in the manufacturing process and have not yet reached completion.

work ticket A document used to record the time a job spends in a specific manufacturing operation.

working capital A measure of solvency, working capital is the difference between current assets and current liabilities and is the net amount of working funds available in the short run. The general equation for working capital is: Current assets minus Current liabilities.

work-in-process inventories Partially completed goods consisting of raw materials that are in the process of being converted into a finished product.

Z

zero-based budgeting A variation of the minimum level approach to budgeting where every dollar of expenditure must be justified.

Index

A

B

C

Note: Exhibits included in the index with e following the page numbers.

D

Note: Exhibits included in the index with e following the page numbers.

Note: Exhibits included in the index with e following the page numbers.

Note: Exhibits included in the index with e following the page numbers.

N

O

P

Note: Exhibits included in the index with e following the page numbers.

Q

R

Note: Exhibits included in the index with e following the page numbers.

S

T

Note: Exhibits included in the index with e following the page numbers.

Note: Exhibits included in the index with e following the page numbers.

Chapter Vignette Sources

CH 1

Kim Bhasin, "ModCloth Plans Huge Expansion Under New CEO," *Bloomberg.Com*, August 31, 2015; Sandra Guy, "ModCloth Hires a Chief Technology Officer," Internetretailer.Com, May 24, 2016; Douglas MacMillan, "At ModCloth, Vintage Fashion Goes Mobile," *Bloomberg Businessweek*, August 8, 2013; Meghan Casserly, "ModCloth Hits $100 Million in Revenue, Gives Social All the Credit," *Forbes*, July 23, 2013; and Bridget Brennan, "The Retailer Winning the Battle for Millennial Women," *Forbes*, November 16, 2012.

CH 2

www.SquareUp.com; Michal Lev-Ram, "Jack Dorsey: The Pride of St. Louis," *Fortune*, September 19, 2013; Greg Bensinger, "Square Takes on PayPal Online," *Wall Street Journal*, June 26, 2013, p. B5; Tomio Geron, "Square Launches Stand, A New Point of Sale Device," *Forbes*, May 14, 2013; Danielle Kucera, "Square Introduces Hardware to Convert iPads into Cash Registers," *Bloomberg Businessweek*, May 14, 2013; Danielle Kucera, "Square Debuts Mobile Gift Cards in Challenge to PayPal," *Bloomberg Businessweek*, December 10, 2012; and Amir Efrati and Annie Gasparro, "Starbucks Invests in Square," *Wall Street Journal*, August 8, 2012, p. B8.

CH 3

Parija Kavilanz, "Next for Razor after massive recall: Hovertrax 2.0," *CNN Money*, July 7, 2106; Matt Malmlund, "Are Hoverboards Safe to Ride Yet? The Razor Hovertrax 2.0 Is," Heavy.Com, December 13, 2016; Bloomberg.com 2017; and Razor.com 2017.

CH 4

Eric Newcomer, "Uber's Loss Exceeds $800 Million in Third Quarter on $1.7 Billion in Net Revenues," *Bloomberg Technology*, December 19, 2016; Jessi Hempel, "Hey, Taxi Company, You Talkin' to Me?" *Fortune*, September 23, 2013; Joshua Brustein, "From Google, Uber Gets Money and Political Muscle," *Bloomberg Businessweek*, August 26, 2013; Josh Linkner, "Uber's Borrowed Creativity," *Forbes*, August 19, 2013; and Andy Kessler, "The Transportation Trustbuster," *Wall Street Journal*, January 26, 2013, p. A13.

CH 5

Tim Worstall, "Why Samsung Beats Apple or Perhaps Vice Versa," *Forbes*, September 9, 2013; and Sam Grobart, "How Samsung Became the World's No. 1 Smartphone Maker," *Bloomberg Businessweek*, March 28, 2013.

CH 6

Unilever 2012 Annual Report; Paul Sonne and Simon Zekaria, "Unilever Tallies Hefty Sales Gain," *Wall Street Journal*, January 24, 2013, p. B6; Matthew Boyle, "In Emerging Markets, Unilever Finds a Passport to Profit," *Bloomberg Businessweek*, January 3, 2013; and Paul Sonne, "Unilever Takes Palm Oil in Hand," *Wall Street Journal*, April 12, 2012, p. B3.

CH 7

Julie Jargon, "The Battle for the Organic Shopper," *Wall Street Journal*, August 22, 2013, pp. B1–B2; Clair Suddath, "Whole Foods Local Forager Elly Truesdell Is a Grocery Tastemaker," *Bloomberg Businessweek*, May 2, 2013; Annie Gasparo, "Whole Foods Lifts Outlook as Sales Rise," *Wall Street Journal*, February 9, 2012, p. B4; and Katie Agin, "Lean Manufacturing 2.0," *Whole Foods Magazine*, January 2010.

CH 8

AP News, "Roku Raises $60M from Hearst, News Corp, Others," *Bloomberg Businessweek*, May 29, 2013; Kyle Stock, "Roku Sales Hit 5 Million Units, Thanks to Amazon, Netflix," *Bloomberg Businessweek*, April 11, 2013; Larry Magid, "Roku Reaches Milestone as Networks Consider Dropping Free Broadcast," *Forbes*, April 10, 2013; Larry Magid, "Review of Roku 3: Could It Kill Cable and Satellite TV?" *Forbes*, April 1, 2013; Walter Mossberg, "Roku 3: Easier Streaming and Remote Headphones," *Wall Street Journal*, March 6, 2013, pp. D1–D3; and Robert Hof, "Could TiVo and Roku Beat Apple to TV Nirvana?" *Forbes*, February 27, 2013.

CH 9

Robert Hof, "Pinterest: Here Come the Ads (But They'll Be Tasteful)," *Forbes*, September 19, 2013; Lydia Dishman, "J. Crew's Smart Pinterest Play: Move Beyond Inspiration to Make a Sale," *Forbes*, August 20, 2013; Kyle Stock, "Nordstrom Racks Now Powered by Pinterest," *Bloomberg Businessweek*, July 2, 2013; Jessi Hempel, "CEO Outlines the Future of Pinterest," *Fortune*, May 30, 2013; Eric Spitznagel, "Dude! The Battle to Become the Male Pinterest!" *Bloomberg Businessweek*, April 10, 2013; and Pui-Wing Tam and Spencer Ante, "As Pinterest Grows, Startup Seeks $2.5 Billion Valuation," *Wall Street Journal*, February 6, 2013, pp. B1–B2.

CH 10

Micah Solomon, "Customer Service: What Southwest Knows and You Don't (Hint: Being Nice Isn't Enough)," *Forbes*, September 22, 2013; Alanna Petroff, "Airlines Rake in $27 Billion in Customer Fees," *CNN Money*, September 19, 2013; Scott McCartney, "Airlines Mergers and Aggravations," *Wall Street Journal*, July 18, 2013, pp. D1–D3; Scott McCartney, "Dear Airline, Here's the Problem ...," *Wall Street Journal*, April 4, 2013, pp. D1–D4; and Scott McCartney, "Reality Check: Why Airlines Are Shrinking Flight Times," *Wall Street Journal*, June 14, 2012, pp. D1–D2.

CH 11

Kenneth Rapoza, "Volkswagen Stakes Out Greater Turf in China," *Forbes*, May 14, 2013; Joann Muller, "How Volkswagen Will Rule the World," *Forbes*, April 17, 2013; and Vanessa Fuhrmans and Friedrich Geiger, "A Weaker Outlook in Europe Slams Volkswagen's Stock," *Wall Street Journal*, February 23, 2013, p. B3.

CH 12

Amazon, "Press Release: Amazon to Create More Than 100,000 New, Full-Time, Full-Benefit Jobs across the U.S. over the Next 18 Months," *Amazon.Com*, January 12, 2017; Jenna Amatulli, "A Brick-And-Mortar Amazon Bookstore Is Coming To NYC," *Huffington Post*, January 10, 2017; Kate Abbey-Lambertz, "Amazon's Flying Warehouse Idea Isn't Even Its Biggest Challenge," *Huffington Post*, December 30, 2016; Peter Cohan, "How You Can Use The Three Big Ideas Behind Amazon's Success," *Forbes*, September 4, 2013; Tim Worstall, "Fascinating Number: Amazon Is Larger Than the Next Dozen Internet Retailers Combined," *Forbes*, September 1, 2013; Danielle Kucera, "Why Amazon Is on a Warehouse Building Spree," *Bloomberg Businessweek*, August 29, 2013; Tom Gara, "Amazon Losing Its Price Edge," *Wall Street Journal*, August 20, 2013, p. B2.